Charrier
Polymeric Materials and Processing

Cover:

Top left: Polymeric molecule – polycarbonate (1957)
Top middle: Artificial organ – Jarvik-7 heart (1982)
                     [polyester, polyurethane]
Top right: Aeronautic product – Rutan-Voyager aircraft (1986)
                     [all composite construction, carbon fiber, epoxy resin etc.]
Bottom left: Automotive product – Renault-Espace minivan (1984)
                     [all plastic composite body by resin transfer molding (RTM)]
Bottom right: Automotive product – General Motors Lumina minivan (1989)
                     [all plastic composite body by sheet molding compound (SMC)]

Jean-Michel Charrier

Polymeric Materials and Processing

Plastics, Elastomers and Composites

with 615 Figures

Hanser Publishers, Munich Vienna New York

Distributed in the United States of America and Canada
by Oxford University Press, New York

Distributed in USA and in Canada by
Oxford University Press
200 Madison Avenue, New York, N.Y. 10016

Distributed in all other countries by
Carl Hanser Verlag
Kolbergerstrasse 22
D-8000 München 80

Library of Congress Cataloging-in-Publication Data
Charrier, Jean-Michel,
    Polymeric materials and processing : plastics, elastomer, and composites / Jean-Michel Charrier.
        p. cm.
    Includes bibliographical references and index.
    ISBN 0-19-520854-4
    1. Polymers.   2. Manufacturing processes.   I. Title.
TA455.P58C474   1990
668.9--dc20

CIP-Titelaufnahme der Deutschen Bibliothek
Charrier, Jean-Michel:
Polymeric materials and processing : plastics, elastomers and composites / Jean-Michel Charrier. – Munich; Vienna ;
New York : Hanser ; New York : Oxford Univ. Pr., 1990
    ISBN 3-446-14198-7 (Hanser) Pp.
    ISBN 0-19-520854-4 (Oxford Univ. Pr.)

ISBN 3-446-14198-7 Carl Hanser Verlag, Munich, Vienna, New York
ISBN 0-19-520854-4 Oxford University Press

Foreword

The Society of Plastics Engineers (SPE) is pleased to sponsor and endorse this new volume, "Polymeric Materials and Processing." For many years Jean-Michel Charrier has been one of the preeminent instructors in SPE's Educational Seminar Programm. His cours "Fundamentals of Plastics Materials and Processing" has served as the base upon which the contents of this book was developed.

Thus, the volume makes available at a substantially reduced cost and in a far more extensive format information previously imparted only to seminar registrants. This broad base provides a background for an understanding to plastics materials and elements of processing – a base upon which more specialized books can cover in greater detail.

SPE, through its Technical Volumes Committee, has long sponsored books on various aspects of plastics. Its involvement has ranged from identification of needed volumes to recruitment of authors and peer review and approval of new publications.

Technical competence pervades all SPE activities, not only in the publication of books, but also in other areas such as sponsorship of technical conferences and educational programs. In addition, the Society publishes periodicals including – *Plastics Engineering, Polymer Engineering and Science, Polymer Processing and Rheology, Journal of Vinyl Technology* and *Polymer Composites* – as well as conference proceedings and other publications, all of which are subject to rigorous technical review procedures.

The resource of some 34,000 practicing plastics engineers has made SPE the largest organization of its type worldwide. Further information is available from the Society at 14 Fairfield Drive, Brookfield, Connecticut 06804, U.S.A.

Technical Volumes Committee
Robert E. Nunn, Chairmann
University of Lowell

Robert D. Forger
Executive Director
Society of Plastics Engineers

Preface
OBJECTIVES, READERSHIP, AND ACKNOWLEDGEMENTS

Natural polymeric materials have always been around, but synthetic (man-made) polymeric materials (plastics, rubbers and composites) have had a significant impact on our lives only since World War II. The subsequent growth has been very rapid, though, and plastics, rubbers, and composites are now found everywhere with many types increasingly used in sophisticated technical applications where they have earned the prestigious title of "engineering materials."

Polymeric materials initially tended to be viewed as a chemistry specialty, but they are now strongly associated with engineering as well, through the design, fabrication, and testing of products. Many books on polymeric materials written by authors with a chemistry background have a certain emphasis on chemistry-related topics such as the chemical manufacture of the resins. People dealing primarily with engineering problems can find these books difficult to read and not sufficiently related to their occupations.

Another characteristic of many books is that they tend to fall into one of two distinct categories: elementary descriptive books and books that emphasize fundamental considerations, requiring a theoretical background that many potential readers have never acquired or have not retained. Authors of the two types of books generally have very different backgrounds and interests.

My objective is to offer an original and effective compromise, by covering a wide range of important subjects related to polymers that are not normally found in a single book, and by presenting the material in a simple, yet technically sound and industrially relevant manner. A detailed list of the book contents and a discussion of the methodology used are presented in subsequent sections of Chapter 1. The broad, balanced, and uniform coverage of the subjects in this book should be a useful contribution toward the recognized need for effective ways of promoting and facilitating interdisciplinary as well as multilevel technical communication in the field of polymers.

The general style of this book is intended to be that of an educational textbook rather than an encyclopedia. The book is geared to those who want to acquire knowledge of polymeric materials for long-term benefit, rather than those who seek specific elements of information for the short-term solution of problems. While individual sections can be read independently, a knowledge of the preceding material will help the reader derive maximum benefit, and it is actually essential to understand and appreciate many fine points.

This textbook was written with a diverse readership in mind and also as a tool for facilitating communication between people with varied backgrounds but a common interest in contributing toward making better plastic, rubber, and composite products. I encountered such wide variety of background in my teaching of professional short courses where it was a difficult challenge to deal with the subject in a style and at a level that was acceptable to the entire audience. Extensive discussions with short-course attendees over the years convinced me that there was need for a book that could be a complement to professional short courses on a variety of polymer-related subjects.

Backgrounds and interests in educational institutions can vary widely from trade and vocational institutions, technical institutions, or undergraduate and graduate higher-education institutions. This book could be suitable for specialized programs in any such institution. In higher-education institutions, it would have to be supplemented by a more advanced discussion of scientific and engineering principles associated with the field, and suited to chemistry, physics or the various types of engineering students.

Backgrounds and interests can also vary widely in the work place. In a somewhat simplistic manner, one can distinguish four categories of people who may deal with polymers in the work place. Resin manufacturers are responsible for the supply of materials and are normally expected to advise on their proper use. Product designers are normally responsible for the choice of suitable materials and fabrication processes for products. Product fabricators are responsible for converting materials into products, using appropriate processing equipment. Finally, product users are normally the ones who need the products and will assess their performance. This book should help resin manufacturers, particularly in their dealings with downstream product designers, product fabricators, and product users. It should help product fabricators in their dealings with upstream resin manufacturers, parallel product designers, and downstream product users. It should help product designers in their parallel dealings with resin manufacturers, product fabricators, and product users. In the industrial environment of either resin manufacturers or product fabricators, people in a range of positions could benefit from the book in different ways, all contributing to an im-provement to the chain of communication. These positions include operators, foremen, technicians, supervisors, engineers, chemists, managers, and salesmen. In the professional, nonindustrial environment, examples of potential users of the book could include industrial designers, architects, and health professionals, who increasingly have to deal with polymer-based products.

I am indebted to many people whose influence, advice, and support gave me the will to undertake and complete this endeavor. They include my former teachers at all levels, past and current colleagues in academia and in industry, and my university students or attendees of my short courses. Special thanks are due to the colleagues who kindly agreed to preview sections of the book and to the persons, most notably Pat Fong, who converted the manuscript into a formal text. The book is particularly dedicated to my parents for their example of commitment to education.

Table of Contents

Chapter 1

GENERAL INTRODUCTION

1.1 CONTENTS AND SECTION INDEXING

This book covers a broad range of topics associated with the use of polymeric materials in products. A detailed table of contents is given at the beginning of the book. Reference to the compact detailed table of contents readily shows the section order with page numbers corresponding to specific sections.

A number of topics in this book do not seem to have been covered, or at least not to the same extent, in other single-authored books of this kind. They include additives in Chapter 2, elastomers in Chapter 3, a thorough review of standard tests in Chapter 4, an extensive coverage of composite materials in Chapter 5, and a detailed case study of an application and a broader focused survey of applications in Chapter 6.

1.2 METHODOLOGY

1.2.1 Introduction

Since this book is intended as an educational tool rather than just a conventional source of information, I have carefully considered its methodology and have introduced a number of features that are not common in similar books. Although such features may initially surprise some readers, it is felt that adjustment should not be difficult and benefits should accrue as study proceeds. Major features are discussed in subsequent sections.

1.2.2 Features

1.2.2.1 Writing Style

In all cases, the information presented in the book was sought from multiple sources and synthesized in my own style.

A special effort was made to discuss the many topics in a logical way, and, in particular, to make a rational use of sentences and paragraphs to separate them. In many cases, the nature of the topics led to a juxtaposition of short and long sentences or short and long paragraphs; this was considered inevitable.

The terminology in this evolving multidisciplinary field is not always uniquely established. Instead of making a somewhat arbitrary selection of term in each specific case, I chose to add synonyms or near-synonyms in parentheses. This feature is considered worthwhile in particular for readers who are not perfectly familiar with North American English.

The writing of the many polymer names brought something of a dilemma. I initially had a preference for the following uniform style: poly(ethylene), poly(vinyl chloride), and poly(methyl methacrylate). Such style, however, has disadvantages associated in particular with the use of parentheses and in the case of poly(amide), for example, is not quite rational. It was decided instead to use single-word names throughout, such as polyethylene, polyvinylchloride, polymethylmethacrylate, and polyamide. Readers may find it useful to mark the conventional subdivision on their text in the following manner: poly'vinyl'chloride, poly'methyl'methacrylate. Such style has been employed in the index of chemical names and in the associated *chemplates* (see section 1.2.2.3).

Also used frequently in the text are abbreviations commonly encountered in the field. Repetition of the abbreviations, along with full names, should facilitate their assimilation by newcomers.

A general consideration for the layout of the text was to present it in a compact yet readable manner so that the reader would have a good perspective on the topic and could easily go back and forth for a better understanding.

1.2.2.2   Figures

Over 250 schematic figures were developed to complement the text. These figures are all cited in the text. Most of the figures are diagrams; a few are schematic graphs.

The basic guideline was to keep the diagrams simple, excluding any feature not discussed in the text. Since it was considered desirable to have the figures near the relevant portion of the text, and in view of the previously stated desire to present the text in a compact manner, small figures were essential.

Small figures made it impractical to label figure elements with full terms, and a system of single character symbols was developed. To facilitate the association of symbols and terms, when possible the first letter of a term was chosen as the character symbol. I used some logic in the method by choosing the first letter of the French or Spanish equivalent term, when necessary. A key to symbols is provided in each figure caption, along with the figure title. Physical elements are normally associated with symbols in circular boxes (or parentheses); ensembles, stages in processes, etc. are associated with symbols in square boxes (or square brackets); and coordinates in graphs are associated with diamond-shaped boxes (or arrow-shaped brackets). Basic elements that appear in many diagrams are systematically given the same symbols, which should quickly become familiar to readers [examples include (S) for test specimen, (T) for tool, (P) for product, (E) for SI unit scale, (E′) for British unit scale, etc.].

A notable feature of the diagrams which involves cross sections is that crosshatches normally found in technical drawings are not represented. Including them would have complicated their drafting, and it is felt that readers can readily adapt to this figure style.

In schematic figures depicting stages in a specific process, the material flow or the stage sequence is systematically represented as proceeding from left to right. It should be noted that this is sometimes contrary to the way an operator sees the material flow when facing a machine, as shown in photographic illustrations.

1.2.2.3 Chemplates

This book places no emphasis on chemistry, but a minimum reporting of chemical facts is essential to help readers perceive the differences between polymer types. Chemical information is reported in the form of *chemplates* described below. Over 200 such *chemplates* are given in Chapter 3.

For each polymer type discussed in this book, the chemical formula of what is defined in Chapter 2 as the repeat unit is systematically represented, along with an abbreviation or *name code* and, when available or applicable, the glass transition temperature T_g or the melting temperature T_m as defined in Chapter 3. Representative temperatures for the unmodified polymers are given in degrees Celsius and Fahrenheit (°C and °F), as well as the range of reported temperatures found in the literature in °C. The fact that the repeat unit is part of a polymeric chain is reflected by links crossing the square brackets that limit the repeat unit. For chemicals which are not polymeric but which take part in the formation of polymers, the molecular formula is represented, along with a name code. In all cases, the arrangement of atoms of C, H, O, N, Cl, S, F, and other elements is represented in a simplified two-dimensional manner, showing single and double chemical bonds. Classical phenyl rings are represented in the conventional manner, as simple hexagons, omitting the associated C and H atoms and double bonds. In a few cases, saturated cyclohexane rings are represented in a similar way with the letter s (saturated) in the center of the hexagon.

Name codes given in *chemplates* correspond, in most cases, to widely accepted abbreviations. A key to all name codes is given in the index of terms. The writing style for the full names has been discussed earlier in this chapter.

1.2.2.4   Photographic Illustrations

Although the text and the associated figures form the essence of this educational book, it was felt that newcomers in particular would benefit from photographic illustrations, which could help them develop a feel for industrial reality. To keep with the previously stated goal of text compactness, to have a good variety of illustrations, and to avoid an undue increase of pages, the illustrations, in relatively small format, are presented in sets at the end of sections. They were selected for their technical significance, rather than for their photographic quality, and were obtained primarily from company-issued documents. Permission to reproduce was sought in all but a few cases where the source could not be traced. Detailed captions allow easy reference to the text. Source acknowledgements are given in square brackets.

1.2.2.5   Supplier and Tradename Listings

The author feels strongly that even in an educational book, a strong connection to the industrial reality must be established. It is thus important to tie the many materials, tests, and fabrication processes to companies supplying these materials, as well as testing or processing equipment. These companies will have to be approached by anyone wanting to become involved in the field. It is also important to realize that materials, which are described in this book in a general manner, are often referred to in industry by tradenames (Plexiglas, Lexan, Delrin, Rilsan, Viton, etc.). Lists of suppliers and tradenames are thus systematically given at the end of chapters. The lists are representative of the North American situation in the 1980s and include European and some Japanese information as well. Tradenames marked with an asterisk indicate cases where they are used for different distinct materials (eg., Bakelite*, Victrex*, Teflon*). No overall index of tradenames is given, and comprehensive lists should be sought in trade publications. Juxtaposed suppliers' names reflect associations, mergers, changes of ownership or takeovers (e.g., Union Carbide/Amoco, Hercules/Montedison/Himont, Celanese/Hoechst), which have recently been quite common and tend to complicate the picture. No attempt has been made, however, to be absolutely up to date on this question, and the reader is referred to current issues of appropriate trade journals for the latest status.

1.2.2.6 Property Data

This book does not contain any table of property data. I feel strongly that such tables can be very misleading in view of the wide range of grades for any material that is associated with topics presented in Chapter 2. Examples of property levels considered high and low are given in the text throughout Chapter 4, and qualitative statements are made throughout Chapter 3. Realistic property data for specific resins should be sought in specialized encyclopedias or handbooks, and, better still, in company literature.

1.2.2.7 Units

When property data or other numerical data are given, the recommended SI system of units, as well as the British system for the benefit of American readers, are used simultaneously. The associated conventional symbols are normally used with a few adjustments that should be easy to figure out. For example, tons are sometimes abbreviated as "tf" to indicate a unit of force, and the distinction between metric and other tons that is not essential is not normally made. To avoid reporting very large or very small numbers, standard prefixes are used that include pico (p) for 10^{-12}, nano (n) for 10^{-9}, micro (μ) for 10^{-6}, milli (m) for 10^{-3}, kilo (k) for 10^{3}, mega (M) for 10^{6}, and giga (G) for 10^{9}. Thus, a micron (μm) is 10^{-6} meters, a kpsi is 10^{3} psi, and a GPa is 10^{9} Pa.

1.3 ASSOCIATED SCIENTIFIC AND ENGINEERING PRINCIPLES

As stated earlier, this book was intentionally written in a descriptive manner, totally avoiding the use of mathematical tools to discuss fundamental or other concepts. It is essential to realize, however, that the field of polymeric materials and processing has long evolved from a practical and descriptive status, and that the analytical (mathematical) modeling of numerous subjects associated with it has greatly helped scientists and engineers in their rational understanding of those subjects, with countless beneficial effects on the development of polymeric materials, processes, and products.

Mathematical modeling is based on fundamental chemistry, physics, and engineering principles that have been quantified, that is, put in mathematical form, and are used in the analysis of specific problems. Mathematical modeling can have different degrees of complexity with solutions that can sometimes be expressed in simple analytical form or may require computer-based numerical calculations.

By comparing the style of papers presented at conferences or published in technical journals in the 1960s, to that of current ones, one sees now much more frequent reference to scientific and engineering principles and to the associated analytical (mathematical) formulation of these principles. To benefit from published technical writing, it becomes increasingly important for people associated with polymeric materials, processes, and products, to have at least a basic knowledge of relevant scientific and engineering principles and their analytical formulation.

A comprehensive list of topics that are closely related to polymeric materials, processes, and products, and lend themselves to analytical formulation, is given in Appendix 1. References to existing books and journals that deal with these topics are given in Appendix 7.

I am currently working on a second book, to be entitled *Polymeric Materials And Processing - Scientific And Engineering Principles*, which will review the topics listed in Appendix 2. Mathematical complexity will be kept to a minimum and frequent reference to the descriptive material of the first book should make the second book a natural complement to this one, even to people who do not have a strong scientific or engineering background.

1.4   APPENDIX 1

Polymeric Materials and Processes Scientific and Engineering
Principles

1. CHEMICAL PRINCIPLES
Chemical Structure/Physical Chemistry
► Monomer(s)
► Polymeric chains
    Basic Molecular Unit
    Linear Chains
        Chain Conformation, Motion
        Entanglements
        Intermolecular Interactions
        Isomers
        Stereoregularity
        Copolymers
    Imperfectly Linear Chains,
        Branching, Grafting
    Molecular Networks
        Crosslinking
        Direct Formation

► Molecular Weights, Distribution
    Definitions
    Experimental Determination
        Osmometry, Light Scattering,
        Viscosity, End-Groups
        Gel Permeation Chromatogaphy

Polymerization Principles
► General mechanisms
► Reactive end-groups polymerization
(condensation)
    Reactive Groups, Interunit Linkages
    Kinetics, Conversion, Molecular
Weights
► Chain addition polymerization (addition)
    Free Radicals, Cations, Anions
    Kinetics, Conversion, Molecular
Weights (Free Radical Case)
► Copolymerization
    Kinetics, Conversion, Composition
        (Free Radical Case)

Polymerization Technology
► Polymerization techniques (thermoplastics)

Bulk
    Solution
    Suspension
    Emulsion
► Polymerization reactions
► Crosslinking of linear polymeric chains
    (rubber vulcanization)
► Direct molecular network formation
    (thermoset curing)

2. PHYSICAL STATES, GENERAL, PHYSICAL BEHAVIOR
Amorphous State
► Glassy state
► Glass transition temperature
► Rubbery state
► Viscous flow
► Methods of investigation
► Molecular orientation

Crystalline State
► Morphology
► Degree of crystallinity
► Crystallization kinetics
► Crystallization thermodynamics
► Methods of investigation
► Morphology - property relationships

Special Systems
► Copolymers (random, block)
► Polyalloys
► Plasticized polymers
► Molecular network polymers
► Filled polymers (composites)

3. VISCOUS FLOW/RHEOLOGY (FLUID STATES)
General Considerations
► Simplest flow modes, viscosity
    Shear
    Elongational

▶Rate/time effects
    Non-Newtonian Behavior, Power Law
▶Temperature effects

▶Other factors
    Pressure
    Molecular Weight

Modeling of Simple Flows
▶Drag flows
    Parallel plate
    Concentric Cylinders
    Cone and Plate
▶Pressure flows
    Uniform Channel
        Capillary (Circular)
        Slit (Thin Rectangular)
    End Effects
    Tapered Channel
    Squeeze Flow

Experimental Determination of Flow Properties
▶Rheometry
▶Melt index

Applications in Thermoplastic Processing
▶Extrusion dies
▶Injection runners and gates

4. MECHANICAL BEHAVIOR (SOLID STATE)
General Tensile Behavior
▶Stress-strain curve
▶Elasticity, yield, fracture
▶Classes of behavior

Linear Elasticity
▶Simplest deformation modes
    Tension, Compression
    Shear
    Hydrostatic compression
▶Non-homogeneous deformations
    Bending
    Torsion
▶Biaxial stresses
    Pressurized Vessels and Pipes
▶Miscellaneous deformation modes

Indentation
▶Composite systems
    Isotropic systems (Particles)
    Anisotropic systems (Fibers)

Non-Linear Elasticity
▶Large deformations of elastomers
▶Theoretical stress-strain relationships
    Molecular basis
    Phenomenological basis
▶Application to inflated structures

Linear Viscoelasticity (Time Effects)
▶Experimental characterization, material constants
    Creep, Stress-relaxation
    Sinusoidal Stresses and Strains
▶Simple parametric models
▶Applications
    Heat generation
    Vibration Damping, Shock Absorption

Time/Temperature Effects
▶Experimental characterization
▶Time/temperature superposition principle
▶W-L-F equation

Mechanical Failure
▶Classical failure criteria
▶Time and temperature effects
▶Elements of fracture mechanics
▶Specific failure modes
    Static (Creep)
    Dynamic (Impact, Fatigue)

Miscellaneous Mechanical Phenomena
▶Tribology (friction, wear)

5. MISCELLANEOUS PHYSICAL PHENOMENA

Heat Transfer
▶Principles
    Conduction
    Convection
    Radiation
▶Modeling of simple problems
▶Multiphase systems

▸Applications
      Processing, Products

Mass Transport
▸Principles
      Materials and Permeants
      Parameters
▸Modeling of simple problems
▸Multiphase systems
▸Experimental characterization
▸Applications
      Processing (Cellular Polymers)
      Products (Barrier Material,
            Controlled Diffusion)

Electrical Properties
▸Principles
      DC and AC Currents
      Parameters, Properties
▸Multiphase systems
▸Applications
      Processing (Dielectric Heating)
      Products (Insulation)

Optical Properties
▸Characteristics of light
▸Reflection, refraction
▸Light scattering
▸Light polarization
▸Applications
      Processing (Morphology)
      Products

Thermodynamics - Equation of State
▸Thermal expansion
▸Compressibility
▸Equation of state (P-V-T)
▸Applications
      Processing (Injection Molding)
      Products (Dimensional Stability)

6. INTRODUCTION TO PROCESS MODELING
General Principles
▸Geometry
▸Material behavior
▸Process parameters
▸Conservation of mass
▸Conservation of energy (heat, momentum)

Examples
▸Extrusion
▸Extrusion Covering
▸Film Blowing
▸Calendering
▸Sheet Thermoforming
▸Blow Molding
▸Coating
▸Rotational Molding
▸Casting
▸Compression Molding
▸Injection Molding

Chapter 2

GENERAL CONCEPTS AND TOPICS

2.1 INTRODUCTION

Polymeric materials are in many ways very distinct from conventional materials such as metals and glasses. The discussion in this chapter of many special concepts associated with their chemical and physical structure should facilitate the appreciation and understanding of the great variety of polymers and grades that are commercially available. The recent emphasis on the modification and/or combination of existing polymers, to tailor their properties to end uses, makes such knowledge even more valuable.

This chapter also contains an extensive presentation of elements or substances that are commonly added to polymers to modify their properties. They include plasticizers, fillers or reinforcements, and additives which are very important to the polymer industry.

2.2 MONOMERS AND POLYMERIZATION

The starting element for the formation of a polymer is a monomer (or monomers). A monomer (M) is a small (low-molecular-weight) molecule with an inherent capability of forming chemical bonds (B) with the same or other monomers in such a manner that long chains (polymeric chains or macromolecules) [P] are formed, as illustrated in Figure 2.1. A typical polymeric chain often involves hundreds or thousands of monomeric molecules. The process of forming polymeric chains is

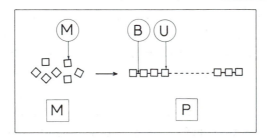

Figure 2.1 · **Polymerization mechanism** · [M] Monomers; [P] Polymeric chain; (M) Monomer; (B) Chemical bond; (U) Repeat unit

referred to as "polymerization" and a material consisting of polymeric chains is called a "polymer." This chemical formation of polymeric chains is routinely carried out by nature to produce biological macromolecules, which are essential parts of living cells. The production of man-made polymers, sometimes referred to as "synthetic polymers," is a relatively recent undertaking traceable to the nineteenth century, and the understanding of the real nature of macromolecules was unclear until the second quarter of this century.

The commercial manufacture of polymers normally involves two stages: (1) the production of the monomer (or monomers) from existing raw materials via chemical or other processes, and (2) the polymerization itself. Polymerization processes are in many respects distinct from regular chemical processes.

There are two basic polymerization mechanisms: addition or chain addition polymerization and condensation or reactive end-group polymerization. A specific polymer is generally associated with one mechanism. The understanding of the mechanisms and, in particular, the evolution of the chemical reaction with time (kinetics) is central to the production of the modern sophisticated types and grades of polymers.

Four methods are primarily used in actual polymerization technology. They are generally referred to as "bulk polymerization," "solution polymerization," "suspension polymerization," and "emulsion polymerization." Some polymers have been produced by all four methods. The desired final form of the polymer, intrinsic characteristics of the polymerization mechanism, and a variety of other considerations determine the choice of method.

In the simplest and most general case, individual macromolecules (polymeric chains) in a polymer, consist of a single characteristic group of atoms closely reminiscent of the monomer (or monomers), which is regularly repeated all along the chain (backbone); such a polymer is referred to as a "homopolymer." The characteristic group is referred to here as the "repeat unit" (U) with roughly equivalent terms being monomeric unit or structural unit. The repeat unit is the most essential characteristic of a homopolymer, and its features are primarily responsible for the physical and chemical properties of the corresponding polymer. Expert chemists have developed a good understanding of the relationship between the molecular structure of the repeat unit and the properties to be expected of the corresponding polymer. In this book, no extensive reference is made to this knowledge, but the chemical formula of the repeat unit of all polymers discussed in Chapter 3 is given, primarily for its essential value as a "fingerprint" or "signature." It allows, in particular, a quick visual assessment of the chemical composition and atom arrangement, which is not always clearly reflected in the chemical name. For newer or more complex polymers there is sometimes uncertainty on some details of the repeat unit, but major features are normally well established.

Polymers are, of course, most commonly identified by a name. Many names, sanctioned by tradition, but that may not always correspond to the most rational terminology are known as "generic names"; examples include polyethylene, polycarbonate, polyester, and polyamide. More specific chemical names sometimes used to further clarify the chemical structure of the polymer tend to be longer; examples include polyethylene terephthalate and Nylon 6. Users of polymers who have to actually purchase polymers from suppliers often go by tradenames, particularly for polymers such as engineering plastics where few and sometimes one single supplier may exist.

In the subsequent discussion of specific commercial polymers, the generic name, a more specific chemical name when desirable or available, the repeat unit, and a representative list of tradenames with associated suppliers names are systematically given. Compilations of tradenames and suppliers' names in alphabetical order are available in specialized publications.

2.3 HOMOPOLYMERS AND POLYMERIC CHAINS

The fact that all polymeric chains in a homopolymer feature a single repeat unit does not generally mean that all chains are identical. Differences concern primarily the dimensions (length) and deviations from the "linear" model discussed earlier (branching). These differences are associated with the statistical nature of the polymerization process and progress in the understanding of the polymerization process, and its kinetics in particular has helped control what will be referred to as the "molecular architecture."

The polymeric chains resulting from most polymerization processes which, at this stage, we assume to be linear chains, vary widely in the number of repeat units involved. The number of repeat units, often called the "degree of polymerization" (DP), is the most logical quantitative way of characterizing a polymeric chain, although in practice, the molecular weight (MW) is more commonly used. When the chemical structure of the repeat unit is known, it is easy to calculate its molecular weight M_1; for example, for polystyrene (PS) M_1 = 104 g per gram-mole, that is for 6.023 x 10^{23} actual repeat units (or just 104 in short). The molecular weight of the polymeric chain is the product M_1 x DP. For a representative value MW = 100,000 for a polystyrene chain, the degree of polymerization is, therefore, about 1000.

If one considers as a vastly oversized model for a polymeric chain a common metal bead key chain where each bead is about 3 mm (1/8 in) long, the total extended length (contour length) of a key chain featuring 1000 beads would be about 3 m (10 ft). The actual polymer chain would be roughly 10 million times smaller.

A polymer consists of a huge number of polymeric chains, typically about 10^{19} chains per cubic centimeter (cm^3, cc, or ml), which differ widely in length. To give a representative indication of the molecular weight of the chains in such a polymer, one must introduce the notion of average. The simplest averaging method is probably the one that would divide the total number of repeat units in a given mass or volume of polymer by the total number of chains. The number obtained would be the number-average degree of polymerization DP_n, and its product by M_1 would be the corresponding number average molecular weight denoted $\bar{M}_n$. Other average quantities are also defined, such as weight-average molecular weight $\bar{M}_w$, z-average molecular weight M_z, viscosity-based molecular weight $\bar{M}_\eta$, and so on. Experimental methods are available which allow the quantitative relative or absolute assessment of average molecular weights. They include osmometry, light scattering and solution viscosity.

Besides time-consuming fractionation techniques, a modern method, gel-permeation chromatography (GPC), is available to assess the actual distribution of chain lengths in a polymer sample. Basically, such distribution reflects the percentage or fraction of chains <F> having their degree of polymerization or molecular weight around a certain level <W> as shown schematically in Figure 2.2, where distributions having a peak around the same average molecular weight (A) are superimposed. Sharp peaks correspond to narrow distributions or low polydispersity (L), with the extreme being a uniform molecular weight (monodisperse sample). Flat curves correspond to broad distributions or high polydispersity (H). Figure 2.3 illustrates how the average molecular weight can vary widely from one grade to another for a given polymer and also shows the bimodal distribution that could result from the mixing of two samples.

While molecular-weight distribution curves represent the best way of characterizing this first aspect of the molecular architecture, they are rarely given in ordinary technical literature. Sometimes an unspecified molecular weight is given (MW), but there is now an increasing trend to give values of both M_n and M_w. The difference between M_n and M_w or the ratio M_w/M_n (polydispersity index PDI) reflects the broadness or sharpness of the distribution with monodisperse samples corresponding to PDI $\approx$ 1 and broad distributions corresponding to large values of PDI.

It is now established that the distribution of molecular weight, not just an average, has a significant effect on many properties, particularly in the areas of processing and ultimate properties, through the fraction of very long or very short chains.

In general, for a given polymer, higher molecular weights tend to improve properties, but by rapidly increasing the resistance to flow (viscosity) in the fluid state, they make processing more difficult and costly. A specific range is generally found most appropriate for each polymer, but different grades corresponding to different levels are often proposed for specific processing or application conditions.

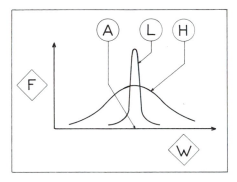

Fig. 2.2

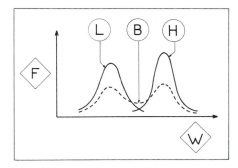

Fig. 2.3

Figure 2.2 · **Molecular weight distributions** · <F> Fraction of chains; <W> Molecular weight; (A) Average molecular weight; (L) Low polydispersity; (H) High polydispersity

Figure 2.3 · **Molecular weight distributions** · <F> Fraction of chains; <W> Molecular weight; (L) Low molecular weight sample; (H) High molecular weight sample; (B) Combined samples

Examples of representative molecular weights (**MW**) or degree of polymerization (**DP**) for a variety of common polymers are as follows: polyethylene (PE): **MW** $\approx$ 300,000, **DP** $\approx$ 10,000 (the extreme case of ultra-high-molecular-weight polyethylene (UHMWPE) corresponds to **MW** $\approx$ 5 x 10^6, **DP** $\approx$ 200,000); polystyrene (PS): **MW** $\approx$ 300,000, **DP** $\approx$ 3000; polyvinylchloride (PVC): **MW** $\approx$ 100,000, **DP** $\approx$ 1500; polyamides (PA) (nylons): **MW** $\approx$ 15,000, **DP** $\approx$ 120; polycarbonate (PC): **MW** $\approx$ 40,000, **DP** $\approx$ 200; polyethylene terephthalate (PET): **MW** $\approx$ 20,000, **DP** $\approx$ 100; acetal (POM): **MW** $\approx$ 40,000, **DP** $\approx$ 1000. These values show that some polymers achieve good properties for very different degrees of polymerization than others.

It should be noted that a number of other quantities for which numerical values are often given in the technical and commercial literature reflect the molecular weight of samples or grades of a given polymer. Examples are the intrinsic viscosity, the **K** value (for PVC primarily), and the melt flow index (MFI).

The other important question, associated with what has been called the molecular architecture, concerns deviations from the "linear" model of repeat units strung along a single line [chain backbone (B)]. During the polymerization, what might be viewed as side or secondary reactions sometimes leads to the growth of side chains or branches. Depending on the nature of the polymer or polymerization conditions, such branches (ramifications) (R) can take different forms, as illustrated in Figure 2.4. One extreme case [L] features few long branches, while another extreme case [S] corresponds to many short branches. Any combination or intermediate case such as [M] can, of course, be encountered.

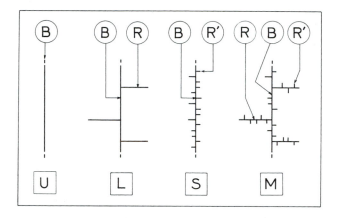

Figure 2.4 · **Molecular architectures** · [U] Unbranched; [L] Long Branching; [S] Short Branching; [M] Mixed Branching; (B) Backbone; (R) Long branch; (R') Short branch

The effect of branching on the properties of a given polymer can be illustrated by comparing the two extreme branching situations [L] and [S] and the linear case [U] in the case of crystallizing polymers. For comparable molecular weights, linear chains [U] are likely to behave differently in a flow situation than the bulkier, less slender chains [L]; hence the melt viscosity or processing characteristics of corresponding polymers could be markedly different. Short branches in chains of type [S] are small but so numerous and so irregularly spaced that they may reduce considerably the ability of portions of linear chains to line up closely to form crystal-like domains; the corresponding polymer would display a lower degree of crystallinity and, thus, a lower stiffness.

Such situations are typical of polyethylene, for example, for which the lower degree of crystallinity in low-density polyethylene (LDPE) is attributed to a high level of short branching, which is often combined with long branching (case [M]). Linear low density polyethylene (LLDPE) appears to have a molecular architecture reminiscent of case [S], although in this case the equivalents of short branches are associated with a copolymerization mechanism.

The polymeric chains discussed thus far involve numerous chemical bonds within each chain (intramolecular chemical bonds), that is within each repeat unit and between repeat units, but the chains are basically chemically independent (no intermolecular chemical bonds).

There are, however, interactions between chains of a less powerful, yet significant, magnitude that corresponds to specific atoms or groups of atoms in the repeat unit. Because of the limited flexibility of the backbone of a polymeric chain, such interactions cannot take place within the repeat unit or even between close neighbors. They involve pairs of repeat units belonging to different chains or perhaps to portions of chains that are widely separated along the backbone. These intermolecular interactions, which range from very weak to relatively strong, play an important role in the properties of the polymers either in the fluid state (melt or solution) or in the solid state (crystallization, in particular). They are generally classified as hydrogen bonding, dipole-dipole interaction or polar bonding, van der Waals forces and ionic bonding.

In addition to the above physical-chemical interactions, the nature of polymeric chains, particularly their length and relatively high flexibility, introduces a purely physical type of interaction that is referred to as "molecular entangling with corresponding entanglements."

Contrary to chemical bonds, which are basically stable below a certain decomposition temperature, physical-chemical interactions and physical entanglements are rather strongly affected by temperature in a somewhat progressive manner. These effects will be discussed later in the text.

2.4 AMORPHOUS STATE

In terms of the shape (conformation) of the polymeric chains they consist of, polymers can, in principle, exist in two states: amorphous or crystalline.

The expression "amorphous," generally indicates the absence (a) of shape (morphous) or, in this case, implies the absence of the characteristic regular arrangement, which will be discussed for the crystalline state. It is applied to a polymer itself or by extension to an individual polymeric chain.

Practically all polymers can be found in the amorphous state at sufficiently high temperatures or in solution, and many commercially important polymers (roughly half of them) exist exclusively in the amorphous state.

The shape of an individual polymeric chain in the amorphous state is thought to be comparable to that of a bead chain (discussed earlier), which would be gathered in a hand and dropped on the floor. It is clear that if one picked it up and dropped it again, the shape would probably be quite different in detail but would have the same general features.

Under certain conditions (high temperature or in the presence of small solvent molecules), the chemical bonds that connect atoms or groups of atoms along the backbone of a polymeric chain allow significant motions, primarily rotations, which can be quite free or somewhat restricted (kinks). The result of this relative freedom is the characteristic random-like conformation [U] depicted in Figure 2.5 and sometimes referred to as "random coil conformation."

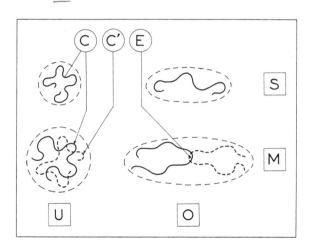

Figure 2.5 · **Molecular conformations** · [U] Unoriented (random); [O] Partially oriented; [S] Single chain; [M] Multiple chains; (C),(C′) Individual chains; (E) Entanglement

As discussed further in a section on thermoplastics, above a characteristic temperature zone for each polymer, molecular (Brownian) motion is very significant and allows relatively long range displacement of segments (portions) of polymeric chains and, in particular, their interpenetration. Previously mentioned intermolecular interactions and physical entanglements [(E) in Fig. 2.5] assure a rather strong cohesion of the polymeric chains which is responsible for the very special properties of polymers in the fluid-like state in particular.

At low temperatures and in the absence of solvent molecules, the polymeric chains of exclusively amorphous (noncrystallizing) polymers retain their random-like conformation, but molecular motion is considerably reduced, preventing long-range displacement of segments of chains and giving solid-like behavior.

Amorphous polymers at high temperatures are sometimes compared to a mass of live and active snakes, while low temperature would correspond to the same frozen or, at least, inactive reptiles.

It is important to note that the application of a load to an exclusively amorphous polymer in the fluid-like state may cause a significant amount of orientation [O] (Fig. 2.5). Release of the load causes a relatively rapid return to the random conformation, which is the most preferred conformation. However, a partial "amorphous" orientation can be frozen in if the polymer is cooled, while under load, to a temperature such that molecular motion is no longer significant. Such molecular orientation has obvious effects on the properties of the polymers, and techniques such as birefringence can be used to detect it in transparent materials.

Specific examples of commercially important, exclusively amorphous (noncrystallizing) polymers will be discussed in Chapter 3 (sections on thermoplastics, thermosets, and elastomers).

2.5 CRYSTALLINITY

While many commercially important polymers exist exclusively in the amorphous state, many others are capable of forming zones (regions, domains) where the random conformation of polymeric chains is replaced by a regular (ordered) conformation reminiscent of that found in regular crystals of low-molecular-weight chemicals.

In a linear homopolymer, the regular succession of identical repeat units along the backbone of each polymeric chain evokes the possibility of at least portions (sections) of the same or different chains piling up regularly, as illustrated in Figure 2.6, with all atoms and groups of atoms imbricated in a manner characteristic of ordinary crystals with a specific unit cell for each polymer. Such an arrangement, however, is possible and stable only if sufficiently strong intermolecular forces can be developed and maintained to overcome the tendency of polymeric chains to adopt a random conformation. Low temperatures favor such arrangement, but it is primarily the makeup of the repeat unit which determines whether a polymer will crystallize.

It is important to realize that it is practically impossible to achieve perfect crystallization of polymers in bulk (no solvent or other low-molecular-weight diluent).

Polymers capable of significant crystallization will be referred to as "crystallizing polymers," and their state of partial or imperfect crystallization will be referred to as the "semicrystalline state."

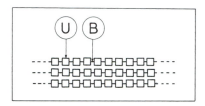

Figure 2.6 · **Crystalline order in polymers** · (U) Repeat unit; (B) Chemical bond

The description of the arrangement of polymeric chains and crystalline regions in a semicrystalline polymer is referred to as the "morphology" (morpho = shape, logy = science), or sometimes as the "microstructure," and is important in the understanding of the properties of crystallizing polymers. The early concept of molecular arrangement described in Figure 2.7 and often referred to as the fringed micelle model [M] has given way to the folded-chain-model (pattern) [F] which has been demonstrated to correspond to most situations. Perhaps surprisingly, chains appear to fold regularly and many chains or portions of chains become involved in thin entities reminiscent of single crystals, which are sometimes referred to as "lamellae" and are schematically represented in Figure 2.8. Representative dimensions of (W) ≈ 10,000 Å (1 μm) and (T) ≈ 100 Å (0.01 μm) indicate that tens or hundreds of repeat units may be involved in one fold and many thousands of molecules in a lamella. Figure 2.7 indicates that a polymeric chain may not be exclusively involved in one

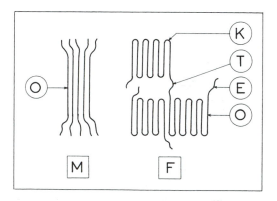

Figure 2.7 · **Crystal models for polymers** · [M] Fringed micelle model; [F] Folded chain model; (O) Ordered region; (K) Kink; (T) Tie section; (E) Loose end

lamella; instead many molecular connections (ties) exist between lamellae, which are sometimes referred to as "interlamellar links," and contribute to the cohesion of the material.

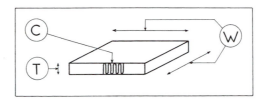

Figure 2.8 · **Folded chain lamella** · (C) Polymeric chain; (T) Thickness (≈ 100 Å or 0.01 μm); (W) Width (≈ 10,000 Å or 1 μm)

A semicrystalline polymer is not merely a collection of lamellae. The crystallization process, illustrated in Figure 2.9, implies that when a polymer melt is cooled below its crystallizing temperature range, crystallization starts around disseminated (discrete) points called "nuclei" (N), and semicrystalline material, in the form described earlier, grows around nuclei to form what is referred to as "spherulites" (S). Spherulites, which can generally be observed by polarized optical microscopy, eventually meet and the crystallization process is soon completed. The last polymeric chains involved may become part of two adjacent spherulites and thus contribute to the formation of inter-spherulitic links, which play a role similar to interlamellar links in assuring the cohesion of the material.

Crystallization is a time-dependent process and several factors affect not only the speed at which it takes place (kinetics), but also the resulting morphology which can

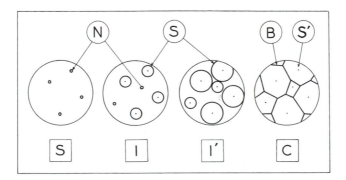

Figure 2.9 · **Crystallization process** · [S] Start; [I] First intermediate stage; [I′] Second intermediate stage; [C] Completion; (N) Nucleus; (S) Growing spherulite; (S′) Fully grown spherulite; (B) Interspherulitic boundary

be studied by suitable techniques. Figure 2.10 illustrates of the different morphologies that may be found in the same polymer. A coarse morphology [C] (few large spherulites) is normally associated with slow cooling and a fine morphology [F] (many small spherulites) is associated with fast cooling. Generally, the former morphology gives a stiffer but more brittle and less transparent material.

Several quantitative ways of characterizing the degree of crystallinity of semicrystalline polymers can be used and the simplest one is briefly presented here. It is based on the not quite realistic hypothesis (assumption) that the semicrystalline polymer consists of two distinct phases (regions); a purely amorphous phase (subscript a) with a low density d_a and a purely crystalline phase (subscript c) with a high density d_c. A mass balance shows that the volume fraction of the purely crystalline phase [called here the "degree of crystallinity" (DC)] is proportional to the easily measured density d of a sample, and the relationship is shown schematically in convenient graphical form in Figure 2.11. The densities d_a and d_c for DC = 0 (or 0%) and DC = 1 (or 100%), respectively, have been reported for many polymers.

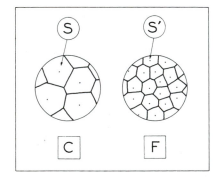

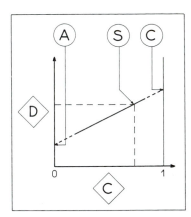

Fig. 2.10   Fig. 2.11

Figure 2.10 · **Spherulitic morphologies** · [C] Coarse morphology; [F] Fine morphology; (S) Large spherulite; (S′) Small spherulite

Figure 2.11 · **Crystallinity/density relationship** · [D] Density; [C] Degree of crystallinity; (A) Purely amorphous; (S) Semi-Crystalline; (C) Purely crystalline

Crystallization does not always take place exactly as described above, when the melt is under stress or deformation while crystallizing (nonquiescent crystallization); spherulites may not be evident and other features (shishkebab, etc.) may be present. Also the process and morphology of crystallization may also be affected by additives, such as nucleating agents or plasticizers.

Specific examples of commercially important crystallizing polymers will be discussed in Chapter 3 (sections on thermoplastics and polymeric fibers).

2.5.1   Liquid Crystal Polymers (LCP)

A number of polymers with outstanding mechanical and thermal properties have been introduced relatively recently, which possess molecular order of a kind different from that found in conventional crystallizing polymers. They are generally referred to as "liquid crystal polymers" (LCP).

While molecules in liquids are normally disordered, certain low-molecular-weight liquids have been known to form ordered regions under certain conditions, and this characteristic is involved in the operation of liquid crystal displays (LCD) in electronic devices.

Polymeric liquid crystals are associated with polymeric chains that are basically stiff (rigid), most commonly as a result of the presence of aromatic (phenyl, etc.) rings and include aromatic polyamides and polyesters.

Liquid-crystal-forming polymers are divided into lyotropic and thermotropic types. In lyotropic types, liquid crystal formation involves a solution of the polymer in a suitable solvent; products made by such "wet" processing are most commonly fibers. The first commercial liquid crystal polymer, Kevlar (du Pont), an aromatic polyamide, corresponds to this type. In thermotropic types, liquid crystal formation simply involves cooling of the melt, and "dry" processing, similar to that of conventional thermoplastics is possible, if the thermal stability is sufficient; Exxcel (Carborundum), Xydar (Dartco) and Vectra (Celanese), all aromatic polyesters, are examples of early commercial thermotropic LCPs.

If a thermotropic-type liquid-crystal-forming polymer is cooled from a molten state (disordered, potentially clear liquid), it undergoes a transition around T_e when liquid crystals (mesophase) form within the melt that involve a high degree of molecular order (anisotropy) and the melt becomes cloudy (opalescent). Several types of liquid crystals are reported (nematic, smectic, and chlolesteric). The nematic type (NLC) appears to be the most common. Its domains are thought to consist of stacks of parallel straight (extended, rod-like) molecules or molecular segments (Fig. 2.12) with low intermolecular attractions. These fiber-like domains can easily be globally oriented in the same direction, particularly in the presence of an elongational flow field in a processing operation.

Further cooling leads to solidification of the material, through the development of intermolecular attractions (at a temperature T_m), with the crystalline state reported to involve very small crystals. Liquid crystal polymers are also reported to have a detectable glass transition temperature T_g. Representative characteristic temperatures for aromatic polyester LCPs are $T_g \approx 100°C$ ($\approx 200°F$) and $T_m > 200°C$ ($\approx 400°F$). Two very notable features associated with liquid crystal polymers are a very low viscosity in the region (T_m - T_e) and a very small contraction (shrinkage) on solidification; these, in addition to high temperature and chemical resistance, make them very suitable for the production of small precision parts for demanding applications.

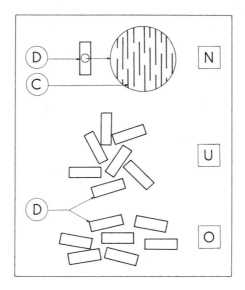

Figure 2.12 · **Liquid crystal polymer morphology** · [N] Nematic mesophase; [U] Unoriented domains; [O] Oriented domains; (D) Domain; (C) Polymeric molecule

The mechanical properties of highly oriented liquid crystal polymers in the direction of molecular orientation are outstanding, ranging from a modulus of about 15 GPa ($\approx$ 2 Mpsi) and a tensile strength of about 200 MPa ($\approx$ 30 kpsi) for a molded sample to a modulus of about 100 GPA ($\approx$ 15 Mpsi) and a tensile strength of about 350 MPa ($\approx$ 50 kpsi) for a fiber. Examples of commercial polyester-based liquid crystal polymers (LCP) are given in Appendix 3.

2.6   CROSS-LINKING AND MOLECULAR NETWORKS

Up to this point, a polymer has been viewed as a collection of individual (independent) polymeric chains with chemical bonds found only within each chain (intramolecular chemical bonds).   The basically nonpermanent physical-chemical interactions between chains are relatively weak and diminish or vanish with increasing temperature to the point where individual chains can move fairly freely relative to each other over long distances, a characteristic of the fluid-like state.   This type of polymer is referred to as a "thermoplastic," or sometimes as a "linear polymer," and specific commercial thermoplastics are discussed in a subsequent chapter.

Another class of polymeric materials exists where, instead of individual polymeric chains, the whole material consists of polymeric sections that are fully interconnected through chemical bonds to form what is referred to here as a "three-dimensional molecular network," as illustrated in Figure 2.13.

If relatively few repeat units are involved in the polymeric section (I) (interlink chain) between interconnections (C) (interchain links), the network is termed "tight" or "dense" [T]; in the opposite case, one talks about loose or light network [L] (Fig. 2.14).   The rigidity of a network polymer depends on the nature of the repeat units involved and is affected by temperature, but generally tight networks correspond to stiffer materials, while loose networks are more likely to be associated with rubbery materials.   In all cases, network polymers cannot be found in a fluid-like state.

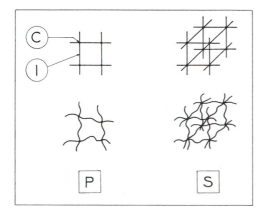

Fig. 2.13

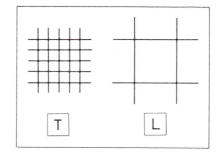

Fig. 2.14

Figure 2.13 · **Polymeric molecular networks** · [P] Plane representation; [S] 3-D representation; (C) Interchain link (crosslink); (I) Interlink chain

Figure 2.14 · **Network density** · [T] Tight; [L] Loose

There are two basic mechanisms for forming network polymer. The first mechanism, referred to here as the "two-step network formation," first involves the polymerization [P] of a monomer (or monomers) (M) to individual (independent) fully polymeric chains (P) and the subsequent introduction of chemical bonds between points of the initial polymeric chains (Fig. 2.15). These chemical interchain links (C) will be referred to as "chemical cross-links" and, the second step, as "cross-linking" [C]. The networks formed by this mechanism are generally loose networks with rubber-like properties. This mechanism has constituted the basis of the conventional rubber industry where terms such as "vulcanization" or "curing" are used for the reactions which correspond to cross-linking. Vulcanizable rubbers and their processing will be discussed further in Chapter 3. Suitable chemicals and/or energy sources are used to form the chemical cross-links.

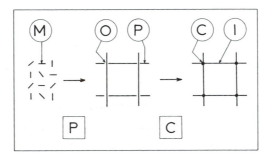

Figure 2.15 · **Two-step network formation** · [P] Polymerization step; [C] Crosslinking step; (M) Monomer; (O) Chain overlap; (P) Polymeric chain; (C) Crosslink; (I) Interlink chain

The second mechanism, referred to here as the "direct network formation," generally implies monomer molecules or slightly polymerized prepolymer molecules that are capable of simultaneously forming polymeric sections and connecting them in network fashion (Fig. 2.16). Network polymers corresponding to this mechanism tend to have

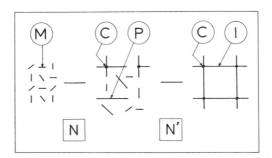

Figure 2.16 · **Direct network formation** · [N] Early stage; [N′] Later stage; (M) Monomer; (C) Crosslink; (P) Polymeric chain; (I) Interlink chain

tighter networks and, consequently, behave as rigid solids. The mechanism corresponds primarily to the processing of thermosetting resins into thermosets, which will be discussed further in Chapter 3.

All network polymers are the result of a physically irreversible process and no physical change can return the materials to a state resembling the initial state and, in particular, to a fluid-like state. Chemical processes that could destroy the cross-links or interchain links would probably cut the interlink chains as well and would have no real practical value.

Cross-linked gels, such as polyacrylamide gels, are three- dimensional polymeric networks swollen by a solvent.

2.6.1   Interpenetrating Polymeric Networks (IPN)

A number of commercial polymeric systems claiming to use the so-called interpenetrating network (IPN) technology have appeared, and many modified conventional polymers may be based on such technology.

As discussed in the section on blends and alloys, when macromolecules of two distinct types are mixed, the resulting mixture rarely involves the extent of dispersion at the molecular level represented in Figure 2.17 [O], and relatively large separate phases (domains) tend to form in a manner that is dependent on processing conditions.

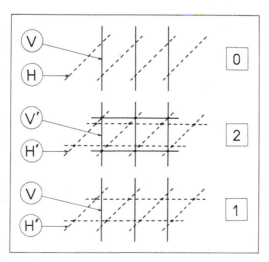

Figure 2.17 · **Interpenetrating polymeric networks** (IPN) · [O] No network; [2] Full IPN; [1] Semi IPN; (H) First type macromolecule; (H′) First type network; (V) Second type marcromolecule; (V′) Second type network

One way to stabilize the molecular dispersion of distinct macromolecules is to cross-link each type in the configuration illustrated in Figure 2.17 [2], forming two interpenetrating (interwoven, intertwined, interlocked) networks. Such configuration is reminiscent of the arrangement of the flexible organic phase and the rigid inorganic phase in natural sponges before the latter is removed, and it is generally referred to as "full IPN" or simply "IPN." A situation where only one polymer is present as a network is illustrated in Figure 2.17 [1] and often referred to as "semi (pseudo)-IPN" or "SIPN." While chemical networks involve stable chemical bonds or cross-links, physical networks can sometimes be formed that disappear at high temperatures. In the first case, the polymeric system is basically of the thermoset type, while thermoplastics can result if physical networks are involved.

A full IPN system can be formed by the simultaneous formation of the two networks or by sequential formation, with one network formed first and a monomer then added and, subsequently, polymerized and cross-linked.

Commercial IPN or SIPN systems cannot always clearly be associated with the simple categories discussed above, however.

Many IPN-related systems are commercially available. Some involve silicone networks in combination with thermoplastics (PA, PET, PBT, PP, PMO, etc.), conventional elastomers (EPDM, ethylene-acrylate, EVA, etc.), thermoplastic elastomers (TPE) or thermosets (polyurethanes). Others involve urethanes combined with acrylics, epoxy or polyester resins, PS, etc., and in some cases, three-component systems. Isocyanates and dicyanates have been combined with acrylics, PC, PESU, and polyester carbonates. Epoxy resins are used with PSU, PESU, and PEI. Thermoplastic elastomers (TPE) are associated with thermoplastics such as PA, PMO and polyurethanes (TPU).

2.7 COPOLYMERS

When a monomer (or monomers) used in a polymerization process corresponds to a single repeat unit in the polymer chain, the resulting polymer is referred to as a homopolymer.

It is sometimes possible, although not generally as easy as one might think, to polymerize two or more monomers corresponding to different repeat units and to have these different repeat units incorporated in the same polymeric chain. The material corresponding to such mixed structure is referred to as a "copolymer."

The mechanism of copolymerization and the resulting structure are not as simple as they might appear and several situations that may arise and that illustrate the complexity of the problem, are described below.

Monomers corresponding to repeat units A and B (squares and circles, respectively, in Fig. 2.18) are considered. Corresponding homopolymers, denoted here PA and PB, are sketched as [H]; copolymers are denoted here P(A-B). In all examples shown, it has been assumed here that comparable numbers of A and B repeat units are involved in each copolymer.

The first copolymer type [R] features repeat units A and B randomly distributed along the chain, for instance, as a result of a random (statistical) incorporation of A or B to a growing chain. The resulting structure is called a "random copolymer" and denoted here "P(A-B)$_r$." The lack of a regular repetition of A or B repeat units may have important consequences. Characteristic properties of PA or PB may not be found in P(A-B)$_r$. A classical example is that of ethylene and propylene, where both

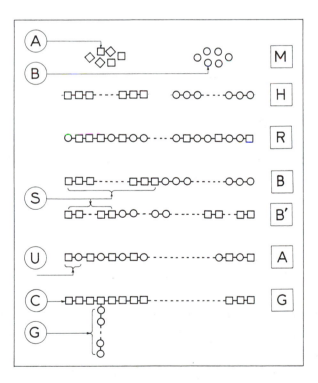

Figure 2.18 · **Copolymer structures** · [M] Monomers; [H] Homopolymers; [R] Random copolymer; [B] Di-block copolymer; [B'] Multi-block copolymer; [A] Alternating Copolymer; [G] Grafted polymer; (A) Type-A monomer; (B) Type-B monomer; (S) Segment (block); (U) Repeat unit; (C) A-backbone; (G) B-graft

homopolymers are of the crystallizing type, giving solid plastics at ambient temperature, while a 50/50 random copolymer does not crystallize and behaves as a rubber (ethylene-propylene rubber).

The second type ([B] or [B']) features relatively long segments (blocks) of repeat units A and repeat units B that are attached to form the chain. This corresponds to "block or segmented copolymers," denoted "P(A-B)$_b$." Each block is sufficiently long to impart to the copolymer the characteristics of the corresponding homopolymer, and the overall behavior is that of a mixture, but one where the components are extremely well dispersed (distributed) down to the molecular level. Type [B] or [B'] could result, in principle, from a sequential (one at a time) addition of the monomers to the reactor.

The third type ([A]) corresponds to regularly alternating **A** and **B** repeat units. It is clear that this can be viewed as a homopolymer whose repeat unit is **A-B** and the properties are likely to be characteristic of a homopolymer. "Alternating copolymers" are denoted here "P(A-B)$_a$."

There are a number of techniques used to determine the fine structure of copolymers. The examination of the effect of temperature on certain physical properties, in particular, can be helpful.

Controlled copolymerization, as difficult as it is, provides almost endless possibilities of slightly or drastically modifying the properties of conventional polymers. A majority of commercial polymers feature at least small amounts of a so-called comonomer that can be viewed as a modifier rather than a full-fledged component. Many commercial polymers contain comparable amounts of two or more comonomers. The term "terpolymer" is sometimes used when three repeat units are involved.

Many specific examples of copolymers will be discussed throughout Chapter 3. A related mode of polymer modification ([G] in Fig. 2.18) involves the attachment to a polymeric chain **A** of segments (blocks) **B** referred to as "grafts." The main backbone chain consisting of **A** repeat units is not modified. Such graft copolymers, denoted here "P(A-B)$_g$," are normally produced in two stages, with homopolymer PA chains being first polymerized and grafts being subsequently polymerized from or attached to sites along the backbone. This technique allows, in particular, the incorporation of small amounts of a modifying polymer in a perfectly dispersed manner that cannot be subsequently altered through processing stages. It has been used, for instance, for the rubber modification of brittle plastics; an interesting advantage of grafting over regular copolymerization, in this case, is that rubber blocks, often susceptible to chemical attack and rupture (chain scission), by not being part of the backbone, would not be responsible for a reduction of molecular weight of the plastic chains. Grafts with polar characteristics have also been used to enhance the adhesion of non-polar polymers to substrates. Since grafts are similar to branches, considerations of branch length and frequency discussed earlier may be applicable.

A number of homopolymers are chemically modified through the replacement of a relatively small number of atoms (usually hydrogen atoms) by other atoms or groups of atoms. The replacement (substitution) does not affect all repeat units and may even affect different repeat units to a different extent. The modified polymer, thus, may no longer have a single, uniquely defined repeat unit (homopolymer) or two distinct repeat units (copolymer). In addition to the term "modified polymer," the expression "polymer derivative" is sometimes used. Examples include modified polyethylenes (CPE and CSPE) and polyvinylchloride (CPVC) or cellulose derivatives (CN, CA, CAP, CAB, EC) as discussed in Chapter 3.

2.8 POLYALLOYS

In the search for polymeric materials closely suited to the wide range of applications, it is natural to consider mixtures of the relatively large but limited number of commercially important homopolymers or copolymers. Cost, properties, and processability are major considerations in the assessment of potential benefits. Mixtures are defined here as combinations of materials not involving chemical reactions (i.e., no formation or rupture of chemical bonds).

It is essential to realize that mixing two polymers to a fine level is seldom easy. Many pairs of polymers are almost impossible to mix or disperse into one another, and attempts to do so yield, at best, rather useless coarse aggregates with little or no cohesion between phases. Polystyrene and polypropylene, for example, are reputed to behave in this manner. Such pairs of polymers are often referred to as "incompatible."

A relatively limited number of pairs of polymers are miscible, that is, capable of forming potentially useful homogeneous (one-phase) mixtures in which molecules of the two types are really mixed, down to the molecular level. This implies a high level of intermolecular interaction related to the chemical structure of the repeat units involved. Such mixtures are in many ways analogous to solutions of simple liquids, and factors such as temperature or concentration can play a role in the "solubility." Classical examples include polyvinylchloride and nitrile rubber; the homogeneous mixture is denoted here "M(PVC/NBR)" or "polyphenylene oxide" and "polystyrene M(PPO/PS)." Other cited examples are given in Appendix 2.

Miscibility or immiscibility of polymers, as in the case of low-molecular-weight compounds, is commonly discussed in scientific terms through thermodynamic considerations.

A third class of pairs of polymers behave in a somewhat intermediate manner. Under certain conditions, a dispersion of small particles (domains) of one of the polymers into a matrix of the other polymer, and sometimes an interpenetrating arrangement of two phases, can be achieved where the combination of a reasonable interaction between phases (cohesion or adhesion at the interface or boundary) and a uniform dispersion yield a potentially useful material. The polymers in such pairs are said to be compatible.

Miscible and compatible pairs are referred to here as "homogeneous" (one-phase) and "heterogeneous" (two-phase) polyalloys, respectively, or "polyalloys," in general, and denoted here "A(PA/PB)." The term polyblends is also used with the same general meaning. Intermediate polyalloys can be found where there are identifiable separate (discrete) regions of each constituent, but the interfacial zone, involving a high degree of molecular interaction and mixing, forms a loosely defined boundary (diffuse interface).

For heterogeneous polyalloys, the arrangement in space (structure) of the discrete regions (P) (domains) in the continuous matrix (M) often has a major effect on the properties. In discussing the structure, it is convenient (see Fig. 2.19) to distinguish between the dispersion [D] (fine to coarse) of the domains, which reflects primarily their size and number and their distribution [D'] [good to poor (agglomerates)] which, in turn, reflects the uniformity throughout a sample. A number of direct and indirect

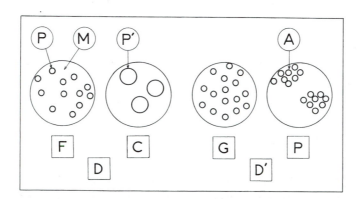

Figure 2.19 · **Phase dispersion and distribution** · [D] Dispersion; [F] Fine dispersion; [C] Coarse dispersion; [D'] Distribution; [G] Good distribution; [P] Poor distribution; (M) Matrix (first phase); (P) Small particles (second phase); (P') Large particles (second phase)

methods are available to characterize the structure of heterogeneous polyalloys. Such considerations also apply to the case of fillers.

The structure is determined partly by the nature of the component polymers and partly by the blending procedure and conditions, as well as the final processing.

Four basic techniques are used to achieve a degree of dispersion of the molecules or the discrete phase prior to the melt processing stage.

Solution blending, normally economically feasible only if each polymer is readily available in solution form, as a result of the polymerization process, for example, favors good mixing at the molecular level.

Emulsion blending requires that the components be in emulsion (latex) form as a result of emulsion polymerization. In a latex, very small polymer particles are suspended in, and kept from coalescing by, soapy water (as in latex paints). Mixing of latexes of different polymers and subsequent removal of the water can lead to an excellent dispersion and distribution of the discrete phase. Powder dry blending achieves good initial distribution of the materials, but normally the powder particle size is still larger than the final desired size of the discrete domains.

Pellet dry blending only gives a very coarse initial dispersion. In the case of dry blended polymers, in particular, the final alloy structure is achieved only after the melt processing stage. The flow (rheological) properties of the components, which are strong functions of the speed of deformation, and the temperature play a major role in the formation of the final structure.

It was pointed out earlier that few polymer pairs are readily miscible (homogeneous polyalloys) or even compatible (heterogeneous polyalloys). The development of methods of increasing the compatibility of pairs has lead to the recent proliferation of commercial polyalloys. Copolymerization or grafting of one or both components, with segments of the other component, or coblending with a polymer compatible with both major components (compatibilizer), are among the methods used.

There is a certain parallel between random copolymers and homogeneous polyalloys, on one hand, and block copolymers and heterogeneous polyalloys, on the other hand.

2.9 PLASTICIZERS

The primary role of a plasticizer, as the name indicates, is to reduce the rigidity (stiffness) of a plastic, that is, to render it more flexible. Polyvinylchloride (PVC), for which plasticizers are widely used, can thus be obtained in a wide range of stiffnesses from rigid and somewhat brittle types, to very flexible rubber-like types.

Low cost plasticizing additives, added mainly to reduce the cost of compounds when the level of stiffness is not important, are sometimes referred to as "extenders." They are sometimes used in conjunction with low-cost fillers, discussed subsequently, which play a stiffening role, compensating the softening (plasticizing) role of the extender.

Plasticizers are normally relatively small molecules that are sufficiently compatible with the polymer molecules to penetrate them, much as a solvent would. They form nonchemical attractions (bonds) with polymeric molecules of varying strength or permanence, often associated with polarity. Highly compatible plasticizers remain "locked in," while less compatible ones may gradually migrate towards the surface and cause exudation or blooming; the term "blooming," however, is more commonly used to describe the surface appearance of solid additives.

Sometimes the incorporation of small levels of a primary, very compatible plasticizer allows the addition of relatively large amounts of a less compatible secondary plasticizer, sometimes referred to also as an "extender."

Plasticizers often play a so-called lubricating role in the processing of thermoplastics, largely through a reduction in viscosity, and may be referred to as "internal lubricants."

The number of commercial plasticizers is extremely large and recourse to the experience of polymer manufacturers and plasticizers suppliers is advisable to obtain best results at optimum cost.

Specific chemicals are often referred to by abbreviations, and examples are given below for a variety of classes of plasticizers.

Esters form the largest class and are of the aliphatic (alkyl) or aromatic (aryl) types. Phthalates are esters of difunctional phthalic acid; examples include di-2-ethyl hexyl (octyl) phthalate (DOP), dibutyl phthalate (DBP), butyl benzyl phthalate (BBP), and di phenyl phthalate (DPP), as well as DINP, DIDP, DIOP, DUP, DTDP, DCHP, DMP, DMEP, DOTP, etc. Phosphates are esters of trifunctional phosphoric acid and generally also play a flame retardant role; they include tributoxy ethyl phosphate, tricresyl phosphate (TCP), triphenyl phosphate (TPP) and isodecyl diphenyl phosphate. Adipates are esters of adipic acid and are generally suitable for food contact; they include di-2-ethyl hexyl (octyl) adipate (DOA), as well as DIOA, DIBA, DBEA, DBEEA, DIDA, and NODA. Trimellitates include tri-2-ethyl hexyl (octyl) trimellitate (TOTM). Isobutyrates include TXIB. Other esters include azelates (Z), citrates, glutarates, oleates, ricinoleates, salicylates, sebacates (S), and stearates.

Epoxy derivatives are described as epoxy resins or epoxidized soybean, linseed, or tall oil esters. Low-molecular-weight polyesters include polyethylene adipate and alkyl sulfonyl ester of phenol. Amide-based plasticizers, such as sulfonamides, lauramides, and acetoacetamilide, include n-ethyl o-toluene and p-toluene sulfonamide. Chlorinated paraffin waxes also derive good flame retardancy from the presence of chlorine (Cl) and serve primarily as extenders. Aromatic petroleum products, such as mineral or tar oils, also serve primarily as extenders. Some regular polymers can play a strong plasticizing role; the mechanism is really similar to that concerning polymer alloys. This appears to be the case for ethylene-vinyl acetate (EVA) copolymer and polyisobutylene (PIB).

As a historic note, it should be noted that one of the earliest commercial applications of synthetic plastics (Celluloid) rested on the use of camphor as a plasticizer for cellulose nitrate in the fabrication of billiard balls.

It is noteworthy that plasticizers are used primarily with noncrystallizing polymers; a direct manifestation of their presence is a lowering of the glass transition temperature zone. Their use in crystallizing polymers tends to interfere with the crystallization process.

2.10 FILLERS, REINFORCEMENTS

The intrinsic stiffness of bulk polymers in the glassy state, even with high degrees of crystallinity, is relatively low compared to that of most inorganic solids [typically the modulus of elasticity E is below about 3.5 GPa ($\approx$ 0.5 Mpsi) for polymers, compared to a range of about 70-200 GPa ($\approx$ 10-30 Mpsi) for inorganic solids].

Stiff inorganic materials can often be combined with polymeric materials in the form of composite systems, where the polymeric material forms a continuous phase (matrix) into which the inorganic material is dispersed as a discrete phase. The discrete inorganic components of such composite systems can be classified, according to their shape, into particles [P] (spheres, cubes or similar shapes), short fibers [F] and disks [D] (platelets, flakes), as shown in Figure 2.20, and for very long elements (Fig. 2.21), as continuous fibers [F] or tapes [T].

Inorganic components are normally referred to as "nonreinforcing fillers," or simply "fillers," if their role is primarily to increase the stiffness of the polymeric material, sometimes with an associated cost advantage. In cases where they have a favorable effect on some aspects of the mechanical resistance (strength), they tend to be referred to as "reinforcing fillers" or "reinforcements."

Fillers and reinforcements generally possess such chemical and temperature resistance that they are unaffected by processing with either reactive or thermoplastic polymeric systems.

The degree of adhesion between the polymeric matrix and the discrete components often determines the difference between mere filling and true reinforcing. Discrete components are often surface-treated with chemical coupling agents to enhance adhesion. Organo-silanes, titanates and zirconates are often used as coupling agents.

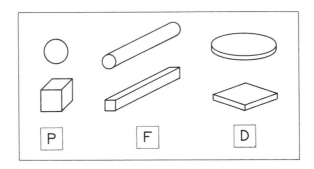

Figure 2.20 · **Discontinuous filler/reinforcement shapes** · [P] Particle; [F] Short fiber; [D] Disk

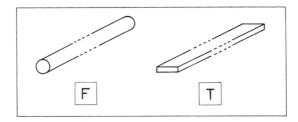

Figure 2.21 · **Continuous reinforcement shapes;** [F] Long fiber; [T] Tape

2.10.1   Particle Class

Fillers and reinforcements primarily in the particle class include calcium carbonate, silica, kaolin, talc, alumina trihydrate, feldspar, baryte, calcium sulfate solid and hollow spheres of glass or other ceramic and carbon black.

Calcium carbonate ($CaCO_3$) is a widely used powdery filler that is generally inexpensive and nonreinforcing. It is available in the so-called natural form as ground limestone in a range of particle sizes down to about 1 μm for fine and ultrafine grades. Another form is the result of physical-chemical processing and is referred to as "precipitated or synthetic calcite" or "aragonite." Its particle size can be as low as 0.1 μm. Treated grades are available for improved adhesion to matrices or reduced water absorption.

Silica (SiO$_2$) is an irregular, sphere-like, generally inexpensive filler with some grades having good reinforcing properties. It is available in amorphous or crystalline (quartz) form and is referred to as "natural" when directly extracted from deposits and just "physically processed," or as "manufactured or synthetic" when subjected to physical-chemical processing. Surface-treated grades are common and crystalline forms, in particular, are quite abrasive.

Kaolin, the major component of clays, basically involves alumina silicates. Drying or calcination lead to solid kaolin or kaolinite or calcined (dehydroxylated or anhydrous) kaolin. Kaolin particles are platelet-shaped (platy) and representative sizes range from 1 to 10 μm.

Talc is a hydrated magnesium silicate primarily used in a platelet-shaped form of sufficiently high aspect ratio to give significant reinforcing properties, particularly with surface-treated grades. This filler has low abrasive effects. Fiber-shaped varieties also exist.

Alumina trihydrate (ATH) is used primarily for its flame-retardant role, but the relatively high loadings required cause it to act as a filler as well.

Feldspar is an anhydrous alkali-aluminum silicate normally of relatively large particle size (20-50 μm). Its transparency and matched index of refraction allows its use with transparent plastics to produce reasonably transparent compounds.

Ground *baryte* (barium sulfate) is a high-density filler that finds special use in sound-deadening compounds.

Anhydrous *calcium sulfate* is offered as a special purpose filler.

Solid glass spheres (beads), also referred to as "microspheres," are available in a wide range of dimensions (5-1000 μm). Their smooth shapes reduce abrasive and viscosity effects, but their manufacturing process tends to make them more expensive than many other sphere-like fillers. Excellent surface treatments are available for enhanced adhesion to polymers.

A disadvantage of most inorganic fillers is their high density compared to that of polymer matrices. Technologies have been developed to produce, at reasonable costs, *hollow glass spheres* (balloons, bubbles) that can have densities as low as 0.15 g/cm^3 ($\approx$ 9 lb/ft^3). For a given external diameter (range 10-500 μm) the density is, of course, a function of the wall thickness, which, in turn, affects the mechanical resistance (particularly to crushing) of the hollow spheres. Low density hollow glass spheres are primarily used in polymers whose processing does not involve high viscosities and high pressures, such as catalyst-activated thermosets. Polymers filled with hollow glass spheres contain entrapped gas, which makes them comparable to foams; the word "syntactic foam," is sometimes used for such cellular materials. Besides density gains, stiffness as well as thermal and acoustical insulation can be significantly improved.

Ceramic-type materials such as fly-ash, a by-product of coal combustion, and temperature resistant polymers, such as phenolics, have been made into solid or hollow spheres.

Carbon black is widely used as a reinforcing filler in rubbers and as a pigment, electrically-conductive filler or shield against UV radiation in plastics. The various reinforcing grades (thermal, furnace or channel) result from the incomplete combustion of hydrocarbons. The small particles (0.03-0.30 μm) have a porous structure and form good bonds with rubbers.

2.10.2   Fiber Class

Fillers and reinforcements in the fiber class include glass fibers, carbon and graphite fibers, metal fibers, asbestos, whiskers and polymeric fibers.

Glass fibers have found very extensive use in plastics, most commonly in continuous form in catalyst-activated thermosetting resins and, in short form, in thermoplastics.

Glass fibers are produced by extruding a glass melt through small orifices, rapidly pulling and, subsequently, cooling the emerging filament. Individual fibers are called monofilaments and commonly have diameters around 10 μm.

In order to protect glass monofilaments from detrimental abrasion, to promote the subsequent adhesion of the polymer to the glass and to help in the handling of strands, a so-called size is applied in liquid form that contains, in particular, the lubricant, the chemical coupling agent and the binder.

Different types of glass are used to make glass fibers for polymer reinforcement. The "E" type (originally developed for electrical purposes) is the least expensive and most common and consists primarily of silica (SiO_2), alumina (Al_2O_3), and lime (CaO). An "S" type is used for advanced composites, and other types (C, etc.) are used for special purposes.

Hundreds of monofilaments spun together form a strand. Groups of tens of strands are referred to as "tows," "yarns," or "rovings," generally untwisted and characterized by their weight-per-unit length. Twisted (spun) or untwisted yarn or roving can be woven into flexible fabrics (cloths) in a variety of patterns to suit reinforcing needs. Fabrics are characterized by their pattern and their weight-per-unit area. Conventional woven fabrics correspond to "biaxial" reinforcement (0-90°). Specially woven fabrics have been introduced that correspond to "triaxial" reinforcement

(0-60-120°). Recently, nonwoven fabric-like reinforcing material has been introduced where rovings are held in place by a stitching method using a polymeric thread. It is the very small diameter of the monofilaments that permits the flexibility of glass strands and fabrics in spite of the brittleness of glass itself. Strands or rovings can be cut into short lengths (3-50 mm or 1/8 to 2 in), and these chopped strands can be dispersed in thermoplastic or thermosetting polymers.

With the use of suitable resin binders, long chopped strands or continuous strands can be made into nonwoven mats that are somewhat intermediates between loose chopped strands and woven fabrics.

Glass fibers can also be reduced to short lengths by a milling procedure, owing to the brittle nature of glass. Milled fibers have a wide distribution of lengths (0.1-5 mm or 1/64-1/4 in) but can be relatively inexpensive and easy to disperse in polymers.

The elastic modulus of glass is about 70 GPa ($\approx$ 10 Mpsi); the tensile strength of filaments can be in the range 1700-3500 MPa ($\approx$ 250-500 kpsi) and the density is about 2.5 g/cm^3.

Even though *carbon* and *graphite* fibers were developed in the late 1950s, their high cost long restricted their use to so-called advanced composites primarily for military or aerospace applications. Their price is now more affordable and their market is rapidly growing.

The distinction between carbon and graphite fibers is not always clear and producers or users sometimes seem to use the names interchangeably. In principle, a graphitic structure has carbon atoms arranged in a characteristic layered structure in which interplane shear or sliding is easy; this is associated with the well-known dry-lubricating properties of graphite powder. In reinforcing fibers, of course, this motion must be restricted and it corresponds to high orientation of the planes achieved during the manufacture. The arrangement of carbon atoms in the so-called carbon fibers appears to be quite different.

In general, carbon or graphite monofilaments are prepared by rather complex processes involving an organic, carbon-rich filamentary material, referred to as the "precursor," which is subjected to combinations of stretching and carbonization in inert atmospheres at high temperatures. The surface of the filaments is often subsequently oxidized to promote adhesion to polymeric matrices. Three types of precursors have been used primarily and resulting fibers are reported to have distinct properties.

Rayon-based fibers are more readily associated with graphite fibers; the graphite structure, being reminiscent of the structure of cellulose-derived rayon, tend to have high modulus but a relatively low elongation at break or tensile strength. Polyacrylonitrile (PAN)-based fibers are considered high- strength fiber; they are also the most expensive. Petroleum pitch-based fibers are less costly and considered high-stiffness fibers.

Much like glass fibers, carbon and graphite fibers are supplied in a variety of forms with monofilament diameters in the range 5-10 μm. Their high rigidity and relatively low elongation at break, however, does not generally give rovings and fabrics as flexible as corresponding glass products.

Carbon and graphite fibers are particularly attractive for their high stiffness and low density, and in certain applications their thermal or electrical conductivity, x-ray transparency, and their low abrasive characteristics are advantageous.

The elastic modulus of carbon and graphite fibers is in the range 200-700 GPa ($\approx$ 30-100 Mpsi); the tensile strength is in the range 2000-5000 MPa (300-700 kpsi) and the density is about 1.75 g/cm^3.

Metal wires have long been used for cables, but the technology of small diameter continuous filaments suitable for polymer reinforcement is relatively recent, and its first major successful application was in tire cords. A number of metals have now been made into filaments (steel, tungsten, molybdenum, etc.), but they have found little use in polymers, partly because of their high density and the relatively large diameter that is achievable.

The elastic modulus of steel is about 200 GPa ($\approx$ 30 Mpsi); a representative value of the tensile strength is about 2500 MPa ($\approx$ 350 kpsi), and the density is about 8 g/cm^3.

Short stainless steel fibers are being used, primarily for their electrical conductivity, in electromagnetic interference (EMI) shielding.

Boron (B) continuous fibers received considerable attention for their very specialized use in early advanced aeronautic or aerospace applications.

Asbestos is a well-known, naturally occurring fibrous mineral with a long history of use as a heat-resistant reinforcement in brake linings, for example. Recent concern with the safety of its handling have, perhaps temporarily, reduced its role. Various types (chrysotile, crocidolite, actinolite, etc.) and various grades exist that are generally in the form of short fibers.

Potassium titanate short fibers are commercially used for the reinforcement of thermoplastics.

Processed mineral fibers are low-cost short fibers made from ceramic (vitreous, glassy)-type slags, which are by-products of coal combustion-related processes.

The so-called refractory or ceramic "whiskers" received much attention in the 1950s and 1960s for their outstanding mechanical properties. They are, in general, short, fiber-shaped, defect-free single crystals based on carbon and oxides, nitrides, or carbides of various metals, such as aluminum (Al), beryllium (Be), boron (B), magnesium (Mg), and silicium (Si). Sapphire (Al_2O_3), silicon carbide, silicon nitride, aluminum nitride, boron carbide, and magnesium oxide, as well as graphite and silicon, are examples. Their price has largely kept them from significantly penetrating the plastics reinforcement field.

A number of polymeric fibers are used for reinforcement. They include conventional polyamide and polyester fibers (aliphatic polyamides and polyethylene terephthalate) and high performance fibers such as aramid fibers (aromatic polyamides, PEEK fibers (polyetheretherketone), and even specially-oriented (extended chain) polyethylene. The corresponding polymers are discussed in Chapter 3.

2.10.3   Disk Class

Fillers and reinforcements primarily in the disk class include mica, glass flakes, and aluminum flakes.

Naturally occurring micas have a variety of chemical compositions and morphologies. Three major types are commercially available for use in polymers: wollastonite, muscovite, and phlogopite. Mica particles are sometimes fiber-shaped, but more commonly platelet or flake-shaped, and their aspect ratio (width-to-thickness ratio) plays an important role in reinforcement. The manufacturing process involves delamination of the raw material by wet or dry grinding and possible subsequent separation according to size and shape (aspect ratio). High aspect ratio (HAR) grades are claimed to give very good reinforcement at reasonable cost, particularly when suitable surface treatment is used.

Glass flakes, which are formed by crushing thin glass tubes, are now commercially available. The well-developed technologies of glass manufacture and glass surface treatment are likely to be positive factors in future use of this filler.

Aluminum flakes are intended primarily as conductive filler for electromagnetic interference (EMI) shielding.

2.11   MISCELLANEOUS ADDITIVES

A wide variety of additives are available to improve specific properties, but they tend to have an effect, often negative, on the other properties. Their cost and efficiency can vary widely. A combination of additives can have a synergistic (enhancing) effect or, in the opposite case, an antagonistic (reducing) effect. Important commercial additives are reviewed in this section.

2.11.1   UV Absorbers and Light Stabilizers

Light in itself would not do much direct harm to polymers, but the radiations, in particular ultraviolet (UV) radiations, tend to initiate or catalyze chemical degradation, such as oxidation, in a process often globally referred to as "photooxidation."

Among the plastics reported to be susceptible to photooxidation are polyethylene (PE), polypropylene (PP), polystyrene (PS), unsaturated polyesters, polyvinylchloride (PVC), cellulose esters (CA, CAB), acrylics and polyethylene terephthalate (PET).

Chemists attempting to elucidate the mechanisms of photooxidation, and its reduction by suitable additives often distinguish between UV absorbers (UA), which reduces the essential factor of the degradation, and light (or photooxidation) stabilizers (LS), which control its progress, although the distinction appears sometimes subtle.

There are many classes of UV absorbers (UA)/light stabilizers (LS) that are generally added in the 0.1-0.6% range. They include the following: benzophenones (primarily UA), for example: 2-hydroxy-4-dodecyloxy benzophenone (DOBP); benzotriazoles (primarily UA), such as 2-hydroxy phenyl benzotriazole (HPBT); acrylic or aryl esters (UA or LS), for example, resorcinol monobenzoate (RMB); "hindered" amines (primarily LS), such as 4-(2,2,6,6-tetramethyl piperidinyl) sebacate; metal salts or organic-metal compounds and complexes involving nickel (Ni), zinc (Zn), copper (Cu) and manganese (Mn), for example, zinc or nickel dibutyl dithiocarbamate; alkylated phenol phosphonate nickel complex. Carbon black (CB) acting as a barrier to UV radiation penetration provides good protection when its color can be tolerated.

Light stabilization is obviously important for any outdoor application of plastics, but particularly for applications associated with recently renewed efforts to harness solar energy.

2.11.2   Antioxidants

Many polymers are susceptible to oxidation, which causes either a reduction in chain length and molecular weight (chain scission), for example, in polyethylene, leading to a loss of stiffness and strength in the first case and embrittlement in the second case. Oxidation can be slow at moderate processing temperatures and its effects are then associated with aging, or quite fast at high processing temperatures, and its effects are then associated with thermal stability. Radiations or impurities such as metal traces can also initiate or catalyze oxidation (photooxidation, metal activation). Antioxidants discussed in this section represent one type of additive that can contribute to the control of oxidation in polymers.

Primary antioxidants that can be used alone are subdivided into two classes. "Hindered" phenolics of low or higher molecular weight operate through reactive OH groups and include butylated hydroxy toluene (BHT) and tetrakis [methylene 3-(3′,5′, di-t- butyl 4′ hydroxyphenyl) propionate] methane. "Hindered" secondary aryl amines operate through reactive NH groups and include substituted para phenylene diamines and diphenyl amines.

Secondary antioxidants engage in synergystic (mutually reinforcing) action with primary antioxidants but would not have a strong role alone. Phosphorus (P)-containing types include organophosphites. Sulfur (S)-containing types include thioesters, such as thiopropionate.

2.11.3   Heat Stabilizers

A form of chemical degradation involves some decomposition at processing temperatures with the evolution of corrosive or toxic chemicals. Polyvinylchloride (PVC) is a classic, and probably the most commercially important case, and the resulting hydrochloric acid (HCl) is a particularly undesirable chemical. Although other polymers require or benefit from suitable heat stabilizers, the term is generally associated with PVC heat stabilization. The quasi-synonym "thermal stabilizer" is sometimes in place of "heat stabilizer."

A majority of heat stabilizers are metal-based. Single metal types involve the following: tin (Sn) as organo-tin compounds, such as butyl tin mercaptides; antimony (Sb), for example, antimony mercaptide; and lead (Pb) in the form of phthalate, sulfate, and carbonate.

Mixed-metal types may correspond to salts and soaps such as stearates and involve the following: calcium (Ca) and zinc (Zn); barium (Ba) and cadmium (Cd); Ba, Cd, and Zn; magnesium (Mg); and aluminum (Al). Secondary or auxiliary stabilizers, such as those involving phosphorus (P) as phosphites or biphenylene diphosphonite, are also available for use with regular (primary) stabilizers.

2.11.4   Flame Retardants

The issue of flammability of polymers is difficult and not yet well understood. Practically all polymers are combustible if sufficient oxygen and heat are available, but there are great variations in the so-called fire or flame resistance measured by tests described in Chapter 4. For many applications, additives must be compounded with the most fire-prone polymers to reduce their flammability [flame retardants (FR)] or to reduce the production of smoke [smoke suppressant (SS) or reducer, inhibitor)].

The many types of flame retardants or smoke suppressants correspond to a wide variety of established or postulated mechanisms. As for most additives, certain types are particularly matched to certain polymers.

A somewhat arbitrary classification distinguishes between two types.

Mineral-based types include the following: alumina trihydrate (ATH), which dehydrates at high temperatures, liberating water and is widely used in unsaturated polyesters for its smoke suppressant role in particular; hydrated magnesium (Mg) sulfate (Epsom salt); boron (B) compounds; such as zinc or aluminum borates; magnesium (Mg) hydroxide; and antimony (tri) oxide (SbO_3).

Organic-related types feature halogens and phosphorus which appear to play a crucial role and include brominated (B) or chlorinated (Cl) aliphatic or cycloaliphatic compounds that tend to produce toxic fumes, such as decabromo diphenyl oxide; and phosphorus-based compounds, such as aromatic phosphate esters with or without halogenation, which have a tendency to be smoke generators.

2.11.5   Antimicrobials

Carbon-scavenging microorganisms, such as bacteria, fungi, and algae, can sometimes grow on the surface of polymers when temperature and humidity conditions are favorable particularly when the polymer compound offers appropriate nutrients, which are often low-molecular-weight additives. Such a situation is important in applications such as humidifiers, air-conditioning filters, or foam mattresses. Microbial growth (bacterial, fungal, algal, spores, or mildew) can be countered with a number of antimicrobial additives available as liquid solutions or in powder form.

Antimicrobials fit into three classes. The first class consists of organometallics, which include tin (Sn)-based types such as trialkyl tin compounds; arsenic (As)-based types, for example: 10,10'-oxybisphenoarsine (OBPA); and copper (Cu) and antimony (Sb)-based types, such as copper-8-quinolinolate. The second class consists of organic sulfur (thio) compounds of the captan or phaltan types. The third class consists of quaternary ammonium compounds. Chloroxylenol has also been mentioned as a suitable antimicrobial.

A number of largely equivalent terms are used for this class of additives, such as antimicrobial agents, bacteriostats, biostabilizers, biocides, fungicides, and preservatives.

2.11.6   Colorants

A major advantage of plastics over metals, for example, is that they can, in most cases, be easily made into products with attractive built-in colors, eliminating secondary finishing operations.

A number of properties and considerations are referred to when discussing colorants: tinting (tinctorial) strength; brilliance (brightness) or dullness; transparency, translucency, or opacity; dispersibility (specks, streaks); migration (bleeding, exudation, blooming, plating-out of tools); toxicity; and chemical and heat resistance; light resistance (fastness). Standard tests for the qualitative or quantitative assessment of a number of these properties will be discussed in a subsequent chapter.

Additives used to impart color to polymers are basically divided into two classes: pigments and dyes.

Pigments are finely divided or powdered solids (0.01-1 μm) that are basically insoluble in the polymer and must be well dispersed and distributed to give maximum coloring effect at the smallest possible concentration, normally less than 1%. They tend to act as nonreinforcing fillers when used in large proportions and thus reduce certain mechanical properties.

Dyes consist of relatively small molecules that are compatible with the polymer molecules, and they are, therefore, basically soluble in the polymer, becoming dispersed at a molecular level.

Pigments can be purchased in powder form or as encapsulates, which are easier to incorporate to polymer in pellet form. It is also quite common to purchase color concentrates where relatively large amounts of pigment (or sometimes dyes) have been compounded into the base polymer. The fraction of concentrate to be added to the pure resin is relatively large, and its physical form is comparable to that of the pure resins.

The pigments are either inorganic or organic. Inorganic pigments consist of two basic types. Carbon black is widely used for black coloration, but also for its radiation screening and reinforcing effect in certain grades. Metal-based pigments, which yield colors generally characteristic of the metal involved, mainly include the following types: oxides (Ti, Fe, Cr), of which white titanium oxide (Ti O_2) is an important example; sulfides (Cd, Hg, Zn); selenides (Cd); sulfates (Ba, Pb); chromates (Pb); molybdates (Pb); and titanates (Ni, Cr). Sr, Ca, Ba and Al are also involved in compounds.

Organic pigments are available in two major classes: azo type and phthalo type (e.g., copper phthalocyanine). Other classes include carbazole, perylene, and aniline types.

Dyes are generally supplied in liquid form. The active ingredient is often in solution in a solvent or oil carrier, to facilitate the incorporation into the polymer. The technique of direct feed in injection molding machines is gaining ground. Dyes are normally used to impart color to transparent plastics, such as styrenics or acrylics.

Dyes are commonly found in three classes: anthraquinone types typically used in automotive tail-lights; nigrosine types, alternatives for carbon black, and oil- or water-soluble azo types. Besides regular colorants whose purpose is just to impart color, other additives are used to produce special appearance-related effects. Fluorescent additives, usually organic dyes, impart the well-known shining effect in relative darkness when exposed to light. Phosphorescent additives, usually inorganic pigments, store light when exposed to a light source and can subsequently shine (afterglow) for a while, in darkness. Pearlescent additives can impart pearl-like sheen mainly to transparent polymers. Metallic powders, primarily aluminum and bronze, are used as an alternative to plating for metal-like appearance or for special effects.

2.11.7   Odorants

Additives are sometimes incorporated into polymers to give products a specific odor (odorants or fragrances) or to control or mask an objectionable odor (deodorants, sanitizers). Sanitizers may also have an antimicrobial role.

2.11.8   Surface-Modifying Additives

A number of additives are used primarily to modify surface (or interface) properties in a desirable manner. The objectives and the corresponding additives are introduced here by considering five distinct cases, with some types of additives playing multiple roles.

The first case involves a molten-polymer-hot-metal interface. It is often desirable to reduce the tendency of molten polymers to stick to hot-metal surfaces during processing (roll mills, extrusion sizing). Additives added to the polymers for this purpose are often referred to as "external lubricants," and their role is clearly different from that of internal lubricants, which primarily affect the viscous flow of the polymer.

External lubricants are particularly important in the PVC industry. They generally involve relatively long, nonpolar, hydrocarbon chains and can be subdivided into the following classes: fatty (carboxylic) acids, such as stearic acid; fatty acid esters such as stearates (e.g., glycerol monostearate); fatty acid alcohols; fatty acid amides or substituted amides, such as stearamide, oleamide, and crucamide (e.g., ethylene bisstearamide or bisoleamide); and fatty acid metallic salts (soaps). The metals are lead (Pb), calcium (Ca), zinc (Zn) magnesium (Mg) or Li, Na, Ba, Cd to a lesser extent, for example, lead stearate, calcium stearate; paraffin waxes of various molecular weights and melting points, either natural or manufactured types, including low-molecular-weight polyethylenes and partially oxidized varieties; silicone fluids or polymers; fluoropolymers in powder form; other polymers for special applications (polyamides (PA), polyvinyl alcohol (PVAl or PVOH); and finally proprietary specialized substances.

The second case involves a solid polymer-metal interface. This corresponds to the detachment of solidified products from metal molding surfaces, and associated additives are often referred to as "internal (mold) release agents." Substances that are applied independently to metal surfaces for the same purpose are often referred to as "external (mold) release agents," "parting agents," or "abherents" (a term opposed to "adherent").

Internal (mold) release agents are, to a large extent, indissociable from external lubricants and, to some extent, from other surface-modifying additives.

The third case involves a solid polymer-solid polymer interface. Solidified polymeric parts or products (films, in particular) often tend to stick to each other in an undesirable manner. Static electrical charges, intimate contact of smooth flexible surfaces, are some reasons for this phenomenon. Additives that reduce this sticking tendency, somewhat equivalent to the tacking tendency of fresh paints or uncured rubber, are referred to as "slip agents" or "antiblocking agents" (antiblocks).

Antistats, discussed later, tend to improve the situation. Inorganic powdered solids, such as silica or silicates, are also claimed to help, possibly by altering the surface flexibility or smoothness. Internal lubricants also play a helpful role.

There are cases where a good degree of polymer-polymer adhesion is desirable as in food wrap films. Suitable additives are referred to as "cling agents."

The fourth case involves static electricity build-up on a solid polymer surface. Static electricity buildup is often the result of friction, particularly at high speeds, and the low volume and surface conductivity of polymers normally prevent the dissipation of electric charges. Static charges can be the cause of sparks and shocks (textile, chemical industries), tend to favor the collection of dust and dirt (records), and contribute to the sticking together (blocking) of polymeric products (films and fibers).

Additives used to reduce static electricity buildup or permanency are called "antistatic agents" or "antistats."

One way of reducing static electricity buildup on polymer surfaces is to provide a conductive path through the bulk of the material, that is, to render it conductive. Large concentrations of carbon black (10-30%) can give acceptable results, which can also be achieved with lower loadings of metallic powders. These solutions are sometimes unacceptable, for instance, when thin films or transparent products are concerned. One then tries to provide a conductive path on the surface. The common way of achieving this goal is to rely on conductive water molecules, which are nearly always present, and trap them on the surface through appropriate molecules featuring water-seeking (hydrophilic) groups, as well as organic groups compatible with the polymeric molecules (surfactant or detergent-type molecules). This implies that the level of relative humidity (RH) plays a major role and the efficacy of the antistat drops as the relative humidity decreases.

Antistatic agents applied externally on products as dilute water or water/alcohol solutions are often referred to as "topical antistatic agents" or "external antistats" and cannot really be considered as additives.

Real antistatic additives (internal antistats) compounded in small amounts (0.1-0.4%) exude or bloom to the surface. They include ethoxylated fatty amines and ethoxylated glycerol esters of fatty acids, also used as external antistats, as well as quaternary ammonium salts of fatty acids.

The fifth case involves a solid polymer-liquid interface. The behavior of liquids in contact with solid surfaces is associated with polarity, surface tension, and contact angle. In some cases, wetting of a polymer is desirable (printing inks, lubrication), while in other cases it is undesirable (staining). An interesting and important case involves the condensation of water on transparent containers, packaging material, or lenses (fogging), which tends to reduce see-through properties. Substances which reduce fogging (antifogging agents or antifogs) can act according to two opposite mechanisms, that is, by favoring the perfect wetting of the plastic leading to the formation of a transparent film or, conversely, by restricting the wetting to the point where few large droplets form and detach from or roll on the surface. Tensioactive substances analogous to detergents or surfactants, usually applied externally (not true additives), correspond to the first mechanism, while hydrophobic exuding or blooming additives promote the second mechanism.

In practice, antifogs are closely related to other surface-modifying agents.

2.12   APPENDIX 2

▶COPOLYMERS (section 2.7)
    OLEFINICS
        P(E-VA), P(E-VAL), P(E-EA), P(E-MA), P(E-AA), P(E-MAA), P(E-P)$_b$
    VINYLICS
        P(VC-P), P(VC-VAC)
    STYRENICS
        P(S-B), P(S-AN), P(S-MMA), P(S-PMS), P(S-AMS), P(S-MLA)
    ACRYLONITRILICS
        P(AN-S), P(AN-MA), P(AN-MMA)
    FLUOROPOLYMERS
        P(E-TFE)$_a$, P(E-CTFE)$_a$, P(TFE-HFP)$_a$, P(VDF-TFE)$_a$, P(VDF-HFI)
    ELASTOMERIC COPOLYMERS
        P(B-S), P(B-AN), P(E-P)$_r$

▶POLYALLOYS (section 2.8)

GENERAL ELECTRIC	NORYL, GELOY, GEMAX, GTX, XENOY
BASF	LURANYL, ULTRANYL, TERBLEND
DUPONT	BEXLOY*
ROHM AND HAAS	ROPET, KYDEX, KYDENE
DOW	PULSE, ZERLON
BORG-WARNER	PREVEX, CYCOVIN, ELEMID, PROLOY
ARCO	ARLOY
MOBAY	BAYBLEND, MAKROBLEND, TEXIN*
MONSANTO	CADON*, TRIAX
CELANESE/HOECHST	DURALOY, VANDAR
UNION CARBIDE/AMOCO	MINDEL, UCARDEL
A(ABS/PA)	TRIAX, ELEMID
A(ABS/PC)	BAYBLEND, PROLOY, CYCOLOY*, PULSE
A(ABS/PSU)	ARYLON*, MINDEL*
A(ABS/PVC)	ABSON, KRALASTIC, CYCOVIN
A(ABS/PU)	PELLETHANE*, CYCOLOY*, ESTANE*
A(PA/PPO)	ULTRANYL, NORYL* GTX
A(PA/TPE)	BEXLOY*, ZYTEL*
A(PBT/PC)	XENOY
A(PBT/PET)	VALOX*
A(PBT/PPO)	GEMAX
A(PC/ASA)	TERBLEND*
A(PC/PET)	MAKROBLEND
A(PC/PS)	ARLOY*
A(PC/SMA)	ARLOY*
A(PC/TPU)	BAYBLEND*, TEXIN*, MERTEX
A(PS/ACR)	ZERLON
A(PS/PPO)	NORYL, LURANYL

▶PLASTICIZERS (section 2.9)

EASTMAN-KODAK	KODAFLEX
FMC	KRONITEX
MONSANTO	SANTICIZER
HALL, C.P.	PLAST HALL
BADISCHE	PALATINOL
EXXON	JAYFLEX
ROHM AND HAAS	PARAPLEX
HARCHEM	EPOFLEX
INTERSTAB	ESTABEX, PLASTOFLEX
SWIFT	EPOXOL
FERRO	PLAS-CHEK
BASF	PLASTOMOLL
BAYER	ULTRAMOLL
EMERY	PLASTOLEIN

▶FILLERS, REINFORCEMENTS (section 2.10)

Particle Class (section 2.10.1)

Calcium Carbonate

PFIZER	MULTIFLEX, ULTRAPFLEX
OMYA	OMYACARB
THOMPSON WEINMAN	ATOMITE, SNOWFLAKE WHITE, DRIKALITE
SYLACAUGA	MICROWHITE
HUBER	HUBERCARB
GEORGIA MARBLE	GAMA-SPERSE
NYCO	NYCARB, CALCOAT
	SILICA
GRACE, W.R.	SYLOID
ILLINOIS MINERALS	IMSILS
CABOT	CAB-O-SIL
DEGUSSA	AEROSIL

Kaolin

THIELE	THIELE
GEORGIA KAOLIN	HYDRITE

Talc

ENGELHARD	EMTAL

Alumina Trihydrate

GREAT LAKES	TECHFILL
AMERICAN MINERALS	HYDROFILL

Baryte

NYCO	NYCOR
THOMPSON-WEINMAN	BARIMITE

Calcium Sulfate
US GYPSUM   TERRA ALBA, SNOW WHITE

Solid Glass Spheres
GREAT LAKES   TECHFILL FS
POTTERS   SPHERIGLASS

Hollow Glass Spheres
P.Q. CORP.   Q-CEL
3-M   GLASS BUBBLE
FILLITE   FILLITE
EMERSON-CUMING   ECCOSPHERE
SILBRICO   SIL-CELL
ZEELEN   ZEEOSPHERES
P.A. IND.   EXTENSOSPHERES
PATENTECH   SPHEREPACK
GREAT LAKES   TECHFILL
NYCO   NYSPHERES

Fiber Class (section 2.10.2)
   Glass
   ST.GOBAIN/CERTAINTEED   VETROTEX
   PILKINGTON   FIBREGLASS
   OWENS-CORNING   FIBERGLAS
   MONTEDISON   VITROFIL

   Carbon and Graphite

   ASHLAND   CARBOFLEX
   UNION CARBIDE/AMOCO   THORNEL
   CELANESE/HOECHST   CELION
   HERCULES   MAGNAMITE
   COURTAULDS   GRAFIL
   MORGANITE   MODMOR
   ROLLS-ROYCE   HYFIL
   TORAY   TORAYCA
   GREAT LAKES CARBON   FORTAFIL

   Metal
   BRUNSWICK   BRUNSMET
   DOW/BASF   LUREX

   Potassium Titanate
   DUPONT   FYBEX
   BIDDLE-SAWYER   TISMO

   Processed Mineral Fiber
   JIM WALTER/NYCO   PMF

Polymeric
ALLIED   COMPET (PA, PET), SPECTRA (PE)
DUPONT   KEVLAR (ARAMID)
ICI   ZYEX (PEEK)

Disk Class (section 2.10.3)
Wollastonite
NYCO   WOLLASTOKUP, NYAD
GREAT LAKES   TECHFILL

Muscovite
US GYPSUM   MUSCOVITE
FRANKLIN-MEARL   ALSIBRONZ
NYCO   NYFLAKE, MICACOAT

Phlogopite
MARIETTA   SUZORITE

Glass Flakes
OWENS-CORNING   FLAKEGLAS

►MISCELLANEOUS ADDITIVES (section 2.11)
UV Absorbers, Light Stabilizers (section 2.11.1)
EASTMAN-KODAK   EASTMAN
BASF   UVINUL
CIBA-GEIGY   IRGASTAB, CHIMASSORB, TINUVIN
3-V CHEM   UVASORB
FERRO   UV-CHEK, PERMYL
CYANAMID   CYASORB,CYASO
BORG-WARNER   SPINUVEX
MONTEFLUOS   SPINUVEX
GOODRICH   GOODRITE
GIVAUDAN   GIVSORB
SANDOZ   SANDUVOR
SYNTHETIC PRODUCTS   SYNPRON

Antioxidants (section 2.11.2)
HOECHST   HOSTANOX
UNIROYAL   NAUGARD
CYANAMID   CYANOX
GOODRICH   GOODRITE
ICI   TOPANOL
ETHYL   ETHANOX
CIBA-GEIGY   IRGAFOS, IRGANOX
SCHNECTADY   ISONOX
VANDERBILT   VANOX
OLIN   WYTOX
BORG-WARNER   WESTON, ULTRANOX
SANDOZ   SANDOSTAB

Heat Stabilizers (section 2.11.3)

M & T CHEM.	THERMOLITE
PENNWALT	PENNMAX
SYNPRO	SYNPRON
ARGUS	MARK
INTERSTAB	STANCLERE
CIBA-GEIGY	IRGASTAB
CYANAMID	CYASTAB
ENVIROSTRAND	ENVIROSTAB
EAGLE-PITCHER	EPITHAL
ASSOCIATED LEAD	DYTHAL, DYPHOS, LECTRO, TRIBASE
MALLINCKROFT	HYDENSE
BASF	SICOSTAB
FERRO	THERMCHEK
KYOWA-MITSUI	ALCAMIZER
SANDOZ	SANTOSTAB

Flame Retardants (section 2.11.4)

ETHYL-SAYTECH	SAYTEX
M & T CHEM.	THERMGUARD
GREAT LAKES	DE
FERRO	PYRO-CHEK
MCGEAN-ROHCO	FYRE BLOC
SOLEM	MICRAL
ALCOA	LUBRAL
MOBIL	ANTIBLAZE
US BORAX	FIREBRAKE
KYOWA-MITSUI	KISUMA
ANZON	ONGARD, TMS, TRUTINT
STAUFFER	FYROL
MONSANTO	PHOSCHECK
SYNTEX/ARAPAHOE	FERROCENE
SUMITOMO/ABBEY	LSV
SHERWIN-WILLIAMS	KEMGARD

Antimicrobials (section 2.11.5)

VENTRON-THIOKOL	VINYZENE

Colorants (section 2.11.6)

CIBA-GEIGY	UVITEX, IRGAZIN, CROMOPHTAL, DRAKENFELD, VIVID
FERRO	CHECKMATE
BASF	THERMOPLAST, HELIOGEN, PALIOGEN, SICOTAN, SICOTRANS
GLIDDEN	ZOPAQUE, CADMOLITH
KERR-MCGEE	TRONOX
MOBAY	INDOFAST
CUSTOM COLOR	ULTRAFLO
SANDOZ	LEUCOPURE

Odorants (section 2.11.7)

MERIX	ADDAROMA
ARMAK-ACCUREL	MODEREX

Surface-modifying Additives (section 2.11.8)

EMERY	EMERWAX
PETROCHEM	PETRAC
HUMKO-WITCO	SLIP-EZE, VYN-EZE, ERAMIDE, SLIP QUICQ, DRAPEX, MARKSTAT, MARKPET, MARKAMIDE, KEMAMIDE, KEMESTER, HYSTRENE, INDUSTRENE, SUNOLITE, EXTRA-DENSE
HOECHST	HOSTALUB
ASSOCIATED LEAD	PLASTIFLOW
TENNECO	NUODEX
EASTMAN-KODAK	EPOLENE
HENKEL-NEYNABER	LOXIOL
ICI	LUBROL, AMTER, SPAN, TWEEN
ROHM AND HAAS	PARAPLEX
CYANAMID	CYASTAT
ISOCHEM	ISOLUBE
INTERSTAB	INTERSTAT
SANDOZ	SANDIN VU
MOBAY	VULKANOL

Chapter 3

CLASSES OF POLYMERIC MATERIALS

3.1 INTRODUCTION

This chapter is primarily a survey of synthetic polymeric materials that have achieved commercial importance. The survey is subdivided into three main parts: thermoplastics, thermosetting resins (thermosets) and elastomers (rubbers). A fourth part discusses selected special polymeric products which include fibers, films, and cellular polymers.

Each main part features some general considerations about the behavior of the corresponding materials, followed by discussion of the various commercial types arranged in appropriate groups (olefinics, acrylics, fluoropolymers, epoxy systems, diene-based rubber, silicone polymers, etc.).

For each polymer or resin system, essential chemical information is given in the form of a *chemplate*, and a representative list of Suppliers and Tradenames is provided in Appendix 3 to illustrate its industrial and commercial significance (see section 1.2.2.4).

Thermoplastic polymers are supplied in a variety of forms: powder (e.g., 1-100 μm), prill, flake, chip, granule, cube, dice, pellet (about 3 mm or 1/8 in), and so on. Certain processing techniques call for specific forms; in other cases, handling or feeding considerations determine the choice. They are shipped packaged in bags (about 25 kg or 50 lb) or groups of bags (pallets or skids), in drums (about 100 kg or 200 lb), in boxes, cartons, or Gaylords (about 500 kg or 1000 lb). They are also shipped in bulk as tanktruck loads (about 15 tons) or rail car loads (about 40-80 tons). Bulk supplies are normally stored in silos (up to 7 m or 21 ft in diameter and 20 m or 50 ft high) and conveyed by pneumatic systems.

Thermosetting resin systems are most commonly supplied in powders for the solid systems and in drums, tanktrucks, and railroad cars for the liquid systems.

Vulcanizable elastomers are most commonly supplied as bales (about 25 kg or 50 lb), but also as powder, chip, crumb, and sheet.

Polymers or polymeric systems, which are fairly widely used, have good although not outstanding properties and are priced at moderate levels, are often referred to as "commodity" (general purpose) plastics or rubbers (PE, PVC, UP, SBR, etc.). The term "engineering" (high performance) plastic or rubber is often used for materials that have a good set of excellent properties (mechanical resistance, temperature limit, etc.). They are normally significantly more expensive (PA, PC, PSU, etc.). Specialty polymers are normally associated with one or more outstanding property (e.g., low friction, electrical), although other properties may be mediocre (PTFE). The classification of commercial polymers as commodity, engineering or specialty materials is somewhat subjective and is thus not emphasized in this textbook.

A total of thirty (30) groups of commercial polymeric materials are discussed in this chapter. Fifteen groups are discussed under thermoplastics, eight under thermosetting resins, and seven under elastomers. It should be noted that the discussion of some groups includes materials associated with other categories. Urethane systems, for example, include thermoplastic and elastomeric materials in addition to thermosetting resins. Imide polymers and silicone polymers are other examples.

An index of major chemical names is given in Appendix 3.

3.2   THERMOPLASTICS

3.2.1   General

3.2.1.1   Introduction

The definition of a thermoplastic polymer (or thermoplastic) can be given in terms of its physical behavior or its molecular structure. In simple terms, a thermoplastic polymer is a material that is solid, that is possesses significant elasticity at room temperature and turns into a viscous liquid-like material at some higher temperature, the change being reversible. Because of their high molecular weight, polymers never become thin fluids, and, contrary to most other substances, the transformation does not necessarily involve the melting of crystals. The concept of a liquid implies molecules that which are not tied by chemical bonds that would prevent relative long range motion, thus cross-links as defined earlier must not be present.

It is essential to realize that this solid-like-to-liquid-like transition, commonly but sometimes rather incorrectly called "melting," can reflect two entirely different mechanisms in two classes of thermoplastic polymers. One class will be referred to as "noncrystallizing thermoplastics" and the other, as "crystallizing thermoplastics."

3.2.1.2 Noncrystallizing Thermoplastics

Noncrystallizing thermoplastics have a molecular structure that makes them incapable of crystallizing, that is of forming regular order in the polymer with molecules or portions of molecules regularly stacked in crystal-like fashion. Molecules can be pictured with a basically random configuration and the material is said to be amorphous. These thermoplastics are often referred to as "amorphous thermoplastics."

At low temperatures, it is thought that the motion of molecules is very small and limited to a very short range. At high temperatures, on the other hand, molecules are very flexible and constantly change conformation. This is the manifestation in polymers of Brownian motion characteristic of ordinary fluids. One might think that such transition should be completely gradual; in fact, it is relatively sudden and a major change in physical behavior occurs over a range of a few degrees to 10 degrees. Physical chemists associate this to the formation of a critical free volume.

A good mental picture of the molecules is, therefore, a random immobile (rigid) configuration below the transition and a random mobile (flexible) configuration above the transition (Fig. 3.1).

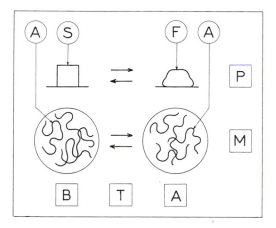

Figure 3.1 · **Noncrystallizing thermoplastics; temperature effect** · [P] Physical state; [M] Molecular conformation; [T] Glass transition; [B] Below transition; [A] Above transition; (A) Amorphous; (S) Solid; (F) Fluid-like

The transition has been called the "glass transition" because the structure and properties of the polymer below it are reminiscent of those of ordinary glass. The transition range is relatively narrow and, as a matter of convenience in the characterization of individual polymers, a specific temperature is often reported and referred to as the "glass transition temperature T_g." It is important to realize that such temperature is not very precisely defined or measured, but it is a most useful characteristic of each homopolymer.

Even though noncrystallizing thermoplastics are discussed specifically here, the concept of glass transition applies to all polymers (crystallizing thermoplastics, rubbers, thermosets, fibers, etc.).

In the following, the concept of glass transition for noncrystallizing thermoplastics is illustrated through schematic graphs. First, a quantity **R** is defined loosely as the resistance to deformation. For a solid material, this corresponds to the stiffness; for a fluid, the viscosity. The effect of the temperature **T** on the quantity **R** is represented schematically in Figure 3.2. Four regions can be defined. On the extreme left, the

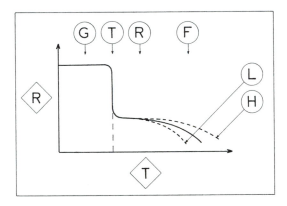

Figure 3.2 · **Noncrystallizing thermoplastics; temperature effect** · <R> Resistance to deformation; <T> Temperature; (G) Glassy region; (T) Glass transition; (R) Rubbery region; (F) Fluid flow region; (L) Low molecular weight; (H) High molecular weight

material is solid and rigid with a modulus of roughly 3500 kPa (500,000 psi); it is the glassy state. In the glass transition region, the material, still largely solid-like, softens considerably. Just above the glass transition, polymers of a sufficient molecular weight retain a good measure of elasticity with a low modulus of 0.7-7 kPa (100-1000 psi) which is characteristic of rubbers. The range of temperature, over which the resistance to deformation does not change, strongly depends primarily on the molecular weight (**MW**) of the thermoplastic (curves L and H). This region is often referred to as the "rubbery plateau." It is thought that the rubbery behavior is associated with molecular entanglements. As the temperature increases, the viscoelastic material becomes increasingly viscous-like (fluid-like).

The change in volume (or specific volume) **v** with the temperature **T** is represented schematically for a noncrystallizing thermoplastic in Figure 3.3. At low temperatures in the glassy state, the slow linear increase of volume indicates a low coefficient of thermal expansion. Above the glass transition, the volume increase is linear again, but with a higher slope, indicating that the mechanism of thermal expansion is now different.

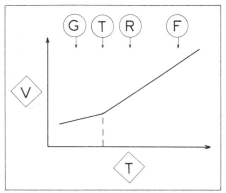

Figure 3.3 · **Noncrystallizing thermoplastics; temperature effect** · <V> Specific volume; <T> Temperature; (G) Glassy region; (T) Glass transition; (R) Rubbery region; (F) Fluid flow region

The glass transition can be detected and measured in a number of ways, including mechanical, thermal, and electrical methods. Examples of representative values of T_g for thermoplastics, which are basically of the noncrystallizing type, are as follows: polystyrene: $T_g \approx 100°C$ ($\approx 212°F$); polyvinylchloride: $T_g \approx 70°C$ ($158°F$); and polycarbonate: $T_g \approx 150°C$ ($\approx 302°F$). Values of T_g are systematically given along with the repeat unit for each thermoplastic homopolymer discussed subsequently.

Noncrystallizing thermoplastics tend to share certain characteristics, such as a potential for transparency and a somewhat lower resistance to chemicals and solvents.

3.2.1.3 Crystallizing Thermoplastics

The concept of crystallinity was introduced earlier, and it was shown that very high crystallinity is rarely achieved in bulk polymers.

The degree of crystallinity in a given semicrystalline polymer is a function of its structure, but also of processing factors, such as the rate of cooling or the deformation prior or during crystallization. It is, therefore, important to realize that crystallizing thermoplastics form a class with characteristics that can be rather close to, or quite different from that of, noncrystallizing thermoplastics.

When a crystallizing thermoplastic is above its melting temperature T_m (comparable to the crystallization temperature), the conformation of the molecules is random and not different from that of noncrystallizing thermoplastics, and the material is in an amorphous state Figure 3.4. Below the melting point, the molecular conformation can be viewed as a mixture of folded chain crystals and basically amorphous regions.

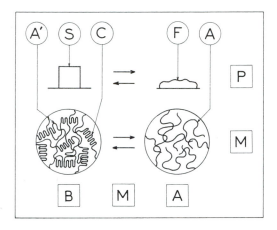

Figure 3.4 · **Crystallizing thermoplastics; temperature effect** · [P] Physical state; [M] Molecular conformation; [M] Melting transition; [B] Below melting; [A] Above melting; (A') Amorphous regions; (S) Solid; (C) Crystalline regions; (F) Fluid; (A) Amorphous

Crystallization is initiated (nucleated) at various locations (nuclei) and semicrystalline solid spherulites start growing around the nuclei; the crystallization process is basically completed when the whole material has been converted into a spherulitic semicrystalline solid. Crystallization is a time-dependent phenomenon with some polymers crystallizing much faster than others. Different polymers cooled under similar conditions can achieve very different degrees of crystallinity.

To parallel the discussion of noncrystallizing thermoplastics, the effect of temperature on the resistance to deformation and the volume is described below.

In Figure 3.5, the resistance to deformation **R** of the solid at low temperatures is shown to be high but comparable to that of glassy noncrystallizing thermoplastics. As the temperature reaches the glass transition temperature T_g of the polymer, a drop in stiffness occurs that basically corresponds to the softening of the noncrystalline (amorphous) parts of the semicrystalline material. The crystalline regions are, in principle, not affected. Further heating below the melting point T_m generally causes no major subsequent softening of the material, and a horizontal or slightly decreasing line is a reasonable representation of the material behavior. When the melting transition or melting point T_m is reached, crystals that held the material together as a solid now melt and the material, far away from its glass transition, is generally quite fluid-like with relatively little rubber-like elasticity unless the molecular weight is very high. The level of the semicrystalline plateau between T_g and T_m is a function of the degree of crystallinity, that is the tendency to crystallize. The upper curve (H) would correspond to a higher crystallinity, while the (L) curve would be for a lower crystallinity. The hypothetical 100% crystalline polymer should, in principle, correspond to curve (H′), while curve (L′) corresponds to the hypothetical 100% amorphous material.

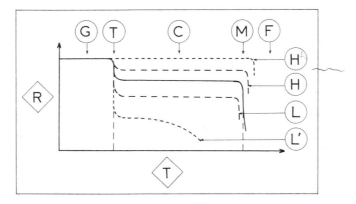

Figure 3.5 · **Crystallizing thermoplastics; temperature effect** · <R> Resistance to deformation; <T> Temperature; (G) Glassy region; (T) Glass transition; (C) Semi-crystalline region; (M) Melting transition; (F) Fluid flow region; (H′) 100% crystallinity; (H) High crystallinity; (L) Low crystallinity; (L′) 0% crystallinity

The change in volume (or specific volume v) is shown in Figure 3.6. If a melt is cooled, its volume decreases linearly with temperature until the first crystals form. As crystals are significantly denser than the amorphous material, the volume drops rather rapidly as the crystallization proceeds below the melting point T_m. In contrast with low-molecular-weight substances, for which crystallization takes place at an essentially fixed temperature, the high viscosity of the melt, combined with the frequent presence of irregularities in the chains, causes a spread of the crystallization range. When all possible crystallization has essentially taken place, the semicrystalline polymer further contracts linearly, primarily through its amorphous regions. If the amorphous content is important (low crystallinity), the glass transition can be detected as a change of slope corresponding to the glass transition (T_g).

The melting transition can also be detected and measured in several ways, including mechanical, thermal, and optical methods. Examples of representative values of T_m

for crystallizing thermoplastics are the following: polyethylene: T_m ≈ 120°C (≈ 248°F); polypropylene: T_m ≈ 175°C (≈ 347°F); and polyamide: T_m ≈ 220°C (≈ 428°F). Values of T_m are systematically given along with the repeat unit for each crystallizing thermoplastic homopolymer discussed subsequently.

Crystallizing thermoplastics are not normally transparent, although they can be translucent, and they tend to have better chemical and impact resistance than noncrystallizing ones.

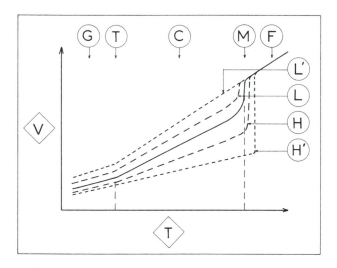

Figure 3.6 · **Crystallizing thermoplastics; temperature effect** · <V> Specific volume; <T> Temperature; (G) Glassy region; (T) Glass transition; (C) Semi-crystalline region; (M) Melting transition; (F) Fluid flow region; (L′) 0% crystallinity; (L) Low crystallinity; (H) High crystallinity; (H′) 100% crystallinity

3.2.2 Commercial Thermoplastics and Related Polymers

3.2.2.1 Olefinics

A group of important commercial plastics features repeat units with carbon (C) and hydrogen (H) atoms exclusively and no ring structures. Although the term "olefin" normally has a broader meaning, this group is often referred to as "polyolefins" or "olefinic resins," and the short term "olefinics" is used here.

Polyethylene (PE)

PE   poly'ethylene (OL)

PE	H H
	
	$\left[\begin{array}{c} \;\;\vert\;\;\;\;\vert\;\; \\ -C-C- \\ \;\;\vert\;\;\;\;\vert\;\; \end{array}\right]$
	
	H H
		PE
		
		T_g -100 °C (-20--180)
		     -148 °F
		
		T_m 120 °C (105-138)
		     248 °F

Regular polyethylene (LDPE, HDPE)

Polyethylene is, by a fairly wide margin, the largest volume plastic. Its discovery in the 1930s was one of the landmarks of the industry. A wide variety of types and grades of polyethylenes are available commercially which share characteristics, such as low price, chemical inertness, good electrical properties, and easy processing.

Although the monomeric unit involves the two carbon atoms reminiscent of the ethylene monomer, the true repeat unit is only CH_2 and the polymer has sometimes been referred to as "polymethylene."

The crystalline melting transition T_m decreases from a maximum around 135°C (275°F) to a low of about 110°C (230°F) as the degree of crystallinity drops. The very low glass transition ($T_g \approx$ -110°C or -166°F) is associated with a good retention of mechanical properties, including flexibility and impact resistance at low temperatures. The first method of production of polyethylene involved very high pressures and led to a highly branched polymer, with a correspondingly low crystallinity and low density. The terms "high pressure," "branched," and "low-density" (LDPE) were, therefore, generally associated with this type of flexible polyethylene (density in the range of 0.910-0.925 g/cm^3). Another method was subsequently developed which required much lower pressures with special catalysts and led to much less branched, that is, linear polyethylene with higher crystallinity and density. The terms "low pressure," "linear," and "high density" (HDPE) became associated with the more rigid polyethylene (density in the range 0.941-0.965 g/cm^3). Now numerous modifications of the methods of preparation, including copolymerization and alloying, and progress in the elucidation of molecular architecture, render this simple classification somewhat insufficient. This is illustrated in particular with LLDPE discussed later.

Density remains a good indicator of the general level of crystallinity, which affects many properties, such as stiffness, resistance to permeation by gases, or resistance to oils and greases, which increase with density.

Polyethylene grades are also classified according to their melt viscosity or melt index, which strongly reflect the molecular weight of the polymer. This is of particular importance for processing where different techniques often call for different melt viscosities. Injection molding, for example, is generally associated with an easy flowing grade, while thermoforming requires a high melt "consistency" or viscosity. Molecular weight does not have such a direct effect on solid state properties, but it is established that high molecular weight is often beneficial, for example, in obtaining adequate environmental stress-cracking resistance. As indicated earlier, the molecular weight distribution is a now recognized important factor.

The properties of polyethylene can be adjusted in a variety of ways besides homopolymerization. Copolymerization and polyalloys are discussed later in the specific case of polyethylene.

Numerous additives have also been developed that can change considerably some properties. For example, high temperature or UV-radiation-induced oxidation can be reduced by stabilizers or antioxidants. Flammability can be controlled through flame retardants. Surface properties can be dramatically modified by the use of slip agents or cling agents or oxidative surface treatment. In some instances, biodegradability or photodegradability has been achieved with suitable modifications.

Polyethylene is used in practically all thermoplastic processing techniques and examples will be discussed later. The applications of polyethylene are numerous and involve many properties that are rated through standard tests.

Linear low density polyethylene (LLDPE)

The low degree of crystallinity of conventional low-density polyethylene is attributed to the frequent short and long branches which are formed during the high pressure polymerization of ethylene monomer.

A new line of polyethylenes is now increasingly popular in which the equivalent of relatively frequent branching is obtained by copolymerizing ethylene at low pressures and in the presence of catalysts with small amounts of so-called α-olefin comonomers (butene, hexene, octene), which play the role of uniform short branches along a nearly linear backbone. It should be noted that the method, first used in Canada in the 1950s, can be used to obtain any density and affords a better control on the molecular architecture and the resulting semicrystalline morphology.

Linear low-density polyethylene, when compared to conventional low-density polyethylene of the same density and melt index in applications, such as films or flexible molded products, is claimed to have better impact, tear, or puncture properties and improved environmental stress-cracking resistance, allowing in particular a downgaging of films. Its processing, however, requires adjustments.

Ultra high molecular weight polyethylene (UHMWPE)

It is possible to produce polyethylene of extremely (ultra) high molecular weight at least 10 times that of regular polyethylenes (3×10^6 to 6×10^6). The polymerization process leads to so-called linear molecules associated with high-density (high-crystallinity) polyethylene, although reported densities (0.93-0.94 g/cm^3) correspond to the usual medium crystallinity range.

The molecular weight must cause such a high degree of physical entanglements that, above the melting point ($\mathbf{T_m} \approx 130°C$ or 266°F), the material behaves in a rubber-like rather than fluid-like manner, causing considerable processing difficulties. Many components are machined from semifinished products supplied by specialized processors. Methods have been developed to produce parts directly from powdered resin by compression molding, forging or stamping, and ram extrusion.

Ultra-high-molecular-weight polyethylene has certain outstanding properties that probably qualify it as an engineering or specialty plastic. Its chemical inertness is almost unmatched and includes environmental stress-cracking (ESC) resistance and resistance to foods and physiological fluids. Its most cited outstanding property is wear or abrasion resistance; it is associated with the chemical inertness, a very low coefficient of friction, excellent impact resistance (toughness), and fatigue resistance. These attributes and a moderate cost explain the growing use of UHMWPE in large scale materials handling equipment (chemical, mining, etc.), as well as in many specialized applications (pen tips, prosthetic wear surfaces, gears, etc.).

Cross-linked polyethylene (XLPE)

The introduction of chemical cross-links into polyethylene has some desirable effects on its chemical and temperature resistance. This can be achieved by the addition of small amounts of organic peroxides (dicumyl peroxide, etc.), which obviously must not cause significant cross-linking before the polymer has acquired its final shape in processing.

A process, such as rotational molding, is suited to this cross-linking method. Another method involves the irradiation of finished products in high-energy fields. It is used particularly for extruded products, such as films (shrink wrap film in particular), pipes, and electrical wire, and cable insulation.

Polyethylene-containing polyalloys

Although polyethylene is not generally easy to blend with other polymers, successful polyalloys with polyamides and polycarbonate, for example, have been reported. Blending of different polyethylene grades or blending with ethylene-based copolymers is common.

Ethylene-vinylacetate copolymers (EVA)

The incorporation of vinylacetate repeat units in polyethylene chains has several effects. Polyvinylacetate (PVAC) is discussed in Section 3.2.2.2. By reducing the regularity of the chain, it lowers the crystallinity and, consequently, the stiffness of the material. Vinylacetate repeat units, by their polar nature, also change the barrier and surface properties leading, for instance, to films with increased water vapor permeability, oil and grease resistance, and cling (blocking, no slip) tendency. A wide range of EVA materials are available that correspond to vinylacetate contents up to 50%. Applications are in films, as well as flexible molded or extruded products.

Ethylene-vinylalcohol copolymers (EVOH)

Ethylene-vinylalcohol copolymers, containing about equal amounts of the two repeat units, find applications in the growing barrier coextrusions area as barrier layers or as interlayers (tie layers) between poorly compatible materials; vinylalcohol repeat units strongly favoring bonding to substrates. Polyvinylalcohol (PVAL) is discussed in Section 3.2.2.2.

Ethylene acrylates copolymers (EEA, EMA)

Copolymerization, with relatively small amounts of ethylacrylate or methylacrylate, is another way of reducing the crystallinity and introducing polarity, which increase flexibility, environmental stress-cracking resistance, compatibility with fillers and other polymers (alloys). Polyethylacrylate (PEA) and polymethylacrylate (PMA) are discussed in Section 3.2.2.5.

Ethylene-carboxylic acid copolymers (EAA, EMAA)

Copolymers, with relatively small amounts of acrylicacid (AA) or methacrylic acid (MAA) repeat units that feature carboxyl acid groups COOH, are particularly notable for their outstanding adhesion to a variety of polar substrates, including fillers and reinforcements. Tackiness, as well as a tendency to corrode metals and to cross-link, require special precautions in processing. Such copolymers can be modified to form the so-called ionomers. Polyacrylic acid (PAA) and polymethacrylic acid (PMAA) are discussed in Section 3.2.2.5.

Ionomers (IO)

Ionomers are modified ethylene-methacrylic acid copolymers where some of the carboxyl acid groups are converted into the corresponding metallic salts (metal methacrylate); the most common metals (M) are sodium (Na) or zinc (Zn). Since the remaining acid groups are anionic and the metal salt groups are cationic, ionic interchain links (bonds) can form that play a role similar to that of cross-links at low temperatures but are reversibly reduced or suppressed at higher temperatures.

Ionomers possess many of the useful general properties of polyethylenes. The presence of carboxyl groups and the metals increase the polarity, allowing good adhesion to substrates including metals and good paintability, as well as a better resistance to fats and oils. Ionic bonds compensate a low level of crystallinity, giving good film properties and clarity as well. The gradual reduction of ionic bonding at high temperatures allows the retention of good melt strength, which is desirable for forming or coating processes. Flex, puncture, impact, and abrasion properties are retained at low temperatures. Cited notable applications include golf balls or bowling pin covers, ski boot outer shells, and food packaging film components.

Ethylene-propylene copolymers [P(E-P)]

A very small proportion of polypropylene-type repeat units can be used to lower the crystallinity of linear polyethylene. Polypropylene (PP) is discussed later in this section. When larger amounts of comonomer are used, two commercially important copolymers result that are often referred to as "polyallomers" and "EP rubbers," respectively.

Polyallomers

Polyallomers are block copolymers, and the size of the blocks allows crystallization to take place, although seemingly slower than in either HDPE or PP, which affords an easier control of the crystalline morphology resulting from processing. Properties are quite similar to those of HDPE and PP.

Ethylene-propylene rubbers

Random copolymerization of ethylene and propylene, by suppressing regularity along the chains, prevents crystallization of the chains. The resulting polymers are amorphous and having low glass transition temperatures intermediate between those of PE ($\approx$ -110°C or -166°F) and PP ($\approx$ -20°C or -4°F), they are rubbery at room temperature. Their chemical inertness, among other things, made them attractive, and since modifications were introduced to allow their conventional vulcanization, they have become major commercial rubbers (see section 3.4.2.1).

Modified polyethylene

Chlorinated polyethylene (CPE)

The substitution of chlorine (Cl) atoms for some hydrogen (H) atoms in the polyethylene chains affects the crystallinity and can improve the fire and oil resistance of polyethylene. High substitution, of course, leads to polyvinylchloride and related chlorine-containing homopolymers.

Chlorosulfonated polyethylene (CSPE)

When a suitable proportion of hydrogen atoms are replaced by chlorine (Cl) and sulfonyl chloride groups (SO₂ Cl), the result is a vulcanizable rubber with some outstanding properties (see section 3.4.2.3).

Polypropylene (PP)

PP   poly'propylene (OL)

| PP | $\begin{array}{cc} H & H \\ | & | \\ \!-\!C\!-\!C\!-\! \\ | & | \\ H & CH_3 \end{array}$ | PP T_g −20 °C (−5−−24) −4 °F T_m 175 °C (165−180) 347 °F |

Polypropylene, one of the four very high volume plastics, is in many respects similar to medium- or high-density polyethylene. Its higher crystalline melting transition (T_m about 175°C or 347°F) gives it, however, a better temperature resistance, which allows, for example, its heat sterilization. Its emergence is associated with the discovery of polymerization techniques, which allow the control of the relative position in space of adjacent repeat units (stereospecificity and tacticity), which is required for crystallization.

In contrast with polyethylene, there is no significant variation in the crystallization tendency between grades. Additives (nucleating agents) and processing conditions (cooling, deformation) can have a strong effect, however, on the crystalline structure and orientation, and the resulting properties.

In general, nonpolar polypropylene has outstanding chemical resistance. It can be slightly affected (swollen) by some nonpolar hydrocarbons and is also sensitive to oxidative degradation with heat or radiations (ultraviolet UV), but can be protected by suitable additives.

Mechanical properties generally correspond to a moderately stiff and tough material. Creep resistance is particularly good in comparison with corresponding polyethylene. The unmodified homopolymers, however, tend to be brittle at low temperatures, a fact associated with the relatively high glass transition (T_g about -20°C or -4°F) of polypropylene. A number of modifications lead to toughness improvements; they include copolymerization, usually with small amounts of ethylene, or the blending with small amounts of butyl or ethylene-propylene rubbers.

Contrary to polyethylene, polypropylene is not normally subject to environmental stress-cracking.

Polypropylene is used in many of the common processing techniques (injection, extrusion, etc.). Notable special applications include the formation of long-lasting integral hinges, biaxially oriented packaging film (OPP film), fibers, and tapes (ribbons) made from slit film subsequently oriented and often woven for bag fabrication.

Properties of filled or reinforced polypropylene are enhanced when suitable adhesion-promoting repeat units are chain or graft copolymerized (coupled polypropylene).

Polybutylene (PBl)

PB1   poly'butylene   (OL)

PB1	H H	PB1	
	$-\left[\begin{matrix} C - C \end{matrix}\right]-$	T_g	-25 °C / 13 °F
	HH-C-H	T_m	125 °C (98–135) / 257 °F
	CH₃		

Polybutylene is based on butene-1 monomer and is also referred to as "polybutene-1." It may contain small amounts of comonomers. It undergoes a rather peculiar crystal-to-crystal transition over a period of several days after processing, which leads to a stable semicrystalline structure. Its melting point is comparable to that of polyethylene, while its glass transition is closer to that of polypropylene. Polybutylene offers a somewhat unusual combination of good creep resistance, even at relatively high temperatures, and flexibility. It also has a very good environmental stress-cracking resistance. Various grades are suited to applications that are primarily in the pipe and film areas.

Polymethylpentene (PMP)

PMP   poly'methyl'pentene (OL)

PMP

$$\left[\begin{matrix} H & H \\ | & | \\ -C & -C- \\ | & | \\ H & H\text{-}C\text{-}H \\ & | \\ & H_3C-C-CH_3 \\ & | \\ & H \end{matrix}\right]$$

PMP

T_g 30 °C (18–40)
       86 °F

T_m 240 °C (230–250)
       464 °F

Polymethylpentene (PMP) or, more specifically, poly 4-methyl pentene-l, is often referred to by the tradename of its current sole manufacturer, "TPX." This polyolefin-type polymer is somewhat of an oddity in that, in spite of the presence of rather bulky side group in the repeat unit, it crystallizes to high degrees (40-60%) and unexpectedly remains highly transparent (90% transmission). It has been postulated that close refractive indices of amorphous and crystalline regions and a very fine crystalline structure may prevent the scattering (diffusion) of light which normally makes highly crystalline polymers translucent to opaque. The density of 0.83 is also remarkably low for a polymer, in general, and especially for a crystallizing type. Commercial grades are reported to involve comonomers, probably as a small fraction.

High transparency is one of the notable properties of PMP. Its mechanical properties are said to be generally comparable to those of polyolefins, such as polypropylene, but stable to higher temperatures up to about 200°C (392°F). Creep resistance is claimed to be better than that of polyolefins and it has a lower permeability to gases and vapors.

Chemical resistance is generally good and is, in particular, unaffected by cold or hot water. Polymethylpentene is, however, attacked by oxidizing agents and affected by light hydrocarbon solvents. It appears sensitive to environmental stress-cracking (ESC). It is not recommended for use in the presence of high energy radiations or sunlight (UV) and is quite flammable.

Electrical properties are generally excellent and said to be comparable to those of PTFE. PMP is primarily processed by injection and blow molding.

Applications generally utilize the high transparency of the plastic and include lighting elements (diffusers, lenses, reflectors), liquid level and flow indicators.

PMP is very suitable for use in food packaging, processing, and service, as cook-in (bake-in, boil-in) containers, trays, or bags. It is compatible with conventional (hot-air) or microwave ovens. Appropriate parts of appliances, such as coffee makers are also made of PMP. It is also used for laboratory and medical ware (hollow ware, syringes, test tubes, connectors, etc.).

Electrical applications include wire covering, coil formers, and coaxial cable connectors.

Various uses of olefin polymers are shown in figures 3.7 to 3.17.

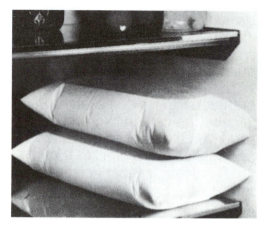

Figure 3.8 · 1.5 - Quart milk pouches (polyethylene LLDPE) **[DU PONT CANADA]**

Figure 3.7 · T-Shirt grocery bag (polyethylene HMW/HD PE)

Figure 3.9 · 55-Gal drums (polyethylene HDPE)

Figure 3.10 · Artificial skating surface (polyethylene) **[BASF]**

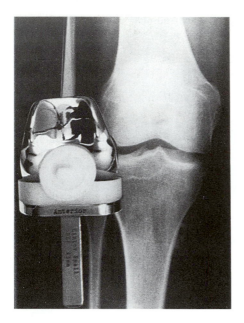

Figure 3.12 · Mechanical gear (polyethylene HMWPE) **[HERCULES]**

Figure 3.11 · Artificial bone joint, metal-
plastic combination (polyethylene UHMWPE)

Figure 3.13 · Lawn/patio furniture (polypropylene
PP) **[ICI]**

Figure 3.14 · Latex paint pail
(polypropylene PP) **[BAPCO]**

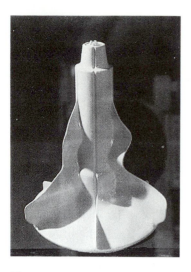

Figure 3.16 · Bicycle wheels (polypropylene PP + coupled glass fiber) **[THERMOFIL]**

Figure 3.15 · Clothes washer agitator (polypropylene PP + 40% glass fiber) [HIMONT]

Figure 3.17 · Hot water piping (polybutylene PB1); valve and fittings (acetal PMO); copper crimp rings **[DU PONT]**

3.2.2.2 Vinylics

A number of commercially important polymers are discussed here as a group, referred to as "vinylics," because of certain similarities in their chemical structure and the presence of the word "vinyl" in their common name. The major polymer in the group is polyvinylchloride.

Polyvinylchloride (PVC)

PVC   poly'vinyl'chloride (VI)

| PVC | H   H
$\left[\begin{array}{cc} \; & \; \\ -C-C- \\ \; & \; \end{array}\right]$
H   Cl | PVC
T_g 70 °C (70-90)
158 °F |

Polyvinylchloride is one of the four major, highest-volume thermoplastics. The homopolymer has a glass transition around 70°C (158°F) and its high consistency above the glass transition has sometimes been partly associated with the presence of a certain ordered structure, although there is no evidence of semicrystalline character.

As with other polymers, high molecular weights, often characterized by the K-value, tend to improve many properties, but create processing difficulties.

Polyvinylchloride has good general chemical resistance. However, some polar organic solvents allow easy solvent joining. Weatherability can be excellent, especially with the incorporation of suitable additives, which explains its widespread exterior use in construction.

The presence of chlorine atoms in the repeat unit is associated with the intrinsic resistance to combustion and its classification as self-extinguishing or flame resistant.

High temperatures cause degradation with formation of hydrochloric acid, which is toxic and can cause severe equipment corrosion. Heat stabilizers are generally used to facilitate processing in particular.

Polyvinylchloride has good insulation properties for low-frequency electrical systems. At high frequencies, dielectric losses are high and, in fact, the associated heat generation is utilized advantageously in dielectric heating or sealing.

One major characteristic of polyvinylchloride is its ability to accept large amounts of "modifiers" that can alter its properties considerably and lead to a wide range of applications. While unmodified polyvinylchloride homopolymer is stiff and relatively brittle (rigid PVC), with suitable plasticizers it can show rubber-like behavior (flexible PVC). The role of plasticizers can be interpreted roughly in terms of a lowering of the glass transition temperature T_g. Stiffness, on the other hand, can be increased, or the cost can be reduced while maintaining good stiffness levels, by using fillers.

In many cases, and in contrast to most other thermoplastics, the best formulation for a given application is compounded by the fabricator from raw materials purchased outside. This requires much experience and often sizable compounding equipment.

Flexible PVC is used in flexible films, wire insulation and jacket, hoses, shoe soles, toys, and other products, while rigid PVC finds applications in sheets, pipes, conduits, home sidings, profiles, and containers.

Polyvinylchloride is also available in liquid-like form as water-based emulsions (latex) or as suspensions of suitable particles in plasticizers (plastisols, organosols) that are used for special coating techniques.

Chlorinated Polyvinylchloride (CPVC)

It is possible to chemically modify polyvinylchloride chains by substituting chlorine atoms for some hydrogen atoms. The chlorine content can thus be increased from 56.8% for PVC to the range 62-72%. Chlorinated polyvinylchloride (CPVC) has improved chemical and temperature resistance and, in particular, can be used in contact with boiling water. It is used in pipe form for hot water distribution.

Vinylchloride-based Copolymers

There are two important copolymers where vinylchloride form the major component.

Vinylchloride-propylene copolymers [P(VC-P)]

From 2-10% of propylene repeat units play a (internal) plasticizing role without leachable plasticizers by reducing the polarity and improve the heat stability for an easier processing. Applications include beverage containers, toys, and medical instruments.

Vinylchloride-vinylacetate copolymer [P(VC-VAC)]

This is another way of internally plasticizing polyvinylchloride with 3-30% of vinylacetate repeat units. Impact properties, in particular, and processing ease are improved. Molded, extruded, or calendered parts often contain 10-15% vinylacetate. Applications include phonograph records and floor covering. Fibers are also made from the copolymer.

Vinylchloride-based Polyalloys

There are several classes of such polyalloys. One corresponds primarily to the desire to improve the impact resistance of rigid PVC and is achieved by blending with compatible rubbery polymers, such as ethylene/vinylacetate copolymer (EVA), nitrile rubber (NBR), and chlorinated polyethylene (CPE), the latter blend has important applications in window and door frames, for example.

Another class involves plastics that are particularly noted for their transparency: polymethylmethacrylate (PMMA) and styrene-acrylonitrile (SAN).

Acrylonitrile-butadiene-styrene (ABS) plastics are also blended with PVC which improves its resistance to combustion.

Polyvinylidenechloride (PVDC)

PVDC poly'vinylidene'chloride (VI)

PVDC	H Cl	PVDC
	$+C - C+$	T_g -18 °C (-40-140) -1 °F
	H Cl	T_m 190 °C (175-205) 374 °F

Polyvinylidenechloride homopolymer, with its symmetrical repeat unit, can crystallize. Its decomposition or degradation temperature is, however, barely above the melting point of about 200°C, which makes it almost impossible to process. Some modifications discussed later are therefore necessary to allow commercial processing.

Polyvinylidenechloride happens to have outstanding barrier properties for such /fluids as oxygen (O_2), carbon dioxide (CO_2), and water (H_2O), which are so important in the packaging of foods in particular. It is also generally chemically inert and has very good combustion resistance.

The most common modification of polyvinylidenechloride, to facilitate its processing and to improve some properties, such as toughness, is copolymerization with 10-15% of vinylchloride (VC), as in Saran material, or acrylonitrile (AN). Acrylate esters, such as ethyl acrylate, are also reported to be copolymerized in amounts up to 50%. Copolymerization reduces the degree of crystallinity to an estimated 35-45% and the melting point to the range 50-175°C. The resulting copolymers P(VDC-VC) or P(VDC-AN) are used for packaging films and film products, such as sterilizable retort pouches, coatings, fibers for textiles or filters, and a variety of containers.

Polyvinylacetate (PVAC)

PVAC poly'vinyl'acetate (VI)

PVAC	H H	PVAC
	$+C - C+$	T_g 30 °C (28-86) 86 °F
	H O	
	O=C—CH$_3$	

Polyvinylacetate homopolymer is noncrystallizing and, because of its low glass transition temperature, it is not used as a plastic. It is widely used, however, as the major ingredient of adhesives and paints in which the polar polymer is finely dispersed in a water-based emulsion (latex) for easy spreading; the water subsequently evaporates. White glue and latex paints are examples of such applications.

Vinylacetate repeat units form the minor component in important copolymers with vinylchloride [P(VC-VAC)] and ethylene (EVA).

Polyvinylalcohol (PVAL)

PVAL   poly'vinyl'alcohol   (VI)

Polyvinylalcohol homopolymer (PVAL or PVOH), highly polar because of its hydroxyl (OH) groups, is crystalline and also water soluble. Since, in practice, it is derived from polyvinylacetate through substitution of hydroxyl (OH) groups for acetyl ($COOCH_3$) groups (hydrolysis), in the partially hydrolyzed form (70-100%) it can be viewed as a random copolymer P(VAC-VAL) with properties quite distinct from those of the polyvinylalcohol homopolymer. Crystallinity and water solubility, for example, can be reduced or suppressed.

In its water soluble form, polyvinylalcohol is used, for example, as a strippable or washable coating (release film for reinforced plastics). Some modified grades have been made into water insoluble fibers and films. Copolymers with ethylene (EVOH) are used in barrier packaging.

Polyvinyl Aldehydics (PVAH)

PVAH   poly'vinyl'aldehydic   (VI)

The reaction of polyvinylalcohol with various aldehydes leads to a class of polymers, referred to here as "polyvinyl aldehydics" but more commonly as "polyvinylacetals," in which all or part of the hydroxyl (OH) side groups are converted into ring-type acetal groups. They differ in the make-up of group R.

Three such polymers have found commercial use:

Polyvinylformal (PVFO)

PVFO   poly'vinyl'formal   (VI)

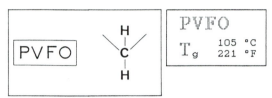

Polyvinylformal, which corresponds to formaldehyde, finds applications as temperature-resistant coatings for containers and electric wires.

Polyvinylacetal (PVACL)

PVACL   poly'vinyl'acetal   (VI)

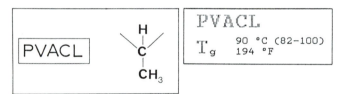

Polyvinylacetal, corresponding to acetaldehyde, has some use as a coating or as an adhesive.

Polyvinylbutyral (PVB)

PVB   poly'vinyl'butyral   (VI)

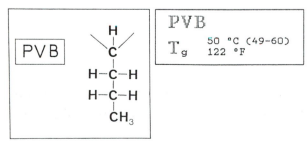

Polyvinylbutyral corresponds to butyraldehyde, and, in a partially converted form that can be viewed as a random copolymer P(VB-VAL) containing 10-15% of vinylal-cohol repeat units, it has long been used in plasticized form for the adhesive interlayer of laminated (triplex) safety glass, which requires toughness, transparency, weatherability, and excellent adhesion to glass.

Polyvinylalkylethers (PVAE)

PVAE   poly'vinyl'alkyl'ether   (VI)

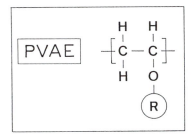

PVME   poly'vinyl'methyl'ether   (VI)

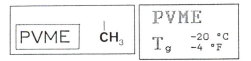

PVEE   poly'vinyl'ethyl'ether   (VI)

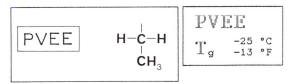

PVIE   poly'vinyl'isobutyl'ether   (VI)

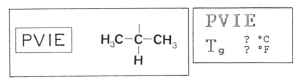

A series of vinyl-type polymers possess a characteristic ether feature (-O-) in the side group and differ in the make-up of group R. Three polyvinylalkylethers are of some commercial interest.

Polyvinylmethylether (PVME) (or polymethylvinylether) is water soluble, while polyvinylethylether (PVEE) and polyvinylisobutylether (PVIE) are not.

Polyvinylalkylethers are used as adhesives, modifiers in polymeric compounds and coatings.

Polyvinylpyrrolidone (PVPO)

PVPO   poly'vinyl'pyrrolidone   (VI)

PVPO		PVPO T_g 175 °C 347 °F

Polyvinylpyrrolidone or poly n-vinylpyrrolidone is not truly a plastic. It is highly polar and water soluble, and finds applications in adhesives and as a water thickener. Water solutions can be used as blood plasma substitute ("artificial blood").

Polyvinylcarbazole (PVCZ)

PVCZ   poly'vinyl'carbazole   (VI)

PVCZ		PVCZ T_g 190 °C (180–210) 374 °F

Polyvinylcarbazole is a true plastic with a high softening point. Cited uses include high frequency dielectrics and photoconductive polymers for xerography.

Polyvinylpyridine (PVP)

P2VP poly'vinyl'pyridine (VI)

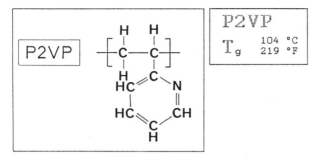

| P2VP | T_g | 104 °C
219 °F |

P4VP poly'vinyl'pyridine (VI)

| P4VP | T_g | 142 °C
288 °F |

Poly 2-vinylpyridine (P2VP) appears to find more applications than poly 4-vinylpyridine (P4VP), primarily as a minor constituent in copolymers used as adhesives. See figures 3.18-3.23 for several applications of vinyl polymers.

Figure 3.18 · Exterior siding, profiles, rain water system (rigid polyvinylchloride PVC)
[FERRO]

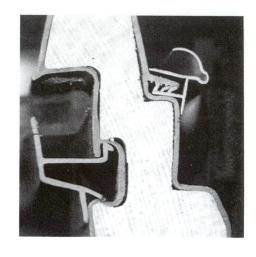

Fig. 3.20

Fig. 3.19

Figure 3.19 · Lawn/patio chair webbing (plasticized polyvinylchloride PVC) **[FERRO]**

Figure 3.20 · Coextruded vinyl-clad window frame (chlorinated PVC substrate, semi-rigid PVC capstock, flexible PVC edging)

Figure 3.21 · Barrier coextrudate/laminate films (with polyvinylidene chloride PVDC layer) **[DOW]**

Fig. 3.22

Fig. 3.23

Figure 3.22 · Coextruded/thermoformed, long shelf life soup container (poly-vinylidenechloride PVDC barrier layer) **[DOW]**

Figure 3.23 · Blow molded squeezable mayonnaise bottle with 6-layer coextruded structure (including polypropylene PP layer and P(E-VOH) barrier layer **[CONTINENTAL CAN]**

3.2.2.3 Styrenics

Several homopolymers feature repeat units that have a similarity in structure and, in particular, feature an aromatic (aryl) ring as a side group.   Polystyrene and a number of other polymers, referred to here as "styrenics," have achieved commercial importance, either in homopolymer form or in copolymer form.

Polystyrene (PS)

PS poly'styrene (ST)

| PS | H   H
┤C — C├
H   ⬡ | PS
T_g 100 °C (70–115)
212 °F |

Polystyrene is one of the four major thermoplastics. Like many plastics, it is commercially available in a wide variety of grades that correspond to variations of many factors.

The homopolymer is of the noncrystallizing type and, below its glass transition temperature T_g, it is a very stiff but brittle and highly transparent (clear) glassy material. Its high gloss and sparkling appearance are associated with a high index of refraction.

Polystyrene has remarkable intrinsic electrical properties. Its nonpolar character corresponds to low dielectric losses over a very wide range of alternating current (AC) frequencies, and the dielectric strength is also exceptional. Polystyrene is widely used in electronics as insulator and capacitor material, sometimes in cross-linked versions.

Processing of polystyrene is generally straightforward. Injection molding, with corresponding easy flowing grades, and extrusion of finished products (profiles, pipes, etc.) or sheets for subsequent thermoforming are the most common processes.

Polystyrene tends to have a rather low intrinsic resistance to weathering, and UV radiation causes yellowing and further embrittlement. Fire resistance is not particularly good. Many organic fluids, such as aromatic and chlorinated hydro-carbons as well as food oils and fats, are either solvents or cause undesirable changes to the material. Properties and dimensions, however, are unaffected by moisture or water.

The brittleness of the unmodified homopolymer is often unacceptable, and modified polystyrene grades have been developed which offer a wide range of impact resistance through chain and graft copolymerization and polyalloying with elastomeric polymers (rubbers). The modification often leads to a reduction or suppression of the transparency and a reduction in stiffness. While the unmodified homopolymer is called "conventional," "normal," "regular," "standard," "general-purpose" (GP), or "crystal polystyrene," impact resistant grades are usually referred to as "high-impact" (HI) or "rubber-toughened polystyrene" and are discussed in some detail later. The impact resistance of noncrystallizing polymers can also be improved through biaxial orientation, and highly transparent, tough polystyrene sheets and films are made that are used in packaging applications, for example.

The many applications of polystyrene include injection molded products, such as low-cost disposable serviceware, cabinets, toys, etc. Extruded products include finished goods, such as profiles or pipes as well as sheets which are subsequently thermoformed into small or large objects.

Polystyrene is also widely used as a cellular material for insulation or packaging applications.

Styrene monomer is generally one of the components of unsaturated polyester resin systems, and polystyrene repeat units form an important part of the network polymer formed through curing.

Polyparamethylstyrene (PPMS)

PPMS poly'para'methyl'styrene (ST)

PPMS	H H $-[C-C]-$ H ⬡ CH$_3$	PPMS T_g 110 °C 230 °F

Poly para(p) methylstyrene homopolymer is fairly similar to polystyrene with a slightly higher glass transition temperature. Commercial production of the monomer has begun recently, and it is claimed to have the potential to become a low-cost alternative for styrene in homopolymers and copolymers.

Polyalphamethylstyrene (PAMS)

PAMS poly'alpha'methyl'styrene (ST)

PAMS	H CH$_3$ $-[C-C]-$ H ⬡	PAMS T_g 160 °C 320 °F

Poly alpha methylstyrene has not achieved much commercial importance as a homopolymer in spite of a relatively high glass transition temperature T_g, which gives it a much better temperature resistance than polystyrene. It finds significant use in copolymers, however.

Rubber-toughened (impact) Polystyrene (HIPS)

Random copolymerization of a small fraction of elastomer-type repeat units with polystyrene does improve the impact properties somewhat, but the associated lowering of the glass transition temperature is normally unacceptable.

Block copolymerization of a small elastomeric component allows the molecular dispersion of the elastomeric regions (blocks), and the glass transition can remain essentially unchanged. The small size of the dispersed regions may have no effect on the light transmission, and transparency can be retained. The chemical manufacture, however, tends to be more complex and costly.

A viable compromise involves the dispersion of independently polymerized small rubbery particles in the polystyrene matrix. Good dispersion and interface adhesion require a good compatibility of the phases, which is often achieved by choosing a styrene-containing rubbery copolymer, such as styrene-butadiene rubber, for the dispersed phase. Dispersion can be conveniently achieved when both phases are blended in finely divided latex form. The resulting system can be viewed as a polyalloy. Rubber particles are thought to play the role of crack arrestors or energy sinks when the toughened polystyrene is subjected to impact loads.

Styrene-based Copolymers

The low cost of styrene monomer and the good processability of the polymer make it an attractive major (dominant) component for a wide range of copolymers that are relatively easy to polymerize. The following discussion will first introduce copolymers that involve only one other type of repeat unit. More complex systems involving more than two types of repeat units (e.g., terpolymers, for example) and polyalloys will be dealt with subsequently.

Styrene-butadiene [P(S-B)]

Styrene and butadiene monomers are relatively easy to copolymerize in a wide variety of ways. Polybutadiene is discussed in section 3.4.2.1. Commercial copolymers tend to be plastic-like (styrene-dominant) or rubber-like (butadiene-dominant). In the first case, polybutadiene contributes primarily in terms of impact resistance (toughness), while in the second case, cost (raw material), compatibility (blends and polyalloys) and processing factors call for the incorporation of styrene.

Styrene-butadiene plastics

Styrene-dominant (about 70%) random copolymers have long been used in emulsion (latex) form to produce coatings (paints). The glass transition is intermediate between those of polystyrene (about 100°C or 212°F) and polybutadiene (about -80°C or -213°F), roughly in proportion to the ratio of repeat units, giving the materials a rather low temperature resistance. Commercial butadiene-styrene plastics, on the other hand, probably correspond to block copolymers.

Styrene-butadiene elastomers

Random copolymers involving about 75% of butadiene repeat units correspond to what is often referred to as the "basic general purpose synthetic rubber" (SBR). (See section 3.4.2.2) Special "tailored" block copolymers form an important class of thermoplastic elastomers.

Styrene-acrylonitrile [P(S-AN) or SAN]

The random copolymerization of, typically, 20-30% of polyacrylonitrile repeat units with polystyrene yields plastics that have many of the useful properties of polystyrene (transparency, surface appearance, ease of processing), as well as improved temperature and chemical resistance. [Polyacrylonitrile (PAN) is discussed in Section 3.2.2.4]. The better resistance to food and body oils makes them prime materials for transparent houseware personal care items. They are also widely used for transparent medical products and for meter or light lenses. Polyvinylchloride and polysulfone, for example, have been used with SAN resins to form commercially important polyalloys [A(SAN/PVC) and A(SAN/PSU)].

Styrene-methylmethacrylate [P(S-MMA) or SMMA)

Copolymerization with some of the more costly methylmethacrylate improves the weatherability and impact properties of polystyrene for transparent applications.

Styrene-paramethylstyrene [P(S-PMS)]

The commercial success of such copolymers depends on the relative cost of the monomers.

Styrene-alphamethylstyrene [P(S-AMS)]

The higher glass transition of alphamethylstyrene gives heat resistant, but also more costly plastics.

Styrene-maleicanhydride [P(S-MLA) or SMA]

Such copolymers, said to contain 6-17% of maleicanhydride repeat units, have a much improved temperature resistance. Maleicanhydride (MLA) is discussed under section 3.3. The combination of cost, processability, impact, and chemical resistance place suitable grades in competition with noncrystallizing engineering plastics.

Several applications of styrene polymers are shown in figures 3.24-3.27.

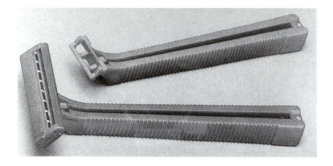

Figure 3.24 · Disposable razors (polystyrene PS) [CACO]

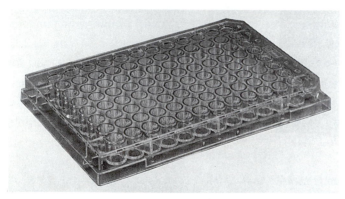

Figure 3.25 · 96 - Well serum/cultures test plate (clear polystyrene PS) [CACO]

Figure 3.26 · Window frame profiles (weatherable polystyrene PS + glass fiber) [THERMOFIL]

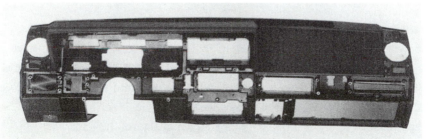

Figure 3.27 · Automotive instrument panel substrate (A(SMA/PC) polyalloy) [ARCO]

3.2.2.4 Acrylonitrilics

Several polymers have repeat units that feature a nitrile side group (C ≡ N).

Polyacrylonitrile (PAN)

PAN poly'acrylo'nitrile (AN)

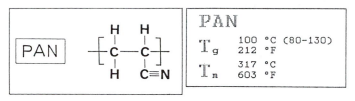

Polyacrylonitrile (or polyvinylcyanide) homopolymer is a polar crystallizing polymer that undergoes chemical decomposition before crystalline melting at temperatures above 300°C (572°F). It is, therefore, not a true thermoplastic material. The almost pure homopolymer, however, can be processed into fibers (acrylic fibers) through its spinning from solutions.

Commercial acrylic textile fibers are reported to contain at least 85% of acrylonitrile, combined, for example, with 5-15% of methylmethacrylate repeat units.

Polyacrylonitrile has a very good resistance to most chemicals, as well as to heat and weathering. It is also a superior barrier material. Acrylonitrile repeat units help confer these properties to thermoplastic copolymers in which they are involved.

Polymethacrylonitrile (PMAN)

PMAN poly'methacrylo'nitrile (AN)

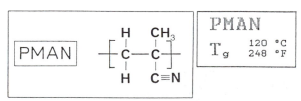

Polymethacrylonitrile homopolymer does not appear to crystallize, and its glass transition temperature is given as 120°C (248°F). Methacrylonitrile repeat units are dominant (90%) in copolymers, involving about 5% of styrene repeat units and also 5% of alphamethylstyrene. Such copolymer is transparent, is an excellent barrier to carbon dioxide (CO_2), and possesses good creep resistance, making it a suitable material for carbonated beverage containers.

Acrylonitrile-based Copolymers

Several commercially important copolymers feature a dominant proportion of acrylonitrile repeat units.

Acrylonitrile-styrene [P(AN-S)] and acrylonitrile-methylacrylate [P(AN-MA)]

Fiber-forming polymers are generally useful for strong, thin container walls or films. Polyacrylonitrile, because of its superior barrier properties, is particularly attractive. Copolymers comprising about 70% of acrylonitrile, between 20% and 30% of either styrene or methylacrylate, and sometimes rubber-like repeat units, such as butadiene (0-10%) or nitrile rubber (NBR), find growing use as food packaging films and containers for carbonated beverages under the name nitrile resins.

Acrylonitrile-methylmethacrylate [P(AN-MMA)]

The use of copolymers involving about 70% of acrylonitrile and 30% of methylmethacrylate repeat units is reported for thick transparent products, such as glazing, which require high-impact properties and good chemical and weathering resistance.

3.2.2.5 Acrylics

A number of commercial polymers involve repeat units whose names feature the term "acryl."

Polyacrylicacid (PAA) and Polymethacrylicacid (PMAA)

PAA   poly'acrylic'acid (AC)

| PAA | H   H
$\begin{bmatrix} & | & & | \\ & C & — & C \\ & | & & | \\ & H & & C-OH \\ & & & \| \\ & & & O \end{bmatrix}$ | PAA
T_g 106 °C
223 °F |

PMAA   poly'methacrylic'acid (AC)

| PMAA | H   CH$_3$
$\begin{bmatrix} & | & & | \\ & C & — & C \\ & | & & | \\ & H & & C-OH \\ & & & \| \\ & & & O \end{bmatrix}$ | PMAA
T_g ? °C
? °F |

Polyacrylicacid and polymethacrylicacid repeat units are characterized by a hydrogen atom (H) and a methyl group (CH_3), respectively, opposite to the acid group. Both repeat units are polar and the corresponding polymers are water-soluble. The repeat units are involved in copolymers, with ethylene repeat units in particular. They are also essential in the formation of ionomers (IO).

Poly-R Acrylates and Poly-R Methacrylates

PRA   poly'R'acrylate   (AC)

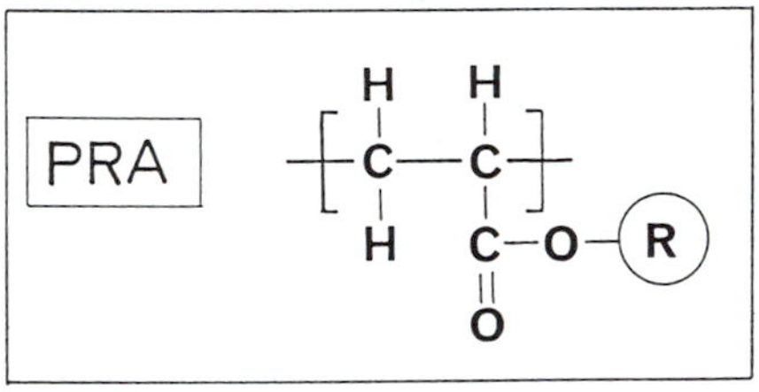

PRMA   poly'R'methacrylate   (AC)

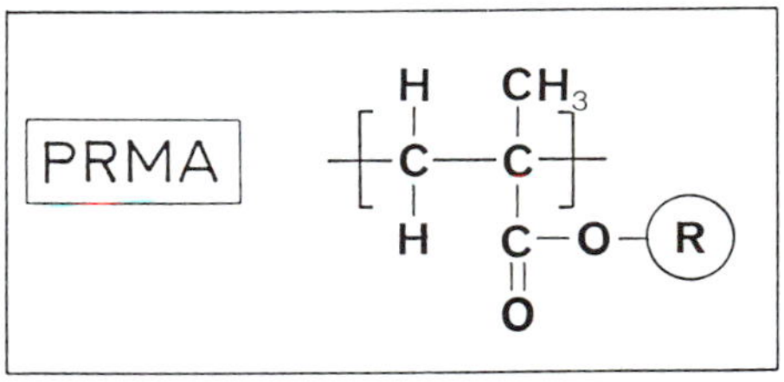

Esters of acrylic or methacrylic acids involve **R** groups that can be methyl, ethyl, butyl, or similar.

Polymethylmethacrylate is really the only homopolymer in the series with a sufficiently high glass transition temperature to form a useful plastic. Repeat units of the other types are used, however, in commercially important copolymers and also in near homopolymer form in paints, adhesives, and other products. Ethylacrylate repeat units form the major component in acrylate rubbers.

Polymethylacrylate (PMA)

PMA   poly'methyl'acrylate   (AC)

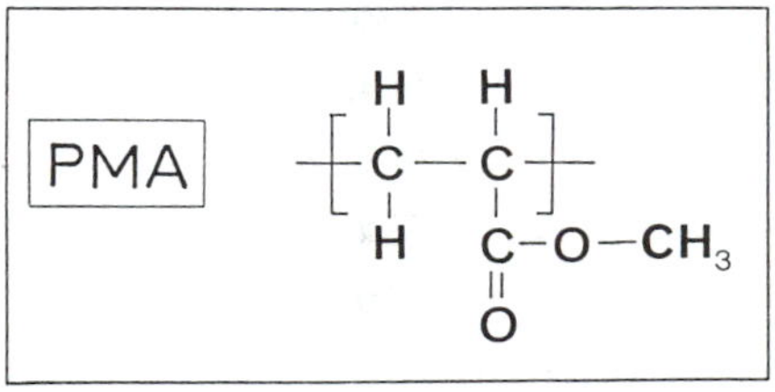

PMA

T_g 9 °C (0-25)
        48 °F

Polyethylacrylate (PEA)

PEA　poly'ethyl'acrylate　(AC)

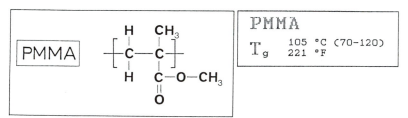

PEA

$$T_g \quad \begin{matrix} -22 \ °C \ (-24--5) \\ -7 \ °F \end{matrix}$$

Polybutylacrylate (PBA)

PBA　poly'butyl'acrylate　(AC)

PBA

$$T_g \quad \begin{matrix} -45 \ °C \ (-55--35) \\ -49 \ °F \end{matrix}$$

Polymethylmethacrylate (PMMA)

PMMA　poly'methyl'methacrylate　(AC)

PMMA

$$T_g \quad \begin{matrix} 105 \ °C \ (70-120) \\ 221 \ °F \end{matrix}$$

The best known and remarkable property of polymethylmethacrylate is probably its excellent transparency. Its optical properties, in general, are supported by good rigidity and acceptable impact and abrasion resistance, outstanding weatherability, and good general chemical resistance except for a number of organic solvents.

It is primarily used in clear or colored and transparent or translucent form to make such diverse objects as hard contact lenses, automotive tail-light lenses, safety and security glazing, skylights, illuminated signs, and optical fibers. It is also used for coatings, such as floor waxes, and in emulsion (latex) paints, although acrylates are more common in this latter application. Methylmethacrylate monomer is also an important ingredient in certain polyester thermosetting systems.

Processing methods include casting from the monomer, for optimal optical properties, extrusion from thermoplastic resins to produce sheets that may be subsequently thermoformed, or injection molding for small complex parts.

Polymethylmethacrylate is also used in copolymer form; for example, the higher glass transition temperature of alphamethylstyrene homopolymer (PAMS) is associated with the fact that the copolymerization of AMS repeat units in polymethylmethacrylate improves its temperature resistance without significantly reducing its transparency.

Polyethylmethacrylate (PEMA)

PEMA   poly'ethyl'methacrylate   (AC)

PEMA

$$\left[\begin{array}{cc} H & CH_3 \\ | & | \\ C - C \\ | & | \\ H & C-O-C-CH_3 \\ & \| \quad | \\ & O \quad H \end{array}\right] \quad H$$

PEMA

T_g 65 °C
         149 °F

Cyanoacrylate Resins (CNA)

CNA   cyano'acrylate'resin   (AC)

CNA

$$\left[\begin{array}{cc} H & C \equiv N \\ | & | \\ C - C \\ | & | \\ H & C-O-(R) \\ & \| \\ & O \end{array}\right]$$

Strong cements (glues, contact adhesives, etc.) based on cyanoacrylate repeat units have appeared in the marketplace. The repeat unit features a nitrile group ($C \equiv N$) opposite an ester group (COOR), where **R** can be methyl, ethyl, propyl, or butyl. The monomers are reported to polymerize with water moisture acting as a catalyst. The absence of significant contraction on polymerizing and the strongly polar nature of the polymer are associated with the outstanding adhesive (bonding) strength.

Hydroxyethylmethacrylate (HEMA)

HEMA   hydroxy'ethyl'methacrylate   (AC)

HEMA

$$\left[\begin{array}{cc} & H \quad CH_3 \\ & | \quad\; | \\ -&C-C- \\ & | \quad\; | \\ & H \quad C-O-C-C-OH \\ & \quad\quad \| \quad\; | \;\; | \\ & \quad\quad O \quad H \;\; H \end{array}\right]$$

2-Hydroxyethylmethacrylate homopolymer (HEMA) is water-soluble, but when it is polymerized in the presence of ethylene glycol dimethacrylate (EGDMA), which acts as a cross-linking agent through its four available links, a network polymer is formed. The network polymer is no longer soluble in water, but can be swollen to an extent controlled by the degree of cross-linking to form what is referred to as a "hydrogel." The soft hydrogel possesses the combination of properties (including good oxygen permeability) required to produce soft contact lenses.

Polyacrylamide (PAM)

PAM   poly'acryl'amide   (AC)

PAM

$$\left[\begin{array}{cc} H \quad H \\ | \quad\; | \\ -C-C- \\ | \quad\; | \\ H \quad C-NH_2 \\ \quad\quad \| \\ \quad\quad O \end{array}\right]$$

MBAM   methylene'bis'acryl'amide   (AC)

MBAM

$$\begin{array}{ccccccccc} H & H & O & H & H & H & O & H & H \\ | & | & \| & | & | & | & \| & | & | \\ C- & C- & C- & N- & C- & N- & C- & C- & C \\ | & & & & | & & & & | \\ H & & & & H & & & & H \end{array}$$

Polyacrylamide is strongly polar, water soluble polymer. When high molecular weight polyacrylamide is cross-linked, it forms a network polymer. Relatively lightly cross-linked polyacrylamide can be swollen with water to form rubber-like gels that are widely used for the separation of small molecules (gel chromatography). Methylene bisacrylamide (MBAM) is often used as the cross-linking agent.

See figures 3.28 and 3.29 for two applications of acrylic polymers.

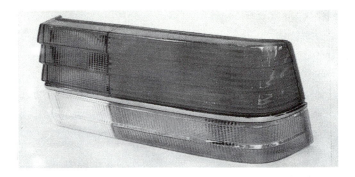

Figure 3.28 · Automotive tail light lenses (acrylic PMMA) **[SIGNALVISION]**

Figure 3.29 · Multi-wall glazing for greenhouses (acrylic PMMA) **[ICI]**

3.2.2.6 Miscellaneous Copolymers and Polyalloys

Commercial polymer systems can become very complex when the many possibilities of tailoring the chemical and physical structure are used and manufacturers, understandably, do not generally publicize the structure of their specific resins and grades. As a consequence, the information given is often not complete or firmly established, but nevertheless the discussion of the following systems should have a useful indicative value.

Acrylonitrile-butadiene-styrene Systems (ABS)

The important ABS plastics, featuring three types of repeat units in significant amounts, were first introduced in the late 1940s.

The proportions of the three repeat units vary according to grade with representative ranges, such as acrylonitrile 20-30%, butadiene 20-30%, and styrene 40-60%.

In a largely oversimplified manner, one can view the major role of the individual repeat units as the following: acrylonitrile for chemical and temperature resistance, butadiene for impact resistance, and styrene for cost and processability.

The method of manufacture of the resins can result in significantly different chemical or physical structures for given proportions, and thus commercial resins correspond to a very wide spectrum of materials.

One process involves the copolymerization of styrene and acrylonitrile monomers in the presence of polybutadiene. While most of the styrene and acrylonitrile copolymerize to form styrene-acrylonitrile copolymer as the dominant phase, a fraction appears to form styrene-acrylonitrile grafts on some polybutadiene chains. These grafts favor a good dispersion of polybutadiene domains in the styrene-acrylonitrile matrix, as well as good adhesion between phases.

Another process involves the independent preparation of two copolymers: styrene-acrylonitrile (SAN) discussed earlier (typically 70:30 proportions) and butadiene-acrylonitrile (typically 65:35 proportions), which is comparable to nitrile rubber (NBR) discussed in the elastomer section. The two copolymers are then mixed (blended) in latex form, or in bulk, at processing temperatures. The presence of acrylonitrile repeat units in both phases favors a good dispersion of the rubber particles and good interfacial adhesion.

ABS resins are very versatile in their applications, which include extruded and molded rigid pipes and fittings for the construction industry, thermoformed refrigerator door liners, and small boat hulls, and telephone and business machine housings. Some grades are claimed to qualify as engineering plastics. The modest intrinsic resistance to weathering can be improved through the use of suitable stabilizers.

ABS-based polyalloys

ABS resins, although already complex in structure, have been combined with other plastics to form commercially important polyalloys. Polyvinylchloride improves flame resistance and chemical resistance in A(ABS/PVC) polyalloys. Polycarbonate improves temperature and impact resistance in A(ABS/PC) polyalloys. The resilience and wear properties of thermoplastic polyurethane are sought in A(ABS/TPU) polyalloys. Other ABS-based polyalloys involve polysulfone [A(ABS/PSU)].

Acrylonitrile-chlorinated polyethylene-styrene Resins (ACS)

These resins appear similar to some types of ABS resins, with chlorinated polyethylene now playing the role of butadiene or nitrile rubber in ABS. Flame retardancy is associated with the presence of chlorine and good weatherability with the absence of butadiene unsaturations.

Olefin-styrene-acrylonitrile Resins (OSA)

These resins appear to be polyalloys of SAN resin with an olefinic thermoplastic elastomer.

Acrylonitrile-ethylene-styrene Resins (AES)

Such resins appear to be polyalloys of SAN resin with graft-copolymerized styrene and acrylonitrile on an ethylene-propylene elastomeric backbone. Their composition, if not their detailed structure, would thus be comparable to that of OSA resins.

Methylmethacrylate-butadiene-styrene Resins (MBS)

These resins are reported to be transparent with a structure similar to that of ABS resins. Some sources appear to give methylacrylate rather than methylmethacrylate as the acrylic component.

Acrylonitrile-styrene-acrylate Resins (ASA)

These resins appear to be polyalloys of SAN resins with a polyacrylate (acryl ester, acrylic) elastomer, which serves as the nitrile elastomer in some ABS resins. The resins are claimed to have a much improved resistance to light (outdoor weathering). The abbreviation "ASA" has also been used for systems referred to as aryl-styrene-acryl resins.

Two applications of ABS resins are depicted in figures 3.30 and 3.31.

Figure 3.30 · Business machine body elements (ABS resin)

Figure 3.31 · Refrigerator inner liner and door liner (ABS resin) **[BORG-WARNER]**

3.2.2.7 *Cellulosics*

Cellulose (CEL)

CEL   cellulose (CE)

CEL

Cellulose, a carbohydrate polymer, is a very common natural material. It is a major constituent of wood ($\approx 50\%$) and cotton fibers ($\approx 100\%$). The repeat unit features a ring structure with three characteristic hydroxyl (OH) groups, which are associated with hydrogen bonds and the high crystallinity of the polymer. Before cellulose crystals can be melted, chemical degradation occurs, and thus cellulose does not have thermoplastic properties or a measurable melting temperature T_m.

A chemical treatment can lead to the destruction of the crystalline structure, and a cellulose-based fluid can then be shaped into films or fibers. A subsequent treatment returns the molecules to their original cellulose structure and the material to a crystalline state. The classical intermediate fluid is often referred to as "viscose" and the final product as "regenerated cellulose."

Regenerated cellulose film is commonly known as "cellophane," the first transparent packaging or wrapping film. Cellophane is rather strongly affected by moisture, but not by food fats and oils. Regenerated cellulose fibers are known as rayon.

Thermoplastic Cellulose Derivatives

CELD   cellulose′derivatives   (CE)

The infusibility of cellulose crystals can be overcome in a permanent way if the hydrogen atom (H) of all or part of the hydroxyl groups (OH) are replaced by other groups, denoted here R (or R-substituent), in general. This is relatively easy, because of the intrinsic reactivity of hydrogen in OH groups. The so-called cellulose derivatives (CELD) are associated with esterification (nitrate, acetate, etc.) or etherification (ethylcellulose, etc.), and it is essential to realize that the substitution, in many cases, involves only a fraction of available OH groups. Degrees of substitution are defined as either the average number of R-substituent groups per unit (0-3) or the weight percentage of R-substituent (0-50% or even higher).

Partially substituted cellulose derivatives have properties that suggest that little or no crystallinity is present. The irregularity of the resulting polymeric chains explains the loss of crystallinity and, at the same time, suggests that they may not have a clear glass transition (T_g) temperature zone; little seems to have been reported regarding this issue.

In general, the properties of cellulose derivatives depend on the type and degree of substitution. Since cellulose derivatives are often plasticized, it is difficult to make very general statements on their mechanical properties. They tend to be moisture sensitive and to have good resistance to petroleum products, as well as food oils and fats.

Cellulose esters
Cellulosenitrates (CN)

CN   cellulose'nitrate   (CE)

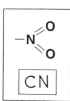

The **R**-substituent in cellulosenitrates is NO_2. Cellulosenitrate, an inorganic ester, is often considered the first synthetic or man-made plastic, and was introduced around the midnineteenth century as a solution (Collodion) or a plasticized plastic (Parkesine, Celluloid). The properties depend primarily on the degree of nitration (reported nitrogen content varies between 11% and 14%), but also on the amount or type of plasticizer, such as camphor. Cited advantages include toughness, water repellency, and good surface appearance, but it is highly flammable and difficult to process by modern methods. Early applications have survived, such as ping-pong balls and frames for prescription or sunglasses.

Celluloseacetates (CA)

CA   cellulose'acetate   (CE)

$$-\overset{\displaystyle}{\underset{\displaystyle O}{C}}-CH_3$$

CA

The **R**-substituent in celluloseacetate is the acetyl group $COCH_3$. Celluloseacetates, organic esters, achieved commercial importance at the beginning of the twentieth century.

The fully substituted derivative or triacetate (44.8% substitution), much like cellulose itself, is not thermoplastic. As other crystalline polymers, it can be made into fibers. Transparent films are also made, which have good resistance to oils, fats, and greases. Optically clear sheets are used for audiovisual purposes (acetate transparencies, photographic film, etc.).

Less substituted derivatives or secondary acetates, with reported substitutions around 40%, are true thermoplastics and are easily molded or extruded. Contrary to cellulosenitrate, the acetates are not highly flammable (slow-burning to self-extinguishing). Common cited applications include toys, and tool or cutlery handles.

Mixed cellulosic organic esters

CP   cellulose'propionate   (CE)

```
        H
        |
   -C - C - CH₃
   ‖    |
   O    H
   ┌──────┐
   │  CP  │
   └──────┘
```

CB   cellulose'butyrate   (CE)

```
        H  H
        |  |
   -C - C - C - CH₃
   ‖    |  |
   O    H  H
   ┌──────┐
   │  C B │
   └──────┘
```

Mixed cellulosic organic esters generally involve propionyl **R**-substituents (COC_2H_5) for propionate (**P**) or butyryl **R**-substituents (COC_3H_7) for butyrate (**B**), along with acetyl **R**-substituents.

Cellulose acetate-propionate (CAP)

Reported ranges of substitution for cellulose acetate-propionate are 2-9% for **A** and 39-47% for **P**.

Cellulose acetate-butyrate (CAB)

Reported ranges of substitution for cellulose acetate-butyrate are 12-15% for **A** and 26-39% for **B**.

Cellulose acetate-propionate and cellulose acetate-butyrate are generally mechanically tougher than celluloseacetate and easier to process.

Applications include many parts or housings, which involve skin contact (tool handles, portable appliances, steering wheels, glass frames, ballpoint pens, typewriter keys, etc.), and small or large transparent or translucent thermoformed parts (blister packages, outdoor signs, skylights, etc.), as well as metallized decorative parts.

Cellulose ethers

A variety of ether-type cellulose derivatives have found important commercial applications. Several of these polymers, however, are water soluble and thus not real plastics. They involve methyl (CH_3), ethyl (C_2H_5), sodium carboxymethyl (CH_2COONa) or hydroxyethyl (C_2H_4OH) R-substituents.

Methylcellulose (MC)

MC   methyl'cellulose   (CE)

Methylcellulose is water-soluble and harmless for external body contact or ingestion (edible). It is used in creams or foods as a thickening agent.

Ethylcellulose (EC)

EC   ethyl'cellulose   (CE)

Ethylcellulose is reported to involve a 45-48% substitution and is a genuine thermoplastic that finds applications particularly for its mechanical properties, especially toughness, at low temperatures, and for its superior resistance to alkalis (bases) relative to that of other cellulosics. It is also used as a coating and adhesive.

Carboxymethylcellulose (CMC)

CMC   carboxy'methyl'cellulose   (CE)

Sodium carboxymethylcellulose is water-soluble. On the average, seven CM groups are substituted for every 10 repeat units. Its applications are similar to those of methylcellulose.

Hydroxyethylcellulose (HEC)

HEC   hydroxy'ethyl'cellulose   (CE)

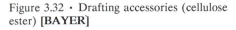

Hydroxyethylcellulose is water-soluble. Figures 3.32-3.34 relate to cellulosics.

Figure 3.32 · Drafting accessories (cellulose ester) [BAYER]

Figure 3.33 · Telephone stand and handset covers (cellulose ester) [BAYER]

Figure 3.34 · Hemodyalisis cartridge housing (cellulose propionate CP); FILTER
(cellulose triacetate CA) **[BAYER]**

3.2.2.8 *Polyamides*

PA–R   general'poly'amide (PA)

| PA-R | $\left[R - \underset{\overset{\|}{O}}{\overset{O}{C}} - \underset{H}{N} \right]$ |

PA–(R1,R2)   general'poly'amide (PA)

| PA-R₁,R₂ | $\left[R_1 - \underset{O}{C} - \underset{H}{N} - R_2 - \underset{H}{N} - \underset{O}{C} \right]$ |

A relatively broad class of polymers involves the formation, in the course of
polymerization, of characteristic amide linkages or groups -CO-NH-. These polymers
are referred to as "polyamides" (PA) or "nylons." The amide groups, also found in
natural proteins, confer the potential for strong intermolecular bonding and also cause
a certain affinity for polar molecules, such as water.

The general form of the repeat unit involves either a group of atoms denoted **R** and
an amide group or a group R_1, an amide group, a group R_2 and a second amide
group. It is the specific composition of the **R** groups that determines differences
between polyamide types.

The most common polyamides are the so-called aliphatic polyamides in which **R** groups consist of CH_2 units. Aromatic polyamides, sometimes referred to as "aramids," involve aromatic rings in **R** groups. There are also commercial polyamides of a mixed (aliphatic-aromatic) type.

Aliphatic Polyamides

PA—n   aliphatic′poly′amide (PA)

PA-n	$\left[\left(C\right)_{n-1} C - N\right]$

PA—4
- T_g 72 °C / 162 °F
- T_m 263 °C (262-265) / 505 °F

PA—11
- T_g 47 °C / 117 °F
- T_m 187 °C (179-194) / 369 °F

PA—6
- T_g 50 °C (20-60) / 122 °F
- T_m 220 °C (215-230) / 428 °F

PA—12
- T_g 40 °C / 104 °F
- T_m 179 °C (175-180) / 354 °F

PA—7
- T_g 60 °C / 140 °F
- T_m 225 °C (223-235) / 437 °F

Aliphatic polyamides are, by far, the most common polyamides, and the class is often referred to simply as "polyamides" or "nylons." Aliphatic polyamides are named here "PA-n" or "PA-(n_1,n_2)" according to the number and distribution of C atoms in the repeat unit.

The relatively short CH_2-based **R** groups (3-ll units) are reminiscent of polyethylene. They are quite flexible and confer a relatively low glass transition temperature T_g, while allowing easy crystallization enhanced by the strong interaction between amide groups of adjacent chain sections. As a general rule, higher amide/CH_2 ratios correspond to higher melting points T_m, as well as increased water absorption.

The molecular weight of commercial polyamides is relatively low (about 10,000-30,000), and polyamide melts generally have a rather low viscosity. This, and the

PA–(n1,n2)   aliphatic'poly'amide (PA)

$$\mathrm{PA\text{-}(n_1,n_2)} \quad \left[\left(\begin{array}{c} H \\ | \\ C \\ | \\ H \end{array}\right)_{n_1}\!\!\!-N-\overset{O}{\overset{\|}{C}}-\left(\begin{array}{c} H \\ | \\ C \\ | \\ H \end{array}\right)_{n_2-2}\!\!\!\overset{O}{\overset{\|}{C}}-N\right]$$

PA–(4,6)

T_g ? °C
    ? °F

T_m 295 °C
    563 °F

PA–(6,10)

T_g 40 °C
    104 °F

T_m 220 °C (210–227)
    428 °F

PA–(6,6)

T_g 50 °C (35–90)
    122 °F

T_m 260 °C (215–265)
    500 °F

PA–(6,12)

T_g ? °C
    ? °F

T_m 210 °C (206–217)
    410 °F

PA–(6,8)

T_g ? °C
    ? °F

T_m 225 °C (220–240)
    437 °F

characteristic sharp melting transition, call for special processing considerations (screw, nozzle, mold design, etc.).

The tendency for most polyamides to absorb significant amounts of water (up to about 8.5%) is associated with amide groups. Polyamides 11 and 12 are much less water sensitive than other commercial types. It is generally an unwelcome, but manageable characteristic, which negatively affects electrical properties and dimensional stability, in particular, and requires precautions in processing (predrying). In terms of mechanical properties, water plays a plasticizing role, promoting a ductile behavior. A polyamide is generally considered dry when less than about 0.2% of water is present.

It is important to realize that polyamides, like all polymers, and engineering polymers in particular, can be modified in numerous ways, and suppliers offer a wide variety of grades adapted to specific applications.

Aliphatic polyamides have a rather high degree of crystallinity and are normally translucent (milky) to opaque in natural form. A tendency to form coarse spherulitic structures, associated with lower impact strength, is countered by the use of nucleating agents that can also have beneficial effects on the speed of crystallization (solidification) for fast production rates.

The success of polyamides as a major class of engineering plastics is associated with a very good balance of properties.

Basic mechanical properties are in the high range although somewhat dependent on the water content. Fatigue and creep resistance are very good. Impact strength is generally good, although polyamides are considered to be notch-sensitive. Polyamides are readily machinable for single or small production parts. Polyamides are noted for excellent frictional properties (self-lubrication) and good wear and abrasion resistance.

The chemical resistance is generally good. The effect of water has been noted. Strong acids, oxidizing agents, some salt solutions (e.g., zinc chloride) can have a detrimental effect. At processing temperatures, oxidative degradation and hydrolysis can occur, although suitable additives can help counter these tendencies. Resistance to hydrocarbons, fungi, bacteria, and food chemicals is particularly good. Very few solvents are known. Polyamides have a fair resistance to UV light (weathering) and additives (UV absorbers, carbon black) are recommended for outdoor applications. Flame resistance is generally good, although the use of glass fiber reinforcement, for example, may call for the use of flame retardants.

Polyamides are used in a variety of thermoplastic processing techniques (injection, extrusion, blow molding, rotomolding, coating, etc.). Its sometimes unconventional behavior, which has been noted earlier, can be handled readily by following processing recommendations made available by suppliers.

The numerous applications of polyamides include a wide variety of mechanical components where mechanical properties, moldability, and self-lubrication are essential factors. Examples include slides and guides, gear trains, bearings, valves, impellers, propellers, and housings. Hydrocarbon resistance is a major consideration for gas tanks, automotive tubing and lines, etc.

Good resistance to oxygen permeation, as well as oils or greases has opened the film packaging market for cheese, bacon, meats, and other foods, and the temperature resistance offers good prospects in the expanding area of boil-in or bake-in bags or pouches.

The use of polyamides as fibers is well known. Monofilaments are used for ropes, tire cords, fishing lines, tennis strings, surgical sutures, brush bristles, and artificial hair and fur. Chopped and spun yarn is used in conventional textiles.

Aromatic Polyamides

P̶M̶P̶I̶   poly'm'phenylene'isophthal'amide   (PA)

PMPI		
T_g	? °C	
	? °F	
T_m	375 °C	
	689 °F	

P̶P̶P̶T̶   poly'p'phenylene'terephthal'amide   (PA)

PPPT		
T_g	>300 °C	
	>572 °F	
T_m	500 °C	
	932 °F	

The chemical composition of commercial polymers in the relatively new class of aromatic polyamide materials (aramids) tends to be complex and proprietary. Two relatively simple repeat units, however, are often associated with this class: poly m-- phenylene isophthalamide (PMPI) and poly p-phenylene terephthalamide (PPPT). In both cases, aromatic rings in the backbone correspond to high chain rigidity and high glass transition temperature.

Aromatic polyamides are not currently used as moldable thermoplastics; they are produced as fibers by unconventional spinning processes which are associated with liquid crystal polymer (LCP) technology. As all polymeric fibers, aramid fibers are highly crystalline, but the crystalline structure differs significantly from that of conventional polymeric fibers and involves extended (straight) chain crystals.

The first commercially important aramid fiber was introduced around 1961 as HT-1 nylon or Nomex and is associated with PMPI. It was particularly noted for its temperature and flame resistance and its good electrical properties and is used in paper-like sheet form as electrical insulation for transformers, electric motors, and generators, as well as in woven form for fire- and temperature-resistant protective clothing, gloves, conveyor belts, etc.

A second type of aramid fiber was introduced around 1972. It is generally associated with PPPT, with mechanical properties as its most outstanding feature. Kevlar 29 (DP-01 or Fiber B) was developed as a textile fiber and is used in products such as tire cord, ropes, cables, protective fabrics, and coated fabrics for inflatable structures.

Kevlar 49 (PRD 49) was introduced primarily as a reinforcing fiber for thermosetting resins.

Aramid fibers have the typical low density of polymeric materials, but remarkably high levels of modulus and strength, comparable with those of glass, carbon fibers or metals give them outstanding "specific" properties (modulus/density or strength/density ratios).

Specific applications of aramids in woven fabric or composite form include radial tire belts; ballistic protection items, such as vests, jackets, helmets, and armor plates; and sports equipment, such as skis, tennis rackets, and fishing rods. They are used extensively in high-performance marine or aerospace applications. Their heat resistance has permitted their use in brake lining materials, as well as for certain gaskets and packings.

Transparent Polyamides

PA-(6,3,T)   poly'amide (PA)

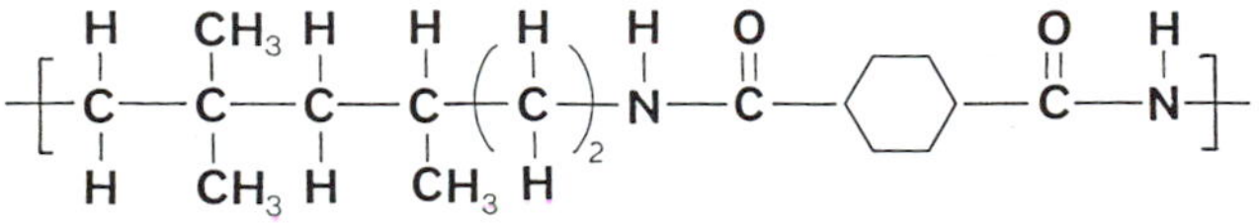

PA-(6,3,T)

T_g ? °C
? °F

PA-(6,T)   poly'amide (PA)

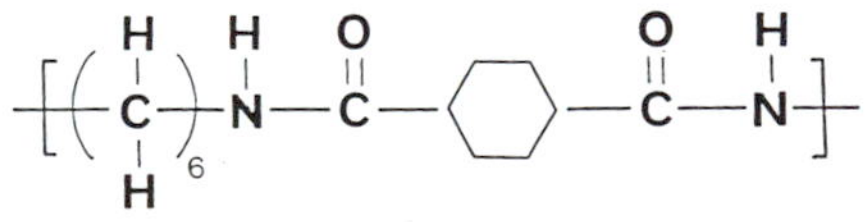

PA-(6,T)

T_g 120 °C / 248 °F
T_m 370 °C (210-370) / 698 °F

PA-(MD,12)   poly'amide (PA)

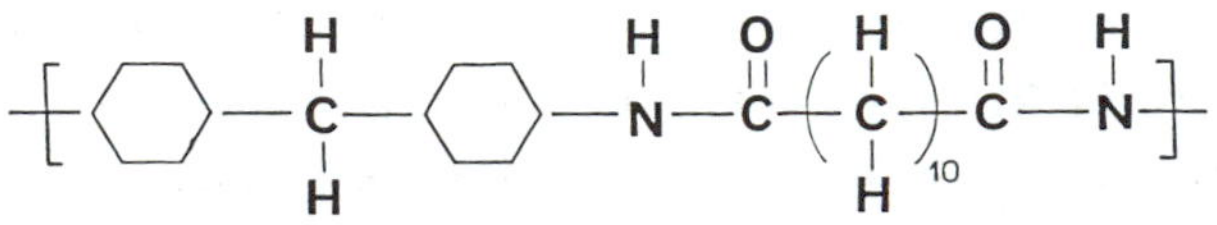

PA-(MD-12)

T_g 135 °C / 275 °F
T_m 205 °C / 401 °F

PA−(MX,6) poly'amide (PA)

PA−(MX,6)

PA−(MX−6)

T_g ? °C
        ? °F

T_m ? °C
        ? °F

There is an important market for transparent engineering plastics that conventional moldable polyamides (aliphatic polyamides) cannot share because of their high crystallinity in the solid state. Conventional noncrystallizing engineering plastics, however, often lack certain aspects of chemical resistance, which polyamides can offer, in particular the resistance to hydrocarbon chemicals often found in engine environments.

A number of transparent polyamides are now commercially available, which appear to be the results of a variety of technologies. In all cases, crystallization has to be suppressed or at least retarded and reduced. An acceptable temperature resistance must now be associated with a higher glass transition temperature than that of conventional aliphatic polyamides. This can be achieved by the incorporation in the repeat unit of aromatic groups that stiffen the chains. At the same time, the introduction of side groups can impede the crystallization. This approach is illustrated in the case of the polymer referred to as "PA-(6,3,T)." Commercial transparent polyamides are also reported to involve copolymers based on PA-6 or PA-12.

Because of the variety of chemical structures involved, the properties and, in particular, the chemical resistance of transparent polyamides, can vary significantly. As stated earlier, hydrocarbon resistance is generally good, but some types may be adversely affected by alcohols and hot water, for example. Prolonged exposure to high temperatures may also trigger crystallization and the associated clouding of parts.

Other Polyamide Types

A number of crystallizing polyamides suitable, in particular, for fiber manufacture, have been developed that involve aliphatic and aromatic groups between amide groups (R_1 or R_2 groups). In PA-(6,T), for example, the R_2 group is of the terephthalic type. In PA-(MD,12) (QIANA fiber), the R_1 group is of the methylene diphenyl (MD) type. In PA-(MX,6) (MXDA fiber), the R_1 group is of the m-xylylene (MX) type.

See figures 3.35-3.41 for several applications of polyamides.

Figure 3.35 · Mechanical gears (polyamide PA-6) [BAYER]

Figure 3.36 · Roller skate sole plate and trucks; ice hockey skate blade support
(toughened polyamide PA) [DU PONT]

Figure 3.37 · Fluidized bed-coated butterfly valve for the chemical process industry
(polyamide PA-11) [ATO]

Figure 3.38 · Coated stirrers (polyamide PA-12) **[EMSER]**

Figure 3.39 · Filter bowl (transparent polyamide PA) **[EMSER]**

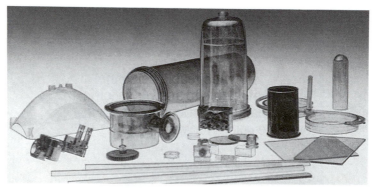

Figure 3.40 · Miscellaneous items (headlamp reflector, filter bowls etc...) (transparent polyamide PA) **[UPJOHN]**

Figure 3.41 · Rotameter elements (Transparent polyamide PA) **[DYNAMIT-NOBEL]**

3.2.2.9 Thermoplastic Polyesters, Polycarbonate

TP-R general'thermoplastic'poly'ester (TP)

TP-(R1,R2) general'thermoplastic'poly'ester (TP)

A class of thermoplastic polymers, referred to as the "thermoplastic polyesters" (TP), involves the formation, during polymerization, of characteristic ester linkages or groups -CO-O. Groups of atoms R or R_1 and R_2 interspersed between ester linkages determine differences between thermoplastic polyester types. These groups play a major role in interactions between molecules, or sections of molecules, which are involved in crystallization. Ester linkages can be destroyed in the presence of water molecules at high temperatures (hydrolysis) and thermoplastics polyesters must thus be processed in a very dry state. In general, polyesters are not affected by water at low (room) temperatures and, in particular, the low water absorption level (less than 0.4%) contributes to their good dimensional stability.

The most common thermoplastic polyesters involve both aliphatic (alkyl) and aromatic (aryl) groups, while some polyesters are wholly (fully) aromatic.

Polyalkylene Terephthalates (PAT)

PAT poly'alkylene'terephthalate (TP)

PBT   poly'butylene'terephthalate (TP)

PBT	$\left[\left(\underset{H}{\overset{H}{C}}\right)_4 O - \underset{O}{\overset{O}{C}} - \langle \rangle - \underset{O}{\overset{O}{C}} - O\right]$	PBT
		T_g 50 °C (40-60) 122 °F
		T_m 245 °C (224-267) 473 °F

Two high volume polyesters involve terephthalate groups and either ethylene or butylene groups. The first type is referred to as polyethylene terephthalate (PET) or (PETP), while the second type is most commonly called "polybutylene terephthalate" (PBT) or (PBTP), although the equivalent name polytetramethylene terephthalate (PTMT) is sometimes used. In general, those polyesters can be referred to as "polyalkylene terephthalates" (PAT).

Polyethylene terephthalate (PET)

PET   poly'ethylene'terephthalate (TP)

PET	$\left[\left(\underset{H}{\overset{H}{C}}\right)_2 O - \underset{O}{\overset{O}{C}} - \langle \rangle - \underset{O}{\overset{O}{C}} - O\right]$	PET
		T_g 70 °C (60-81) 158 °F
		T_m 265 °C (245-271) 509 °F

The flexible, but short, $(CH_2)_2$ groups tend to leave the chains relatively stiff and PET is particularly noted for its very slow crystallization outside a relatively narrow temperature range centered around 190°C (374°F). When cooled reasonably rapidly from the melt to a temperature below the glass transition T_g, PET solidifies in amorphous form, that is, it can be highly transparent. If the amorphous solid is subsequently heated above T_g, crystallization takes place (to about 30% crystallinity), although, as stated above, reasonable rates of crystallization require fairly high temperatures, normally above 120°C. In many of its applications, PET is first preshaped in the amorphous state and then given a uniaxial (fibers or tapes) or biaxial (film, containers) crystalline orientation. Through injection molding, PET can yield amorphous transparent objects (cold mold) or crystalline opaque objects (hot mold).

PET was initially introduced in the form of fibers, and this market is still very active. PET is also used in uniaxially oriented tape form, for strapping.

Another large market, which generally involves biaxial orientation, is that of films and sheets. Applications involve photographic and x-ray films, magnetic tapes, electrical insulation, drafting sheets, and food packaging films, including boil-in bags and retort pouches.

A rapidly growing market was recently opened by the introduction of new grades suitable for the fabrication of containers by a blow-molding process. One-step injection blow molding is used for small containers (vials, etc.), while, in view of the relatively low melt strength of present grades, large containers tend to be made by a two-step process involving the injection molding of an amorphous preform (cold mold), followed by its heating above T_g and its blowing to the final shape. Alcoholic beverages and edible liquids, in general, are increasingly packaged in PET containers. Biaxially oriented PET has a sufficiently low permeability to carbon dioxide (CO_2) to be a choice material for holding carbonated beverages; its strength and impact resistance being also suitable for such pressurized containers.

Polybutylene terephthalate (PBT)

Longer, more flexible $(CH_2)_4$ groups are generally associated with the fact that PBT can crystallize much faster than PET, and PBT is not normally encountered in amorphous solid form. The properties of the fairly highly crystalline PBT (as much as 60% crystallinity) are fairly similar to those of unoriented crystalline PET. PBT is not as conveniently oriented as PET, however, and it is normally used primarily in injection-molded applications, where fast cycles can be achieved with minimal precautions other than a thorough drying of the resin (less than 0.005% of water). Suitable grades tend to have a rather sharp melting transition, with a relatively low melt viscosity, allowing the molding of intricate shapes. The rapid crystallization and the high degree of crystallization, however, are often associated with warpage problems.

A good combination of properties makes PBT alone, or filled grades (glass, minerals, etc.), very suitable choices for many engineering applications. Mechanical properties are very good at reasonable temperatures, frictional and wear properties are among the best; electrical properties are good and stable; the very low water absorption and small thermal expansion, particularly with fillers, give very good dimensional stability. The chemical resistance, favorably affected by the crystallinity, is generally good, with some limitations including strong bases and hot water (above 60°C or 140°F).

Applications include electrical connectors, fuse boxes, coil bobbins, motor housings and brush holders, distributor and ignition coil caps, automotive body panels, exterior mirror housings, power tool housings, cookware handles, pumps and meters housings, rotors and valves, motion-transmitting gears, and windshield wiper blade frames. Many of these applications involve glass-filled grades (RTP), PBT is particularly compatible with glass fibers.

PET-based or PCT-based Copolyesters

Poly cyclohexanedimethanol terephthalate (PCT)

PCT   poly'cyclohexane'di'methanol'terephthalate   (TP)

PCT

T_g 75 °C (60-90)
          167 °F

T_m 292 °C (290-295)
          558 °F

CHDM   cyclo'hexane'di'methanol   (TP)

The polymer resulting from the reaction of cyclohexanedimethanol (CHDM) and terephthalic acid (TA) is reminiscent of PET, but features a saturated aryl-type group C_6H_{10} (s) between the two alkyl groups CH_2 (cyclohexylenedimethylene group). This thermoplastic homopolyester, referred to as "poly cyclohexanedimethanol tere-phthalate" and abbreviated as "PCT," is noted as less water sensitive than PET, but does not appear to be a commercial plastic.

Acid-modified PCT (PCTA)

The use of another difunctional acid, to replace some of the terephthalic acid in the polymerization of PCT, introduces chain irregularity, and useful polymers can result, which display little or no crystallizing tendency. These polymers are generally referred to as "acid-modified, PCT-based, copolyesters" (PCTA). Such materials are extruded as transparent films or sheets that are very suitable for many packaging applications (frozen meats shrink bags, blister packages, etc.).

Glycol-modified PET (PETG)

The substitution of a certain fraction of ethylene glycol by glycols, such as cyclohexanedimethanol (CHDM) in the polymerization of PET, also introduces chain irregularity and thus amorphous characteristics. Corresponding polymers are often referred to as "glycol-modified, PET-based, copolyesters" (PETG). A combination of properties, such as clarity, toughness, and melt strength, make such materials very suitable for blow-molded containers, thermoformed blister packages, and similar products.

Polyarylesters

A number of specialty plastics have repeat units that feature only aromatic-type groups (phenyl or aryl groups, etc.) between ester linkages. They are often referred to as "wholly aromatic polyesters." Polyarylesters is a general name for this class of polymers.

The simplest polyarylester is probably the homopolymer (homopolyester) based solely on p-hydroxybenzoyl acid. It is referred to as "poly p-hydroxybenzoyl acid" (PHBA).

Other wholly aromatic polyesters are based on a combination of suitable chemicals, most commonly p-hydroxybenzoic acid, terephthalic acid, isophthalic acid, bisphenol-A, and other bisphenols. They are generally classified as aromatic copolyesters and some of them are referred to as "polyarylates."

Poly p-hydroxybenzoyl acid (PHBA)

PHBA   poly'p'hydroxy'benzoyl'acid   (TP)

PHBA		
T_g	?	°C
	?	°F
T_m	550	°C
	1022	°F

The repeat unit of poly p-hydroxybenzoyl acid (PHBA) corresponds to a very stiff and regular chain, which explains the high crystallinity of the polymer and the temperature stability of the structure. Thermal degradation starts to occur at about 450°C before true melting, although a crystal-crystal transition around 350°C allows a special type of processing. This specialty polymer appears to be used primarily in blends with fluoropolymers for high-temperature wear applications (coatings, bearings, seals, etc.).

Polyarylates (PAR)

BA   bisphenol'A   (TP)

TA   terephthalic'acid   (TP)

$$\boxed{TA} \quad H-O-\overset{\overset{O}{\|}}{C}-\langle\hexagon\rangle-\overset{\overset{O}{\|}}{C}-O--H$$

IA   isophthalic'acid   (TP)

$$\boxed{IA} \quad H-O-\overset{\overset{O}{\|}}{C}-\langle\hexagon\rangle-\overset{\overset{O}{\|}}{C}-O--H$$

Polyarylates are often defined as copolyesters involving bisphenol-A (BA) and a mixture of terephthalic acid (TA) and isophthalic acid (IA), resulting in two distinct repeat units. This source of irregularity along the chains prevents crystallization, yielding amorphous polymers that are thus naturally transparent. The aryl groups are associated with stiff chains giving high glass transition temperatures with reported values of $T_g \approx 185°C$ (173-190) or 365°F for a commercial polyarylate. Besides having a very good resistance to heat, steam, and radiations, polyarylates are noted for their good weatherability and good fire resistance, even without additives. As other polyesters, they require thorough drying before processing. Reported applications include high-performance outdoor transparent parts, microwave cookware, and electrical or electronic parts. Materials marketed as polyestercarbonate or polyphthalatecarbonate appear to fit in this category.

Other aromatic copolyesters

DHB   di'hydroxy'bisphenol   (TP)

$$\boxed{DHB} \quad H-O-\langle\hexagon\rangle-\langle\hexagon\rangle-O-H$$

High-temperature-resistant aromatic copolyesters involving, for example, dihydroxybisphenol (DHB) and p-hydroxybenzoic acid, as well as either terephthalic acid or isophthalic acid, have become commercially available for injection or compression molding. The resulting chains allow crystallization and, in the case of injection grades, a definite melting point exists (T_m over 300°C or 572°F), above which thermoplastic processing is possible. Applications correspond primarily to very high temperature special situations. Such polymers were initially marketed under the tradename "EKKCEL" (Carborundum/Kennecott/ Sohio).

Much activity is currently taking place for the development and commercialization of so-called, liquid crystal polymers (LCP), which are discussed in this book in the section on crystallinity. Most thermoplastic liquid crystal polymers appear to be aromatic copolyesters.

Polycarbonate (PC)

PC   poly'carbonate   (TP)

PC	structure		PC		
	$-[-\langle\bigcirc\rangle-\underset{\underset{CH_3}{|}}{\overset{\overset{CH_3}{|}}{C}}-\langle\bigcirc\rangle-O-\underset{\overset{\|}{O}}{C}-O-]-$		T_g	150 °C (143–156) / 302 °F	
			T_m	230 °C (200–267) / 446 °F	

Polycarbonates can be viewed as polyesters of carbonic acid. In addition to a characteristic carbonate linkage O-CO-O, general purpose polycarbonate features a group resulting from the use of bisphenol-A. Special purpose grades appear to be proprietary copolymers, which may involve side groups different from the CH_3 groups of bisphenol-A, and possibly more carbon atoms between the aromatic groups.

The aromatic groups and the side groups are associated with relatively rigid chains and a minimal tendency to crystallize. The glass transition temperature T_g is consequently rather high. Above T_g, polycarbonates exhibit a rubbery to viscous behavior, since the crystalline melting temperature T_m does not correspond to a well-marked transition. When good melt flow is desired, it is recommended to process the melt above T_m. Despite relatively low molecular weights (25,000 to 50,000), the melt viscosities at moderate temperatures tend to be rather high, requiring high injection molding pressures and appropriate mold designs.

Current efforts to systematically use copolymerization and blending (polyalloys) of major polymers, to tailor polymeric systems to specific applications, have resulted in successful polycarbonate-containing copolymers and polyalloys.

Polycarbonates can be produced with a high level of purity and, owing to their basically noncrystalline structure, they can be highly transparent in unpigmented, unfilled grades.

Polycarbonates are particularly known for their outstanding toughness (impact resistance), which is superior to that of most rigid plastics, especially transparent ones; good stiffness and excellent creep resistance also contribute to making polycarbonates good engineering plastics for structural (mechanical) applications.

The noncrystalline nature of polycarbonates is associated with low molding shrinkage, allowing close product tolerances. The dimensional stability of parts is very good, with very little moisture absorption.

General-purpose polycarbonate is self-extinguishing, and special grades are available that are basically nonflammable. Grades based on the bromination of side groups can generate toxic fumes, however, and other fire-retarded grades are sometimes preferable.

The chemical resistance of polycarbonates, although not bad, is not one of its very strong points. Aromatic hydrocarbons (high-octane gasoline), chlorinated hydrocarbons, esters, ketones, amines, and strong bases (alkaline detergents, ammonia compounds), can severely affect the properties of PC. Subtle effects, characteristic of many noncrystallizing polymers, result in the formation of cracks or crazes in the simultaneous presence of stresses and of certain fluids; solvent stress-cracking or crazing must be watched for when solvent-based adhesives, paints, and inks are used; annealing, or the application of coatings, can reduce the problem. At elevated temperatures, hydrolysis may cause a chemical degradation. Continuous water exposure above 60°C, or short exposure to high processing temperatures, of insufficiently dried polycarbonate containing traces of water (more than about 0.02%), are damaging to the material. Polycarbonates are resistant to oxidation in air at elevated temperatures.

A tendency to absorb UV radiations may cause surface discoloration upon exposure to sunlight, but little structural damage results. Coatings are often used for weather protection of sheets and also provide scratch or mar resistance.

Electrical insulation properties are generally good and unaffected by moisture. Like many other thermoplastics, polycarbonates are used with reinforcing fillers (glass, etc.) in nontransparent, stiffness-critical applications. Good stiffness/weight compromises can be obtained in structural foamed parts.

Among the numerous applications of polycarbonates, many involve the combination of transparency and toughness. Safety glazing for public places, windshields, guards, street lighting globes, automotive lenses, mirrorized sheets, and double extrusions for solar energy collection are examples of such applications.

The nontoxicity and general biocompatibility of polycarbonates have opened numerous markets in the houseware and food industries (returnable milk and water cooler bottles, beer pitchers, microwave ovenware, etc.) and for medical applications.

Toughness and temperature resistance are generally strong factors in power tools and portable appliances housings, pump impellers, and a number of automotive applications.

Tolerances, dimensional stability, fire retardancy, toughness and electrical insulation may be particularly desirable in miscellaneous applications, such as camera bodies, modular phone connectors, capacitor film, ski slalom poles, and drafting films.

Various uses of thermoplastic polyesters and polycarbonates can be seen in figures 3.42-3.56.

Fig. 3.42   Fig. 3.43

Figure 3.42 · Outboard motor propeller (glass fiber-reinforced thermoplastic polyester PET) **[DU PONT]**

Figure 3.43 · Vacuum cleaner motor housing (thermoplastic polyester PET) **[ALLIED]**

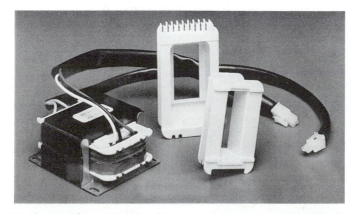

Figure 3.44 · Nesting transformer bobbins (thermoplastic polyester PET) **[DU PONT]**

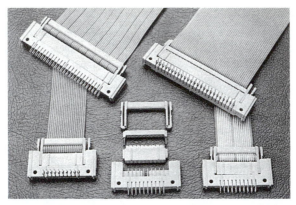

Figure 3.45 · Flat cable terminals (thermoplastic polyester PBT + glass fiber) [AKZO]

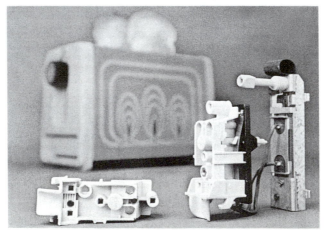

Figure 3.46 · Toaster switches and terminal plate (thermoplastic polyester PBT + glass fiber) [AKZO]

Figure 3.47 · Dual ovenable dish (liquid crystal polymer LCP) [DARTCO]

Figure 3.48 · Tri-pack column packing for the chemical process industry (liquid crystal polymer LCP) [DARTCO]

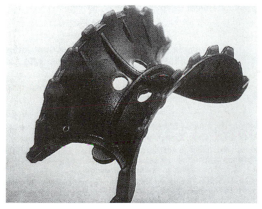

Figure 3.49 · Saddle column packing for the chemical process industry (liquid crystal polymer LCP) [NORTON/CELANESE/HOECHST]

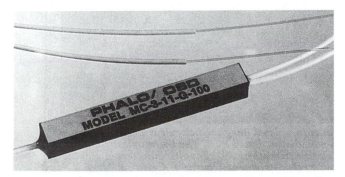

Figure 3.50 · Fiber optic coupler (liquid crystal polymer LCP) [CELANESE]

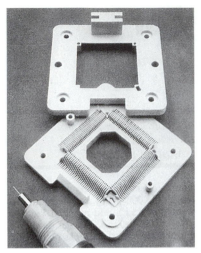

Fig. 3.51   Fig. 3.52

Figure 3.51 · Microchip carrier (liquid crystal polymer LCP) [DARTCO]

Figure 3.52 · Motorcycle helmet shell and windshield (polycarbonate PC) [BAYER]

Figure 3.53 · Sunglasses lenses (polycarbonate PC + anti-scratch silicone coating) [CEBE]

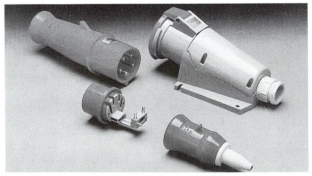

Figure 3.54 · Shrouded plugs and sockets (A(PC/ABS) polyalloy) [BAYER]

Fig. 3.56

Fig. 3.55

Figure 3.55 · Coffee maker stand, water tank and filter (polycarbonate PC) **[BAYER]**

Figure 3.56 · Street lamp body and lens (polycarbonate PC) **[BAYER]**

3.2.2.10 Sulfone Polymers

DPSU di'phenyl'sulfone (SU)

```
┌──────────────────────────────────────────────────┐
│                           O                        │
│                           ‖                        │
│  ┌──────┐      ┌─◯─┐      S      ┌─◯─┐             │
│  │ DPSU │   ──┤     ├──  ──  ──┤     ├──           │
│  └──────┘      └───┘      ‖      └───┘             │
│                           O                        │
└──────────────────────────────────────────────────┘
```

A new class of polymers emerged in the mid-1960s, which is referred to as the "sulfone polymers," because of the characteristic -SO_2- (sulfone) group, which is, in fact, always flanked along the chain backbone by two phenyl groups. The expressions "diphenylsulfone" (DPSU) or "diarylsulfone" characterize the complete group.

The diphenylsulfone group contributes rigidity, thermal, oxidative, and hydrolysis resistance to a chain, and sulfone-based polymers differ through the types of other groups completing the repeat unit. The other groups include phenyl rings, as well as carbon atoms or oxygen atoms (ether) in the backbone; the latter two contribute to the chain flexibility.

Most of these polymers are relatively new and produced by few chemical companies on a proprietary basis, and the names and chemical structure of the various commercial materials are often uncertain. The names "polysulfone" (PSU), "polyethersulfone" (PESU), and "polyphenylsulfone" (PPSU) or "polyarylsulfone" (PASU), which are sometimes used interchangeably, are commonly employed.

Polybisphenolsulfone (PBSU) or Polysulfone (PSU)

PBSU   poly'bisphenol'sulfone (SU)

PBSU	PBSU

T_g 190 °C (175-190)
         374 °F

The repeat unit of the polymer, referred to here as "polybisphenolsulfone" (PBSU), or simply as "polysulfone" (PSU), is reported to consist of a bisphenol-A residue featuring two ether linkages -O-, two phenyl rings and an aliphatic isopropylidene linkage -C(CH₃)₂-, in addition to the diphenylsulfone group. The chain is generally stiff, giving a high glass transition temperature. The material is noncrystalline, and transparent light amber-tinted grades are available.

PBSU has good mechanical properties (rigidity, creep resistance, and toughness, in particular), which are little affected by large temperature changes. Electrical properties are also good and stable.

The hydrolysis resistance is particularly effective and PBSU can undergo repeated steam sterilization. The resistance to chemicals (including detergents, oils, gasoline, and alcohols) is generally good, although strongly polar solvents, in particular, have a detrimental effect. Like other noncrystallizing polymers, PBSU can be subject to environmental stress-cracking (ESC).

The resistance to UV radiations (sunlight) is not too good, and adequate protection is recommended for outdoor exposure. PBSU is effective for fire-sensitive applications; it is rated as self-extinguishing, with low smoke and toxic fumes generation.

Injection molding requires predrying to avoid vapor formation, but the melt is very stable at the high processing temperatures (up to 370°C or 700°F). The viscosity remains quite high, and mold temperatures are around 95°C (203°F). Extrusion is used to produce thin films or sheets which can be thermoformed.

Applications, which include many transparent items, are varied; in the medical field, where steam sterilization is required; in the food industry and for appliances (piping and fittings, coffeemakers, microwave ware); in the electrical-electronic industry (connectors, fuse boxes, coil bobbins, capacitor films, structural circuit boards); in the chemical processing industry (electroplating tanks, pumps and piping, tower packing, membranes); in aerospace (astronaut helmets and face shields); and in transportation (aircraft cabin interior panels and trim).

Polyethersulfone (PESU)

PESU   poly'ether'sulfone (SU)

| PESU | $\left[\!\!\begin{array}{c} O \\ \| \\ O-\!\!\bigcirc\!\!-\!\!S-\!\!\bigcirc \\ \| \\ O \end{array}\!\!\right]$ | PESU T_g 221 °C (210-230) 430 °F |

The commercial polymers, referred to as "polyethersulfone" (PESU or PES), appear to involve a simple ether-diphenylsulfone repeat unit. The glass transition T_g is high but manageable for thermoplastic processing, and since the materials do not crystallize, they have the potential for being transparent.

PESU is claimed to be rigid, strong, and tough with very low creep over a wide range of temperature reaching over 150°C (302°F).

It is very resistant to hydrolysis and also to high-temperature oxidation, a feature associated with the absence of aliphatic groups, such as the isopropylidene group $-C(CH_3)_2-$ present in bisphenol-A residues.

It is unaffected by many chemicals but may be attacked by esters, ketones, and some aromatic or halogenated solvents. As a noncrystallizing polymer, it can be sensitive to environmental stress-cracking (ESC). It is not very resistant to UV radiations and must be protected for outdoor use.

It has good flame resistance and is classified as self-extinguishing, with little smoke or toxic gases emitted during combustion. It is reported to be resistant to high energy radiations. It can be used in contact with foods.

Applications normally involve high temperature situations encountered in appliances such as ovens, dryers, irons, heaters, electrical terminal blocks (soldering), high-intensity lamp sockets, reflectors and lenses, and steam-sterilizable medical equipment.

Polyarylethers (PAE)

An engineering polymer was introduced in the mid-1970s, under the general name "polyarylether" (PAE) and tradename "Arylon" and apparently withdrawn around 1980. The name implies that phenyl(aryl) rings and ether linkages are major features of the repeat unit. A number of repeat units have been reported in textbooks or review articles, but it appears now that the polymer was really an ABS/PSU polyalloy. Another similar polyalloy (Mindel) is now offered by another supplier, along with a SAN/PSU polyalloy (Ucardel). The ABS or SAN component may be introduced to facilitate processing and to lower the cost.

ABS/PSU polyalloys should normally be nontransparent, while transparency could be expected in SAN/PSU polyalloys. Both alloys must be noncrystallizing, as their components. A glass transition temperature of about 150°C or 302°F was reported for PAE, that is, about 40°C lower than that of PBSU.

PAE is reported to have a particularly high impact strength, with the good temperature and chemical resistance associated with ABS and PBSU. Processing is said to be very straightforward. Applications include temperature-resistant automotive or appliance parts, particularly those that require oven-baked painting.

Polyphenylethersulfones (PPESU)

PPESU–A   poly'phenyl'ether'sulfone   (SU)

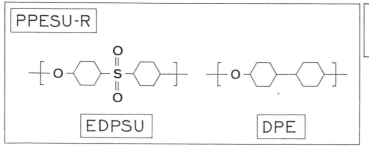

PPESU–R   poly'phenyl'ether'sulfone   (SU)

Two sulfone-related commercial polymers, with chemical structures reported to be different from those already described, have been referred to as "polyphenylsulfone" or "polyarylsulfone." The term "polyphenylethersulfone" (PPESU) is used here, with PPESU-A associated with the Astrel type and PPESU-R associated with the Radel type.

PPESU-A has been reported to feature ether-diphenylsulfone groups (EDPSU) and diphenylsulfone groups (DPSU), possibly in a copolymer-type fashion, with the DPSU group forming the major component. A reported glass transition temperature $T_g \approx$ 288°C (550°F), higher than that of polyethersulfone, reflects the presence of the more rigid DPSU group.

PPESU-R appears to have a repeat unit featuring an ether-diphenylsulfone group (EDPSU) and a diphenylether group (DPE). A reported glass transition temperature $T_g \approx$ 220°C (428°F), comparable to that of PESU, suggests that the DPE group is about as rigid as the EDPSU group.

The properties of PPESU are generally similar to those of common polysulfone (PBSU). The temperature resistance is higher and they are claimed to be less sensitive to environmental stress-cracking (ESC) and to oxidative attack.

See figures 3.57-3.59 for three applications of sulfone polymers.

Fig. 3.57

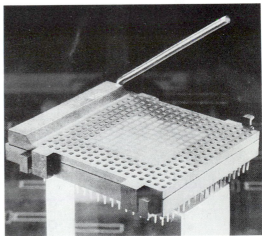

Fig. 3.58

Figure 3.57 · Artificial heart casing (polysulfone PSU) [UNION CARBIDE/AMOCO]

Figure 3.58 · VLSI pin grid array socket (A(ABS/PSU) polyalloy) [UNION CARBIDE/AMOCO]

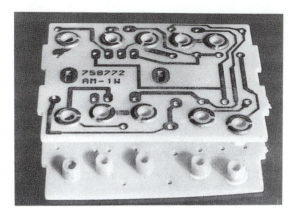

Figure 3.59 · 3-D molded circuit board (polyethersulfone PES) **[ICI]**

3.2.2.11　Imide Polymers

PI—R　general'poly'imide　(IM)

$$PI-R \quad \left[N \underset{\underset{O}{\overset{\parallel}{C}}}{\overset{\overset{O}{\overset{\parallel}{C}}}{}} R \right]$$

PI—(R1,R2)　general'poly'imide　(IM)

$$PI-(R_1,R_2) \quad \left[N \underset{\underset{O}{\overset{\parallel}{C}}}{\overset{\overset{O}{\overset{\parallel}{C}}}{}} R_1 \underset{\underset{O}{\overset{\parallel}{C}}}{\overset{\overset{O}{\overset{\parallel}{C}}}{}} N - R_2 \right]$$

A family of temperature-resistant polymers involves imide rings in the repeat unit. Such rings are sometimes termed "heterocyclic rings" because they contain an atom (nitrogen N) other than the usual carbon C. They correspond to the reaction of certain acid anhydrides with amines just as amide groups correspond to the reaction of certain acids with amines. Polyimides of types PI-R or PI-(R_1,R_2) can be formed, where the Rs are characteristic groups.

The first imide polymers were of the thermosetting type (TSPI), and many of the current high-performance commercial resins are still of this type. Their processing involves a chemical reaction and some knowledge of the reactants and their reactions is thus important.

Some imide resins have been introduced which can be processed as thermoplastics by injection molding or extrusion, for example (TPPI). They include commercial materials referred to by their suppliers as polyamideimides (PAI) and polyetherimides (PEI).

Thermosetting and Thermoplastic Polyimides (TSPI AND TPPI)

TMA   trimellitic'acid'anhydride   (IM)(EP)

PMA   pyro'mellitic'di'anhydride   (IM)(EP)

MLA   maleic'anhydride   (IM)(UP)

BPA   benzo'phenone'anhydride" (IM)

BPA

O
‖
C
O=C   C=O
  ⟨   ⟩—C—⟨   ⟩
O=C   ‖   C=O
C   O   C
‖   ‖
O   O

MDA   methylene'di'aniline (IM)(UR)

MDA

H   H   H
 \ | /
  N—⟨   ⟩—C—⟨   ⟩—N
 / | \
H   H   H

PEA   di'amino'di'phenyl'ether (IM)

PEA

H   H
 \   /
  N—⟨   ⟩—O—⟨   ⟩—N
 /   \
H   H

MPA   m'phenylene'di'amine (IM)(EP)

MPA

H   H
 \   /
  N—⟨   ⟩—N
 /   \
H   H

PPA   p'phenylene'diamine (IM)

PPA

H   H
 \   /
  N—⟨   ⟩—N
 /   \
H   H

PAA   poly'amic'acid (IM)

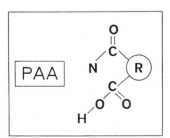

In the formation of polyimides, one reactant is generally a multifunctional acid and/or acid anhydride featuring a characteristic group R_1 (trimellitic acid/anhydride (TMA), pyromellitic dianhydride (PMA), benzophenone tetracarboxylic anhydride (BPA), maleic anhydride (MA), etc.) The other reactant is a difunctional aromatic amine featuring a characteristic group R_2 such as 4,4' diamino diphenyl methane (MDA), 4,4' diamino diphenyl ether (PEA), m-phenylene diamine (MPA), benzidine or p-phenylene diamine (PPA), and, sometimes, aromatic diisocyanates, for example 4,4' diisocyanato diphenyl methane (MDI).

The processing (molding, coating, etc.) is sometimes conducted in a fluid state (elevated temperature or solvent) at an intermediate stage of reaction with a so-called polyamic acid (PAA) precursor, the actual closing (cyclization) of the imide rings taking place during the subsequent curing (baking).

A distinction is often made between condensation-type thermosetting polyimides, which give off (evolve) gaseous by-products during cure, and addition-type polyimides, which are easier to process into good solid parts, although often not quite as temperature-resistant.

The actual type of polyimide is sometimes reflected in names such as PMR polyimide (pyromellitic resin or polypyromellitimide), and PABM polyimide (polyaminobismaleimide).

The properties of commercial polyimides naturally depend on the exact chemical nature of the repeat unit and the absence or presence and degree of cross-linking (thermoplastics or thermosets). There are many general characteristics, however, which tend to be common to all polyimides.

A major advantage of polyimides is their high temperature resistance. They maintain acceptable properties at temperatures as high as 250-300°C (482-572°F) for prolonged exposure or even 500°C (932°F) for short exposure. This is associated with the stiffness of the chains (high glass transition temperature T_g) and their resistance to chemical degradation (oxidative stability, etc.).

Polyimides are generally chemically inert, although not as much as fluoropolymers. They resist attack by most chemicals but are known to be affected by concentrated acids, alkalis (bases), oxidizing agents, and, in some cases, steam. They are reported to be highly resistant to ionizing radiations, allowing their use in the nuclear industry, but are not considered to have good weathering properties. Their fire resistance is excellent.

Mechanical properties are generally good, with outstanding creep resistance at high temperatures, low friction, and high wear resistance over a wide temperature range. Suitable additives can further enhance the frictional properties.

Electrical properties are also very good and stable with temperature although affected by a significant tendency to absorb water.

The processing of regular polyimides is rather complex, and sometimes handled by the resin suppliers themselves. The risk of rapid oxidation at processing temperatures may require nitrogen blankets. The need to drive off solvents or condensation by-products often calls for special molding techniques (powder sintering, etc.), although compression or transfer molding can sometimes be used with suitable resin systems. Stock items (rods, sheets, etc.) can also be machined to shape. Polyimides can be used as matrices for fiber reinforcements, often in preimpregnated ("prepreg") form, and subsequently oven cured.

Application of these costly, high-performance resins are growing in demanding areas, particularly those involving high temperatures.

Mechanical components include unlubricated bearings, bushings, thrust washers, piston rings, gears, ball-bearing cages (retainers), valve seats, gaskets, compressor vanes, and turbine blades.

Sometimes modified with silanes, polyimides are used as temperature resistant adhesives, binders (diamond abrasive wheels) and matrices (composites), as well as coatings (varnishes, enamels). Porcelain-like resistant and nonsticking coatings can be baked on cooking utensils.

Temperature-resistant electrical applications include wire and cable insulation and a variety of components, such as solder-resistant printed circuit boards and encapsulation for integrated circuits.

Polyimides are available in film and fiber form for applications such as high-temperature electrical insulation, filters, and temperature and flame-resistant fabrics.

Polyamideimide (PAI)

PAI   poly'amide'imide (IM)

PAI
T_g 275 °C
      527 °F

The reaction of trimellitic acid/anhydride (TMA) with aromatic diamines can lead to thermoplastics with repeat units featuring both amide and imide groups, which are referred to as "polyamideimides" (PAI). Temperature resistance is primarily associated with the aromatic and imide groups, while the degree of flexibility required for a practical thermoplastic behavior is associated with the amide group.

PAI is reported to retain good mechanical properties, creep and impact resistance in particular, at temperatures as high as 275°C (527°F). It is resistant to hydrocarbons, solvents, and solutions of acids and bases but can be attacked at elevated temperatures by alkalis (bases), some acids, and steam. The amide groups also allow a significant water absorption, and pre-drying is thus required prior to processing.

Processing is primarily by injection molding at high temperatures (343°C or 650°F) in hot molds (232°C or 450°F). Demolded parts achieve better property levels when gradually postcured to 260°C (500°F).

Applications, primarily in high-performance areas, include electrical-electronic and mechanical parts in automotive, aircraft, and aerospace, where they strongly compete with metal parts. For example, PAI parts have been used extensively in an experimental internal combustion engine (Polimotor).

Polyetherimide (PEI)

PEI   poly'ether'imide (IM)

The reported repeat unit of polyetherimide (PEI) features two imide rings separated by an m-phenylene diamine residue, as well as a bisphenol-A residue, also found in several other engineering thermoplastics, which comprises two ether linkages -O- and contributes enough flexibility to the chain to make it a true thermoplastic. The amorphous character of the resin gives it good dimensional stability and inherent transparency.

The mechanical properties are good with a tensile strength for the unreinforced resin claimed to be unsurpassed among thermoplastics. These properties are little affected over a wide temperature range, allowing, for example, hand or wave soldering on printed-circuit boards.

Chemical resistance, generally good and including resistance to most corrosive automotive fluids, is claimed to be comparable to that of good crystalline polymers. UV stability (weathering) is also claimed to be good. The resins should be less affected by water and steam than the polyamideimides.

PEI is reported to have an exceptionally high inherent flame resistance with the highest oxygen index of all engineering plastics and very low smoke evolution. It is thus well suited to construction and transportation regulations.

Electrical properties are good, with a low dissipation factor, allowing microwave applications and a high dielectric strength.

Present applications are found in the electrical-electronic area, such as for transparent parts (filter bowls, fiber optic connectors), in aircraft engine components, and in high intensity lighting systems (plated reflectors). Thin films can be made, which have very good dimensional stability.

Several uses of imide polymers are shown in figures 3.60-3.63.

Fig. 3.60   Fig. 3.61

Figure 3.60 · Tape for semi-conductor chip bonding (polyimide PI) [RODGERS]

Figure 3.61 · Pump impeller and distributor (polyamideimide PAI) [AMOCO]

Figure 3.62 · Sterilizable home ventilator manifold (polyetherimide PEI) [GENERAL ELECTRIC]

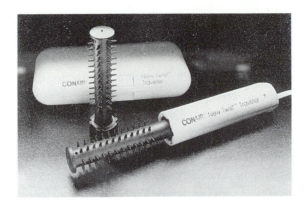

Figure 3.63 · Styling comb/curler brush for high heat personal care electrical appliance (polyetherimide PEI) [GENERAL ELECTRIC]

3.2.2.12   Ether-Oxide Polymers

The common names of a number of industrially important polymers specifically include the words ether or oxide, which reflect the presence of an ether or oxygen linkage -O- in the backbone of the repeat unit. The rest of the repeat unit may feature aliphatic (methylene, ethylene, propylene) or aromatic (phenylene) groups.

Polymethyleneoxides (PMO) or Acetals

PMO   poly'methylene'oxide   (EO)

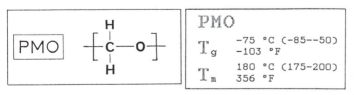

PMO	$\begin{array}{c} H \\ | \\ -C-O- \\ | \\ H \end{array}$	PMO		
		T_g	-75 °C (-85–-50) -103 °F	
		T_m	180 °C (175–200) 356 °F	

This structurally simple polyether is also frequently referred to as "polyoxymethylene" (POM), "polyformaldehyde," polyacetal or simply "acetal."

Straight polymerization gives a material with a strong tendency for depolymerization at high temperatures, making it very difficult to process. The first practical way of countering this problem involves end-capping, that is, a suitable modification of chain ends (acetylation, methylation), with corresponding commercial materials known as "PMO homopolymers" (PMOH). Another method involves a random copolymerization, introducing a small fraction (about 2%) of ethyleneoxide-type repeat units, whose C-C bonds are thought to impede depolymerization; the term "copolymer" is used to specify those polymethyleneoxides (PMOC).

Polymethyleneoxides have a fairly high degree of polymerization (over 1000), and the simple regular chains crystallize to a high degree (about 75-80%). The high density (over 1.4) reflects the tight packing of the crystallized chains. Copolymerization tends to lower slightly the crystallinity and melting temperature T_m. The reported glass transition temperatures are very low in comparison with those of other crystallizing engineering plastics. Both types of polymethyleneoxides share an assortment of excellent properties that ranks them among the very best of engineering plastics.

PMO resins are in many ways comparable to polyamides 6 and 6-6, although their density (over 1.4) is significantly higher and there are differences in their resistance to chemical environments.

The stiffness, hardness, and strength of PMO are among the highest of all thermoplastics and stable over a good temperature range. Outstanding creep and fatigue resistance contribute to making the resin suitable for applications requiring springiness. Toughness is good, particularly under repeated impact. Contact properties (friction and wear) are excellent for such stiff and strong material, which calls for applications such as bearings, slides, gears, and cams.

PMO resins can decompose with the formation of toxic formaldehyde gas if overheated during melt processing.

The resins are little affected by water, with a much smaller moisture absorption than most polyamides and a correspondingly good dimensional stability. They have excellent resistance to hot water (82°C or 180°F for indefinite times), and some PMO applications which involve boiling water contact.

PMO resins are resistant to most organic compounds, such as solvents, lubricants, and gasoline, as well as many other chemicals, but are degraded in the presence of strong acids or strong alkalis (bases), although the copolymers (PMOC) fare much better in the second case.

Resistance to radiations is not particularly good, and UV stabilization is required to reduce the effects of sunlight in outdoor exposure. The intrinsic burning tendency of the resins is comparable to that of polyethylene.

PMO resins are processed primarily by injection molding. When precautions are taken to avoid prolonged overheating, the molding is relatively easy with good resin flow and fast cycles. The high degree of crystallinity corresponds to high mold shrinkage, but the resins are not noted for causing special warpage problems normally associated with oriented crystallization. Small pressure containers are produced by blow molding, and extrusion is used primarily to produce semifinished products (rods, bars, plates, etc.), from which prototype parts, for example, can easily be machined.

Applications of PMO resins generally involve relatively small parts that must perform an important mechanical function, require close dimensional tolerances, and often involve motion and contact. In many cases, they have competed with, and replaced, die cast zinc and aluminum alloys, stamped steel, and brass.

The automotive industry, for example, makes use of PMO gears, bearings, slides, cams, and ratches. The resistance to gasoline justifies the use of PMO for caburetor and fuel pump parts.

PMO has long been used in the fabrication of aerosol containers (container itself, stem valve, and spray nozzle) and the reservoir (tank) of disposable lighters.

Resistance to cold and hot water, in particular, has been a key factor in the use of PMO in plumbing applications for fixtures or fittings (toilet ball cock valves, shower heads, valves, pumps, faucets, sink baskets, etc.).

A number of applications in the food industry and for housewares have been reported (milk pumps, coffee spigots, kettle body, etc.).

It is noteworthy that, contrary to most other crystallizing thermoplastics, PMO does not appear to have been used to make either fibers or films. The very high crystallinity and, perhaps, the low glass transition temperature may have been among the negative factors.

Polyethyleneoxide (PEO)

PEO   poly'ethylene'oxide (EO)

PEO

$$\left[\begin{array}{c} \overset{\displaystyle H}{\underset{\displaystyle H}{\mid}}\!\!C\!-\!\overset{\displaystyle H}{\underset{\displaystyle H}{\mid}}\!\!C\!-\!O \end{array}\right]$$

The repeat unit of polyethyleneoxide (PEO), also referred to as "polyoxyethylene" or "polyethyleneglycol," is similar to that of polymethyleneoxide, but PEO is water-soluble, which precludes its use as a plastic. It is widely used as a water thickener. Its characteristic temperatures have been reported as T_g = -67°C (-89°F) and T_m = 66°C (151°F).

Polypropyleneoxide (PPRO)

PPRO poly'propylene'oxide (EO)

Polypropyleneoxide (PPRO) can be produced in atactic or isotactic form. The irregular atactic form does not crystallize and, with a low glass transition temperature $T_g \approx -72°C$ ($\approx -98°F$), it forms the basis for a commercial specialty elastomer. The regular isotactic form can crystallize with a reported melting point $T_m \approx 74°C$ ($\approx$ 165°F), which is too low for a commercial plastic.

Polyphenyleneoxides (PPO), Polyphenyleneethers (PPE)

UPPO unsubstituted'poly'phenylene'oxide (EO)

SPPO substituted'poly'phenylene'oxide (EO)

PPO poly'phenylene'oxide (EO)

PPO

T_g 210 °C (204-234)
       410 °F

The term polyphenyleneoxide (PPO) or poly 1,4 phenyleneoxide should normally be used for the polymer featuring only an unsubstituted phenyl ring and an oxygen in the repeat unit. Polyphenyleneoxide is now used, however, to designate the polymer involving the substitution of two methyl groups and the correct name should thus be poly 2,6 dimethylphenyleneoxide. The abbreviation "PPO" will be used here for the second type, while "UPPO" will refer to the unsubstituted type. Other possible 2,6 substitutions (halogens, ethyl, isopropyl, etc. as groups R_1 and/or R_2) correspond to polyphenyleneoxides referred to here as "SPPO," but they do not appear to have led to commercially important homopolymers.

Polyphenyleneoxide is a polyether through the -O- group in the repeat unit and thus the term "polyphenyleneether" (PPE) is sometimes used.

Pure PPO has a high glass transition temperature T_g. It is capable of crystallizing between T_g and the melting point T_m (around 260°C or 500°F). Such narrow range probably contributes to the fact that the polymer is normally considered amorphous. Its cost, and certain processing difficulties associated with a high melt viscosity, have led to the introduction of blends (polyalloys) of PPO with polystyrene (PS) or high-impact polystyrene (HIPS). The components are very miscible, and the resulting blends feature a single glass transition temperature. A balanced blend (50/50) is reported to have a T_g around 150°C (302°F) and cited T_g values for commercial grades range from 100 to 135°C (230°F-275°F). These blends are often referred to as "modified polyphenyleneoxide" (MPPO).

Polyphenyleneether-based copolymers, possibly involving styrene, have recently been introduced.

The mechanical properties of MPPO are generally good, with a high stiffness and low creep over a good temperature range. Good toughness extends to low temperatures. Excellent dimensional stability is associated with the noncrystalline structure, a low coefficient of thermal expansion, and very low moisture absorption. The density of about 1.06 is among the lowest of engineering thermoplastics. In spite of its noncrystalline character and the high miscibility of the components, MPPO is not available in transparent grades.

Electrical properties are generally good and unaffected by moisture. Dielectric properties, in particular, are good and stable.

MPPO is classified as self-extinguishing and nondripping, which favors fire-regulated applications, such as in transportation.

The most notable aspect of the resistance of MPPO to chemical agents is its resistance to water, including hot water and steam (hydrolytic stability). MPPO can be repeatedly sterilized in steam autoclaves. It is, however, attacked by some inorganic chemicals, such as strong acids and alkalis (bases), and is swollen or dissolved by many hydrocarbons (aromatic, halogenated, etc.). As a noncrystalline polymer, it can be affected by environmental stress-cracking, although it is considered to be paintable with solvent-based paints, particularly when parts are stress-annealed. Weatherability is considered adequate.

Injection molding is the most commonly used process, and MPPO exhibits good flow, low shrinkage, and little warpage associated with its noncrystalline nature and the presence of polystyrene. Molds are normally kept at a high temperature (around 100°C or 212°F), and the molding requires certain precautions spelled out by the suppliers. Parts can easily be painted, or metallized. Thermoforming of such noncrystalline polymer is quite straightforward but involves fairly high temperatures.

The high hydrolytic stability is associated with applications in hot water systems (valves, pumps, fittings, plumbing fixtures, etc.) and for medical supplies requiring steam sterilization.

Many applications in the automobile industry involve interior parts (dashboard) or exterior parts (grilles, wheel covers), which are often painted or metallized.

Resistance to dilute aqueous acid solutions is a factor in the use of MPPO for photographic processing tanks.

Several applications of ether-oxide polymers are demonstrated in figures 3.64-3.69.

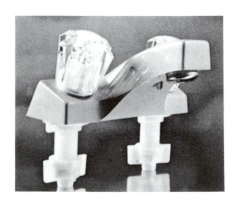

Fig. 3.64

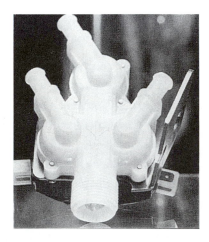

Fig. 3.65

Figure 3.64 · Hot water-resistant pumbing fitting (acetal PMO) [CELANESE]

Figure 3.65 · Clothes washer electromagnetic valve (acetal PMO) [HOECHST]

Fig. 3.66   Fig. 3.67

Figure 3.66 · Molded/sonic-welded butane lighter reservoir/body (acetal PMO)
[DU PONT]

Figure 3.67 · Electrical load management box (modified polyphenyleneoxide PPO) **[GENERAL ELECTRIC]**

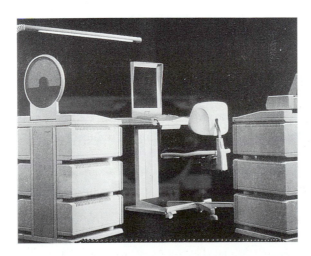

Figure 3.68 · Structural foam molded elements for office workstation units (modified polyphenyleneoxide PPO or polycarbonate PC) **[BORG-WARNER]**

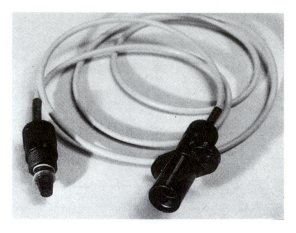

Figure 3.69 · Fiber optic connectors (modified polyphenyleneether PPE) [BORG-WARNER]

3.2.2.13 Ketone Polymers

PAEK poly'aryl'ether'ketone (KE)

| PAEK | $-\!\!\left[O-\!\!\bigcirc\!\!-\overset{\overset{O}{\|}}{C}-\!\!\bigcirc\!\!\right]\!-$ | PAEK T_g 154 °C / 309 °F T_m 367 °C / 693 °F |

A number of recently introduced polymers feature ketone groups -CO-, phenyl (aryl) rings, and ether linkages -O- in the chain backbone. A simple combination, referred to here as "polyaryletherketone" (PAEK) and featuring two aryl rings in the repeat unit, has a high glass transition temperature T_g and a very high melting point T_m. The combination, featuring two ether linkages and three aryl rings, corresponds to the repeat unit reported for the original PEEK commercial plastic (polyetheretherketone), which we refer to here as "polyaryletheretherketone" (PAEEK or PEEK-1). A variety of other commercial ketone polymers is being introduced.

Polyetheretherketone-1 (PEEK-1)

PEEK—1 poly'ether'ether'ketone (KE)

| PEEK-1 | $-\!\!\left[O-\!\!\bigcirc\!\!-O-\!\!\bigcirc\!\!-\overset{\overset{O}{\|}}{C}-\!\!\bigcirc\!\!\right]\!-$ | PEEK-1 T_g 143 °C (142–144) / 290 °F T_m 335 °C (332–342) / 635 °F |

The pair of ether linkages -O- in the chain backbone confer to the chains of polyetheretherketone-1 (PEEK-1) enough flexibility for a true thermoplastic behavior and the ability to crystallize (25-50% crystallinity). The high glass transition temperature T_g and the high melting temperature T_m, combined with high temperature chemical stability, rate this polymer among the most temperature-resistant thermoplastics. As with other crystallizing thermoplastics, crystallinity can develop only at temperatures between T_m and T_g, a fact that must be taken into account for processing (injection, extrusion, etc.).

PEEK-1 retains good mechanical properties at high temperatures, such as 200°C or 392°F, for prolonged periods of time. Its chemical resistance is excellent and it is practically insoluble in any solvents; only very strong chemicals such as concentrated sulfuric acid have a severe effect. It is particularly resistant to hydrolysis by steam or high temperature pressurized water, and absorbs little moisture. It is noted for its excellent resistance to nuclear radiations. As other crystallizing engineering plastics, it is resistant to environmental stress-cracking. Electrical properties are suitable for use as an insulating material. A low flammability and very low smoke and toxic gas emission, make it very promising for critical applications, such as encountered in aeronautical and aerospace areas.

PEEK-1 can be injection molded at high temperatures (up to 400°C or 752°F), into hot molds (up to 180°C or 356°F), to favor crystallization. Despite the low water absorption of the resin, predrying is required. Extrusion is also used to produce fibers and films.

Applications are rapidly expanding in volume and diversity. The excellent mechanical properties at high temperatures are superior to those of other temperature-resistant polymers, such as fluoropolymers, for wire and cable covering in critical applications (aerospace, nuclear industry, etc.). Pump impellers, valve parts, electrical connectors, for example, are injection molded. Films can be used for printed circuits or as barrier membranes. Fibers woven into fabrics have been used as filters and conveyor belts in high temperature situations. Much interest is shown for the use of the polymer as a matrix for high performance composites, its thermoplastic character allowing new fabrication methods to be considered.

Other Ketone Polymers

The supplier of the original commercial ketone polymer (PEEK-1) is now supplying, under the general name "PEEK," a variety of high-temperature thermoplastics with a range of crystallizing tendencies. PEEK-HTA is basically amorphous ($T_g \approx 260°C$ or 500°F), PEEK-HTC can crystallize to a moderate degree ($T_g \approx 205°C$ or 401°F) and PEEK-HTX can be highly crystalline ($T_g \approx 70°C$ or 158°F and $T_m \approx 210°C$ or 410°F). These ketone polymers are probably copolymers with varying degrees of regularity.

Other suppliers offer ketone polymers with a range of crystallizing tendencies. They are sold under the names polyketone (PK), polyetherketone (PEK) and poly-aryletherketone (PAEK).

See figures 3.70-3.72 for three uses of ketone polymers.

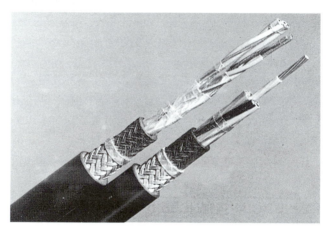

Figure 3.70 · Offshore control cable insulation (polyetheretherketone PEEK) **[ICI]**

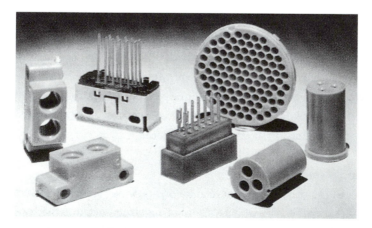

Figure 3.71 · Electrical connectors for aerospace and oil industries (polyetheretherketone PEEK) **[ICI]**

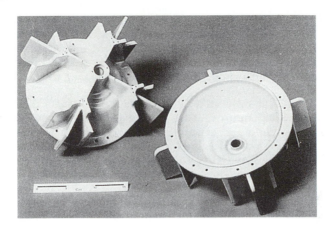

Figure 3.72 · Electrostatically-sprayed chemical resistant coating on centrifuge housing (polyetheretherketone PEEK) **[ICI]**

3.2.2.14   *Fluoropolymers*

A family of carbon chain polymers features fluorine atoms that form very strong bonds with carbon atoms (C-F). These polymers are referred to as "fluoropolymers," and the members, which have a characteristic plastic-like behavior, are often called "fluoroplastics," while those with a rubber-like behavior are called "fluoroelastomers." A more specific discussion of fluoroelastomers is presented in the Elastomers section.

Seven major characteristic repeat units are involved in commercial fluoroplastics. Five of them correspond to commercially available homopolymers, while the remaining two appear to be used exclusively in copolymers. Copolymers sometimes involve an ethylene (E) repeat unit in addition to fluorinated repeat units.

There are significant differences between the various types of fluoroplastics, which will be discussed in some detail subsequently, but there are also many characteristics that tend to be common to all of them.

The strong carbon-fluorine (C-F) chemical bond, the crystalline structure at the molecular level where fluorine atoms may form a sheath-like protection for the carbon backbone, and the relatively weak interaction between chain segments in the crystals, contribute to the characteristic properties of fluoroplastics.

Fluoroplastics are noted for their excellent resistance to a wide variety of chemicals over a wide range of temperatures. They are unaffected by water and do not decompose or become oxidized until subjected to very high temperatures. Their weathering resistance is generally outstanding. Some do not burn, others burn very slowly.

Some of their physical properties are exceptional for certain specific applications and remain stable up to rather high temperatures. They tend to have low coefficients of friction and good antistick characteristics. They are durable and maintain toughness and flexibility at low temperatures. They are generally highly impermeable to gases and vapors. Their electrical properties (insulation, dielectric, arcing resistance, etc.) are generally excellent and stable.

Most fluoroplastics, however, have rather mediocre mechanical properties, when assessed at room temperature in mild environments, and do not measure up to so-called engineering plastics. Stiffness and strength are relatively low and the materials are easily scratched or cut through. Creep (cold flow) is often a problem, although it is sometimes taken to advantage, such as in sealing applications. The closely packed crystalline structure corresponds to unusually high densities for polymers. High coefficients of thermal expansion are sometimes associated with dimensional stability problems. A few specific chemicals, as well as high-energy radiations, can attack specific types of fluoroplastics.

The most desirable properties are often obtained at the cost of processing ease. Standard thermoplastic techniques are sometimes unusable, or melt and mold temperature, metal requirements, and safety precautions are demanding.

As in the case of most plastics, various additives, fillers, and other agents can modify the properties of fluoroplastics quite considerably. A general discussion, however, has to be limited to the unmodified polymers.

Polytetrafluoroethylene (PTFE)

PTFE   poly'tetra'fluoro'ethylene   (FP)(FE)

		PTFE	
PTFE	$-\left[\begin{array}{c} F \\ \| \\ C \\ \| \\ F \end{array} - \begin{array}{c} F \\ \| \\ C \\ \| \\ F \end{array}\right]-$	T_g $-130\ °C\ (-150--112)$ $-202\ °F$ T_m $327\ °C\ (327-330)$ $621\ °F$	

Polytetrafluoroethylene (PTFE) can probably be viewed as the standard of fluoroplastics, the material that typifies the remarkable properties of the whole class.

PTFE has a very simple and regular molecular structure. In the amorphous configuration, the chains are very flexible with a low glass transition temperature.

Solid PTFE, however, is highly crystalline (50-75%) and, consequently, opaque. Above the crystalline transition point T_m, the high-molecular-weight polymer (500,000-5,000,000) fails to behave as a true thermoplastic, becoming very rubbery (gel-like) in a manner reminiscent of ultra-high-molecular-weight polyethylene (UHMWPE) with the possibility of chemical decomposition at higher temperatures. Processing requires special techniques discussed later.

The chemical resistance of PTFE over a wide range of temperatures surpasses that of any other polymer. Very few chemicals, such as unusual fluorinated solvents, molten alkalis (sodium hydroxide NaOH), or molten alkali metals (Na), have an effect on PTFE.

PTFE has exceptional resistance to UV radiations and weathering in general. It is totally unaffected by cold or hot water and will not decompose or be oxidized at high temperatures in the solid state. This has been associated, in particular, with a shielding effect of the fluorine sheath surrounding the carbon backbone. PTFE, however, is reported to deteriorate rapidly when exposed to high energy radiations. PTFE has inherent flame retardancy. It will not burn and will only decompose at very high temperatures with little residue.

PTFE is well known for its extremely low coefficient of friction (0.05) and it will not stick to, or even be wetted by, practically any substance. For such reasons, it is often referred to as "self-lubricating," "antistick," "nonadhesive," etc. Depending on the exact conditions, it can have high to low resistance to wear and abrasion.

PTFE is definitely not a good structural plastic, having rather low rigidity and strength and, perhaps most importantly, being subject to cold flow (creep), which has been associated also with a low level of interaction between chain segments in crystals. The mechanical properties, however, are rather stable over a wide range of temperatures from cryogenic temperatures (-268°C or -450°F) to over 250°C (482°F). PTFE, with its very compact crystalline structure, has the highest density of commercial plastics (2-2.3).

PTFE also has outstanding electrical properties as insulator or dielectric material. A low and stable dissipation factor and high arcing resistance over a wide range of temperatures, have long made PTFE a choice material for demanding applications in spite of average mechanical properties.

PTFE calls for special processing techniques. Molding of parts, sheets, plates, and similar materials is done by the sintering, at high temperatures (around 370°C or 698°F) and under pressure, of preforms made from powdered resin. Rods, tubes, profiles, wire coatings, and fibers can be produced by special ram extrusion processes using long dies, high pressures, high temperatures (400-450°C or 752-842°F) and, sometimes, resin particles in a lubricating medium (naphta). Tapes can be sliced (skived) from solid stock. Coatings can be made fom dispersions that can undergo a coagulation-like process. Chemical etching and special adhesives now allow the attachment of PTFE to substrates.

Applications of chemically resistant PTFE are numerous in the chemical process industry as liners for reactors and a variety of components (pipes, seals, gaskets, valve and pump parts, filter media, etc.) and for laboratory ware (seals, spigots, etc.).

Flame and weather resistance, in particular, explain the use of PTFE as a binder and coating for glass or other fabrics used for tent-like structures (covered stadiums, etc.).

Antistick and self-lubricating properties are called for in such applications as coatings for home cookware, industrial food processing equipment, tool blades, snow shovels, conveyor parts, chutes, and hoppers and in slip expansion joints, bridge bearing pads, and piston rings. These properties, and a degree of cold flow, are involved in the well-known pipe thread tape sealants.

PTFE in micro-size powder form is used as filler for thermoplastics and thermosets, and in aerosol sprays for lubrication purposes.

Electrical and electronic applications include high temperature wire and cable insulation and critical coaxial wire spacers for high-frequency applications in particular.

Polychlorotrifluoroethylene (PCTFE)

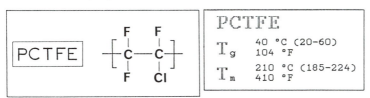

PCTFE   poly'chloro'tri'fluoro'ethylene   (FP)(FE)

PCTFE

T_g 40 °C (20-60)
       104 °F

T_m 210 °C (185-224)
       410 °F

The repeat unit of polychlorotrifluoroethylene (PCTFE) differs from that of PTFE by the replacement of a fluorine atom by a chlorine atom, which reduces the flexibility of the chains (higher glass transition temperature T_g), their tendency to crystallize (maximum 40-65%) and the melting point T_m. PCTFE, in fact, can be made optically clear, an amorphous-like characteristic, in thicknesses as high as 3 mm (1/8 in). The reduced melting point and a generally lower molecular weight (100,000-200,000) make PCTFE a true thermoplastic.

PCTFE has better mechanical properties than PTFE (stiffer, stronger, etc.), but its frictional properties do not come near those of PTFE.

Chemical resistance is generally good, although not comparable to that of PTFE and other fully fluorinated fluoroplastics. Chlorinated solvents, in particular, can affect PCTFE, and it can be subject to stress-cracking at elevated temperatures. It is claimed to have a good resistance to liquid oxygen, which explains its use in some special areas (aerospace, medical), as well as a better resistance to high-energy radiations than PTFE.

The presence of chlorine atoms, noted to enhance flame retardancy, keeps PCTFE in the nonburning category with PTFE. It causes, however, a serious increase in dielectric losses, particularly at high frequencies.

The processing of PCTFE can involve injection and compression molding, extrusion, blowing, etc. Processing temperatures are rather high, and any degradation of the material can cause severe corrosion and environmental problems. PCTFE crystallizes on slow cooling, while quenching, for films in particular, can yield transparent products.

Applications of PCTFE include wire and cable insulation, protective shrink sheaths, electronic flexible printed circuits (PC), etc. In the chemical process industry, it appears as gaskets, O-rings, seals, valve seats, and instrument windows. Its extremely low water vapor transmission, even as thin transparent film, and its thermosealability explain its use as a packaging material, in the pharmaceutical industry in particular (strip and blister packs for tablets and capsules).

Polyvinylfluoride (PVF)

PVF   poly'vinyl'fluoride (FP)

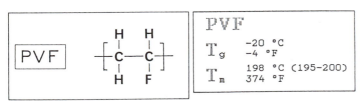

Polyvinylfluoride (PVF) involves regular chains capable of crystallizing to a high degree, but many of the most common products, films and sheets, are reported to be transparent.

PVF products are strong and tough, with good abrasion and staining resistance up to fairly high temperatures (100-150°C or 212-302°F), and they are classified as slow burning. They are generally less chemically resistant than fully fluorinated plastics but show excellent UV resistance and good color retention and are not affected by water. Their excellent weatherability has made them a choice material for exterior applications, such as coatings for metals (sidings, gutters, etc.), plywood finishes, architectural sheets, lighting panels, and glazing for solar energy collection. Other applications include electrical wrapping tape and parting layers for laminates.

Polyvinylidenefluoride (PVDF)

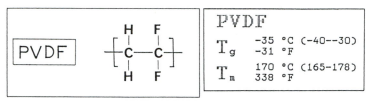

PVDF   poly'vinylidene'fluoride (FP)(FE)

PVDF		
T_g	−35 °C	(−40–−30)
	−31 °F	
T_m	170 °C	(165–178)
	338 °F	

Polyvinylidenefluoride, often abbreviated as "PVDF but also as "PVF$_2$," features a symmetrical repeat unit corresponding to a flexible chain. It is normally highly crystalline (65%). As with other crystallizing polymers, transparent films can also be produced.

PVDF is reported to be strong, tough, and abrasion resistant. In terms of stiffness and cold flow (creep), it is much better than fully fluorinated plastics (PTFE, PFEP, PPFA) and comparable to some copolymers discussed later [P(E-TFE), P(E-CTFE)].

Like other fluoroplastics, it has an outstanding weathering resistance and is also resistant to high energy radiations. It is not generally as chemically resistant as fully fluorinated plastics, however. PVDF will burn but is classified as self-extinguishing and nondripping.

PVDF supplied as pellets, powder or dispersions can be processed as a thermoplastic by injection molding, extrusion, fluidized bed coating, etc. and is used in a wide variety of applications. The chemical process industry is a major market.

Coatings or finishes are applied to metal surfaces such as aluminum siding and roofing. Colors are easily incorporated and are stable. Low oxygen and water vapor permeability contribute to providing long-term protection. Electrical components (resistors, diodes) can be encapsulated in PVDF.

Molded parts include seals, gaskets, packings, diaphragms, valve parts, pump impellers, pipe fittings, and coil bobbins (spools).

Extruded products include pipes (tubing, ducting), wire insulation, and jacketing, as well as semifinished forms (slabs, rods) that can serve to make thermowelded liners for chemical reactors or to machine parts. Monofilaments are woven into fabric for use as filters.

An interesting application, where PVDF is in competition with other somewhat similar materials such as UHMWPE, is the fabrication of porous pen tips which must be tough, as well as abrasion and ink resistant.

Polyperfluoroalkoxy (PPFA)

PPFA   poly'per'fluoro'alkoxy (FP)(FE)

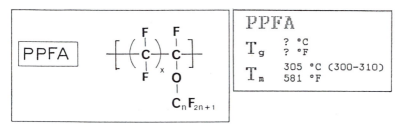

The introduction of perfluoroalkoxy (PFA) side-groups in polytetra-fluoroethylene-like molecules has led to a so-called fully fluorinated plastic, which has properties quite close to those of PTFE while being a true thermoplastic. The PFA sidegroups have the general composition $-O-C_nF_{2n+1}$ with n often reported to be 2. In order to preserve the crystallizing ability, the PFA side-groups are likely to be regularly spaced, and **x**, the number of intermediate CF_2 groups, has been reported to be 2-3.

With its high melting point, PPFA has almost the same temperature resistance as PTFE. Its true thermoplasticity is probably associated with a lower molecular weight.

PPFA is claimed to have better creep resistance than PTFE, possibly a result of chain interlocking favored by the PFA side-groups. The same reason, however, may account for its less remarkable frictional properties (coefficient of friction 0.15).

PPFA has the outstanding chemical resistance of other fully fluorinated plastics (PTFE, FEP).

Pellets of PPFA can be injection molded, extruded, blow molded, etc. Processing temperatures are high, however, with a typical melt temperature of 388°C (730°F) and a mold temperature of 232°C (450°F).

Applications often involve extruded products in the form of films, sheets, rods and tubing. PPFA is used as colorable insulation for electrical circuitry and flat cables; heat shrinkable tubing is used for the protection of connections. PPFA liners and flexible tubings are used in the chemical process industry.

Polyhexafluoropropylene (PHFP)

PHFP   poly'hexa'fluoro'propylene   (FP)(FE)

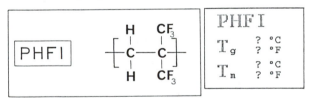

PHFP		
T_g	11	°C
	52	°F
T_m	?	°C
	?	°F

Although polyhexafluoropropylene (PHFP) homopolymer does not seem to be commercially available, its repeat unit appears in an important fluoroplastic copolymer, PFEP, which is discussed later. The repeat unit corresponds to a fully fluorinated polypropylene repeat unit and is significantly more rigid than the PTFE repeat unit with a glass transition temperature T_g around 11°C (52°F).

Polyhexafluoroisobutylene (PHFI)

PHFI   poly'hexa'fluoro'isobutylene   (FP)

PHFI		
T_g	?	°C
	?	°F
T_m	?	°C
	?	°F

The repeat unit of polyhexafluoroisobutylene (PHFI) also appears in a commercial fluoroplastic copolymer, which is discussed later. The repeat unit of PHFI features the relatively bulky CF_3 group in a symmetrical manner, a favorable situation for crystallization.

Fluoroplastic Copolymers

As indicated earlier, commercial fluoroplastic copolymers involve primarily ethylene (E), tetrafluoroethylene (TFE), chlorotrifluoroethylene (CTFE), hexafluoropropylene (HFP), and vinylidenefluoride (VDF) repeat units. P(E-TFE), P(E-CTFE), P(TFE-HFP), P(VDF-TFE), and P(VDF-HFI) are offered as thermoplastics, while P(VDF-CTFE) and P(VDF-HFP), for example, are rather elastomeric (see section 3.4.2.4).

Since the mechanical properties of fluoroplastics are associated with crystallinity, fluoroplastic copolymers must have a regular molecular structure capable of crystallizing, commonly a 50/50 alternating arrangement. Fluoroelastomers, on the other hand, besides having a low glass transition temperature, must not be capable of crystallizing. Their structure is thus normally of the random copolymer type.

P(E-TFE)

P(E-TFE) copolymer (FP)

	E	TFE	P(E-TFE)

P(E-TFE)	H H
	│ │
	─C─C─
	│ │
	H H
		F F
		│ │
		─C─C─
		│ │
		F F
			T_g ? °C
			   ? °F
			T_m 271 °C (270-271)
			   520 °F

Copolymers involving ethylene (E) and tetrafluoroethylene (TFE) repeat units [P(E-TFE), PETFE, or simply ETFE] have been reported to correspond to a 50/50 alternating arrangement, suitable for crystallinity, as well as a 25-75 ratio.

These thermoplastic copolymers are reported to be tough and to have good abrasion and cut-through resistance. Their electrical properties are very good. They have a better resistance to high energy radiations than PTFE but are not as chemically resistant, being attacked, in particular, by strongly oxidizing agents. They are also combustible. P(E-TFE) is noted for its good compatibility with glass reinforcement, leading to truly reinforced materials. Processing is relatively easy by injection or extrusion, melt and mold temperatures are around 3l5°C (600°F) and 93°C (200°F), respectively. Melt flow is reported to be excellent.

Applications include valve components, tower packings, and liners in the chemical process industry, molded labware, wire insulation in mass transit equipment in particular, electrical connectors, and coil bobbins. P(E-TFE) is also widely used in the nuclear industry.

P(E-CTFE)

P(E-CTFE) copolymer (FP)

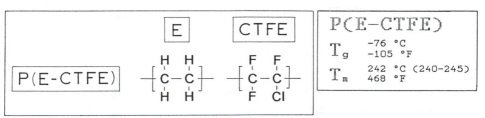

	E	CTFE	P(E-CTFE)

P(E-CTFE)	H H
	│ │
	─C─C─
	│ │
	H H
		F F
		│ │
		─C─C─
		│ │
		F Cl
			T_g -76 °C
			   -105 °F
			T_m 242 °C (240-245)
			   468 °F

Copolymers reported to involve a 50/50 alternating arrangement of ethylene (E) and chlorotrifluoroethylene (CTFE) repeat units [P(E-CTFE), PECTFE, or ECTFE] are crystalline. For their stiffness, strength, and toughness, they are claimed to be comparable to good engineering plastics such as polyamide-6 (PA-6).   Good mechanical properties are retained at cryogenic temperatures or at temperatures as high as 177°C (350°F). Flame resistance is excellent, the materials are classified as nonburning.

Processing is reported to be fairly straightforward by injection or extrusion. Applications are numerous in the chemical process industry (tower packings, valve and pump components, etc.). Laboratory uses include tubing, bottles, carboys, and drums, and P(E-CTFE) is also used for medical packaging. Electrical applications include regular or heat-shrinkable insulation. Monofilaments are converted into mats or fabrics for filters or mist eliminators, as well as braided sleeving.

P(TFE-HFP) or PFEP

PFEP   poly'fluorinated'ethylene'propylene'copolymer   (FP)

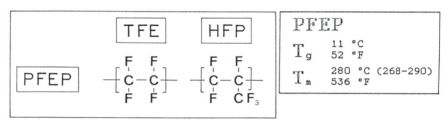

A copolymer, reported to feature a 90-10 or a 50-50 alternating arrangement of tetrafluoroethylene (TFE) and hexafluoropropylene (HFP) repeat units, is somewhat less crystalline than PTFE with a lower melting point T_m. This is partly associated with the presence of CF_3 side-groups. Since the copolymer can be viewed as a fully fluorinated ethylene-propylene copolymer, it is often referred to as "fluorinated ethylene-propylene" (FEP) or "PFEP."

Because it is fully fluorinated, PFEP has nearly the same outstanding chemical resistance as PTFE. Its lower melting point gives it a somewhat lower temperature resistance than PTFE, but it is a true thermoplastic with a moderate melt viscosity, probably associated with a lower molecular weight.

Mechanical properties are reported to be similar to those of PTFE, but frictional properties are not as remarkable.

Processing is commonly done by injection and extrusion. Melt temperature is around 357°C (675°F).

Applications are, in many respects, similar to those of PTFE, but the processing convenience generally allows the fabrication of a wider range of products. In the electrical-electronic area, coil bobbins, wire and cable insulation, and jacketing are cited. In the chemical process industry, valves, gaskets, packings, linings and pipes involve PFEP. Transparent films can be produced with suitable control of the cooling and the ensuing crystallization; their use is cited in the manufacture of glazing for solar energy collectors. Shrinkable tubular film can also be produced, which finds use as antistick roll cover, for example.

P(VDF-TFE)

P(VDF-TFE) copolymer (FP)

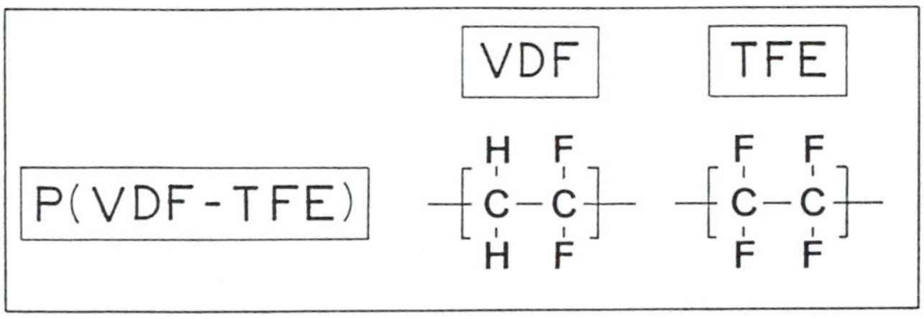

P(VDF-TFE)

T_g ? °C, ? °F

T_m 154 °C, 309 °F

A commercial copolymer, with vinylidenefluoride (VDF) and tetrafluoroethylene (TFE) repeat units [P(VDF-TFE)] in a 50/50 alternating arrangement, is reported to have a relatively low melting point for its very simple and regular structure. This corresponds to rather easy processing but limited temperature resistance. The fully fluorinated nature of the copolymer corresponds to excellent chemical resistance.

P(VDF-HFI)

P(VDF-HFI) copolymer (FP)

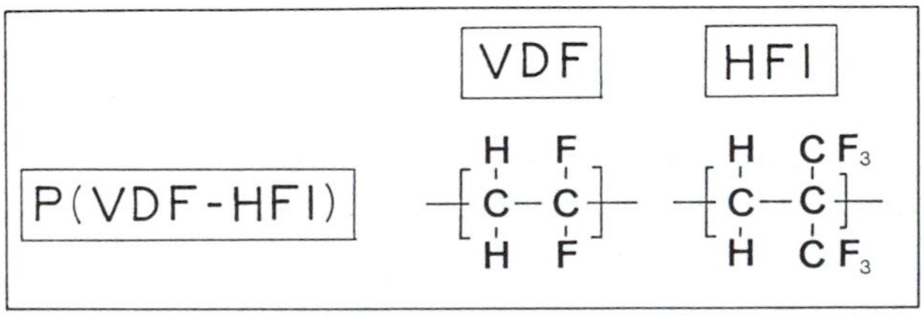

P(VDF-HFI)

T_g ? °C, ? °F

T_m 327 °C, 621 °F

A 50/50 alternating copolymer with vinylidenefluoride (VDF) and hexafluoroisobutylene (HFI) repeat units [P(VDF-HFI)] involves the relatively bulky CF_3 groups in an otherwise regular and symmetrical structure.

This highly crystalline copolymer is reported to be hard and rigid, with good abrasion and scratch resistance and a good creep resistance, particularly at high temperatures, which is generally missing in fully fluorinated fluoroplastics.

Figures 3.73-3.80 depict various applications of fluoropolymers.

Fig. 3.73

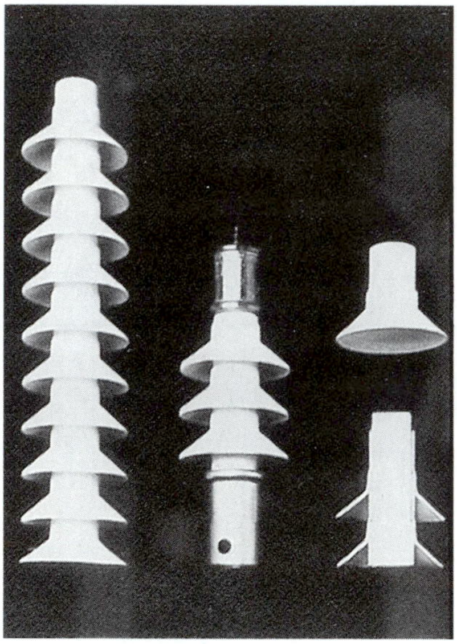

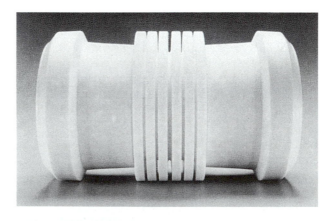

Fig. 3.74

Figure 3.73 · No-stick cookware (polytetrafluoroethylene PTFE) **[TEFAL]**

Figure 3.74 · High voltage insulating boots (polytetrafluoroethylene PTFE) **[ICI]**

Figure 3.75 · Machined flexible pipe coupling for the chemical process industry (polytetrafluoroethylene PTFE) **[HOECHST]**

Figure 3.76 · Turned seals for the food industry (polytetrafluoroethylene PTFE) [HOECHST]

Figure 3.77 · Fluoropolymer-lined chemical process equipment (polytetrafluoroethylene PTFE) [ICI]

Figure 3.78 · Fluoropolymer sintered lining and concertina packing for a control valve (polytetrafluoroethylene PTFE + carbon filler) [HOECHST]

Figure 3.79 · Body, cover and impeller of
certifugal pump (polyvinylidenefluoride PVDF)
[PENNWALT]

Figure   3.80   ·   Dual-laminated   chemical   process   equipment   (chemically   resistant
polyvinylidenefluoride PVDF inner layer and mechanically resistant glass fiber + polyester resin
outer layer) **[PCUK]**

3.2.2.15 Miscellaneous Heterochain Polymers

Polyphenylenesulfide (PPS)

PPS   poly'phenylene'sulfide   (HP)

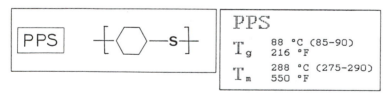

Polyphenylenesulfide (PPS), also referred to as "polyarylenesulfide" (PAS) or "poly
p-phenylenesulfide," features a simple symmetrical repeat unit with a phenyl group and
a sulfur atom (-S-) in the backbone. The phenyl group confers chain rigidity for a
relatively high glass transition temperature T_g, and both the symmetry and the absence
of bulky side groups, allow the chains to crystallize. The melting point T_m is very high.
High crystallinity (45-65%) is obtained at temperatures in the range T_g to T_m (hot

mold or annealing), but rapid solidification in cold molds can produce a much lower crystallinity (15%).

PPS is a temperature-resistant engineering plastic. Mechanical properties are moderately affected by temperature, and little chemical degradation in air (oxidation) occurs up to temperatures as high as 230°C ($\approx$ 450°F). Higher temperatures (above about 360°C or 680°F) can cause cross-linking.

Resistance to chemicals is reported to be very good, with no known solvents at temperatures below about 180°C (356°F). It tends, however, to be affected by oxidizing chemicals, such as nitric acid. Chlorinated solvents may also induce environmental stress-cracking (ESC). PPS is insensitive to moisture and is reported to have good weatherability, as well as good resistance to high energy radiations. It has good inherent flame resistance. PPS is a stiff and strong material with a tendency to be brittle and notch sensitive. It is noted as particularly compatible with glass fiber reinforcement, as a result of good wetting and bonding, and it is used primarily in reinforced grades (RTP), which are markedly tougher. Its use as coating relies partly on its good resistance to abrasion.

Electrical properties are reported to be good from the insulation or dielectric points of view. PPS is basically transparent to microwaves.

Processing of this thermoplastic is mostly by injection and also using coating technologies. Extrusion is reported to be rather impractical, possibly as a result of melt oxidation and a low melt viscosity.

Injection molding of PPS is claimed to be easy in spite of the high temperatures involved (about 320°C or 608°F for the melt and 135°C or 275°F for the mold). The low melt viscosity allows fast cycles and thin wall moldings. Precautions must be taken, however, to control mold corrosion and environmental hazards.

PPS is widely used as coatings, which can be applied by electrostatic, fluidized-bed, or slurry techniques. Coatings are often "baked" at about 357°C (675°F) to induce cross-linking. Special formulations reported to be "antistick" or "nonstick" may be PPS/PTFE polyalloys.

PPS resins are used where temperature and chemical resistance are called for. In the chemical process industry, PPS has been used in construction of pump housings and impellers, valves, metering devices, tower packings, and other products; etch tanks, for example, are coated with PPS. Other applications include lamp sockets, coil bobbins, gears, bushings, carburetor parts, and personal-care and household appliances (propellers or turbines for fan heaters or dryers, coatings for washing machines, microwave-compatible cookware, release coatings for cookware, etc.).

PPS has also been used as an adhesive and as a laminating resin.

Parylenes (PPX)

PPX−N   parylene (HP)

PPX-N	PPX−N
$\left[\!\!\begin{array}{c} H \\ \mid \\ C \\ \mid \\ H \end{array}\!\!-\!\!\bigcirc\!\!-\!\!\begin{array}{c} H \\ \mid \\ C \\ \mid \\ H \end{array}\!\!\right]$	T_g 100 °C 212 °F T_m 400 °C (400–405) 752 °F

PPX−C   parylene (HP)

PPX-C	PPX−C
$\left[\!\!\begin{array}{c} H \\ \mid \\ C \\ \mid \\ H \end{array}\!\!-\!\!\bigcirc\!\!-\!\!\begin{array}{c} Cl\ H \\ \mid \\ C \\ \mid \\ H \end{array}\!\!\right]$	T_g 60 °C 140 °F T_m 290 °C (280–300) 554 °F

PPX−D   parylene (HP)

PPX-D	PPX−D
$\left[\!\!\begin{array}{c} H \\ \mid \\ C \\ \mid \\ H \end{array}\!\!-\!\!\bigcirc\!\!-\!\!\begin{array}{c} Cl\ H \\ \mid \\ C \\ \mid \\ Cl\ H \end{array}\!\!\right]$	T_g ? °C ? °F T_m ? °C ? °F

Parylenes (PPX) are polymers of p-xylylene (xylene), also referred to as "parylene-N" (PPX-N), or substituted derivatives where either one or two hydrogen atoms H of the phenyl ring are replaced by chlorine atoms Cl [monochloro-substituted parylene-C (PPX-C) or dichloro-substituted parylene-D (PPX-D)].

The polymers have a high degree of polymerization (several thousand) and are highly crystalline with high melting points. Since they are sensitive to thermal and thermooxidative degradation and are practically insoluble, conventional processing is not possible. Instead, they are conveniently used as protective coatings deposited *in situ* on parts, such as encapsulated microelectronic components (transistors, resistors, capacitors, printed and integrated circuits, etc.).

The deposition corresponds, in fact, to a vapor phase polymerization, taking place on the cool surface of the part to be coated (substrate), in a vacuum environment. The process is, of course, relatively complex, but is well suited to relatively small electrical-electronic parts and yields remarkably uniform and strongly adhering thin coatings.

Parylene coatings have a good resistance to moisture and gas permeation, as well as good electrical characteristics. They are unaffected by most chemicals and solvents, and their highly crystalline structure contributes to their good environmental stress-cracking resistance. They are sensitive, however, to thermooxidative and UV (sunlight) degradation.

See figures 3.81-3.83 for 3 applications of heterochain polymers.

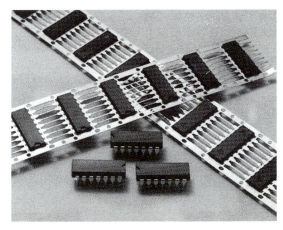

Fig. 3.81   Fig. 3.82

Figure 3.81 · Test socket for integrated circuit (polyphenylenesulfide PPS) **[PHILLIPS]**

Figure 3.82 · Encapsulated integrated circuits for automated assembly (polyphenylenesulfide PPS) **[PHILLIPS]**

Figure 3.83 · Chemical process equipment elements (polyphenylenesulfide PPS) **[PHILLIPS]**

3.3   THERMOSETTING RESINS (THERMOSETS)

3.3.1   GENERAL

3.3.1.1   Introduction

Thermoplastic resins are most commonly supplied by resin manufacturers in polymerized form, and processors do not normally have to deal with any chemical reaction; only physical changes being involved in what we refer to as "physical processing."

The processing of conventional rubbers involves the moderate cross-linking of already polymerized molecules, often referred to as "vulcanization," which corresponds to relatively limited chemical reactions.

In contrast, major chemical reactions take place in the course of the processing of thermosetting resins, which generally undergo a complex combination of polymerization and cross-linking, converting low- or relatively low-molecular- weight molecules into tight or relatively tight three-dimensional molecular networks. The expressions setting or curing are generally used for this conversion, and we refer to the corresponding processing as "reactive processing."

The chemical reactions involved in the course of the reactive processing of thermosetting resins are often complex and sometimes incompletely understood or considered confidential by resin manufacturers. Resin manufacturers can generally provide extensive technical assistance, particularly when they supply complete systems with detailed instructions for their use. A basic understanding of the major chemicals and reactions involved is helpful, but a detailed discussion is beyond the scope of this book.

The discussion of thermosetting resins is subdivided here into three types that reflect some major differences in processing methods. This subdivision is, otherwise, somewhat arbitrary and most of the conventional classes of thermosetting resins have systems fitting more than one of our types.

Our three types are titled temperature-activated, catalyst-activated, and mixing-activated systems, respectively.

Even though the traditional name "thermosetting resins" (or "thermosets") seems to imply that heating must be involved (thermo), it is now generally used for all reactive systems (room or elevated temperatures).

When dealing with reactive systems leading to three-dimensional molecular networks, one must consider a number of concepts. The shelf life of the resin or the resin system components reflects their stability before heating, the addition of a catalyst, or mixing. Pot life and gel time reflect the time available to shape the resin before significant cross-linking prevents fluid-like deformation of the material.

Changes in the physical state [P] of the materials [liquid (L), fluid (F) or solid (S)] or in their molecular configuration [M] [low molecular weight (L), molecular network (N)] are illustrated schematically for the three thermosetting resin types in Figures 3.84 to 3.86.

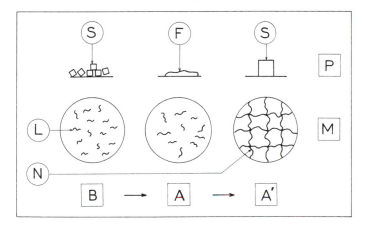

Figure 3.84 · **Temperature-activated thermosetting resin systems** · [P] Physical state; [M] Molecular conformation; [B] Before heating; [A] After heating; [A′] Final stage; (S) Solid; (F) Fluid; (L) Low molecular weight; (N) Molecular network

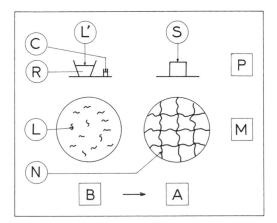

Figure 3.85 · **Catalyst - activated thermosetting resin systems** · [P] Physical state; [M] Molecular conformation; [B] Before catalyst addition; [A] Final stage; (R) Resin; (C) Catalyst; (L′) Liquid; (S) Solid; (L) Low molecular weight; (N) Molecular network

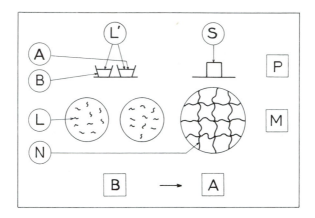

Figure 3.86 · **Mixing-activated thermosetting resin systems** · [P] Physical state; [M] Molecular conformation; [B] Before mixing; [A] Final stage; (A) First component; (B) Second component; (L′) Liquid; (S) Solid; (L) Low molecular weight; (N) Molecular network

The evolution of the resistance to deformation <R> with reaction time or duration <D> is illustrated in Figure 3.87. The material changes from a fluid (F) to a solid (S) through an intermediate gel state (G). The effect of higher (H) or lower (L) temperatures, catalyst levels, or component reactivities is also illustrated in Figure 3.87.

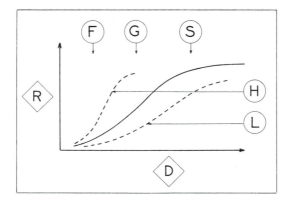

Figure 3.87 · **Thermosetting resins; time effect** · <R> Resistance to deformation; <D> Reaction time; (F) Fluid; (G) Gel; (S) Solid; (L) Slow reaction; (H) Fast reaction

3.3.1.2   Temperature-Activated Systems

A number of thermosetting resin systems are supplied in solid granular or powder form ([S] in Fig. 3.84). The first or short-term effect of a temperature rise is a softening of the material which allows it to flow and, therefore, to be molded [F]. Prolonged exposure to a sufficiently high temperature triggers the chemical reaction which forms, by cross-linking, a tight three-dimensional molecular network that corresponds to a now rigid plastic [S'].

Those thermosetting resin systems are generally heated by conduction, with viscous heating and dielectric heating sometimes used as well. The need for relatively high temperatures (typically 150°C or 300°F) and high molding pressures can call for relatively expensive processing machinery and tooling.

The most typical temperature-activated systems are probably the formaldehyde-related resin systems (FOR), which include phenoplasts (PF resins) and aminoplasts (UF and MF resins). Certain types of unsaturated polyester (UPR), vinyl ester (VER), alkyd (AKR), allyl (ALR) and furan (FUR) resin systems, as well as some epoxies (EPR) and polyimides (PIR), are also associated with this type.

3.3.1.3   Catalyst-Activated Systems

Some thermosetting resin systems are supplied in stable liquid form [(R) in Fig.3.85]. After a suitable and normally small amount of liquid chemical, most commonly called "catalyst" (C), is added to the liquid resin, a chemical reaction starts that eventually leads to the formation of a solid material having a three-dimensional molecular network structure [A]. The nature and amount of the catalyst allow a control of the speed at which the reaction takes place (Fig. 3.87).

Many such systems can set (cure) at room temperature; this and their low initial viscosity makes them attractive for casting purposes and for the formation of composite materials in association with reinforcing fibers in the form of continuous roving, woven cloth, etc. Unsaturated polyester liquid resin systems (UPR) are most representative of this type.

3.3.1.4   Mixing-Activated Systems

There are thermosetting resin systems that consist primarily of two liquid chemicals [(A) and (B) in Fig. 3.86] that are stable when kept separate but react to form three-dimensional molecular networks when generally comparable amounts are mixed. Elevated temperatures can speed up the reaction but are not needed in principle.

Some systems with relatively low reactivity are suitable for batch mixing and subsequent casting, for example. Mixing can also be carried out in a semi-continuous way, allowing the mixing and dispensing of specific amounts. Very reactive systems have recently been introduced, which are rapidly mixed and injected into mold cavities to allow fast molding cycles for large and thin parts; such processes are often referred to specifically as RIM (reaction injection molding).

Polyurethane resin systems (PUR) are major representatives of this type, along with some epoxy (EPR) and other resin systems.

3.3.2 Commercial Thermosetting Resin Systems and Related Polymers

3.3.2.1 Formaldehyde Systems

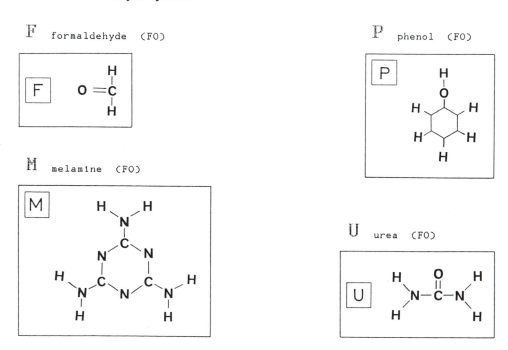

A series of thermosetting polymers involves the reaction of formaldehyde (F) with three hydrogen-containing chemicals: phenol (P), urea (U), or melamine (M) to form three-dimensional molecular networks. In a somewhat oversimplified manner, the mechanism can be viewed as the oxygen (O) from the formaldehyde condensing, with two hydrogens (H) from two different molecules of P, U, or F in the form of H_2O, leaving a chemical link between the two molecules. In practice, the chemistry of the reactions can be quite complex. The discussion of one-stage systems, associated with resols, or two-stage systems, associated with novolacs prepolymers, precursors, or additional curing agents, is beyond the scope of this book.

Formaldehyde-related thermosets are frequently compounded with a variety of fillers such as wood flour, α-cellulose fibers, and minerals.

For molding purposes they are generally supplied in powder or granular form or sometimes compacted as preforms (pills). The uncured resin can be preheated rather rapidly using high-frequency (radio frequency or microwave) methods, or hot plasticized slugs can be prepared with an extruder-like device.

Molding temperatures are in the range 125-200°C ($\approx$ 250-400°F) and molding pressures are in the range 2000-8000 psi ($\approx$ 14-56 MPa) for compression molding and can be as high as 20,000 psi ($\approx$ 140 MPa) for injection molding. In order to face increasing competition from thermoplastics, systems suitable for relatively fast injection molding had to be developed.

Formaldehyde-related thermosets are also widely used in conjunction with other materials for a variety of important applications where they can act as binder, adhesives, coatings, surface treatments, etc.

Phenoplasts (phenolics, phenolic resins, PF resins) are based on phenol (P) and formaldehyde (F). They were among the very first commercial polymers to be introduced at the turn of the century under the tradename Bakelite.

These low cost thermosets have a good assortment of properties which include high rigidity, dimensional stability up to fairly high temperatures, and low flammability. They are, however, generally brittle and can be obtained only in dark colors (brown, black).

Applications through molding include temperature-resistant insulating parts for appliances (knobs, handles, etc.), electrical components (connectors, distributor caps, sockets, etc.) and bottle closures. They serve as binder (matrix) in abrasive (grinding) wheels, brake linings, clutch faces, wood particle boards (chipboards), molds and cores in modern foundry work, or adhesive in plywood fabrication and furniture assembly. An important application is in decorative laminates (counter or table tops, etc.) where phenoplast-impregnated kraft paper is pressed into heat-resistant, dimensionally stable sheets; the surface layer is made of colorable aminoplast, discussed later. Fire-resistant rigid foams are also produced for insulation or structural purposes.

Aminoplasts (amino resins, UF or MF resins) comprise resins based on urea (U) and formaldehyde (F) or melamine (M) and formaldehyde (F). Both urea and melamine feature amino (NH_2) group, hence the name amino resins. Aminoplasts, contrary to phenoplasts, can be made translucent or in light colors and are thus suitable where aesthetic considerations are important.

Urea-formaldehyde (UF) resins are used for many of the same applications as PF resins when color requirements justify the higher cost. A castable foam system suitable for home insulation has been developed that, however, requires good process control to avoid undesirable formaldehyde formation.

Melamine-formaldehyde (MF) resins are noted for their excellent water resistance. They are used for dishwater-safe molded dinnerware which can be decorated with molded-in paper overlays; they form the surface layer of decorative laminates (Formica, Arborite); they serve as adhesives for water-resistant plywood (marine, exterior) and in the treatment of papers and textiles to improve their water resistance, in particular.

3.3.2.2 *Furan Systems*

FUN   furan (FU)

FUN
H-C — C-H
H-C   C-H
O

FUL   furfural (FU)

FUL
H-C — C-H
H-C   C-C = O
O   H

Furan (FUN), furfuryl aldehyde [furfural (FUL)] and furfuryl alcohol feature a ring structure which can be opened (cleaved) to yield polymeric molecules. With the unsaturations present, the formation of three-dimensional molecular networks is possible.

Furan resin systems are often combined with formaldehyde-related thermosetting resins. They are used as binder for sand in foundry work or abrasive particles in grinding wheels, as well as adhesives and matrix for reinforced plastics used in the chemical process industry, where corrosion resistance is important.

3.3.2.3 Allyl Systems

AA allyl'alcohol (AL)

AA $H-O-\overset{\displaystyle H}{\underset{\displaystyle H}{C}}-\overset{\displaystyle H}{C}=\overset{\displaystyle H}{\underset{\displaystyle H}{C}}$

DAP di'allyl'phthalate (AL)(UP)

DAP $\overset{\displaystyle H}{C}=\overset{\displaystyle H}{C}-\overset{\displaystyle H}{\underset{\displaystyle H}{C}}-O-\overset{\displaystyle O}{\overset{\displaystyle \|}{C}}\quad\overset{\displaystyle O}{\overset{\displaystyle \|}{C}}-O-\overset{\displaystyle H}{\underset{\displaystyle H}{C}}-\overset{\displaystyle H}{C}=\overset{\displaystyle H}{\underset{\displaystyle H}{C}}$

DAIP di'allyl'isophthalate (AL)

DAIP $\overset{\displaystyle H}{C}=\overset{\displaystyle H}{C}-\overset{\displaystyle H}{\underset{\displaystyle H}{C}}-O-\overset{\displaystyle O}{\overset{\displaystyle \|}{C}}\quad\overset{\displaystyle O}{\overset{\displaystyle \|}{C}}-O-\overset{\displaystyle H}{\underset{\displaystyle H}{C}}-\overset{\displaystyle H}{C}=\overset{\displaystyle H}{\underset{\displaystyle H}{C}}$

DEGBAC di'ethylene'glycol'bis'allyl'carbonate (AL)

DEGBAC

$H-\overset{\displaystyle H}{C}-\overset{\displaystyle H}{\underset{\displaystyle H}{C}}-O-\overset{\displaystyle O}{\overset{\displaystyle \|}{C}}-O-\overset{\displaystyle H}{\underset{\displaystyle H}{C}}-\overset{\displaystyle H}{C}=\overset{\displaystyle H}{\underset{\displaystyle H}{C}}$

$H-\overset{\displaystyle H}{C}-\overset{\displaystyle H}{\underset{\displaystyle H}{C}}-O-\underset{\displaystyle O}{\overset{\displaystyle \|}{C}}-O-\overset{\displaystyle H}{\underset{\displaystyle H}{C}}-\overset{\displaystyle H}{C}=\overset{\displaystyle H}{\underset{\displaystyle H}{C}}$

The manufacture of allyl resin monomers involves the reaction of a monofunctional unsaturated alcohol, allyl alcohol (AA), with a difunctional acid. Ester linkages are thus formed, but the resulting molecules are not polymeric. The presence of two unsaturations (C = C) per monomer permits the formation of a three-dimensional molecular network (cure) through the use of suitable catalysts (benzoyl peroxide or tert-butyl perbenzoate) and elevated temperatures (above about 150°C or 300°F).

The most common allyl monomers are diallylphthalate (DAP) or diallylorthophthalate and diallylisophthalate (DAIP) or diallylmetaphthalate.

Thermoplastic prepolymers are available that can be cured through remaining allyl unsaturations; they involve very low cure shrinkage.

Allyl resin systems are used as high performance molding compounds, frequently incorporating reinforcements, for high heat and humidity electrical applications, for example. They are also used in the fabrication of heat-cured laminates, including preimpregnated fiber systems (prepregs).

Although the chemistry and the mechanism of cure of allyl resin systems is quite different from that of conventional unsaturated polyester resin systems, the two types are not always identified as distinct resins.

A special type of allyl monomer, diethylene glycol bis-allylcarbonate (DEGBAC) or allyldiglycolcarbonate (ADC), has found an important application in the casting of optical components (prescription and other lenses). The cure of this thermosetting resin can be achieved with benzoyl peroxide at moderate temperatures (about 180°F or 80°C). It is marketed under the tradename CR-39.

3.3.2.4 Alkyd Systems

The name "alkyd" appears to have been derived from alcohol (alk) and acid (yd). The "reaction" of difunctional alcohols (glycols) and difunctional acids or anhydrides gives polyesters, and alkyd resins are thus related to this class of polymers.

Alkyd resins were long used primarily as coatings (paints, varnishes, lacquers). They involved ethylene glycol or glycerol and phthalic anhydride with various fatty acids based on linseed, soybean, and tung oils. Glycerophthalic (Glyptal) coatings, for example, involved glycerol and phthalic anhydride.

Thermosetting molding compounds, now referred to as "alkyd molding compounds, appear to be unsaturated polyester resin systems (UPR) where the cross-linking monomer is diallylphthalate (DAP).

3.3.2.5 Unsaturated Polyester Systems

The first major constituent of unsaturated polyester resin systems, referred to here as "UPR" and also called simply "polyester resins," consists of relatively short polymeric chains (oligomers) resulting from the controlled reaction between a difunctional acid

MLA maleic'anhydride (IM)(UP)

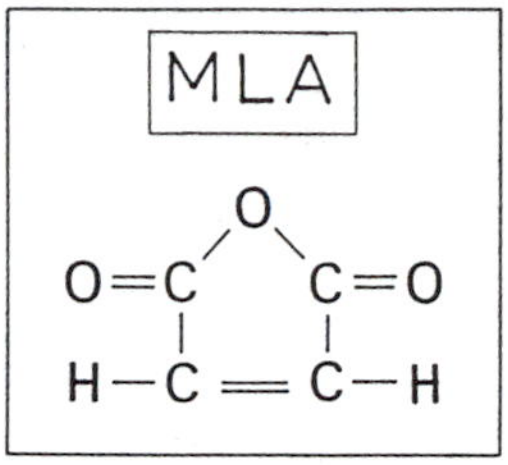

MLA

$$O=C \overset{O}{<} C=O$$
$$H-C = C-H$$

PTA phthalic'anhydride (UP)(EP)

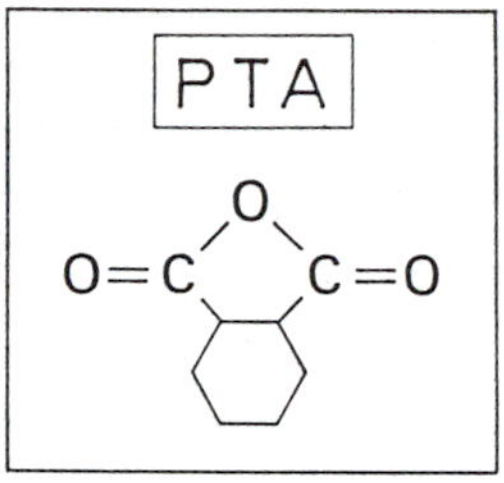

PTA

$$O=C \overset{O}{<} C=O$$

EG ethylene'glycol (UP)

EG

$$H-O-\overset{H}{\underset{H}{C}}-\overset{H}{\underset{H}{C}}-O-H$$

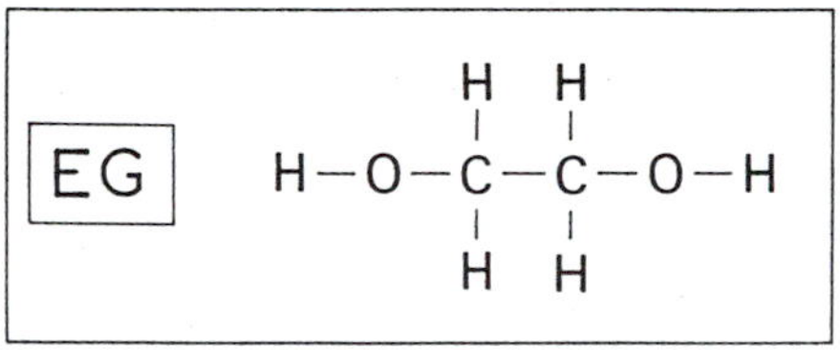

(or anhydride) and a difunctional alcohol (glycol). Characteristic ester linkages are formed, hence the name "polyester." At least some of the acid (or anhydride) features double bonds between adjacent carbon atoms (unsaturations), which are required for the subsequent cross-linking of the systems into three-dimensional molecular networks. This first constituent is thus called "unsaturated polyester." The typical molecular weight of the corresponding molecules is 1000-3000. The acids or anhydrides include maleic acid or anhydride (MLA) and fumaric acid (unsaturated) or phthalic (orthophthalic) anhydride (PTA), isophthalic acid, terephthalic acid, and adipic acid (saturated). The glycols include ethylene glycol (EG) or diethylene glycol, propylene glycol or dipropylene glycol, and glycerol.

The other major constituent is a monomer capable of polymerizing, as well as reacting with the unsaturations in the polyester molecules to form interconnections and thus molecular networks. The proportion of monomer used in commercial systems

S styrene (UP)

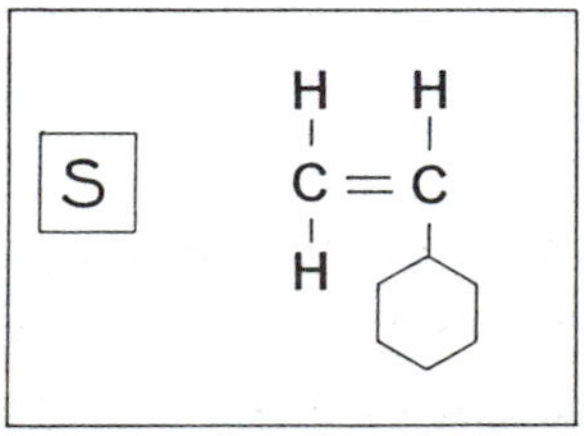

S

$$\overset{H}{\underset{H}{C}} = \overset{H}{C}$$

AMS alpha'methyl'styrene (UP)

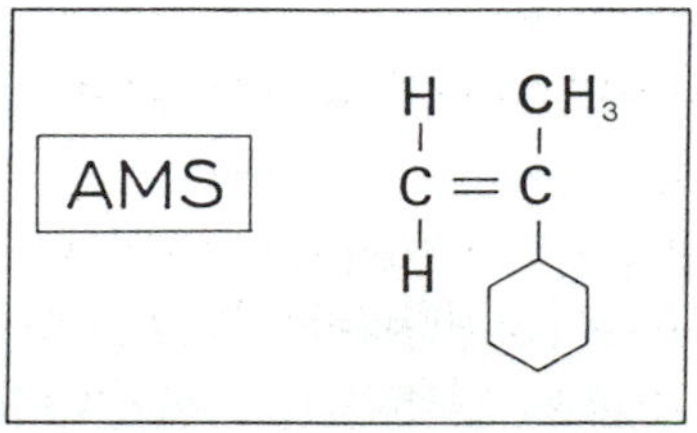

AMS

$$\overset{H}{\underset{H}{C}} = \overset{CH_3}{C}$$

PMS para'methyl'styrene (UP)

| PMS |

$$
\begin{array}{cc}
H & H \\
| & | \\
C & = C \\
| & \\
H & \bigcirc \\
& | \\
& CH_3
\end{array}
$$

MMA methyl'methacrylate (UP)

| MMA |

$$
\begin{array}{cc}
H & CH_3 \\
| & | \\
C & = C \\
| & | \\
H & C-O-CH_3 \\
& \| \\
& O
\end{array}
$$

DAP di'allyl'phthalate (AL)(UP)

| DAP |

$$
\begin{array}{c}
H \quad H \quad H \quad \overset{O}{\underset{\|}{}} \quad \overset{O}{\underset{\|}{}} \quad H \quad H \quad H \\
C=C-C-O-C \qquad C-O-C-C=C \\
H \quad H \qquad \bigcirc \qquad H \quad H
\end{array}
$$

TAC tri'allyl'cyanurate (UP)

| TAC |

$$
\begin{array}{c}
H \quad H \quad H \qquad N \qquad H \quad H \quad H \\
C=C-C-O-C \qquad C-O-C-C=C \\
H \quad H \quad N \quad N \quad H \quad H \\
C \\
| \\
O-C-C=C \\
H \quad H
\end{array}
$$

ranges from about 30 to 50%. Low viscosity monomers also serve as diluent for the higher viscosity polyester molecules. Examples of suitable monomers include styrene (S), the least expensive and most commonly used one, alpha-methylstyrene (AMS), vinyltoluene [mixed isomers, including para-vinyltoluene also called "para-methyl styrene" (PMS)], methylmethacrylate (MMA), particularly when weathering is important, diallylphthalate (DAP), and triallylcyanurate (TAC).

The density of unsaturations in the unsaturated polyester resins, as well as the proportion of polymerizable monomer, determine the final cross-link density, or the "tightness" of the molecular network and, hence, its stiffness and hardness.

Resin systems are normally supplied with an additive (inhibitor) that prevents or retards premature cross-linking (cure), allowing a suitable "shelf life." Hydroquinone and tertiary butyl catechol are examples of inhibitors.

Heat or radiations (UV, etc.) alone can often trigger the cross-linking reaction (cure), but, generally, additives known as catalyst (or initiator) and accelerator (or promoter) are involved. The chemistry of these systems is quite complex, but, in a somewhat oversimplified way, one can view the initiator as being the active element; the accelerator not having a direct effect on the resin system, but simply helping the initiator play its role.

Catalysts (initiators) include methylethylketone (MEK) peroxide, benzoyl peroxide, and cumene hydroperoxide. Accelerators (promoters) include metallic soaps, such as cobalt naphthenate and cobalt octoate or tertiary amines, such as dimethyl aniline and diethyl aniline.

Unsaturated polyester resin systems may be subdivided into two groups: those that can cure at room temperature and those that require higher curing temperatures.

Room temperature curing systems correspond to our "catalyst-activated systems." The accelerator is often incorporated into the resin system and the catalyst (initiator) is added just prior to use. The nature of the resin system and the amount of catalyst determine the speed of cure. These systems are particularly convenient for use as a matrix for reinforced plastics, since the low viscosity of the resins allows an easy combination with the reinforcement (primarily glass roving, cloth or mat), and the fabrication and curing of products at ambient temperatures is particularly convenient for large parts. Applications of these systems correspond primarily to the so-called fiber-reinforced plastics (FRP) widely used now to make pipes, tanks, containers, structural elements (beams, posts, springs, etc.), hulls, architectural panels, etc.

Other systems are compounded with all ingredients (catalyst and accelerator, as well as extenders, fillers, etc.) but are relatively stable at room temperature. They are then subjected to the high temperature of a heated mold (typically 150°C or 300°F). They correspond to our "temperature-activated systems." Bulk molding compounds (BMC) and sheet molding compounds (SMC) belong to this category. They are processed by injection molding (BMC) or compression molding (BMC and SMC) into relatively small parts (BMC) or large body-type parts (SMC).

In general, the properties of parts made with unsaturated polyester resin systems are highly dependent on the chemical composition of the system, as well as the fillers or reinforcements. Good weathering, high flame retardancy, or good toughness and fatigue resistance, for example, can be achieved, but normally at an increased cost and sometimes to the detriment of other properties.

3.3.2.6 Vinylester Systems

DGEBA   di'glycidyl'ether'of'bisphenol'A   (VE)(EP)

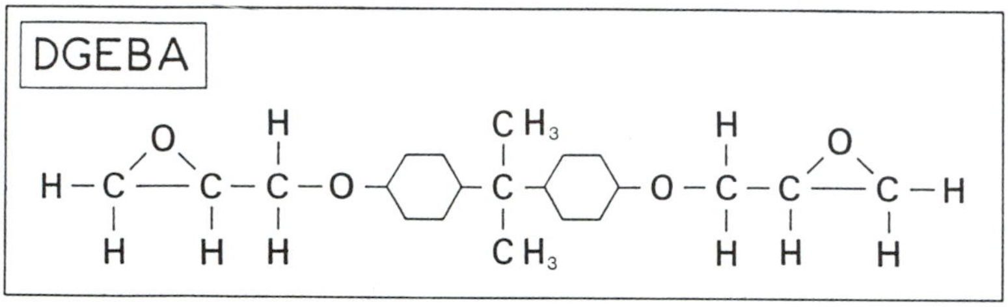

MAA   methacrylic'acid   (VE)

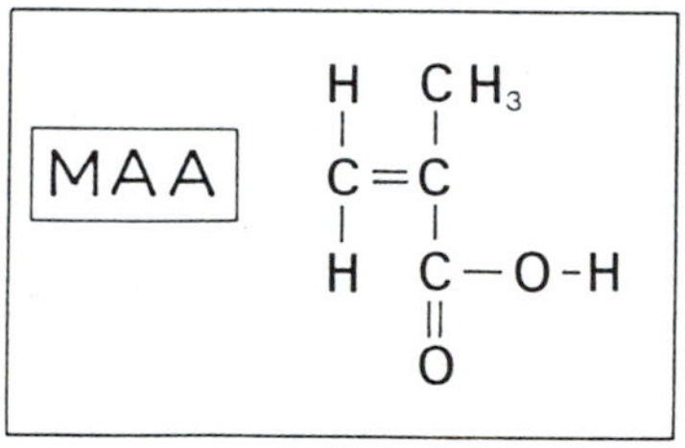

Vinylester resins (VER) consist of short linear molecules resulting from the reaction of epoxide group-terminated molecules, such as diglycidyl ether of bisphenol-A (DGEBA) with unsaturated acids, such as methacrylic acid (MAA). They feature ester linkages and vinyl-type unsaturations, hence their name "vinylester resins." Their cross-linking into three-dimensional networks requires, like regular unsaturated polyester resins, a monomer such as styrene.

Vinylester resins are primarily used as the matrix for fiber reinforced plastics (FRP). They are noted for their very good adhesion to glass and for the high corrosion resistance they impart to the composites. Chemical process equipment (piping, tanks, coatings, etc.) forms a large market for these resins.

3.3.2.7 Epoxy Systems

E   epoxide'group   (EP)

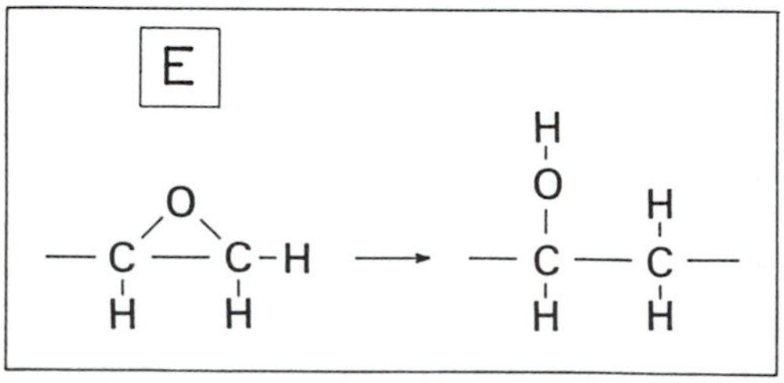

ECH   epi'chloro'hydrin   (EP)

A class of thermosetting resins, the epoxy resin systems, feature a type of reactive group, referred to as "epoxide groups" or "oxirane ring" (E). This group can react with active hydrogen atoms (H) of amines or acid anhydrides, for example, to form chemical links (cross-links) that are the basis of the curing of these resins.

Epoxy resins are often the result of the reaction between epichlorohydrin (ECH) and multifunctional acids, amines or alcohols. The reaction is sometimes called "glycidylization" and the epichlorohydrin residue is referred to as a "glycidyl group" (G).

DGEBA   di'glycidyl'ether'of'bisphenol'A   (VE)(EP)

TGMDA   tetra'glycidyl'methylene'di'aniline   (EP)

PNP   poly'nuclear'phenol'epoxy   (EP)

CA   cyclo'aliphatic'epoxy (EP)

HY   hydantoin'epoxy (EP)

The most common epoxy resin is based on bisphenol-A and, in its simplest form, is often referred to as "diglycidyl ether of bisphenol-A" (DGEBA). It is sometimes used in a slightly polymerized form that features hydroxyl (OH) groups.

Other epoxy resins include brominated versions of DGEBA for fire retardancy, tetraglycidyl methylene dianiline (TGMDA), polynuclear phenol epoxy (PNP), epoxy phenol novolac and epoxy cresol novolac, cycloaliphatic epoxies (CA) that are used

DETA   di'ethylene'tri'amine (EP)

TETA   tri'ethylene'tetr'amine (EP)(UR)

particularly in electrical applications, and hydantoin epoxies (HY), which are very compatible with aramid fibers.

MPA   m'phenylene'di'amine (IM)(EP)

DADPS   di'amino'di'phenyl'sulfone (EP)

DCDA   di'cyan'di'amide (EP)

PTA   phthalic'anhydride (UP)(EP)

TMA   trimellitic'acid'anhydride (IM)(EP)

PMA   pyro'mellitic'di'anhydride (IM)(EP)

PMA

The formation of the three-dimensional network (curing) can take place at room temperature or at elevated temperatures. The required chemicals, referred to as "catalysts," "hardeners," "hardening agents," "cross-linking agents," or "curing agents," include polyfunctional aliphatic or aromatic amines, such as diethylene triamine (DETA or DTA), triethylene tetramine (TETA) or hexamethylene tetramine, m-phenylene diamine (MPA), diamino diphenyl sulfone (DADPS or DDS), and dicyandiamide or cyanoguanidine (DCDA), as well as acid anhydrides such as phthalic anhydride (PTA), pyromellitic dianhydride (PMA), and trimellitic acid anhydride (TMA). The active hydrogen atoms of these curing agents react primarily with epoxide groups, but also occasionally with hydroxyl groups (OH) present in partially polymerized resins. As much as 10-15% of curing agent must generally be added to the epoxy resin.

The properties of epoxy resin systems (EPR) naturally depend on their exact chemical composition and cure, but they are generally superior to those of less expensive resins systems, such as unsaturated polyesters (UPR).

Epoxy resin systems can be hard, tough, strong and fatigue resistant. They are known for their excellent adhesion to most materials, including metals, as well as low cure shrinkage. They have good electrical properties with a low dissipation factor.

They have a good thermal and chemical (corrosion) resistance. Their resistance to salt water and weathering makes them particularly suitable for tough marine environments. Fire retardancy is enhanced in brominated resin systems.

Epoxy resin systems can be processed in a variety of ways and cured at low or elevated temperatures. Low-viscosity resins can be cast or used to impregnate reinforcements. Molding compounds can be injection-, compression-, or transfer-molded. Fast reacting systems are reportedly used in the reaction injection molding (RIM) process.

Applications of epoxy resin systems fall into several categories.

Protective coatings are widely used for industrial, architectural, marine, and other applications. Solvent-based, as well as solventless systems (water-based or powders), are used for pipe, tank, drum, and can linings.

Electrical and electronic applications range from the encapsulation (potting) of small components, such as transistors or the manufacture of laminated printed circuit (PC) boards or integrated circuits (IC) to large outdoor insulators.

Epoxy resins serve as binder for sand-filled industrial floorings or as matrix for fiber-reinforced plastics (FRP) used in the manufacture of items, such as pressure pipes and tanks, rocket motor casings, and aerospace structural components.

Epoxy adhesives, often available as convenient two-component systems, are now used for major structural joints in aerospace, automotive, and construction applications. With the increased use of composites, conventional joining procedures often have to be replaced by adhesive bonds which correspond to a more favorable stress distribution.

3.3.2.8 Urethane/Urea Systems

UT   urethane'linkage   (UR)

UA   urea'linkage   (UR)

IC   isocyanurate'linkage   (UR)

Urethane resin systems (URR) or polyurethanes form a broad group of polymeric materials that contain urethane chemical groups and are associated with isocyanate chemistry. They include liquid thermosetting resin systems, either offered as complete packages with appropriate technical assistance by certain suppliers or developed by part manufacturers, as well as solid thermoplastics generally produced by large chemical companies and, subsequently, converted into parts by conventional thermoplastic processing methods.

The chemistry of polyurethane or isocyanate-based resins is very complex, and the variety of ingredients and specific systems precludes here anything but the statement of very general principles that are necessarily somewhat oversimplified. A basic reaction involves isocyanate (NCO) and hydroxy (OH) end-groups and leads to urethane linkage groups (UT), from which the name to this class of materials was derived. Isocyanate (NCO) and primary amine (NH_2) end-groups lead to urea linkage groups (UA) and some resin systems are sometimes referred to as "polyurea resin systems" (UAR). Isocyanurate linkage groups (IC) are sometimes involved. Another reaction that plays an important role involves isocyanate (NCO) end-groups and water molecules (H_2O) and produces carbon dioxide (CO_2), which serves as a blowing agent for certain cellular products.

In simple terms, the macromolecular formation of polyurethane plastics or elastomers can be viewed as taking place according to either one of two distinct mechanisms.

If difunctional (two reactive groups) components (isocyanates and polyols) are involved, "linear" macromolecules are formed; the absence of chemical bonds between chains corresponding to a thermoplastic behavior. The highly polar urethane groups are capable of relatively strong intermolecular attractions that, however, disappear at sufficiently high temperature. When remaining portions of the chains are rigid (high glass transition temperature T_g) or when they are capable of crystallizing below a sufficiently high melting point T_m, the thermoplastic can be a rigid plastic. Elastomeric thermoplastic polyurethanes appear to consist of molecules featuring relatively long flexible sections (soft blocks), as well as sections capable of strong intermolecular interactions below a certain softening temperature (hard blocks) that then act as "physical" cross-links.

When multifunctional molecules (three or more reactive groups) are present in the components (e.g., polyols or curative agents), molecular networks can be formed. The chemical cross-links are now permanent and the resulting materials are thermosets. The rigidity or crystallizing tendency of the chains between cross-links and the frequency of cross-linking (cross-link density) determine the stiffness of the thermoset, which can range from a hard plastic to a soft elastomer.

The two major ingredients of polyurethane resin systems are liquid isocyanates and polyols.

TDI 2,4 toluene'di'isocyanate (UR)

TDI 2,6 toluene'di'isocyanate (UR)

MDI methylene'di'phenyl'di'isocyanate (UR)

PMDI polymeric'MDI (UR)

HMDI   hydrogenated'MDI   (UR)

HMDI $O=C=N-\langle S \rangle - \overset{\overset{\displaystyle H}{\displaystyle |}}{\underset{\underset{\displaystyle H}{\displaystyle |}}{C}} - \langle S \rangle -N=C=O$

Isocyanates feature the chemical groups NCO and are generally difunctional (diisocyanates). Common examples include toluene (or tolylene) diisocyanate in two isomeric forms (2,4 and 2,6) which is abbreviated as "TDI" and "methylene di (or bis) phenyl diisocyanate (MDI)," also used in polymeric form (PMDI). There are also aliphatic isocyanates, such as hydrogenated MDI (HMDI), which tend to be highly toxic but impart a better resistance to sunlight than aromatic ones; this is an important consideration for coatings.

PEEG   poly'ethylene'ether'glycol   (UR)

PEEG $H-O\left[\left(\overset{\overset{\displaystyle H}{\displaystyle |}}{\underset{\underset{\displaystyle H}{\displaystyle |}}{C}}\right)_2 O\right]_n H$

PBEG   poly'butylene'ether'glycol   (UR)

PBEG $H-O\left[\left(\overset{\overset{\displaystyle H}{\displaystyle |}}{\underset{\underset{\displaystyle H}{\displaystyle |}}{C}}\right)_4 O\right]_n H$

PPEG   poly'propylene'ether'glycol   (UR)

PPEG $H-O\left[\overset{\overset{\displaystyle H}{\displaystyle |}}{\underset{\underset{\displaystyle H}{\displaystyle |}}{C}} - \overset{\overset{\displaystyle H}{\displaystyle |}}{\underset{\underset{\displaystyle CH_3}{\displaystyle |}}{C}} - O\right]_n H$

BOH   hydroxyl'terminated'butadiene   (UR)

BOH $H-O-\left[\begin{array}{c} H \\ | \\ C \\ | \\ H \end{array} - \begin{array}{c} H \\ | \\ C \end{array} = \begin{array}{c} H \\ | \\ C \end{array} - \begin{array}{c} H \\ | \\ C \\ | \\ H \end{array}\right]_n O-H$

IBOH   hydroxyl'terminated'isobutylene   (UR)

IBOH $H-O-\left[\begin{array}{c} H \\ | \\ C \\ | \\ H \end{array} - \begin{array}{c} CH_3 \\ | \\ C \\ | \\ CH_3 \end{array}\right]_n O-H$

Polyols, also referred to as "macroglycols," feature hydroxyl groups (OH) as end-group and side-group. Their molecular weights (chain length) can range from about 300 to about 5000, and the frequency of occurrence of OH groups (functionality or reactivity) can vary by a factor of 10. Flexible polyurethanes are associated with low functionality and long chains, while rigid ones correspond to high functionality and short chains. Polyols are generally divided into polyether types, which have a greater resistance to hydrolysis (water-associated degradation), and polyester types which have a better resistance to oils and hydrocarbons, in general. Examples of polyether polyols include polyethylene ether glycol (PEEG), polytetramethylene (or butylene), ether glycol (PTMG or PBEG), and polypropylene ether glycol (PPEG).

Some hydroxyl-terminated hydrocarbon polymers (OH end-groups) can react with suitable isocyanates to form three-dimensional molecular networks (thermosets). They include unsaturated (C=C) butadiene (BOH) and saturated isobutylene (IBOH) types.

HMDA   hexa'methylene'di'amine   (UR)

HMDA $H_2N-\left[\begin{array}{c} H \\ | \\ C \\ | \\ H \end{array}\right]_6 NH_2$

TETA   tri'ethylene'tetr'amine   (EP)(UR)

$$\text{TETA} \qquad H_2N-\left(\underset{H}{\overset{H}{C}}\right)_2-N-\left(\underset{H}{\overset{H}{C}}\right)_2-N-\left(\underset{H}{\overset{H}{C}}\right)_2-NH_2$$

MDA   methylene'di'aniline   (IM)(UR)

$$\text{MDA} \qquad H_2N-\langle\ \rangle-\underset{H}{\overset{H}{C}}-\langle\ \rangle-NH_2$$

MOCA   methylene'bis'ortho'chloro'aniline   (UR)

$$\text{MOCA} \qquad H_2N-\underset{}{\overset{Cl}{\langle\ \rangle}}-\underset{H}{\overset{H}{C}}-\underset{}{\overset{Cl}{\langle\ \rangle}}-NH_2$$

BD   butane'diol   (UR)

$$\text{BD} \qquad H-O-\left(\underset{H}{\overset{H}{C}}\right)_4-O-H$$

DEG   di'ethylene'glycol   (UR)

$$\text{DEG} \qquad H-O-\left(\underset{H}{\overset{H}{C}}\right)_2-O-\left(\underset{H}{\overset{H}{C}}\right)_2-O-H$$

TMP tri'methylol'propane (UR)

```
 TMP        H
            |
            O
            |
        H—C—H
     H      |      H
     |      |      |
 H₃C—C——————C——————C—O—H
     |      |      |
     H      |      H
        H—C—H
            |
            O
            |
            H
```

Polyurethane-type resins often feature other chemicals that play a role in the complex and varied chemical reactions. A discussion of their individual roles is beyond the scope of this book. These chemicals may be called extenders, chain-extending agents, curative agents, cross-linking agents, or even catalysts and they are used in relatively small amounts. They include aliphatic amines, such as hexamethylene (or triethylene) diamine (HMDA) and trimethylene tetramine (TETA), as well as aromatic amines, such as methylene (diphenyl) diamine (or dianiline) (MDA) and 4,4′ methylene-bis-ortho (or 2) chloroaniline (MOCA). They also include diols containing hydroxyl (OH) groups, such as diethylene glycol (DEG) and 1,4 butanediol (BD), as well as trimethylol propane (TMP).

Chemicals such as organic tin compounds (dibutyltin dilaurate) or tertiary amines are often involved in the recipes as true catalysts for the reactions. Nucleating agents may also be present to help control the homogeneity of foams, along with surface active agents, such as silicone oils. Phosphorus-based or halogenated additives may also be involved to improve the fire retardancy of foams, in particular.

Isocyanurate resins, sometimes referred to as "PIR" or "trimer resins," are also based on isocyanate and polyol reactions with an excess of isocyanate resulting in ring trimerization [isocyanurate (IC)]. Rigid isocyanurate foams are now widely used for their greater inherent fire resistance.

The properties of polyurethanes can vary widely, depending on the exact system considered. Among the mechanical properties, abrasion resistance is one that generally stands out. It has been pointed out that polyester-based systems tend to have better oil and fuel resistance, while polyether systems resist better hydrolysis (water-related degradation, particularly at high temperatures).

Many mechanically demanding parts are made of solid (unfoamed) polyurethane by a molding process that may involve a thermoplastic resin with high molding pressures (conventional injection molding) or a reactive system with much lower molding pressures (casting, pouring) but usually a longer cycle time. The stiffness can range from that of a soft rubber to that of an engineering plastic. Examples of such applications include pump liners and impellers, gears, sprocket wheels, bushings, shock mounts, O-rings, seals and gaskets, solid tires or wheel covers, roller covers (printing, paper industry), sports boots (ski, hockey), conveyor belts, and chute liners.

A relatively new process, reaction (or reactive) injection molding (RIM), was initially developed with urethane resin systems. It permits, in particular, the economical fabrication of large thin parts, such as automobile body component. The products are very slightly cellular and relatively flexible unless a stiff reinforcement is used (RRIM).

Some polyurethane resins can be processed exactly as conventional rubbers. They generally feature unsaturations in the chains, to allow conventional vulcanization, and are referred to as "solid millable gums."

Flexible polyurethane foams are widely used for cushioning purposes, in home and office furniture, as well as in transportation. Topper pads in spring mattresses or entire mattresses are now made of polyurethane foam; these, as well as cushions for upholstery, are normally cut from foamstock. Automobile seat cushions are currently either made from foamstock or molded to shape. Seats for motorcycles, snowmobiles, and small water crafts, which are unprotected, are often molded with an integral skin. Semiflexible, higher density, polyurethane foams are used as protective, impact-absorbing, materials in automobiles, in particular. Crash pads may be of the integral skin type or they may consist of a thermoformed PVC shell filled with foam. Fragile instruments may be packaged in rigid or flexible polyurethane foam or a combination of them.

Rigid and semiflexible polyurethane foams are widely used for buoyancy purposes. Positive flotation is conferred to small water crafts by filling compartments or ballast with low density closed cell foam. Personal flotation devices (PFD) often involve semiflexible self-skinned foam elements. In both cases, a water and fungus-resistant resin system is used.

Applications related to textiles include artificial (synthetic) fibers; elastomeric fibers (Spandex generic name), which generally are made of wet spun, segmented (block) copolymers and are widely used in foundation garments, swimsuits, and surgical hoses; foamed textile backings are heat-bonded to fabrics and often play a thermal insulation role; carpet backings (underlays) play a cushioning and, often, a tuft-locking role, etc.

Urethane-related coatings are offered in the form of finishes, paints, lacquers, and varnishes. Some solvent-based coatings are unreactive, but many undergo curing after application through a variety of mechanisms (air, moisture, heat, chemical effects, UV, electron-beam, microwave radiations, etc.). Applications may be by dipping, spraying, brushing, etc. Powder coatings are also available for fluidized bed coating, in particular. Applications include metal corrosion protection (marine, pipelines), electrical insulation (wires), waterproofing (fabrics, concrete), and mechanical protection (optical surfaces, indoor flooring).

A number of adhesives are based on urethanes. They include rigid structural adhesives, as well as flexible adhesives, particularly suited for use with elastomers or flexible elements. Reactive systems involve one or two components, while nonreactive systems are solvent-based or of the hot melt type.

Polyurethanes are widely used as sealants, in the form of caulking compounds, as well as membranes (moisture barrier films, flexible tank liners, roofing membranes, and even meteorological balloons).

Special applications of polyurethanes include artificial (synthetic) leather (poromeric material), which is reported to consist mainly of polyester (PET) fibers, web-embedded in a porous polyurethane matrix, and artificial (synthetic) sponges which are flexible open cell foams or "reticulated" foams which feature a very highly open structure and find applications as air filters and humidifier drum bands.

Various applications of thermosetting resins are demonstrated in figures 3.88-3.100.

Fig. 3.88

Fig. 3.89

Figure 3.88 · 1932 Billiard balls (phenolic resin PF)

Figure 3.89 · Molded circuit for auto headlight pod switch (phenolic resin PF + reinforcement) **[RODGERS]**

Figure 3.90 · Automotive ignition elements: caps and rotors (phenolic resin PF) **[DUREZ]**

Figure 3.91 · 12-Bar commutator in electric motor (Phenolic resin PF) **[RODGERS]**

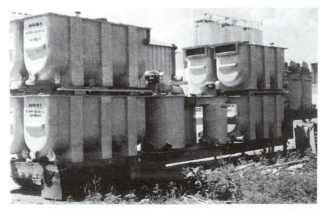

Figure 3.92 · Solvent extraction units (vinylester resin + glass fiber) **[DOW/MESA]**

Fig. 3.93

Fig. 3.94

Figure 3.93 · Telecopier gears (polyurethane PU + PTFE + glass fiber) [XEROX]

Figure 3.94 · Molded sprocket wheels (thermosetting polyurethane TSPU) [MOBAY]

Fig. 3.95

Fig. 3.96

Figure 3.95 · Electric cable sheathing (thermoplastic polyurethane TPPU) [BAYER]

Figure 3.96 · Window frame section (aluminum tube embedded in foam core/integral skin thermosetting polurethane TSPU) [BAYER]

Fig. 3.98

Fig. 3.97

Figure 3.97 · Molded gear crown (thermoplastic polyurethane TPPU) [UNIROYAL]

Figure 3.98 · Sprayed-on foam insulation for storage tank (thermosetting polyurethane TSPU) [PCUK]

Fig. 3.99

Fig. 3.100

Figure 3.99 · Downhill ski boot (thermoplastic polyurethane TPPU bottom shell, polyamide PA front flap, polyethylene PE rear flap) [NORDICA]

Figure 3.100 · Downhill ski innerboot (inner polyamide PA jersey, soft polyurethane PU foam liner, PU film, denser cast PU foam with integral skin) [SALOMON]

3.4   ELASTOMERS (RUBBERS)

3.4.1   General

3.4.1.1   Introduction

Elastomers can perhaps best be defined as materials capable of large or fairly large elastic deformations. Such a definition does not imply any special chemical structure. In practice, however, it is now established that such special mechanical behavior is associated with polymeric molecules in a rubbery state (above their glass transition temperature T_g) that resist deformation from a preferred random-like conformation.

Elastomeric or rubber-like elasticity is displayed over short periods of time by any noncrystallizing thermoplastic polymer above T_g, and it is thought that molecular entanglements are responsible for the transmission of loads to individual sections of molecules. Such entanglements, however, are not permanent and stress-relaxation effects prevent such materials from being truly elastic.

Permanent attachments or links between molecules or molecular sections are required to achieve a satisfactory degree of "permanent" elasticity, and there are several ways of achieving this goal.

The following discussion of elastomers (rubbers) considers three types: the conventional (vulcanizable) elastomers, the reactive system elastomers, and the thermoplastic elastomers, which are associated with different principles.

3.4.1.2   Vulcanizable Elastomers

One method for producing a material with good elastomeric properties (rubber) involves the formation of chemical cross-links between high-molecular-weight linear molecules. The starting polymer (raw rubber) must be of the noncrystallizing type, and its glass transition temperature T_g must be well below room temperature to ensure a rubbery behavior. The chemical cross-links must not be too numerous, typically every hundred carbon atoms in a carbon backbone chain. This formation of chemical cross-links is commonly referred to as "vulcanization" or "curing."

Physical changes [P] and molecular changes [M] taking place in the processing of vulcanizable elastomers are illustrated schematically in Figure 3.101.

Conventional vulcanization of the most common rubbers generally involves sulfur-based chemical systems and relies on the presence of carbon-carbon ($C = C$) double bonds or unsaturations in the chains. Other chemical systems can be used

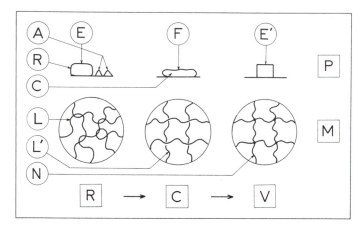

Figure 3.101 · **Elastomer vulcanization (cure)** · [P] Physical state; [M] Molecular conformation; [R] Unvulcanized rubber; [C] After compounding; [V] After vulcanization; (R) Raw (gum) rubber; (A) Vulcanization additives; (E) Semi-elastic state; (F) Semi-fluid state; (C) Compound; (E′) Fully-elastic state; (L),(L′) Polymeric chains; (N) Molecular network

(organic peroxides, etc.), but they are generally more costly. The incorporation of the vulcanization ingredients into the raw rubber is carried out at moderate temperatures in an operation generally referred to as compounding. The compounds are then shaped into products (extrusion, molding, etc.) and heated to a relatively high temperature (typically 150°C or 300°F) to induce the cross-linking. Vulcanization temperature and duration are functions of the chemical systems used.

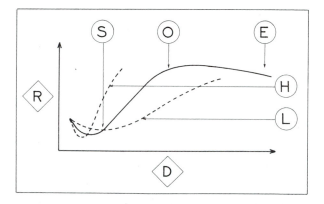

Figure 3.102 · **Elastomer vulcanization (cure); time effects** · <R> Resistance to deformation; <D> Heating time; (S) Scorch time; (O) Optimum cure; (E) Excessive cure; (H) Higher temperature; (L) Lower temperature

The change in the resistance to deformation <R> of the compound as a function of time (duration) of cure <D> is illustrated in Figure 3.102. The scorch time (S) is somewhat analogous to the gel time in liquid thermosetting resins (onset of molecular network formation), and times (E) in excess of the optimum cure time (O) may have a detrimental effect on the properties of the vulcanizates. Curves (H) and (L) illustrate the effect of higher or lower cure temperatures.

A number of other additives are often compounded into rubbers. They include antioxidants, antiozonants, oil extenders to reduce cost or soften the rubber, fillers to reduce cost or stiffen the rubber, and reinforcing fillers.

Suppliers of raw rubbers suggest suitable compounds for specific applications and processing methods, as well as corresponding vulcanization conditions. Experienced rubber processors develop their own recipes that sometimes involve blends of raw rubbers.

3.4.1.3 Vulcanizable Elastomeric Compounds

A number of components are normally mixed (compounded) to obtain compounds suitable for conventional vulcanization into practical elastomeric products.

The polymer (elastomer) is generally the major component, and the amounts of other components are usually given as weight per hundred weight of rubber (phr).

Sulfur usually amounts to a few phr and certainly less than about 10 phr for true elastomers. Sulfur alone reacts too slowly at practical temperatures (about 150°C or 300°F), and combinations of accelerators and activators are used. Examples of accelerators include hexamethylene tetramine (HMTA), diphenylguanidine (DPG), mercaptobenzothiazole disulfide (MBTS), tetramethylthiuram disulfide (TMTD), and zinc diethyl dithiocarbamate. Many of them feature combined sulfur (thio). Common activators include zinc oxide (ZnO) and stearic acid.

Protective agents are used to suppress or reduce the deteriorating effect of oxygen and ozone. Examples include phenyl betanaphthylamine (PBNA) and alkyl paraphenylene diamine (APPD).

The most common reinforcing filler is carbon black, with channel, furnace, and thermal varieties. Silica is used when light colors are required or with certain elastomers (silicone elastomers). Many nonreinforcing (inert) fillers, such as calcium carbonate, clay, and kaolin, are also used, particularly for inexpensive compounds.

A number of fluids are often employed to help reduce the stiffness of elastomers or for other purposes, including processing ease, and low cost. They include components referred to as "pepticizers," "plasticizers," "lubricants," "factices," and "oils," such as paraffin waxes, mineral, and other oils.

A typical tire tread compound has the following composition: natural rubber smoked sheet (100), sulfur (2.5), sulfenamide (0.5), MBTS (0.1), stearic acid (3), zinc oxide (3), PNBA (2), HAF carbon black (45), and mineral oil (3).

The major ingredients of a typical shoe sole compound are SBR (100) and clay (90), while a typical electric cable cover features polychloroprene (100), kaolin (120), FEF carbon black (15), and mineral oil (12), in addition to the vulcanization and protective agents.

3.4.1.4   Reactive System Elastomers

Materials with good elastomeric properties (rubbers) can also be produced in a single step from low-molecular-weight reactive chemicals. The mechanism is similar to that described for thermosetting plastics, but since relatively infrequent cross-linking is required for elastomers, chain polymerization is favored over cross-linking in the overall chemical reaction.

Certain types of polyurethane and silicone elastomers fall into this category. The starting chemicals are normally in liquid form and thus easy to mold, and the reaction can be triggered by heat, catalysts, or mixing as in the case of thermosetting plastics.

3.4.1.5   Thermoplastic Elastomers

The rapidly growing and relatively new class of thermoplastic elastomers (TPE) differs markedly from the previous two classes of elastomers, in that the processing of TPE does not involve any chemical reaction. The links between flexible molecules, which are required for rubber-like elasticity, appear to be the result of physical interactions that operate at use temperatures, but can be suppressed for processing by raising the temperature, or with the use of a suitable solvent and restored upon cooling or drying.

The various types of thermoplastic elastomers can generally be made in a wide range of stiffness (hardness) and thus bridge the gap between soft plastics and elastomers. Few of them, however, are available in very soft, highly elastic grades.

Because of their thermoplastic nature, thermoplastic elastomers can be processed by many processes, including injection molding, extrusion, blow molding, film blowing, and rotational molding.

The number of applications, which is rapidly increasing as they often displace conventional vulcanizable elastomers and elastomeric thermosetting resins, includes injection-molded soles in footwear, adhesives (pressure sensitive, contact and hot melt), solution coating of fabrics, wire and cable covering, and plastic modification (impact, stress-crack resistance).

Thermoplastic elastomers have many advantages over conventional vulcanizable elastomers, but they are still generally inferior in a number of important properties, such as creep, set, and resilience.

The major thermoplastic elastomers are often classified into four types: olefinics, styrenics, polyurethanes, and polyesters. In terms of mechanisms responsible for the soft or relatively soft, rubber-like behavior, however, two major principles appear to be involved.

In the first case, linear elastomeric molecules or cross-linked (vulcanized) very small elastomeric particles, most frequently ethylene-propylene (EPR) or (EPDM), are blended with a compatible thermoplastic [most commonly polypropylene (PP)] in ratios that determine the stiffness of the resulting elastomer (a 80/20 EPDM/PP ratio gives a fairly soft elastomer). This class is often referred to as the "olefinic thermoplastic elastomers" (OTPE).

The so-called styrenic thermoplastic elastomers (STPE) most commonly consist of long triblock copolymer molecules with an elastomeric central block (butadiene, isoprene, ethylene-butene, etc.) and end blocks (styrene, etc.), which tend to agglomerate to form "hard" domains at temperatures below their glass transition or melting temperature. These hard domains play the role of cross-links at use temperature but lose their cohesion at processing temperatures.

Several other types of thermoplastic elastomers are reported to consist of multiblock (segmented) molecules with alternating hard and soft blocks (segments). The "soft" blocks are flexible and confer the rubbery character, while the "hard" blocks are capable of strong intermolecular interactions at use temperatures, to provide the physical cross-linking effect. Urethane (UTPE), etherester (EETPE), and etheramide (EATPE) thermoplastic elastomers belong to this category.

In urethane thermoplastic elastomers, the soft blocks correspond to the polyol involved in the polymerization and can be ether-based or ester-based, giving differences in oil or water resistance. The hard blocks correspond to the isocyanate and chain extender.

In the so-called etherester or copolyester thermoplastic elastomers, the soft blocks, which contain ether groups, are amorphous and flexible, while the hard blocks can consist of crystallizing polybutylene terephthalate (PBT).

In the recently introduced etheramide or polyetherblockamide thermoplastic elastomers, the hard blocks consist of a crystallizing polyamide.

The structure of triblock [T] and multiblock [M] thermoplastic elastomers is illustrated in Figure 3.103.

The properties and cost of thermoplastic elastomers can vary widely as a function of the type and specific composition. Styrenics and olefinics are generally the least expensive.

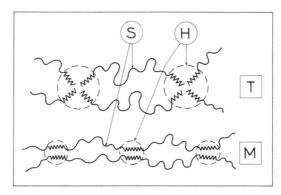

Figure 3.103 · **Thermoplastic elastomers; block copolymer types** · [T] Triblock type; [M] Multiblock type; (S) "Soft" block (matrix); (H) "Hard" block (domains)

3.4.2   Commercial Elastomers and Related Polymers

3.4.2.1   *Diene and Related Elastomers*

A number of polymers, widely used as commodity rubbers, are often associated with the term diene, which is itself related to the presence of carbon-carbon (C = C) double bonds, suitable for conventional vulcanization.

Polyisoprene, Natural Rubber (PI)

PI−C   cis'poly'isoprene (DE)

| PI-C | H H CH$_3$ H $\left[\begin{array}{c} C-C=C-C \\ H \qquad\qquad H \end{array}\right]$ | PI−C T_g −70 °C (−75−−68) −94 °F |

PI−T   trans'poly'isoprene (DE)

| PI-T | H H H $\left[\begin{array}{c} C-C=C-C \\ H \qquad CH_3 H \end{array}\right]$ | PI−T T_g −70 °C (−75−−70) −94 °F T_m 68 °C (60−74) 155 °F |

Cis-1,4-Polyisoprene (PI-C), the major component of natural rubber, is now produced as a synthetic polymer. In the absence of stress, it is only capable of very slow and slight crystallization at temperatures between its melting point ($T_m \approx 28°C$ or $\approx 82°F$) and its glass transition temperature. When highly stretched, however, it crystallizes readily, and this strain-crystallization is associated with its excellent mechanical resistance, even in the absence of reinforcing filler (gum rubber).

Trans-1,4-Polyisoprene (PI-T), a major component of balata or gutta- percha has about the same glass transition temperature as cis-1,4 PI, but it crystallizes quite readily below its melting point ($T_m \approx 68°C$ or $\approx 155°F$). It was one of the first plastics used.

Natural rubber (NR) consists primarily of high-molecular-weight cis-1,4-polyisoprene molecules. A latex of the polymer (emulsion in water) is tapped from Hevea trees, then subjected to several processing operations (coagulation, milling, drying, smoking, etc.), and generally sold in bale form.

Natural rubber was first cross-linked into a highly elastic network by Charles Goodyear (vulcanization, 1837). Sulfur cure using the unsaturations (C = C) of the chain is still the major cross-linking method.

Natural rubber is particularly noted for its high tensile and tear strengths, high resilience (low hysteresis); resistance to cold flow (low compression set); and resistance to wear, abrasion, and fatigue.

Natural rubber does not have a good intrinsic resistance to sunlight, oxygen and ozone, heat aging, and oil and fuels.

Natural rubber in unfilled form is widely used for products requiring very large elastic deformations or very high resilience, such as pharmaceutical or medical devices, tires, gaskets, and shock absorption devices.

Polybutadiene (PB)

PB   poly'butadiene   (DE)

Cis-1,4-Polybutadiene or simply polybutadiene (PB) is used primarily as a component in copolymers (SBR, NBR, etc.) or in blends with other rubbers (NR, SBR). Processing difficulties are cited for not using it alone. Polybutadiene can help improve, in particular, low-temperature properties, resilience, and abrasion or wear resistance of compounds.

Mixtures of cis-1,4, trans-1,4 and even cis-1,2 polybutadiene are reported to be involved in the fabrication of ABS plastics.

Polychloroprene (CR)

CR   poly'chloroprene'rubber   (DE)

CR

$$\left[\begin{array}{c} H \quad H \quad Cl \quad H \\ | \quad | \quad | \quad | \\ C-C=C-C \\ | \qquad \qquad | \\ H \qquad \qquad H \end{array}\right]$$

CR

T_g $\begin{array}{l} -50 \ ^{\circ}C \ (-50--46) \\ -58 \ ^{\circ}F \end{array}$

Polychloroprene (CR) or neoprene was one of the very first synthetic rubbers produced. The strain-crystallization associated with its molecules is responsible for its excellent mechanical properties, comparable to those of natural rubber; however, crystallization can also be a problem in prolonged exposure to low temperatures.

Because of its polar nature, associated with the presence of chlorine atoms Cl, polychloroprene has a relatively good resistance to oils. It is also flame-resistant and has very good ozone and weather resistance.

Applications include automotive products (fuel hoses, cable covers, protective boots, etc.) bridge pads, roofing membranes, fabric coatings, and adhesives.

Polyisobutylene, Butyl Rubbers (PIB)

PIB   poly'isobutylene   (DE)

PIB

$$\left[\begin{array}{c} H \quad CH_3 \\ | \quad | \\ C-C \\ | \quad | \\ H \quad CH_3 \end{array}\right]$$

PIB

T_g $\begin{array}{l} -65 \ ^{\circ}C \ (-70--50) \\ -85 \ ^{\circ}F \end{array}$

Polyisobutylene (PIB) is remarkably different from most common rubbers in two respects. It has a very low gas permeability and very high damping properties (energy absorption). Since the molecules do not contain unsaturation (C = C), they cannot be cross-linked by the most conventional methods. On the other hand, networks have good weathering, ozone, and heat aging resistance. Polyisobutylene is capable of strain-crystallization and can have good mechanical resistance. Resistance to oils and fuels is not good.

If isobutylene is copolymerized with a small fraction of isoprene (1-2%), the isoprene unsaturations can be used for conventional vulcanization. Such isobutylene-isoprene copolymer is referred to as butyl rubber (IIR).

A major limitation of butyl rubber is its poor compatibility with other common rubbers and generally low adhesion properties. Partial chlorination or bromination brings a marked improvement and also allows faster cure. Such modified butyl rubbers are referred to as "chlorobutyl rubber," "bromobutyl rubber" or "halobutyl rubbers," in general.

Uses of butyl rubbers include inflatable products (tire innertubes or innerliners), curing bags or bladders, steam hoses, and shock and vibration absorption devices.

3.4.2.2 Elastomeric Copolymers

Styrene-butadiene Rubber (SBR)

SBR   styrene'butadiene'rubber   (EC)

Styrene-butadiene rubber (SBR) was developed in Germany under the name "BUNA-S" and in North America, during World War II, as "GR-S" (government rubber-styrene). It is a random copolymer of butadiene (67-85%) and styrene (15-33%). Butadiene is reported to be primarily in trans-1,4 configuration. The glass transition temperature of a typical 75/25 composition is about -60°C ($\approx$ -76°F). Butadiene rubber (BR) is not capable of crystallizing under strain and, consequently, does not have good mechanical properties in gum form (no reinforcing filler). With carbon black reinforcement, its mechanical properties are adequate for many common applications.

SBR is one of the least expensive rubbers and generally processes easily. When compared to natural rubber, which it initially sought to replace in reinforced form, it is inferior in most mechanical properties except wear, but it is somewhat better in heat aging, ozone resistance, weathering resistance and resistance to oils.

Applications of SBR are numerous including tires, footwear, wire and cable insulation, industrial rubber products, adhesives, paints (latex or emulsion).

Acrylonitrile-butadiene Rubber (NBR)

NBR nitrile'rubber (EC)

Acrylonitrile-butadiene rubber or nitrile rubber (NBR), a copolymer with 20-50% of acrylonitrile, was developed as a general purpose, oil-resistant rubber. The presence of polar nitrile groups (C ≡ N) is responsible for the drastically increased resistance to oils, fuels, and solvents, which is superior to that of polychloroprene (CR). Heat aging is quite good, and abrasion resistance is high. Cost is moderate. Ozone and weathering resistance, however, is not very good, and low-temperature flexibility is quite limited in some grades. Because of its polar nature, NBR shows high dielectric losses.

Applications include fuel and oil tubing and hose, gaskets and seals, conveyor belting, and printing rolls and pads.

The introduction of 2-10% of carboxyl side groups (COOH) in nitrile rubber confers improved ozone resistance, and low-temperature flexibility, as well as outstanding abrasion and wear resistance to the so-called carboxylated nitrile rubbers (COX-NBR).

Nitrile rubber (NBR) and polyvinylchloride (PVC) form one of the relatively few pairs of distinct, but miscible, polymers and can thus form homogeneous blends or polyalloys. This is attributed, in part, to their common polar nature. The addition of about 30% of PVC improves considerably the ozone resistance of nitrile rubber and the blends process easily; fire resistance is also increased because of the presence of chlorine atoms. Balanced A(NBR/PVC) blends (50/50) with about 15% of plasticizer process as thermoplastics and can be viewed as thermoplastic elastomers.

Ethylene-propylene Rubber (EPR)

EPR ethylene'propylene'rubber (EC)

	E	P	HD

| EPR | $\begin{array}{c} H \quad H \\ \mid \quad \mid \\ \!\!-\!\!\big[C-C\big]\!\!-\!\! \\ \mid \quad \mid \\ H \quad H \end{array}$ | $\begin{array}{c} H \quad H \\ \mid \quad \mid \\ \!\!-\!\!\big[C-C\big]\!\!-\!\! \\ \mid \quad \mid \\ H \quad CH_3 \end{array}$ | $\begin{array}{c} H \quad H \\ \mid \quad \mid \\ \!\!-\!\!\big[C-C\big]\!\!-\!\! \\ \mid \quad \mid \\ HH-C-H \\ \mid \\ C-H \\ \| \\ C-H \\ \mid \\ CH_3 \end{array}$ |

While both polyethylene (PE) and polypropylene (PP) are crystallizing plastics, random copolymers of ethylene and propylene are noncrystallizing, and the low glass transition temperature of the copolymer is suitable for its use as a rubber. The percentage of ethylene and propylene repeat units is one of the factors determining the properties of the copolymers (reported values are in the range 67/33 to 50/50 for ethylene and propylene, respectively). The glass transition temperature for a 67/33 copolymer is reported to be about -60°C ($\approx$ -76°F).

Since neither ethylene nor propylene repeat units feature unsaturations (C = C), E-P copolymers, referred to as "EPR," are unsaturated. This makes them resistant to ozone, weathering, and heat aging, but does not allow conventional vulcanization with sulfur-based systems.

The incorporation of a small fraction of a third monomer containing unsaturations (diene D), which now allows conventional vulcanization, corresponds to EPDM rubbers, also sometimes referred to as "EPT rubbers" (terpolymers). Dienes most commonly used include 1,4-hexadiene (HD), 5-ethylidene-2-norbornene (ENB), and dicyclopentadiene (DCPB); they all feature unsaturation in a side (pendant) group, preventing chain scission if left-over unsaturations are attacked by ozone, for example. EPDM rubbers thus retain the excellent ozone and weathering resistance and the good heat aging of EPR rubbers.

As stated earlier, EP rubbers rank high in ozone, weather, and heat resistance. They also have good electrical properties. Their limitations are mostly associated with a low resistance to oils and fuels, poor adhesion to many substrates or reinforcements (tire cords), and a generally low compatibility with other rubbers. EP rubbers are widely used for exterior automotive and construction parts, including solid and cellular (foam or sponge) weather strips, wire and cable insulation (jacketing) and general electrical insulation, hose and belt products, and coated fabrics. Through blending, they are used to improve the weather resistance of other rubbers or the low temperature impact resistance of polypropylene.

3.4.2.3 Ethylene-Related Elastomers

Chlorinated Polyethylene (CPE)

The moderate random chlorination of polyethylene suppresses crystallinity and yields a rubber-like material that can be cross-linked with organic peroxides. Such rubber is referred to as "chlorinated polyethylene" (CPE or CM). The chlorine (Cl) content is in the range 36-42%, compared to 56.8% for polyvinylchloride (PVC). Such rubber has good heat, oil, and ozone resistance. It is also used as a polymeric plasticizer for PVC.

Chlorosulfonated Polyethylene (CSPE)

CSPE   chloro'sulfonated'poly'ethylene   (EE)

Chlorosulfonated polyethylene (CSPE or CSM) corresponds to the moderate random chlorination of polyethylene (24-43% Cl) and the incorporation of infrequent chloro-sulfonic groups (SO_2Cl) as preferred cross-linking sites. It is reported that the sulfur content is in the range 1-1.5%, i.e about one chlorosulfonyl group per hundred ethylene units.

CSPE rubber is noted for its excellent weathering resistance even in light colors. It has a good resistance to ozone, heat, chemicals and solvents, good electrical properties, low gas permeability for a rubber, and good adhesion to substrates.

CSPE rubber is used for hose products, roll covers, tank linings, wire and cable covers, footwear, and building products.

Ethylene-vinylacetate Copolymer (EVA)

EVA   ethylene'vinyl'acetate'copolymer   (EE)

Random copolymers of ethylene (E) and vinylacetate (VA) can be amorphous, and thus elastomeric, for vinylacetate contents in the range 40-60%. Commercial EVA rubbers contain about 40-45% of vinylacetate. They can be cross-linked through the use of organic peroxides. They are reported to have good heat, ozone, and weather resistance.

Ethylene-acrylate Copolymer (EAR)

EAR   ethylene'acrylate'rubber   (EE)

Copolymers of ethylene (E) and methylacrylate (MA) have been introduced, which also contain carboxylic side groups (COOH) as cure sites. They are reported to be highly resistant to ozone and to be even better energy absorbers than butyl rubbers.

3.4.2.4 *Fluoroelastomers*

PVDF   poly'vinylidene'fluoride (FP)(FE)

| PVDF | H F
$-[\!-C\!-\!C\!-]\!-$
H F | PVDF
T_g $\quad$ -35 °C (-40--30)
$\quad\quad$ -31 °F |

PCTFE   poly'chloro'tri'fluoro'ethylene (FP)(FE)

| PCTFE | F F
$-[\!-C\!-\!C\!-]\!-$
F Cl | PCTFE
T_g $\quad$ 40 °C (20-60)
$\quad\quad$ 104 °F |

PHFP   poly'hexa'fluoro'propylene (FP)(FE)

| PHFP | F F
$-[\!-C\!-\!C\!-]\!-$
F CF_3 | PHFP
T_g $\quad$ 11 °C
$\quad\quad$ 52 °F |

PTFE   poly'tetra'fluoro'ethylene (FP)(FE)

| PTFE | F F
$-[\!-C\!-\!C\!-]\!-$
F F | PTFE
T_g $\quad$ -130 °C (-150--112)
$\quad\quad$ -202 °F |

PPFA   poly'per'fluoro'alkoxy (FP)(FE)

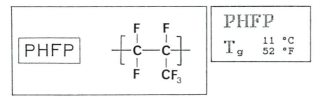

$-[\!-(\!-C\!-)_x\!-C\!-]\!-$ with F, F, F, O, C_nF_{2n+1}

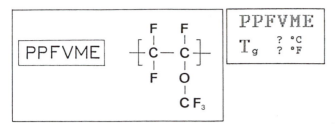

PPFVME   poly'per'fluoro'vinyl'methyl'ether   (FE)

| PPFVME | $\begin{bmatrix} F & F \\ | & | \\ C & C \\ | & | \\ F & O \\ & | \\ & CF_3 \end{bmatrix}$ | PPFVME $\quad T_g \quad \begin{array}{l} ? \ °C \\ ? \ °F \end{array}$ |

PPFBA   poly'per'fluoro'butyl'acrylate   (FE)

| PPFBA | $\begin{bmatrix} F & F \\ | & | \\ C & C \\ | & | \\ F & C-O-C_4F_9 \\ & \| \\ & O \end{bmatrix}$ | PPFBA $\quad T_g \quad \begin{array}{l} ? \ °C \\ ? \ °F \end{array}$ |

PHFPO   poly'hexa'fluoro'propylene'oxide   (FE)

| PHFPO | $\begin{bmatrix} F & F \\ | & | \\ C & C-O \\ | & | \\ F & CF_3 \end{bmatrix}$ | PHFPO $\quad T_g \quad \begin{array}{l} ? \ °C \\ ? \ °F \end{array}$ |

The general principle for making fluoroelastomer chains is to suppress the crystallinity associated with the chains of fluoroplastics, discussed in the section on thermoplastics, by random copolymerization and to provide a mechanism for cross-linking, sometimes by terpolymerization.

The most common fluoroelastomers involve the following monomers: vinylidenefluoride (VDF), chlorotrifluoroethylene (CTFE), hexafluoropropylene (HFP), tetrafluoroethylene (TFE), and perfluoroalkoxy (PFA) or perfluoroalkylvinyls, such as perfluorovinylmethylether (PFVME). Specific examples include P(VDF-CTFE), P(VDF-HFP), P(TFE-PFA) and P(VDF-HFP-TFE). Other types being developed include polyperfluorobutylacrylate (PPFBA) and polyhexa-fluoropropyleneoxide (PHFPO).

Fluoroelastomers are generally expensive, but possess a number of outstanding properties. They offer exceptional resistance to chemicals, in general, and to oils and solvents (including chlorinated solvents), in particular. They can withstand high temperatures. They offer excellent weathering (UV resistance) and ozone resistance. They have good barrier properties (low permeability to gases and vapors). Their mechanical properties can be quite good, but they are not normally suitable for low temperature elastomeric applications.

These specialty elastomers are used for demanding applications in the chemical, petroleum, automotive, and aerospace industries. Examples of applications include mechanical seals, packings, O-rings, gaskets, diaphragms, expansion joints and connectors, hose liners, roll covers, and wire and cable insulation.

The fluoroelastomers discussed above are sometimes referred to as "fluorohydrocarbon elastomers" since they contain only F, H, and C atoms (and oxygen in some cases). Two other classes of elastomers include fluorinated types. Fluorosilicone elastomers (FSIE) remain flexible at very low temperatures, and fluorinated polyorganophosphazenes (FPZE) are noted for a good combination of low-temperature flexibility with oil and fuel resistance.

3.4.2.5 Silicone Polymers

PDMS   poly'di'methyl'siloxane (SI)

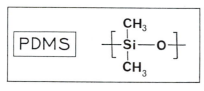

MPDMS   modified'PDMS (SI)

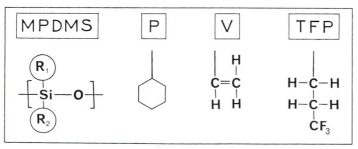

A class of polymers, generally referred to as "silicone polymers" or "polysiloxanes," is based on polymeric chains featuring the very stable, alternating combination of silicon (Si) and oxygen (O) atoms in the backbone and a variety of organic side groups attached to the silicon atoms. The most common side groups are two methyl (CH_3) groups, and the corresponding polymer is referred to as "polydimethylsiloxane" (PDMS).

Unmodified PDMS has very flexible chains corresponding to a very low glass transition temperature T_g. Its regular structure allowing crystallization below the melting point T_m reduces its potential as a low temperature elastomer. The substitution of a small fraction (5-10%) of bulky side groups R_1 or R_2, such as phenyl groups P (phenylmethylsiloxane (PMS) or diphenylsiloxane (DPS), can be used to reduce or suppress crystallization. Substituents, such as vinyl groups V featuring double bonds (unsaturations), can be introduced in small amounts (about 0.5%) to facilitate cross-linking (vinylmethylsiloxane (VMS). Trifluoropropyl TFP side groups enhance the resistance to solvent swelling (fluoromethylsiloxane FMS); corresponding polymers being called "fluorosilicones."

In the linear form (uncross-linked), polysiloxane chains correspond to degrees of polymerization ranging from 200-1000 for low consistency resins to 3000-10,000 for high-consistency resin. The use of polysiloxanes as fluid-like, uncross-linked materials, although important, is not within the scope of this book. Solid-like behavior is obtained through cross-linking and because of the very low glass transition temperature T_g and melting point T_m, the room temperature behavior is rubber-like (elastomeric) except for very high degrees of cross-linking.

The mechanism of cross-linking (vulcanization, curing) can be based on the presence of above-mentioned unsaturations (vinyl) or reactive end-groups (alkoxy, acetoxy). Some details are given in the subsequent discussion of polysiloxanes processing.

Silicone polymers, which are mostly elastomeric, possess a number of useful properties, some of them unusual.

As elastomers, they tend to have rather mediocre tear properties, but special grades, including those with special silica fillers, are suitable for mechanically important applications. Mechanical properties are little affected by temperature over a very wide range [from about -90°C (-130°F) to as high as 250°C (482°F)].

Surface properties are generally characterized by a very low surface energy (surface tension) giving good slip, lubricity, and release properties (antistick), as well as water repellency, to cured parts. Excellent adhesion, however, can also be obtained when curing occurs in contact with a substrate (caulking compounds, sealants).

Silicone elastomers have a good chemical inertness but are more sensitive to swelling by hydrocarbon solvents than fluoroelastomers, for example. They have good resistance to oils and greases. They are resistant to weather (UV radiations) and high energy radiations (nuclear industry). They have a good intrinsic flame resistance without additives.

Electrical properties of silicone polymers (insulation, dielectric, etc.) are excellent and stable.

A low index of reflection gives silicone coatings a useful combination of high transmission and low reflectance.

Suitable grades of silicone polymers can be biologically (physiologically) inert and, with a low toxicity, are well tolerated by body tissues and are thus used as implants.

As stated earlier, silicone polymers discussed here are normally cross-linked, i.e. their processing involves a vulcanization or curing stage. It is customary to distinguish four distinct groups: low-consistency-room-temperature curing resins (RTV), low-consistency-high temperature curing resins (LIM, LSR), high-consistency-high temperature curing resins (HTV, HCE), and rigid resins.

Low-consistency-room-temperature vulcanizing (RTV) elastomers involve low-molecular weight polysiloxanes and generally rely on reactive end-groups for cross-linking (cure) at, or only slightly above, room temperature. The so-called one-component (one-package, one-part) systems rely on atmospheric moisture for curing and normally correspond to relatively thin parts, coatings, etc. Two-component (two-package, two-part) systems use a catalyst and require a mixing stage; small exotherms generally allow the molding of thick parts.

Liquid silicone resins (LSR) also involve low molecular weight polysiloxanes, but a different curing system requires relatively high curing temperatures [typically 150°C (302°F) for a fast cure (10-30 s)]; the mixed system is largely unreactive at room temperature (long "pot life"). Such systems are thus suitable for the high-speed liquid injection molding (LIM) process which is increasingly used for small complex and precise parts.

High-molecular-weight, high-consistency resins containing unsaturations are suitable for conventional rubber processing. These heat-curable elastomers (HCE) are cross-linked through high temperature vulcanization (HTV), normally through the use of peroxides.

Finally, special polysiloxane systems can be cross-linked into such tight networks that they become quite rigid. The uncross-linked systems, however, are stable only in appropriate solutions, and their use seems to be limited to paints, varnishes, coatings, and matrices for laminates, the cross-linking taking place when the solvent evaporates. Oven curing at moderate to high temperatures is often recommended to complete the reaction. Silicone-epoxy systems used for electrical encapsulation seem to fall into this category.

Most applications of silicone polymers involve elastomeric forms. The flexibility (hardness) of the elastomer can be adjusted over a wide range.

Many electrical applications involve high-voltage and high or low temperatures (power cable insulation, high voltage leads and insulator boots, ignition cables, spark plug boots, etc.). In the electronic industry, semi-conductors are often encapsulated in silicone resins (potting).

Mechanical applications requiring low- and high-temperature flexibility and chemical inertness include O-rings, gaskets, seals (aircraft doors and windows, freezers, ovens and appliances), diaphragms, flapper valves, protective boots and bellows, and printing rolls.

Silicone elastomers are used to make casting molds and patterns for polyurethane, polyester, or epoxy parts.

Silicone sealants and caulking agents are outstanding for their weathering resistance, adhesion to substrates, and permanent flexibility.

Suitable silicone compounds can have desirable shock and vibration damping characteristics. This is perhaps well illustrated by the peculiar bouncing ("silly") putty, which is an uncrosslinked, high-molecular-weight PDMS-based compound, modified with fillers and plasticizers, capable of highly elastic or perfectly viscous behavior depending on the speed or temperature of loading.

Silicone compounds are widely used in the biomedical field for their biological inertness. Prosthetic devices, in particular, can be conveniently made by casting techniques and their flexibility precisely adjusted to the needs. Silicone membranes are also used in artificial organs, such as kidneys (blood dialyzers).

Hard silicone coatings have recently been introduced that, when applied to the surface of clear plastics such as acrylics or polycarbonates and cured at moderate temperatures, provide scratch, wear, and abrasion protection, as well as improved resistance to weathering and environmental stress-cracking.

3.4.2.6 Miscellaneous Other Elastomers

Acrylic Rubber (AR)

AR acrylic'rubber (ME)

Acrylic or acrylate rubbers (AR or ACM) often consist primarily of polyethylacrylate (PEA) copolymerized with a small amount ($\approx 5\%$) of 2-chloroethylvinylether CEVE, for example, which serves as a cure site. The glass transition temperature of polyethylacrylate is about -22°C (-7.6°F), and acrylic rubber is not suitable for low temperature applications. A similar polyacrylate, polybutylacrylate (PBA), can be used, which has a lower glass transition temperature of about -45°C (-49°F).

Acrylic rubbers are resistant, in particular, to high temperatures, lubricating oils, including so-called sulfur-bearing oils, which often cause the hardening of other oil-resistant rubbers, such as nitrile rubbers. Applications thus include seals, gaskets, and hoses.

Epichlorohydrin Rubber (ECHR)

ECHR   epi'chloro'hydrin'rubber   (ME)

Epichlorohydrin rubber (ECHR or CO) results from the polymerization of epichlorohydrin (ECH) with a repeat unit PECH. The presence of chlorine contributes to its excellent resistance to oils and fuels and to a good flame resistance. It is also resistant to heat aging and ozone.

The relatively high glass transition temperature of polyepichlorohydrin limits its low-temperature use, but copolymers with more flexible ethyleneoxide (EO) repeat units ($T_g \approx$ -67°C or $\approx$ -88.6°F) are offered which are suitable down to about -40°C (-40°F).

Applications include seals, gaskets, diaphragms, wire and cable covers, and protective boots.

Polysulfide Rubbers (SR)

SR   poly'sulfide'rubber   (ME)

Polysulfide rubber (SR, ET, or EOT) was one of the first synthetic rubbers. In its original form (polyethylenesulfide PES or Thiokol A), it consists of adjacent ethylene and sulfide units, giving a relatively stiff chain with a reported glass transition temperature of -27°C (-16.6°F). The low temperature flexibility is increased by the juxtaposition of ethylene oxide units (T_g ≈ -67°C or -88.6°F) in the so-called polyethyleneethersulfide PEES (Thiokol B).

The mechanical properties of polysulfide rubbers are not generally good, but they are used for their outstanding resistance to many oils or solvents and to weathering, as well as for their low permeability to gases.

Applications include those involving contact with fuels, paints and printing inks, and outdoor exposure (caulking, mastics, putty).

Propyleneoxide Rubber (PROR)

PROR propylene'oxide'rubber (ME)

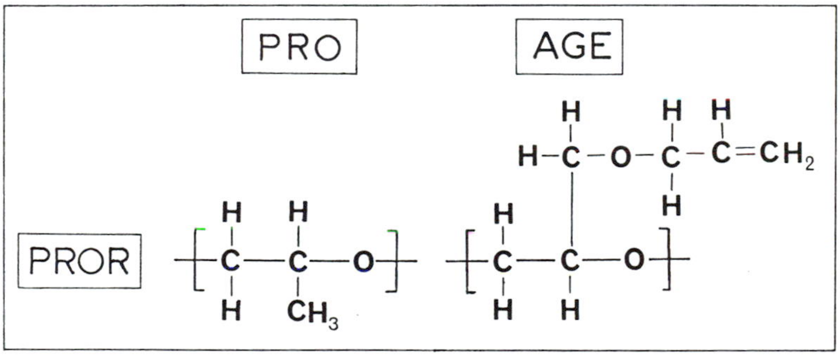

Polypropyleneoxide does not crystallize in its atactic form and has a low glass transition temperature (T_g ≈ -72°C or -98°F). Its copolymer with allylglycidylether (AGE) allows conventional vulcanization. Propyleneoxide rubber (PROR) is claimed to have excellent dynamic properties (resilience, etc.).

Polynorbornene (PNB)

PNB poly'norbornene (ME)

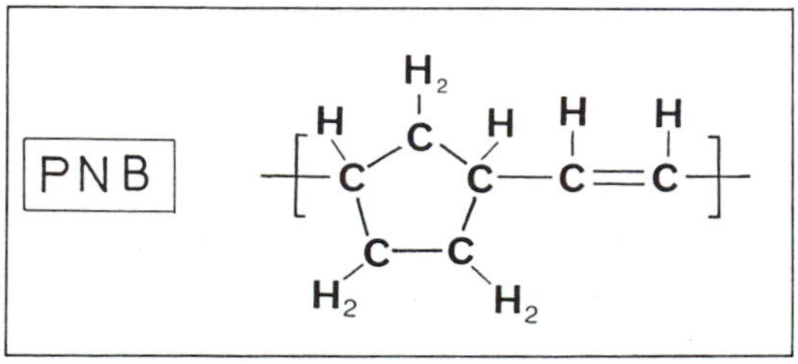

Norbornene (bicyclo-2,2,1-heptene-2) polymerizes into high molecular-weight polynorbornene PNB (1,3 cyclopentylenevinylene). Although the pure polymer is a plastic ($T_g \approx 35°C$ or 95°F), it can easily be plasticized with large amounts of oil and, subsequently, vulcanized into an elastomer with a low service temperature (-65°C or -85°F). The damping properties of the elastomer can be conveniently adjusted and major applications are currently in this area.

Polyorganophosphazenes (PPZ)

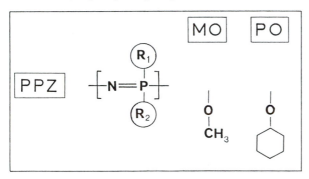

Polyorganophosphazenes (PPZ) form an example of a new class of polymeric materials involving inorganic chains. In this case, atoms of nitrogen (N, azo) and phosphorus (P) form the chain and a variety of organic side groups R_1 and R_2 can be attached to the phosphorus atom. The side groups may include halo (Cl or F), amino (NH_2 or NHR), alkoxy [methoxy MO, ethoxy, etc.], aryloxy or phenyloxy (PO) and fluoroalkoxy groups.

The resulting high-molecular-weight chains are often flexible (low glass transition temperature T_g) and thus suitable as elastomers, but types with higher T_g and crystallizing types are reported to have good potential in applications such as coatings, fibers, and biomedical materials.

Inherent fire resistance, weatherability, and water and oil repellency can be achieved within this class of materials.

3.4.2.7 Thermoplastic Elastomers

Thermoplastic elastomers (TPE) have been discussed earlier in a general manner. Many grades are now commercially available in each of five main types: olefinic

(OTPE), styrenic (STPE), urethane (UTPE), etherester (EETPE) and etheramide (EATPE).

See figures 3.104-3.111 for several applications of elastomers.

Figure 3.104 · Simple adhesive-bonded rubber/metal mounts for vibration/shock control [LORD]

Figure 3.105 · Complex adhesive-bonded rubber/metal mounts for vibration/shock control [LORD]

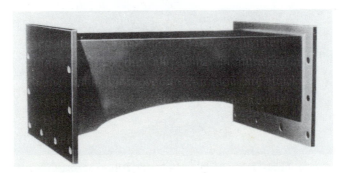

Figure 3.106 · Large marine fender [LORD]

Figure 3.107 · Tanker loading hose: rubber lining and cover (lining in nitrile rubber NBR) **[GOODRICH]**

Figure 3.108 · Chemical-resistant centrifugal pumps lining (fluoroelastomer P(HFP-VDF)) **[PCUK/3M]**

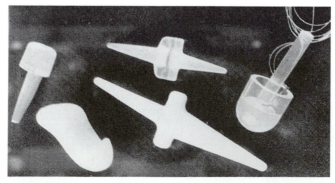

Figure 3.109 · Artificial bone joint implants (silicone elastomer PDMS) **[DOW CORNING/WRIGHT]**

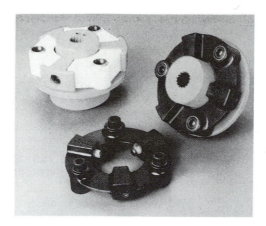

Figure 3.110 · Mechanical coupling flexible element (thermoplastic elastomer EETPE) **[DU PONT]**

Figure 3.111 · Cross-country ski boot sole (thermoplastic elastomer EATPE) **[SALOMON/ATO]**

3.5   SELECTED SPECIAL POLYMERIC PRODUCTS

3.5.1   Polymeric Fibers

3.5.1.1   General

There are many naturally occurring polymeric fibers, which can be subdivided into fibers of animal origin (wool, mohair, or angora, camel, fur, silk, cashmere, alpaca, vicuna, llama, etc.) and fibers of vegetable origin (cotton, flax or linen, sisal, etc.). These fibers are either protein or cellulose-based.

Polymeric fibers, which are the result of major, man-controlled chemical reactions or transformations, are referred to as "man-made," "synthetic" or "artificial fibers." They are more than polymeric materials; they are, to a large degree, products in finished or semifinished form. It is felt, however, that they should be discussed, at least briefly, as a class in this book.

Polymeric fibers are used in a variety of applications, including filters, cords, and cables and, of course, fabrics.

Fabrics frequently require that the man-made fibers undergo a process which gives them a texture, reminiscent of that of most natural fibers (Fig. 3.112). Continuous monofilament tows or yarns are cut into staples which are subjected to a process often referred to as "yarn spinning." Yarn spinning separates the monofilaments and tangles them with a twist or spin into a spun yarn consisting of the relatively short filaments whose mechanical interlocking give a reasonable strength, while the loose ends afford a bulkier, less silky feel and appearance.

The manufacture of fabrics is a subsequent operation conducted in weaving, knitting, or other mills. There are many types of fabrics. Woven fabrics or clothes are either

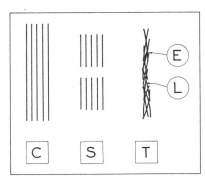

Figure 3.112 · **Fiber texture** · [C] Continuous filaments; [S] Staple filaments; [T] Spun staple filaments; (E) Loose ends; (L) Filament interlocking

plain, patterned (dobby or jacquard), or loop-type (terry or cut loop pile). Knitted fabrics are either circular (weft knit) or flat (warp knit, such as tricot or raschel). Tufted fabrics are produced as cut or uncut pile. Stitch-bonded fabrics rely on a secondary fiber to hold the primary yarns in a given pattern. Nonwoven fabrics are subdivided into bonded webs that make use of a polymeric binder to hold continuous or staple yarn together, and needle punch felts which involve a mechanical-type interaction.

Fiber-forming polymers are normally of the crystallizing, uncross-linked type, but besides crystallization, strong orientation of molecules and crystalline units is an essential feature.

3.5.1.2 Characterization

The long-established textile industry has developed specific methods of characterization of fibers and associated units.

Fiber dimensions are often reported as titer in denier (mass in g of 9000 m of monofilament or multifilament yarn); such method is particularly suitable in the case of somewhat irregular cross-sections. Typical titers for monofilaments range from about 3 to 15 denier. For a representative specific gravity of 1.3, a titer of 10 denier corresponds approximately to a diameter of 0.030 mm ($\approx$ 0.001 in). Hosiery often involves monofilaments of 15-denier titer; apparel may involve 12-filament twisted yarn with a global 50-denier titer; tire cord may involve 136-filament twisted yarn with a global 840-denier titer; cordage may involve 2448-filament untwisted yarn with a global 15,000-denier titer.

Fiber strength is often reported as tenacity in force (gf) per unit titer (denier). For a representative specific gravity of 1.3, a tenacity of 6 gf/denier corresponds to a tensile strength of about 100 kpsi ($\approx$ 700 MPa). The tenacity of common synthetic polymeric fibers is generally in the range 3-9 gf/denier, corresponding to tensile strengths between 30 and 150 kpsi ($\approx$ 200-1000 MPa). Elongations at break are often in the range 25-50%.

Fiber moduli are commonly reported in gf/denier with values commonly in the range 30-50 gf/denier, corresponding to about 0.3-1 Mpsi ($\approx$ 2-7 GPa).

3.5.1.3 Processing

The formation of monofilaments involves two basic steps which are often conducted in rapid sequence (Fig. 3.113). The first step, referred to as "filament spinning" itself, is the formation of a monofilament, referred to as the "as-spun monofilament," which is semicrystalline, but basically nonoriented. The second step, referred to as "cold drawing" or simply "drawing," confers most of the orientation through a stretching, yielding, and drawing process that takes place in the solid state, but above the glass transition temperature of the crystallizing polymer to facilitate molecular motion and rearrangements. The monofilament in final form is referred to as the drawn monofilament.

Filament spinning can be achieved in several ways. It sometimes involves a chemical reaction during the fiber-forming stage, but in the majority of cases, the transformation or changes are only physical, involving heat or mass transfer.

One process is referred to as "wet" spinning (Fig. 3.114). It involves the extrusion of a liquid-like fluid through the small holes (orifices) of a spinneret in a bath containing another fluid with which the extruded strand interacts, either chemically or through a molecular exchange (mass transfer). After a sufficient interaction (residence) time, the strand becomes the solid, as-spun monofilament.

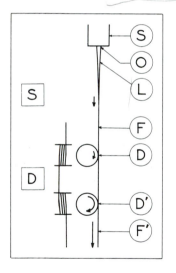

Fig. 3.113

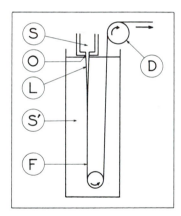

Fig. 3.114

Figure 3.113 · **Monofilament formation** · [S] Spinning step; [D] Drawing step; (S) Spinneret; (O) Orifice; (L) Liquid strand; (F) As-spun filament; (D) Slower take-up drum; (D′) Faster drawing drum; (F′) Drawn filament

Figure 3.114 · **"Wet" spinning** · (S) Polymeric solution; (O) Spinneret orifice; (L) Liquid strand; (S′) Spinning bath fluid; (F) As-spun filament; (D) Take-up drum

The so-called "dry" spinning process (Fig. 3.115) involves the extrusion of a concentrated polymer solution through small spinneret holes. The emerging strands are then dried (the solvent is evaporated by a cross-flow of air) to a final solid state.

In most cases, the difficulty of such process is related to the handling and separation of solvents.

Melt spinning (Fig. 3.116) involves the extrusion of the molten polymer through relatively large spinneret holes and its cooling and solidification in a cross-flow of air. The difficulty here often concerns the thermal stability of the melt and its high viscosity.

In all cases, but particularly in the case of melt spinning, the strands are rapidly pulled (elongated) as they emerge from the spinneret holes, primarily in order to reduce their diameter. The fluids must be able to withstand this rapid elongation.

Acrylic and acetate fibers are either wet- or dry spun, while polyamides, polyolefins and polyesters are most commonly melt spun.

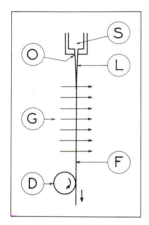
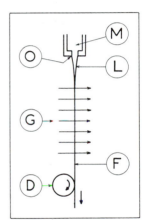

Fig. 3.115   Fig. 3.116

Figure 3.115 · "Dry" spinning · (S) Polymeric solution; (O) Spinneret orifice; (L) Liquid strand; (G) Drying gas crossflow; (F) As-spun filament; (D) Take-up drum

Figure 3.116 · "Melt" spinning · (M) Polymeric melt; (O) Spinneret orifice; (L) Viscous; liquid strand; (G) cooling gas crossflow; (F) As-spun filament; (D) Take-up drum

3.5.1.4 Commercial Types

There are six major types of conventional polymeric fibers: rayon, acetates, olefinics, vinylics, acrylics, nylons and polyesters.

Rayon or viscose rayon fibers are marketed as regular, cross-linked, or high-wet-modulus (polynosic) types.

Acetate or triacetate fibers are based on cellulose acetate.

Olefinic fibers include polyethylene (PE) and polypropylene (PP).

Vinylics are based on polyvinylchloride (PVC), but often involve copolymerization with vinylacetate (AC) or vinylidenechloride (VDC), for example.

Acrylics or modacrylics are based on polyacrylonitrile (PAN), but generally involve copolymerization with polyvinylchloride (PVC), for example.

Polyamides or *nylons* involve aliphatic polyamides.

Polyesters involve polyethyleneterephthalate (PET).

In addition, a number of special-purpose or high performance fibers have been commercialized, including polyurethanes, aramids, extended chain polyethylene, PBI, and PEEK.

3.5.2   Polymeric Films

3.5.2.1   General

Polymeric materials are widely used in the form of wide products of uniform thickness (gauge). For relatively soft materials, the term "film" is generally associated with thicknesses between about 40 μm (0.04 mm) or $\approx$ 0.001 in (1 mil) and 400 μm (0.4 mm) or $\approx$ 0.010 in (10 mils). Thicker products (heavy gauge) are usually referred to as "sheet," particularly for relatively stiff materials. Dry-cleaning garment covers, which are among the thinnest soft material films, consist of low-density polyethylene LDPE, about 13 μm or $\approx$ 0.5 mils thick. The thickness of ultra thin high-density polyethylene HDPE film can be as low as about 7 μm or $\approx$ 0.28 mils, and the term "tissue" is sometimes used in this case.

Plastic films can be manufactured by several processes, including flat extrusion on chill rolls (film casting) which is basically a calendering process, and tubular (bubble) extrusion blowing. Mechanical skiving from blocks is occasionally used for materials that are difficult to process. Uniaxial or biaxial molecular orientation, which can be promoted by a flat stretching device or through the bubble process, tends to improve certain important properties as in the case of oriented polypropylene (OPP) film.

Because of their special geometry and applications, films are the subject of a number of standard tests, somewhat different from those used to characterize polymeric materials in general, and sometimes associated with the paper industry (TAPPI) or with the Packaging Institute (PI). They include burst resistance (Mullen), tear resistance (Elmendorf, Graves), puncture resistance (Union Carbide), folding endurance (MIT, Schopper), slip, curl, and sealability. Mass transport (permeability) properties are essential in many packaging applications.

Many polymers are used in film form. The most commercially important ones are briefly mentioned below, together with the abbreviated names used elsewhere in this section. Regenerated cellulose or cellophane (CEL) has long been used, often coated with a thermoplastic for heat sealing. Cellulose nitrate (CN) and cellulose acetate (CA) were also among the early films. Low-density (LDPE) and high-density (HDPE) polyethylenes are by far the most common film materials. Polypropylene is generally used as oriented polypropylene (OPP). Ionomers (IO) (Surlyn tradename) are olefin-related film materials. Polyvinylchloride (PVC) is commonly used in plasticized form. Polyvinylidenechloride (PVDC) is often known as Saran (a tradename) and is generally used in copolymer form, for example with 10-15% of acrylonitrile (AN). Ethylene-vinyl acetate (EVA) and ethylene-vinyl alcohol (EVOH) copolymers are also used. Polyethylene terephthalate (PET), a thermoplastic polyester, is widely used in film form. Polystyrene (PS) is sometimes used in biaxially oriented form. Polycarbonates (PC), polysulfones (PSU), polyethersulfones (PESU), polyimides (PI), polyetherimides (PEI), and several fluoropolymers, such as PTFE, and FEP, are also used for specialty (engineering) applications. All of these materials are discussed in other sections of Chapter 3.

Composite films can be defined as combinations of parallel layers of different materials designed to offer a set of properties not possessed by any one of the individual materials. The coating or lamination of materials, such as paper or aluminum foil, with polymers has long been used with a calendering-like process. Multilayer all-polymer films are now generally made by coextrusion. Typically, for a food packaging application, different layers will have the following major roles: mechanical strength (PET, etc.), sealing (PE, etc.), and barrier (PVDC, EVOH, etc.). Since different polymers generally do not form a good interlayer bond, additional tie-layers (adhesives) must be included. Scrap of composite films is sometimes reground and incorporated as an additional "fill" layer. Complex coextrusion dies, capable of handling over ten layers, are used for either flat or tubular extrusion.

3.5.2.2 Applications

In the case of food packaging, for example, films must provide a suitable control of the in and out movement of gases and vapors, in particular, and the expression "barrier" packaging is used in this case. Many applications of films in packaging, however, call primarily on the mechanical resistance of the films. We refer to this case as "mechanical" packaging.

"Barrier" packaging is of particular importance in the case of foods. Traditional packaging in glass or metal containers, is being increasingly displaced by polymeric containers and film packaging, in particular, is now making strong progress. Economic as well as functional reasons support the use of polymeric film packaging.

In some cases, the entire package is flexible (bags, pouches), while in other cases it may be relatively rigid ("cups" for yogurt, "cans" for soup, "tubs" for margarine, "trays" for TV dinners, etc.) with a mechanical closure (cover, lid) or a sealed film closure. Many liquid, semifluid and solid particulate foods are now automatically packaged in form/fill/seal bags (milk, frozen peas, etc.).

Packaging plays a role in transit, warehouse storage, and shelf or display counter storage. Refrigeration or freezing impose certain constraints. Packaging is essential for sanitary and conservation reasons. Appropriate packaging should economically retard the deterioration (spoilage) of foods in the form, for example, of discoloration (red meats), staleness (bread), rancidness (ham), or downright decay.

"Barrier" packaging involves primarily the control of the transmission (transport) of oxygen (O_2), carbon dioxide (CO_2) and water vapor or moisture (H_2O), but food characteristics, such as odor, scent, or aroma and other food components, such as oils and fats, must often be considered.

Special consideration is increasingly given to a number of new food packaging developments. These include heat-resistant packaging (boil-in, cook-in, and bake-in bags or wraps, ovenable frozen food, etc.) where different constraints are associated with conventional, convection, and microwave ovens; sterilizable packaging (retortable pouches for steam sterilization, around 120°C or $\approx$ 250°F, or radiation sterilization); aseptic packaging of foods or pharmaceuticals; and controlled-atmosphere packaging (O_2, N_2, and CO_2).

Liquid foodstuff includes primarily soup, which requires heating, and beverages. Beverages can be subdivided into vegetable and fruit juices, non-carbonated (flat) alcoholic beverages which include wine, and hard liquors and carbonated beverages (carbon dioxide CO_2), which include soft drinks and beer. Milk is generally discussed as a dairy product. Carbonated beverages, which can develop pressures of 3.5-7 atm (50-100 psi), require rigid containers particularly resistant to CO_2 permeation, but the use of flexible bags for the packaging of other liquid foodstuff is rapidly growing.

Semi-fluid foodstuff includes condiments, such as salad dressing, mayonnaise, relishes and tomato ketchup, sauces (barbecue, pasta, etc.); and jelly, jam, marmalade, or preserves. The traditional glass containers are gradually being replaced by polymeric semirigid containers or flexible pouches.

Most solid foods are candidates for all plastic packaging, but there are large differences in the requirements that are associated with the nature of the food and the intended use.

Animal products include fresh (wet) fish which requires odor control; fresh red meat, which requires high H_2O barrier and controlled O_2 permeation for color retention (PVC); fresh or frozen poultry, which is often shrink-wrapped; luncheon meats; and ham and bacon with high fat content. Cooked or frozen products call for different packaging requirements.

Dairy products include milk, which is now sold in rigid plastic containers (PC, PET), as well as flexible film pouches (LDPE). Cheese wraps must provide high moisture retention.

Fresh produce wrapping is often associated with a "respiration" problem, that is a CO_2/O_2 exchange with the atmosphere, and the evolution of water (H_2O). Films must allow a reasonable exchange (PS), or suitable holes must be provided to prevent fogging or even rotting in the case of carrots or potatoes, for example.

Bakery products (sliced bread, cakes, pies) must be wrapped with suitable H_2O barriers to prevent premature drying.

Dry foods include cereals, biscuits, coffee, and snack foods, such as potato chips. In all cases, a sufficient moisture barrier is required. Oxygen must be kept out of many snack foods, and, in the case of coffee, aroma must be kept in.

Confectionery includes chocolate products whose high oil content may require oil-resistant acrylonitrile-based films to compete with the current aluminum foil, and sweets, high in sugar, which must be isolated from water or moisture sources.

Tobacco, although not a food, involves similar packaging constraints similar to those for foods to maintain its critical moisture content and to lock in the aroma. Heat-sealable coated cellulose film is now increasingly replaced by oriented polypropylene (OPP).

"Mechanical" film packaging applications include thick-gauge industrial sacks for powdered or granular products (LDPE); garbage (trash) bags (LDPE); general merchandise, paper-like, thin gauge bags (HDPE); supermarket grocery check-out (carry-out) bags of the flexible T-shirt type (LDPE) or more rigid free-standing type (HDPE); very thin gauge dry-cleaning garment covers (LDPE); gift or florist wrap; or ultrathin tissue-like film (HDPE). Relatively thick-gauge film is used for skin or blister packaging of dry goods, such as hardware items.

A growing area of application concerns the use of heat- shrinkable films (biaxially stretched and quenched films) fitted closely to the contours of an object or a set of objects to provide protection or to keep the objects together. Shrinking of the films (PVC, LDPE, PP, etc.) is achieved through hot water, hot air convection or radiation heating. Objects such as cans, jars, and bottles are collated and shrink-wrapped on trays or pallets. Such transit packaging is sometimes referred to as "unitizing."

Protection and unitizing can also be achieved by winding a thin plastic tape under some controlled tension (stretch wrapping).

Besides packaging applications, there are many other important uses for polymeric films.

In construction and public works, they are used as construction coverings for weather protection of wet concrete and workers (LDPE), as industrial liners, and as roof liners.

In agriculture and horticulture, they serve as crop silo covers, water reservoir liners, seed-bed covers and mulch substitutes and greenhouse covers (LDPE). In many cases, a controlled transmission of solar radiations can be achieved.

In electrical and electronic areas, films are found in applications such as condenser (capacitor) dielectrics (PS), in membrane switches, as wire insulation tape (PVC, PI), and as audio/video tape (PET).

Suitable polymeric films are now used as selective diffusion (semipermeable) membranes for chemicals separation, water desalination (desalting), blood dialysis or oxygenation, etc.

Other miscellaneous applications of films include photographic and cinematographic substrates (cellulose nitrate CN, the original "film" material, was superseded by much less flammable cellulose acetate CA, and now PET); typewriter ribbon (LDPE), specialty moisture-proof printing or typing paper and envelopes (HDPE), high altitude balloons or sail material.

3.5.3   Cellular Polymers

3.5.3.1   General

The methods of production and fabrication of polymeric materials allow the incorporation of various amounts of gas in the form of voids, cells, and similar; the resulting lighter material is referred to as "cellular," "blown" or "expanded polymer," "foam," "sponge."

In view of the great variety of cellular polymers corresponding to numerous different applications, several different bases or criteria can be used for rational classifications as discussed below.

On the basis of elastic properties of the polymeric material, referred to as the "matrix" (subscript m), one can distinguish between elastomeric foams, when the matrix is an elastomer or rubber capable of large elastic deformations; flexible foams, involving a soft plastic matrix, such as plasticized polyvinylchloride (PPVC), low-density polyethylene (LDPE) and certain polyurethane plastics (PU); and rigid foams involving rigid matrices, such as polystyrenes (PS), unsaturated polyesters, phenolics (PF), and certain polyurethane plastics.

The type of polymeric matrix, thermoplastic or thermosetting, can also form the basis for a classification and is closely associated with the processing.

The amount of gas incorporated is reflected in the density ρ_c (or the specific gravity) and is best expressed as a volume fraction V_p. With ρ_m taken as the density of the matrix material, $V_p = 1 - \rho_c/\rho_m$. Light foams correspond to densities in the approximate range 0.01-0.10 g/cm^3 ($\approx$ 1-6 lb/ft^3), while dense foams correspond to a range 0.4-0.6 g/cm^3 ($\approx$ 25-40 lb/ft^3).

The arrangement and distribution of the gas in the cellular polymer corresponds to the structure or morphology of the composite system. A basic distinction is made between closed-cell systems, where spherical or roughly spherical voids (cells) are fully separated by matrix material, and open cell systems where there are interconnections between voids (Fig. 3.117). The degree of interconnection can be assessed if a sample is subjected to a moderate vacuum; a liquid is then allowed to fill the interconnected spaces and the weight gain is measured. There are obvious implications in terms of heat transfer and mass transport, in particular. The cell size or average cell size can be an important factor, and a distinction is sometimes made between microcellular foams, which correspond roughly to cells indistinguishable with the naked eye, and macrocellular foams. The cell density (number of cells per unit cross-section area or volume) is also used to characterize the "coarseness" or "fineness" of a foam. Cellular (foamed) parts sometimes feature a deliberately created inhomogeneous (nonuniform) morphology. This is the case when a foamed core is "sandwiched" between solid skins, as in so-called "structural foams," which should perhaps be called structured foams, or in elastomeric parts with a so-called "integral skin." Occasionally, the foaming process will give an anisotropic structure and corresponding anisotropic properties; in such cases, the cells are, for example, elongated in the direction of foam rise.

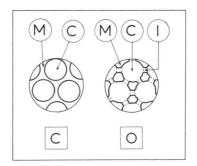

Figure 3.117 · **Cellular polymer structure** · [C] Closed cell; [O] Open cell; (M) Matrix; (C) Cell; (I) Interconnection

In closed-cell cellular polymers, the nature of the entrapped gas may have an effect on certain properties or the suitability for specific applications. Air, nitrogen, water, pentane, methylene chloride, and fluorohydrocarbon vapors or condensates may be present in cells and the composition may change with time due to mass transport through the relatively permeable matrix material.

Another classification can be based on the mechanism used for the formation of the cellular structure. Mechanical agitation is used in some specialized processes to incorporate air into a liquid resin system (latex, reactive system, etc.); such processes are sometimes referred to as "aeration" or "frothing." One of the more common mechanisms involves the use of physical blowing agents (PBA), while the other uses chemical blowing agents (CBA). In some cases, at least some of the gas is evolved as a by-product of a thermosetting reaction (e.g., polyurethane systems).

Physical blowing agents (PBA) include nitrogen (N_2), gas which is generally forced into solution in a polymer melt or in one of the components of a reactive system under a high pressure and comes out of solution to form the cells when the pressure is released. Other physical blowing agents are liquids at room temperature and have a low boiling point T_b. In this case, vaporization of a liquid phase may be induced by heating or by the heat generated by a chemical reaction in a thermosetting system (e.g., polyurethane or unsaturated polyester). Such physical blowing agents (PBA) include aliphatic hydrocarbons, such as pentane C_5H_{12} ($T_b \approx 36°C$ or 97°F), which are flammable; chlorinated hydrocarbons, such as methylene chloride CH_2Cl_2 ($T_b \approx 41°C$ or 105°F) which can be toxic; and fluorohydrocarbons, such as trichloro-fluoromethane CCl_3F or Freon 11 ($T_b \approx 24°C$ or 75°F) which are more costly. The blowing efficiency of physical blowing agents is sometimes rated as the volume of vapor (reduced to standard conditions STP) per unit mass; typical values being between 200 and 300 cm^3 (STP)/g. Nucleating agents in the form of finely divided solids are often used with physical blowing agents to help control the size and density of cells. Surfactants are also used as a way of controlling the degree of interconnections, in particular.

Chemical blowing agents (CBA) are compounds that decompose above a characteristic temperature zone T_d, liberating large amounts of gas. The gas evolved is preferably an inert permanent gas, such as nitrogen N_2 or carbon dioxide CO_2, although other gases or vapors are sometimes acceptable (water H_2O, ammonia NH_3, carbon monoxide CO, hydrogen H_2, etc.). Activators can sometimes be added to lower the decomposition temperature zone, and, in general, the rate and sometimes the extent of decomposition increase with temperature. The nature of the chemical residue is also a factor in the choice of a chemical blowing agent. Early chemical blowing agents were mostly inorganic compounds, such as sodium bicarbonate $NaHCO_3$, which liberates carbon dioxide CO_2 in a temperature range of about 100-140°C ($\approx$ 210-280°F). Other carbonates, nitrites, which liberate nitrogen N_2, and hydrides, which liberate hydrogen H_2, have been used.   Gas yields (blowing efficiencies) generally range from about 200 to 2000 cm^3 (STP)/g; being very high in the case of hydrogen, which, however, diffuses away.   Many commercial organic compounds are now recommended for specific situations, including high decomposition temperatures associated with the expansion of some engineering thermoplastics. They include abbreviated names, such as TSH for toluene sulfonyl hydrazide (T_d $\approx$ 120°C or 250°F), OBSH for oxybis benzene sulfonyl hydrazide (T_d $\approx$ 160°C or 320°F), AFBA for azobisformamide (T_d $\approx$ 210°C or 410°F), TSSC for toluene sulfonyl semicarbazide (T_d $\approx$ 230°C or 450°F), PT for phenyl tetrazole, and THT for trihydrazinatriazine for even higher temperatures.   When chemical blowing agents are in finely divided solid form, they may determine cell nucleating sites. Nucleating agents and surfactants are often used, however, to help control the cellular structure.

3.5.3.2 Examples

  Two examples of commercially important cellular polymeric systems (styrene and urethane foams) and a special type of cellular product (structural foam) are discussed below, which illustrate, in particular, the variety of processing methods involved.
  Polystyrene (PS) is widely used in cellular form and is generally referred to as "expanded polystyrene" (EPS) or sometimes as "Styrofoam," an early tradename (Dow).
  Expanded polystyrene can be made from expandable polystyrene beads, which are small spheres of polystyrene (diameter about 0.3-2.3 mm or 0.012-0.090 in) containing 3-7% of pentane as a physical blowing agent (PBA). The bulk density of the beads, including air spaces between them, is about 0.7 g/cm^3 or $\approx$ 42 lb/ft^3. The beads are first preexpanded, generally through the use of steam around 100°C or 212°F, to a bulk density between about 0.02 and 0.05 g/cm^3 or 1.1-3 lb/ft^3 and, after cooling, they are allowed to reach a state of equilibrium with air permeating into the cells (maturing). Probably through the use of appropriate additives, the preexpanded beads remain free-running, and they can be subsequently molded by completely filling a cavity with the close-packed beads and, again through the use of steam, produce simultaneously the small amount of additional expansion to fill the voids and the fusion of the beads into a basically homogeneous cellular structure (Fig. 3.118). The final structure is primarily of the closed-cell type with cell diameters reported to be in the range of 0.080-0.150 mm or 0.003-0.006 in. The process is used to mold large

blocks from which insulating boards, for example, can be cut, or to mold custom products, such as disposable cups, insulating containers, and protective elements, for packaging.

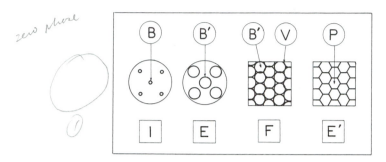

Figure 3.118 · **Expanded polystyrene formation** · [I] Initial stage; [E] Pre-expansion; [F] Mold filling; [E′] Final expansion; (B) Expandable bead; (B′) Pre-expanded bead; (V) Void; (P) Final cellular product

Cellular polystyrene slabs, logs, boards, and sheets can also be made by a modified extrusion process involving the injection of a physical blowing agent (PBA) in the high-pressure zone preceding the die. The blowing agent expands only when the pressure is released at the die exit. Sheets can be thermoformed into items such as meat trays and egg cartons.

Polyurethane resins (UR) are also widely used in cellular form. Since the stiffness of the polyurethane matrix can vary widely from that of a soft elastomer to that of a rigid plastic, a very broad range of foam characteristics can be achieved.

Flexible PU foams generally have a density above 0.080 g/cm^3 ($\approx$ 5 lb/ft^3) and a predominantly open cell structure. They are usually water-blown (carbon dioxide CO_2 is thus the blowing agent). A special formulation produces high-resiliency (HR) foams that are particularly elastic (low compression set). Such foams are used primarily for cushioning purposes.

Rigid PU foams often have a very low density when used for thermal insulation purposes (0.030-0.060 g/cm^3 or $\approx$ 2-4 lb/ft^3); the structure is then predominantly of the closed-cell type to trap the low conductivity blowing agent (Freon 11).

One method of fabrication of rigid or flexible polyurethane foams involves the batch or continuous formation of a large block of foam (log, bun, loaf) in a suitable "mold," using a cross traveling dispensing head to deliver liquid or "frothed" resin. A typical cross-section is 2 m x 1 m ($\approx$ 6 ft x 3 ft), and a typical linear speed of production for a continuous process is 4 m/min ($\approx$ 12 ft/min). The method is referred to here as the "foamstock" (bunstock, slabstock, boardstock) method. Specific products subsequently cut from the foamstock, using hot wires, for example, include parallel-faced slabs, boards, and sheets, as well as other shapes.

Another method of fabrication involves the permanent placement of foam in a cavity of a product. This may be for insulation, buoyancy, structural or combined purposes. This method is referred to here as "in situ (in-place) foaming." It normally requires good adhesion to the cavity walls and may require appropriate treatment (degreasing, corona discharge, etc.).   Precautions must be taken to assure that the pressure generated during foaming does not cause an unacceptable deformation of the product cavity.

In the spray-on (spray-up) method, the liquid or frothed resin is projected against a surface (substrate) but rises freely on the opposite side. The external insulation of tanks, vessels, roofs, and other structures can be done by this method, which avoids joints inherent to the use of slabs or sheets.

When a number of foamed objects of a specific complex shape are to be made, molding in a reusable mold (tool) is normally the appropriate method. For demolding, adhesion to the tool cavity must be suppressed through the use of appropriate release (parting) agents. An appropriate amount of liquid or frothed resin is metered into the closed mold. If the pressure generated during foaming is not adequately controlled, the dimensions of the demolded object may differ significantly from those of the mold, particularly in the case of flexible foams.   The technique can be adapted to the formation of integral skins (self-skinned products) by controlling the heat transfer at the mold surface to favor cell collapse (high temperature) or prevent cell formation (low temperature).   Steering wheel covers and transportation seats, for example, are made by this technique.

The frothing method corresponds to a two-stage expansion. A suitable (low boiling point) physical blowing agent (often dichlorodifluoroethane CCl_2F_2 or Freon 12) is incorporated to the resin system under enough pressure (4-5 atm) to prevent its expansion. The pressure release at the exit of the dispensing nozzle causes the immediate formation of a "froth" (foamed cream), corresponding to a preexpansion ratio of about x10. Subsequent expansion is associated with the curing reaction which causes the vaporization of the other blowing agent (usually trichlorofluoromethane CCl_3F or Freon 11) for a typical further expansion ratio of about x3. The pressure developed in a cavity and temperature variations are lower than in the case of direct liquid feeding and much larger products can be made this way, particularly by successive layer buildups.

Structural foams (or structured foams) featuring a cellular core and solid skins can be based on thermoplastic or thermosetting polymers and can be produced by a variety of methods. A process for molding thermoplastic structural foams, sometimes referred to as the "low-pressure" or "Union Carbide process," forms the foam in an accumulator from which it is transferred into the mold cavity under a moderate pressure of about 35 atm or 500 psi (Fig. 3.119). Tooling is relatively inexpensive, but the surface finish and appearance, in particular, are not very good (swirl patterns, etc.). Another process, often referred to as the "high-pressure" or "USM (United Shoe Machinery) process," involves the conventional injection of the melt containing the physical blowing agent; the high pressure (up to 1500 atm or ≈ 20,000 psi) prevents foaming and allowing excellent surface finish. The mold cavity is then enlarged (expansion mold), allowing the still molten core material to foam (Fig. 3.120). The corresponding tooling can be expensive, and there are obvious shape restrictions. The reaction injection molding (RIM) process can produce thermosetting polyurethane structural foams under low pressures (about 3.5 atm or 50 psi) with good surfaces; it is thus particularly suitable for large parts.

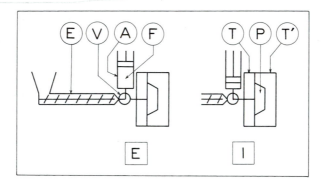

Figure 3.119 · **Low pressure structural foam molding** · [E] Expansion; [I] Injection; (E) Extruder; (V) Valve; (A) Accumulator; (F) Foamed melt; (T),(T′) Mold ; (P) Cellular product

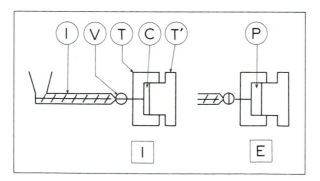

Figure 3.120 · **High pressure structural foam molding** · [I] Injection; [E] Expansion; (E) Extruder; (V) Valve; (T),(T′) Mold; (C) Dense melt; (P) Cellular product

3.5.3.3 *Applications*

Cellular polymers have certain properties that make them ideal choices for many applications.

Their mechanical properties, on a per weight basis, can be excellent, and rigid foams are widely used in structural applications, often as core materials in conjunction with rigid shells and in sandwich constructions.

Their thermal insulation properties are outstanding, and closed-cell foams are widely used as insulation board and for the packaging of frozen or perishable foods, such as ice cream, fish, and produce.

Their very low density makes closed-cell foams ideal buoyancy (flotation) materials; the support (lift) per unit mass is exceptionally high. They are also much safer than empty ballasts.

Cellular polymers are particularly valuable for the protection of sensitive objects against shocks and vibrations and for cushioning purposes. They are widely used in rigid, semirigid, flexible, and elastomeric form for numerous applications in packaging, automotive occupants protection, cushioning, bedding, and fruit and egg packaging.

Suitable cellular polymers can be very efficient acoustic insulation or dampening materials with their use likely to expand with the growing concern about the environment quality.

Open cellular structures are also used in filtering and humidifying applications.

3.6   APPENDIX 3

Alphabetical Lists of Polymeric Materials Suppliers

▶UNITED STATES (US)

AMOCO	GOODYEAR
ARCO	GRACE
BORDEN	GULF
BORG-WARNER	HERCULES
CELANESE	MINNESOTA MINING AND
CYANAMID	MANUFACTURING (3-M)
DIAMOND-SHAMROCK	MOBAY
DOW	MOBIL
DUPONT	NORCHEM
DUREZ	PENNWALT
EASTMAN	PHILLIPS
EL PASO	PLENCO
EMERSON-CUMING	POLYPENCO
ETHYL	REICHHOLD
FIRESTONE	ROHM AND HAAS
FMC	THIOKOL
FREEMAN	UNIROYAL
GENERAL ANILIN AND FOOD (GAF)	USI
GENERAL ELECTRIC (GE)	USS
GENERAL TIRE	
GOODRICH	

▶OUTSIDE THE US

AKZO-ENKA	ISR
ANIC	JSR
ATO	KUREHA
BASF	MITSUI
BAYER	MONTEDISON
BP	NIPPON ZEON
CDF	NOVACOR
CIAGO	PCUK
CIBA-GEIGY	PETROFINA
DAICEL	POLYSAR
DAIKIN KOGYO	RHONE-POULENC
DENKA	SHELL
DSM	SHIN-ETSU
DYNAMIT NOBEL	SIR
EMSER	SNIA
HOECHST	SOLVAY
HULS	SUMITOMO
ICI	UNITIKA

THERMOPLASTICS (section 3.2)
Suppliers and Tradenames

Olefinics (section 3.2.2.1)
POLYETHYLENE (PE)
  Regular polyethylene (LDPE, HDPE)

DOW	DOW, ZETAFIN
EL PASO	REXENE*
DUPONT	ALATHON, SCLAIR, SCLAIRLINK
ALLIED	GREX, PAXON, SUPREL
CELANESE	FORTIFLEX, FORTILENE*
HERCULES	HI-FAX
PHILLIPS	MARLEX*, SIRTENE
UNION CARBIDE	BAKELITE*
GULF	POLY-ETH, GULF, HEX-ONE
EASTMAN KODAK	TENITE*, EPOLENE
USI	PETROTHENE, FLAMOLIN
ALLIED	PAXON
NORCHEM	NPE, NORCHEM*
ARCO	DYLAN
PETROFINA	FINATHENE
CHEMPLEX	CHEMPLEX
RHONE-POULENC	MANOLENE, NATENE
PCUK	NATENE, PLASTYLENE
CDF-CHIMIE	LOTRENE, NORSOPLAST*
ATO	LACQTENE*
HULS	VESTOLEN*
BASF	LUPOLEN
HOECHST	HOSTALEN*G, POLIETILENE
SHELL	CARLONA
DSM	STAMYLAN*
ICI	ALKATHENE
BP	RIGIDEX, NATENE
MONTEDISON	FERTENE, CELENE, MOPLEN*
SIR	SIRTENE
ANIC	ERACLENE
SOLVAY/SOLTEX	FORTIFLEX, ELTEX*
SUMITOMO	SUMIKATHENE, SUMIKON*
MITSUBISHI	BEAURON, YUKALON

  Linear low density polyethylene (LLDPE)

NIPPON	REXLON
MITSUI	HI-ZEX*
CDF-CHIMIE	LOTREX
EXXON	ESCORENE
DOW	DOWLEX
UNION-CARBIDE	G-RESIN
DUPONT	SCLAIR
NORCHEM	NORLIN

UNIFOS CHIMIE	UNIFOS
NOVACOR	NOVAPOL
DSM	STAMYLEX
ESSO	LPX
SOLVAY	SOLTEX*
PHILLIPS	MARLEX*

Ultra high molecular weight polyethylene (UHMWPE)

HOECHST	HOSTALEN GUR
HERCULES	UHMW 1900
POLYMER/	
POLYPENCO	ULTRA-WEAR
MITSUI	HI-ZEX* MILLION

Cross-linked polyethylene (XLPE)

DUPONT	SCLAIRLINK

Polyethylene-containing polyalloys

DUPONT	SELAR
UNIROYAL	ROVEL

Ethylene-vinylacetate copolymers (EVA)

ATO	LACQTEE*V
USI	ULTRATHENE, VYNATHENE
DUPONT	ELVAX
EL PASO	REXENE*
SUMITOMO	EVATATE
BAYER	LEVASINT, LEVAPREN
ICI	EVATANE, ALKATHENE*
ESSO/EXXON	ESCORENE ULTRA
JAPAN CO.	NIPOFLEX
MITSUI	EVAFLEX
REICHHOLD	ELVACE
BASF	LUPOLEN*V

Ethylene-vinylalcohol copolymers (EVOH)

KURARAY/NORCHEM	EVAL
DUPONT	SELAR

Ethylene-acrylates copolymers (EEA, EMA)

DUPONT	VAMEC, VAMAC

Ethylene-carboxylic acid copolymers (EAA, EMAA)

DOW	NUCREL

Ionomers (IO)

DUPONT	SURLYN
UNION CARBIDE	BAKELITE*
MITSUI	HI-MILAN

Ethylene-propylene copolymers (P(E-P)) Polyallomers

EASTMAN	TENITE*

POLYPROPYLENE (PP)

HERCULES/HIMONT	PRO-FAX, PARLON P
ENJAY	ESCON
PHILLIPS	MARLEX*
EASTMAN	TENITE*PP
SHELL	CARLONA P, SHELL PP
ARCO	DYPRO
EL PASO	REXENE*
SOLVAY/SOLTEX	FORTILENE*, ELTEX*P
NORCHEM	NPP, NORTUFF, NORCHEM*
DSM	STAMYLAN*P
BASF	NOVOLEN
HULS	VESTOLEN*P, VESTOPREN
MONTEDISON	MOPLEN*, MOPLEFAN, FERSOLA
HOECHST	HOSTALEN*PP
SUMITOMO	NOBLEN
ICI	PROPATHENE, VULKIDE
ATO	LACATENE*P
BP/RHONE-POULENC	NAPRYL
AVISUN	OLEFAN
CDF-CHIMIE	PRYLENE, NORSOPRYL
ANIC	KASTILENE
CHIMIE-LINZ(A)	DAPLEN*
ALLIED	PLASKON
CIBA-GEIGY	PROCON
CELANESE	PROPYLEN
SIR	SIRTENE P
MITSUBISHI	LINKLON
USI CHEM	NORTUFF

POLYBUTYLENE (PB1)

COSDEN	POLYVIS
SHELL/WITCO/MOBIL	WITRON, DURAFLEX, PB 200
HULS	VESTOLEN*BT

POLYMETHYLPENTENE (PMP)

MITSUI	TPX

Vinylics (section 3.2.2.2)

POLYVINYLCHLORIDE (PVC)

DUPONT	ELVAX
GOODRICH	GEON
CELANESE	CELANESE CT
FIRESTONE	EXON

UNIROYAL	MARVINOL
MONSANTO	OPALON, VYRAM, ULTRON
GENERAL TIRE	VYGEN, BOLTARON, BOLTAFLEX
GOODYEAR	PLIOVIC, PLIOFLEX, PLIOVAC
DIAMOND-SHAMROCK	DALVIN, DACONVIN, DACON, DACOVIN
HOOKER	RUCON
REICHHOLD	BLANE
UNION CARBIDE	BAKELITE*
ORGAVYL/ATO	LUCOVYL, LUCOLENE, LUCOREX, LACQVYL
RHONE-POULENC	VYNAN
SHELL	CARINA
SIR	VIXIR
ICI	WELVIC, CORVIC, FLOVIC, DARVIC
CDF-CHIMIE	GEDEVYL
PCUK/PLASTIMER	EKAVYL
SOLVAY	SOLVIC, BENVIC
DYNAMIT-NOBEL	TROSIPLAST, TROVIDUR, ASTRALON
HOECHST	HOSTALIT
MONTEDISON	VIPLA, SICRON
HULS	VESTOLIT
SUMITOMO	SUMILIT, SUMIKON*
DSM/CRM	VARLAN
GRACE	GRACON
WACKER	VIRMOL
BASF	VINOFLEX
ANIC	RAVINIL
KANEGAFUCHI	KANEVINYL
MARUTO	BELCON

CHLORINATED POLYVINYLCHLORIDE (CPVC)

GOODRICH	TEMPRITE, GEON CPVC
ORGAVYL	LUCALOR
MONTEDISON	EDILAC, EDIVYL
DYNAMIT-NOBEL	RHENOFLEX
SOLVAY	SOLVITHERM

POLYVINYLIDENECHLORIDE (PVDC)

MITSUI	KREHALON
BASF	DIOFAN
DOW	SARAN
ICI	VICLAN
SOLVAY	IXAN

POLYVINYLACETATE (PVAC)

HOECHST	MOWILITH, HOSTAFLEX
BORDEN	LEMAC, CASCOREZ
DUPONT	ELVACET

RHONE-POULENC	RHODOPAS,RHOVYL
MONSANTO	GELVA
FIRESTONE	VELON
MONTEDISON	EDIVIL

POLYVINYLALCOHOL (PVAL)

MONSANTO	GELVATOL
DUPONT	ELVANOL
RHONE-POULENC	RHODOVIOL
HOECHST	MOWIOL
WACKER	POLYVIOL
BORDEN	LEMOL

POLYVINYL ALDEHYDICS (PVAH)

Polyvinylformal (PVFO)

DUPONT	BUTACITE*
RHONE-POULENC	RHOVINAL*F

Polyvinylacetal (PVACL)

DUPONT	BUTACITE*

Polyvinylbutyral (PVB)

MONSANTO	SAFLEX, BUTVAR
DUPONT	BUTACITE*
RHONE-POULENC	RHOVINAL*B, RHOVIFLEX
DYNAMIT-NOBEL	TROSIFOL
HOECHST	MOWITAL

POLYVINYLALKYLETHERS (PVAE)

GAF	ACRONAL
BASF	LUTONAL

POLYVINYLPYRROLIDONE (PVPO)

GAF	KOLLIDON

POLYVINYLCARBAZOLE (PVCZ)

BASF	LUVICAN

Styrenics (section 3.2.2.3)

POLYSTYRENE (PS)

UNION CARBIDE	BAKELITE*
HULS	VESTYRON
EL PASO	REXENE*
BASF	POLYSTYROL
MONSANTO	LUSTRON, LUSTREX
UNIROYAL	KRALON*
DOW	STYRON
BORG-WARNER	MARBON, FYRID
HOECHST	HOSTYREN
FOSTER-GRANT	FOSTARENE

ARCO	DYLENE
AMOCO	AMOCO
AMER. PETROFINA	COSDEN*PS
FINACHEM	FINASTYR
SIR	RESTIROL
SHELL	DURATHRON
SUMITOMO	ESBRITE
AMER. ENKA	REXOLITE
POLYMER	POLYPENCO*
BP	POLYSTYRENE
ATO	LACQRENE
CDF-CHIMIE	GEDEX
MONTEDISON	EDISTIR
LATI	LASTIROL
HITACHI	HITANOL
MITSUBISHI	DIAREX

POLYPARAMETHYLSTYRENE (PPMS)

CYANAMID	CYMAC

POLYALPHAMETHYLSTYRENE (PAMS)

AMOCO	RESIN 18
HERCULES	KRISTAFLEX

STYRENE-BASED COPOLYMERS

Styrene-butadiene (P(S-B)) Styrene-butadiene plastics

PHILLIPS	K-RESIN
UNIROYAL	KRALAC, KRALON*
ARCO	DYLARK*

Styrene-acrylonitrile (P(S-AN) or SAN)

DOW	TYRIL, MAGNUM
SIR	RESTIL
BASF	LURAN*
FOSTER-GRANT	FOSTACRYL
MONSANTO	LUSTRAN*A
HULS ·	VESTORAN
ATO	LACQSAN
RHONE-POULENC	AFCOLENE*A
MONTEDISON	KOSTIL
DAICEL	CEBIAN
PCUK	STYVACRIL
LATI	LASTIL
BAYER	NOVODUR*W
ARCO	DYTHERM

Styrene-methylmethacrylate (P(S-MMA) or SMMA)

DOW	ZERLON
PCUK	AFCOLENE, METACRYLENE

| RICHARDSON | NAS |
| ROHM AND HAAS | PLEXIGLAS ZK |

Styrene-maleicanhydride (P(S-MLA) or SMA)
| MONSANTO | CADON |
| ARCO | DYLARK* SMA |

Acrylonitrilics (section 3.2.2.4)
POLYMETHACRYLONITRILE (PMAN)
| MONSANTO | LOPAC |

ACRYLONITRILE-BASED COPOLYMERS
Acrylonitrile-styrene (P(AN-S)) and acrylonitrile-methylacrylate (P(AN-MA))
| KRAHN | BAREX |
| SOLVAY | SOLTAN |

Acrylics (section 3.2.2.5)
POLY R ACRYLATES AND POLY R METHACRYLATES
Polymethylmethacrylate (PMMA)
DUPONT	LUCITE, ELVACITE
CYANAMID/CYRO	ACRYLITE, CYANACRYL
ROHM AND HAAS	PLEXIGAS, IMPLEX, CRYSTALEX, KORAD, PLEXIDUR
CYRO	CYROLITE, EXOLITE
UNION CARBIDE	BAKELITE*
ICI	PERSPEX, DIAKON, ASTERITE
MONTEDISON	VEDRIL, CRILAT
USS	SWEDCAST
MITSUBISHI	SHINKOLITE
SWEDLOW	ACRIVUE
SUMITOMO	SUMIPEX
ALTULOR	ALTUGLAS
BASF	ACRONAL
RICHARDSON	RSA, NOAN
CHEMACRYL	ROHAGLAS, ACRYLITE

CYANOACRYLATE RESINS (CNA)
HUGHSON LORD	CYLOK
DEVCON	ZIPGRIP
TESCOM	ZIPBOND
3-M	SCOTHWELD
EMERSON-CUMING	ECCOBOND KWIK
SUMITOMO	CYANOBONE

POLYACRYLAMIDE (PAM)
| UNION CARBIDE | SEPARAN |

Miscellaneous Copolymers and Polyalloys (section 3.2.2.6)

ACRYLONITRILE-BUTADIENE-STYRENE SYSTEMS (ABS)

ATO	LACQRAN
CDF-CHIMIE	NORSQRAN
EL PASO	REXENE*
DSM	RONFALIN
BORG-WARNER	CYCOLAC
UNIROYAL	KRALASTIC, ROYALITE
MONSANTO	LUSTRAN*
BAYER	NOVODUR*
BASF	TERLURAN
DOW	TYBRENE, MAGNUM*
MITSUBISHI	SHINKOLAC,DIAPET,SANREX
MONTEDISON	UTRAL, EXTIR
PCUK/CDF	UGIKRAL, LORKARYL
RHONE-POULENC	AFCORYL
ARCO	DYLEL
SIR	RESTIRAN
SCHULMAN	POLYMAN*
KANEGAFUCHI	KANE-ACE
GOODRICH	ABSON
MITSUI	LITAC
LATI	LASTILAC
ANIC	KRASTILENE
ENICHEM	URTAL, RAVIKRAL

ACRYLONITRILE-CHLORINATED POLYETHYLENE-STYRENE RESINS (ACS)

SHOWA-DENKA	ACS

OLEFIN-STYRENE-ACRYLONITRILE RESINS (OSA)

UNIROYAL	ROVEL

ACRYLONITRILE-ETHYLENE-STYRENE RESINS (AES)

JSR	JSR-AES

ACRYLONITRILE-STYRENE-ACRYLATE RESINS (ASA)

BASF	LURAN S
STAUFFER/GE	GELOY*1000
MONSANTO	CENTREX

Cellulosics (section 3.2.2.7)

CELLULOSE (CEL)

DUPONT	CELLOPHANE

THERMOPLASTIC CELLULOSE DERIVATIVES

Cellulose esters

Cellulosenitrates (CN)

BX PLASTICS	XYLONITE

CELANESE	CELLULOID
HERCULES	HERCULOID

Celluloseacetates (CA)

FABELTA/AKZO	SETILITHE
DUPONT	PLASTACEL
EASTMAN	TENITE*, KODACEL
BAYER	CELLIDOR*
CELANESE	FORTICEL*CA
RHONE-POULENC	RHODIALITE, RHODEX, RHODANITE, RHODOID, RHODOPHANE
BIP	BEXOID

Mixed cellulosic organic esters
Cellulose acetate-propionate (CAP)

CELANESE	FORTICEL*CAP
BAYER	CELLIDOR*CP
EASTMAN	TENITE*

Cellulose acetate-butyrate (CAB)

CELANESE	FORTICEL*CAB
EASTMAN	TENITE*, UVEX
BAYER	CELLIDOR BSP
TEIJIN	TENEX

Cellulose ethers
Methylcellulose (MC)

DOW	METHOCEL

Ethylcellulose (EC)

DOW	ETHOCEL

Polyamides (section 3.2.2.8)
ALIPHATIC POLYAMIDES

FABELTA	FABELNYL, TUBIMIDE
BASF	ULTRAMID
MONTEDISON	RENYL, NAILONPLAST
AKZO-ENKA	AKULON
BAYER	DURETHAN, NYDUR
ATO	ORGAMIDE, RILSAN
DUPONT	DARTEK, ZYTEL, ELVAMIDE, MINLON
ICI	MARANYL
RHONE-POULENC	TECHNYL
ALLIED	CAPRON, PLASKON, NYPEL, CAPRAN
HOECHST	FOSTA
CELANESE	CELANESE
HULS	VESTAMID
MONSATO	VYDYNE
POLYMER	NYLATRON
EMSER-WERKE	GRILAMID, GRILON

FIRESTONE	NYLON
SNIA	SNIAMID
DYNAMIT-NOBEL	TROGAMID
ASHLEY	ASHLENE
TORAY	AMILAN
DAICEL	DAIAMID
HITACHI	HITAMIDE
ASAHI	LEOTEL
MITSUBISHI	NOVAMID
DSM	STANYL
WELLMAN	WELLAMID

AROMATIC POLYAMIDES

DUPONT	NOMEX, KEVLAR, VESPEL, VESTREL
AKZO-ENKA	ARENKA, TWARON
SOLVAY	IXEF

TRANSPARENT POLYAMIDES

DYNAMIT-NOBEL	TROGAMID
UNION CARBIDE	AMIDEL
EMSER-WERKE	GRILAMID*TR 55,GRILON*TR 27
UPJOHN	ISONAMID
DUPONT	ZYTEL*, BEXLOY*C
ALLIED	CAPRON*C-100

Thermoplastic Polyesters, Polycarbonate (section 3.2.2.9)
POLYALKYLENE TEREPHTALATES (PAT)

CIBA-GEIGY	CRASTINE
BASF	ULTRADUR, ULTRADEX
GE	VALOX
DUPONT	RYNITE, MYLAR, CRONAR
ALLIED	PETRA, VERSEL
MOBAY	PETLON
BAYER	POCAN
EASTMAN	TENITE, KODAPAK
HOECHST	HOSTADUR, HOSTAPHAN, ALBERTOL
AKZO	ARNITE, ARLASTIC
ICI	MELINEX, MELINAR, DEROTON, MELINITE, CARODEL
DYNAMIT-NOBEL	DYNALIT
CELANESE	CELANEX, CELANAR, PETPAC, IMPET
AMCEL	KELANEX
GOODYEAR	CLEARTUFF, TRAYTUF, CPET
GAF	GAFITE, GAFTUF
DOW	LUREX
RHONE-POULENC	TERPHANE, TECHSTER, RHODESTER
ATO	ORGATER
HULS	VESTODUR
ROHM AND HAAS	CARODEL

MONTEDISON	PIBITER
SNIA	SNIALEN
MITSUBISHI	NOVADUR

PET-BASED OR PCT-BASED COPOLYESTERS
| EASTMAN | KODAR, EKTA |

POLYARYLESTERS
Poly p-hydroxybenzoyl acid (PHBA)
| CARBORUNDUM | EKONOL |

Polyarylates (PAR)
AMOCO	ARDEL
CELANESE/	
HOECHST	DUREL
SOLVAY	ARYLEF
BAYER	APEC
DUPONT	ARYLON
GE	LEXAN*PPC

POLYCARBONATE (PC)
GE	LEXAN
MOBAY	MERLON
BAYER	MAKROLON, ANDORAN, MAKRISOL
ROHM AND HAAS	TUFFAK
DOW	CALIBRE
ATO	ORGALAN
ALTULOR	ALTUCHOC
MITSUBISHI	JUPILON, NOVAREX
TEIJIN	PANLITE
ANIC/ENI	SINVET

POLYESTER-BASED LIQUID CRYSTAL POLYMERS (LCP)
DARTCO/AMOCO	XYDAR
CELANESE/	
HOECHST	VECTRA
BASF	ULTRAX
ICI	VICTREX*SRP
GRANMONT	GRANLAR

Sulfone Polymers (section 3.2.2.10)
POLYBISPHENOLSULFONE (PBSU)
| AMOCO | UDEL, UCARDEL, MINDEL*A |

POLYETHERSULFONE (PESU)
| ICI | VICTREX*PES |
| BASF | ULTRASON*E |

POLYARYLETHERS (PAE)
    UNIROYAL   ARYLON*T

POLYPHENYLETHERSULFONES (PPESU)
    3M   ASTREL
    AMOCO   RADEL

Imide Polymers (section 3.2.2.11)
THERMOSETTING AND THERMOPLASTIC POLYIMIDES (TSPI AND TPPI)
    DUPONT   VESPEL, KAPTON, PYRALIN, PYRRONE, K-
                                                POLYMER
    RHONE-POULENC   KINEL, KERIMID*, NOLIMID
    ROHM AND HAAS   KAMAX
    DIXON   MELDIN
    UPJOHN/DOW   POLYIMIDE 2080
    CIBA-GEIGY   P13-N, XU-218, MATRIMID
    GE   GEMON
    RAYCHEM   POLYIMIDAL
    ROGERS   ENVEX
    NATIONAL STARCH   THERMID

POLYAMIDEIMIDE (PAI)
    AMOCO   TORLON
    RHONE-POULENC   KERIMID*, RHODEFTAL, KERMEL

POLYETHERIMIDE (PEI)
    GE   ULTEM

Ether/Oxide Polymers (section 3.2.2.12)
POLYMETHYLENEOXIDES (PMO) OR ACETALS
    DUPONT   DELRIN
    CELANESE   CELCON
    AMCEL   KEMATAL
    HOECHST   HOSTAFORM
    BASF   ULTRAFORM
    DAICEL   DAICEL
    POLYPLASTIC   DURACON
    ASAHI   TENAC

POLYETHYLENE OXIDE (PEO)
    UNION CARBIDE   POLYOX

POLYPHENYLENEOXIDES (PPO), POLYPHENYLENEETHERS (PPE)
    GE   NORYL
    BORG-WARNER   PREVEX
    ASAHI-DOW   XYRON
    AKZO   ARNOX
    HULS   VESTORAN

Ketone Polymers (section 3.2.2.13)
POLYETHERETHERKETONE-1 (PEEK-1)
    ICI   VICTREX*, STABAR*

OTHER KETONE POLYMERS
    UC/AMOCO   KADEL
    ICI   VICTREX*, PEK, PEEK*
    RAYCHEM/BASF   STILAN, ULTRAPEK
    HOECHST   HOSTATEC
    DUPONT   KADEL

Fluoropolymers (section 3.2.2.14)
POLYTETRAFLUOROETHYLENE (PTFE)
    GAF   GAFLON
    MONTEDISON   ALGOFLON
    DUPONT   TEFLON
    ALLIED   HALON
    PCUK   SOREFLON
    ICI   FLUON
    HOECHST   HOSTAFLON*TF
    PENNWALT   TETRAN
    DAIKIN-KOGYO   POLYFON
    ASAHI   AFLON*

POLYCHLOROTRIFLUOROETHYLENE (PCTFE)
    3M   KEL-F*
    ALLIED   PLASKON*CTFE, ACLAR, ACLON
    PCUK   VOLTALEF*
    DAIKIN-KOGYO   DAIFLON
    HOECHST   HOSTAFLON*
    CHEMPLAST   CHEMFLUOR

POLYVINYLIDENEFLUORIDE (PVDF)
    DYNAMIT-NOBEL   DYFLOR*
    PCUK   FORAFLON
    PENNWALT   KYNAR
    SKW   VIDAR
    KWICKA   KF
    SOLVAY   SOLEF

POLYPERFLUOROALKOXY (PPFA)
    HOECHST   HOSTAFLON*TFA
    DUPONT   TEDLAR, TESLAR, TEFLON*PFA
    DYNAMIT-NOBEL   DYFLOR*
    ASAHI   AFLON*

FLUOROPLASTIC COPOLYMERS P(E-TFE)
    DUPONT   TEFZEL

DAIKIN-KOGYO	NEOFLON
HOECHST	HOSTAFLON*ET

P(E-CTFE)
ALLIED	HALAR, DURASAN

P(TFE-HFP) or PFEP
DUPONT	TEFLON*FEP

P(VDF-HFI)
ALLIED	CM-1

Miscellaneous Heterochain Polymers (section 3.2.2.15)
POLYPHENYLENESULFIDE (PPS)
PHILLIPS/TORAY	RYTON
BAYER	TEDUR
CELANESE/HOECHST	FORTRON
GE	SUPEC

PARYLENES (PPX)
UNION CARBIDE	PARYLENE

THERMOSETTING RESINS (THERMOSETS) (section 3.3)
Formaldehyde Systems (section 3.3.2.1)
Phenoplasts
ALLIED	PLASKON*
ICI	MOULDRITE
REICHHOLD	PLYOPHEN, VARCUM
BORDEN	CASCOPHEN
MONSANTO	RESINOX
UNION CARBIDE	BAKELITE*
HOOKER/OCCIDENTAL	DUREZ
PLENCO	PLENCO*
GE/PLENCO	GENAL
SIR	SIRFEN
CIBA-GEIGY	AZOLONE
MONTEDISON	CHERATOLO
CDF-CHIMIE	NORSOPHEN, GEDELITE
HOECHST	HOSTASET, PHENODUR, VULKARESEN
RHONE-POULENC	PROGILITE, REZOPHENE
PCUK	ERVADUR, ERVAPHENE
BASF	LUPHEN, PHENUREN
SUMITOMO	SUMIKON
DYNAMIT-NOBEL	TROLITAN
ROGERS	ROGERS
FUDOW	FUDOWHITE
FENDS	CELORON
BAYER	DESMOPHEN

Aminoplasts
UREA-FORMALDEHYDE RESINS (UFR)

DYNAMIT-NOBEL	ULTRAPAS*
MONTEDISON	GABRITE
CYANAMID	BEETLE
ICI	MOULDRITE*
MONSATO	RESIMENE*
ROHM AND HAAS	RHONITE, UFORMITE
ALLIED	PLASKON*
FMC	SYLPLAST
SIR	SIRIT, SIRITLE
REICHHOLD	BECKAMINE
CIBA-GEIGY	CIBANOIDE, CIBADOINE, CIBAMINE
HOECHST	RESAMINE*
BASF	KAURIT

MELAMINE-FORMALDEHYDE RESINS (MFR)

ICI	MOULDRITE*
SIR	MELSIR
CIBA-GEIGY	MELANTINE, MELOLAM
MONSANTO	RESIMENE*
MONTEDISON	MELBRITE, LAMELITE
CYANAMID	FORMICA, MELMAC, CYMEL
DYNAMIT-NOBEL	ULTRAPAS
BIP	MELMEX
ROHM AND HAAS	UFORMITE
ALLIED	PLASKON
REICHHOLD	DIARON, SUPER, BECKAMINE
PCUK	ERVAMINE
HOECHST	MAPRENAL, RESAMINE*
MITSUI/TOATSU	MELMIGHT
DSM/CYANAMID	AMEL

Furan Systems (section 3.3.2.2)

QUAKER OATS	QUACORR
ASHLAND	HETRON*

Allyl Systems (section 3.3.2.3)

ROGERS	DAPEX
HOOKER/OCCIDENTAL	DUREZ*
FMC	DAPON
ICI	ATLAC*
GOODRICH	KRISTON
ALLIED	PLASKON, DIALL
PPG	CR-39

Alkyd Systems (section 3.3.2.4)

ROHM AND HAAS	DURAPLEX
SHERWIN-WILLIAMS	DYAL

| GE | GLYPTAL |
| ALLIED | PLASKON |

Unsaturated Polyester Systems (section 3.3.2.5)

BAYER	LEGUVAL
MOBAY	MULTRON
GENERAL TIRE	GENPOL, GLYDON
CYANAMID	CYPOR
REICHHOLD	POLYLITE, STYRESOL
UNIROYAL	VIBRIN
ROHM AND HAAS	PARAPLEX
ALLIED	PLASKON*, ACTOL
SIR	SIRESTER
RHONE-POULENC	STRATYL
ICI	ATLAC*
PCUK	UGIKAPON, ERVAPON, ERVAMIX
CDF-CHIMIE	NORSODYNE, NORSOMIX
SNIA	SNIATRON
BP	EPOK
HULS	VESTOPAL
ASHLAND	AROPOL, HETRON*
HOOKER	RUCO, DUREZ*
HITACHI	POLYSET
FREEMAN	STYPOL
HOECHST	HOSTASET
KOPPERS/ICI	DION, CORRES
PPG	SELECTRON
GOODYEAR	VITEL
ARCO	KOPLAC
MONTEDISON	GABRASTER
BASF	PALATAL
URACHEM SHEBY	URALAM
BIP	INJAK
BXL	DSR
SCOTT BADER	CRYSTIC
OCF	ATRYL

Vinylester Systems (section 3.3.2.6)

DOW	DERAKANE
SHELL	EPOCRYL
REICHHOLD	CORROLITE
ASHLAND	HETRON*
ICI/KOPPERS	ATLAC*, DION-VER*

Epoxy Systems (section 3.3.2.7)

SHELL	EPON, EPIKOTE
REICHHOLD	EPOTUF, POLYOX
CIBA-GEIGY	ARALDITE, ARACAST, HYDANTOIN
UNION CARBIDE	BAKELITE*, UNOX

DOW	DER
BAYER	LEKUTHERM
EMSER	GRILONITE, GRILONIT
BASF	EPOXIN
HOECHST	BECKOPOX, BECKIPOX
CELANESE	EPI-REZ
SIR	EPOSIR
ARCO	KOPOX
CDF-CHIMIE	LOPOX
PLENCO	PLENCO
RSA	REPOX
SHOWA	RIPOXY
SUMITOMO	BAKELITE SUMIKON

Urethane/urea Systems (section 3.3.2.8)

DUPONT	ADIPRENE, LYCRA
GOODRICH	ESTANE, TUFTANE
CYANAMID	CYANAPRENE
UNIROYAL	ROYLAR, VIBRATHANE, SPANDEX
GENERAL TIRE	GENTHANE
GOODYEAR	VITHANE
MOBAY	TEXIN, MULTRATHANE, MONDUR, MULTRANOL
UPJOHN	ISOPLAST, PAPI, ISONATE, PELLETHANE, ISONAL, CURITHANE, CASTETHANE
DOW	VORANOL,SPECTRIM
POLAROID	POLATHANE
BASF	LUVIPREN, LUPRANAT, LUPRANOL, LUPRAPHEN, UROFLEX, UROPAC
BAYER	BAYDUR, BAYFLEX*, DESMODUR, DESMOPAN, DESMOFLEX, DESMOPHEN
PCUK	EKAMERE, EKANATE, UGIPOL, LILENE
RHONE-POULENC	SCURANE, SKURANE
SOLVAY	IXOL
CIBA-GEIGY	UREOL
SHELL	CARADOL, CARADATE
AKZO	ELATE
FABELTA	FABELTAN
AVEBE-SCHOLTEN	RESINOL-URESTYL

THERMOSETTING URETHANE ELASTOMERS (TSU)

CYANAMID	CYANAPRENE*
DUPONT	ADIPRENE, SPANDEX, LYCRA
GOODRICH	ESTANE
BAYER	UREPAN, VULKOLLAN
MOBAY	TEXIN, MULTRATHANE
CONAP	CONOTHANE
UPJOHN	CASTETHANE, RIMTHANE
THIOKOL	ELASTOTHANE,SOLITHANE

HOOKER	RUCOTHANE
GENERAL TIRE	GENTHANE
POLAROID	POLATHANE
ALLIED	ARCON
ELASTOGRAN	ELASTOLLAN*, CAPROLAN
QUINN	Q-THANE
UNIROYAL	VYRENE, VIBRATHANE

THERMOPLASTIC URETHANE ELASTOMERS (TPU)

FABELTA	FABELTAN
CYANAMID	CYTOR, CYANAPRENE*
UNIROYAL/GOODRICH	ROYLAR
BAYER	DESMOPAN
ICI	DATAMOULD
UPJOHN	PELLETHANE
THIOKOL	PLASTOTHANE
ELASTOGRAN/BASF	ELASTOLLAN*
GOODRICH	ESTANE
HOOKER	RUCOTHANE

ELASTOMERS (RUBBERS) (section 3.4)

Diene and Related Elastomers (section 3.4.2.1)

POLYISOPRENE, NATURAL RUBBER (PI)

GOODRICH	AMERIPOL* SN
GOODYEAR	NATSYN
SHELL	ISOPRENE, CARIFLEX* IR
HARDMAN	ISOLENE
ANIC	EUROPRENE*IP
JSR	JSR-IR
NIPPON-ZEON	NIPOL* IR
POLYSAR	TRANSPIP
FIRESTONE	HARTEX
MOBAY/BAYER	THERBAN

POLYBUTADIENE (PB)

GENERAL TIRE	DURAGEN
GOODYEAR	BUDENE
GOODRICH	AMERIPOL* CB, HYCAR*
POLYSAR	TAKTENE
ANIC/ENICHEM	EUROPRENE* CIS PB
AM.SYNTH.RUBB.	CISDENE
FIRESTONE	DIENE
TEXAS-US	SYNPOL
COLORADO	RICON
PHILLIPS	SOLPRENE*, BUTAREZ
BAYER	BUNA CB
SHELL	CARIFLEX* BR
ISR	INTENE
HULS	BUNA CB

THIOKOL	THIOKOL HC
NIPPON SODA	NISSO
ARCO	POLY-BD
UBE	UBEPOC
JSR	JSR-BR
NIPPON ZEON	NIPOL* BR

POLYCHLOROPRENE (CR)

DUPONT	DUPRENE, NEOPRENE
PETRO-TEX	CHLOROPRENE
DENKA	DENKA, NEOPRENE
BAYER	PERBUNAN* C, BAYPREN
DISTUGIL/SCHULMAN	BUTACLOR
SHOWA	NEOPRENE W
TOYA SODA	SKYPRENE

POLYISOBUTYLENE, BUTYL RUBBERS (PIB)

GOODRICH	HYCAR*
HARDMAN	KALENE
POLYSAR	POLYSAR*
PETRO-TEX	PETRO-TEX
CITY-SERVICES	BUCAR
CFR	TOTAL
AMOCO	INDOPOL
EXXON/ESSO	VISTANEX, EXXON
NAPHTA-CHIMIE	NAPVIS
BASF	OPPANOL B

Elastomeric Copolymers (section 3.4.2.2)
STYRENE-BUTADIENE RUBBER (SBR)

ISR	INTEX, INTOL
FIRESTONE	BUTAPRENE
GOODYEAR	PLIOLITE, PLIOFLEX
AM.SYNTH.RUBB.	SBR
COPOLYMER	COPO
GENERAL TIRE	GENTRO, GENTAC
HULS	BUNA* SL, EM
GOODRICH/GULF	AMERIPOL* SBR
ASHLAND	BAYTOWN
ICI	BUTAKON* S
SYNPOL	SYNPOL, NAUGATOC
HULES MEX	HUMEX*
SHELL	CARIFLEX* S
SIR	SIREL
SUMITOMO	SUMITOMO SBR
POLYSAR	KRYLENE, KRYNOL
ANIC/ENICHEM	EUROPRENE* SBR

JSR	JSR-SBR
NIPPON ZEON	NIPOL* SBR
ASAHI CHEMICAL	TUFDENE, SOLPRENE
BAYER	BAYSTAL
PHILLIPS	SOLPRENE

ACRYLONITRILE-BUTADIENE RUBBER (NBR)

HULES MEX	HUMEX*
POLYSAR	KRYNAC*, TORNAC
FIRESTONE	FR-N
ANIC	EUROPRENE* N
UNIROYAL	PARACRIL*, NITREX
PCUK	BUTACRIL
COPOLYMER	NYSYN
GOODRICH	HYCAR*
MONTEDISON	ELAPRIM*
BAYER	PERBUNAN* N, THERBAN
ICI	BUTAKON* N
GOODYEAR	CHEMIGUM, CHEMINIC
BP	BREON
NIPPON ZEON	HYCAR, NIPOL* NBR, ZETPOL
JSR	JSR* NBR
COX-NBR	
GOODRICH	HYCAR*

A(NBR/PVC)

POLYSAR	POLYSAR*
UNIROYAL	PARACRIL* OZO
JSRJSR	NV
NIPPON ZEON	NIPOL*
GOODRICH	HYCAR*

ETHYLENE-PROPYLENE RUBBERS (EPR)

UNIROYAL	ROYALENE, ROYALTHERM
COPOLYMER	EPSYN
MONTEDISON	DUTRAL*
DUPONT	NORDEL*
GOODRICH	EPCAR
POLYSAR	POLYSAR*
SHELL	SHELL KMT
EXXON/ESSO/ENJAY	VISTALON
ISR	INTOLAN
ATO	TOTAL EP
HULS	BUNA* AP
MITSUI	EPT
JSR	JSR-EP
SUMITOMO	ESPRENE
DSM	KELTAN*

Ethylene-Related Elastomers (section 3.4.2.3)
CHLORINATED POLYETHYLENE(CPE)

DOW	TYRIN, PLASKON
BAYER	BAYER CM
ICI	HALOTHENE
HOECHST	HOSTALIT Z
BASF	LUTRINGEN

CHLOROSULFONATED POLYETHYLENE (CSPE)

DUPONT	HYPALON

ETHYLENE-VINYLACETATE COPOLYMER (EVA)

USI	VYNATHENE
BAYER	LEVAPREN

ETHYLENE/ACRYLATE COPOLYMER (EAR)

DUPONT	VAMAC

Fluoroelastomers (section 3.4.2.4)

3-M	KEL-F*, FLUOREL*
DUPONT	VITON*, KALREZ
MONTEDISON	TECHNOFLON*
DAIKIN-KOGYO	DAI-EL*, SKF
ASAHI GLASS	AFLAS
PCUK	VOLTALEF*
USSR	SKF

P(VDF-CTFE)

3-M	KEL-F*
PCUK	VOLTALEF*

P(VDF-HFP)

PCUK/3-M	FLUOREL*
MONTEDISON	TECHNOFLON*
DAIKIN-KOGYO	DAI-EL*
DUPONT	VITON*

Silicone Polymers (section 3.4.2.5)

DOW-CORNING	SILASTIC*, SYLGARD
RHONE-POULENC	RHODORSIL
GE	SE, SS, PSE, GENSIL, BLENSIL, TUFEL,FSE
EMERSON-CUMING	ECCOSIL
SWS SILICONES	SWS
BAYER	SILOPREN
OLIN	DEXSIL
ISOCHEM	EPOSILRUB, ISOCHEMSILRUB

Miscellaneous Other Elastomers (section 3.4.2.6)
ACRYLIC RUBBER (AR)

GOODRICH	HYCAR* 4000
HUGHSON-LORD	CHEMLOCK
MONTEDISON	ELAPRIM* AR
CYANAMID	CYANACRIL C,R,L
POLYSAR	KRYNAC*
THIOKOL	THIAKRIL
BORDEN	AKRYLON
UNIROYAL	PARACRIL* OHT
NIPPON ZEON	NIPOL-AR

EPICHLOROHYDRIN RUBBER (ECHR)

GOODRICH	HYDRIN
HERCULES	HERCLOR (C)
OSAKA-SODA	EPICHLOROMER
NIPPON-ZEON	HYDRIN

POLYSULFIDE RUBBERS (SR)

THIOKOL	POLYSULFIDE (FA), THIOKOL LP

PROPYLENEOXIDE RUBBERS (POR)

HERCULES	PAREL

POLYNORBORNENE (PNB)

CDF-CHIMIE	NORSOREX

POLYORGANOPHOSPHAZENES (PPZ)

FIRESTONE	PNF
ETHYL	EYPEL-F

Thermoplastic Elastomers (section 3.4.2.7)
THERMOPLASTIC ELASTOMERS (NON-URETHANE-BASED) (TPE)

SHELL	KRATON D-G, CARIFLEX* TR, ELEXAR TBE
PHILLIPS	SOLPRENE*
ANIC(ENICHEM)	EUROPRENE* SOL T
FIRESTONE	STEREON TBE
DUPONT	HYTREL, SOMEL (OE), NORDEL* (OE), ALCRYN, SURLYN, BEXLOY* V
AKZO	ARNITEL
UNIROYAL/REICHHOLD	ROYALITE, TPR
BAYER	LEVAFLEX EP
MONSANTO	SANTOPRENE, GEOLAST
SCHULMAN	POLYTROPE
ALLIED	ET POLYMER
GOODRICH	TELCAR
ISR	UNIPRENE (OE)
HULS	VESTOPREN TP

EXXON/REICHHOLD	VISTAFLEX
CIBA-GEIGY	REN-FLEX (OE)
DSM	KELTAN* TP
CPT	C-FLEX
HOECHST	HOSTAPREN
GAF/CELANESE	GAFLEX, PTE
MONTEDISON	DUTRAL* TPO (OE), PIBIFLEX
GE	LOMOD
ATO/RITSAN	PEBAX
RHONE-POULENC	DYNYL
UPJOHN/DOW	ESTAMID
GOODYEAR	ELASTUF
ASAHI	TUFPRENE
EASTMAN	EDCEL, EKTAR* TO
NIPPON ZEON	ELASTAR XLNBR/PVC
CELANESE/HOECHST	RITEFLEX TPE

POLYMERIC FIBERS (section 3.5.1)

Rayon

COURTAULDS	VINCEL, LIRELLE
	FMC, AMERICAN VISCOSE AVISCO*,
	AVRIL
SNIA	TRITAL
ENKA	ZANTREL
DUPONT	CORDURA

Acetate

COURTAULDS	DICEL, TRICEL
CELANESE	FORTISAN, ARNEL

Olefinic

HERCULES	HERCULON
COURTAULDS	COURLENE
VECTRA/	
CHEVRON/ENJAY	VECTRA
FMC,	
AMERICAN VISCOSE	AVISCO*
PHILLIPS	MARLEX

Vinylics

RHODIACETA	RHOVYL
GOODRICH	DARLAN
FIRESTONE	VELON

Acrylics

DUPONT	ORLON
CHEMSTRAND/	
MONSANTO	ACRILAN
CYANAMID	CRESLAN

COURTAULDS	COURTELLE
CRYLOR	CRYLOR
DOW/BADISCHE	ZEFRAN
EASTMAN	VEREL
UNION CARBIDE	DYNEL

Nylons

DUPONT	ANTRON
BRITISH NYLON SPINNERS	BRI
CHEMSTRAND/ MONSANTO	BLUE-C*
CELANESE	CELON
ALLIED	CAPROLAN
BAYER	PERLON
ICI	BRULON, SUTRON
MONSANTO	ASTROTURF, CADON
PHILLIPS	STRYTON

Polyesters

CEL-CIL	TERYLENE
DUPONT	DACRON
TEIJIN	TETORAN
FIBER IND./ CELANESE	FORTREL
EASTMAN	KODEL
BEAUNIT	VYCRON
HYSTRON	TREVIRA

Chapter 4

PROPERTIES AND STANDARD TESTING

4.1 INTRODUCTION

Any product application involving a material is associated with requirements referred to here as "constraints." Constraints may involve the shape and size of the product (for aesthetic or functional reasons), the cost of the product (material and processing costs), and the service performance of the product. The service performance is a function of the product shape and or size, as well as the material properties.

A wide assortment of distinct material properties has been established, which is relevant to polymeric materials and products.

A rigorous assessment of the performance of a material, with respect to a specific property, would ideally require a thorough scientific study, which would be long and difficult and would require a well-qualified researcher.

Standard testing, on the other hand, can be viewed as a convenient shortcut, which allows the rapid generation of quantitative information on material properties. Such information is often used to rank materials for the property associated with a test.

This chapter discusses a majority of the standard tests developed and widely used for plastics. The development of standard tests is normally the work of committees and is based on experience and consensus. Each standard test is the subject of a document, written in such a way that a good technician, with access to appropriate commercial equipment, will find all the information needed to carry out the test and to obtain results that should not depend significantly on human factors.

The development and follow-up work on standard tests is the responsibility of private or public, national or international organizations, such as those listed at the end of this introduction. Most of the standard tests discussed in this chapter are associated with the American Society for the Testing of Materials (ASTM).

Each standard test is given a code number by the sponsoring organization (e.g., ASTM D790 or ISO 178 for similar flexural tests). A list of code numbers for similar or related tests is provided in Appendix 4.

Since most tests require the use of commercial testing equipment, representative examples of U.S. and foreign suppliers are also given when appropriate. As discussed in Chapter 1, no tables of property data are presented in this book, but qualified examples of numerical values, for high and low levels in particular, are systematically given in the text.

4.1.1   Standards and Organizations

AFNOR	Association Française de Normalisation
ANSI	American National Standards Institute
ASTM	American Society for the Testing of Materials
BGA	Bundesgesundheitsamt
BNQ	Bureau de Normalisation du Québec
BSI	British Standards Institution
CSA	Canadian Standards Association
DIN	Deutsche Industrie Normen (Deutsches Institut für Normung)
DNA	Deutsche Normen Ausschuss
FAA	Federal Aviation Agency
FDA	Food and Drug Administration
ISO	International Standards Organization
IEC	International Electrical Commission
MIL	U.S. Military Specifications
N	Niederländishe Norm
NEMA	National Electrical Manufacturers Association
NSF	National Sanitation Foundation
SAE	Society of Automotive Engineers
SPI	Society of the Plastics Industry
UL	Underwriter's Laboratory
UNIPLAST	Ente Nazionale Italiano di Unificazione
VDE	Verband Deutscher Elektrotechniker

4.2   MATERIALS AND TEST SPECIMENS

4.2.1   Test Specimen Preparation

Most standard tests require the use of test specimens of specific geometry (shape and dimensions). The method of preparation (fabrication) of test specimens depends on a number of factors, including the type of polymer and the form in which the material is available.

In the case of rigid plastics, test specimens can be molded into the desired shape. Injection molding is a rapid way of obtaining many test specimens, but these specimens can feature a nonhomogeneous structure, as well as orientation (anisotropy), and the properties can be affected significantly by the process parameters. Compression molding, a relatively slow process, tends to give homogeneous and isotropic test specimens, but the process is not representative of most commercial fabrication processes for thermoplastics. Compression and transfer molding methods are most convenient for thermosetting plastics and vulcanizable or reactive elastomers.

The preparation of test specimens from rigid plastics in stock form may involve machining (sawing, milling, etc.). High-speed routering, using a suitable guide or template, is a convenient way of machining test specimens from rigid flat stock (plaques).

In the case of soft or thin plastic or elastomeric flat stock (films, sheets, etc.), test specimens can be stamped out (die-cut) with a suitable sharp cutter.

In general, one must realize that the testing of test specimens does not always precisely reflect the actual properties of fabricated objects, because of differences in factors such as structure (morphology), orientation, or residual or internal stresses. This is particularly important for crystallizing thermoplastics.

4.2.2 Test Specimen Conditioning

The properties of polymeric materials tend to be strongly affected by temperature, and it is, therefore, important to specify the temperature of the material during a test. A number of polymeric materials (polyamides, cellulosics, etc.) can absorb small amounts of water (moisture), which affects many of their properties. Polymeric materials have a low thermal conductivity and the movement of water molecules in polymers is also slow. Reaching thermal and moisture equilibrium can, therefore, be a relatively long process (1-4 days), which is referred to as "test specimen conditioning."

Two parameters are generally controlled in conditioning: the temperature and the relative humidity (RH) of the external atmosphere. A most common standard atmosphere corresponds to 23°C (73.4°F) and 50% RH and is sometimes referred to as "23/50." Conditions such as (27/65) or (20/65) are also used for so-called normal temperatures. There are also preferred subnormal (low) and above-normal (elevated) temperatures. At high temperatures, the humidity factor may become irrelevant.

Conditioning is often conducted in suitable preconditioning cabinets, and the actual testing in suitable test chambers.

Two examples of test specimens are shown in figures 4.1 and 4.2.

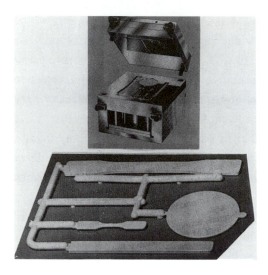

Fig. 4.1

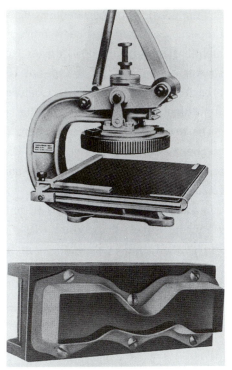

Fig. 4.2

Figure 4.1 · Injection molding of test specimens (mold cavity and molded set) **[MUD]**

Figure 4.2 · Die cutting of test specimens (stamping press and die cutter)

4.3 SHORT-TERM CONVENTIONAL MECHANICAL TESTING

Fabricated parts can be subjected to steady or unsteady, simple or complex loadings, and the testing of materials or parts under actual conditions of use, while obviously ideal, can be time-consuming or difficult. A number of mechanical tests have thus been developed that can be carried out quickly, require fairly simple equipment (universal testing machine and simple accessories), and provide quantitative data, allowing at least a preliminary ranking of materials for mechanical applications. Such tests are often referred to as "short-term conventional mechanical tests," and include primarily tensile and flexural testing but also compression, torsion, shear, tear, and biaxial stressing.

4.3.1 Universal Testing Machines

A number of standard mechanical tests are performed on so-called universal testing machines, fitted with appropriate accessories. Such machines basically consist of a rigid frame (F) and a movable crosshead (C) (Fig. 4.3). The crosshead motion, and the force involved, can be set or recorded during a test. Some machines are electro-mechanically driven ([M]), while others are servo-hydraulically operated ([H]). The speed of deformation, or the rate of loading, can be controlled, as these parameters are known to have a rather strong effect on the mechanical behavior of polymeric materials. The range of speeds or rates on universal testing machines is, however, relatively limited, and very slow or very fast testing (creep, stress-relaxation, impact) is normally carried out on specialized equipment.

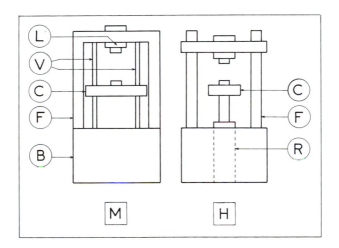

Figure 4.3 · **Universal testing machines** · [M] Mechanical; [H] Hydraulic; (L) Load cell; (V) Screws; (C) Crosshead; (F) Frame; (B) Base; (R) Ram (cylinder)

4.3.2 Testing Modes

4.3.2.1 Tensile

Tensile testing (ASTM D638 and equivalents) requires dumbbell (dogbone) test specimens (Fig. 4.4 [S]). Such test specimens feature a straight zone of uniform cross section (gauge zone) (G), over which the deformation and corresponding stress are uniform, and two end tabs (T) of larger cross-section, over which the test specimen is held (dumbbell or dogbone shape). For polymeric materials, test specimens usually have a uniform thickness and the tabs are pinched in no-slip jaws (clamps, grips) attached to the testing machine. Standard ASTM D638 tensile test specimens of types I, IV and V are represented in Figure 4.2.

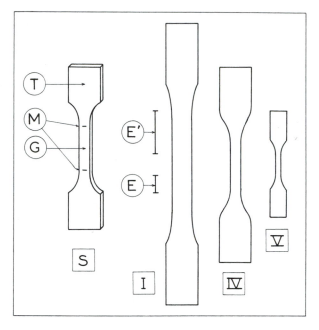

Figure 4.4 · **Tensile test specimens** · [S] Dumbbell test specimen; [I] ASTM type I; [IV] ASTM type IV; [V] ASTM type V; (T) End tab; (M) Gauge mark; (G) Gauge zone; (E) 1 cm scale; (E′) 1 in scale

When a dumbbell tensile test specimen is pulled, the displacement of the jaws is not exactly proportional to the tensile deformation in the gauge zone, even for small deformations. Extensometers have been developed, which allow the recording of the deformation between gauge marks (M). Some clip-on types are particularly suitable for rigid test specimens, and no-contact types use optical principles to follow the displacement. Strain gauges, common for metals, are not generally used for polymers.

In view of the known effect of speed on the mechanical behavior of polymeric materials, the strain rate must be specified. For a given test specimen, it corresponds to specified movable jaw speeds. Typically, 5 mm/min or 0.25 in/min, for a test specimen with a 100 mm (4 in)-long gauge zone, is referred to as a "moderate speed" and the corresponding test as a "short-term (quasi-static) test." The tensile behavior of polymeric materials can vary widely   as a function of the type of polymeric system, as well as the temperature or speed of testing and other factors. A full stress-strain curve is the ideal way of reporting the tensile behavior, but specific quantities are generally reported, which include the tensile (Young's) modulus E, the tensile yield stress σ_y when applicable, the tensile strength (ultimate or at break) σ_b and also the elongations at yield (ϵ_y) and at break (ϵ_b).

The tensile modulus E, a measure of the material stiffness, is commonly reported in mega- or gigapascals (MPa or GPa) and kilo-or megapounds per square inch (kpsi or Mpsi) (1 Mpsi $\approx$ 6.9 GPa). The stiffest unreinforced plastics correspond to $E \approx$ 3.5 GPa or $E \approx$ 500 kpsi. For most engineering plastics, E is in the range 2-3.5 GPa (300-500 kpsi); for polyethylene PE, E ranges from about 70 MPa (10 kpsi) for LDPE to 700 MPa (100 kpsi) for HDPE. For elastomers, E is in the range 0.7-7 MPa (0.1-1 kpsi). In comparison, the tensile modulus of metals is much higher ($E \approx$ 200 GPa or 29 Mpsi for steel and $E \approx$ 69 GPa or 10 Mpsi for aluminum); their density, however, is also much higher. Glass, a common reinforcement for polymers, has a high tensile modulus ($E \approx$ 69 GPa or 10 Mpsi), and for composites with unidirectional glass fiber reinforcement the modulus can reach $E \approx$ 35 GPa or 5 Mpsi, while for short glass-fiber-reinforced engineering thermoplastics it can reach $E \approx$ 15 GPa or 2 Mpsi.

The tensile yield stress σ_y of a ductile material, which corresponds to the onset of significant permanent deformation, is often the limiting stress for applications, rather than the tensile strength (at break) σ_b which corresponds to the actual rupture of the test specimen. Values of σ_y or σ_b for unreinforced engineering plastics range from about 50 MPa or 7.5 kpsi to 90 MPa or 13 kpsi and can reach about 150 MPa or 22 kpsi for short glass fiber-reinforced grades. Corresponding values for polyethylenes PE are about 7 MPa or 1 kpsi for LDPE and 35 MPa or 5 kpsi for HDPE. For comparison, corresponding values for aluminum alloys are in the range 40-500 MPa (6-75 kpsi). The range is about 40-2000 MPa (6-300 kpsi) for steels.

Elongations at break ϵ_b range from lows of 0.01 (1%) for brittle plastics, such as polystyrene PS, to highs of 6 (600%) for ductile LDPE. For most engineering plastics, the range is about 0.15-1 (15-100%).

Tensile tests provide a convenient way of assessing the anisotropy (orientation) of a plaque by machining test specimens in perpendicular (orthogonal) directions. Other effects, such as weld (knit) line strength, can be assessed with dumbbell test specimens injection molded in cavities double-gated at opposite ends.

Another property related to tensile loading, Poisson's ratio, can be determined (ASTM E132). It is of fundamental rather than practical interest.

4.3.2.2 Flexural

Flexural testing is most commonly carried out in the three-point bending mode (ASTM D790) illustrated in Figure 4.5. It is generally more convenient than tensile testing to assess the stiffness of rigid materials, but less convenient for strength measurements.

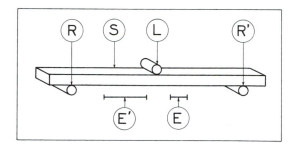

Figure 4.5 · **Three-point bending** · (R),(R′) Supports; (S) Test specimen; (L) Loading; (E) 1 cm scale; (E′) 1 in scale

The deformations and corresponding stresses in a test specimen, subjected to flexural testing, are highly nonuniform. In particular, across the thickness, the deformation changes gradually from a compressive mode to a tensile mode. Analysis of the overall deformation of a test specimen is often done using classical strength of materials assumptions, yielding such quantities as flexural modulus E_f and flexural strength σ_{bf}. It must be realized, however, that such quantities may not correlate well with corresponding tensile quantities, such as tensile modulus E_t or tensile strength σ_{bt}, if the test specimens feature a variation of structure across the thickness, a common fact in injection molded thermoplastics, particularly the crystallizing or short fiber-reinforced types, or if the tensile and compressive behaviors of the material are significantly different.

Test specimens for three-point bending tests must be slender to ensure the validity of the strength of materials analysis, which neglects shear, and a span to thickness ratio of 16 to 40 is normally used. The recording of the load as a function of the central deflection is used to calculate the flexural modulus, as well as a flexural strength if the material fails in the test. The flexural strength corresponds to the calculated maximum stress in the test specimen at the onset of failure, which the strength of materials analysis predicts to occur on the surface ("outer fiber"), in the cross-section subjected to the maximum bending moment, i.e. the central point where the load is applied.

In four-point bending tests, the test specimen is still supported near its ends, but the load is applied at two intermediate points, reducing the load concentration.

For quick flexural stiffness assessments, other methods are sometimes used. One such method (ASTM D747) uses a test specimen clamped at one end and bent in a cantilever mode, allowing large flexural deformations (Fig. 4.6). Measurements of torque and angular deformation are made. The method is used primarily for comparative assessment of flexural stiffness and strength; it is often associated with the names of corresponding testing equipment suppliers (Tinius-Olsen, Teledyne Taber, Suter). Another method (DIN 51230) uses relatively small test specimens bent in a four-point mode (Dynstat).

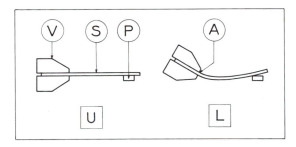

Figure 4.6 · **Cantilever bending** · [U] Unloaded; [L] Loaded; (V) Vise; (S) Test specimen; (P) Fixed support; (A) Axis of vise rotation

Reported values of flexural moduli (E_f) are generally somewhat higher than corresponding tensile (E_t) values, but a meaningful comparison would be possible only if identical test specimen were used. Reported flexural strength values are practically always significantly higher than corresponding tensile values, most frequently about 50% higher and sometimes over 100% higher. This probably reflects a higher resistance to compression. It must be emphasized that the role of the strength-of-materials assumptions is critical in the computation of flexural strength values, which are best viewed as "apparent" values, more useful for comparative purposes for test specimens of identical geometries, than as intrinsic material properties.

4.3.2.3 Compression

Compression testing of polymeric materials is not as widely done as tensile or flexural testing, partly because it is not very easy to perform and to analyze.

The most common test (ASTM D695) uses small test specimens in the form of square prisms (parallelepipeds) or right cylinders, as illustrated in Figure 4.7. The test specimens are compressed between parallel plates (anvil faces) at a small rate (usually 0.05 min^{-1} or 5%/min). The compression (compressive) modulus E_c can be determined for very small deformation and should normally be equal to the tensile modulus E_t. Rigid and brittle polymers may fracture (shatter) at a certain compressive stress, which is then referred to as the "compressive strength" σ_{bc} and is generally significantly higher than the corresponding tensile strength σ_{bt} (sometimes by a factor 2 or 3). Rigid and ductile materials may display a clear compressive yield behavior, allowing the determination of a compressive yield stress σ_{yc}. For some materials, the deformation gradually leads to a severely distorted shape, and the compressive stress at a moderate arbitrary (reference) strain level, such as 0.1 or 10%, is sometimes used as an indication of the resistance to compression loading for comparison purposes.

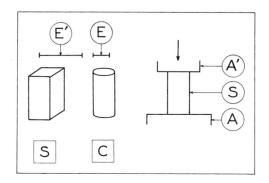

Figure 4.7 · **Compression testing** · [S] "Square" test specimens; [C] "Circular" test specimens; (A),(A′) Anvils; (S) Test specimen; (E) 1 cm scale; (E′) 1 in scale

Polymeric material do not generally fail in a compression mode, but they are often subjected to compressive loads for long periods of time and their deformation should not become excessive. A compression test designed to assess time effects (ASTM D621) is discussed in section 4.8.1.

4.3.2.4 Torsion

Torsion is a mode of loading that involves a nonuniform shear deformation. A shear modulus **G** can be determined from a torsion test, from the knowledge of the moment (torque) applied, and from the small angular deformation and test specimen dimensions, using classical strength of materials formulas. The most logical test specimen geometry (Fig. 4.8) is a right cylinder (bar) [C]. One end is held in a stationary chuck-like clamp, while the other end is held in a clamp that can be rotated.

Since polymeric materials are more commonly available in flat form (plaques), the test specimen for some of the standard torsion test (ASTM D1043) is a parallelepiped (bar) [R].

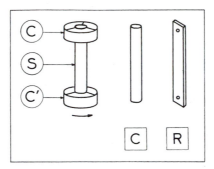

Figure 4.8 · **Torsion testing** · [C] Circular cross-section; [R] Rectangular cross-section; (C),(C') Clamps; (S) Test specimen

The shear modulus **G** of a simple material is a function of the tensile modulus **E** as well as the Poisson's ratio μ, but since μ is a weak factor, **G** is roughly proportional to **E**.

Torsion testing is a convenient way of assessing the effect of temperature on the modulus (stiffness, rigidity) of polymeric materials and also their dynamic properties.

4.3.2.5 Shear

A number of applications of polymeric materials, and several fabrication techniques, involve the failure of the material under shear deformations and tests have been developed to assess the resistance to shear.

A punch-type shear test (ASTM D732) uses disk-shaped test specimens (S) clamped in a stationary block [(C) and (C')] over a circular hole (die), as illustrated in Figure 4.9. A movable punch (P) is used to shear off the central portion of the test specimen. The force required is recorded and, when divided by the sheared area, gives a shear strength τ_b. Because of the complex deformation that may actually take place during a test, however, the shear strength may be a significant function of the test specimen thickness, and therefore, not a true material property. Reported shear strength values for engineering plastics are in the range 40-50 MPa or about 6-8 kpsi.

A similar test, often referred to as a "double shear test," is particularly convenient for materials that can be easily obtained as cylindrical bars (Fig. 4.10). A shear strength can also be calculated.

Shear tests are also very appropriate to assess the strength of adhesive bonds between adherent substrates. They are referred to as "lap shear test" [S] or "double lap shear test" [D] which are particularly convenient because of the symmetry involved (Fig. 4.11).

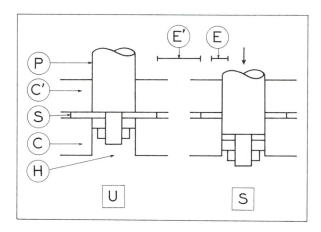

Figure 4.9 • **Punch shear test** • [U] Unloaded; [S] After shearing; (P) Circular punch; (C′) Upper clamp; (S) Test specimen; (C) Lower clamp; (H) Hole; (E) 1 cm scale; (E′) 1 in scale

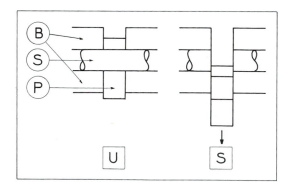

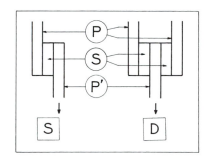

Fig. 4.10   Fig. 4.11

Figure 4.10 • **Double shear test** • [U] Unloaded; [S] After shearing; (B) Holding block; (S) Test specimen; (P) Shear plate

Figure 4.11 • **Lap shear tests** • [S] Single lap; [D] Double lap; (P) Stationary plate(s); (S) Test specimen(s); (P′) Moving plate

4.3.2.6 Tear

Flexible plastics and elastomers, in sheets and film form, often fail in a tearing mode, and their resistance to tearing is often inadequately reflected by such properties as tensile strength. The question of tear resistance is very complex, and, as a result, no single, simple test is very satisfactory.

Standard tearing tests involve a variety of test specimen geometries (angle tear, trouser tear, etc.), which are illustrated in Figure 4.12. They are conducted either on universal testing machines or on specialized equipment (Elmendorf, etc.). They generally involve a cut, slit, or nick, which is made before or during the test itself (razor or other blade, pointer, or needle). The quantitative determination of a tear resistance is often associated with a somewhat subjective interpretation of the test results.

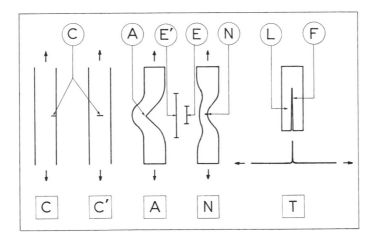

Figure 4.12 · **Tear tests** · [C] Edge cut; [C′] Center cut; [A] Angle tear; [N] Crescent tear [T] Trouser tear; (C) Cut; (A) Sharp corner; (N) Nick; (L) Leg; (F) Slit; (E) 1 cm scale; (E′) 1 in scale

4.3.2.7 Biaxial Stress

A biaxial state of stress is developed when a circular diaphragm, pipe, or container is subjected to pressure (Fig. 4.13). This is the basis for a number of quick-burst tests (ASTM D774, D1599). The pressure at failure (rupture), or the stress calculated from such pressure, is reported. It must be noted that, in the case of pipes, the quick-burst situation may be encountered in accidental pressure surging, but the evaluation of the long-term resistance to lower sustained pressures is generally more representative and is the subject of several test methods in the pipe industry.

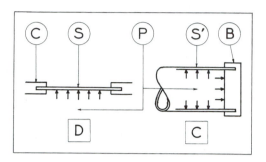

Figure 4.13 · **Biaxial stress testing** · [D] Pressurized diaphragm; [C] Pressurized cylinder; (C) Annular clamp; (S) Flat test specimen; (P) Pressure; (S′) Tubular test specimen; (B) End caps

Several examples of short-term conventional mechanical testing are shown in figures 4.14-4.19.

Figure 4.14 · Universal testing machine and control console (screw drive type) **[INSTRON]**

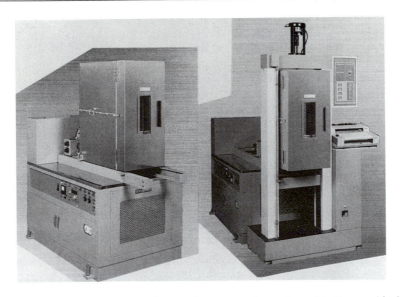

Figure 4.15 · Environmental chamber (on stand or mounted on universal testing machine) **[TOYO SEIKI]**

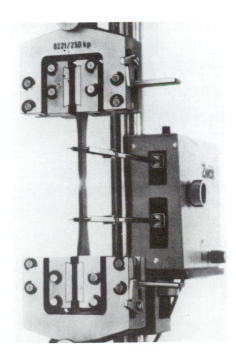

Figure 4.16 · Recording extensometer
[ZWICK]

Figure 4.17 · Stiffness tester (flexure)
[TINIUS OLSEN]

Figure 4.18 · Three-point and four-point flexural tests **[ZWICK]**

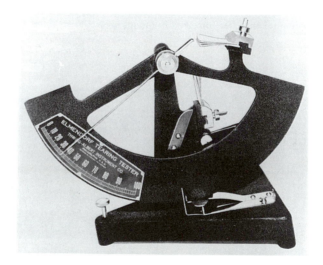

Figure 4.19 · Elmendorf tearing tester **[THWING-ALBERT]**

4.4 HARDNESS

The rapid assessment of the stiffness or rigidity of materials is a very desirable objective, which is partially met by hardness tests.

Hardness tests normally involve the quantitative assessment of the resistance to penetration (indentation) of a material by an indentor (impresser), which can have a variety of shapes (sphere, pyramid, cone, etc.). While flat and relatively thick test specimens, used in conjunction with bench-top instruments, are normally recommended, local measurements can often be performed on parts of complex shapes with hand-held instruments.

For polymeric materials in particular, the interpretation of results in terms of conventional mechanical characteristics is generally difficult, as a result of the combination of elastic and plastic nonhomogeneous deformations and the time dependence of the mechanical properties. The results of different tests are also often difficult to compare, and the relationships or correlations between scales, which appear in publications, are only very approximate. The various tests, however, can be very valuable, particularly for comparing generally similar materials. Hardness measurements are often indicative of scratch, wear, and abrasion resistance, machinability, etc., but any such relationship should be considered with caution.

Hardness measurements basically involve the surface of test specimens, and since it is established that many polymeric materials and processing techniques lead to structural inhomogeneities, particularly near the surface of parts, results should be interpreted in the appropriate context.

4.4.1   Rockwell Hardness

The Rockwell hardness test (ASTM D785) uses a spherical steel indentor of diameter **d** (Fig. 4.20 [R]). A minor dead load F_m (usually 10 kgf or 98 N or 22 lbf) is first applied to ensure good contact, followed by the major dead load F_M and a return to the minor load F_m; the whole procedure taking about 45 s. The difference in depth of indentation between the second and third step is the basis for defining the Rockwell hardness number. For polymeric materials, only two conditions are normally used: condition **R**, for softer materials, corresponds to **d** = 1/2 in (12.7 mm) and F_M

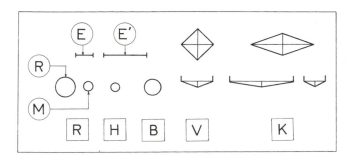

Figure 4.20 · **Hardness test indentors** · [R] Rockwell; [H] Ball; [B] Brinell; [V] Vickers; [K] Knoop-tukon; (R) Rockwell R indentor; (M) Rockwell M indentor; (E) 1 cm scale; (E′) 1 in scale

= 60 kgf (589 N or 132 lbf) for a range R20 to R120; condition M, for stiffer materials, corresponds to **d** = 1/4 in (6.35 mm) and F_M = 100 kgf (981 N or 220 lbf) for a range M20-M140.   Overlap covers approximately the range R100-R120 or M20-M30.   Because of the relatively large size of the indentor, a minimum test specimen thickness of 6 mm (1/4 in) and an area over 6 cm^2 (1 in^2) are recommended; stacking of suitable thin specimens is possible.

Rigid thermosets often give Rockwell hardnesses in the range of M100-M120. Engineering thermoplastics are often in the range R110-R120.

4.4.2   Shore Hardness

The Shore hardness test (ASTM D2240) is associated with the Durometer instrument.   It features pin-shaped indentors of two types (A or D), illustrated in Figure 4.21 [S], which protrude from a flat surface and are loaded by a calibrated spring.   The instrument is pressed against the test specimen until the surfaces come in close contact.   The indentor penetration is related to a Shore (Durometer) hardness number.   The A scale, using the blunt indentor, is suitable for soft materials, such as elastomers, and covers the range 20A-95A.   The D scale, with the pointed indentor, is intended for harder materials, such as soft plastics, and generally covers a range 40D-90D; 40D corresponds approximately to 90A.

Soft rubbers are in the range 20A-30A, and include examples such as rubber bands and soft erasers.   Tire treads are in the range 55A-70A.   Typewriter rolls correspond to about 90A.   Soft plastics, such as low density polyethylene (LDPE), correspond to about 45D, while high density PE and other medium stiffness plastics correspond to about 65D.   Bowling balls correspond to about 90D.

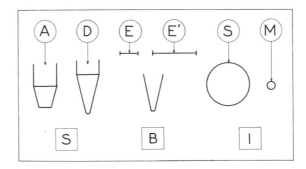

Figure 4.21 · **Hardness test indentors** · [S] Shore; [B] Barcol; [I] IRHD; (A) Shore A indentor; (D) Shore D indentor; (S) IRHD standard indentor; (M) IRHD micro indentor; (E) 1 mm scale; (E′) 0.1 in scale

4.4.3 Ball Hardness

The ball indentometer method, commonly used in Europe, uses a spherical indentor of diameter d = 5 mm (0.2 in) (Fig. 4.20 [B]), with a load F = 36.5 kgf (358 N or 80 lbf). Results are reported in stress or pressure units (N/mm^2 or MPa), often under the abbreviation "HK." Typical values for relatively soft and stiff engineering plastics are HK ≈ 100 N/mm^2 and HK ≈ 150 N/mm^2, respectively.

4.4.4 International Rubber Hardness

The international rubber hardness method (ASTM D1415) bears some similarity with the Rockwell hardness method. The standard test uses a spherical indentor (ball) of diameter d ≈ 2.5 mm (≈ 1 in) and a major (high) load F_M I 5.6 N (≈ 1.25 lbf), while the micro-test corresponds to a d ≈ 0.4 mm (≈ 0.015 in) and F_M ≈ 0.15 N (≈ 0.035 lbf) (Fig. 4.21 [I]). In both cases, the minor load is about 5% of the major load. The ball penetration is related to international rubber hardness degrees (IRHD), which correspond approximately to Shore A values. For highly elastic rubbers, a fairly good correlation is found between IRHD readings and the Young's modulus E of the material.

4.4.5 Barcol Hardness

The hardness of rigid plastics, particularly that of reinforced thermosetting plastics, is often reported in Barcol hardness units (ASTM D2583). The Barcol (Barber and Coleman) impresser, uses an indentor similar to that used in the Shore D method, except for a flat tip instead of a rounded one (Fig. 4.21 [B]). The minimum recommended test specimen thickness is about 1.5 mm (≈ 1/16 in). As in the Shore methods, the indentor protrudes from a surface that is pressed against the test specimen. The indentor is loaded with a calibrated spring and its penetration is related to a Barcol hardness number. The usual range is about 50B-90B. Barcol 60B is roughly equivalent to Shore 80D and to Rockwell M100.

4.4.6 Miscellaneous Methods

Several methods for assessing the hardness of metals, in particular, are based on the impression left into the material by an indentor after its removal. It thus reflects primarily a permanent plastic deformation. Since most polymeric materials are viscoelastic, recovery is progressive and complex, and these methods are often difficult to use.

The Brinell test involves a spherical indentor of diameter $d = 10$ mm (≈ 0.4 in) (Fig. 4.20 [B]), and the area of the impression is measured. Results are reported in stress (pressure) units. An acetal, for example, is reported to have a Brinell hardness of 205 N/mm² HB.

The Vickers test involves a square pyramidal indentor of angle 136° (Fig. 4.20 [V]). Results are also reported in stress (pressure) units. A reported value for an acetal is 185 N/mm² HV. The pyramidal shape is also used in a common micro-hardness instrument (Wallace).

The Knoop-Tukon test (ASTM D1474) involves an elongated pyramidal indentor (Fig. 4.20 [K]). The asymmetrical shape of the Knoop indentor is claimed to have certain advantages over the regular pyramid, and it appears to have a potential for detecting material anisotropy, through comparison of measurements corresponding to different indentor orientations.

A method, occasionally used for the quick assessment of the hardness of plastics, involves the observation of the trace or scratch left by sharp pencils of standard hardnesses (4H, H, HB, B, etc.), which are run across the surface. Pencil hardness determination is rather subjective, but it is practical and relevant for coatings, in particular.

A related method, developed by geologists and mineralogists, is also based on the observation that harder materials scratch softer ones. It has led to the Mohs hardness scale (1-10). Fingernail, a handy standard, rates about 2 on the scale and polymers, in general, are in the range 1 to slightly over 2.

See figures 4.22-4.24 for three examples of hardness testing.

Figure 4.22 · Hardness tester (Durometer) **[SHORE]**

Figure 4.23 · Hardness tester (IRHD) [ZWICK]

Figure 4.24 · Hardness tester (Barcol impressor) [GARDNER]

4.5   FRICTION, WEAR, AND ABRASION

The study of the frictional characteristics of materials is sometimes referred to as "tribology" and the corresponding properties as "frictional," "tribological," and even "tribonetic" properties.

Tribological characteristics are involved in such applications as sleeve or rolling element bearings, bushings, thrust plates, bearing pads, cams, vane tips, seals, piston rings, and gears.

4.5.1   Coefficient of Friction

The primary tribological characteristic is the coefficient of friction between two surfaces. The coefficient of friction μ is defined as the ratio of the sliding force F_s to the normal force F_n or the ratio of the shear stress S (sliding force divided by area of contact) to the normal pressure P_n. For many pairs of materials, such as metals, the coefficient of friction is well defined and largely independent of experimental factors. For polymeric pairs, or pairs involving a polymer and another material, the measured coefficient of friction μ tends to be a significant, and sometimes strong, function of several parameters.

The nature of each material in the pair can be important and thus the coefficient of friction is not strictly a material property. Comparisons should normally correspond to a standard (reference) mating surface (heterofriction) or to the same material (homofriction).

A basic distinction must generally be made between the static (starting) coefficient μ_s and the dynamic (kinetic, sliding) coefficient μ_d, the former being generally higher than the latter. This question can be associated, in particular, with stick-slip, squeaking, and chattering. In the case of dynamic friction, the velocity V can be a significant factor. A typical testing velocity is 25 cm/s ($\approx$ 50 ft/min).

The normal or contact pressure P_n (load) can also be a significant factor; a typical practical value being about 0.2 MPa ($\approx$ 30 psi).

The surface finish (roughness) of rigid mating surfaces, in particular, can also have an effect on friction. In the case of metals, it is often characterized by an averaged peak-to-valley distance, determined with a profilometer, and expressed in micrometers μm (RMS) or microinches (μin) (RMS); a typical value for smooth steel is about 0.25 μm (RMS) or $\approx$ 10 μin (RMS).

The presence of a lubricating fluid at the interface tends to lower the friction. A number of additives can also contribute to reducing the friction of polymeric materials.

They include fluorocarbon polymers, bronze, brass, graphite and carbon, and molybdenum sulfide (moly).

One simple method for the determination of the static and dynamic coefficients of friction μ_s and μ_d uses an inclined plate (Fig. 4.25 [G]); gravity being responsible for the sliding force F_s, as well as the normal force F_n.

Another method uses a horizontally towed sled (Fig. 4.25 [T]), more suitable for assessing velocity effects, at least within a reasonable range.

Representative values, for the coefficient of friction μ of polymeric materials against metals, range from about 0.05 for fluorocarbon polymers (PTFE) to 2.5 for some rubbers. It is generally below 0.3 for engineering plastics suitable for frictional applications such as acetal PMO and polyamides PA.

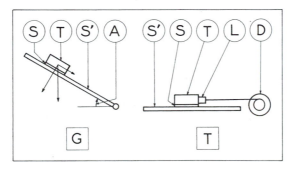

Figure 4.25 · **Coefficient of friction measurement** · [G] Inclined plate method; [T] Towed sled method; (S) Test specimen surface (sled); (S′) Mating surface (plate); (T) Sled; (A) Angle of plate inclination; (L) Load cell; (D) Sled drive

4.5.2 Wear

The term "wear" is usually employed to describe a progressive damage at the interface of two sliding surfaces. A distinction is sometimes made between adhesive wear and abrasive wear. The former expression is associated with a tendency for the surfaces to bond locally, followed by a breakage of the bonded area, and it normally corresponds to smooth surfaces. The latter expression is associated with the removal of fragments torn off from the softer surface, and it normally corresponds to a rough, hard, i.e. abrading, second surface.

Two major factors affecting the wear of sliding surfaces are the relative velocity V at the interface and the contact (normal) pressure P_n (or just P). The quantitative assessment of the wear characteristics of materials is complex, and only basic principles are presented here.

Even at low velocities **V**, excessive pressures **P** will prevent the proper operation of sliding mechanisms involving polymeric materials. Conversely, very high velocities **V** will cause unacceptable temperature rises, even at low pressures **P**. It has further been shown experimentally that if the product **PV** does not exceed a limiting value (**LPV** or **PV** limit), for a given system, the operation is basically satisfactory and only reasonable wear occurs. Under such conditions, the rate of wear, expressed as the thickness reduction per unit time, is roughly proportional to the product **PV**, and the proportionality constant is called the "wear factor" **K**. It thus becomes possible to characterize quantitatively the resistance to wear of a sliding system, and if a reference surface is used (for example, stainless steel with a specified finish), the wear resistance of different polymers can be compared.

Representative results for a fluorocarbon polymer (PTFE), which has outstanding sliding properties (lubricity), are the following: maximum static pressure: about 17 MPa ($\approx$ 1000 psi); maximum speed under low load: about 50 cm/s ($\approx$ 100 ft/min); **PV** limit for continuous service: about 0.7 (MPa · cm/s) or $\approx$ 200 (psi · ft/min); wear factor **K**: about 2500 (inch/h, psi · ft/min).

Corresponding results for strong engineering plastics widely used for sliding mechanisms (acetal POM or polyamide PA) are the following: maximum static pressure: about 35 MPa ($\approx$ 5000 psi); maximum speed under low load: about 150 cm/s ($\approx$ 300 ft/min); **PV** limit for continuous service: 3.5 (MPa · cm/s) or $\approx$ 1000 (psi · ft/min); wear factor **K**: 50 (inch/h, psi · ft/min).

For an inexpensive thermosetting plastic (phenolic PF), the PV limit for continuous use would be about 0.35 (MPa · cm/s) or $\approx$ 100 (psi · ft/min), and the wear factor **K** about 1000 (inch/h, psi · ft/min).

Wear tests are conducted on devices featuring a variety of modes of sliding and geometries (Fig. 4.26). These include unidirectional or alternating (reciprocating) motion, pin-cylinder [P], bar-cylinder [B], pin-disk [D], and thrust washer [W].

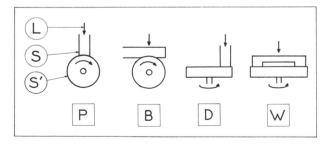

Figure 4.26 · **Wear tests geometries** · [P] Pin-cylinder; [B] Bar-cylinder; [D] Pin-disk; [W] Thrust washer; (L) Load; (S) Test specimen; (S′) Mating surface

4.5.3 Abrasion

Although severe wear at the interface of sliding surfaces can be sometimes considered as abrasion (abrasive wear), the word "abrasion" is normally used to characterize the rapid removal of matter from a surface through the action of a strongly abrading element (grinding wheel, sand paper, sand jet, metal file, steel wool, slurry, etc.).

The many tests associated with abrasion are often very empirical. They have some value for rough comparison purposes, but the use of specific results as a general measure of the abrasion resistance of a material is often questionable.

One of the best known tests, the Taber rotary test (ASTM D1044), illustrated in Figure 4.27, uses a 10 cm (4 in)-thin, disk-shaped, test specimen (S) and freely rotating standard abrasive wheels (W) (e.g., calibrase CS 17). The load (L) applied to each wheel hub (H), which is adjustable, is often 1000 g ($\approx$ 2 lbf). The abrasion level is generally reported in milligrams (mg) of weight loss per 1000 cycles, typically about 10 mg/1000 cycles for an abrasion-resistant material.

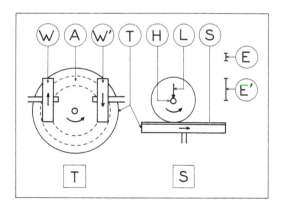

Figure 4.27 · **Taber abraser** · [T] Top view; [S] Side view; (W),(W′) Abrasive wheels; (A) Abrasion track; (T) Turntable; (H) Hub; (L) Load; (S) Test specimen; (E) 1 cm scale; (E′) 1 in scale

Other abrasion tests feature ball mill arrangements (ABBE); twisted metal wires cutting a groove in the material (wire drag tests); sand or other particles falling by gravity, or projected against a test specimen (ASTM D968, D1242, D673); steel wool rubbed against the test specimen (du Pont). A number of tests are used specifically for rubbers (du Pont abrader, Akron abrader, Pico abrader, etc.).

Transparent polymers, in particular, must retain a perfectly smooth surface for optical applications, which often involves contact with a variety of abrading environments. Damage to the surface can take a variety of form and degree (marring, frosting, scuffling, galling, scratching, etc.).   Some tests involve a qualitative comparison of the damage with reference materials such as allyl carbonate lens material CR-39.   Coatings have been developed that dramatically improve the resistance of transparent polymers to surface damage.

Figures 4.28 and 4.29 show testing of slip, wear, and abrasion.

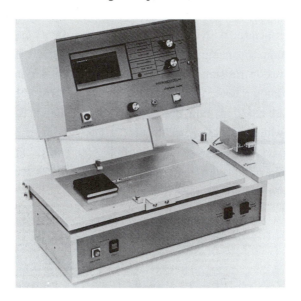

Figure 4.28 · Slip tester (stationary sled type) **[I-MASS]**

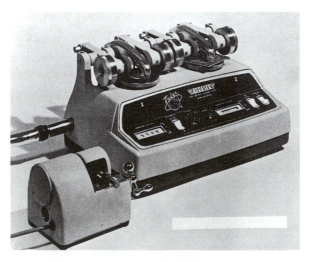

Figure 4.29 · Abrasion tester (two-station type) **[TABER]**

4.6   IMPACT

The impact testing of polymeric materials is recognized as a difficult and controversial subject, and it is accepted that no simple test can offer an unquestionable assessment of the impact resistance of any material. Modern theories of fracture mechanics are now allowing scientists and engineers to develop a better understanding of impact failure, in particular, although the methods of investigation can be much more complex than the conventional standard impact tests discussed here. Conventional impact tests remain useful guides for the development and use of polymeric materials, as long as their limitations are kept in mind.

Impact tests on actual parts, under conditions of speed, environment, and other variables, corresponding to actual use conditions, are naturally recommended. They involve more than just material properties; the parts act as structures, with a complex and changing stress pattern developing in the parts during the impact.

A question that has much practical importance is that of repeated impact. Cumulative damage tends to be serious for some materials, while others appear to recover between blows. No method seems to have been standardized for the assessment of the resistance of polymeric materials to such loading patterns.

An impact failure generally involves a true fracture in a part, or in a test specimen. For materials that are clearly brittle, i.e. stiff and possessing a very low elongation at break in normal moderate speed testing, the mechanism of impact failure is not very different from failure at moderate speeds. Many polymeric materials, however, including engineering plastics, have a stress-strain behavior at moderate speeds and under normal (ambient) temperatures, which indicates a good degree of ductility normally associated with toughness. Under high speed impact conditions, and particularly at low temperatures, however, they fracture in a brittle-like manner. The intrinsic viscoelasticity of the material is a strong factor in this change, which corresponds, in rough terms, to a shift towards a less viscous and more elastic behavior at high speeds and low temperatures.

4.6.1   High Speed Testing

Conventional universal testing machines are capable of a range of crosshead speeds which allow the assessment of the effect of speed on the mechanical behavior, and the strength in particular. The speeds involved, however, are normally much smaller than those which are considered representative of impact situations. They are typically below 5 cm/s ($\approx$ 0.2 ft/s) where slamming a door corresponds to about 3 m/s ($\approx$ 10 ft/s); a very low speed car collision at 5 km/h ($\approx$ 3 mph), to about 1.4 m/s ($\approx$ 4.6 ft/s); a football or hockey collision, to about 30 m/s ($\approx$ 100 ft/s); and a firearm projectile, to about 300 m/s ($\approx$ 1000 ft/s).

4.6.2   Pendulum Flexural Impact Tests

Two widely used impact tests, the Izod and Charpy tests, make use of a swinging pendulum apparatus (Fig. 4.30), with test specimens loaded in a flexural mode. The energy consumed in breaking (fracturing) the test specimen is normally the sole quantity measured. It is expressed, for example, in joules [J (N · m) or feet per pound-foot (ft.lbf) with 1 J = 0.737 ft · lbf. The striking speeds of pendulum hammers are typically around 2.5 m/s ($\approx$ 8 ft/s), and their energy can be in the range 1.4-21.7 J ($\approx$ 1-16 ft · lbf).

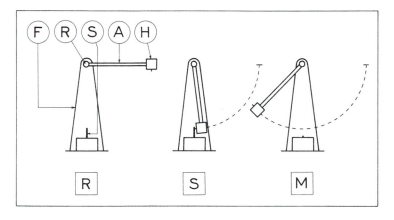

Figure 4.30 · **Swinging pendulum apparatus** · [R] Release; [S] Strike; [M] Maximum swing; (F) Frame; (R) Axis of swing; (S) Test specimen; (A) Arm; (H) Head

In the Izod test (ASTM D256-A), the test specimen (S) is clamped vertically in a vise (V) and struck in a cantilever bending mode (Fig. 4.31 [I]). The most stressed section is subjected to combined flexural and shear stresses, the former being the dominant factor.

In the Charpy test (ASTM D256-B), the test specimen (S) is laid horizontally over two supports (anvils) (A) and struck in a three-point bending mode (Fig. 4.32 [C]). Because of the geometry, true flexural conditions exist in the most stressed central section.

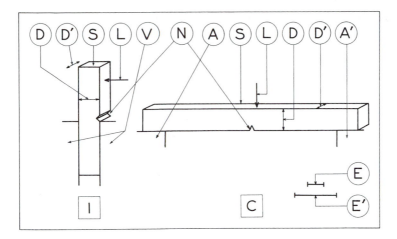

Figure 4.31 · **Izod and charpy test specimens** · [I] Izod test specimen; [C] Charpy test specimen;
(D) Dimension "along"; (D') Dimension "across"; (S) Test specimen; (L) Load;
(V) Vise; (A),(A') Supports; (E) 1 cm scale; (E') 1 in scale

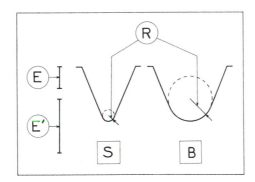

Figure 4.32 · **Notch geometry** · [S] Sharp; [B] Blunt; (R) Notch tip radius; (E) 1 mm scale;
(E') 0.1 in scale

In both Izod and Charpy tests, the flexural span is specified, and it is essential, for comparable results, to use test specimens with the same "along" dimension (D) (such as 12.7 mm or 0.5 in). The energy measured, however, is roughly proportional to the "across" dimension (D') (often referred to as either "thickness," "width," or "length of notch"), which can, therefore, be chosen within a reasonable range (1/8 in or 3.2 mm to 1/2 in or 12.7 mm).

The impact strength is usually quoted as energy per unit dimension (D') for Izod tests (J/m or ft·lbf/in, with 1 kJ/m ≈ 18.7 ft·lbf/in), or energy per unit cross-section (D) x (D') for Charpy tests (J/m^2 or ft·lbf/in^2).

It has long been recognized that the presence of sharp corners in parts reduces their impact resistance, often considerably, through a stress concentration mechanism. Notches are often intentionally put into Izod or Charpy test specimens to assess the so-called notch sensitivity of materials or, sometimes, just to cause the test specimen to fracture rather than just deform.

The most critical characteristic of such notches (Fig. 4.31) is the notch tip radius (R), and it has been demonstrated that the impact energy of many polymeric materials can vary quite appreciably when the radius is changed over a practical range (0.25-2.5 mm or 0.010-0.100 in); this can be a measure of notch sensitivity. A notch tip radius of 0.25 mm (0.010 in) is often used as a standard; it corresponds to a sharp notch, and the associated severe stress concentration.

Naturally, notches are placed in the most stressed section of Izod or Charpy test specimens and on the tensile side, since this is where the fracture begins (Fig. 4.31).

Notches are sometimes molded in but more commonly machined (milled) in straight test specimens. One effect of notching may be the local removal of a layer of material (skin), which may have a structure different from that of the rest of the test specimen. This is probably partly associated with the observation that crystallizing polymers tend to be more notch-sensitive than do noncrystallizing ones. Acetal POM and polyamide PA engineering resins are examples of notch-sensitive plastics. Care in the design of parts, to avoid sharp corners for example, can have a major effect on their resistance to impact loading.

Polycarbonates (PC) generally get the highest notched Izod rating of common structural engineering plastics, with typical values in the range 0.4-0.7 kJ/m ($\approx$ 8-13 ft·lbf/in); polyphenylene oxide (PPO) is in the range 0.13-0.27 kJ/m ($\approx$ 2.5-5 ft·lbf/in); polyamides (PA) and acetals (PMO) correspond to about 0.05-0.08 kJ/m ($\approx$ 1-1.5 ft·lbf/in).

Copolymerization, polyalloying, the use of reinforcing fillers, etc. can often produce grades with improved impact properties [high impact polystyrene (HIPS), super-tough nylons ST PA, etc.]. It can, therefore, be misleading to categorize plastics, even on the basis of a well-defined test. In view also of the frequent lack of correlation between tests, precise ratings, or rankings are of dubious value.

4.6.3 Pendulum Tensile Impact Tests

Dumbbell-shaped test specimens can be subjected to impact loading in a pendulum apparatus (ASTM D1822). As illustrated in Figures 4.33 and 4.34, one tab of the dumbbell test specimen (S) is clamped to the pendulum head (H) and a relatively small T-shaped crosshead clamp (C) is attached to the other tab. After release of the pendulum, the arms of the crosshead clamp hit a double anvil (A) at the low point of the swing, producing a sudden tensile load in the test specimen.

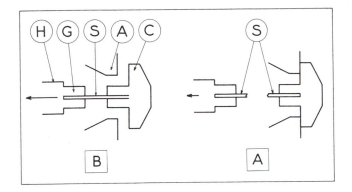

Figure 4.33 · **Tensile impact** · [B] Before impact; [A] After impact; (H) Pendulum head; (G) Grip; (S) Test specimen; (A) Anvil; (C) Crosshead

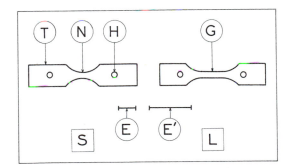

Figure 4.34 · **Tensile impact test specimens** · [S] Short test specimen; [L] Long test specimen; (T) Tab; (N) Neck; (H) Mounting hole; (G) Gauge length; (E) 1 cm scale; (E′) 1 in scale

The energy consumed is recorded, subjected to certain specific corrections, and often reported as an energy per unit cross section area (J/m^2 or $ft \cdot lbf/in^2$). It should be noted that the energy consumed, until the actual localized failure begins, depends on the volume of material involved, and thus, test specimens of type [S] and [L] normally yield different results for the same cross section.

Such a tensile impact test is particularly convenient when the material is only available in relatively thin form, or when orientation effects are to be assessed.

4.6.4   Falling-Weight Impact Tests

A number of tests (ASTM D3029, etc.) assess the impact resistance of rigid plastic through the effect of a striker (ball, dart, tup, missile) of mass (weight) (M) (kg or lb), dropped vertically from a height (H) (m or ft) on a horizontal test specimen (Fig. 4.35). The test specimen (S) is generally a sheet or plate of thickness t held on an annular support (A) of diameter **D**. The geometry of the test specimen and support (t, **D**), and of the striker nose (N) [generally spherical with a radius **r** = 0.25, 0.5 or 2 in ($\approx$ 6.25, 12.5 or 25 mm)], are important parameters in such test.

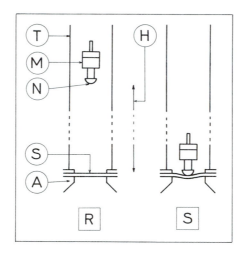

Figure 4.35 · **Falling weight impact** · [R] Release; [S] Strike; (T) Tower (drop tube); (M) Striker weights; (N) Striker nose; (S) Test specimen; (A) Annular support; (H) Drop height

For very brittle materials, the striker can simply be a steel ball, whose mass **M** is a direct function of its radius r [typically 6.25 or 12.5 mm ($\approx$ 0.25 or 0.5 in)]. Damage in the form of cracks, or local shattering, can be limited to the stricken upper surface, or global shattering can occur. The minimum falling height **H**, causing an arbitrarily defined level of damage, is reported as a measure of the impact resistance of the material.

For tougher materials, the striker features a nose of diameter **d** = 12.5 mm ($\approx$ 0.5 in) or 38 mm ($\approx$ 1.5 in) and can carry adjustable weights, usually to a maximum of about 13.5 kg ($\approx$ 30 lb). The impact can cause relatively large deformations, and damage is sometimes most visible on the underside of the test specimen. In the fixed-height mode, the weight is progressively increased until the arbitrarily defined level of damage is achieved in a given fraction of test specimens. In the fixed-weight mode, it is the height that is varied.

In these tests, knowledge of the mass (weight) **M** and the height **H** allows the calculation of the energy **W** (J or ft · lbf). The height **H** is directly related to the initial velocity of impact **V** (m/s or ft/s), a 0.61 m ($\approx$ 2 ft) height corresponding to about 3.4 m/s ($\approx$ 11.3 ft/s).

Some modern instruments use an initial energy above that required to cause a complete failure of the test specimen and monitor the residual speed of the striker after the impact. The speed reduction can be related to the energy involved in the impact failure.

A related test for plastic films involves the circumferential clamping of a test specimen and its perforation (puncture) by the striker, sometimes after a rather large deformation (ASTM D1709). The name Gardner is often associated with falling weight impact tests.

4.6.5 Perforation Impact Tests

Servo-hydraulic systems have been developed, which permit rapid displacements of a plunger at a speed basically unaffected by the load. Such systems are used to punch a hole into, or shatter, sheet or plate-shaped test specimens clamped over a circular opening, in a configuration similar to that used for falling-weight impact tests. A transducer permits the recording of the load on the plunger nose.

A test used for films and sheets uses a ball shot at a velocity of about 50 m/s ($\approx$ 160 ft/s) by a pneumatic device. The speed reduction associated with the perforation (puncture) is converted into an energy, expressed per unit thickness of test specimen (ASTM D3099).

4.6.6 Instrumented Impact Tests

Most simple impact tests provide a single numerical value as the intended measure of the impact resistance of the material. More quantitative information about the actual behavior of the material can be obtained if the displacement of the striker and the force exerted on the test specimen are monitored during the impact test. This is possible with modern transducers, which allow the simultaneous recording (oscilloscope or microcomputer) of displacement and force traces in so-called instrumented tests. It should be kept in mind, however, that the relatively high speeds involved can be associated with vibrations, force waves, and response delays for the instruments.

See figures 4.36-4.42 for examples of impact testing.

Figure 4.36 · Impact testing of pc helmet **[BAYER]**

Figure 4.37 · High rate impact test specimens **[RHEOMETRICS]**

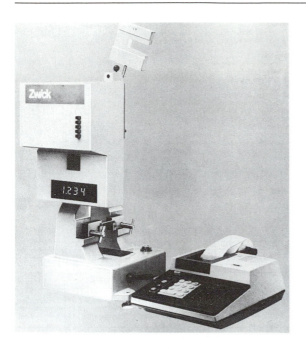

Figure 4.38 · Electronic pendulum impact tester (Charpy mode) [ZWICK]

Figure 4.39 · Drop weight impact tester (with residual energy-measuring device) [KAYENESS]

Figure 4.40 · High rate impact tester [RHEOMETRICS]

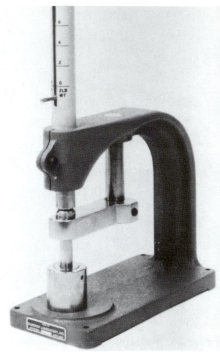

Fig. 4.41 Fig. 4.42

Figure 4.41 · Conventional pendulum impact tester (Izod mode) [ZWICK]

Figure 4.42 · Drop weight impact tester [GARDNER]

4.7 CYCLIC LOADING

The expression "dynamic testing" is often used when a polymeric test specimen is subjected to sudden or repeated (cyclic) loads not intended to cause failure (nondestructive testing). In contrast, impact tests cause the failure of test specimens under sudden loads, and dynamic fatigue tests cause failure under repeated loads.

4.7.1 Dynamic Testing

Dynamic testing is of special importance in the case of polymeric materials because of their well known sensitivity to the speed of loading, a characteristic of viscoelastic materials. The analysis of dynamic tests, particularly those involving repeated loads (sinusoidal testing), is complex and requires a mathematical base. Quantities such as the storage and loss moduli (**E′** and **E″** or **G′** and **G″**) and the loss tangent or loss factor (tan **δ**) are thus defined, measured, and often reported in graphical form. Besides providing useful information for applications involving dynamic loading (high-speed machines, shock and vibration damping, etc.), dynamic testing is widely used as a convenient way of assessing temperature effects, and even for the elucidation of the chemical and physical structure of polymeric systems (copolymers, polyalloys, etc.).

While torsion pendulums operating on the principle of free-vibrations were initially used, modern instruments tend to be of the force-vibration type and feature load and displacement transducers, as well as computers for the analysis of the data.

4.7.2 Dynamic Fatigue

When a material is subjected to a steady load for a long period of time, it may eventually fail, even if the calculated stress is well below the stress determined to cause failure in a short-term, moderate-speed (static) test. This is sometimes referred to as "static fatigue."

A similar phenomenon is encountered if a material is subjected to a fluctuating (cyclic) load, and it is generally referred to as "dynamic fatigue" or, sometimes, simply "fatigue."

In order to properly define a dynamic fatigue test, a number of parameters, or factors, must to be specified. Various stressing modes are possible (tension-compression, flexure, torsion, etc.); flexure is probably the most common for standard tests on polymeric materials. The loading pattern most commonly involves a sinusoidal variation of load or deformation, which may take the form of a relatively small variation around an average level (modulated) or a complete reversal (alternated). The alternated loading pattern, although not necessarily most representative of part loading in service, is generally simpler to carry out and to analyze. For materials that are not purely elastic, in particular, one must distinguish between the case where the maximum load level for each cycle (load amplitude) is set and kept constant throughout the test (constant amplitude of force or stress) and the case where it is the maximum deformation level that is set and kept constant (constant amplitude of deformation or strain). The frequency at which a dynamic fatigue test is conducted has little effect in the case of many highly elastic materials; the number of cycles is the important parameter. For most polymeric materials, however, the effect of frequency should not be discounted without supporting evidence.

The mode of dynamic fatigue failure of most highly elastic materials appears to involve the gradual propagation of cracks, which is associated with local stress concentrations. In the case of polymeric materials, and particularly if the frequency of testing is relatively high, thermal effects associated with the viscoelasticity of the materials and their low thermal conductivity can cause a so-called thermal failure. Thermal failure may involve severe overall temperature increases, or only modest local changes, which may be sufficient to alter the structure and the corresponding mechanical behavior of the materials. Under current standard testing conditions, most glassy thermoplastics and rigid thermosets tend to fail by a crack propagation mode, while many crystallizing thermoplastics fail in the thermal mode.

It is now recognized that a good understanding of the dynamic fatigue phenomenon must involve the microscopic observation of the evolution of the damage throughout the test and its analysis on the basis of fracture mechanics considerations. This is, however, closer to fundamental research work than to standard testing, and several practical tests are in use, which characterize only the point of test specimen failure.

One test (ASTM D671) uses test specimens subjected to flexure in a cantilever mode (Fig. 4.43). In order to generate a reasonably uniform stress across the plane,

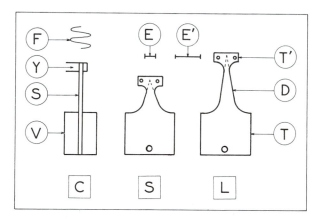

Figure 4.43 · **Dynamic fatique test** · [C] Cantilever mode; [S] Short test specimen; [L] Long test specimen; (F) Applied force; (Y) Yoke; (S) Test specimen; (V) Vise; (T),(T') End tabs; (D) Deformed region; (E) 1 cm scale; (E') 1 in scale

the deformed region (D) of the test specimen (S) has a roughly triangular shape. The alternated sinusoidal force (F), of constant amplitude, can be generated mechanically by an unbalanced rotating mass (eccentric), or through an electro-magnetic device. Tests involving a constant amplitude of deflection, generated by an eccentric mechanism, generally involves cantilever-mounted test specimens (Fig. 4.44). A half tensile test specimen [T] has been used, with the tab mounted in a vise and the other end deflected through a roller arrangement; failure is likely to occur at point (F), towards the end of the gauge zone. Other test specimens are symmetrical around a region of reduced cross section (F) where failure is expected to occur; this reduction can be accomplished by machining the sides to a scalloped shape [S], machining a transverse groove (V-notch [N]), or drilling a hole [H]. In all cases, special care must be taken to use test specimens with a good and reproducible finish.

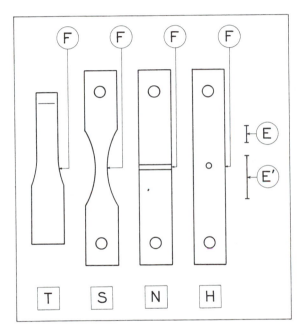

Figure 4.44 · **Dynamic fatique test specimens** · [T] Half tensile; [S] Scalloped; [N] Notched; [H] Holed; (F) Failure region; (E) 1 cm scale; (E') 1 in scale

All of the practical tests are useful for quality control or rough comparison purposes, but care must be taken not to draw hasty conclusions concerning actual service performance.

In the case of a constant amplitude of force test on a cantilever-mounted specimen, for example, individual tests are carried out for different force levels, and the number of cycles at failure **N** is recorded in each case. The maximum stress **S** in the test specimen for each force level is calculated using classical strength of materials considerations. Results are plotted as so-called **S-N** (Wöhler, fatigue life) curves (Fig. 4.45), where **S** is normally on a linear scale <S>, while **N** is on a logarithmic scale

$<N'>$. As stated earlier, the frequency **f** of the test may be a factor, and a check of its effect is recommended; low frequencies, less likely to produce thermal effects, also correspond to long tests, and forced cooling may be an answer in some cases.

Experimental **S-N** curves often correspond to one of two types (Fig. 4.45). In one case (C), after an initial drop, the **S-N** curve tends asymptotically toward a constant stress level. This indicates that for maximum stresses lower than this limit, dynamic fatigue failure never occurs under the conditions of the test. This stress level, corresponding to an infinite fatigue life, is sometimes referred to as the "fatigue limit" (L) and is obviously only a fraction of the conventional flexural strength, typically between 1/5 and 1/30. In another case (C′), the **S-N** curve drops regularly, with no sign of stabilization for a reasonable number of cycles. No fatigue limit (L) can thus be defined, but the stress level for an arbitrary reference fatigue life (e.g., 30×10^3, 10^6 or 10^7 cycles) is sometimes reported as "fatigue endurance." For a typical engineering plastic that fits this type of behavior, the fatigue endurance can go from about 1/2 of the flexural strength for 30×10^3 cycles to about 1/4 for 10^7 cycles. Specific plastics are often associated with class I (C) or class II (C′) behavior, but in view of the complexity of the phenomenon, such classification should be used with caution.

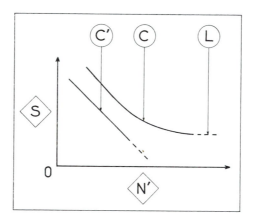

Figure 4.45 · **Dynamic fatique S-N curves** · $<S>$ Maximum stress (lin. Scale); $<N'>$ Cycles at failure (log. Scale); (C) Case I; (C′) Case II; (L) Fatigue limit

Examples of applications requiring a good resistance to fatigue-type stressing, and that normally require special tests, include integral or "living" hinges that must resist repeated, but generally slow, large-amplitude flexing, as well as rubber parts, particularly in shock or vibration damping systems, which are often subjected to relatively large deformations.

4.8   LONG-TERM STATIC LOADING

Many products made of polymeric materials are expected to offer a satisfactory mechanical response to loads over a long period of service. This response may involve sustained, moderate, or high loads or deformations.

The long-term mechanical response of polymeric materials to sustained moderate loads or deformations is associated with their viscoelastic character of these materials. The so-called linear viscoelasticity theory provides a convenient mathematical base for the corresponding characterization of materials. Its principles, however, imply very small loads or deformations, smaller than those often encountered, even in mild service conditions. Consequently, practical tests, usually referred to as "creep" or "stress-relaxation tests," can make only a limited use of the theoretical concepts for the rationalization of results.

The long-term mechanical response to sustained high loads or deformations eventually leads to failure (yield or ductile-type failure or brittle-type failure). This case is sometimes referred to as "static fatigue."

4.8.1   Creep and Stress-Relaxation Tests

The principle of a creep test, sometimes referred to as "cold flow test," is that a test specimen is subjected to a constant load, corresponding to a certain stress or stress distribution, and the resulting gradually increasing deformation, corresponding to a strain or strain distribution, is measured (monitored) as a function of time.

In contrast, a stress-relaxation test involves a constant deformation (strain) and the measurement of the gradually decreasing load (stress) as a function of time.

The theory of linear viscoelasticity suggests the definition of such quantities as creep compliance, stress relaxation modulus, and retardation and relaxation spectra and, through appropriate models, allows the correlation of creep, stress relaxation and even dynamic testing data. As stated earlier, however, these considerations do not hold well for the levels of stresses and strains that are normally of interest to engineers.

Practical creep or stress-relaxation tests are conducted on test specimens subjected to tensile, compressive, or flexural loads or deformations. In the case of tensile deformations, an extensometer capable of accurate measurements of small deformations is normally required. For each of the loading modes, characteristic stresses or strains are calculated from the measured loads or deformations using classical strength-of-materials equations, as in the case of short-term testing.

In creep tests, weights (gravity force) are normally used to impose the constant load. For such long-term tests, relatively infrequent deformation readings are made, and dial gauges are often sufficient for manual data gathering. Stress-relaxation tests tend to require more costly equipment (force transducers, etc.). In all cases, the duration of the tests and the need to establish the reproducibility of results impose the use of dedicated, multispecimen instruments.

Creep or stress-relaxation of polymeric materials is rather strongly increased when the temperature of the test specimen is raised. The effect may be more drastic than expected from short-term stiffness (modulus) data, and thus often requires investigation, particularly for engineering plastics intended for continuous use at high service temperatures.

Most polymeric materials subjected to creep or stress-relaxation tests under moderate loads tend to show a relatively instantaneous (elastic) major response, followed by a time-dependent minor response. A certain equilibrium may eventually be reached, particularly with cross-linked materials under very moderate loads. If the load or deformation is suppressed, a relatively instantaneous major recovery occurs, followed by a progressive (delayed, protracted) minor recovery; again an equilibrium may eventually be reached, although different from the initial state.

Creep data are collected as deformation as a function of time for a given load, and converted into strain as a function of time for a given stress. Typical levels of constant stress for engineering plastics range from 3.5 MPa ($\approx$ 500 psi) to 15 MPa ($\approx$ 2000 psi). Typical test durations can be 100 h (4.17 days), 1000 h (41.7 days), and, less frequently, 10,000 h (417 days, i.e. over one year). Since the response of the material is better perceived in units of stiffness, and in view of its use in strength-of-materials equations, an apparent modulus, or creep modulus, is often calculated by dividing the fixed stress by the time-dependent strain. When the creep modulus for a given stress is plotted versus time on logarithmic scales ($<M'>$ and $<T'>$ in Fig. 4.46), data often fall on a reasonable straight line (C). An extrapolation of such line to longer times (C') provides a way of predicting longer-term behavior. Such extrapolation procedure should be used with caution, however, particularly for relatively high stress levels. Creep data are also sometimes manipulated to produce stress-strain relationships corresponding to a fixed time, for example, 1 h or 1000 h, which are referred to as "isochronous stress-strain curves."

Stress-relaxation data can be handled in an analogous way, with a stress relaxation modulus for a given strain plotted versus time. Typical fixed strain levels are around 1-2%. No exact relationship exists between creep and stress relaxation data, although, of course, they tend to agree in qualitative terms.

A fundamental principle for the correlation of time and temperature effects on viscoelastic material (the time-temperature superposition principle), can often be applied with reasonable success to creep and stress relaxation data to reduce the number of tests.

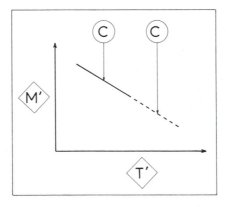

Figure 4.46 · **Creep data representation** · $<M'>$ Creep modulus (log. Scale); $<T>$ Time (log. Scale); (C) Experimental range; (C') Extrapolated range

ASTM D2990 discusses, in particular, general considerations for tensile, compressive, and flexural creep testing. ASTM D2991 deals with stress relaxation testing. ASTM D621 concerns compressive testing in a creep mode, but for rather short times (10 s to 24 h); it applies to rigid plastics (method A) or to flexible ones (method B), in which case it also assesses the recovery after unloading; the stress in the first case is about 7-28 MPa ($\approx$ 1000-4000 psi), while in the second case it is only 0.7 MPa ($\approx$ 100 psi).

4.8.2   Static Fatigue

Either creep or stress-relaxation tests can be conducted at such high levels of load or deformation, or for such a long time, that the test specimens eventually show evidence of unacceptable damage (failure). Failure can be in the form of large irreversible deformations (yield or necking for ductile-type failure), which are normally associated with a change in the microstructure that may include the formation of crazes (crazing). Failure can also be in the form of visible cracks, which may lead to overall rupture (brittle-type failure).

Practical tests often involve creep in the tensile mode (ASTM D2990), and a relationship between the fixed stress imposed, and the time to failure, can be obtained, which bears some similarity with the **S-N** curves of dynamic fatigue. In the same way, a static fatigue limit may exist in some cases, and the curves corresponding to actual experiments can sometimes be extrapolated, with caution, to longer times.

See figures 4.47 and 4.48 for examples of long-term static loading.

Figure 4.47 · Bending fatigue test system (four-station model) **[FDI]**

Figure 4.48 · Dead-weight creep apparatus (21- station model in environmental chamber) **[NA]**

4.9 HIGH-TEMPERATURE SOFTENING

It is well known that temperature has a rather strong effect on the properties of polymeric materials and, in particular, on their mechanical properties.

At high temperatures, chemical reactions within the polymer, or between the polymer and the environment, may cause a gradual change in the properties through modifications to the molecular structure. Such effects are discussed in the section on thermal degradation.

The effect of high temperatures can also be purely physical, i.e. without modifications to the chemical structure of either the individual polymeric molecules for thermoplastics, or the three-dimensional molecular network for cross-linked systems. One must further distinguish between gradual effects, which are associated with creep, stress-relaxation, fatigue, etc., and relatively immediate (short-term) effects. The latter case is the subject of this section.

As indicated earlier, any properties can, in principle, be measured rapidly at a number of temperatures, and numerical results can be presented as a function of temperature in tabular or graphical form.   Such characterization, however, is time-consuming. Standard tests for the rapid evaluation of short-term temperature effects are available, which are based on a quick assessment of the response (resistance) of materials to a moderate load, an indication of the material stiffness.

Two of the best known tests involve a flexural deformation (HDT and Martens), and a third one (Vicat) involves the penetration of an indentor. In all three methods, a loaded test specimen is gradually heated from room temperature and the deformation is monitored. The temperature at which an arbitrary level of deformation is reached is reported, as an indication of the short-term temperature "resistance" of the material. Such tests are widely used throughout the industry.

4.9.1 Heat Deflection Temperature

For this test (ASTM D648), a bar-shaped test specimen (S) (Fig. 4.49) is loaded in the three-point bending mode. The constant load is chosen to produce a maximum stress (fiber stress or surface stress) in the test specimen, of either 0.455 MPa ($\approx$ 66 psi) or 1.82 MPa ($\approx$ 264 psi), as calculated from basic strength-of-materials considerations. The temperature is then raised at a specified rate of 120°C/h ($\approx$ 216°F/h). The temperature at which the central deflection has increased by 0.254 mm ($\approx$ 0.010 in) is reported as the heat deflection temperature (HDT) or deflection temperature under load (DTUL). The temperature obtained depends on the stress level, for example, for a polycarbonate PC the reported HDT is 130°C ($\approx$ 265°F) under 264 psi and 140°C ($\approx$ 285°F) under 66 psi. The difference is larger for a crystallizing polyamide PA: 65°C ($\approx$ 150°F) under 264 psi and 182°C ($\approx$ 360°F) under 66 psi.

Representative HDT values, under 264 psi for some engineering plastics, are around 90°C ($\approx$ 200°F) for polyamides 6-6 (PA 6-6), 120°C ($\approx$ 250°F) for acetals (PMO), 150°C ($\approx$ 300°F) for polycarbonate (PC), 180°C ($\approx$ 350°F) for polysulfone (PSU) and 340°C ($\approx$ 650°F) for polyimides.

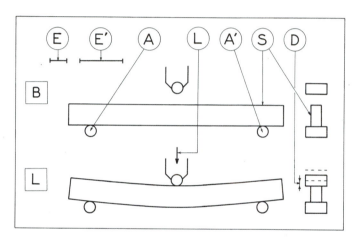

Figure 4.49 · **Heat deflection temperature test** · [B] Before loading; [L] Under load; (A),(A') Supports; (L) Applied load; (S) Test specimen; (D) Deflection; (E) 1 cm scale; (E') 1 in scale

4.9.2   Martens Heat Stability Temperature

For this German test (DIN 53458), a bar-shaped test specimen (S) (Fig. 4.50) is loaded in a four-point bending mode between a stationary grip (G) and second grip (G') attached to a deflection-magnifying arm (A). A mass (M) is adjusted on the arm to produce a maximum stress in the test specimen of 4.9 MPa ($\approx$ 712 psi), as calculated from strength-of-materials considerations. The temperature is raised at the rate of 50°C/h ($\approx$ 90°F/h). The temperature at which the second grip has rotated a certain amount, which corresponds to a certain deflection at the end (E) of the arm, is reported as the Martens heat stability temperature (MHST).

The loading and the arbitrary deformation in the HDT and Martens tests are different, and results are not thus directly comparable. For a polyamide (PA), for example, the HDT under 66 psi is reported to be 200°C (390°F), while the MHST is only 60°C (140°F).

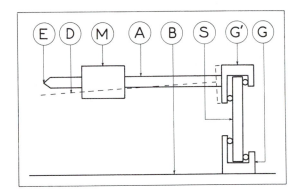

Figure 4.50 · **Martens heat stability test** · (E) Arm end; (D) Displaced arm axis; (M) Adjustable mass; (A) Arm; (B) Base; (S) Test specimen; (G′) Upper grip; (G) Stationary grip

4.9.3   Vicat Softening Point

For this test (ASTM D1525), a small flat test specimen (S), thicker than 3.2 mm (1/8 in), is used (Fig. 4.51).   A flat-ended cylindrical rod (needle) (N) of diameter 1.143 mm ($\approx$ 0.045 in), i.e. a cross-section area of 1 mm^2, is pressed vertically against the test specimen surface, under a force of 9.81 N, corresponding to a mass of 1 kg and an average pressure of 9.81 MPa ($\approx$ 1 420 psi).   The temperature is then raised

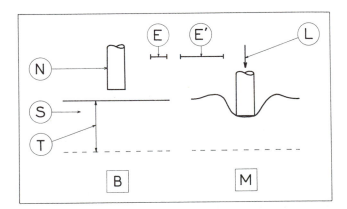

Figure 4.51 · **Vicat softening point test** · [B] Before loading; [M] Maximum penetration; (N) Needle indentor; (S) Test specimen; (T) Minimum thickness; (L) Applied load; (E) 1 mm scale; (E′) 0.1 in scale

at a rate of either 50°C/h (same as Martens test) or 120°C/h (same as HDT test). The temperature at which the needle penetration (indentation) has increased by 1 mm is reported as the "Vicat softening temperature" (VST) or the "Vicat softening point."

The complex loading mode does not lend itself to a simple quantitative interpretation in terms of modulus, but the deformation reflects the stiffness of the material.

The Vicat test is generally considered more suitable than the HDT or Martens tests for materials that are relatively soft.

4.9.4   Transition Temperatures

Emphasis has been placed on the important role played by the glass transition temperature T_g for all thermoplastics, rubbers, and a number of thermosetting resins and by the melting temperature T_m for crystallizing thermoplastics. These quantities have a more fundamental value than do the temperatures determined through the tests just described, which involve arbitrary choices of experimental parameters.

The glass transition temperature T_g, also often referred to as a "second-order transition," and the melting temperature T_m, also often referred to as a "first-order transition" or "crystalline melting," can be determined in a variety of ways. Dynamic mechanical testing, sometimes referred to as "thermo-mechanical analysis," is discussed in this section.   Dilatometry techniques are based on the monitoring of thermal expansion as a function of temperature.   Differential thermal analysis (DTA) and differential scanning calorimetry (DSC) are based on the monitoring of thermodynamic quantities (heat capacity or specific heat) as a function of temperature.   The measurement of electrical properties can also provide ways of assessing the transition temperatures.

The crystalline melting transition, which involves a phase change, can often be detected through direct observation or a variety of optical techniques.   The hot plate method (Fisher-Johns) (ASTM D789, D1457, D2116, D2133), the polarizable microscope hot-stage method (Kofler) (ASTM D2117), the capillary tube (Thiele) method, and the Durrans method, are examples of such techniques.

Although, for simplicity and clarity, it has been implied that the transition temperatures were uniquely defined, it is important to keep in mind that, in reality, for polymeric materials, the transitions occur over a certain temperature range and that the range is affected by factors such as the time scale of the experiments.

A systematic comparison of reported HDT and T_g or T_m values permits some general observations.   For noncrystallizing thermoplastics, there is relatively little difference between HDT (66 psi), HDT (264 psi), and T_g; HDT (264 psi) is, at most, 20°C (36°F) below T_g and HDT (66 psi) is quite close to T_g. For crystallizing thermoplastics, HDT (264 psi) can be as much as 100°C below HDT (66 psi), which can be as much as 200°C below the melting temperature T_m. This indicates that, for these materials, there is a gradual softening between T_g and T_m, which depends on variables such as the nature of the material and its crystalline structure.

The addition of reinforcing fillers, such as short glass fibers, to crystallizing thermoplastics, is known to raise significantly the heat deflection temperature, while it has little effect in the case of noncrystallizing thermoplastics. In both cases, of course, the stiffness is increased at room or higher temperatures.

4.9.5 Dynamic Mechanical Testing

If test specimens of polymeric materials are subjected to small amplitude sinusoidal (dynamic or cyclic) loads or deformations, the simultaneous monitoring of the load and the deformation (stress and strain) allows the determination, through the theory of linear viscoelasticity, of two basic quantities: 1) the storage modulus E' or G', which tends to reflect the elastic response of the material; and 2) E'', G'', or tan δ, which tend to reflect the viscous response. Since the measurements are quick, a broad temperature range can be scanned in a short time and, with modern instruments, the storage modulus, for example, can be plotted as a function of temperature, giving a very clear indication of the short-term effect of temperature on the stiffness. Creep

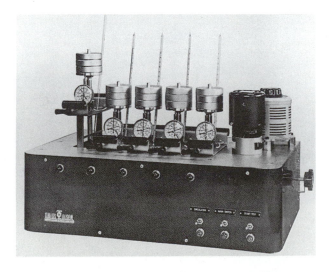

Figure 4.52 · High temperature softening tester (five-station model) [TINIUS OLSEN]

effects, often a limitation in the use of polymeric materials, especially at elevated temperatures, are not assessed, however, through such measurements. Glass transition (T_g) or melting (T_m) temperatures are now frequently determined through dynamic mechanical testing.

Testing of high-temperature softening is shown in figures 4.52-4.54.

Figure 4.53 · Vicat softening point test (loading jig) [TINIUS OLSEN]

Figure 4.54 · Martens heat stability temperature test (loading jig) [ZWICK]

4.10 LOW TEMPERATURE STIFFENING

Many polymeric materials are used in applications such as films, and fabric coatings, which require high flexibility (low stiffness). Rubbers (elastomers) and thermoplastics such as low density polyethylene (LDPE) or plasticized polyvinylchloride (PVC) are examples of materials that are very flexible at room or elevated temperatures. At lower temperatures, however, such materials can stiffen up as a result of a change in the role of the plasticizer, a change in crystallinity, or the transition to a glassy state for amorphous materials or for the amorphous regions of semicrystalline materials.

An increase stiffness at low temperatures may become unacceptable for the application and it may also render the material, or the part, excessively brittle when subjected to impact loadings. While standard tests for stiffness or impact properties, described earlier, can be conducted at progressively lower temperatures, and the results provided in tabular or graphical form, the procedure is time-consuming, and several simple tests have been devised to determine a representative temperature below which an arbitrary level of stiffness or brittleness is exceeded.

4.10.1 Stiffness

Several standard tests established to assess the stiffening of flexible plastics or elastomers at low temperatures are based on the torsion of rectangular test specimens.

One method (ASTM D1043) describes a general test for the determination of the shear modulus **G** of polymeric materials as a function of temperature. One end of the test specimen (S) is held in a stationary clamp (C), while the other end is in a clamp (C') that can rotate (Fig. 4.55). The torque and the angle of rotation of the second clamp can be measured and, with the dimensions of the test specimen, a representative value of the shear modulus G can be calculated. When plotted versus temperature in the low range, it indicates the stiffening region.

The Gehman test (ASTM D1053) is based on a similar principle, but uses a calibrated torsion wire (F) to assess the torque applied to the test specimen (S) (Fig. 4.56). The test specimen is often cut from a standard 2 mm ($\approx$ 0.080 in) thick, press-cured, rubber sheet.

A commonly used method, the Clash and Berg test, is also based on the same principle, and defines a so-called cold flex temperature as the temperature at which a specific test specimen, subjected to an arbitrary torque, deflects to a specific degree.

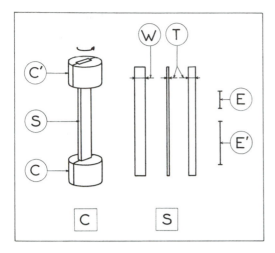

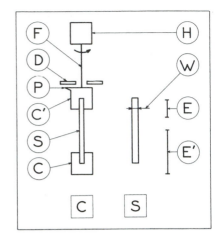

Fig. 4.55   Fig. 4.56

Figure 4.55 · **Torsion test** · [C] Test configuration; [S] Test specimens; (C) Stationary clamp; (C′)
Rotary clamp; (S) Test specimen; (W) Width; (T) Thickness (mini, maxi); (E) 1 cm scale; (E′) 1
in scale

Figure 4.56 · **Gehman test** · [C] Test configuration; [S] Test specimen; (F) Torsion wire;
(D) Dial; (P) Pointer; (C′) Upper clamp; (S) Test specimen; (C) Stationary clamp; (H) Rotary
head; (W) Width; (E) 1 cm scale; (E′) 1 in scale

4.10.2   Static Brittleness

The cold bend test (BS2782-104A) involves the helical winding (21.5° angle), around
a 5.1-mm (≈ 0.2-in) diameter mandrel (M), of a 4.8-mm (≈ 0.2-in) wide test specimen
strip (S) of thickness 1.27 mm (0.050 in), as shown in Figure 4.57. The procedure

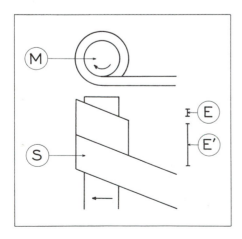

Figure 4.57 · **Cold bend test** · (M) Mandrel;
(S) Test specimen; (E) 1 mm scale; (E′) 0.25
in scale

imposes a specific flexural deformation in the strip. The temperature around which test specimens start to fracture or to show signs of surface cracking is termed the "cold bend temperature."

4.10.3 Dynamic Brittleness

One test (ASTM D746) involves small test specimens (S) (Fig. 4.58), normally die-cut from 1.91-mm ($\approx$ 0.075-in) thick sheets. The test specimens are clamped at one end or over the tab (T) and hit once in a cantilever mode by a mechanically or electrically operated striker, at a velocity of about 2 m/s ($\approx$ 6.5 ft/s). Tests are generally carried out at a given temperature, on a set of 10 test specimens mounted side by side and hit successively. The test specimens are then replaced and the temperature is lowered by increments. The brittleness temperature corresponds to the temperature at which 50% of a set of test specimens fail in a brittle manner (total break, partial break, crack, fissure, etc.). The presence of surface flaws (nicks, etc.), or intentionally placed notches, can severely affect the results as in the case of Izod or Charpy impact testing.

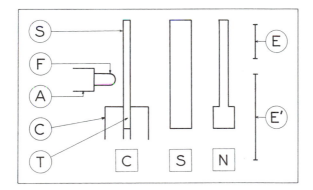

Figure 4.58 · **Brittleness temperature test** · [C] Test configuration; [S] Straight test specimen; [N] Narrow test specimen; (S) Test specimen; (F) Striker; (A) Activator; (C) Clamp; (T) Tab; (E) 1 cm scale; (E') 1 in scale

Another test (ASTM D1790) is suited to plastic films (less than 0.25 mm or 0.010 in). A test specimen (S), in the form of a strip, is folded to form a loop (L) (Fig. 4.59). The free ends are stapled to a card, and the loop is crushed between an anvil (A) and a swinging hammer (H), i.e. subjected to severe impact bending. The velocity and energy of the hammer are about 2 m/s ($\approx$ 6.5 ft/s) and 2.6 J ($\approx$ 1.9 ft.lbf), respectively. The brittleness (cold crack) temperature corresponds to 50% brittle failure in sets of test specimens.

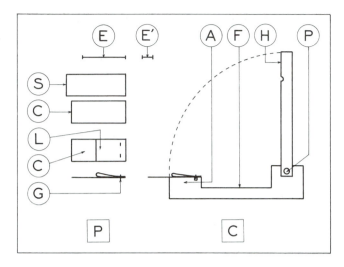

Figure 4.59 · **Film brittleness temperature test** · [P] Test specimen preparation; [C] Test configuration; (S) Test specimen strip; (C) Card holder; (L) Loop; (G) Staple; (A) Anvil; (F) Frame; (H) Hammer; (P) Pivot; (E) 10 cm scale; (E′) 1 in scale

4.11 CHEMICAL ENVIRONMENT

4.11.1 General Considerations

When polymeric materials are exposed to an aggressive (hostile, harmful) chemical environment, the effects may only involve basically physical changes, but chemical changes may also take place.

In the case of purely physical effects, the molecular structure of the polymer remains unchanged. Brief exposure may cause surface tackiness or, in severe cases, the chemicals may truly dissolve the molecules of a thermoplastic (solvation). The concept of solubility parameter is helpful in characterizing the polymer/solvent affinity, and the polarity of the molecules involved is a major factor. For cross-linked polymers (thermosets, rubbers), for semicrystalline thermoplastics with solvation-resistant crystalline regions and for cases where there is a low polymer/solvent affinity, partial absorption may occur, which results in a certain degree of swelling, associated with dimensional changes and softening (plasticizing). In some cases, chemicals that have little effect on a pure polymer may extract additives with a resulting stiffening effect or reduced chemical resistance for plasticizers and stabilizers, respectively.

Truly chemical effects are those involving the breaking and/or formation of chemical bonds. In the case of the breakage of bonds in independent polymeric chains (backbone scission), the molecular weight is reduced. In some cases, further polymerization may result, as well as branching, grafting, or cross-linking. The chemical reaction mechanisms may involve hydrolysis, i.e. the reversal of a condensation reaction in the presence of water molecules (ester, amides, etc.). Oxidation may result from the presence of oxygen or other oxidizing chemicals (polyolefins, etc.). Pyrolysis corresponds to the exposure to high temperatures in the absence of other chemicals. Low- or high-energy radiations can also promote chemical changes (vinyls, fluorocarbon polymers. etc).

4.11.1.1 Assessment

The global characterization of the degree of resistance of a polymeric material to a specific chemical is not a simple matter, since different properties may be affected differently and any given application tends to involve primarily a specific set of properties. The general environment (temperature, radiations, other chemicals, etc.), and other factors, also play a role in the process.

A screening of polymeric materials considered for use in contact with a specific chemical can often be made through the use of published general ratings (handbooks or commercial literature), such as excellent resistance (no effect), very good or good resistance (minor, slight or little effect), poor resistance (softening or swelling, i.e., serious effect), and no resistance at all (severe deterioration, degradation, or solvation). Such ratings may be based on a visual assessment of surface effects (low ratings) or on actual testing, but this is often unspecified, and the use of such general ratings can therefore be misleading. It is normally preferable to know the specific criteria used for the assessment or rating.

Performing specific property tests on samples (or test specimens) after exposure to a chemical and comparing the results to the case of nonexposed samples, allows a quantitative assessment, which can be expressed as a percent retention or percent loss of property.

Surface effects are probably easiest to detect and are often important for applications; they may involve loss of gloss, etching, tackiness, discoloration, staining, clouding, crazing, cracking, or bubbling. Dimensional or weight changes are indications of, at least, physical effects. Some mechanical or electrical properties, such as impact strength, arc-tracking resistance, etc., are particularly sensitive to the exposure to chemicals, and are thus often chosen to assess the effect.

Physico-chemical methods of analysis of the molecular structure, such as molecular weight determination, the characterization of the degree of cross-linking, and infrared (IR) spectroscopy have the advantage of shedding some light on the mechanism involved.

4.11.1.2 Factors

When planning chemical resistance tests, or when evaluating published information on the chemical resistance of specific polymeric materials, it is important to keep in mind that many factors can affect the occurrence, or severity, of chemical effects.

The nature of the chemical involved is obviously a primary factor, but its form (liquid, vapor), and its concentration (dosage), if it is not in pure form, can play an important role as well.

When two or more chemicals are involved simultaneously, the effect can be quite different from that of each chemical alone (synergistic effects). A thorough evaluation of such effects can be, of course, an enormous task.

The temperature of exposure is generally an important factor, because it affects the rate of penetration of the chemical (mass transport), as well as the kinetics of any chemical reaction. Higher temperatures normally have an accelerating effect. Exposure is normally done around room temperature (20°C-25°C or 68°F-77°F), and at one or several higher temperatures (50°C or ≈ 120°F, 70°C or ≈ 160°F, 93°C or ≈ 200°F).

The duration of exposure is also an important factor for reasons similar to those given for temperature. Short time exposure can be appropriate for the quick screening of materials and for cases where contact is expected to be incidental (accidental spillage, etc.). Most commonly, prolonged (long-term) exposure is necessary, with typical durations being 24 h, 1 week, 16 weeks, and even years.

The geometry of the sample or test specimen can be a factor, particularly in terms of the depth of penetration of the chemical (surface/volume ratio). This is especially important when chemical effects are rated in terms of dimensional changes.

The physical structure (morphology) of the sample or test specimen is often affected by processing. Higher degrees of crystallinity or testing in a direction of molecular orientation, for example, are often associated with a higher resistance to chemicals.

It has been demonstrated that many polymeric materials are more affected by aggressive chemicals when they are under external or internal stress, than when they are merely immersed in the absence of any external or internal stress. This phenomenon is often referred to as environmental (or sometimes solvent) stress cracking (or crazing) and is discussed specifically in another section.

Finally, it is essential to realize that the effect of many aggressive environments on polymeric materials can be effectively retarded, or suppressed, through the use of suitable additives. Other additives that are incorporated for other purposes (color pigments, fillers, processing aids) may interfere positively, or negatively, with the chemical resistance of polymeric materials, and since most commercial grades now contain additives, the selection of materials based on general information must be handled with caution.

4.11.1.3 Potentially Aggressive Chemicals

It is appropriate to distinguish between what is referred to here as "general chemicals," which are, obviously, extremely numerous and can be classified in terms of certain classical chemical characteristics (functions), and a number of specific fluids (as well as solids or gases in a few cases), which are commonly used for important applications and are referred to here as "application chemicals."

General Chemicals

The knowledge of the effect of general chemicals on polymeric materials is of special importance to the chemical process industry (CPI), in view of the use of plastics, rubbers, and composites in the construction of chemical process equipment (piping, linings, gaskets, packing, etc.).

Among the numerous general chemicals, only about 50 laboratory reagent-grade (quality) chemicals are normally used by polymeric materials producers in the evaluation of the chemical resistance of their products.

Since the effect of chemicals on polymeric materials is associated with specific chemical characteristics (chemical functions), it is useful to classify these chemicals according to such characteristics, although, unless one can rely on a strong chemistry background, it can be risky to generalize the effect of a chemical to other chemicals in the same class.

It is convenient to distinguish between "active" chemicals, which are often involved in chemical reactions, and solvents, which are normally rather neutral and tend to have "physical" effects on polymeric materials.

"Active" chemicals are most commonly in liquid form and frequently in aqueous (water) solutions. They are sometimes in vapor form and they also include a number of "permanent" gases.

Acids are often subdivided into mineral acids (sulfuric H_2SO_4, hydrochloric HCl, etc.) and organic acids (acetic, formic, stearic, oleic, etc.). There is also an important difference between nonoxidizing acids and oxidizing acids, such as nitric acid HNO_3 and hypochlorites. A distinction is also made between strong acids and weak acids. Acid anhydrides and chlorides are often associated with this class.

Alkalies (or bases) comprise weak bases such as ammonia NH_4OH, and strong bases such as sodium hydroxide (caustic soda) NaOH.

The class of alcohols is also associated with glycols, phenols, cresols, etc.

Another class generally groups esters such as acetates or phthalates; ketones such as acetone or methyl ethyl ketone (MEK); aldehydes; ethers or ether oxides such as tetrahydrofurane (THF) or diethylether (DEE); nitrogen compounds, such as amines and nitriles, including hydrazine or pyridine; and amides.

The class of strong oxidants includes examples, such as potassium permanganate ($KMnO_4$), sodium hypochlorite (NaOCl), hydrogen peroxide (H_2O_2), and wet chlorine.

Aqueous salt solutions involve sodium chloride (NaCl), calcium chloride ($CaCl_2$), and zinc chloride.

Gaseous chemical elements or compounds include oxygen (O_2), halogens such as chlorine (Cl_2) and nitrogen oxides (NO_x) associated with pollution in particular, and ozone (O_3), which is very aggressive to many rubbers in particular and which may be present as traces in air (0.01-0.05 ppm).

Solvents are often subdivided into aliphatic hydrocarbons, including examples such as n-pentane, hexane, n-heptane, and octane; aromatic hydrocarbons such as benzene, toluene, and naphthalene; halogenated solvents such as methylene chloride, trichloroethane, chloroform, carbon tetrachloride, and perchloroethylene. An important distinction is made between nonpolar solvents, which tend to have more effect on nonpolar polymers, and polar solvents, which affect polar polymers and include examples such as dimethylformamide (DMF) or dimethylsulfoxide (DMS).

Application Chemicals

Application chemicals, which include a number of so-called industrial chemicals, can be grouped by general areas of application. In many cases, they are specific solutions or mixtures, and they often contain small amounts of specific additives.

Fuels are particularly associated with the automotive industry. They are primarily hydrocarbon-based, but often contain additives. Examples of polymeric materials, which are generally compatible with fuels, include acetals (PMO), polyamides (PA), and nitrile rubber (NBR). Reference fuels (ASTM A,B,C) are simply isooctane (paraffin hydrocarbon), or mixtures with toluene (aromatic hydrocarbon). The standard fuel (Indolene) is primarily paraffinic, while "spiked" fuels contain a higher fraction of aromatics (toluene); aromatic fractions help control knocking, a role once played by tetraethyl lead additives (leaded fuels). "Sour" fuels contain hydroperoxides resulting from oxidation in recirculated fuels typical of fuel-injected engines. Gasohols are blends (mixtures) of regular fuels with alcohols (methanol, in particular). Diesel fuels are quite different in composition from regular gasoline. Fuel effects are most commonly assessed at room temperature, but higher testing temperatures, such as 50°C (122°F), tend to play an accelerating role. Swelling is the most common problem, but oxidation or other chemical degradation can also take place in some of the fuels. The use of the new, or special fuel types, often involves the reconsideration of polymeric materials for parts, tubings, tanks, seals, etc.

Lubricants for mechanical devices comprise mineral oils and greases, which are generally hydrocarbon-based, but often contain additives involving sulfur-, phosphorus- or lithium-based compounds. Lubricants are characterized through SAE (Society of Automotive Engineers) or ASTM Standards. Lubricating oils include engine oils, such as ASTM oils 1, 2, and 3, and are sometimes modified with sulfur compounds; testing normally involves temperatures of up to 100°C (212°F). Manual transmission oils are often tested to 130°C (266°F), and automatic transmission oils to 150°C (302°F); the latter sometimes contains polar phosphate ester additives; typical tradenames include Mobil, Dexron, Tranself, and Skydrol. Other hydraulic fluids include Pydraul, Sunbis, and Ucon. Greases are less likely to cause swelling but are known to induce degradation, such as stress-cracking, in some plastics.

Hydraulic brake fluids often contain high-molecular-weight glycols, to control viscosity and vaporizing tendency, and such tensio-active additive can cause stress-cracking.

Antifreeze engine coolants used to about 100°C (212°F) are generally 50/50 mixtures of water and ethylene glycol, with anticorrosion additives (Prestone). Polyamides-11 (PA-11), high density polyethylene (HDPE), and polypropylene (PP) are often used with such fluids.

Windshield washer fluids are typically 90/10 mixtures of water and ethyl or methyl alcohol, sometimes with a detergent. Stress cracking of plastics may be a problem.

Lead storage battery electrolyte consists of dilute sulfuric acid (32° Baumé).

Refrigeration fluids, such as those used in automotive air-conditioning systems, are generally fluorine-based (Freon); the most common type is dichlorodifluoromethane (R 12). Other fluids include Dowtherm.

Saline solutions are solutions of certain salts in water, and testing may involve complete immersion, or spraying (salt spray), which is often more aggressive.

Polymeric materials are normally known to have a good resistance to such environments, which are generally very aggressive to metals. Sea water is a dilute solution (about 3%) of sodium chloride NaCl in water, and it is known that corrosion can occur inland, quite a distance from shore, through wind-carried elements (marine atmosphere). Ice control or removal from sidewalks, streets, and highways often involves calcium chloride ($CaCl_2$). Road salt and water sometimes combine with zinc alloys to form zinc chloride which, for example, is harmful to some polyamides. Refrigeration brines are also salt solutions.

A variety of cleaning (cleansing) agents tend to be aggressive to some polymeric materials. They include liquid or powder detergents, often based on phosphate esters, which operate through tensio-active (surfactant) effects. Some dishwasher detergents are known to be highly alkaline. Other agents, associated with laundry and dishwashing, include soap solutions, rinse agents, and antistatic agents, which must be checked for their long-term effects on materials at the appropriate temperature. Bleaches (Javex) may involve chlorine and peroxide, for example, about 12.5% of active chlorine. Dry-cleaning solvents include perchloroethylene or trichloroethylene.

Many types of waxes and polishes used for furniture, floors, car bodies, and other materials often involve a solvent base and can be aggressive to polymeric materials.

Foods involve natural fats and oils (esters of fatty acids), of animal or vegetal origin, as well as numerous other chemical compounds that can have superficial, appearance-related, effects (staining), or may reduce the load-bearing capacity of parts through swelling, stress-cracking, etc. Staining agents include beverages (coffee, tea, wine, fruit juices, etc.), foods (mustard, vinegar, ketchup or catsup, jelly or jam, etc.), cosmetics (lipstick, skin creams, nail polish, nail polish remover, etc.), and a variety of miscellaneous items, such as shoe polish, crayons, and marking (felt) pens.

A number of potentially aggressive agents are also associated with the medical field. They include physiological fluids, anaesthetics, sterilizing and antiseptic media (ethylene oxide, steam, benzalkonium chloride, ethanol, chlorine water, and formaldehyde (formalin)).

4.11.1.4 General Chemical Resistance Testing

The easiest and most common standard procedure for assessing the effect of chemicals on polymeric materials (ASTM D543) involves the exposure, by immersion, of a large number of suitable test specimens to the chosen chemical. Test specimens are then periodically removed, cleaned, examined, and subjected to suitable tests. This procedure, which does not involve the application of a load on the test specimens during exposure, is often referred to as the "immersion procedure." Property data, percent loss, or percent retention, can be reported for specific exposure times (1 day, 1 week, 1 month, etc.), or the data can be plotted as a function of exposure time in view of possible extrapolations.

4.11.2   Special Cases

Several important subjects that involve the effect of the environment on polymeric materials are discussed in this section.

4.11.2.1   Mechano-Chemical Effects

Environmental Stress-Cracking (ESC)

It has long been recognized that many polymers, which appear to be unaffected by certain chemicals through the normal (unstressed) immersion procedure, can be seriously affected if stresses are present in the test specimens during their exposure to the chemicals.

The stresses can be the result of external (applied) loading, and are then sometimes referred to as "active" stresses. Stresses may also be present in an unloaded part or test specimen, often as a result of thermal effects when processed or used, or because of the presence of inhomogeneities, fillers, metallic inserts, etc.; such stresses are sometimes referred to as "passive" stresses (also "internal," "residual," "frozen in," "molded in." etc.).

The adverse effect of aggressive chemicals on stressed material is most commonly evidenced in the form of cracks in regions under tensile stresses, which can grow until catastrophic failure occurs.   The phenomenon is thus often referred to as "environmental stress-cracking" (ESC). A certain analogy with a phenomenon affecting metals has also led to the occasional use of the expression "stress-corrosion" for polymers, although it seems less appropriate. Since many polymeric materials can undergo stress-induced local structure changes, known as "crazing," the expression "environmental stress-crazing" is also used when crazing is strongly favored by a chemical. In many cases, it is recognized that crazing and cracking coexist, crazing preceding cracking in the crack tip zone; the term "environmental cracking/crazing" is then used.

One of the serious effects of even relatively mild environmental stress-cracking can be to change the mode of failure of a material from a normally ductile mode to a brittle mode, thus making a normally tough and strong part turn brittle and weak.

The mechanism of environmental stress-cracking or crazing is the object of much scientific investigation because of its importance in the performance of polymeric parts, and many questions remain to be answered.

Environmental stress-cracking agents are most commonly liquids, although vapors and semisolid substances such as greases can be active, too. They are generally polar and can be either hydrophilic (such as alcohols) or hydrophobic (such as silicone oils) or mixed (tensioactive). When the agents have some limited solvent effect, the expression "solvent stress-cracking" is sometimes used. Examples of chemicals that can have strong stress-cracking effects on specific polymers include aqueous solutions of zinc chloride for polyamides (PA 6-6) and toluene-propanol mixtures for polycarbonate (PC). Such chemicals can even be used for the rapid detection of residual stresses in polymeric parts, with cracks forming almost instantly in tension-stressed regions. Potential stress-cracking fluids for polyethylene include oils, greases, soaps, detergents, wetting agents, and surfactants. A widely used standard stress-cracking fluid, described as a highly polar nonionic liquid [nonyl phenoxy poly (ethylene-oxy) ethanol or aryl-alkyl polyethylene glycol], is known under the tradename "Igepal" or "Antarox" (GAF). It is used pure (full strength) or as water solutions (typically 5-25% Igepal). Solutions are often more aggressive, due to more favorable viscosity and surface tension.

Environmental stress-cracking effects are generally more prevalent in noncrystallizing (amorphous) polymers. Semicrystalline polymers can also be affected through their amorphous regions in particular.

In general, environmental stress-cracking effects are more severe at higher temperatures. This is probably associated with the higher mobility of the molecules involved.

ESCR Tests

Tests for environmental stress-cracking resistance (ESCR) can be divided into two classes, according to the mode of imposition of the load or deformation. The mode where the load [and corresponding stress(es)] is kept basically constant is related to creep, and it is referred to here as "imposed load." The mode where the deformation [and corresponding strain(s)] is basically constant is related to stress-relaxation, and it is referred to here as "imposed deformation." A distinction is important in view of the strong viscoelastic character of polymeric materials in particular. Imposed load tests tend to be more severe but are also more difficult to perform.

The determination of the boundary between susceptibility and resistance to environmental stress-cracking/crazing is obviously dependent on the choice and interpretation of a criterion, which can be somewhat subjective when no catastrophic failure occurs. The fracture mechanics approach, although much more elaborate, offers a good potential for the fundamental understanding of this complex phenomenon.

A standard test corresponding to the imposed load mode is often known as the "environmental stress rupture" or "Lander test" (ASTM D2552). Tensile test specimens (S) of 1-mm ($\approx$ 0.04 in) thickness (Fig. 4.60) are subjected to a constant load, through a dead weight (W) and lever (L) arrangement while immersed in the agent (A). The time to rupture of test specimens, subjected to a specific tensile stress somewhat lower than the conventional tensile strength [typically around 10 MPa ($\approx$ 1.45 kpsi) for a polyethylene], is reported. The relationship between applied stress and rupture time is of special interest, and, in some cases, a critical (threshold) stress is determined, below which environmental stress-cracking never seems to occur.

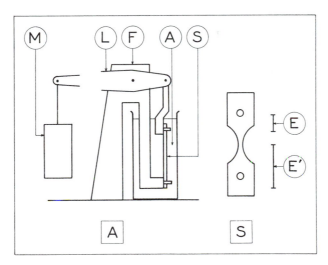

Figure 4.60 · **Tensile ESCR test** · [A] Apparatus; [S] Test specimen; (M) Weight; (L) Lever; (F) Frame; (A) Aggressive fluid; (S) Test specimen; (E) 1 cm scale; (E′) 1 in scale;

A simple test known as the bent strip or Bell Labs test, which corresponds to the imposed deformation mode, has long been used for polyethylene (ASTM D1693). A rectangular test specimen (S) (Fig. 4.61) of a specified thickness (for instance, 3.2 mm or 0.125 in) is bent back through about 180° and held in a U-shaped holder (H). The outer surface is under a high tensile strain of the order of 50%. A longitudinal notch (N), cut (nicked, scored) in the undeformed test specimen with a sharp blade, serves as a controlled "imperfection," favoring the reproducible formation and growth of cracks or crazes. Groups of ten test specimens are immersed in a standard stress-cracking agent, generally at a somewhat elevated temperature (50°C or 122°F). The time at which visible cracks or crazes, or fracture, has occurred in 50% of the test specimens is reported as the **F$_{50}$** time, which can range from minutes to months. The negative effect of low-molecular-weight fractions, or the positive effect of modifying polyethylenes with butylene or isobutylene, for example, can be demonstrated with the test.

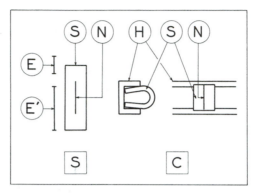

Figure 4.61 · **Bent strip ESCR test** · [S] Test specimen; [C] Test configuration; (S) Test specimen; (N) Notch; (H) Holder; (E) 1 cm scale; (E′) 1 in scale

Another test, corresponding to the imposed deformation mode and known as the "Rader test," is used in the plastic pipe industry. It involves the squeezing of rings, cut from pipes, with a stress-concentrating notch in the region of maximum tensile deformation.

A class of tests involves the imposition of a specific strain at the edge of a hole. Such tests are often referred to as the "Pohrt" ball (or "pin") indentation tests. A hole (H) is drilled and reamed in a test specimen (S) (Fig. 4.62) and an oversized ball (B)

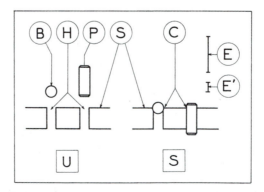

Figure 4.62 · **Ball/pin ESCR test** · [U] Unstressed; [S] Stressed configuration; (B) Ball; (H) Hole; (P) Pin; (S) Test specimen; (C) Hole edge; (E) 1 cm scale; (E′) 1 in scale

(or pin (P)) is pressed into the hole. The strain involved can be of the order of 1%. The system is immersed into the aggressive fluid medium, and the area around the hole edge (E) is monitored for cracking or crazing. Test specimens of suitable shapes can also be subsequently tested in tension or flexure after removal of the ball or pin. The presence of cracks around the hole leads to a reduction in strength, particularly under impact conditions. Such a test is particularly suitable for use in specific areas of complex parts.

Several tests have been used that impose a range of strain or stress on a rectangular test specimen of uniform thickness. The Dow test uses an elliptic jig (J) (Dow profile) as a guide for bending the test specimen (S) (Fig. 4.63 [E]), and the local strain can be calculated through geometric considerations. In the cantilever beam test (Fig. 4.63 [C]), the test specimen (S) held in a clamp (C) is subjected to a weight (W) at its free end, and the local stress can be calculated through mechanical considerations. In both cases, the aggressive fluid can be applied on the tensile surface, through a soaked piece of blotting paper, for example, and the point that cracks reach in a reference time is recorded and used to estimate the corresponding critical strain or stress.

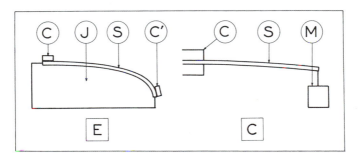

Figure 4.63 · **Flexural ESCR tests** · [E] Elliptic jig test; [C] Cantilever test; (C),(C′) Clamps; (J) Elliptic jig; (S) Test specimen; (M) Weight

4.11.2.2 High-Energy Radiations

High-energy or ionizing radiations are associated with radioactivity. Some radiations (α, β) are of particulate nature and have a relatively low penetrating power in solids. Highly penetrating electromagnetic gamma (γ) radiations are of particular concern, or interest, in the case of polymeric materials. These radiations can trigger unwanted detrimental chemical reactions such as bond rupture, chain scission, and undesirable cross-linking. In some cases, however, they can be put to good use to help achieve polymerization, cross-linking, and grafting.

Gamma radiations are produced in atomic piles, through electron beam units, and from radioisotopes such as cobalt 60. They are characterized by a very short wavelength (0.005-0.28 Å) [(10,000 Angstroms (Å) = 1 μm)], and an energy that is typically around 2 MeV (0.32 pJ or 0.32 x 10^{-12} J). When a material is exposed to gamma radiations, the total dose is usually expressed in RAD (radiation adsorbed dosage) or energy per mass of material irradiated (100 RAD = 1 J/kg). The Rep (Roentgen equivalent physical) is approximately equal to the RAD. Typical total doses, involved in testing of the radiation resistance of polymeric materials, are in the range 1-10 MRAD. The radiation exposure (flux, dose) rate is expressed in RAD/h, with typical values around 0.1 RAD/h.

The resistance of polymeric materials to high energy radiations is important, in view of their application as insulating materials for electrical systems, as well as seals and gaskets, in the nuclear industry or in equipment involving radiation sources (cancer treatment units, sterilization systems, thickness gauges, etc.). Some otherwise excellent polymers are known to be rather strongly affected by high energy radiations [polyvinylidenechloride (PVDC), polymethylmethacrylate (PMMA), polytetra-fluoroethylene (PTFE), butyl rubber (IIR), etc.]. Radiation exposure is commercially used to make heat shrinkable films [irradiated polyethylene (PE) film].

X-ray radiations, of a longer wavelength (0.03-20 Å), may have some effect on some polymeric materials.

4.11.2.3 Microorganisms and Animals

Polymeric materials may be susceptible to attack by microorganisms, which include bacteria, actinomycetes (actinomyces), and fungi (mushroom, mould, mildew, alga). They can attack polymers, and particularly their low molecular weight additives such as plasticizers, through the production of enzymes. Their action can be a function of several factors, such as humidity, oxygen (aerobic vs anaerobic conditions), temperature (generally a relatively low and narrow range), pH (acidity), and the presence of chemicals such as inorganic salts. Microbial attack is of particular concern in the food industry and in construction or civil engineering. Testing can involve soil burial tests (e.g., 120 days) or accelerated tests with agar-agar in Petri dishes.

Additives can be incorporated into polymeric materials to suppress or retard microbial attack.

Certain animals can cause serious damage to polymeric parts. They include rodents, insects such as termites, and insect larvae. Poisonous additives can help control their action.

4.11.2.4 Water Absorption

Polymeric materials that are soluble in water are important, particularly in the biological field, but they are normally unsuitable for parts intended for structural applications. Most commonly used plastics and elastomers are insoluble in water, but they can absorb small amounts, which can alter a number of properties. Electrical properties are generally strongly affected by even small amounts of water. Water tends to play a plasticizing role and can raise the impact resistance of some brittle plastics. When water absorption is relatively large, dimensional changes may cause tolerance problems in close-fitting situations such as gears or shaft-bearing systems. While absorbed water normally does not react chemically with the polymers at room or low temperature, reactions can occur at processing temperatures and lead to chemical degradation. Processing temperatures can also cause the formation of water vapor bubbles and unacceptable parts.

The determination of the degree of water absorption (ASTM D570) normally involves 3.2-mm (1/8-in) thick molded disks or strips, cut out of sheets. The test specimens are first thoroughly dried in an oven at 50°C ($\approx$ 120°F) for at least 24 hours, wiped dry, and weighed. The water absorption is expressed as the percent by weight of water absorbed in the test. Redrying is sometimes carried out to check the possibility of the water extraction of soluble matter (additive, etc.). While standard water absorption data correspond to room temperature absorption, data are sometimes reported for water absorption under specific temperature and humidity conditions.

Fluorocarbon polymers absorb practically no water. Olefin polymers such as polyethylene and polypropylene absorb only slightly over 0.01%. Thermoplastic polyesters (PET, PBT) also have very low absorption ($\approx$ 0.02). Polystyrenes can be in the range 0.03-0.10; polyphenylene oxides 0.05-010; polycarbonates, 0.15-0.20; acetals (PMO), 0.20-0.25; polyamides (PA-6 and PA-6,6), around 1.50; and cellulose acetate (CA) over 1.70. All the above figures corresponding to room temperature absorption.

4.11.2.5 Weathering

The term "weathering" normally refers to the effect of prolonged outdoor exposure on materials. Polymeric materials are often affected by such exposure. The environmental factors that contribute to weathering effects are varied, and their combination can produce synergistic results.

A major factor that distinguishes weathering from other environmental exposure is the role of solar radiation. The complex energy spectrum of solar radiation, at ground level, includes visible light (390-800 nm or 3900-8000 Å wavelength), as well as ultraviolet (UV) radiation (under 390 nm) and infrared (IR) radiation (over 800 nm). The absorption of IR radiation can cause a significant temperature rise in exposed samples (20°C or 36°F for light colors and 40°C or 72°F for dark colors are typical of such heat build up). The absorption of UV radiation can induce or accelerate chemical reactions, which generally lead to a degradation of the material. The UV region of the spectrum, particularly around 310-325 nm, is the most aggressive. An intensity of exposure is sometimes expressed in Watts per square meter (W/m^2) and the total energy received over a period of time in kilojoules per square meter (kJ/m^2) or langleys (1 ly = 1 cal/cm^2 and 1 J/m^2 ≈ 2.39 kly). Methods of quantitative characterization of the degree of exposure include the use of a radiometer. A 4-year exposure to Florida sun, for example, is reported to correspond to about 20 kJ/m^2.

Other factors influencing the resistance of polymeric materials to outdoor exposure include oxygen, which is, of course, always present in air; ozone, present in variable concentration; water vapor (humidity); condensed water (dew); moving air (wind) or water (rain), which can alter the temperature, have some leaching effect and carry aggressive agents (sand, salt spray, minerals, acids, etc.).

The effect of natural outdoor exposure obviously depends on climatic conditions, with New Jersey, for example, corresponding to a temperate climate, Florida to a hot and humid environment, and Arizona to hot and dry conditions. Samples, generally in the form of sheets, strips, or specific test specimens are oriented in an optimal manner (45°, south), and commonly exposed over a period of 1-3 years; the duration of exposure is obviously suited to the expected resistance of the material and its intended application. The assessment of weathering effects is often limited to the exposed surface (gloss, color, etc.), but a variety of properties can also be measured, as suited to the intended use.

Attempts to "accelerate" outdoor exposure by concentrating solar rays with mirror devices while using adequate ventilation to keep the temperature down, do not appear to have been very successful.

The most common procedures for accelerating weathering effects involve so-called indoor or artificial weathering. Solar radiation is replaced by radiation from sources that include fluorescent (Q-Panel) or incandescent sun lamps, mercury vapor or arc sources, carbon arcs, and Xenon arcs (Xenotest), and are often used with appropriate filters to try to match the critical UV region of the solar spectrum. The UV-associated energy corresponding to Xenon arcs has been reported to be of the order of 0.5 kJ/m^2

per hour of exposure. The alternation of day and night, and even rainfalls, is simulated at an accelerated rate, with samples mounted on a rotating carousel (Weatherometer).

Although precise correlations between natural and artificial weathering are elusive, when sufficient experience with the type of material considered exists, accelerated testing can be very useful in the development of new grades, or the assessment of protective additives, which are widely used in commercial resins. Artificial weathering is commonly reported to correspond to an accelerating factor between about 5 and 20 and occasionally up to several hundred times.

The intrinsic susceptibility of polymeric materials to weathering and, in particular, to degradation associated with UV radiation (photodegradation), is determined by molecular features such as the presence of certain hydrogen atoms allowing oxidation (polyethylene and polypropylene), hydrogen and chlorine atoms allowing dehydrochlorination (polyvinylchloride) chain unsaturation allowing chain scission (C=C in certain elastomers), etc. Polymeric materials noted for their good intrinsic resistance to weathering include acrylics, fluorocarbon polymers, cellulose esters, and silicone rubber. With suitable additives, many other polymers can be used successfully for outdoor applications. For certain applications, such as some agricultural films, it may be desirable to have a progressive disintegration of the material, calling for a photodegradable polymer. Examples of weathering are shown in figures 4.64-4.66.

Figure 4.64 · Direct outdoor exposure

Figure 4.65 · Accelerated weathering (Weather-ometer) [ATLAS]

Figure 4.66 · Accelerated weathering (Q-U-V tester) [Q-PANEL]

4.11.2.6 Thermal Degradation

All polymeric materials have a limited resistance to high (elevated) temperatures. Effects of elevated temperatures that do not involve the breakage or formation of chemical bonds were discussed earlier. Truly chemical effects may take place rapidly, at sufficiently high temperatures, and correspond to short-term thermal degradation. Chemical effects can be much slower, at somewhat lower temperatures, and thus correspond to long-term thermal degradation (thermal aging). The resistance to thermal degradation is often referred to as "thermal stability" or "thermal endurance."

It should be noted that certain physical changes may also be associated with thermal degradation (loss of volatile components, changes in crystalline structure, etc.).

Short-Term Thermal Degradation

Short-term thermal degradation typically corresponds to heating rates of the order of 40°C (72°F) per minute. For thermoplastics, it normally occurs well above the glass transition (T_g) or melting (T_m) temperatures and is thus associated with processing that involves relatively short exposure times (residence time in the equipment). The absence or the presence of oxygen (nitrogen or air atmospheres, respectively) can be a major factor and one should distinguish between thermal and thermo-oxidative degradation.

The most common method of assessment of short-term thermal degradation is by thermo-gravimetric analysis (TGA), which involves the precise monitoring of the mass (weight) of a small sample, as it is steadily heated in a controlled atmosphere. The decrease, or occasional increase, of weight tends to reflect a chemical reaction, a sign of degradation.

Thermal degradation and the associated chemical reactions can also be assessed through differential thermal analysis (DTA) or differential scanning calorimetry (DSC), which can detect, in particular, reaction exotherms or endotherms.

Polymeric materials can often be protected against short-term thermal degradation by suitable additives.

Long-Term Thermal Degradation

The long-term effects of elevated temperatures on polymeric materials can be assessed in a variety of ways, but two basic procedures are mainly used: creep rupture tests and the determination of a temperature index.

Creep rupture tests correspond to a testing procedure described earlier. They are particularly recommended for parts continuously or frequently subjected to relatively high stresses at elevated temperatures. The need to apply relatively high loads to a large number of tests specimens, for long periods of time, requires special equipment and attendance, and the effects of temperature exposure correspond to the specific loading mode and level.

The determination of a temperature index, sometimes also referred to as a "continuous use temperature index," basically involves the exposures of a large number of suitable test specimens to several selected elevated temperatures in the absence of external loads and the periodic withdrawal of some of the test specimens for testing, normally at room temperature. The degree of retention of property can thus be assessed as a function of the temperature and duration of exposure. In many cases, the thickness of the test specimens proves to be a significant factor and must thus be specified.

The specific procedure, for the analysis of corresponding data to assign a temperature index, involves a number of arbitrary choices, and the results have a comparative, rather than absolute value. The first choice is that of the property, or properties, to be monitored. Tensile or flexural strength, Izod or tensile impact strength and electrical properties, such as dielectric strength, are common choices for their sensitivity to thermal degradation. The percent property retention <P> is plotted versus the exposure duration <E> (Fig. 4.67), for each of several high exposure temperatures (T). The maximum exposure duration, corresponding to an

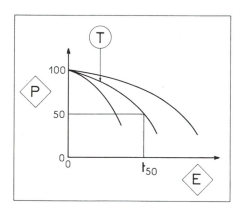

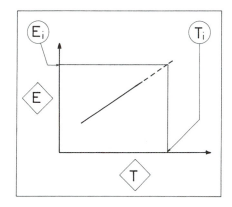

Fig. 4.67   Fig. 4.68

Figure 4.67 · **Long term thermal degradation** · <P> Percent property retention; <E> Exposure time; (T) Exposure temperature

Figure 4.68 · **Temperature index determination** · <E′> t_{50} time (log. Scale); <T′> (absolute temperature)$^{-1}$; (E′$_i$) Endurance time rating; T_i Temperature index

arbitrary acceptable percent property retention (t_{50} for 50% retention is used here as an example), is determined for each temperature. If several properties are monitored, the lowest t_{50} is chosen. The data are then processed in the light of Arrhenius principles (log maximum exposure duration $<E'>$ versus inverse absolute temperature $<T'>$, as shown in Fig. 4.68). By linear extrapolation, the temperature (T_i), which corresponds to an arbitrary "safe life" or "endurance rating time" (E'_i), is determined and referred to as the temperature index. Test exposures are usually limited to less than a year (8760 h) and extrapolations may involve endurance rating times of 11,000 h (1.25 years), 60,000 h (6.85 years), and even 100,000 h (11.4 years). Such temperature index ratings are conducted by Underwriters Laboratories under UL 746 (associated "yellow card").

The knowledge of the exact criteria used in the determination of a temperature index is a prerequisite for its use as a guide for material selection. In general, the concept is best suited to situations where exposure to elevated temperatures is continuous or frequent, but where parts are only infrequently (occasionally) subjected to high loads.

Very conservative temperature indices are also issued for generic types of polymeric materials, which are based on records of actual field performance of parts.

It should be noted that additives for thermal protection tend to become inefficient over very long periods.

4.12   FLAMMABILITY AND COMBUSTION

Most polymeric materials, which are organic chemicals and generally contain a large proportion of carbon atoms C and hydrogen atoms H, will burn under certain conditions.

The mechanism of burning (combustion) is complex but generally involves several characteristic layers or regions in a direction perpendicular to the surface of a sample. Closest to the unaffected material, there is a heated layer, followed by a degradation (pyrolysis) layer, generally featuring tar or char. Immediately beyond the material surface, gaseous degradation products first mix with air and subsequently burn in the flame region; the next region corresponds to combustion products.

The importance of the ability to assess at least the relative resistance of polymeric materials to combustion is clear, in view of the many applications where combustion would have serious consequences, such as children's sleepwear; electrical insulation in construction wiring; wall, ceiling and floor paneling and insulation; upholstery, bedding, and draperies; tanks and containers for flammable liquids; and interior elements in transportation.

A number of standard tests are commonly used to assess characteristics, such as the ease of ignition (ignitability), the flame spread or propagation (burning rate), the fuel contribution (heat release), and the evolution of combustion products (smoke, toxic gases). It has long been recognized that results of laboratory tests may not be sufficient to describe or appraise the fire hazard or fire risk of materials, products, or assemblies under actual fire conditions, and ASTM requests that such statement (caveat) be included in test reports. It should be noted, too, that many elements can affect the performance of specific polymeric materials in laboratory tests or real fire situations; they include the thickness and shape of test specimens or parts, the presence of additives and modifiers such as plasticizers, fillers, colorants, and, of course, fire retardants.

A number of organizations are involved in flammability and fire matters, and their acronyms often appear in the literature. They include NBS (National Bureau of Standards), DOT (Department of Transportation), FAA (Federal Aviation Administration), UMTA (Urban Mass Transit Authority), NFPA (National Fire Protection Association), MVSS (Motor Vehicle Safety Standard), FTMS (Federal Test Method Standard), UL (Underwriters Laboratories), and FM (Factory Mutual).

Most of the important standard methods used for product development or regulatory purposes are reviewed in this section.

4.12.1 Oxygen Index

A widely used test, referred to as the "oxygen index test" (ASTM D2863) or, sometimes, as the "Fenimore-Martin method," determines the minimum concentration of oxygen O_2 in an oxygen/nitrogen (O_2/N_2) mixture, which supports flaming combustion. A heat-resistant glass tube (T) (column) is partially filled with glass beads (B) to homogenize the upward flow of the O_2/N_2 mixture (G) fed at the base (Fig. 4.69). The total linear gas flow rate is specified ($\approx$ 4 cm/s or 1.6 in/s) and the individual volumetric gas flow rates can be adjusted. Self-supporting test specimens (S), 2-3 mm thick ($\approx$ 0.080-0.120 in), or sheet or film material (S') held in a frame (F), are placed in an upright position in the column, and the upper end is ignited with a gas flame igniter (I) (candle-like burning). Criteria of duration (3 min) or extent (50 mm) of burning are used to determine a critical volumetric (molar) oxygen concentration above which the test specimen continues to burn and below which it extinguishes. The concentration, on a percent basis, is referred to as the "oxygen index" (OI) or "limiting oxygen index" (LOI). Since the volumetric oxygen concentration in standard air is about 21%, materials with an oxygen index above 21 should, in principle, be self-extinguishing, and materials with OI smaller than 21 should burn in air. Combustion involves complex mechanisms, however, and depends on the specific conditions.

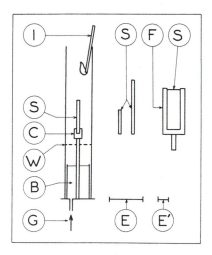

Figure 4.69 · **Oxygen index test** · (G) Gas mixture; (B) Glass beads; (W) Wire screen; (C) Clamp; (S) Test specimen; (I) Igniter; (F) Holding frame; (S′) Film or sheet; (E) 10 cm scale; (E′) 1 in scale

Polytetrafluoroethylene (PTFE), polyvinylidenechloride (PVDC) and polyarylsulfone (PASU), for example, are rated above 50. Polyvinylchloride (PVC), polyvinylidene fluoride (PVDF), polyphenylene sulfide (PPS), polyethersulfone (PESU), polyimides (PI), polyphenylene oxide (PPO), polycarbonate (PC) and polyamides (PA) are generally rated between 50 and 21 in the order given. Polystyrene (PS), polyethylene (PE), polypropylene (PP), polymethylene oxide or acetal (PMO) and cellulose acetate (CA) are generally rated below 21. It should be recognized, however, that the presence of fire retardant additives or other modifications can markedly modify the rating of polymeric materials.

4.12.2   Horizontal/Vertical Burning

One of the most frequently used tests, for the characterization of the flammability of rigid (self-supporting) plastics involves a horizontal cantilever-held test specimen (ASTM D635). The thickness of the test specimen (S) can be in the range 1.25-5 mm ($\approx$ 0.050-0.250 in); its longitudinal axis is horizontal, but it is tilted to an angle of 45° (Fig. 4.70). A 10-mm-barrel bunsen burner, set to give a blue flame, is used as the igniter (I); it is applied to the free end (B) of the test specimen for 30 s, and then removed. Depending on the burning mode, data are reported as average burning rate (ABR) in centimeters per minute (cm/min), i.e. the distance to the gauge mark (M) divided by the time for the flame or glow to reach it, or the average time of burning (ATB) in minutes and the average extent of burning (AEB) in millimeters when combustion ceases before reaching the gauge mark; the material is sometimes referred to as "self-extinguishing" in this case.

Materials or samples that are not stiff enough to be self-supporting in a cantilever test (sheets and films less than 1.25 mm or 0.050 in, for example) can be tested in a vertical position (ASTM D568). In this case (Fig. 4.71), the bunsen burner igniter (I) is applied to the low free end (B) until the test specimen ignites, but not longer than 15 s. The average burning rate (ABR), when combustion proceeds to the gauge mark (M), or the average time of burning (ATB) and the average extent of burning (ATB) are also reported. In such vertical upward burning test, the heat of combustion preheats the yet-unignited material most efficiently.

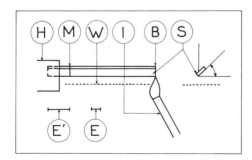

Fig. 4.70

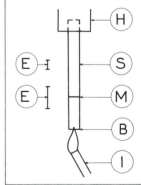

Fig. 4.71

Figure 4.70 · **Horizontal burning test** · (H) Holder; (M) Gauge mark; (W) Wire screen; (I) Igniter; (B) Free end; (S) Test specimen; (E) 1 cm scale; (E′) 1 in scale

Figure 4.71 · **Vertical burning test** · (H) Holder; (S) Test specimen; (M) Gauge mark; (B) Free end; (I) Igniter; (E) 1 cm scale; (E′) 1 in scale

4.12.3 UL Flammability Ratings

Underwriter Laboratories (UL) subject test specimens to flammability tests somewhat similar to ASTM D635 (horizontal) and ASTM D658 (vertical) and issue ratings for materials satisfying certain criteria (UL 94).

For the horizontal test, the test specimen (S) geometry and positioning (Fig. 4.72) are the same as for ASTM D635. The methane blue flame of an igniter (I) is applied to about 6 mm (1/4 in) of the free end, for a maximum of 30 s. If the flame propagates along the test specimen, the burning rate between the 1 in (25.4 mm) (M) and 4 in (101.6 mm) (M') gauge marks is determined. The material is rated HB (or 94 HB) if the burning rate is less than 1.5 in/min (38.1 mm/min) for test specimens 0.120 in ($\approx$ 1/8 in or 3mm) thick or thicker, or less than 3 in/min (76.2 mm/min) for test specimens thinner than 0.120 in (normally not thinner than about 0.030 in or 1/32 in, to be self-supporting). Materials now rated HB (horizontal-burning) were formerly rated SB (slow-burning).

For the vertical tests, normally applied to more fire resistant materials, bar-shaped or plaque-shaped test specimens are most commonly used (Fig. 4.73). For the least stringent ratings, the low end of the bar-shaped vertical test specimen (S) is subjected to the igniting flame (I) for 10 s; the flame is then withdrawn briefly and reapplied for

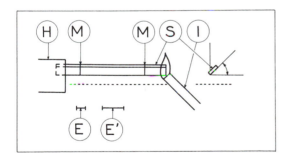

Fig. 4.72

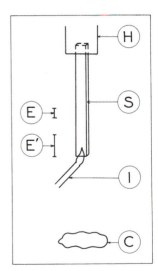

Fig. 4.73

Figure 4.72 · **UL horizontal flammability rating test** · (H) Holder; (M'),(M) Gauge marks; (S) Test specimen; (I) Igniter; (E) 1 cm scale; (E') 1 in scale

Figure 4.73 · **UL vertical flammability rating test** · (H) Holder; (S) Test specimen; (I) Igniter; (C) Cotton; (E) 1 cm scale; (E') 1 in scale

10 s. A rating V-O (most stringent), V-1, or V-2 is issued on the basis of criteria, including the flaming time (10 s, 30 s), the afterglow time (30 s, 60 s), and the tendency for flaming drips to ignite dry absorbent (surgical) cotton (C) placed 12 in (30.5 cm) below the test specimen. Materials now rated V-0 to V-2 were formerly rated SE-0 to SE-2 (self-extinguishing). A more stringent rating for bar-shaped test specimens involves five successive 5-s applications of the hottest part of the igniting flame, interspersed by 5-s withdrawals. Flaming or glowing combustion must not persist for over 60 s after the last flame application, with no dripping, for the material to be issued a 5V rating. In the case of plaques, the flame is applied in five different ways (Fig. 4.74). Materials now rated 5V were formerly rated SE-1A.

Thin materials (TM) samples require a special set-up (Fig. 4.75). Strip-shaped test specimens (S) are wrapped around a 12.5-mm (0.5 in)-diameter mandrel (R), and the testing leads to ratings VTM-0 (most-stringent), VTM-1, and VTM-2 according to the same procedure and criteria used for V-0 to V-2 ratings, except for flame applications of only 3 s.

Materials such as epoxy resins (ER), polyvinylchloride (PVC) and polytetrafluoroethylene (PTFE), are often rated 94 V-0, while polymethylene oxide or acetal (PMO) and polyurethane (PU) are often rated 94 HB. Fire retardant additives and other modifications can significantly change the ratings of polymeric materials.

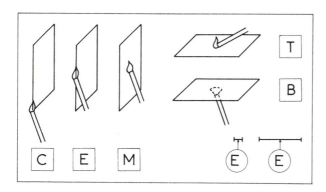

Fig. 4.74

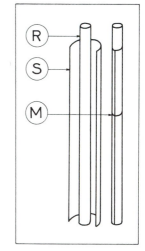

Fig. 4.75

Figure 4.74 · **Flame application for plaques** · [C] Corner; [E] Edge; [M] Center; [T] Top; [B] Bottom

Figure 4.75 · **Thin material flammability rating** · (R) Mandrel; (S) Test specimen; (M) Gauge mark

4.12.4   Ignition Temperature

The tendency for materials to catch fire (ignite) in air, at high temperatures, can be assessed through a small-scale test using a so-called hot-air ignition furnace or Stechkin (Setchkin) apparatus (ASTM D1929). The furnace (Fig. 4.76) consists of two concentric ceramic tubes; the outer tube (O) is surrounded by electric heating elements (H), capable of heating the furnace to a maximum temperature of about 750°C ($\approx$ 1 382°F). The inner tube (C), a bottom, and a lid with an opening form the chamber. A small amount (about 3 g or 0.1 oz) of test material (S) is placed on a support in the chamber, and a metered flow of air (A) is fed in the space between the ceramic tubes and then introduced at the bottom of the chamber. The minimum temperature required to produce gases that can be ignited with a pilot (igniter) flame (I), placed over the lid opening, is referred to as the "flash ignition temperature" (FIT).

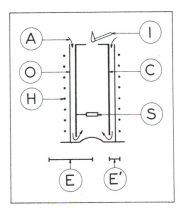

Figure 4.76 · **Hot air ignition furnace** · (H) Heating elements; (O) Outer tube; (A) Air inlet; (I) Igniter; (C) Inner tube; (S) Test specimen; (E) 10 cm scale; (E′) 1 in scale

The minimum temperature required to cause the spontaneous ignition of the test specimen is referred to as the "self-ignition temperature" (SIT). Ignition may correspond to an explosion, flame, or sustained glow.

The two ignition temperatures can be close, for example, FIT $\approx$ 341°C (645°F) and SIT $\approx$ 349°C (660°F) for a polyethylene (PE); significantly different, for example, FIT $\approx$ 390°C (735°F) and SIT $\approx$ 455°C (850°F) for a polyvinylchloride (PVC); or quite different, for example, FIT $\approx$ 350°C (680°F) and SIT $\approx$ 496°F (925°F) for a polystyrene (PS). High SIT values are reported for a polypropylene (PP) (570°C or 1058°F), a polycarbonate (PC) (580°C or 1076°F) and a polyamide (PA) (530°C or 986°F).

4.12.5   Incandescent Contact

The assessment of the resistance of rigid plastics to contact with an incandescent surface (ASTM D757) is of special importance for applications involving electric heating elements and concerns, particularly, materials used for insulation purposes. A horizontal silicon carbide (SiC) rod (R), heated to a temperature of 950°C or 1742°F (cherry red) by an electric current, is used as the incandescent surface (Fig. 4.77). The horizontal test specimen (S) is gently pressed against the rod (force (F) of about 275 N or 1/16 lb) for a period of 3 min. The test specimen may burn, fuse, char, or shrink. Depending on the burning mode, results are reported as average burning rate (ABR) in mm/min, average time of burning (ATB) in min, or average extent of burning (AEB) in mm.

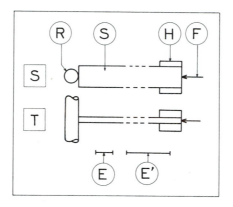

Figure 4.77 · **Incandescent contact test** · [S] Side view; [T] Top view; (R) Heated rod; (S) Test specimen; (H) holder; (F) Pressing force; (E) 1 cm scale; (E') 1 in scale

4.12.6   Radiant Panel Test

The surface flammability of plaques can be assessed in a small-scale test (ASTM E162), often referred to as the "radiant panel test." The test apparatus (Fig. 4.78)) features a radiant panel (P), kept at a temperature of about 670°C (1238°F) and usually gas-fired. The test specimen (S) faces the radiant panel, but at an angle of 30°. A pilot burner (igniter) (I), at the upper end of the test specimen, can be used to ignite combustion gases; in this case, the flame front progresses downward, along the test specimen. Gases evolved are channeled through a stack (C) that can be fitted with temperature sensors (T) and a filter to collect smoke particles. Data can be analyzed and reported in terms of flame spread factor (FS), heat evolution factor (Q), and flame spread index (FSI).

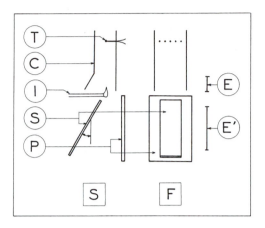

Figure 4.78 · **Radiant panel test** · [S] Side view; [F] Front view; (T) Temperature sensor; (C) Stack; (I) Igniter; (S) Test specimen; (P) Radiant panel; (E) 10 cm scale; (E′) 1 ft scale

4.12.7 Tunnel Fire Test

The tunnel test, or Steiner tunnel test (ASTM E84), is intended to provide a comparative assessment of the surface burning characteristics of materials on a relatively large scale. The fire test chamber (Fig. 4.79) is a long, insulated, horizontal duct with a removable lid (L). The fire end (F) features an air intake and a gas burner (B) rated at about 5.3 MJ/min ($\approx$ 5000 Btu/min). The chamber is equipped with observation windows (W) along its length. The vent end (V) features a temperature sensor, an optical device (O) to record the obscuration associated with the smoke generated (vertical light path), and a draft device to establish a specific gas flow rate in the tunnel. Test specimens (S), about 50 cm ($\approx$ 20 in) wide and 7.3 m ($\approx$ 24 ft) long, are held horizontally between the lid and the chamber walls. They may consist of joined sections and may be supported by a suitable open structure (wire mesh, etc.).

After the gas burner is turned on, the propagation of the flame front is monitored through the windows for the duration of the test (maximum 10 min). The burner and draft conditions correspond to a flame spread time of about 5.5 min for the maximum spread distance of about 6 m ($\approx$ 19.5 ft), in the case of the reference flooring-grade red oak. Data of flame spread distance versus time for other materials are used to determine a flame spread index (FSI), which is 0 for incombustible asbestos-cement board and 100 for red oak. FSI values below about 25 correspond to materials normally rated as incombustible; examples of other ratings are as follows: 25-50 (fire resistant), 50-75 (slow burning), 75-200 (combustible) and over 200 (highly combustible).

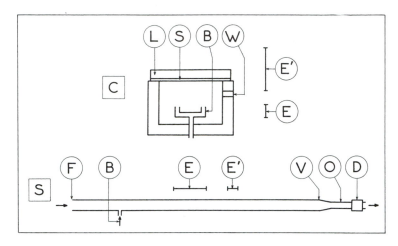

Figure 4.79 · **Tunnel fire test** · [S] Side view; [C] Cross view; (F) Fire end; (B) Gas burner; (V) Vent end; (O) Optical device; (D) Draft device; (L) Lid; (S) Test specimen; (W) Window; (E) 1 m scale (side view); (E′) 1 ft scale

4.12.8   Smoke/Toxic Gases Generation

Burning or smoldering polymeric materials usually generate (evolve) smoke, which is generally undesirable, but which also often serves to trigger fire detection devices.

Several standard tests are designed to provide a quantitative measurement of the amount of smoke generated by the combustion of polymeric materials.

The ASTM smoke density test (ASTM D2843) involves a smoke density chamber (Fig. 4.80) featuring a horizontal test specimen (S) holder, a propane-fueled burner (I), an optical device (O) to record light transmitted over a horizontal light path across the chamber, and a standard "exit" sign on the back panel. After a test specimen is ignited in the chamber, which is closed except for small vents at the bottom, the percent light absorption (obscuration) is monitored for 4 min and presented as a specific smoke density D/time T curve. Data are often reported as D_{90} (90 sec), D_4 (4 min), D_M (maximum level), or as total smoke produced (smoke density rating), which corresponds to the area under the curve. A blower (B) is used to purge the chamber after a test. The Rohm and Haas XP-2 chamber is associated with this test.

The NBS smoke test uses a somewhat different chamber with the test specimen held vertically and subjected to an electric radiant panel (2.5 W/cm^2). The light path of the optical device used to record the light absorption is vertical to circumvent smoke stratification problems. Data are often reported as maximum specific optical density ($\mathbf{D_M}$), visibility reduction time (VRT) which corresponds to 25% reduction, smoke obscuration number (SON) or smoke obscuration index (SOI). The chamber is sometimes referred to as the "Aminco/NBS chamber."

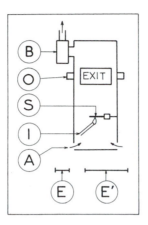

Figure 4.80 · **Smoke density chamber** · (B) Blower; (O) Optical device; (S) Test specimen; (I) Igniter; (A) Air inlet; (E) 10 cm scale; (E′) 1 ft scale

A test referred to as the "Arapahoe/Syntex test" determines the mass of smoke particles collected on a filter (gravimetric method) when the smoke generated by a short exposure to a flame (30 s) is vacuum-suctioned.

All smoke tests are controversial as to their absolute value, but they allow useful comparisons between materials tested under identical conditions.

There is often a significant difference between the amounts of smoke generated under smoldering or flaming conditions. Under smoldering conditions, polyvinylchloride (PVC) and polyethylene (PE) are among the highest smoke producers, while polycarbonate (PC) or polyamides (PA) are low; ABS resins are fairly low also. Under flaming conditions, ABS resins and polystyrene (PS) are high, polyamides (PA) remain low, but polycarbonate (PC) is substantially higher.

Besides smoke, which reduces visibility in fire situations, there is generally much concern regarding the toxicity of gases produced during combustion (noxious fumes), although fire casualties are perhaps more often the result of a lack of oxygen than fumes toxicity. Chemical analysis is required to determine the composition of combustion fumes.

Real large-scale fires, such as room fires, involve many factors, such as ventilation, turbulence, heat losses, and radiation-related ignition of contents, which are not easily controlled in simple standard tests. Attempts are made to develop mathematical models of fires, which could allow at least the rough assessment of the effect of many factors, and consequently reduce the amount of experimentation required.

Some devices used for flammability and combustion testing are shown in figures 4.81-4.84.

Figure 4.81 · Oxygen index apparatus (Stanton Redcroft) [TARLIN]

Figure 4.82 · Radiant panel apparatus [CSI]

Figure 4.83 · Smoke density chamber (NBS type)

Figure 4.84 · Smoke density chamber (Rohm and Haas type)

4.13 ELECTRICAL PROPERTIES

Polymers are widely used in electrical and electronic applications. In most cases, they play an insulating role and require some structural (mechanical) resistance. Electrical properties are associated with static electrical charges, direct electrical currents (DC currents), and alternating electrical currents (AC currents). Major variables include the voltage (difference of potential), expressed in volts (V); the current, expressed in amperes or amps (A); and, in the case of AC currents, the frequency, expressed in cycles per second or hertz (Hz). Voltages may be just microvolts (mV) in electronic applications or kilovolts (kV) in power distribution. Frequencies are normally 50 or 60 Hz for power distribution, but the electromagnetic spectrum covers a very wide range of frequencies, with typical sub-ranges, including audio frequencies (about 3-15 kHz), radio frequencies RF (about 15kHz to 3000 MHz), hyperfrequencies, or microwaves (about 3000 kHz or 3-300 GHz). Radar frequencies, for example, are typically around 10 GHz. Electromagnetic waves can also be characterized by their wavelength, expressed in meters (m), millimeters (mm), or micrometers (μm).

There are several fundamental electrical properties that are basically material properties; they include volume resistivity and permittivity. Other properties, which are important in some types of applications, include dielectric strength, and arc resistance and are the subject of standard tests.

4.13.1   Electrical Resistance

When a DC voltage is applied, through suitable electrodes, to a polymeric test specimen in such a way that a uniform current flows through the material, the volume resistivity p_v of the material can be determined and expressed, for example, in units of ohms $\cdot$ centimeters ($\Omega \cdot cm$). The inverse of the volume resistivity is the volume conductivity σ_v expressed in siemens per centimeter (S/cm). Highly conductive metals have volume conductivities as high as 0.6×10^6 S/cm or 0.6 MS/cm, while the lowest volume conductivity is probably around 10^{-19} S/cm for paraffins; corresponding volume resistivity are about 1.6×10^{-6} $\Omega \cdot cm$ and 10^{19} $\Omega \cdot cm$, respectively.

ASTM D257 discusses specific methods for the assessment of the electrical resistance of insulating materials for a variety of test specimen shapes and dimensions and corresponding electrodes.

The volume resistivity of polymeric materials can be a function of a variety of factors. A relatively minor factor is the electrification or polarization time, which reflects a certain delay in the establishment of a steady current and is generally set at 60 s. The voltage is also a minor factor, in a reasonable range, and is generally set at 500 V (DC). The presence of impurities, additives, plasticizers, or fillers can have a strong effect on the volume resistivity; normally insulating polymers can, in fact, be made fairly conductive by the addition of relatively small amounts of metallic or carbon black powders or special additives. When a polymer is capable of absorbing significant amounts of water, humidity conditions and the corresponding conditioning are very important and must be specified. The volume resistivity of polymers normally drops markedly when the temperature increases, unless it is associated with a moisture content reduction.

Fluorocarbon polymers (PTFE) and polystyrene PS are generally the most resistive (insulating) plastics ($\approx 10^{18}$ $\Omega \cdot cm$); polyethylenes (PE) are often in the range 10^{15}-10^{16} $\Omega \cdot cm$; polyvinylchlorides (PVC) can be in the range 10^{11} to 10^{15} $\Omega \cdot cm$, depending on the degree of plasticization; phenolics are commonly in the range 10^{10}-10^{12} $\Omega \cdot cm$. Volume resistivity in the approximate range 10^7-10^{13} $\Omega \cdot cm$ are associated with polymers referred to as "antistatic," and the range 10^3-10^6 $\Omega \cdot cm$ is associated with so-called static-dissipating polymers. Polymeric systems are considered conductive when their volume resistivity drops in the range $1\text{-}10^3$ $\Omega \cdot$ cm, and applications include situations where static electricity build up must be prevented, as well as electromagnetic interference (EMI) shielding. Highly conductive polymeric systems (over 1 S/cm) are being investigated as lightweight alternatives for battery electrodes, for example; they are based on polyacetylene, poly p-phenylene, polyphenylene sulfide (PPS), and other compounds.

In many applications of polymeric materials, a form of electrical conduction, referred to as "surface conduction" or sometimes "surface leakage," can occur. Such conduction can be strongly affected by factors such as the presence of contaminants on the surface, which may help provide a conductive path. When such factors are eliminated, a surface resistivity p_s, which is characteristic of the test specimen surface, can be determined. The normal unit for surface resistivity is the ohm (Ω), but to distinguish it from the volume resistance, it is often referred to as ohm per square (Ω/sq).

The determination of volume or surface resistivity, which are basically material properties, is done for test specimens of convenient shape and dimensions. The measurement of the resistance between conductors separated by a specific insulating part, does not normally allow the determination of a material property, but it can be valuable either to rank materials or for quality control purposes. The inverse of the resistance is called the "conductance."

4.13.2 Dielectric Properties

Polymers are widely used in situations involving alternating (AC) currents. Their primary role is often that of an insulator, but they can also be the dielectric material in capacitors, and, in some cases, AC currents are actually used to heat polymers through dielectric effects.

The characterization of the dielectric characteristics of a materials involve the analysis of a sinusoidal AC voltage, and the corresponding sinusoidal current passing through test specimens of certain shapes and dimensions (ASTM D150). Two basic materials properties can be determined, which are often referred to as the "dielectric constant" and the "dissipation factor."

In the context of the static charge of a capacitor, the dielectric constant (or permittivity) ϵ_0 of a material is defined as the ratio of the capacitance of the capacitor, with the material as the dielectric, to the capacitance of the same capacitor, with a vacuum between the electrodes. It is, therefore, a dimensionless quantity.

The definition of a dielectric constant (or permittivity) ϵ' for an AC current is more complicated and may depend significantly on the frequency. It is also a dimensionless quantity, and tends toward ϵ_0 for low frequencies. The dielectric constant ϵ' is often reported at 50 or 60 Hz (power distribution frequency), and at much higher frequencies, such as 10^3 Hz (1 kHz) and 10^6 Hz (1 MHz).

The dielectric constant of dry air is approximately 1, i.e. close to that of vacuum; it is approximately 80 for water. For polymeric materials, it is generally in the relatively narrow range 2-10. Some fluorocarbon polymers, (PTFE), polyethylene, (PE) and polystyrene (PS), have low dielectric constants (slightly over 2), which are also almost independent of frequency. Polymers with the highest dielectric constants include cellulose acetates (CA), phenolic and amino resins, some polyamides, (PA) and some fluorocarbon polymers (PVDF).

The dielectric constant is not generally a strong function of temperature. The characterization of the dielectric behavior of insulators, or dielectrics, under AC current loads also requires the knowledge of a second dimensionless quantity, which can have widely different values for different materials, and reflects most directly the power dissipation that can take place in the insulator or dielectric. Such quantity can be the phase angle ϕ (radians), the power factor cos ϕ, the loss angle δ (radians), which is the complement of the phase angle ($\delta + \phi = \pi/2$), and the loss tangent or dissipation factor tan δ, which is the most commonly used quantity. The power dissipated in a dielectric is proportional to the product of the dielectric constant by the dissipation factor, which is referred to as the "loss index" or "loss factor" $\epsilon'' = \epsilon'$ tan δ. A certain analogy is found with dynamic mechanical testing.

Since the dielectric constant ϵ' does not vary very much, the dissipation factor tan δ tends to reflect the tendency of a material to dissipate energy in AC fields. Such dissipation is generally undesirable, but it is used to advantage to heat certain polymers.

There are several mechanisms which can be responsible for dissipation in polymeric systems; a major one being associated with dipoles. Polar materials have a much higher dissipation factor than nonpolar ones. The dissipation factor can be a rather strong function of the frequency, with changes by a factor 10 for the range 60 Hz to 1 MHz not uncommon. It can also be a significant function of temperature.

Representative values, for the low dissipation factor of polyethylenes (PE), polypropylenes (PP) and some fluoropolymers (PTFE), are in the range 0.0001-0.0005; in this case, data are sometimes reported as "loss angle δ in microradians (μrad)," with δ in radians being approximately equal to tan δ. Intermediate dissipation levels correspond to 0.0010 to 0.0100. Polymers, such as polyamides (PA), acrylics (PMMA), and some fluoropolymers (PCTFE), can have dissipation factors above 0.0100.

4.13.3   Dielectric Strength

When insulating or dielectric materials are subjected to sustained AC fields, power dissipation may occur and cause a temperature rise in the material. The temperature may stabilize as a result of external cooling, for example (thermal equilibrium), or a situation of thermal runaway may develop.

Very strong AC fields (high voltages) can cause the short-term failure of insulating or dielectric materials, associated with erosion, or the formation of a conducting track through the thickness of the material, which is referred to as "electrical or dielectric breakdown." Standard tests are designed to allow the determination of the minimum voltage causing the breakdown (dielectric breakdown voltage) and the dielectric strength (voltage per unit thickness of material between electrodes). The breakdown voltage is expressed in volts (V) and the dielectric strength in volts per cm (V/cm) or volts per mil; 1 mil is equal to 0.001 in or 0.00254 cm, 1 kV/mil ≈ 394 kV/cm. The ASTM D149 test involves cylindrical electrodes with rounded edges placed on opposite faces of films, sheets or plates of material (Fig. 4.85). Power distribution frequency (60 Hz) is normally used for the AC voltage. Since the specific conditions of application of the voltage have an effect on the results, three short-term methods are described (short time, slow rate of rise, and step by step). In the short time method, for example, a uniform rate of voltage rise is specified (0.1 kV/s-3 kV/s). Breakdown normally corresponds to a sudden current surge and to rupture or local decomposition of the material. Precautions must be taken to avoid undesirable flashover or corona edge effects. The dielectric strength is not completely independent of the thickness of the test specimen and is generally higher for very thin films.

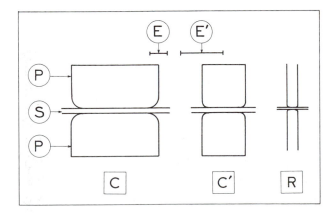

Figure 4.85 · **Electrodes for dielectric strength test** · [C],[C′] Cylinders; [R] Rod; (P),(P′) Electrodes; (S) Test specimen; (E) 1 cm scale; (E′) 1 in scale

High short-term dielectric strengths are reported for some fluoropolymers (PFA), about 800 kV/cm ($\approx$ 2 kV/mil), and for polyvinylchloride (PVC), about 400 kV/cm. Polystyrene (PS) corresponds to about 250 kV/cm, polyethylene (PE) to about 200 kV/cm; phenolic resins (PF) to about 120 kV/cm, and another fluoropolymer (PVDF) to about 100 kV/cm.

4.13.4   Arc Resistance

Insulating materials are often subjected to arcs arising from the opening and closing of circuits in switches, circuit breakers, connectors, and distributor caps, for example. The surface characteristics of the insulator may become altered to the point where it shows unacceptable surface conduction or leakage, often referred to as "tracking" or "surface tracking," which is normally associated with a form of degradation of the material (carbonization, formation of ignitable gases, etc.).   In some cases, unacceptable removal of material (erosion) may occur.

The characterization of the arc resistance of insulating polymers is a complex problem, in view of the many parameters involved, and standard tests provide only some limited information. Tests can be divided into dry or wet tests.

ASTM D495 describes a dry test involving a high voltage (12.5 kV), low-current (maximum of 40 mA) arc, produced between two electrodes. Thin stainless steel strip electrodes or tungsten rod electrodes can be used. The arc is produced between the corner of the rectangular strip [S] electrodes or between the tips of the chisel-shaped rod [R] electrodes (Fig. 4.86). A rather complicated scheme is used to gradually increase the severity of the test. For the first 240 s (4 min), an intermittent (inter-

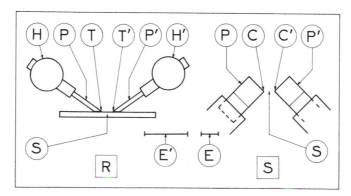

Figure 4.86 · **Electrodes for arc resistance test** · [R] Rod; [S] Strip; (H),(H′) Holders; (P),(P′) Electrodes; (T),(T′) Tips; (C),(C′) Corners; (S) Test specimen; (E) 1 cm scale; (E′) 1 in scale

rupted) arc is applied under 10 mA. For the following 180 s (3 min), the arc is applied continuously under a current increasing to 40 mA. Tracking is detected by observation, or by a major change in the current. The time corresponding to the onset of tracking is reported as the arc resistance time in seconds. It should be noted that, since this is basically a surface phenomenon, any surface contamination (moisture, dust, finger marks, etc.) can have a significant effect on the results.

Polytetrafluoroethylene (PTFE) has a very high dry arc resistance (over 200 s). Among thermosets frequently used as insulators, alkyds, and melamine resins are reported to be superior to phenolics. Polyethylenes (PE) have a relatively high arc resistance (around 150 s), while polystyrenes (PS) and polyvinylchlorides (PVC) have a relatively low arc resistance (around 70 s).

The arc resistance can also be assessed in the presence of a liquid medium that can be a conductive solution (electrolyte), applied drop by drop between two electrodes in contact with a test specimen. Tracking is again associated with a current rise, and a comparative tracking index (CTI) can be defined, which is associated with the number of drops required for tracking. A number of other names are associated with tests of this type, such as "inclined plane-tracking," and "differential wet tracking."

The flammability of polymeric materials exposed to arcs is often an important concern. Long-term effects of mild arcs on polymeric materials must also be considered when designing electrical components for long life.

4.14 GAS OR VAPOR PERMEABILITY

Compared to other materials, such as metals or glass, polymers are relatively permeable to the molecules of liquids or gases. The motion of such molecules through a polymer, is often referred to as "mass transport." It is a rather complex process that may involve several mechanisms. Diffusing (penetrant) molecules may be those of a "permanent" gas, such as oxygen (O_2), nitrogen (N_2) or carbon dioxide (CO_2), or those of a chemical that may be in liquid form under normal conditions (e.g., water or gasoline).

The quantitative assessment of the "ease" of penetration (permeation, transport, transmission) of diffusing molecules, through polymers, is important in view of the numerous applications which involve this phenomenon. Such applications include the packaging of a wide variety of products, often in the form of films; the protection of substrates, such as metal structures or electronic components from chemical attack (coatings, linings, encapsulation). In those cases, important diffusing substances include O_2 (food spoiling, metal oxidation, etc.), CO_2 (carbonated beverages, plant metabolism, etc.) and H_2O (moisture content or dryness of packaged articles, etc.).

An important area involving the motion of small molecules, through polymeric materials, is that of membrane separation and filtration, with specific examples, such as desalination (desalting) of brackish and sea waters, wastewater treatment (reclamation of domestic, municipal, or industrial effluents), blood dialysis and oxygenation, food processing, and preparative biochemistry. They are associated with pressure-driven techniques, such as microfiltration (MF), ultrafiltration (UF), hyperfiltration (HF), reverse osmosis (RO), gas separation, and voltage-driven electro-dialysis.

Another growing application involves the controlled permeation of substances through the wall of either microcapsules (microencapsulation), associated with contraceptives, parasite diseases control, selective ion removal, living tissues encapsulation, *in situ* catalysis, etc., or larger capsules (fertilizers, pesticides, etc.)

4.14.1   Gas Transmission

Gas "permeability" (GP) is determined by subjecting a thin test specimen of thickness h and area a to a pressure difference Δp. The transmission rate is generally expressed as the volume of gas Δv, under standard temperature and pressure conditions (STP), which is transmitted over an interval of time Δt. Reported permeabilities correspond to the reduction of actual data to specific reference conditions, based on fundamental principles. A set of specific reference conditions, commonly used in association with the British system of units, corresponds to h = 1 mil (0.001 in), a = 1 in^2, Δp = 1 atmosphere (14.7 psi or $\approx$ 0.1 MPa), and Δt = 24 h (1 day), with Δv expressed in cm^3 (cc or ml). One metric set of reference conditions involves h = 1 cm, a = 1 cm^2, Δp = 1 Pa, and Δt = 1 s, with Δv in cm^3. The rational, SI-based, unit of permeability should correspond to h = 1 m, a = 1 m^2, Δp = 1 Pa, and Δt = 1 s with the mass Δm in kg or, better, in kg-moles given, rather than Δv (STP).

The measurement of the gas transmission rate (GTR) of "permanent" gases through polymeric films or sheets is the subject of ASTM D1434, which discusses two procedures (manometric and volumetric procedures). In both cases (Fig. 4.87 and 4.88), a disk-shaped test specimen (S), typically 10 cm ($\approx$ 4 in) in diameter, is tightly sealed around its periphery, through the use of a suitable gasket (G), to form a barrier between a high-pressure zone (H) [gas inlet (I)], and a low-pressure zone (L). The gas permeates through the film from (H) to (L). A porous medium (A) (filter paper or sintered material) helps support film specimens without hindering the gas flow.

The principle of the manometric procedure (Fig. 4.87) (Dow cell) is to evacuate the low pressure cavity [chamber (L)] of the permeability cell through a port (O), and to monitor the subsequent pressure rise as the permeating gas enters it. When a mercury manometer is used, the movement of the mercury meniscus (M) in the capillary tube (T) is followed visually (cathetometer), or through the change of resistance of a platinum wire. Pressure transducers, which do not cause any change of volume of the low-pressure cavity, facilitate the analysis of results. The initial volume of the low pressure cavity (L) can be modified through the use of solid or hollow volume adaptors (V) for low- or high-permeability films. Pressure in the high-pressure zone (H) can also be a variable.

In the volumetric procedure (Fig. 4.88), the low-pressure side (L) is maintained under atmospheric pressure, and the volumetric flow rate of gas across the film is monitored through the movement of a short slug (index) (R) of a suitable liquid [e.g., methyl isobutyl ketone (MIK)], in a capillary tube (T) (diameter 0.25 - 1 mm).

For both procedures, the gas transmission rate (GTR) and the permeability, in the case of homogeneous test specimens, are calculated from data corresponding to steady state permeation. For heterogeneous, layered, test specimens, consisting of several different materials, the gas transmission rate (GTR) associated with the specific test specimen structure is reported.

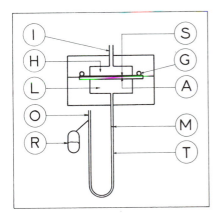

Fig. 4.87

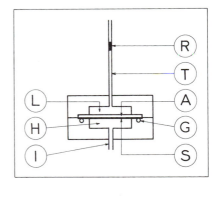

Fig. 4.88

Figure 4.87 · **Gas transmission test; manometric procedure** · (R) Overflow reservoir; (O) Port; (L) Low pressure zone; (H) High pressure zone; (I) Inlet; (S) Test specimen; (G) Gasket; (A) Porous support; (M) Mercury meniscus; (T) Capillary tube

Figure 4.88 · **Gas transmission test; volumetric procedure** · (I) Inlet; (H) High pressure zone; (R) Liquid slug; (T) Capillary tube; (A) Porous support; (G) Gasket; (S) Test specimen

4.14.2   Water Vapor Transmission

Water vapor transmission (WVT), or moisture vapor transmission rate (MVTR), can be determined by subjecting one face of a flat test specimen to the action of a dehydrating agent desiccant, that is, a very low relative humidity (RH ≈ 0), and the other face to an atmosphere of a specific relative humidity RH. In this case, the transmission rate under steady state conditions is expressed as the mass   m of water having permeated across the test specimen, which corresponds to the weight increase of the desiccant, during an interval of time **Δt**. The set of specific reference conditions, commonly used for films in the British system of units, corresponds to h = 1 mil (0.001 in), **a** = 1 in^2, and **Δt** = 24 h (1 day), with **Δm** expressed in grams. One metric set of reference conditions involves h = 1 cm, a = 1 cm^2, and **Δt** = 1 s, with **Δm** in grams. The rational, SI-based unit should be the same as in the gas transmission case.

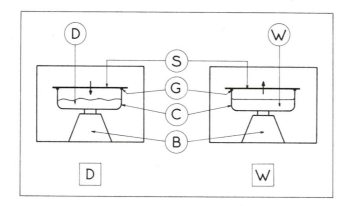

Figure 4.89 · **Water vapor transmission test** · [D] Dessicant method; [W] Water method; (D) Dessicant; (S) Test specimen; (G) Seal; (C) Dish; (B) Scale; (W) Water

ASTM E96 deals with the measurement of the water vapor transmission of sheet material by two methods (desiccant and water methods). In each case, a test specimen (S) (Fig. 4.89) is placed over an impermeable aluminum or glass dish (cup, pan) (C), and a tight seal (G) is provided around the edge (gasket, cement, wax, etc.). The weight of the assembly can be monitored [scale (B)] and is placed in a controlled atmosphere (A); the temperature and relative humidity RH are typically 32°C (90°F) and 50% RH or 38°C (100°F) and 90% RH for low and high humidities, respectively. In the desiccant method [D], the dish (C) contains a desiccant (D) (RH ≈ 0%), such as anhydrous calcium chloride $CaCl_2$ or silica gel, and, in this case, the water molecules move across the test specimen (S), from the controlled atmosphere (A) (source) to the desiccant (D) (sink), the assembly gaining weight. In the water method [W], the dish contains distilled water (W) (RH $\approx$ 100%) and the water molecules move across the test specimen (S), from the dish (C) (source) to the controlled atmosphere (A) (sink); the assembly loses weight. For each method, after an "induction" period, a steady-state permeation regime is reached, which corresponds to a linear increase or decrease of weight of the assembly with time; data can be converted into water vapor transmission (WVT) or permeance.

Gas and vapor transmission through polymers is a relatively strong function of temperature; the transmission rate generally increases at higher temperatures. A number of polymers can absorb significant amounts of moisture, which is often present in the environment, and the rate of transmission of gases through hygroscopic polymers generally increases with increasing moisture content. Polymers in a rubbery state tend to have higher transmission rates than in a glassy state, since the increased mobility of the polymer chains favors the motion of the penetrant molecules. The motion of penetrant molecules is strongly impeded in the crystalline regions of crystallizing polymers, and the permeability decreases with increasing degree of crystallinity.

In view of the confusing variety of units used in the literature for reporting gas or vapor transmission rates or permeabilities, and of the fact that relatively large differences, associated with molecular modifications or additives, exist within classes, it has appeared convenient to give examples in terms of the ratio of permeability to that of widely used low density polyethylene LDPE (e.g., x 10), with the understanding that these are only rough representative figures.

In the case of oxygen (O_2) permeability, few polymers have a permeability higher than that of low density polyethylene and they are normally elastomeric materials: ratios are $\approx$ x 100 for silicone rubber, $\approx$ x 4 for natural rubber. The ratios are $\approx$ x 0.3 for high density polyethylene (HDPE), about the same for oriented polypropylene (OPP), $\approx$ x 0.5 for polystyrene (PS), $\approx$ x 0.2 for butyl rubber and $\approx$ x 0.006 for polyamides (PA). Polyvinylidenechloride (PVDC) is an outstanding oxygen barrier material (ratio $\approx$ x 0.001).

For CO_2 permeability, representative ratios are $\approx$ x 50 for silicone rubber, $\approx$ x 5 for natural rubber (NR), $\approx$ x 15 for butyl rubber, $\approx$ x 0.15 for HDPE, $\approx$ x 0.006 for polyamides (PA), $\approx$ x 0.004 for polyethylene terephthalate (PET) and $\approx$ x 0.001 for polyvinylidenechloride (PVDC).

For H_2O transmission, representative ratios are $\approx$ x 100 for cellulose acetate (CA), $\approx$ x 50 for silicone rubber, $\approx$ x 40 for ethylene-vinyl alcohol (EVAL), $\approx$ x 15 for natural rubber (NR), $\approx$ x 10 for polyamides (PA), $\approx$ x 5 for polystyrene (PS), $\approx$ x 3 for polycarbonate (PC), ≈ x 1 for polyethylene terephthalate (PET), ≈ x 0.05 for HDPE and PP and ≈ x 0.02 for polyvinylidenechloride (PVDC).

Gas and water transmission testing is shown in figures 4.90 and 4.91.

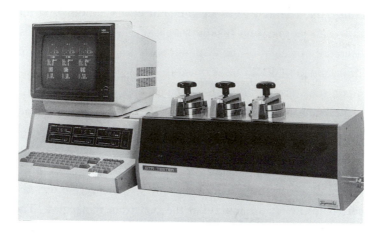

Figure 4.90 · Gas transmission rate tester (three-cell model) [TOYOSEIKI]

Figure 4.91 · Water vapor transmission tester [THWING-ALBERT]

4.15   OPTICAL PROPERTIES

Most polymeric materials are intrinsically capable of transmitting electromagnetic radiations in the wavelength range corresponding to visible light ($\approx$ 3900-8000 Å or 390-800 nm). Light sources (sunlight, incandescent, vapor-arc, and arc lamps) have a characteristic radiation spectrum, and filters can be used to enhance certain wavelengths such as violet ($\approx$ 410 nm), yellow ($\approx$ 580 nm), or red (650 nm). Standards have been set by the Commission Internationale de l'Eclairage (CIE).

Noncrystallizing pure polymers (sometimes referred to as "amorphous polymers") often allow high levels of light transmission and can thus be referred to as "transparent polymers." They include many styrenics (PS, etc.), acrylics (PMMA, etc.), cellulosics (CA, etc.), as well as engineering plastics, such as polycarbonate (PC), polysulfone (PSU), also thermosets, such as unsaturated polyester, epoxy and urethane resins (UP, EP, UR) and unfilled, specially compounded elastomers (polyisoprene PI, silicone, urethane, etc.). The presence of crystalline regions in crystallizing polymers tends to reduce the level of light transmission, and pure semicrystalline polymers in moderate thicknesses are generally translucent. They include olefinics (PE, PP, etc.), polyamides (PA 6, PA 6-6, etc.), and thermoplastic polyesters (PET, PBT, etc.). There are, however, examples of crystallizing polymers that can be made into highly transparent, relatively thick, objects; they include polymethylpentene (PMP) and polyethyleneterephthalate (PET). Films of many crystallizing polymers, particularly oriented films, can also be transparent.

The presence of additives, particularly colorants and fillers, can reduce or suppress light transmission through any polymer.

The transparency or translucency of polyalloys is influenced by the size of the domains; transparency is lost when the average domain size is significantly larger than the wavelength of light ($\approx$ 1 μm).

The orientation of the polymeric chains in polymeric materials causes optical anisotropy, which can be characterized or detected by techniques, including birefringence measurements, or X-ray diffraction in the case of semicrystalline polymers.

Classical optical theory is geometrical in nature and does not account for the fact that light rays are diffused (scattered) by the media and interfaces. Polymeric light-transmitting solids, however, correspond to a wide range of optical behavior, from transparent (crystal-clear, water-clear, etc.) to diffusing (translucent, hazy, cloudy, milky, opalescent, etc.). Some materials may appear translucent under certain conditions (distant viewing) but clear under other conditions (contact-clarity).

The practical characterization of the optical properties of polymeric solids is a complex subject. It involves the definition and measurement of quantities such as index of refraction, transparency, gloss, haze, and yellowness index.

Transparent polymers and, in some cases, translucent polymers have found many applications where their optical properties match those of glass, the traditional alternative. They are superior, however, in other respects (weight, impact resistance, moldability, etc.).

Transparent protective and decorative applications include large parts, such as flat glazing, corrugated panels, skylights, domes, canopies, cockpit covers, blisters or bubbles for airplanes and helicopters, solar collectors, and mirrorized sheets; smaller parts include windshields, face shields, and safety glasses. Large translucent panels are used for internally lighted signs.

Excellent optical quality is required for certain applications, such as automotive lenses (taillights, headlights), prescription and sunglasses lenses, and even camera lenses.

Thin polymeric coatings (acrylic, urethane or silicone) are used on polymeric or inorganic transparent parts to protect them against chemicals or abrasion, or to alter their surface characteristics (anti-glare coatings).

Applications involving fluid sighting include fluid level indicators, syringes, filter bowls, flowmeters, pressure gauge lenses, and seethrough tubing and piping.

Electrical applications include transparent cable connectors, fuse carriers and covers, and relay casings and covers.

Lighting applications are associated with translucent or transparent diffusers and globes in fixtures.

A growing field of application concerns optical fibers used for light piping or communications.

4.15.1   Refraction

The characterization of highly transparent materials, from the point of view of classical geometrical optics, involves concepts of reflection (angle of reflection equal to the angle of incidence) and refraction (angle of refraction r different from angle of incidence i). Figure 4.92 illustrates the refraction concept. The index of refraction or refractive index n is defined as the ratio of the speed of light in vacuum [or approximately in air (A)] to the speed of light in the solid material (M) and can be calculated from the angles i and r of the incident (I) and refracted (R) rays, respectively, through the expression n = sin i/sin r.

Two methods are suitable for transparent polymers (ASTM D542). One method uses an Abbé refractometer with a contacting liquid of high refractive index to ensure a good contact between the test specimen and the refractometer prisms. The other method uses an optical microscope, which is first focused on the upper surface of the test specimen, and then on the lower surface; the index of refraction is the ratio of the actual test specimen thickness to the length of travel of the microscope lens tube (apparent thickness).

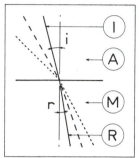

Figure 4.92 · **Refraction concept** · (I) Incident ray; (A) Air; (M) Material; (R) Refracted ray

The index of refraction **n** is an essential characteristic of transparent materials. For conventional optical glass (crown, flint), it is in the approximate range 1.50-1.60. Fluoropolymers tend to have the lowest index of refraction ($\approx$ 1.35); silicones ($\approx$ 1.43), cellulosics ($\approx$ 1.46-1.50), polymethylpentene (PMP) ($\approx$ 1.46), acrylics ($\approx$ 1.49), and allylics ($\approx$ 1.49) have relatively low indices of refraction. Styrenics ($\approx$ 1.56-1.60), polycarbonate (PC) ($\approx$ 1.58) and polysulfone (PSU) ($\approx$ 1.63) have higher indices of refraction.

Low indices of refraction tend to reduce surface or back reflection and are thus desirable for certain applications such as anti-glare coatings. High indices of refraction tend to correspond to higher part brilliance and thinner optical lenses for a given focal distance.

4.15.2   Specular Transmission

The transmission of light across clear and colorless test specimens, within a very narrow angle, is the subject of a relatively simple standard test (ASTM D1746). A green-yellow light source (L) (Fig. 4.93) and a collimator (C) are used to produce a parallel beam perpendicular to the test specimen (S). The light emerging within a very narrow angle (less than $\approx$ 0.1°) is measured through a photodetector (D). A specular transmittance T_s is defined as the ratio of the light intensities, with and without the test specimen in the beam, or the corresponding percentage. Highly transparent polymeric test specimens correspond to values as high as 94% (acrylics) and commonly around 90% (polycarbonate PC, styrenics, cellulosics, etc.), which are comparable with those for glass. It must be noted that the specular transmittance is associated with a test specimen of a specific thickness. The specular transmittance T_s is directly associated with the image-forming characteristics of the test specimen, or the material itself if similar thicknesses are considered. Expressions, such as "transparency," "clarity," "see-through clarity," and "image resolution," are used in this context.

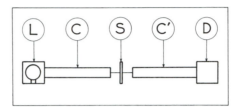

Figure 4.93 · **Specular transmission test** · (L) Light source; (C),(C′) Collimators; (S) Test specimen; (D) Photodetector

4.15.3   Reflection, Gloss

A standard test concerns the quantitative characterization of what is loosely defined as the reflection of light over a material surface, in a mirror-like fashion. The property measured is specifically referred to as specular gloss (ASTM D523) and is associated with expressions, such as gloss, sparkle, shine, sheen, luster, and glare. Opposite expressions include adjectives, such as dull, matte or mat, flat and lusterless. The specular gloss measurement (Fig. 4.94) involves a light source (L) and a collimator (C) to produce a parallel beam impinging on the test specimen surface at an incident angle **i**. The light reflected within a narrow viewing angle **v** equal to **i** is

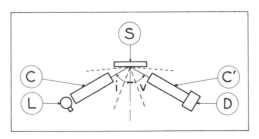

Figure 4.94 · **Specular gloss test** · (L) Light source; (C),(C′) Collimators; (S) Test specimen; (D) Photodetector

measured through a photodetector (D). Highly polished black glass, the primary reference standard, is assigned a specular gloss of 100, and secondary reference standards such as white mat surfaces are used for calibration. Specular gloss measurements can be made at low incident angles (such as 20°) for high gloss test specimens, or at high angles (such as 85°) for low gloss cases, but the angle of 60°, recommended for intermediate gloss, is most commonly used. Specular gloss is a complex function of the optical characteristics of the material such as the index of refraction, as well as the smoothness (or roughness) of the surface. Wear, abrasion, chemical attack, weathering, etc., which affect the surface of polymeric materials, rapidly reduce the gloss.

4.15.4   Transmission, Haze

When a parallel beam of light impinges normally (90°) on a test specimen of a material which is not highly transparent and clear, a' significant fraction of the transmitted light is deviated in directions between 0° and 90° to the normal. This is often referred to as forward diffusion (it seems preferable to reserve the expression scattering for the case of polarized light). Two concepts associated with this form of light transmission, i.e. haze and luminous transmittance, are the subject of a relatively complex standard test (ASTM D1003). One procedure uses an apparatus referred to as a hazemeter (Fig. 4.95) which consists of a light source (L), a collimator (C) and a hollow sphere (B) featuring an entrance port (I), an exit port (O), and a photoelectric detector (D). The inner surface of the sphere is coated with a highly reflecting mat white substance, and any light impinging on the reflective surface eventually reaches the photoelectric detector; the sphere is thus referred to as the integrating sphere. By leaving the entrance port (I) unobstructed, or inserting a test specimen (S) of a partially transparent material, and by fitting the exit port (O) with either a light trap (T), or a highly reflecting mat white reference standard (R) ([l] to [4]), a total luminous transmittance T_t and a diffuse luminous transmittance T_d, which excludes the light transmitted within a relatively narrow angle ($\approx$ 2.5°), can be determined. The haze H is defined as the ratio T_d/T_t or the corresponding percentage. The method is considered suitable for haze values less than about 30%; beyond that, other tests such as ASTM E166 (goniophotometry) must be used. Typical haze values for highly transparent plastics are in the range 1-3%. It should be noted that, because of different reference angles ($\approx$ 2.5° vs. $\approx$ 0.1°), there is no simple relationship between T_t, T_d, or H on the one hand, and the previously defined specular transmittance T_s on the other hand. Another procedure associated with ASTM D1003 involves the use of a recording spectrophotometer (ASTM E308).

Many applications of plastics as clear materials (e.g., glazing) require low haze and correspondingly high specular or luminous transmittance. For some applications (diffusers in lighting fixtures, or panels in internally-lighted signs), a combination of high total luminous transmittance and haze is desirable.

As is the case of reflection, diffusion can have its source in the material itself, as well as in its surface if it is not extremely smooth. Surface frosting, in fact, can turn a highly transparent sample into a translucent one.

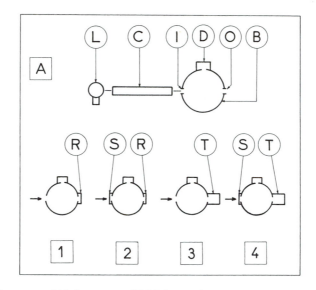

Figure 4.95 · **Haze test** · [A] Apparatus; [1]-[4] Successive arrangements; (L) Light source; (C) Collimator; (I) Entrance port; (D) Photodetector; (O) Exit port; (R) Reference standard; (S) Test specimen; (T) Light trap; (B) Integrating sphere

4.15.5 Luminous Reflectance

The normal or quasi-normal impingement of a light beam on a sample, which is not perfectly clear and does not have a perfectly smooth surface, can also produce backward diffusion in directions between 0 and 90° to the normal. A spectrophotometer (ASTM D1003, E308) can be used to determine a luminous reflectance. As illustrated in Figure 4.96, a light beam entering the integrating sphere (B), through the entrance port (I), impinges on the test specimen (S) with a small angle of incidence **i** ($\approx$ 6°). The mirror-like reflection can be counted or discounted by placing a reflecting plug or a light trap at the exit port. A symmetrical arrangement allowing the shift of the beam to a reference standard (R) is used for convenience.

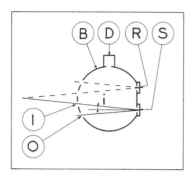

Figure 4.96 · **Luminous reflectance test** · (O) Exit port; (I) Entrance port; (B) Integrating sphere; (D) Photodetector; (R) Reference standard; (S) Test specimen

4.15.6   Color

An important aspect of the optical properties of polymeric materials is that of color, particularly since polymeric parts are often colored in the bulk through the use of appropriate colorants (pigments and dyes).

Human color perception is affected by the lighting (white light vs. colored light), as well as the selective absorption characteristics of the material. Since the visual assessment or comparison of colors (hues, shades, tinges, tints, etc.) is a rather subjective question for a human observer, quantitative, instrument-based, colorimetry methods have been developed. The International Commission on Illumination (CIE) coordinates efforts in this area and has set up a system known as "CIE 1931," which is based on the composition of any color from three primaries. The principles and standard procedures, which are described in ASTM E308 in particular, are rather complex and feature terms such as color matching functions, tristimulus values **X, Y,** and **Z;** chromaticity coordinates; and trichromatic coefficients. The instruments involve standard light sources, such as CIE source **C** for example, and are referred to as "spectrophotometer" or "recording spectrophotometer," "spectrocolorimeter," or "tristimulus colorimeter." Color evaluation, comparison, matching, or specification systems and the corresponding instruments are associated with names such as Munsell, MacAdam, Hardy, etc.

A case of special interest is associated, in particular, with a tendency for many initially colorless or white, transparent or translucent polymers to develop an undesirable yellowish color (discoloration), with aging in particular. A standard method (ASTM D1925), based on the use of a recording spectrophotometer (ASTM D308) for transmittance and reflectance measurements, permits the determination of a yellowness index (YI) from tristimulus values, using a yellow source (570-580 nm). A reference reflectance standard (magnesium oxide or Vitrolite white glass) is also involved, which corresponds to zero yellowness. Negative values of the yellowness index are sometimes associated with the term "blueness."

Some devices for measuring optical properties can be seen in figures 4.97-4.100.

Figure 4.97 · Gloss meter (specular gloss) [GARDNER]

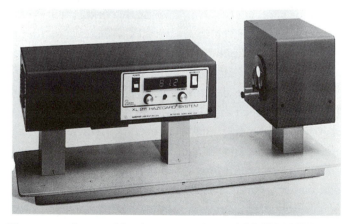

Figure 4.98 · Haze meter (haze and luminous transmittance) [GARDNER]

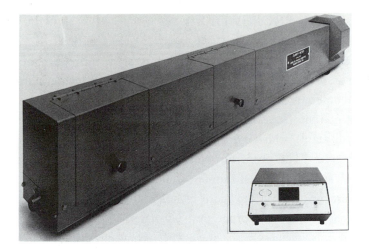

Figure 4.99 · Clarity meter (specular transmission) **[GARDNER]**

Figure 4.100 · Spectrocolorimeter **[HUNTER LAB]**

Transient - that, unistal *(handwritten annotation in top margin)*

4.16 THERMAL PROPERTIES

The transfer of heat across a material requires a difference of temperature (temperature gradient). If a flat plate, initially at a uniform temperature, is subjected to a certain temperature difference between its faces, the temperature first changes as a function of time (transient stage), and then a sort of dynamic equilibrium is reached (steady state), which corresponds to a permanent temperature distribution across the sample. The property, referred to as the "thermal conductivity" **k**, is associated with steady-state heat transfer, while other properties such as the thermal diffusivity **α** are involved in the more complex analysis of transient heat transfer. Other important concepts and properties, associated with the heating and cooling of polymeric materials, include the specific heat C_p, convective (fluid-material interface) and contact (solid-material interface) heat transfer coefficients, generally associated with the symbol **h**, and infrared heat emission and absorption.

Thermal expansion (or contraction) is another important phenomenon associated with the heating (or cooling) of polymeric materials.

4.16.1 Thermal Conduction

The thermal conductivity **k** corresponds, in the case of a sample of uniform thickness, to the power (heat per unit time) crossing an element of unit area and unit thickness, when the temperature difference is unity. In the SI system of units, the thermal conductivity is expressed in **W/(m · K)**; in a frequently used metric system of units, **k** is expressed in cal/(cm · s · °C); in the British system, **k** is generally expressed in (Btu · in)/(ft^2 · h · °F), the area being in square feet and the thickness in inches. One British unit of thermal conductivity, abbreviated here as BU unit, is approximately equal to 0.144 SI unit. The numerical value of the thermal conductivity expressed in the above British unit is sometimes referred to as the "K factor" and its inverse (1/K), as the "R factor."

One standard method for the determination of the thermal conductivity of polymeric materials in sheet form (ASTM C177) uses a symmetrical device represented schematically in Figure 4.101. Two disk-shaped test specimens (S) are sandwiched between an electrically heated plate (heater) (H) and metal plates (heat sinks or cold sinks) (P). Thermocouples (T) and (T′) allow the measurement of the test specimen surface temperatures. A guard heater (G) compensates for lateral heat losses through the insulation (I).   The electric power and the temperature difference, under steady-state conditions, together with the dimensions of the area of the test specimen facing the heater, permit the calculation of the thermal conductivity. Another method (ASTM C518) uses thin calibrated heat flow sensors on the surface of a test specimen sandwiched between an electric heating plate and a heat sink.

The best thermally conductive materials are metals, such as copper (≈ 400 SI or ≈ 2800 BU), aluminum (200-300 SI or 1400-2100 BU), and steel (20-40 SI or 140-280 BU). Reported values for cement or concrete are around 10 SI or 70 BU; for glass, they are around 0.8 SI or 5.5 BU. Most "pure" polymeric materials have thermal conductivities in the range 0.1-0.5 SI or 0.7-3.5 BU. Semicrystalline plastics generally have a higher thermal conductivity than do amorphous ones. Representative examples include polystyrene (PS) (≈ 0.15 SI or ≈ 1 BU), polycarbonate (PC) (≈ 0.2 SI or ≈ 1.4 BU), polyamides (PA) (≈ 0.25 SI or ≈ 1.75 BU); and polyethylenes (PE) (≈ 0.33 SI or ≈ 2.3 BU). The presence of fillers or reinforcements, which generally have a higher thermal conductivity (carbon and metals in particular), has a strong effect on the overall conductivity of the resulting composite. Since gases, and air in particular, have a lower thermal conductivity than polymers, in the absence of convection (about 0.04 SI or 0.28 BU for air), closed-cell cellular polymers (foams) are good thermal insulators, with thermal conductivities in the range 0.015-0.15 SI or 0.1-1 BU, i.e. R-factors in the range 1-10. A typical expanded polystyrene (EPS), for example, has a reported thermal conductivity of 0.035 SI or 0.24 BU, i.e. R-factor ≈ 4.15. This, combined with the low density of foams and their reasonable mechanical properties, makes them prime insulating materials.

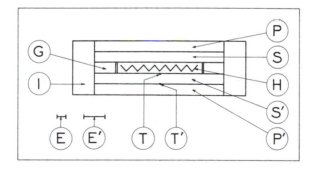

Figure 4.101 · **Thermal conduction test** · (I) Insulation; (G) Guard Heater; (P),(P′) Heat sink plates; (S),(S′) Test specimens; (H) Heated plate; (T),(T′) Thermocouples; (E) 1 cm scale; (E′) 1 in scale

4.16.2   Thermal Expansion

The dimensional change, associated with an increase in temperature (thermal expansion), is an important and often limiting characteristic of polymeric materials in solid state applications. Thermal expansion is a major factor in the dimensional stability of parts; other factors include water absorption and post-curing phenomena in thermosets.

Applications where thermal expansion can play an important role include large parts, such as piping, exterior siding, and glazing, for which offsets or expansion joints must often be used; close-fitting moving elements, such as slides, bearings, and gears, for which seizure or excessive friction can be a problem; tight-fitting assemblies, such as inserts, and press fits, for which loosening or excessive stresses must be avoided; optical components (lenses), for which the geometry is critical; and adhesive bonds between dissimilar materials where high shear stresses may develop.

Thermal expansion is characterized either by the coefficient of linear thermal expansion, referred to here by the symbol α_L, or by the coefficient of volumetric (cubic) thermal expansion α_V, with the approximate relationship $\alpha_V \approx 3\,\alpha_L$. These coefficient are normally, fairly constant over a range of temperature corresponding to solid state applications. The unit for the coefficients would be simply an inverse temperature, but α_L, for example, is often reported as (length/length)/temperature, such as $(m/m)/°K$ in the SI system or $(in/in)/°F$ in the British system. Since its value in those units is quite small, it is convenient to report it as $(\mu m/m)/°K$ or $(\mu in/in)/°F$, which corresponds to a factor 10^6; these units are used here for the examples given with the symbols μSI and μBU, respectively.

A standard method for the measurement of the coefficient of linear thermal expansion (ASTM D696) uses a quartz dilatometer. The apparatus (Fig. 4.102) features a long, low expansion vitreous silica (fused-quartz) tube (T) and a rod (R) of the same material. A test specimen (S), at least 5 cm ($\approx$ 2 in) long, is placed between the tube base and the bottom end of the rod (R), and the rod top contacts a device (D) capable of accurate displacement measurements (dial gauge, displacement transducer). A suitable length of the tube (T) is immersed in a temperature-controlled bath (B), and the temperature is slowly raised.

The coefficient of cubic thermal expansion (ASTM D864) can be measured with a mercury dilatometer (Fig. 4.103), which resembles a mercury thermometer. The test specimen (S) is immersed in the mercury within the reservoir (R), and the expansion is derived from the rise of the mercury in the capillary tube (C), when the temperature of the bath (B) is raised.

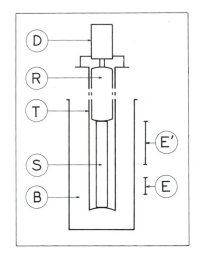

Fig. 4.102

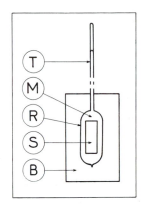

Fig. 4.103

Figure 4.102 · **Quartz dilatometer** · (B) Temperature-controlled bath; (S) Test specimen; (T) Quartz tube; (R) Quartz rod; (D) Displacement-measuring device; (E) 1 cm scale; (E′) 1 in scale

Figure 4.103 · **Mercury dilatometer** · (B) Temperature-controlled bath; (S) Test specimen; (R) Glass reservoir; (M) Mercury; (T) Capillary tube

A few materials, such as graphite or glass-bonded mica, have an extremely low coefficient of linear thermal expansion α_L of about 0.1 μSI ($\approx$ 0.05 μBU). Vitreous silica (fused quartz) corresponds to $\alpha \approx$ 0.05 μSI ($\approx$ 0.27 μBU). Metals range from about 1.2 μSI ($\approx$ 0.7 μBU) for Invar to about 22 μSI ($\approx$ 12 μBU) for aluminum, with steel around 12 μSI ($\approx$ 6.5 μBU). "Pure" polymers range from about 15 μSI ($\approx$ 8 μBU) for certain thermosets, such as phenolic or amino resins, to about 300 μSI ($\approx$ 170 μBU) for silicone elastomers, with acrylics (PMMA) around 50 μSI ($\approx$ 28 μBU); polystyrene (PS) around 60 μSI ($\approx$ 33 μBU); polyamides (PA), thermoplastic polyesters (PET), and acetals (PMO) around 80 μSI ($\approx$ 45 μBU); fluoropolymers (PTFE) around 100 μSI ($\approx$ 55 μBU); polyethylenes (PE) around 100-160 μSI ($\approx$ 55-90 μBU); and natural rubber (NR) around 220 μSI ($\approx$ 120 μBU).

The addition of stiff inorganic fillers and reinforcements can reduce considerably the thermal expansion and thus increase the dimensional stability of polymeric systems. Mica and short glass fibers, in particular, are widely used for this purpose; advantage is taken of their lower thermal expansion and their mechanical ability to restrain the expansion of the polymeric matrix.

The anisotropy of materials, always significant when fibrous fillers are used, is associated with different expansions in different directions and is often responsible for warpage problems.

4.17 DENSITY

The determination of the density of polymeric materials is important for several reasons, which include design considerations when weight is a factor, the identification of unknown materials, and the assessment of the structure (crystalline, cellular, etc.) of the material in a product.

Density is reported in mass per unit volume (1 g/cm^3 or g/ml $\approx$ 62.4 lb/ft^3 or 0.036 lb/in^3). Specific gravity, defined as the ratio of the mass of a given volume of material to that of the same volume of water, both at 23°C (1 73.4°F), is dimensionless. The density of water at 23°C is about 1 g/cm^3.

Polymeric materials generally have a low density compared to most other solid materials. For pure polymers, the specific gravity (almost equal to the density in g/cm^3) ranges from about 0.83 [polymethylpentene (PMP)] to about 2.14 [polytetrafluoroethylene (PTFE)]. The range 0.83-1.00, besides PMP, also includes polypropylene (PP) and polyethylene (PE). The range 1.00-1.25 includes polystyrene (PS) and other styrenics, polyurethanes (PU), polyamides (PA), acrylics (PMMA), and polycarbonate (PC). The range 1.25-1.50 includes many vinyls (PVC), polyesters (PET, PBT), acetal POM, polyimides, phenolics, etc. Above 1.5, one finds highly chlorinated or fluorinated polymers (PVDC, PVDF, PTFE, etc.), and silicone polymers.

The conventional determination of the density can be made by weight and volume measurements (ASTM D792). One method, suitable for relatively large test specimens, is based on Archimedes' buoyancy principle (Fig. 4.104). It involves weighing the test specimen alone [S], and then determining the apparent weight of the test specimen (S), held by a fine wire (W), and submerged in a liquid (L). The other method, suitable for small test specimens as well as finely divided materials, involves

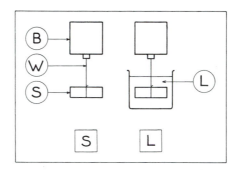

Figure 4.104 · **Density measurement; buoyancy method** · [S] Solid weighing; [L] Immersed solid weighing; (S) Test specimen; (W) Wire; (B) Scale; (L) Liquid

the use of a pycnometer (Fig. 4.105), which consists of a flask (F) and a cap (C), with a thin overflow tube (T). Flask and cap fit through a precise ground glass tapered connection. The pycnometer is weighted when filled with liquid alone [L] and when containing the test specimen immersed in the liquid [S].

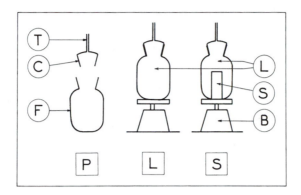

Figure 4.105 · **Density measurement; pycnometer method** · [P] Pycnometer; [L] Liquid weighing; [S] Liquid/solid weighing; (F) Flask; (C) Cap; (T) Overflow tube; (L) Liquid; (S) Test specimen; (B) Scale

A special method, based on buoyancy, is widely used for polymers, particularly to assess very small differences in density (ASTM D1505). It involves the preparation of a density gradient column as illustrated in Figure 4.106 [P]. Two miscible liquids of different density [liquids (H) and (L) of high and low densities, respectively] are

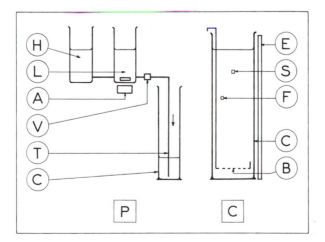

Figure 4.106 · **Density measurement; density column** · [P] Density column preparation; [C] Density column; (C) Transparent column; (T) Tube; (V) Valve; (A) Stirrer; (L) Light liquid; (H) Heavy liquid; (E) Density scale; (S) Test specimen; (F) Calibrated float; (B) Lifting basket

placed in connected identical containers; the downstream container is fitted with a gentle stirrer. Through a control valve (V) and a thin tube (T), the liquids are very slowly fed to the bottom of the cylindrical column (C). This set up leads to a continuous density gradient in the column; the first fed, almost pure, light liquid (L) ends up at the top, while the last fed, almost pure, heavy liquid (H) is at the bottom. Calibrated glass floats (F) can be used to establish a density scale (E) and small test specimens (S), gently introduced at the top, sink to the level corresponding to their density. Test specimens can be periodically lifted out, through a very slowly moving basket (B), and such columns can be stable for months. Alcohol-water columns (specific gravity range about 0.80-1.00) are widely used for polyethylene. Broad-range columns, such as ethanol-carbon tetrachloride (about 0.80-1.60), can be used for resin identification, while intrinsically dense or filled materials may require combinations such as carbon tetrachloride-bromoform (about 1.60-2.90).

All of these methods can only employ liquids that do not affect the test specimens, and care must be taken to avoid air entrapment.

A density measurement apparatus is shown in figure 4.107.

Figure 4.107 · Two-column density measuring apparatus [DAVENPORT]

4.18   APPENDIX 4

List of Related ASTM and ISO Standards

▶MATERIALS AND TEST SPECIMENS (section 4.2)

Test Specimen Preparation
    ASTM   D1928, D1897, D641, D1248
    ISO   293, 294, 2818

Test Specimen Conditioning
    ASTM   D618, D3222, E171, D1708, D759
    ISO   291, R483

Also
    ASTM   D15, D832
    ISO   295, 2557, 3167, 471, 4648, 4661

▶SHORT-TERM CONVENTIONAL MECHANICAL TESTING (section 4.3)

Testing Modes

Tensile
    ASTM   D638, D882, E111, E132,
                                D1708, D229,D651,D412
    ISO   R527, R1184, 37

Flexural
    ASTM   D790, D747, D797
    ISO   178, TR 4173

Compression
    ASTM   D695
    ISO   604

Torsion
    ASTM   D1043
    ISO   R458, 537

Shear
    ASTM   D732
    ISO   1827

Tear
    ASTM   D1004, D1938, D1922,
                                D2582, D624
    ISO   6383, 34, 816, 6133

Biaxial stress
    ASTM   D1599, D774, D1598

►HARDNESS (section 4.4)
    Rockwell Hardness
        ASTM   D785, D530
        ISO   2039

    Shore Hardness
        ASTM   D2240, D676, D1706
        ISO   R868, 2039

    Ball Hardness
        ASTM   D531
        ISO   2039

    International Rubber Hardness
        ASTM   D1415
        ISO   48, 1400, 1818

    Barcol Hardness
        ASTM   D2583

    Miscellaneous Methods
        ASTM   E10, E140, D1474

►FRICTION, WEAR, ABRASION (section 4.5)
    Coefficient of Friction
        ASTM   D1894, D3028
    Abrasion
        ASTM   D1044, D1242, D968, D673, D2228, D1630

►IMPACT (section 4.6)
    Pendulum Flexural Impact Tests
        ASTM   D256, D3998
        ISO   R180, R179

    Pendulum Tensile Impact Tests
        ASTM   D1822

    Falling Weight Impact Tests
        ASTM   D3029, D2444, D1709

    Also
        ASTM   D3099
        ISO   2897

►CYCLIC LOADING (section 4.7)
    Dynamic Testing
        ASTM   D945
        ISO   TR4137, 2856, 4662, 537, 4663, 4664

Dynamic Fatigue
    ASTM   D671, D813, D1052
    ISO   132

►LONG-TERM STATIC LOADING (section 4.8)
    Creep and Stress-Relaxation Tests
        ASTM   2990, 2991, 621, 674, D395, D1229
        ISO   899, 815, 1653, 2285, 3384, 6056

    Static Fatigue
        ASTM   D2990
        ISO   R899

►HIGH TEMPERATURE SOFTENING (section 4.9)
    Heat Deflection Temperature
        ASTM   D648
        ISO   75

    Vicas Softening Point
        ASTM   D1525
        ISO   306

    Transition Temperatures
        ASTM   D3418, D789, D2117, D3222, D1457, D795,
                                    D2116, D2133
        ISO   1218, 3146

►LOW TEMPERATURE STIFFENING (section 4.10)
    Stiffness
        ASTM   D1043, 1053
        ISO   R812, 1432

    Dynamic Brittleness
        ASTM   D746, D1790, D2137
        ISO   974

►CHEMICAL ENVIRONMENT (section 4.11)
    General Chemical Resistance Testing
        ASTM   D543, C581, D380, D1239,
                                    D1203, D471, D1149
        ISO   R175, R462, 176, 177,
                                    1817, 1431
    Mechano-Chemical Effects
        ASTM   D1693, D2552, D2561,
                                    D2648
        ISO   DIS4600, 6252

    High Energy Radiations
        ASTM   D1672

Micro-Organisms/Animals
    ASTM   D2676, D1924, D3083,
                                            G21, G22
    ISO   846

Water Absorption
    ASTM   D570, D756
    ISO   62, R117, R960

Weathering
    ASTM   D1435, G24, E187, G23,
                                            G26, G43, E42, D1499,
                                            D1501, D2565, D1494
    ISO   4582, 4607, 877, 4892,
                                            R878, R879, 877

Thermal Degradation
    ASTM   D756, D794, D1870,
                                              D2115, D793, D2951,D1299,
                                          D865, D573, D454, D592, E95
    ISO   2578, 1137, 4611, R182,
                                          188

►FLAMMABILITY/COMBUSTION (section 4.12)
Oxygen Index
    ASTM   D2863

Horizontal/Vertical Burning
    ASTM   D635, D568, D1692, D1433, D229
    ISO   R1210, R1326

Ignition Temperature
    ASTM   D1929
    ISO   871

Incandescent Contact
    ASTM   D757
    ISO   181

Radiant Panel Test
    ASTM   E162

Tunnel Fire Test
    ASTM   E84

Smoke/Toxic Gases Generation
    ASTM   D2843, E662

▶ELECTRICAL PROPERTIES (section 4.13)
    Electrical Resistance
        ASTM   D257
        ISO   3915, 1853, 2878, 2882, 2883

    Dielectric Properties
        ASTM   D150

    Dielectric Strength
        ASTM   D149

    Arc Resistance
        ASTM   D495, D2132, D2302, D2303, D3638

    Also
        ISO   1325

▶GAS/VAPOR PERMEABILITY (section 4.14)
    Gas Transmission
        ASTM   D1434

    Water Vapor Transmission
        ASTM   E96, C355, D1653, D2684, D814
        ISO   2556, 1399, 2782

▶OPTICAL PROPERTIES (section 4.15)
    Refraction
        ASTM   D542
        ISO   R489

    Specular Transmission
        ASTM   D1746, D1003, E308
        ISO   2556

    Reflection, Gloss
        ASTM   D523, D2457

    Transmission, Haze
        ASTM   D1003, E166, E308

    Luminous Reflectance
        ASTM   D1003, E308

    Color
        ASTM   D1535, D1729, D2244, E308, D1925, E313

▶THERMAL PROPERTIES (section 4.16)
    Thermal Conduction
        ASTM   C177, C518

Thermal Expansion
ASTM   D696, D864

►DENSITY (section 4.17)
ASTM   D792, D1182, D1505
ISO   R1183, 1675, R60, 823, 2781

Alphabetical List of Testing Equipment Suppliers

ACCEL
ACCO
ADAMEL LHOMARGY
AMERICAN ULTRAVIOLET
AMES
APPLIED TEST SYSTEMS (ATS)
APPLIED COLOR SYSTEMS
ATLAS ELECTRIC DEVICES (ATLAS)
BRABENDER, C.W.
CARVER
CEAST
CUSTOM SCIENTIFIC INSTRUMENTS
(CSI)
DAVENPORT
DOHRMANN/ENVIROTECH
DUPONT
DYNATUP
EMERSON
FATIGUE DYNAMICS (FD)
FISHER SCIENTIFIC
GARDNER/PACIFIC SCIENTIFIC
GOTTFERT, W.G.
HAAKE BUCHLER
HARVEY, R.J.
HERACEUS
HOUNSFIELD
HUNTERLAB
ICITACS
INSTRON
INSTRUMENT FOR THE MATERIALS
AND STRUCTURAL SCIENCES (IMASS)
KAYENESS
LAW, K.J.

LLOYD, J.J.
METLAB
METRAVIB
METTLER
MOREHOUSE
MORGAN, M.M.
MTS SYSTEMS (MTS)
MULLEN
PERKIN-ELMER
PLASTECHON
POLYMER LABORATORIES
PRECISION SCIENTIFIC
Q-PANEL
RAPRA
REOS
RHEOMETRICS
SATEC
SCHENCK
SHEEN
SHIMADZU
SHORE
SOUTH FLORIDA TEST SERVICE/ATLAS
STANTON REDCROFT
TABER/TELEDYNE
TARLIN
TENSILKUT
TESTING MACHINE INC. (TMI)
THERMOTRON
THWING-ALBERT
TINIUS-OLSEN
TOYOSEIKI
WALLACE, H.W.
ZWICK

Testing Equipment Suppliers by Subject

▶Materials and test specimens (section 4.2)
TENSILKUT
CSI
ZWICK
CARVER

▶Short term conventional mechanical testing
(section 4.3)
TINIUS OLSEN
ZWICK
THWING-ALBERT
HOUNSFIELD
LLOYD
INSTRON
TOYOSEIKI
MTS
ATS
TMI
SCHENCK
CSI
GARDNER
HARVEY
DAVENPORT
MONSANTO
WALLACE
TABER
IMASS

▶Hardness (section 4.4)
CSI
TMI
SHORE
ADAMEL LHOMARGY
GARDNER
SHIMADZU
ZWICK
WALLACE
SCHENCK
TOYOSEIKI

▶Friction, wear, abrasion (section 4.5)
CSI
HARVEY
GARDNER
DAVENPORT
TABER
ZWICK

ADAMEL LHOMARGY
TMI
WALLACE

▶Impact (section 4.6)
TMI
TINIUS OLSEN
CSI
ZWICK
RHEOMETRICS
GARDNER
IMASS
SCHENCK
SATEC
DYNATUP
MTS
TOYOSEIKI
KAYENESS
CEAST
METLAB
ICITACS

▶Cyclic loading (section 4.7)
MTS
TMI
INSTRON
SCHENCK
FD
TINIUS OLSEN
ATS

▶Long term static loading (section 4.8)
ATS
CSI
SCHENCK
WALLACE
INSTRON
TINIUS OLSEN
TMI
LLOYD

▶High temperature softening (section 4.9)
TINIUS OLSEN
CSI
CEAST
ZWICK
TMI

DAVENPORT
DUPONT
PERKIN-ELMER
TOYOSEIKI

►Low temperature stiffening (4.10)
CSI
TINIUS OLSEN
TMI

►Chemical environment (section 4.11)
General Chemical Resistance Testing
ADAMEL LHOMARGY
TMI
ACCEL

Mechano-Chemical Effects
CSI
TMI
TOYOSEIKI

Water Absorption
TMI
DUPONT
GARDNER
BRABENDER

Weathering
CSI
TMI
ATLAS
Q-PANEL
SOUTH FLORIDA TEST SERVICE
TOYOSEIKI

Thermal Degradation
PERKIN-ELMER
CSI
ATLAS
TMI
WALLACE

►Flammability/combustion (section 4.12)
CSI
TMI
STANTON REDCROFT
TARLIN
TOYOSEIKI

►Electrical properties (section 4.13)
CSI

►Gas/vapor permeability (section 4.14)
DOHRMANN
CSI
HARVEY
THWING-ALBERT
TMI
MOCON

►Optical properties (section 4.15)
TMI
THWING-ALBERT
GARDNER
HUNTERLAB
MINOLTA
APPLIED COLOR SYSTEMS
GENERAL ELECTRIC
TOSHIBA
PHOTOVOLT

►Thermal properties (section 4.16)
CSI

►Density (section 4.17)
ADAMEL LHOMARGY
TOYOSEIKI
TMI
DAVENPORT
GARDNER
CSI
BRABENDER

Chapter 5

PROCESSING TECHNIQUES

5.1 INTRODUCTION

The processing of polymeric materials - plastics, elastomers and composites - is characterized by a wide variety of distinct methods or techniques.

These techniques are discussed in this chapter in an order corresponding to the following classification: Techniques involving the continuous manufacture of a product having a basically uniform cross section, which include extrusion, extrusion covering, film blowing and calendering; techniques involving the shaping of a deformable polymer preform against a mold surface, which include sheet thermoforming and blow molding; techniques involving the gradual build-up of a polymer layer against a mold surface, which involve coating and rotational molding; and, finally, techniques which involve the complete filling of a mold cavity, and include casting, compression molding, transfer molding, injection molding and reaction injection molding.

For each technique, the discussion is subdivided into principle, equipment, tooling (product-specific), auxiliaries (secondary equipment, often product type-specific), materials (most commonly used), products (most commonly made) and related processes (often extensions of the basic process).

A discussion of composite materials, and their processing and typical products is also presented in this chapter. Some processing techniques for composite materials are very distinct from the other techniques discussed for regular polymeric materials.

All diagrams illustrating the processing techniques have been prepared so that the polymeric material systematically moves from left to right. Illustrations show that, in practice, operators often face the equipment in the opposite way.

The forms in which the polymeric materials are supplied by their manufacturers are described in the introduction to Chapter 3 (Section 3.1).

Some economic aspects of polymer processing (cost of equipment and tooling) are discussed in Chapter 7.

5.2 EXTRUSION

5.2.1 Principle

The extrusion process basically consists in continuously shaping a fluid polymer through the orifice of a suitable tool (die), and subsequently solidifying it into a product (extrudate of constant cross section).

In the case of thermoplastics, the feed material, in powder or pellet form, is now most commonly heated to a fluid state and pumped into the die, through a screw extruder; it is then solidified by cooling after exiting from the die. Unvulcanized rubbers and some thermosetting resins can be extruded, and subsequently solidified by heat curing, for example.

Extrusion products are often subdivided into groups that include filaments of circular cross-section, profiles of irregular cross section, axisymmetric tubes and pipes, and flat products such as films or sheets.

The extrusion process is also used to cover continuous substrates with a polymeric layer (extrusion covering process) and is a major element of the blow molding process and of the film blowing process. These processes are described in subsequent sections.

Mixtures of polymers, fillers, additives, etc. (compounds) are often prepared in extruders.

5.2.2 Equipment

A conventional single screw extruder consists of several important elements, as illustrated in Figure 5.1. The screw (S) rotates in the cylindrical barrel (B); the material enters the extruder through a feed hopper (F) and exits through the die (tool) (T), which is fitted to the extruder itself through an adapter (A). The mechanical drive system normally features a variable speed electric motor (M) and a speed reduction device (R).

The barrel of a conventional extruder has a circular cylindrical bore. Extruders are generally rated by the barrel bore diameter. This diameter can be as low as about 3/4 in ($\approx$ 20 mm) for laboratory extruders and quite commonly around 2½-6 in ($\approx$ 65-150 mm) for commercial extrusion. Diameters as large as 600 mm ($\approx$ 24 in) are used in polymer manufacturing plants, with a corresponding length of almost 15 m ($\approx$ 48 ft).

Barrels are often cooled around the feed port to facilitate the entry of the solid feed, and subsequently heated by controlled electric band heaters (H). A representative heating power for a 2 in ($\approx$ 50 mm) extruder is about 10 kW. Air or liquid coolers (C) are generally incorporated, for temperature sensitive materials in particular.

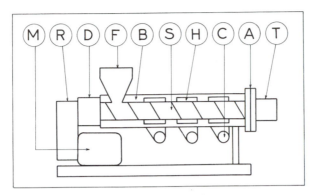

Figure 5.1 · **Single screw extruder** · (M) Electric motor; (R) Speed reduction device; (D) Thrust bearing; (F) Feed hopper; (B) Barrel; (S) Screw; (H) Heater; (C) Cooler; (A) Adapter; (T) Tool (die)

Barrels are normally designed to withstand a maximum pressure of about 10,000 psi ($\approx$ 700 atm) and feature a very hard bore surface (nitriding, Xaloy, Hastelloy, etc.).
The screw is an element of the extruder that can be changed and matched to the specific material being extruded or to the product being made.

A simple screw is illustrated in Figures 5.2 and 5.3. The flight (F) defines the flow channel between the screw root (R) and the barrel (B), since little material can flow over the small clearance of the flight land (L). The flight helix angle (A) is often around 17.8°, which corresponds to a pitch (P) equal to the barrel diameter (square screw). A screw may feature more than one flight (double flight screw in Fig. 5.4).

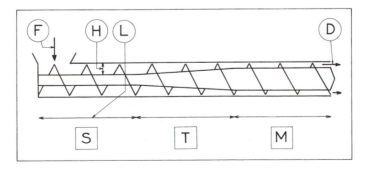

Figure 5.2 · **Simple extruder screw** · [S] Solid-conveying zone; [T] Transition zone; [M] Melt-conveying zone; (H) Channel depth; (L) Zone length

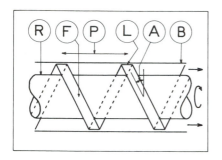

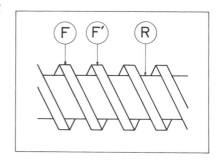

Fig. 5.3   Fig. 5.4

Figure 5.3 · **Single flight screw** · (R) Root; (F) Flight; (P) Pitch; (L) Land; (A) Flight angle; (B) Barrel

Figure 5.4 · **Double flight screw** · (F) First flight; (F′) Second flight; (R) Root

Along its length from the feed port (F) to the discharge point (D), the simple screw of Figure 5.2 features three zones which correspond roughly to three stages in the process. Zone [S] is associated primarily with the conveying of the solid material and features a relatively deep channel (depth H_s). Zone [M] is associated primarily with the metering and pressurizing (1000-3000 psi or 70-200 atm) of the molten material and features a shallower channel (depth H_m). Most melting takes place over the intermediate (transition) zone [T]. The ratio of the total screw length to the barrel diameter (L/D) is usually referred to as the "screw aspect ratio" and is often around 24 (range 20-30). The ratio of channel depths H_s/H_m is called the "compression ratio" and is often around 3 (range 2-6). Zone lengths are often comparable, but some materials may call for very short (PA) or very long (PVC) transition zones.

It is often desirable to remove gases that may be entrapped, or evolved, during the melting stage. This can be accomplished with an appropriate barrel/screw combination, as illustrated in Figure 5.5. The first part of the screw is analogous to the previous type, and pressure is developed at the end of the melt zone [M]. An increase of the channel depth in the venting zone [V] causes a decompression, and gases can be vented (atmospheric pressure) or extracted (vacuum) through a vent port (V). A subsequent reduction of the channel depth permits the recompression of the melt in the pressurizing zone [P] preceding the die.

The speed of rotation of extrusion screws can generally be varied continuously over a fairly wide range ($\approx$ 20-200 rpm); large screws have a somewhat lower maximum speed. The output and outlet pressure are interdependent and are functions of the screw geometry and speed, as well as the melt viscosity.

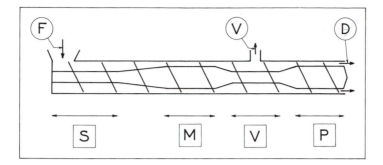

Figure 5.5 · **Vented extrusion** · [S] Solid zone; [M] Melt zone; [V] Decompression (venting) zone; [P] Recompression (pumping) zone; (V) Vent

Screws are machined, and subsequently hardened and sometimes chrome-plated. Some are cored to allow the cooling or heating of appropriate zones. Some extruders feature two screws (twin-screw extruders) which may be of the co-rotating or counter-rotating types (Fig. 5.6). They are widely used for shear-sensitive materials (e.g., PVC) and for compounding purposes. Their mode of operation involves a more thorough mixing of material elements, and their performance is more reminiscent of volumetric pumps. A commercial type of extruder features a large main screw and four smaller satellite screws (planetary extruder).

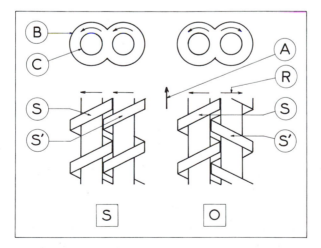

Figure 5.6 · **Twin-screw extrusion** · [S] Co-rotating screws; [O] Counter-rotating screws; (B) Barrel; (C) Screw core; (S) First screw; (S′) Second screw; (A) Axial material motion; (R) Rotary screw motion

A number of screwless extruders appear to have had limited success, but the use of gear pumps, located between conventional extruders and dies, is becoming increasingly popular, in the case of coextrusion in particular; it allows a precise control of the melt flow rate.

The mechanical drive of the screw generally involves a variable-speed DC motor, belt-coupled to a two-stage gear reducer for an overall reduction ratio of about 10. A representative drive power for a 2 in ($\approx$ 50 mm) extruder is about 20 hp ($\approx$ 15 kW); the corresponding maximum screw torque being about 1000 ft·lbf ($\approx$ 1400 N·m).

The pressure developed in the extruder head produces a strong axial force on the screw, which requires a high capacity thrust bearing (D) (Fig. 5.1).

The downstream end of an extruder (extruder head) normally features a rigid plate bored with small holes (breaker plate), which supports wire meshes (screen pack). The breaker plate helps straighten out the flow in the axial direction, and the screen pack plays a filtering and homogenizing role. For continuous operation, shuttle or continuous screen changing devices are used.

The extruder head also features an adapter (A) for attaching the die (T) (Fig. 5.1). In many cases, the product (extrudate) (P) exits the die "in-line" with the screw axis (case [I] in Fig. 5.7), but it is sometimes necessary or preferable to have an angle (cross) head arrangement [C] or an offset head arrangement [O] as in the case of extrusion covering discussed in the next section.

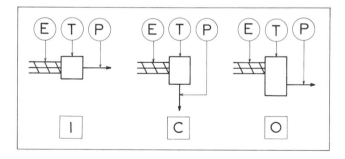

Figure 5.7 · **Extruder/die configurations** · [I] In-line die; [C] Cross die; [O] Offset die; (E) Extruder; (T) Die; (P) Product

A representative production output for a 2 in ($\approx$ 50 mm) extruder is about 100 lb/h ($\approx$ 50 kg/h), while an output as high as 20,000 lb/h ($\approx$ 10,000 kg/h) has been reported for a very large extruder.

5.2.3 Tooling

The shaping tool associated with extrusion is usually called the die. Widely different die designs are associated with filaments, profile products, tubes or pipes, and films or sheets.

Filaments are often made from plate dies featuring multiple orifices with streamlined (tapered) entrances. Profiles without hollow sections are also made from plate dies, as illustrated in Figure 5.8. A suitable transition piece or adaptor (I) is used between the extruder exit (E) and the die plate (T). The orifice may be machined from a one-piece plate [O] (Fig. 5.9) by spark erosion or electrical discharge (EDM) techniques, for example, or the die plate may be split to facilitate machining ([S]). It is important to try to equalize the flow rate of the material exiting from all areas of a profile die, i.e. to prevent "channeling"; this is illustrated in Figure 5.10 with transverse [T] and axial [A] cross sections, for a profile with nonuniform leg thickness ([N]).

The formation of a hollow extrudate, such as a tube or a pipe, requires the use of a mandrel (M) to form the inner surface, while a bushing (B) forms the outer surface (Fig. 5.11). The mandrel is commonly held in place by a spider (S), featuring flow channels between streamlined legs; one of the legs is bored to allow the injection of air (A) for start-up and/or sizing. A sufficient downstream channel length must be provided to avoid weak weld-lines.

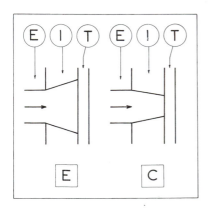

Fig. 5.8

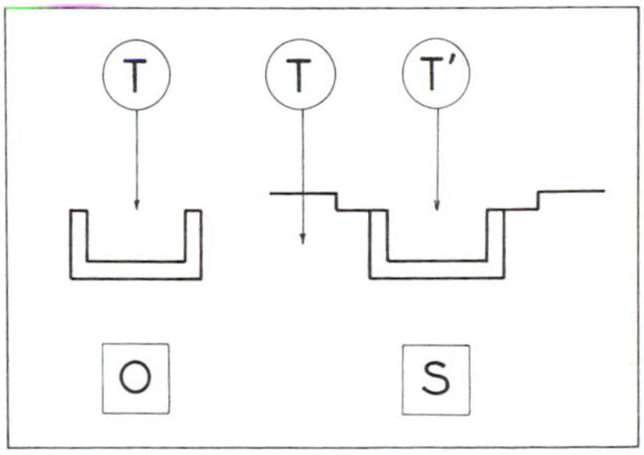

Fig. 5.9

Figure 5.8 · **Plate die configurations** · [E] Expanding transition; [C] Contracting transition; (E) Extruder exit; (I) Transition piece (pre-land); (T) Die plate (land)

Figure 5.9 · **U-profile die plate alternatives** · [O] One-piece; [S] Split; (T),(T′) Die plate or elements

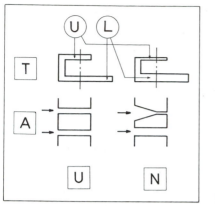

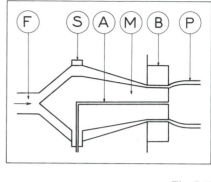

Fig. 5.10

Fig. 5.11

Figure 5.10 · **J-profiles die plates** · [T] Transverse cross-section; [A] Axial cross-sections; [U] Uniform leg thickness; [N] Non-uniform leg thickness; (U) Upper leg; (L) Lower leg

Figure 5.11 · **Tubing die** · (F) Feed; (S) Spider; (A) Air channel; (M) Mandrel; (B) Bushing; (P) Product

There are several possible slot (slit) die configurations for the formation of films or sheets (Fig. 5.12). T-Shaped dies [T] feature a simple circular manifold (M) which channels the material sideways from the feed zone (F), after which it flows axially

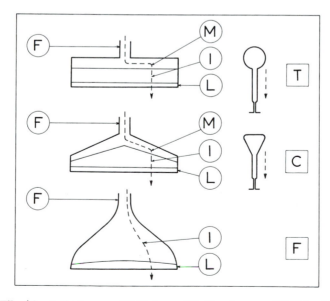

Figure 5.12 · **Film/sheet die types** · [T] T-shape; [C] Coat-hanger; [F] Fishtail; (F) Feed; (M) Manifold; (I) Pre-land; (L) Land

through the intermediate pre-land (I) and land (L). Coat-hanger dies [C] feature a slanted, tear drop (pear, banjo) shaped manifold, to minimize material hold-up or stagnation. In some cases, complex fishtail dies [F] have been designed for a gradual flow transition, from the circular cross section at the extruder exit to the thin rectangular cross section at the die exit. It is very difficult to design and build a film or sheet die that will give a uniform product thickness across the entire width. Two types of devices, which are used to adjust the gap thickness in operation, are illustrated in Figure 5.13; choke bars (restricter bars) (R) and flexible lips (L) have a large number of adjusting screws across the width, which permit local adjustments.

Coextrusion of products consisting of two or more distinct materials extruded through a single die, is becoming increasingly common. Two methods of coextrusion are illustrated in Figures 5.14 and 5.15, in the case of flat extrusion. Multiple manifold coextrusion (Fig. 5.14) may feature a primary manifold (M) to form the core (C), and secondary manifolds (M') to form surface layers (S), with restricter bars (R) to adjust the flows; such coextrusion die is complex but tolerant to the flow properties of the materials. A method taking advantage of the laminar flow of viscous polymer melts (Fig. 5.15) combines the materials fed by a primary extruder (E) and satellite extruders (E'), in the appropriate configuration, through a relatively simple feedblock (B), and the multilayered stream is then fed to a conventional die (T), through which it retains its layered structure. This versatile system has some restrictions associated with material flow properties.

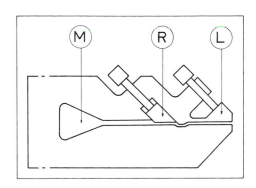

Fig. 5.13

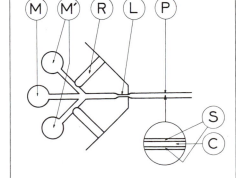

Fig. 5.14

Figure 5.13 · **Film/sheet die thickness adjustment** · (M) Manifold; (R) Restrictor bar; (L) Flexible lip

Figure 5.14 · **Multiple manifold film/sheet coextrusion** · (M) Primary manifold; (M') Secondary manifold; (R) Restrictor bar; (L) Land; (P) Product; (S) Skin; (C) Core

In general, the design of extrusion dies is complicated by the phenomenon of die swell, which is very pronounced for most polymeric melts (Fig. 5.16). Die swell [S], which may involve a two- or three-fold increase in cross-dimensions, depends on resin characteristics, as well as flow conditions. For simple geometries, drawdown [D] can be used to correct the dimensions, but this is not generally sufficient for complex shapes such as encountered in profiles.

Extrusion outputs are sometimes limited by flow instabilities producing rough surfaces (shark skin) or periodic fluctuations, but the cooling of thick extrudates is often the major limiting factor because of the low thermal conductivity of polymers.

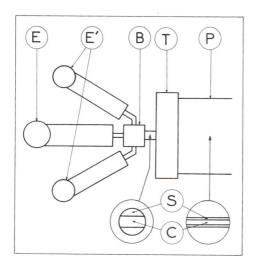

Fig. 5.15

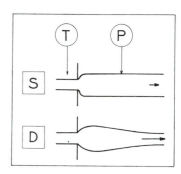

Fig. 5.16

Figure 5.15 · **Feedblock film/sheet coextrusion** · (E) Primary extruder; (E′) Satellite extruder; (B) Feedblock; (T) Conventional die; (P) Product; (S) Skin; (C) Core

Figure 5.16 · **Die exit phenomena** · [S] Die swell; [D] Extrudate drawdown; [T] Die; [P]Extrudate

5.2.4   Auxiliaries

Although the die is the major element in the formation of the extruded product, downstream auxiliaries are often essential to meet product specifications, while maximizing the output.

Auxiliaries include cooling, sizing, post forming, and haul-off, as well as cutting and/or winding devices (Fig. 5.17 to 5.24).

Cooling can be achieved by air convection, a relatively inefficient method, in the case of thin extrudates (film blowing). Water convection (immersion) in a tank (trough), or evaporation (spray), a more efficient method, is used widely for pipes and profiles (Fig. 5.17 and 5.18). In the case of flat extrudates (films or sheets), conduction cooling on chill rolls is commonly used. Cooling of the extrudate is often the limiting factor for extrudate speed. This is related to the low heat conductivity of polymers and problems associated with the formation of a solid skin and subsequent shrinkage of the inner material.

Sizing depends strongly on the shape and dimensional specifications of the products. In the case of tubes and pipes, for example, if the external diameter is crucial (Fig. 5.19 and 5.20), the emerging tubing is forced against an external sleeve or a ring-like

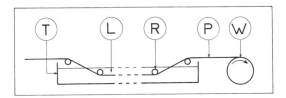

Figure 5.17 · **Immersion cooling (flexible extrudate)** · (T) Tank; (L) Load; (R) Guide roll; (P) product; (W) Winder

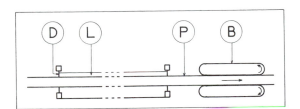

Figure 5.18 · **Immersion cooling (rigid pipe)** · (D) Rubber diaphragm; (L) Cooling water; (P) Product; (B) Haul-off belts

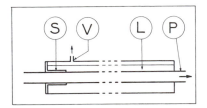

Fig. 5.19

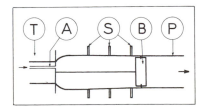

Fig. 5.20

Figure 5.19 · **External vacuum pipe sizing** · (S) Sizing sleeve; (V) Vacuum port; (L) cooling water; (P) Product

Figure 5.20 · **Internal pressure pipe sizing** · (T) Die; (A) Air pressure inlet; (S) Sizing rings; (B) Sealing plug; (P) Product

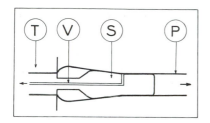

Fig. 5.21

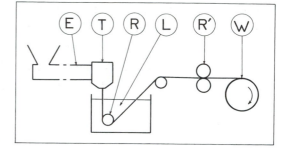

Fig. 5.22

Figure 5.21 · **Internal vacuum pipe sizing** · (T) Die; (V) Vacuum channel; (S) Sizing mandrel; (P) Product

Figure 5.22 · **Water bath film/sheet casting** · (E) Extruder; (T) Cross die; (R) Guide roll; (L) Cooling water; (R') Haul-off rolls; (W) Winder

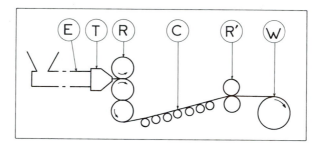

Figure 5.23 · **Chill roll film/sheet casting** · (E) Extruder; (T) in-line die; (R) Roll stand; (C) Conveyor; (R') Haul-off rolls; (W) Winder

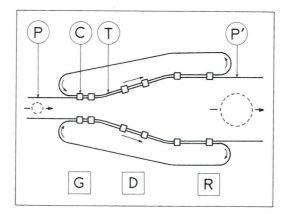

Figure 5.24 · **Biaxial film/sheet orientation** · [G] Grip zone; [D] Drawing zone; [R] Release zone; (P) As-extruded product; (C) Clip; (T) Track; (P') Oriented product

sizing jig (S), by external vacuum (V) (Fig. 5.19), or by internal pressure (A) (Fig. 5.20). If it is the internal diameter that is important (Fig. 5.21), an internally cooled mandrel-like sizing jig (S), in combination with internal vacuum, may be used. In both cases, the thickness can be controlled through the amount of axial pull (drawdown). The thickness of sheets and films may be controlled by the amount of drawdown or by the gap between rolls (calendering).

The thickness of extruded sheets, pipes, and other materials can now be monitored continuously with a variety of gauges (nuclear, infra red, ultrasonic, magnetic reluctance, etc.)

Post forming is normally associated with profiles and may involve, for example, the parallelism of the legs of a U-channel. Jigs, fingers, shoes, and rollers are used to gradually straighten out distorted emerging extrudates as they cool.

The solidified extruded product must be pulled at a velocity related to the average velocity of flow of the material through the die. The devices required for take-off (haul-off) may involve DC motor-driven rubber rolls, caterpillar flat or cleated belts (Fig. 5.18) and, sometimes, winding drums.

Flexible extrudates may be wound (Fig. 5.18), while rigid ones may be cut to length by fly cutters, featuring fast-rotating blades or knives, or by traveling cut-off circular saws, which follow the extrudate during the cutting sequence.

Flat films or thin flexible sheets can be extruded (cast) vertically into a water quench bath (B), as illustrated in Figure 5.22, and then pulled around a guide roll (R), through haul-off rolls (R'), to a winder (W). A higher velocity can normally be achieved with chill roll extrusion (casting), as illustrated in Figure 5.23; the cooling/finishing roll stand (stack) (R) may feature an embossing roll to produce a surface pattern on the product. Uniaxial machine direction orientation (MDO) may be produced between two sets of pulling rolls; the outlet rolls rotate faster than the inlet rolls. Biaxial orientation may be produced through the use of a tentering frame device, as illustrated in Figure 5.24; the edges of the as-extruded product (P) are gripped by clips (C), which are accelerated along tracks (T), producing both machine direction (MD) and cross-direction (CD) orientation in the drawn product (P').

5.2.5 Materials

Practically all thermoplastics can be processed by extrusion, but in order for the emerging extrudates to maintain their shape until they solidify, extrusion grades tend to have relatively high molecular weights associated with high viscosity and melt strength.

Polyethylene (PE) is widely used for films and pipes, either as LDPE (flexible) or HDPE (rigid). Polypropylene (PP) is often used as oriented film (OPP). Polyvinylchloride (PVC) is used in rigid form (RPVC), as well as in flexible or plasticized form (PPVC), commonly with twin screw, corrosion-resistant extruders. Several engineering plastics are extruded into rodstock or slabstock for subsequent machining into parts. Very viscous polymers, such as PTFE or UHMWPE, are often processed by screwless (ram) extrusion.

As indicated earlier, conventional rubbers and, to a much smaller extent, thermosets, are extruded to form profiles, for example, but they must be subsequently cured.

5.2.6   Products

Fibers and monofilaments are extruded from a number of thermoplastics (PA, acrylics, polyesters) at speeds in the range 250-2000 m/min ($\approx$ 800-6000 ft/min).

Profiles are extruded in a wide variety of shapes, from flat strips or simple channels to very complex shapes, including hollow sections; vinylic, styrenic, and olefinic resins are among the most common profile materials. Some profiles feature a cellular (foam) core and a solid skin, or a rigid structural section with integral flexible sealing strips produced by coextrusion. Typical application include exterior wall siding, window or door tracks and frame elements, jamb liners, handrail covers, corner, edge and joint moldings, and weatherstripping. Production speeds are typically 3-20 m/min ($\approx$ 10-60 ft/min) for flexible profiles, and 1-5 m/min ($\approx$ 3-15 ft/min) for rigid ones.

Extruded tubular products can range in size from tiny tubing, used for separation purposes (e.g., artificial kidneys) or drinking straws, to pipes as large as 63 inches in diameter ($\approx$ 1.6 m) and 3/4 inch thick ($\approx$ 2 cm) made of HDPE. Typical production speeds for intermediate sizes are about 1-13 m/min ($\approx$ 3-40 ft/min) for rigid pipes and about 10-20 m/min ($\approx$ 30-60 ft/min) for flexible ones, while typical large outputs are about 2000 lb/h ($\approx$ 1000 kg/h). Stiff, but light, pipes are made by coextrusion with a cellular (foam) core. Longitudinally flexible, but transversely rigid, pipes for drainage purposes, for example, are made with corrugations produced in a post forming operation. Very large tubes are made by helically winding, and then bonding or mechanically interlocking a suitable extruded profile, a method that does not require a very costly investment. Flexible reinforced tubing is made by extruding an inner liner, braiding around it a fiber reinforcement, and subsequently extruding over it a cover (jacket). Polyvinylchloride (PPVC or RPVC) and polyethylene (LDPE or HDPE) are widely used as tubing or pipe resins.

Flat products are usually subdivided into films, when thinner than 0.010 in ($\approx$ 0.25 mm), and sheets above that. Production speeds can be as high as 1500 ft/min ($\approx$ 450 m/min) for thin films, with outputs of 3000 kg/h ($\approx$ 6000 lb/h); for thicker sheets, it is typically in the range 15-30 ft/min ($\approx$ 5-10 m/min) for outputs smaller than 500 kg/h ($\approx$ 1000 lb/h). Widths as large as 13 ft ($\approx$ 4 m) have been reported and the thickness of slabs can be as high as 0.5 in ($\approx$ 12.5 mm). Corrugated sheets, featuring high longitudinal rigidity, are made by a post forming operation. Stiff, but light, glazing panels, which feature two thin panels connected by multiple longitudinal ribs, are produced in a single extrusion step; they offer good thermal insulation properties. Similarly structured products made from ductile polyethylene are used as water-resistant replacements for corrugated cardboard.

Figures 5.25-5.42 demonstrate extrusion equipment.

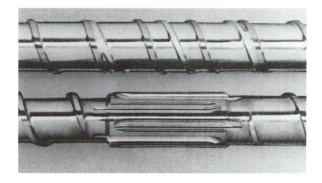

Figure 5.25 · Special purpose screw designs

Figure 5.26 · Planetary screw extruder [BATTENFELD]

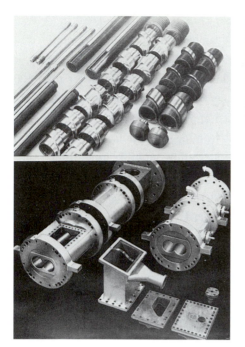

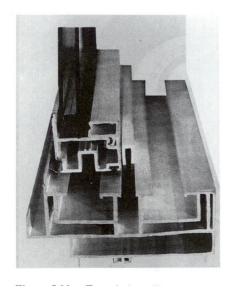

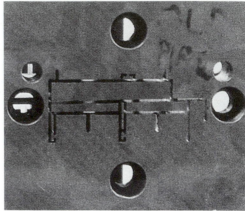

Figure 5.28 · Plate die for profile

Figure 5.27 · Modular twin-screw extruder (screw and barrel elements) **[BERSTORFF]**

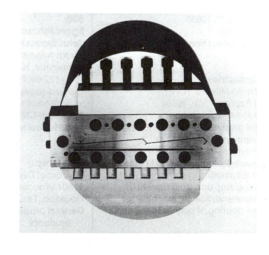

Figure 5.29 · Extruded profile

Figure 5.30 · Die for exterior wall siding

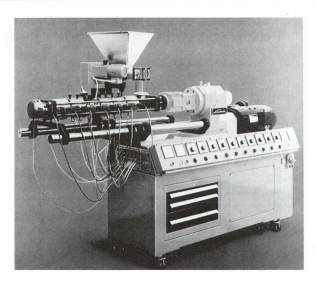

Figure 5.31 · Modular small extruder **[LEISTRITZ]**

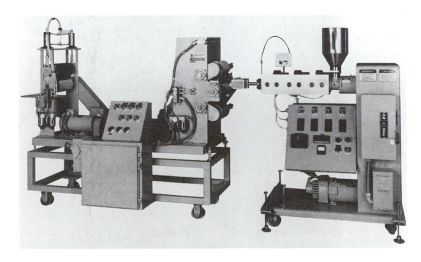

Figure 5.32 · Laboratory sheet line **[KILLION]**

Figure 5.33 · Sheet die with single screw extruder (90 mm or 3.5 in.) **[OMIPA]**

Figure 5.34 · Large extruder (200 mm or 8 in.) **[BERSTORFF]**

Figure 5.35 · Large homogenizing extruder (600 mm or 24 in.) [BERSTORFF]

Figure 5.36 · Large sheet coextrusion set-up (one 6 in., two 3.5 in. and one 2.5 in. extruders; 5 ft or 150 mm wide die) [WELEX]

Fig. 5.37

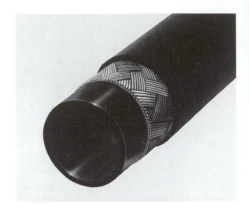

Fig. 5.38

Figure 5.37 · Feedblock for coextrusion line **[WELEX]**

Figure 5.38 · Braid-reinforced hose (liner extrusion, braiding, jacket extrusion)

Fig. 5.39

Fig. 5.40

Figure 5.39 · Corrugated pipe/conduit (post-extrusion forming) **[CORMA]**

Figure 5.40 · Tubing die (bushing, mandrel and spider) **[BATTENFELD]**

Figure 5.41 · Large tubing die (1400 mm or 55 in. diameter) **[BATTENFELD]**

Figure 5.42 · Controlled sizing of extruded pipe (diameter and wall thickness) **[BATTENFELD]**

5.3   EXTRUSION COVERING

5.3.1   Principle

The expression "extrusion covering" is used here for a process which fully surrounds a continuous substrate with a cover of polymeric material. Its most common use is for the formation of an insulating layer or a protective jacket on power or communication electrical wires and cables.

5.3.2   Equipment

An extrusion covering line (Fig. 5.43) comprises a substrate (S) pay-off (input) system, a substrate preheater (H) [typically to around 100°C ($\approx$ 200°F)], an extruder fitted with an appropriate extrusion covering tool (T), a cooling device (C), and a take-up (output) system for the product (P). Instruments for the continuous testing of dimensions or properties are often incorporated before take-up. Input and output systems often include devices such as tension controllers, capstans, and dancer columns.

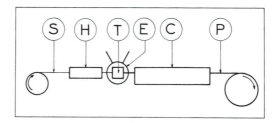

Figure 5.43 · **Extrusion covering line** · (S) Substrate; (H) Preheater; (T) Tool (die); (E) Extruder; (C) Cooler; (P) Product

5.3.3   Tooling

In its simplest form for the case of wire coating, an extrusion covering die (Fig. 5.44), mounted with its extrusion axis perpendicular to the extruder axis (crosshead die), comprises a tapered guider or core tube (G) for the substrate (S), and a suitable channel to direct the covering fluid polymer (C), from the extruder exit to an annular gap between a bushing (B) and the continuously moving substrate.

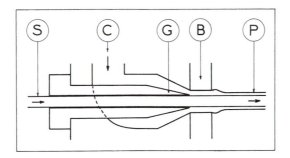

Figure 5.44 · **Extrusion covering die** · (S) Substrate; (C) Covering material; (G) Substrate guider; (B) Bushing; (P) Product

Figure 5.45 illustrates the difference between two basic methods of formation of the cover. In pressure covering [P], the cover is formed in a land (L) between the stationary die and the moving substrate, with the advantage that high pressure (up to 5000 psi or ≈ 350 atm) favors good contact, but with difficulties associated with backflow of the covering material and cover thickness uniformity, which depends on the substrate dimensions and centering. In tube-on covering [T], the annular cover (C) is formed in a land (L), between the stationary die and the guider, and subsequently brought against the substrate (S) by a suitable speed differential or by internal vacuum; the method allows a better control of the cover thickness uniformity and is widely used for thin covers.

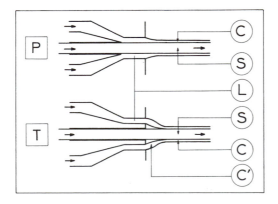

Figure 5.45 · **Methods of cover formation** · [P] Pressure covering; [T] Tube-on covering; (C) Cover; (S) Substrate; (L) Die land; (C′) Extruded tube

Figure 5.46 illustrates the formation of a thick cover [E], or a thin cover [M], with a pressure-type covering die by adjusting the flow rate of the cover material (C) and the travel velocity of the substrate (S).

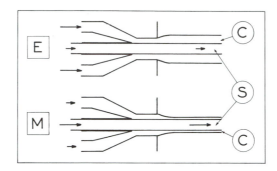

Figure 5.46 · **Cover thickness control** · [E] Thick cover; [T] Thin cover; (C) Cover; (S) Substrate

5.3.4   Materials

Plasticized polyvinylchloride (PPVC) and polyethylene (PE) are the most widely used thermoplastic cover materials, but other plastics such as polyamides, fluoropolymers, and cellulosics are used for demanding applications in wire insulation, or where transparency is desirable. For conventional rubber covering, an unvulcanized cover is applied, followed by continuous vulcanization (curing) through steam, molten salt, or high frequency heating.

5.3.5   Products

Wire and cable coating, sheathing, and jacketing is the most common application for extrusion covering. It includes single conductor (wire) or multiple conductor (cable) covering, the formation of flat ribbon (tape) multiconductor cables, including appliance cords and TV antenna cables, and multilayer covering. Production speeds as high as 10,000 ft/min or ≈ 100 mph (≈ 3000 m/min or 175 km/h) are reported.

Another area of application, sometimes referred to as "metal profile embedment," concerns the fabrication of decorative trim elements, with polished brass, polished aluminum, or chrome-plated substrates embedded in a protective, transparent cover. Plastic bag ties also involve the extrusion covering of a ductile wire.

Several examples of extrusion covering equipment are shown in figures 5.47-5.50.

Figure 5.47 · Die for building wire insulation **[NOKIA]**

Figure 5.48 · Die for coaxial cable expanded insulation **[NOKIA]**

Figure 5.49 · Guider for cable covering die

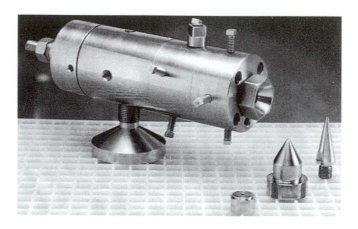

Figure 5.50 · Wire and cable coextrusion crosshead [B + H]

5.4   FILM BLOWING

5.4.1   Principle

The film blowing process basically consists of extruding a tube of molten thermoplastic and continuously inflating it to several times its initial diameter, to form a thin tubular product that can be used directly, or slit to form a flat film.

5.4.2   Equipment

The first element of a conventional film blowing line (Fig. 5.51) is the extruder (E), which supplies one, and sometimes two or more, tubular dies (T), described subsequently in the section on tooling.

The molten tube (I), emerging from the die, is subjected to both a moderate internal air pressure via an air inlet (A) running through the die mandrel, and a longitudinal force via take-off rolls (R'). The tube is simultaneously cooled by air from an external air ring (R). The molten tube gradually deforms into a stable solid cylindrical bubble (B) beyond the frost (freeze) line (F).

The bubble is gradually flattened in the collapsing device (tent frame) (C), which consists of a pair of converging, ladder-like sets of idler rolls or wood slats, and beyond the pinch (nip) rolls (R') it is handled as a thin flat product.

Internal bubble cooling sometimes involves the circulation of air inside the trapped volume via ducts in the die mandrel.

External [E] or internal [I] sizing and/or cooling of the bubble is sometimes achieved by contact with the surfaces of baskets (B) or mandrels (M), as illustrated in Figure 5.52.

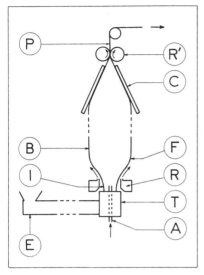

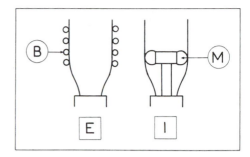

Figure 5.52 · **Bubble sizing techniques** · [E] External sizing; [I] Internal sizing; (B) Basket; (M) Inflatable mandrel

Figure 5.51 · **Film blowing line** · (E) Extruder; (I) Molten tube; (B) Bubble; (P) Product; (R′) Pinch/take-off rolls; (C) Collapsing device; (F) Freeze line; (R) Cooling air ring; (T) Tool (die); (A) Air inlet

Start-up of the film blowing operation normally involves the pulling of the uninflated extruded tube, with the help of a cable, until it becomes pinched between the nip rolls. Internal air pressure is subsequently applied to form the bubble.

The blow-up ratio (BUR), defined as the ratio of bubble to die diameters (or circumferences), is normally in the range 1.5-4, large values requiring high melt strengths. The air pressure in the bubble, which is responsible for the blowing, is normally in the range 0.05-0.2 atm ($\approx$ 1.5-3 psi). Machine direction drawdown is associated with the take-off velocity. As illustrated in Figure 5.53, a combination of high internal air pressure (A) with low take-off speed (V) leads to preferential cross (transverse) orientation [C], while the opposite promotes machine direction orientation [M]. It is normally possible to achieve a balanced orientation [B] with suitable settings.

The most common film blowing line configuration involves vertical upward extrusion and cooling; vertical downward extrusion has been reported, particularly when rapid liquid cooling is desired (PP, PVDC), as well as horizontal in-line extrusion and blowing for relatively small sizes and heat sensitive materials (PVC).

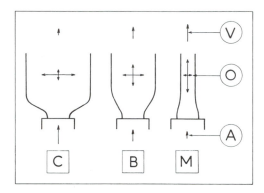

Figure 5.53 · **Operating conditions and orientation** · [C] Cross orientation; [B] Balanced orientation; [M] Machine direction orientation; (V) Take-off speed; (O) Orientation; (A) Internal pressure

5.4.3   Tooling

The extrusion die that produces the tube of molten polymer is the key element of the process. It is essential to achieve an excellent uniformity of the gap thickness and flow rate around the entire die circumference, as well as to minimize material inhomogeneity; this now involves very sophisticated designs.

Crosshead dies of the bottom-fed/spider-type tend to cause problems with weld-lines, while it is difficult to obtain flow rate uniformity with side-fed/spiderless types. Modern film blowing dies are increasingly of the bottom-fed/spiral mandrel type, which is illustrated schematically in Figure 5.54. The mandrel (M) features several spiral grooves (S), such as the one shown which has a decreasing cross section (depth), while the clearance (C) between mandrel and bushing (B) increases to the pre-land region (I), to become smaller again in the land (L).

Dies for coextruded, multilayer blown films feature several concentric spiral groove

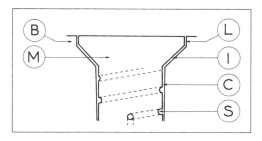

Figure 5.54 · **Spiral mandrel die** · (M) Mandrel; (B) Bushing; (L) Land; (I) Pre-land; (C) Clearance; (S) Spiral groove

systems with associated clearances, leading to individual pre-lands and the common die land.

Die diameters as large as about 2.5 m ($\approx$ 8 ft), are used. The land gap thickness is often in the range 0.4-1 mm ($\approx$ 0.015-0.040 in), and the material flow rate (extruder output or line throughput), often quoted per unit length of die orifice circumference, is in the range 2-30 lb/h/in or $\approx$ 0.4-6 kg/h/cm.

In order to distribute across the width of the final wound product the inevitable circumferential thickness variations in the extruded tube or the blown bubble, a slow continuous or oscillatory rotation of the mandrel, the bushing, the entire die, and even the haul-off tower, are used.

5.4.4 Auxiliaries

While the normal output of a film blowing line is a tubular, lay-flat product (T) (Fig. 5.55), the introduction of slitters, cutters, punches, gusseting and sealing devices, and other instruments can allow in-line production of slit-open or lay-flat products (S), and gusseted products (G), as well as a variety of bags including T-shirt bags with cutouts.

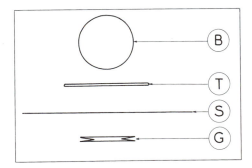

Figure 5.55 · **Blown film product configurations** · (B) Bubble; (T) Tubular lay-flat; (S) Slit-open lay flat; (G) Tubular gusseted

5.4.5 Materials

Polyethylenes of various types (LDPE, LLDPE, HMWHDPE, etc.) are by far the most common film blowing resins. Other resins used alone, or in combination with polyethylene for barrier purposes, include polyamides (PA), ionomers, polyvinylidene-chloride (PVDC), polyvinylalcohol (PVAL) or (PVOH), and copolymers such as (EVOH) and (EVA).

5.4.6   Products

Films produced by the film blowing process are widely used in many areas.

"Thick gauge," heavy-duty films are often in the range 0.004-0.008 in or ≈ 0.1-0.2 mm and can be as thick as 0.020 in or ≈ 0.5 mm). They are used for agricultural, construction, and industrial applications, including covers for silage, greenhouses, chemical/solar ponds, flat cars, etc., or liners for reservoirs, ponds, pits, and ditches, and are often associated with irrigation. Agricultural mulch films are also increasingly used.

Films are also widely used for a variety of packaging applications, which include wrap, can lining, fabricated bags such as garbage bags, gusseted (V-tucks, W-folds) fashion bags, and T-shirt bags (sacks) for groceries, and very thin garment bags or covers (about 0.3 mils or 0.003 in or ≈ 7.5 μm), which feature one or several seals.

Blown films can produce a moderate amount of heat-induced contraction (about 50%) and thus find applications as shrink films.

Multilayer (multi-ply) coextruded blown films, which contain from 3 to 11 layers, are increasingly used for barrier packaging, in particular. Examples in Figure 5.56 illustrate possible structures that may feature structural (S), barrier (B) and regrind (R) layers with intermediate tie (adhesive) layers (A).

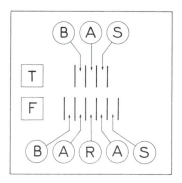

Figure 5.56 · **Multilayer film structures** · [T] Three-layer; [F] Five-layer; (B) Barrier layer; (A) Tie layer; (S) Structural layer; (R) Regrind layer

Linear production speeds are often in the range 10-45 m/min (≈ 30-150 ft/min) and are reported to be as high as 200 m/min (≈ 600 ft/min) for thin products such as garment bags. Slit-open lay-flat widths (bubble circumference) as high as 20 m (≈ 65 ft) and outputs of 5000 lb/h (≈ 2500 kg/h) have been reported.

See figures 5.57-5.60 for examples of film blowing.

Figure 5.57 · Blown film extrusion line (70 mm extruder) **[REIFENHAUSER-VAN DORN]** ·

Figure 5.58 · Multilayer film blowing die (three materials, fiver layers) **[BRAMPTON]**

Figure 5.59 · External and internal calibration/cooling of film blowing bubble **[DOLCI]**

Figure 5.60 · Single extruder/multiple die film blowing

5.5   CALENDERING

5.5.1   Principle

The calendering process is used for the fast production of flat films or sheets of plastics or rubbers. Its principle is illustrated in Figure 5.61. A suitable amount of plasticated material (M) is regularly fed between two counter rotating heated cylinders (rolls) (R) and (R′). The material is entrained at the surface of the rolls and squeezed in the wedge, and a layer of a thickness corresponding approximately to the shortest distance between roll surfaces (gap) is formed through the nip (N) and entrained on the surface of one of the rolls (R′). An excess of material forms the bank (B). The plasticated material undergoes very severe deformations in the nip region, and the viscoelastic character of polymeric materials imposes limitations on the speed of deformation, as well as the thinness, of the layer formed. The material normally goes through one or more additional inter-roll nips [(N′), (N″)], where the gap becomes progressively smaller, and the roll temperature becomes progressively lower, to attain the desired film or sheet thickness and a solid-like consistency in the product (P).

Alternative methods to produce films or sheets include the film blowing process, film casting, and sheet extrusion, which are discussed in other sections. Sheet extrusion, in particular, involves a post-extrusion finishing operation that resembles calendering.

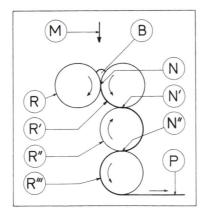

Figure 5.61 · **Calendering process** · (R),(R′) Feed rolls; (R″),(R‴) Gauge/finishing rolls; (M) Feed material; (B) Material bank; (N) Feed nip; (N′) Intermediate nip; (N″) Gauge nip; (P) Product

5.5.2   Equipment, Tooling, and Auxiliaries

Calendering lines correspond to large investments in spite of the apparent simplicity of the process. They are often dedicated to the mass production of a single product.

The diameter of calendering rolls is generally in the range 40-90 cm ($\approx$ 16-36 in) and their length is generally in the range 1-2.5 m ($\approx$ 36-100 in); this corresponds to length: diameter ratios between 2 and 3. The width of finished films or sheets is somewhat smaller than the roll length. Rolls are normally made of cast iron; they are cored for temperature control (steam, oil, water, electric), and their surface plays an essential role (dimensions, finish, hardness).

Calendering units generally feature 3 to 5 rolls (2 to 4 nips), arranged in a variety of configurations (roll axis pattern or sheet path) denoted by letters such as F, I, L, S, W, and Z. Examples, as illustrated in Figure 5.62, correspond to a vertical stack [I], an inverted L [L], and a Z-like configuration [Z]. The configurations differ, in particular, in the circumferential length of contact (active length) on individual rolls.

Roll speeds are normally individually adjustable. Different circumferential speeds for two adjacent rolls increase the deformation in the material. The speed ratio (friction ratio) may be as high as 1.5, but is normally closer to 1 in the gauge nip (N″). Linear line speeds are generally in the range 30-120 m/min ($\approx$ 100-400 ft/min). Powers can be very large (168-500 kW or $\approx$ 550-750 hp).

The thickness (gauge) of the product is controlled by adjusting the gap in the gauge nip (N″). This is normally done by screw-down mechanisms acting on the bearing boxes. For small nip gaps in particular, a high nip pressure builds up, which corresponds to nip forces in the range 20-100 mtf/m ($\approx$ 1000-5000 lbf/in); the resulting flexural deformation of the rolls [O] in Figure 5.63 causes unacceptable variations of thickness across the width (barrel-shaped wound product packages). Corrections for roll flexure are of three types: roll crowning [C], corresponds to deliberate noncylindrical roll geometries; roll crossing [X], involving a small angle between roll axes; and roll bending [B] involving the application of countering flexural forces (F) to auxiliary bearing boxes (B'), on roll extensions beyond the major bearing boxes (B).

The last roll, or pair of rolls, in the calendering stack determines the surface finish of the product. A smooth polished roll gives a glossy surface, while matt or textured surfaces (pattern, grain) are produced by engraved rolls; embossing (the creation of relatively large off-plane deformations) can be achieved with matching positive and negative rolls or with a single embossing roll coupled with a rubber-covered pressure roll.

The plasticated material is fed to the feed nip in the form of a full-width sheet (extruder fitted with slot die), in the form of a strand or rope (traversing die on swiveling extruder), and in the form of a traversing strip or ribbon (Banbury-type internal mixer and roll mill).

Post-calender trains include chill rolls (cooling drums), scanning thickness gauges (ß-ray type), electrostatic control devices, edge trimmers, and winders. Cold drawing or stretching is sometimes used and results in orientation and lighter gauge. In the case of vulcanizable rubbers, a set of heated drums may be used for curing the product.

Typical calender outputs are in the range 0.5-5 mt/hr ($\approx$ 1000-10,000 lb/hr).

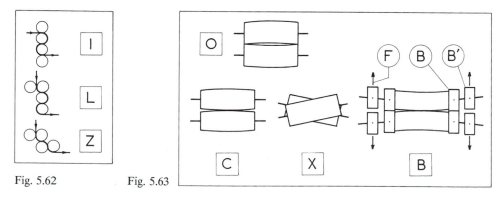

Fig. 5.62   Fig. 5.63

Figure 5.62 · **Calendering rolls configuratons** · [I] Vertically aligned; [L] Inverted L; [Z] Z-Like

Figure 5.63 · **Roll flexure compensation** · [O] Uncompensated flexure; [C] Roll crowning; [X] Roll crossing; [B] Roll bending; (F) Applied force; (B) Major bearing box; (B') Auxiliary bearing box

5.5.3   Materials and Products

Vinyl thermoplastics (PVC and copolymers), and vulcanizable rubbers, are the most commonly calendered materials. Other thermoplastics, such as polyethylene and ABS, are also used.

Film thicknesses are not normally below about 0.05 mm ($\approx$ 0.002 in): a typical example is vinyl baby pants film (about 0.08 mm or $\approx$ 0.003 in). Sheets can be as thick as about 6 mm ($\approx$ 0.250 in); floor tiles, for example, are often around 2.5 mm ($\approx$ 0.100 in) thick. Product widths have been reported as large as about 3.4 m ($\approx$ 135 in), but it is more commonly about 1.5 m ($\approx$ 60 in) for rigid PVC (RPVC) and about 2.5 m ($\approx$ 96 in) for plasticized PVC (PPVC).

As stated earlier, the calendering process involves large investments, but is capable of large outputs and is well suited to the production of textured products, as well as laminated and coated substrates.

Examples of applications include vinyl films made into products such as baby pants, inflatable toys, shower curtains, tablecloths, pool liners, wall covering, and veneered panels as well as vinyl sheets for credit cards, blister packaging, floor tiles, and floor covering (linoleum). Cured rubber membranes are widely used for waterproofing, and calendering is the standard method for making unvulcanized cord-reinforced rubber plies, which are the basic elements for the construction of many rubber-based products (conveyor belts, tires, inflatable boats, etc.).

Calendering equipment is shown in figures 5.64-5.66.

Figure 5.64 · Roll drive and control on large production calender **[BERSTORFF]**

Figure 5.65 · Laboratory calender (four 6 in. x 13 in. rolls in inverted "L" configuration) **[FARRELL]**

Figure 5.66 · Large production calender **[REPIQUET]**

5.6   SHEET THERMOFORMING

5.6.1   Principle

Sheet thermoforming, or simply thermoforming, involves the heating of a flat thermoplastic sheet to a softened state (above the glass transition temperature $\mathbf{T_g}$ for noncrystallizing thermoplastics or near the melting temperature $\mathbf{T_m}$ for crystallizing ones), followed by the deformation (forming) of the softened sheet into a desired shape by pneumatic or mechanical means, and finally its solidification (freezing) into this shape by cooling.

In the case of noncrystallizing thermoplastics in particular, the deformation takes place in the rubbery region where the material is highly elastic. The deformation, frozen in by cooling, is generally highly recoverable if a thermoformed part is reheated above $\mathbf{T_g}$; the softened part will thus tend to return to its original flat configuration.

Thermoforming transforms a flat sheet (blank), of uniform thickness, into a contoured product of variable thickness resulting from the nonuniform biaxial stretching. At any stage of the forming process, most sheet deformation takes place in areas that have not yet come in contact with the cold tool. For a typical cup-like product, such as [P] illustrated in Figure 5.67, regions such as the edge (E), the side (sidewall, rim, crown) (S), the corner (C), the bottom (cap, disk) (D), the apex (A) and the flange (F) have thicknesses that can be substantially less than that of the blank [B] or web (W). The material also retains a high degree of biaxial orientation, which may have a positive effect on properties. The severity of the deformation is often characterized by a drawdown ratio that, in the case of a cup, could be the ratio of the height (or depth) of the cup to its diameter, or the ratio of the total area of the cup to the corresponding initial area on the blank.

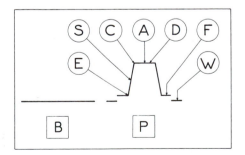

Figure 5.67 · **Typical cup-like product** · [B] Blank; [P] Product; (E) Edge; (S) Side; (C) Corner; (A) Apex; (D) Bottom; (F) Flange; (W) Web

Thermoforming normally involves a one-surface (single surface) tool, and it is convenient to distinguish between negative (female, cavity) tools, which are basically concave and into which the sheet is formed (drawn), and positive (male, plunger) tools, which are basically convex and over which the sheet is formed (draped). If the typical product shown in Figure 5.67 is made against a negative tool, its external surface will normally reflect the surface finish of the tool, while the internal surface will normally correspond to the surface finish of the sheet stock (blank). In the case of a positive tool, the inverse occurs; this has important practical implications as discussed in Chapter 6 (section 6.2.3.1).

A number of techniques and variations are used to make products that can combine high drawdown ratios with acceptable thickness distributions. Such methods involve pneumatically and/or mechanically induced deformations.

Pneumatic deformation is most commonly done by vacuum (suction), with the maximum pressure differential thus about 1 atm; surge tanks are normally used to permit fast evacuation rates. Positive air pressure, often used in conjunction with suction, can be helpful for thick products or to reproduce fine tool surface textures. It is essential for some techniques discussed later.

Mechanical deformation tends to be used primarily for pre-forming or pre-stretching, before final vacuum or air pressure forming. Corresponding auxiliary tools are referred to as assist devices (plug, former, etc.).

The simplest thermoforming technique is perhaps that referred to as "straight vacuum thermoforming" (Fig. 5.68). The blank (M), held in a clamping frame (C), is

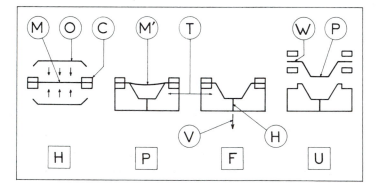

Figure 5.68 · **Straight vacuum thermoforming** · [H] Heating; [P] Positioning; [F] Forming; [U] Unloading; (M) Blank; (O) Oven; (C) Clamp; (M′) Softened blank; (T) Tool (mold); (V) Vacuum; (H) Vacuum hole(s); (W) Web; (P) Product

heated in an oven (O) (stage [H]). The clamp and the softened blank (M′) are positioned over a negative tool (T) (stage [P]). A vacuum (V) is pulled between the blank and the tool surface through one or several suitably placed small holes (H) (forming stage [F]). After contacting the surface of the cooled tool, the material solidifies and the product (P), still surrounded by a web (W), can be unloaded (stage [U]). When made by this technique, products such as the typical product shown in Figure 5.67 tend to have very thin walls in regions (C) and (D) and only moderate drawdown ratios can be achieved. Figure 5.69 shows how a pressure box (B) and positive air pressure (A) can be used in conjunction with the previous technique; simple venting on the tool side is less effective than evacuation.

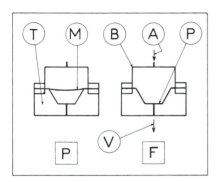

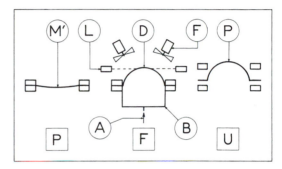

Fig. 5.69   Fig. 5.70

Figure 5.69 · **Air pressure thermoforming** · [P] Positioning; [F] Forming; (T) Tool (mold); (M′) Softened blank; (B) Pressure box; (A) Air pressure; (P) Product; (V) Vacuum

Figure 5.70 · **Free forming** · [P] Positioning; [F] Forming; [U] Unloading; (M′) Softened blank; (L) Optical level detector; (D) Dome; (F) cooling fans; (P) Product; (A) Air pressure; (B) Pressure box

The technique of free forming used for some special products, such as transparent domes, canopies, and skylights, is illustrated in Figure 5.70. The heated blank (M′) is inflated (blown) until the top of the dome (D) reaches a certain height. An optical level detector (L) can be used to control the air pressure while the dome is cooled, usually with the help of suitably placed fans (F), to give the solid desired product (P). The uniformity of heating is very critical since the final shape, not only the thickness, depends on the deformability of the softened sheet.

Thermoforming over a positive tool is often referred to as "draping." The simplest draping technique is illustrated in Figure 5.71. Most of the deformation is mechanically induced when the positive tool (T) moves against the softened sheet (M′) (straight draping), but the application of a vacuum (V) through suitably placed holes (H) is often required to help make the sheet conform to the tool. Straight or vacuum-assisted draping leads to thick bottom (D) and thin sidewall (S) in a typical product (Fig. 5.67). The thickness distribution can be improved in the technique referred to here as "snap-back draping," as illustrated in Figure 5.72. The softened sheet (M′) in Figure 5.72 is pneumatically pre-stretched (pre-blown) in the form of a bubble (dome) (D) before the positive tool (T) moves in, and vacuum (V) is applied to the tool, with atmospheric or positive air pressure now acting in the box (B) to cause the "snap-back" of the pre-blown sheet against the tool surface.

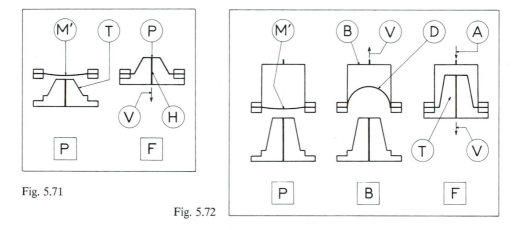

Fig. 5.71

Fig. 5.72

Figure 5.71 · **Vacuum-assisted draping** · [P] Positioning; [F] Forming; (M′) Softened blank; (T) Tool (plug); (P) Product; (V) Vacuum; (H) Vacuum hole(s)

Figure 5.72 · **Snap-back draping** · [P] Positioning; [B] Pre-blowing; [F] Final forming; (M′) Softened blank; (B) Vacuum/pressure box; (V) Vacuum; (D) Dome; (A) Air pressure; (T) Tool (plug); (V) Vacuum

Direct contact between the positive tool (T) and the softened sheet (M′) can be avoided during the initial stage of the draping process by using the so-called air slip technique, as illustrated in Figure 5.73. Air pressure (A), applied through the top of the tool, forms a cushion of flowing air (S) between sheet and tool, which allows the unhindered deformation of the sheet. The same principle can be used with plug assists.

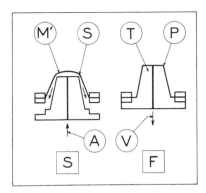

Figure 5.73 · **Air slip forming** · [S] Pre-stretching; [F] Final forming; (M′) Deformed blank; (S) Air slip; (T) Tool (plug); (P) Product; (A) Air pressure; (V) Vacuum

A technique that combines the use of pneumatic and mechanical pre-stretching (pre-forming) is illustrated in Figure 5.74; such a technique, which is sometimes referred to as "pillow" (or "billow") forming, helps achieve deep draws with fairly uniform wall thickness. The softened sheet (M′) is first blown into a bubble (dome) (D) by positive air pressure (A) applied through the negative tool (T). The mechanical assist device (plug or form) (F) is then pushed against the sheet while some air pressure is maintained in the tool cavity; the situation is reminiscent of an air mattress (or pillow) resisting indentation, hence the use of the word "pillow" (O). Forming is completed when vacuum (V) in the tool cavity finally draws the softened sheet against the surface to form the product (P).

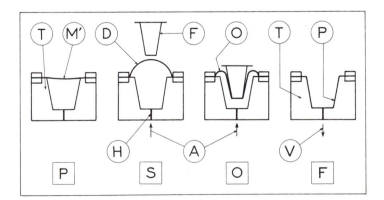

Figure 5.74 · **Pillow forming** · [P] Positioning; [S] Pre-stretching; [O] Pillow pre-forming; [F] Final forming; (T) Tool (mold); (M′) Softened blank; (D) Dome; (F) Assist device (plug); (O) Pillow; (P) Product; (H) Hole(s); (A) Air pressure; (V) Vacuum

5.6.2 Equipment

The equipment used to thermoform parts depends very much on the size of the parts and the rate of production desired.

The simplest commercial type is probably the single station shuttle thermoformer, illustrated in Figure 5.75 with front (right) and side (left) views. A machine frame (B) supports horizontal tracks (R), as well as two vertically moving, air-actuated platens (P) and (P′) carrying the tool and assist devices. A clamping frame (C) holding the cut sheet (M) can shuttle horizontally from the loading/forming/unloading (work) station, under the machine frame (B) to the heating oven (O). The two-station (double end) shuttle thermoformer (Fig. 5.76) is a variation which uses a single oven (O) with two work stations, the associated clamping frames (C) and (C′) taking turns in the oven. In some cases, particularly for large parts, the heating elements may shuttle over the stationary clamping frame.

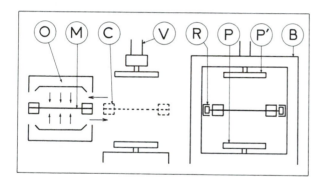

Fig. 5.75

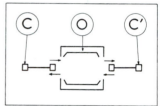

Fig. 5.76

Figure 5.75 · **Single station shuttle thermoformer** · (O) Oven; (M) Blank; (C) Clamp; (V) Air cylinder; (R) Rack; (P),(P′) Platens; (B) Frame

Figure 5.76 · **Two-station shuttle thermoformer** · (C),(C′) Clamps; (O) Oven

Rotary thermoformers (Fig. 5.77) feature three clamping frames (C), mounted on a carrousel, which are indexed into the loading/unloading station (L), the heating oven (O) and the forming station (F).

For the mass production of relatively small thin-wall parts, such as packaging containers, and disposable cups, roll-fed, in-line thermoformers featuring rows of cavities across the direction of motion are particularly convenient. Inintermittent

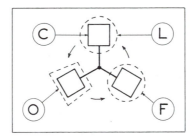

Figure 5.77 · **Rotary thermoformer** · (C) Clamp; (L) Loading/unloading station; (F) Forming station; (O) Oven

in-line thermoformers (Fig. 5.78), the roll-fed material (M), after being heated in the oven (O), is formed in the tool cavity (T) in stop and go (intermittent) motion, synchronized with the stroke of a trimming cutter (C) that separates the parts (P) from the web (W). In continuous in-line thermoformers (Fig. 5.79), the tool cavities (T) are built into a large diameter drum (D) that rotates at a steady speed. Suitable configurations of in-line thermoformers can allow immediate in-line filling and sealing of containers (form/fill/seal machines).

Thermoformers capable of handling cut sheets are as large as about 3 m x 9 m (≈ 10 ft x 30 ft), and holding tools as heavy as 20 mt (≈ 40,000 lb), have been built.

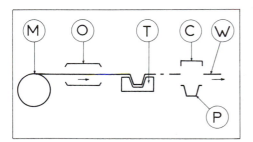

Fig. 5.78

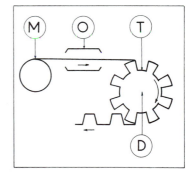

Fig. 5.79

Figure 5.78 · **Intermittent in-line thermoformer** · (M) Roll-fed material; (O) Oven; (T) Tool; (C) Cutter; (W) Web; (P) Product

Figure 5.79 · **Continuous in-line thermoformer** · (M) Roll-fed material; (O) Oven; (T) Tool; (D) Drum

5.6.3   Tooling

Tools for thermoforming are not normally subjected to high stresses since the pressure differential is often limited to one atmosphere in vacuum forming or 3-4 atmospheres in pressure forming. They are often made from cast or machined aluminum for small and medium sizes. Epoxy and polyester resins, with fiber reinforcement and a heat conductive filler, are suitable for the relatively slow production of large parts.

Tools are generally water-cooled to temperatures in the range 40-95°C ($\approx$ 100-200°F), while mechanical assist devices (plugs) are kept at somewhat higher temperature (60-150°C or $\approx$ 140-300°F).

Thermoforming tools are one-surface tools. When the important product surface is not that in contact with the tool, the tool surface does not require a good finish. In fact, for materials such as the polyolefins (PE, PP), a sand (grit)-blasted tool surface facilitates a complete air evacuation.

Vacuum is applied through fine holes, slots, or ports (0.5-1 mm or $\approx$ 0.020-0.040 in) that do not leave significant marks on products.

The extraction of products from tools requires larger taper ($\approx$ 5°) for positive tools than for negative tools ($\approx$ 2°), because of material shrinkage. Small corner radii are generally difficult to form or cause excessive thinning.

5.6.4   Auxiliaries

Heating of the sheet stock (blank) is most commonly done with radiant electric heaters (nichrome wire, calrod, ceramic, quartz, etc.), which correspond to electric power densities around 15-25 kW/m$_2$ ($\approx$ 10-15 W/in^2). The absorption of the radiant energy depends on the sheet material and color. Heaters are located on one or both sides of a sheet at a distance of 7.5-20 cm ($\approx$ 3-8 in), and heating times, which depend strongly on sheet thickness, can range from about 1 s to as long as 10 min. The sagging of a sheet during heating is related to its thermal expansion, as well as to creep under its own weight; it is often a difficult problem for large blanks. Convection ovens and contact heating on hot plates are occasionally used.

After forming, products must be separated from the surrounding web by a trimming operation. For small products, this is often done by shearing off (punching off), using the punch and die principle; a trimming edge is sometimes incorporated in the tool design and activated after forming (trim-in-place), or a trim press is used subsequently (post-trim). For large products, contour sawing or routering is often more appropriate.

Web scrap, which may correspond to as much as 50% of the material in the case of cups, requires extensive recycling.

5.6.5 Materials

Noncrystallizing thermoplastics are normally easier to thermoform than crystallizing ones, because of their highly elastic behavior over a fairly wide range of temperature above T_g. They include styrenics such as high-impact (HI) or crystal polystyrene (PS), and copolymers such as ABS. Nitrile resins are used in packaging applications for their barrier properties. Acrylics (PMMA, etc.) and cellulosics (CA, CAB, etc.) are also used, particularly when transparency is desired. Crystallizing olefinics, such as high-density polyethylene (HDPE) or polypropylene (PP) and polyamides (PA), are occasionally used, but they require accurate control of the blank temperature. Thermoplastic polyesters (PET) are increasingly thermoformed, for food packaging in particular; they may be processed in the amorphous state (APET).

The thermoformability of thermoplastics is often associated with their "melt strength"; it requires a good resistance of the melt to low stresses (sag during heating) but high extendibility under higher stresses (forming stage).

The process of thermoforming requires material in semi-fabricated form (cut sheet flat stock, or sheet and film roll stock). For packaging applications in particular, coextruded sheet or film stock is increasingly used. Cellular sheet stock is also widely used (meat trays, egg containers, etc.). Preprinted or even textured sheet stock can be used, but the deformation during forming causes pattern changes.

5.6.6 Products

Products made by sheet thermoforming fall into two distinct categories. Small products made in high output machines, often of the roll-fed, in-line type, using multicavity tools, are associated primarily with packaging and disposable items such as those used in the food industry and for medical applications. They include skin and blister packs (PE, PP, PVDC, PVC, CA, CAB, CP, PS, etc.), individual containers for jelly or cream, vials, cups, tubs, trays, and lids. As many as millions of parts per day can be produced with a single tool featuring several hundred cavities.

Larger products are generally made from cut sheets at much slower rates; the heating stage often is the limiting factor. Medium-sized products include machine covers and housings, light diffusers, furniture facings, refrigerator main liners and inner door panels, shower stalls and trays, sinks, and bath tubs. Translucent illuminated advertising or display signs are conveniently custom-made, as single units or in small numbers, at low tooling costs. Transparent products, such as contoured windows, skylights and cockpit canopies, are often made by free forming of acrylic or other transparent sheets. Large parts, such as interior panels or exterior body panels for recreational vehicles, watercraft hulls (canoes, sailboards, dinghies as long as 6 m or 20 ft), and pre-fabricated construction panels, can be reinforced with a fiber-reinforced plastic backing (FRP-rigidized thermoformings). In this case the thermoformed element plays the dual role of tool (mold) and gel coat.

Small and medium-sized products can have relatively complex shapes, the use of refined techniques allowing a reasonably good control of the thickness. Large parts normally have relatively simple shapes corresponding to moderate drawdowns and are generally made by a basic technique.

5.6.7   Related Process

Hollow products can be made in one operation by a process referred to as twin sheet (dual sheet, clam shell) thermoforming, as illustrated in Figure 5.80. Two parallel heat-softened sheets (M) and (M′) are first vacuum-formed in tools (T) and (T′) (stage [F]), and the two half shells are then fusion-bonded at the point of contact

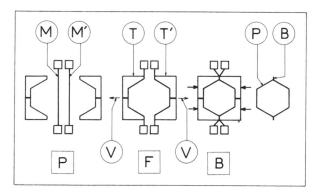

Figure 5.80 · **Twin sheet thermoforming** · [P] Positioning; [F] Forming; [B] Bonding; (M),(M′) Softened blanks; (T),(T′) Tools (molds); (P) Product; (B) Bond

when the tools are brought together (bonding stage [B]). The product (P) features a bead or ledge (B) corresponding to the bonded area. This technique also permits the insertion of an element such as a preformed cellular (foam) core in the hollow shell. Heated sheet stock or sheets extruded directly between the tools can be used. The second case is closely related to the blow molding process discussed later.

Several thermoforming devices are demonstrated in figures 5.81-5.86.

Figure 5.81 · Large shuttling oven thermoformer [SHUMAN]

Figure 5.82 · Small single station
thermoformer [AAA]

Figure 5.83 · Thermoforming of
ABS refrigerator liner

Figure 5.84 · Roll-fed, in-line thermoformer **[GABLER]**

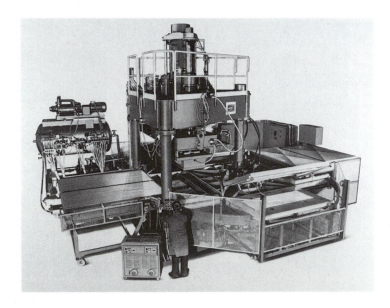

Figure 5.85 · Rotary thermoformer **[RIET]**

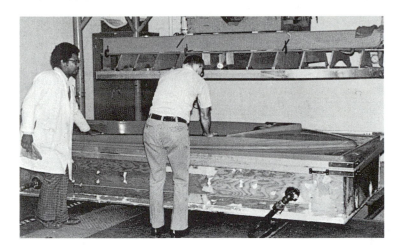

Figure 5.86 · Thermoforming of sailboat deck

5.7 BLOW MOLDING

5.7.1 Principle

The basic principle of the blow molding process is to inflate a softened thermoplastic hollow preform against the cooled surface of a closed mold, where the material solidifies into a hollow product. The process is called "extrusion blow molding" (EBM) when the preform is produced by extrusion or "injection blow molding" (IBM), when the preform is injection molded.

The extrusion blow molding (EBM) process, as illustrated in Figure 5.87, involves an extruder (E) fitted with a die or die head (D) which produces the preform by extruding downward a tube of thermoplastic generally called preform or parison (F) at stage [E]. While the preform is still soft, it is then pinched (stage [P]) between the two halves of a mold (T); the bottom is pinched shut (sealed), while the top is pinched around a metal tube or blow pin (B) protruding from the die core. At the following stage [B], the soft preform is blown against the cooled mold surfaces by air (A) injected through the blow pin (B). After the thermoplastic material has solidified, the mold is opened and the product (P) is pulled out (demolded) at stage [D]. Typical circumferential blow-up ratios (product diameter over parison diameter) are in the range 3-4.

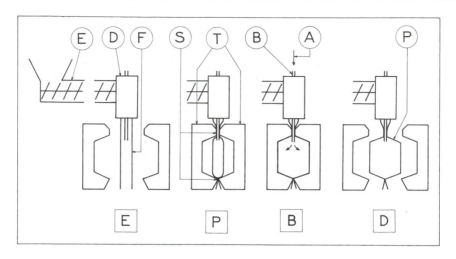

Figure 5.87 · **Extrusion blow molding** · [E] Extrusion; [P] Pinching; [B] Blowing; [D] Demolding; (E) Extruder; (D) Die; (F) preform; (S) Squeezed area; (T) Tool; (B)Blow pin; (A) Air pressure; (P) Product

The injection blow molding (IBM) process, as illustrated in Figure 5.88, first involves an injection stage [I], during which the thermoplastic material is injected into an injection mold (T) featuring two important elements, a split neck ring (R) and a core pin (C). Upon demolding [D], the preform (F) remains attached to the neck ring and core pin, but the injection mold is replaced by a blow mold (T′) (stage [P]). Air (A) is subsequently injected through a valve (V) in the core pin, to blow the soft

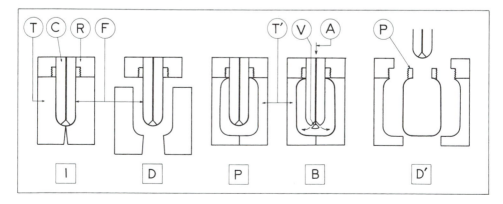

Figure 5.88 · **Injection blow molding** · [I] Preform injection; [D] Preform demolding; [P] Tool replacement; [B] Product blowing; [D′] Product demolding; (T) Injection tool; (C) Core pin; (R) Neck ring; (F) Preform; (T′) Blowing tool; (V) Air valve; (A) Air pressure; (P) Product

preform against the cooled blow mold surface, to form the product (P). The core is retracted and the neck ring and the mold simultaneously split open to demold the product. Injection molded preforms are sometimes demolded after solidification, stored, and subsequently reheated for blowing; the process is then referred to as "reheat IBM."

In conventional extrusion blow molding, and to a large extent in injection blow molding as well, the material deformation is primarily circumferential, leading to an unbalanced orientation in products. A technique referred to as "stretch blow molding" (SBM), illustrated in Figure 5.89 for an injection molded preform, permits the achievement of a more favorable biaxial orientation. The core (C) features a stretching rod and plug (S), which is extended during the stretching stage [S] while the annular core is retracted, causes an axial deformation of the preform. The subsequent blowing stage [B] adds a circumferential deformation.

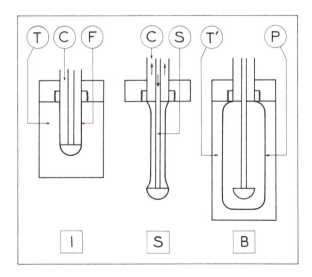

Figure 5.89 · **Injection-stretch blow molding** · [I] Injection; [S] Stretch; [B] Blowing; (T) Injection tool; (C) Core; (F) Preform; (S) Stretching device; (T') Blowing tool; (P) Product

5.7.2   Equipment

Extrusion blow molding (EBM) machines basically consist of two major elements: 1) the parison former, which comprises an extruder, a die, and sometimes a special accumulating device; and 2) the mold handling device (mold carrier).

A class of machines involve the continuous extrusion of the parison. In an arrangement sometimes referred to as the Mills continuous tube EBM (Fig. 5.90), molds (T) mounted on a rotary hold (horizontal-axis ferris-wheel type or vertical axis-table, merry-go-rounds, or carousel types) take turns at the pinching station [P] with subsequent blowing [B], cooling [C] and demolding [D] of the product (P). Another arrangement, illustrated in Figure 5.91, involves the rapid pinching of the parison by a mold (T) and its immediate removal to a blowing and demolding position [B]; a second mold (T') often alternates with mold (T). This arrangement is often referred to as "mold shuttle." It is also possible to have a parison shuttle system in which suitable lengths of parison are quickly cut and mechanically transferred to stationary mold assemblies. Occasionally, swiveling dieheads alternately feed pairs of molds.

Many machines, particularly for large capacities, extrude the parison in a discontinuous manner, using an accumulator. A somewhat smaller extruder can be used, which continuously plasticates the thermoplastic resin while the parison can be extruded relatively rapidly, when needed, by ram or piston action. Three types of

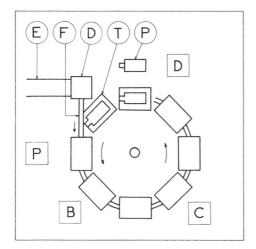

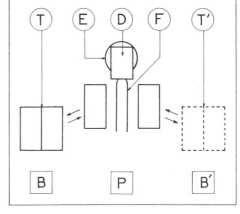

Figure 5.90 · **Continuous tube extrusion blow molding (side view)** · [P] Pinching; [B] Blowing; [C] Cooling; [D] Demolding; (E) Extruder; (F) Preform; (D) Die; (T) Tool; (P) Product

Figure 5.91 · **Mold shuttle extrusion blow molding (front view)** · [B] First blowing position; [P] Pinching position; [B'] Second blowing position; (T) First tool; (E) Extruder; (D) Die; (F) Preform; (T') Second tool

accumulators are represented schematically in Figure 5.92. System [S] uses the same principle as reciprocating screw injection; a charge (C) is first accumulated between the screw tip and a closed valve (V). System [L] uses a three-way valve (V) to transfer a charge (C) into a reservoir (accumulation stage [A]), from which it is extruded (extrusion stage [E]); this system has the disadvantage of large differences in resin residence time, the last material to go in being the first to go out (short time), while the first material in is the last out (long time). System [F] is somewhat more complex but corresponds to a more desirable "first-in first-out" (FIFO) material flow; a typical arrangement involves the retraction of a sealing sleeve (S) and the closing of the valve-shaped die gap (V) during accumulation [A], and subsequent extrusion by the action of the annular piston (P).

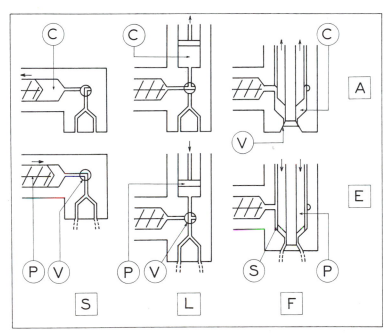

Figure 5.92 · **Accumulating devices** · [S] Reciprocating screw; [L] First in last out (FILO); [F] First in first out (FIFO); [A] Accumulation; [E] Extrusion; (C) Charge; (V) Valve; (P) Plunger, piston; (S) Sealing sleeve

Semi-continuous rotary systems, involving wheel-type and carousel-type mold-holding devices, are illustrated in Figures 5.93 and 5.94, respectively.

Injection blow molding (IBM) machines often feature the rotary system, as illustrated in Figure 5.95, with stationary injection mold (T) as well as blow mold (T′) and a revolving hub (H), which transfers the preform (F) from the injection station [I] to the blowing station [B], and the product (P) to the demolding station [D].

Blowing pressures are often limited to normal plant air pressure (about 120 psi or ≈ 8 atm), and clamping forces are thus relatively small (typically about 1 ton for a bottle and about 50 tons for a shipping drum). For very large products, self-locking molds have been used.

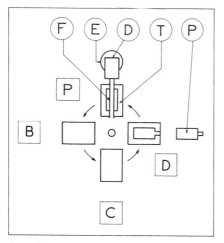

Fig. 5.93

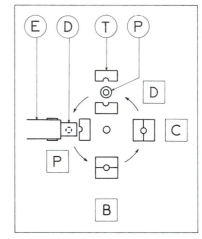

Fig. 5.94

Figure 5.93 · **Rotary vertical wheel system (front view)** · [P] Pinching; [B] Blowing; [C] Cooling; [D] Demolding; (F) Preform; (E) Extruder; (D) Die; (T) Tool; (P) Product

Figure 5.94 · **Rotary horizontal carousel system   (top view)** · [P] Pinching; [B] Blowing; [C] Cooling; [D] Demolding; (E) Extruder; (D) Die; (T) Tool; (P) Product

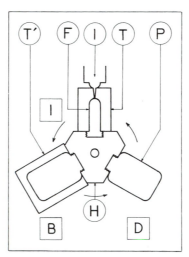

Figure 5.95 · **Rotary injection blow molding (top view)** · [I] Injection station; [B] Blowing; [D] Demolding; (T') Blowing tool; (F) Preform; (I) Injection nozzle; (T) Injection tool; (P) Product; (H) Hub

5.7.3 Tooling

Tooling for a specific extrusion blow molded product involves the mold as well as the die to produce the parison. In the case of injection blow molding, an injection mold is needed for the preform, in addition to the blow mold.

Parison extrusion dies normally feature a 90° configuration, and feed sections are designed to minimize the formation of die weld lines. The orifice region (land), between the bushing (B) and the mandrel or core (M) (Fig. 5.96), features an annular gap (G), which may be straight, converging for small diameter parisons in particular, or diverging (trumpet or valve shape). A diverging gap (Fig. 5.96), associated with an axially adjustable (floating) mandrel (M), can be used for parison thickness programming; a wider gap [W] being used, for example, in the later stage of the extrusion of a long parison to compensate for gravity sag. Figure 5.96 also illustrates the diameter (circumferential) and thickness swells, which increase with the speed of extrusion. These and other factors are associated with problems such as parison pleating, curtaining, folding, and webbing. Technology is now available to produce coextruded parisons involving several layers of different materials with complementary properties.

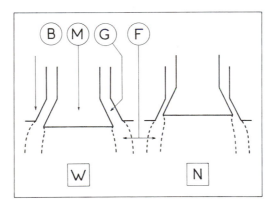

Figure 5.96 · **Extrusion die and parison geometry** · (B) Bushing; (M) Mandrel; (G) Gap; (F) Parison (preform)

Blow molds are subjected to moderate pressures and clamping forces, compared to injection molds; they can thus be constructed more lightly, and aluminum (cast or machined) is often used, which has advantages in terms of weight and heat conductivity. In aluminum molds, pinch regions often feature steel inserts which offer a better wear resistance. For very high volumes, all-steel molds are sometimes required. Other mold materials, such as beryllium-copper and zinc alloys, have also been used.

Depending on the product shape (Fig. 5.97), molds may feature side cores, handle eye-forming sections, off-center neck-forming sections with puncturing blow pins or needles, etc. Air venting requires vent holes or slits, with typical diameter or thickness of about 0.2 mm ($\approx$ 0.010 in) or 0.1 mm (0.005 in), respectively, flash vents, or air evacuation by vacuum.

Mold cooling involves flooding or, more commonly, drilled or cast-in water channels. Inner cooling of the product is sometimes enhanced by using refrigerated blowing air, moist air expansion, or even liquid carbon dioxide or nitrogen vaporization.

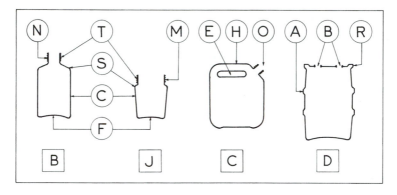

Figure 5.97 · **Blow molded products** · [B] Bottle; [J] Jar; [C] Canister; [D] Drum; (N) Narrow neck; (T) Thread; (S) Shoulder; (C) Body; (F) Base; (M) Wide mouth; (E) Eye; (H) Handle; (O) Off-center neck; (A) Annular rib; (B) Bungs; (R) Ring

5.7.4 Auxiliaries

Extrusion blow molding produces a significant amount of process scrap, which must normally be recycled after regrinding. Process scrap is associated with the flash resulting from the pinching (neck, tail or bottom, handle eye, etc.). Such scrap can amount to as much as 25% for bottles and 50% for toys. Blow molded parts often require finishing operations besides flash removal (deflashing); these may include external trimming, facing of the neck or mouth, and internal reaming.

5.7.5   Materials

The process of blow molding requires a good stretchability of the softened thermoplastic (melt-strength), over a reasonable temperature "window." A relatively high molecular weight (HMW) is normally required, particularly for crystallizing resins.

Polyethylene (HMWPE) is, by far, the most widely used resin for large products; it is also used for high-volume packaging. Polypropylene tends to be used in processes that promote orientation, such as stretch blow molding, and where a higher temperature resistance is required, such as in hot filling.

Polyvinylchloride (PVC) is widely used for bottles, in Europe in particular. The homopolymer, particularly in oriented form (OPVC), can be crystal clear; continuous extrusion is normally preferred, to minimize the risk of thermal degradation.

Thermoplastic polyester (PET) is primarily used in injection blow molding; preforms are injected in a cold mold to an amorphous solid state, and subsequently reheated to slightly over 100°C ($\approx$ 210°F) for blowing.

A variety of other thermoplastic resins that have been blow molded include PETG, Nitrile, SAN, PVDC, PPO, PC, and PA.

It is estimated that the resin accounts for about 85% of the total cost of a mass-produced beverage bottle.

5.7.6   Products

Blow-molded products are associated with certain inherent design limitations, concerning shapes and wall thickness in particular. While the blow molding process normally yields one-piece closed hollow products, pairs of open hollow products have been made by splitting closed moldings. Production lines are sometimes dedicated to a single large volume product, or versatile machines are used for the custom production of suitable parts.

Packaging is the major area of application of small to medium-size disposable (no-return) blow-molded products.

Liquid foodstuffs are increasingly packaged in narrow neck plastic bottles (Fig. 5.62). Mineral water is commonly sold in France in 1.5 l ($\approx$ 50 U.S. fl oz) bottles which weigh about 40 g ($\approx$ 1.5 oz) and are produced at the rate of 12,000/h in 24-cavity dedicated machines, with an estimated total yearly consumption of over 10×10^9 units. Milk is sold in 1/2 or 1 U.S. gallon bottles made of HDPE. Alcoholic beverages are increasingly sold in PET bottles ranging in capacity from 50 ml for single service airline liquor minis to 1.5 l for wine. Carbonated beverages (soft drinks) are also routinely packaged in PET bottles, 2 l bottles weighing only about 80 g ($\approx$ 3 oz) compared to about 1 kg ($\approx$ 40 oz) for corresponding glass bottles. Other liquid foodstuffs packaged in plastic bottles include edible oils, vinegar, seasoning (salad dressing), and catsup.

Solid or nonflowing foodstuffs are increasingly packaged in blow-molded, wide-mouth plastic jars (Fig. 5.62). They include nuts, powdered drinks or coffee, mayonnaise, and peanut butter.

Blow-molded containers, ranging in capacity from small vials to 4-16 oz ($\approx$ 125-500 ml) bottles, are used for cosmetics, toiletries, and pharmaceutical and medical packaging (prescriptions, mouthwash, cough medicine, etc.).

A variety of household products are almost exclusively packaged in plastic bottles (bleach, dishwashing detergent, liquid soap, etc.). New markets are opening, which include paints [1 gal ($\approx$ 4 l) PP cans] or aerosol containers.

A number of important industrial products are now increasingly made of plastics by blow molding, at the expense of traditional materials such as steel or cement. They include shipping drums and stationary storage tanks.

Shipping drums offer a very large market with a current penetration in the U.S. of only about 1.5 x 10^6 units per year, but estimated to grow shortly to about 5 x 10^6 units per year, still only about 10% of the steel drum production. Shipping drums have a capacity of 55 U.S. gal ($\approx$ 45 Imp gal or $\approx$ 205-225 l); they weigh about 20 lb ($\approx$ 10 kg), compared to about 45 lb ($\approx$ 20 kg) for steel equivalents. They are produced at the rate of about 20/h in one-cavity machines. They often feature stiffening annular ribs (A) (Fig. 5.62), as well as a lifting ring (L-ring, chime ring, heat ring) (R) to allow "parrot beak" handling, and bung closure elements (B), which are sometimes injection-molded separately and incorporated during blow molding. They are normally made from HMWPE.

Stationary storage tanks, blow-molded from PE, are now made in volumes as large as 10,000 l ($\approx$ 2500 U.S. gal). They are used for underground residential fuel oil storage, as well as septic tanks.

Other miscellaneous industrial products include mandrel forms for the filament winding of pressure tanks and solid fuel rocket cases, ducts and bellows, and double-walled housings.

A number of blow-molded parts are used in connection with the automotive industry. They include disposable motor oil containers (1 quart or $\approx$ 2 l) produced at rates as high as 4000/h on a single machine; handled disposable windshield washer fluid canisters; handled portable gas canisters (5 U.S. gal or $\approx$ 20 l DOT 34 "jerrycans");

brake fluid reservoirs; liquid coolant overflow tanks (PP), and a relatively recent major innovation, plastic (HDPE) fuel tanks, now produced in about 3 min cycles.

The toy market is also important, with small products such as rattles, or large ones such as riding horses which are generally made of HDPE.

A most interesting application is the float of sailboards, which is possibly the longest item made by blow molding; its length of over 4 m ($\approx$ 12 ft) poses severe parison sag problems. One-piece float shells (hull and deck) are blow-molded and subsequently filled with PU foam. This is further discussed in Chapter 6 (section 6.2.3.1).

Small boat hulls can be made as a one-piece closed product which is subsequently split into two open hulls.

5.7.7   Related Processes

5.7.7.1   Coextrusion Blow Molding

Coextrusion is increasingly used to combine layers of materials that contribute different key properties to products. Chemically resistant barrier and structural layers, generally in combination with intermediate tie layers, may be involved.

5.7.7.2   Compression Blow Molding

In such processes, sometimes referred to as "intrusion" or "displacement blow molding," the preform is compression-molded from a metered charge. The molding temperature can be closer to the blowing temperature and higher viscosity resins can be used.

5.7.7.3   Dual Sheet Blowing

This process, involving the parallel extrusion of two sheets which may be of different materials, grades or colors, is described in the section on thermoforming. Some blow molding techniques are demonstrated in figures 5.98-5.109.

Fig. 5.99

Fig. 5.98

Figure 5.98 · Miscellaneous blow molded products (bins, coolers, toys, canisters etc...)

Figure 5.99 · Carbonated beverage bottles (PET polyester)

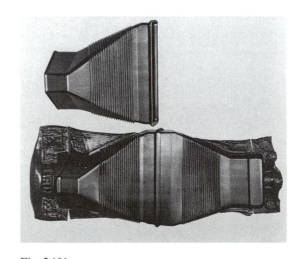

Fig. 5.101

Fig. 5.100

Figure 5.100 · Motor oil canister (with coextruded unpigmented viewing stripe) **[GRAHAM]**

Figure 5.101 · Blow molding of automobile ducts (back to back twin molding)
[KAUTEX]

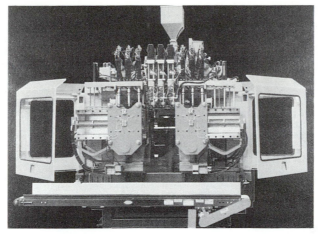

Figure 5.102 · Shuttle blow molding machine (three-parison type) **[HOOVER]**

Figure 5.103 · Blow molding of PE motor oil bottles (four-cavity set-up) **[KAUTEX]**

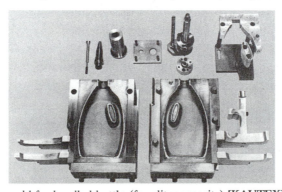

Figure 5.104 · Blow mold for handled bottle (four-liter capacity) **[KAUTEX]**

Fig. 5.105   Fig. 5.106

Figure 5.105 · Injection-stretch blow molding of PET bottles (preforms and finished products) **[BATTENFELD]**

Figure 5.106 · Blow molding of hdpe automobile gas tank (fifty-liter capacity) **[KAUTEX]**

Figure 5.107 · Blow molding of HDPE bunged barrel (sixty-liter capacity) **[KAUTEX]**

Figure 5.109 · Blow molding of heating oil tank (4000-liter capacity, HDPE) [**KAUTEX**]

Figure 5.108 · Blow molding of sailboard shell (HDPE) [**KAUTEX**]

5.8 COATING

"Coating" may be defined as the formation (application) of a layer (coat) of polymer on a substrate. A basic distinction is made here between, what is referred to as "planar coating," for flat film and sheet substrates, and "contour coating," for general three-dimensional objects. Related processes, including the important case of wire coating, are discussed in another section ("Extrusion Covering").

5.8.1 Planar Coating

A variety of flexible flat substrates (webs) are coated with polymers for a variety of reasons, including appearance, waterproofness, electrical insulation, and sealability. These substrates include metal foils, such as aluminum (Al), typically about 0.1 mm (≈ 0.003 in) thick, paperboard (paper or light cardboard), textiles (woven, knit, scrim, and nonwoven), and plastic films or sheets.

The adhesion between substrate and coat is always important, and various methods are used to favor a good bond. They include chemical treatment (primer), exposure to gas flame or corona discharge, and the use of a tie (anchor) layer.

Two basic techniques, as illustrated in Figure 5.110, are used to form the coating and control its thickness. The roller (roll) technique [R] squeezes the fluid coating material (C) against the substrate web (W) in the wedge (nip), between counter-rotating pressure (nip) rolls (R). In the knife technique [K], a blade (doctor blade) (B) holds an excess of coating material (C), allowing the entrainment of a suitable amount through a small gap. In both cases, the fluid coating material can be provided by an extruder (full-width slot die or traversing strand die), or by a calendering device. The coated product (P) may have to be subsequently dried or cooled.

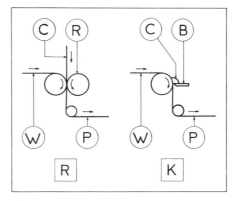

Figure 5.110 · **Planar coating** · [R] Roller technique; [K] Knife technique; (W) Web; (C) Coating material; (R) Pressure rolls; (B) Doctor blade; (P) Product

A related process, referred to here as "planar transfer coating" and illustrated in Figure 5.111, is of particular interest for the fabrication of vinyl or urethane-coated fabrics. It involves the formation of a skin layer of material (S) on a carrier film (R), which has been treated to allow subsequent skin release (e.g., silicone treatment). After conditioning (C) (drying or cooling), a layer of tie material (T) is added, and the fabric web (W) is brought in contact with the fluid tie layer between nip rollers (N). After conditioning, the carrier web (R') is peeled from the product (P). This technique permits the formation of leather-like material, involving a textured compact skin separated from the textile backing by a flexible cellular intermediate layer.

Planar coatings are generally applied in widths in the range 1-4 m ($\approx$ 40-160 in). Coat thicknesses are typically 0.05-0.10 mm ($\approx$ 0.002-0.004 in) for coated metal foils, and weights are normally in the range 50-500 g/m^2 ($\approx$ 0.01-0.10 lb/ft^2) for coated fabrics. Planar coating lines are generally operated at relatively high speed (150-600 m/min or ≈ 500-2000 ft/min), and involve many elements such as guide rollers, accumulators, unwind and rewind systems, tensioning devices, idlers, brakes, and indexing turrets.

Planar coated products include photographic films, magnetic tapes, pressure-sensitive adhesive tape, wall paper, packaging films, tarpaulins, skins for air-supported structures, and flooring.

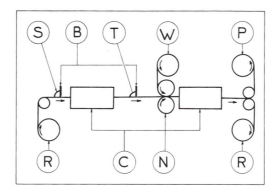

Figure 5.111 · **Planar transfer coating** · (R) Carrier film; (S) Skin material; (B) Doctor blades; (T) Tie material; (W) Fabric web; (P) Product; (N) Nip rollers; (C) Conditioning zones

5.8.2 Contour Coating

Objects of complex shapes can be coated by dipping them in suitable fluids, or by spraying.

As illustrated in Figure 5.112, dipping [D] an object (S) into a liquid polymeric solution or melt (L), followed by drying or cooling [C], is a simple way of producing a coated product (P), but the coat thickness can vary quite considerably, with gravity playing a major role.

By a mechanism similar to that described in another section for slush rotational molding, a heated substrate can be dipped into a PVC plastisol to form a more uniform coating.

An interesting method, referred to as "fluidized bed dip coating" (Fig. 5.113), first involves the formation of a fluidized bed with small thermoplastic particles similar to those used in conventional rotational molding. The compact mass of particles (M)

(stage [U]) can be "fluidized" by forcing a gas (G) through a porous diaphragm (D) at a suitable velocity. The greatly expanded fluid-like bed (F) can now be easily penetrated by a solid object. If a metallic object (S), for example, is heated and then dipped into the fluidized bed, successive particle layers adhere to the substrate by a heat transfer-controlled mechanism similar to the one operating in the conventional rotational molding process. After removal from the bed, the coated product (P) is normally subjected to the elevated temperature of a heated chamber (C) to smooth out the external surface of the coating.

In a modification of the process particularly suitable for thin coatings, fluidized-bed particles are electrostatically charged (negative charge), and if a grounded

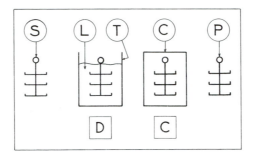

Figure 5.112 · **Liquid dip coating** · [D] Dipping; [C] Conditioning; (S) Substrate; (L) Coating liquid; (T) Tank; (C) Conditioning chamber; (P) Product

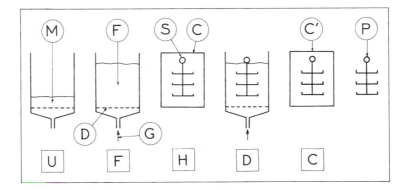

Figure 5.113 · **Fluidized bed dip coating** · [U] Unfluidized bed; [F] Fluidized bed; [H] Substrate heating; [D] Dipping; [C] Conditioning; (M) Powdered coating material; (F) Fluidized particles; (D) Porous diaphragm; (G) Gas inlet; (S) Substrate; (C) Heating chamber; (C') Conditioning chamber; (P) Product

conductive object is brought over the bed, particles are uniformly attracted to its surface. Subsequent heating causes the fusion and coalescence of the particles into a coating. This process is often referred to as "electrostatic bed coating." Electrostatic powder spraying works on a similar principle; charged particles being entrained in an air jet toward the substrate.

Thermal spray coating involves the entrainment of solid particles in a jet of very hot gas (combustion bases in the case of flame coating), which causes their rapid fusion before reaching the substrate.

Atomized solutions, melts, or dispersions (plastisols) can be sprayed onto substrates, much like paints, with drying, cooling, or subsequent heating leading to solid coatings.

Applications of contour coating include plasticized PVC tool handles, fluorocarbon-coated household utensils, dish drain racks, outdoor furniture (PA-11), chemical and electrical equipment, and temporary (strippable) protective coatings for sharp tools (ethylcellulose). In some cases, a flexible product can be stripped from a suitable substrate serving as a positive mold (boots, gloves, etc.).

The purpose of paints is to produce thin protective or decorative coatings. Paint technology is a specialized and complex area. Different classes of liquid systems, applicable by brush, roller, spray or even dipping, are adapted to many applications. Paints are latex-based, solvent-based, or curable. Significant differences exist between primers, top coats, and touch-up paints; exterior paints are different from interior paints; house paints and industrial paints often have widely different purposes. Related liquid systems include lacquers, varnishes, and enamels.

Extrusion coating equipment is shown in figure 5.114.

Figure 5.114 · Extrusion coating of paper with polyethylene

5.9 ROTATIONAL MOLDING

5.9.1 Principle

The process of rotational molding, sometimes also referred to as "rotomolding," is described in Figure 5.115. At the loading stage [L], a suitable powdery thermoplastic material charge (M) is introduced in the open mold [mold halves (T) and (T′)]. The mold is then closed and mounted on a holding device, which permits its double (biaxial) rotation around two orthogonal (perpendicular) axes (R) and (R′) to produce a tumbling action. A heating stage [H] follows, in which the exterior of the mold is subjected to a high temperature in a suitable chamber (C), while being rotated. Heat transfer through the mold wall eventually raises the temperature of the inner mold surface to a level sufficient to cause superficial melting of the thermoplastic particles (tackiness) and their sticking to the mold surface. A single layer of adjacent particles

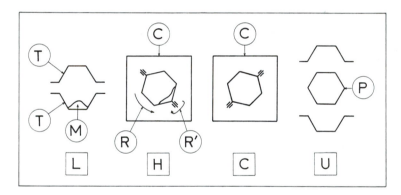

Figure 5.115 · **Rotational molding process** · [L] Loading; [H] Heating; [C] Cooling; [U] Unloading; (T),(T′) Mold halves; (M) Material charge; (R),(R′) Axes of rotation; (C) Conditioning chamber; (P) Product

is thus retained on the mold surface, while other particles tumble away. Further heat transfer through the layer of particles causes their coalescence and raises the temperature of the inner surface enough to cause the retention of a second layer of particles. The relatively low heat conductivity of the polymer is associated with a relatively slow rate of thickness build up, and the tumbling action only assures that powder is regularly brought in contact with the forming polymer shell. When the whole material charge has been consumed, further heating may help consolidate and homogenize the material, through intermolecular diffusion in particular, also producing a smoother inner surface. The cooling stage [C] subjects the exterior surface of the mold to rapid cooling, and reversed heat transfer eventually causes the solidification of the polymeric shell, allowing the unloading [U] of the part (P). The process is characterized by relatively long cycles associated with the thermal cycling.

5.9.2 Equipment

The mold handling (holding) device, capable of imparting double rotation, is the central element of rotational molding equipment. There are two major types of equipment, referred to here as the "shuttle cart system" and the "swing/rotary arm system."

The shuttle cart system, as illustrated in Figure 5.116, features a cart (wagon) (W), incorporating the mold rotation device, which can be rolled in and out of the heating or cooling chamber (bay) (C). This system is used in particular for products of very large dimension such as sailboards, in which case full rotation around the long axis (R') occurs, but only partial rotation (tilting) takes place in the perpendicular direction (R).

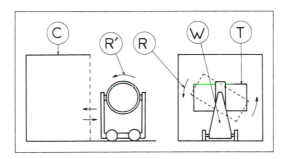

Figure 5.116 · **Shuttle cart rotational molding** · (C) Conditioning chamber; (R') Rotation axis; (R) Tilting axis; (W) Cart; (T) Mold

The swing/rotary arm systems, as illustrated in Figure 5.117, features arms (spindles) (A) that can rotate in a horizontal plane around a hub (pivot) (H). In one-arm machines [O], the single mold-holding arm swings from the loading/unloading station to the oven (O) or cooling chamber (C). In three-arm machines [T], three mold-holding arms take turns at the various stations (indexing), always turning in the same direction (carousel). Chambers are fitted with quick-action doors to minimize heat losses in particular. The mounting of molds at the end of an arm is illustrated

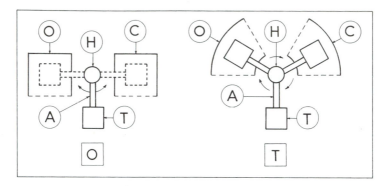

Figure 5.117 · **Swing/rotary arm rotational molding** · [O] One-arm (swing); [T] Three-arm (rotary); (O) Oven; (H) Hub; (C) Cooling chamber; (T) Mold; (A) Arm

in Figure 5.118. In the straight arm arrangement [S], two molds [T] and [T'] are mounted symmetrically on a spider [R'], which imparts one rotation, the spindle [R] imparts the other rotation. The offset arm arrangement [O] is suitable for single, but longer molds. Heating stations (ovens) most commonly use gas or oil-fired furnaces and forced air convection for heat transfer to the molds. Temperatures are often in the range 250-400°C (≈ 500-750°F), with maxima around 480°C (≈ 900°F). Infrared (IR) heating is also used in some cases.

Cooling stations may use blower-forced air, water spray (mist, fog), or water jets, in this order, for increasingly rapid cooling. In the case of crystallizing thermoplastics, cooling rates can affect the properties significantly.

The area where loading and unloading (recharging and demolding) takes place, is referred to as the "work station."

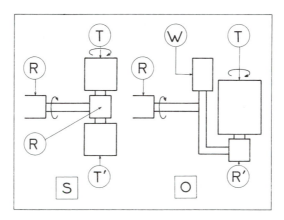

Figure 5.118 · **Mold mounting alternatives** · [S] Straight; [O] Offset; (R) Spindle drive; (R') Spider drive; (T),(T') Molds; (W) Counterweight

5.9.3   Tooling

Molds for rotational molding are normally split (two-half, two-piece) negative molds, with built-in mechanical locking.   The need for rapid heat transfer, and minimum weight to facilitate rotation, calls for relatively thin walls, which are acceptable in view of the low pressures involved.   Most mechanical stresses are associated with the weight of the mold and its material charge.   Tooling costs are thus relatively low for this process.

Large molds are generally fabricated from steel or sometimes aluminum in sheet form.   The thickness of steel sheets is in the range 1-3 mm (1/32 - 1/8 in).   External reinforcing frames are used, which also serve for clamping and holding the shells.

Smaller molds are generally made from aluminum, which is light and heat conductive.   They are often cast in thicknesses around 6 mm (1/4 in), or they can be machined from blocks or fabricated from semifinished elements.   Beryllium-copper and electroformed epoxy-backed nickel constructions are also used.   Occasionally, double-walled (cored, jacketed) molds are used; the constrained heating and fluid circulation can lead to energy and time savings, but such molds are much more expensive.

To prevent pressure build up associated with the thermal expansion of entrapped air, molds must be vented.   Occasionally, a modest degree of internal pressurization is intentionally setup, to improve, in particular, the dimensional accuracy of parts.

5.9.4   Materials

The nature of the process normally calls for the use of a relatively thin powder (200-500 μm or $\approx$ 0.008-0.020 in particles) of a thermoplastic polymer.   Particles featuring sharp edges and corners process better than purely spherical ones, probably because of the rapid softening of those areas.   The "running" properties of the powders and the build up of electrostatic charges are among the important factors to be considered.   Materials that have a relatively sharp softening point, such as crystallizing thermoplastics (T_m), have certain processing advantages.   A sufficiently high molecular weight is always necessary to prevent deformation of the part prior to cooling.

Polyethylene is widely used, particularly in its high-density form (HDPE).   The process also permits the introduction of cross-links (XLPE), if the materials contain a cross-linking agent such as dicumyl peroxide (DI-CUP), whose action is triggered by additional heating after the formation of the part.   Polypropylene (PP) and acetal (PMO) are among other crystallizing thermoplastics occasionally used.   A special technique involves the use of powdered caprolactam, which first melts, and subsequently polymerizes, into polyamide (nylon) PA-6 around 150-180°C ($\approx$ 300-360°F). Noncrystallizing thermoplastics reportedly used in the process include styrenics (HIPS), ABS, polycarbonate (PC), cellulosics (CAB), and thermoplastic polyurethanes (PU). EVA copolymers are also used for flexible items. Thermosetting resins such as epoxies (EP), which melt before curing, are widely used not so much to make parts, but for the internal coating of metal vessels, pipes, and other structures which serve as "molds."

5.9.5 Products

The process is associated with certain part characteristics that are, in some cases, fairly unique.

The part thickness, which is heat-transfer-controlled, can be quite uniform and is usually in the range 3-6 mm ($\approx$ 1/8-1/4 in), although thinner (1 mm or $\approx$ 0.040 in) or thicker walls (25 mm or $\approx$ 1 in) can be obtained. Corners and edges are often thicker as a result of concentrated heat transfer, and, conversely, insulated areas do not become covered with polymer, thus forming openings. Very large parts can be made economically, with current records for PE tanks having a capacity of about 75 m^3 ($\approx$ 20,000 gal) for dimensions about 4 m ($\approx$ 12 ft) in diameter by 10 m ($\approx$ 30 ft) long and a resin weight of about 3 tons. More common sizes are in the 100-1000 l ($\approx$ 25-250 gal) range, which includes the standard 200 l ($\approx$ 55 gal) drum. The process is suitable for making small objects, normally with multicavity molds.

A major advantage of the process is that seamless hollow parts can be made without even the need for a plug. Certain shapes, however, such as flat surfaces, or thin ribs, tend to be difficult to make, because of poor powder spreading or bridging. The part design must naturally be adjusted to the process. It should be noted that semihollow parts can be made in pairs, subsequently split in the plane of symmetry (boat hulls, luggage shells, etc.). Molded-in inserts, either metallic or made of another plastic, are easy to incorporate. The process is not intended for precision parts, and details, such as certain threads, are difficult to reproduce. Parts have the advantage of being largely free of residual (internal) stresses, but porosity problems sometimes occur, and the inner surface tends to be relatively coarse (pucked, grained, orange skin). No scrap results from the process, which is a clear advantage in the case of cross-linked systems.

A particular advantage of the process is the possibility of sequential molding of successive distinct layers (lamination). A variety of combinations have been used, such as a skin backed with a fiber-reinforced inner layer, a cellular core sandwiched between two compact skins, two layers of different colors, and a skin of a material with a high softening point (PA) with a PE inner layer. In all cases, appropriate material charges are added in succession, with suitable temperature adjustments.

Examples of rotationally molded products include open containers such as bins and tote trucks, pipes and ducts, drums and tanks (chemical storage, fuel, septic tanks), road markers and signs, body components (particularly for trucks, tractors, trailers), furniture elements, luggage shells, recreational boat hulls (sailboard, canoe), seamless flotation devices (fishing floats, buoys), toys (balls, dolls, hobbyhorses), and fashion models (mannequins).

5.9.6   Related Processes

5.9.6.1   Slush Rotational Molding

This process uses a liquid material charge called a "plastisol," which is a suspension (dispersion) of finely divided particles of a thermoplastic resin [usually polyvinylchloride PVC] in a plasticizer such as DOP. Double rotation of the mold distributes the plastisol (slush) over the surface of the mold where heating (about 175°C or ≈ 350°F) causes a gelling, that is, the irreversible combination of plasticizer and resin to form a homogeneous layer of plasticized PVC (PPVC). As in the case of powders, heat transfer through the forming PPVC layer determines the rate of retention of plastisol and thus the product thickness.

5.9.6.2   Shell Casting

The process referred to here as "shell casting" is illustrated in Figure 5.119. It is similar to powder or slush rotational molding except that it does not involve the rotation of a mold. An open mold (T) is heated (stage [H]), and then filled (loaded) with either a plastisol or powdery material charge (M). When an appropriate layer (shell) (S) of gelled or fused material has formed, the excess part (E) of the charge is poured out. The mold is often reheated to consolidate the inner surface of the shell in particular, and subsequently cooled before unloading. The process involves the handling of large excesses of material and, even though this excess is reusable, it suggests that the process is better suited to relatively small parts and small runs. Rotational molding equipment is shown in figures 5.120-5.122.

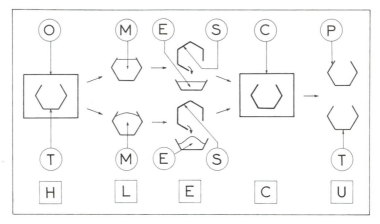

Figure 5.119 · **Shell casting** · [H] Heating; [L] Loading; [E] Excess removal; [C] Conditioning; [U] Unloading; (O) Oven; (T) Mold; (M) Liquid or powdered material; (S) Shell; (E) Excess material; (C) conditioning chamber; (P) Product

Figure 5.120 · Three-arm rotational molding machine

Figure 5.121 · Rotationally-molded hull/deck combination (12-ft boot) **[WEDCO]**

Figure 5.122 · Rotationally-molded septic tank 850 gal. or 4000 l capacity [WEDCO]

5.10 CASTING

5.10.1 Principle, Materials, and Products

A number of related polymer processing methods, generally involving the polymerization of a liquid resin directly into the shape of a product, are often globally referred to as "casting methods" when the resin and the product are subjected to minimal stresses (atmospheric pressure, gravity flow, slow chemical reaction, moderate temperature, etc.). They include cases where inserts (inclusions) are to be partially or totally surrounded by a polymeric matrix (encapsulation, embedment, potting, etc.), to assure positioning, thermal or electrical insulation, environmental protection, etc. Cellular polymers and short fiber or particle-filled polymers are sometimes processed by casting, as discussed in other sections.

In most cases, casting corresponds to the pouring (casting) of the liquid resin system into a mold (gravity or atmospheric pressure casting). Because of the low stresses involved, lightly-built open molds [O] or two-piece molds [T] may be used (Fig. 5.123). The relatively high viscosity of the monomer or reactants, and the need to vent the cavity, often call for mold designs reminiscent of metal die casting [bottom feed runners (F), vents (V), etc.].

In some cases, the chemical reaction taking place during a casting process converts a low-molecular-weight monomer into a high-molecular-weight thermoplastic; the most common examples are acrylics such as PMMA and polyamides. In other cases, polymerization and cross-linking take place simultaneously in the casting process, leading to thermosets; examples include polyurethane resins (UR), unsaturated polyester resins (UP), epoxy resins (EP) and silicone resins (SI).

Problems often associated with the chemical reactions involved in casting include cure shrinkage, which can be as high as about 20% for acrylics, and heat evolution (exothermic reactions), which can lead to runaway situations through auto acceleration, if the chemical systems are very reactive and insufficient provision is made for cooling. Such problems can sometimes be alleviated by casting pre-polymerized fluids (syrups), which, however, have higher viscosities.

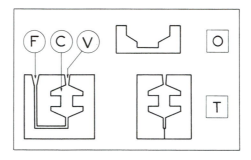

Figure 5.123 · **Casting molds** · [O] Open mold; [T] Two-piece mold; (F) Feed runner; (C) Cavity; (V) Vent

The reactive systems, consisting of one or several chemicals and catalyst-type additives, can be prepared in batches or through continuous mixing. In the case of batches, the gelation time, i.e. the time at which the system ceases to be fluid, must be sufficiently long to allow pouring in the mold. Continuous mixing involves mixing heads that may have to be periodically solvent-cleaned (flushed), to prevent unwanted cure. The special case of fast reacting systems is discussed in another section on RIM.

There is a large market for transparent plastic sheets with high-level optical qualities (distortion-free in particular), which cannot be achieved by thermoplastic extrusion, where even a modest amount of molecular orientation resulting from the flow in the die causes anisotropic optical properties. By contrast, in casting, polymerization starts and proceeds in a medium that is basically in static equilibrium (quiescent).

Acrylic sheets are commercially made by a batch process (cell method), as illustrated in Figure 5.124, which involves a mold (cell) made of two highly polished glass plates (plateglass) (P) separated by a flexible gasket (G), to allow for polymerization shrinkage, and held together by spring clips (C). The resin (R) is gradually poured into the cell, and the slow polymerization process is carried out in carefully controlled air ovens, liquid baths, or even autoclaves, over periods of many hours or even days, depending on the thickness which can be as much as about 10 cm ($\approx$ 4 in) and as thin as about 0.8 mm ($\approx$ 0.030 in). A continuous process has been developed for relatively thin sheets (Fig. 5.125), which uses highly polished carrier and cover stainless steel belts (B) and (B') to constrain the viscous prepolymerized resin (R) while it slowly hardens.

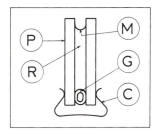

Fig. 5.124

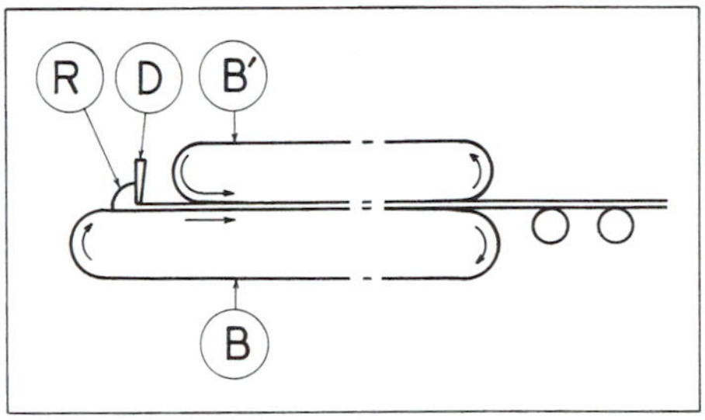

Fig. 5.125

Figure 5.124 · **Cell casting of sheets** · (R) Resin; (P) Plate; (M) Meniscus; (G) Gasket; (C) Spring clip

Figure 5.125 · **Continuous casting of sheets** · (R) Resin; (D) Doctor blade; (B') Cover belt; (B) Carrier belt

Acrylic solid cylindrical shapes (rods, bars) must be made by the gradual polymerization of successive layers of material in a vertical mold which minimizes radial shrinkage.

Acrylic tubes are normally made by centrifugal casting in spinning cylindrical molds; the free inner surface allows unhindered shrinkage.

Many polyurethane products are, or were, made by casting. They include early ski boot or hockey skate shells, as well as roller skate or skate board wheels.

Solid fuel rockets involve the casting, in the rocket case, of a hydrocarbon elastomer that serves as a fuel, as well as a matrix for an oxygen-generating filler.

Biological specimens are routinely embedded in acrylic resins to allow thin sectioning (microtoming) for microscopic examinations. The thermoplastic resin can be subsequently leached out with a solvent.

Marble-like plastic furniture components (sinks, vanity tops, etc.) are conveniently made by casting a viscous resin system, to which a liquid colorant is added to form appropriate streaks (veins).

Polyamide (nylon) cast products are generally limited to prototypes, limited runs or large, bulky parts; they include journal and slide bearings, gears, and sheaves.

Encapsulated products are often associated with the electrical-electronic industry. They include coils, transformers, connectors, terminal blocks, and a variety of electrical casings. The encapsulation of electrical or electronic components is often referred to as "potting."

5.10.2   Related Processes

The word "casting" is also associated with film forming processes that do not involve a chemical reaction. Solvent casting of films, for example, has been used in the case of polyvinylchloride (PVC). It involves the casting on a stainless steel belt of a solution fed from a sheet-type die, and the subsequent evaporation of the solvent. Additives normally required for the melt processing of PVC are unnecessary, and the solution can be thoroughly filtered, prior to casting, to eliminate particles often associated with pinholes in films. The process is also suitable for the coating of thin metal foil.

Three illustrations of the casting process are shown in figures 5.126-5.128.

Figure 5.126 · Polyurethane casting
(flexible silicone mold)
[DOW CORNING]

Figure 5.127 · Polyurethane foam casting

Figure 5.128 · Polyethylene film casting [EGAN]

5.11 COMPRESSION MOLDING

5.11.1 Principle

The compression molding process is used almost exclusively for temperature-activated thermosetting polymers; its occasional use for thermoplastic polymers is discussed later in this section. Compression molding basically involves the pressing (squeezing) of a deformable material charge between the two halves of a heated mold, and its transformation into a solid product under the effect of the elevated mold temperature (conduction heat transfer). Compression molding temperatures are often in the range 140-200°C (≈ 280-400°F); mold pressures can vary from about 35 atm (≈ 500 psi) to 700 atm (≈ 10,000 psi); and setting (curing, vulcanization) times can vary widely from about 1 min for relatively thin phenolic parts to over 1 hour for very thick rubber components. Material charges are often pre-heated to speed-up the initial softening stage and, in some cases, they are even pre-plasticated. Compression molding is characterized by the slow and moderate flow of the very viscous material charge to fill the cavity, and it is not normally suitable for making complicated (intricate) parts, or parts featuring fragile inserts. The chemical reaction (cure, vulcanization) may be associated with material shrinkage, as well as the evolution of gaseous by-products, which may require a special venting operation (breathing, bumping), early in the molding process. Compression molding can be subdivided into several specific techniques (flash, positive, and semi-positive molding) that correspond to different mold geometries and are discussed in the section on tooling.

5.11.2   Equipment

Compression molding molds are used on compression presses (Fig. 5.129), which may be of the downstroking [D] or upstroking [U] types, and are generally slow-acting and hydraulically operated [clamping ram or cylinder (C)]. Large presses tend to feature a frame (F), while smaller ones often use a combination of tie bars (B) and bolster plate (L). Clamping capacities range from about 10 tons for small laboratory presses to several hundred tons for large presses. Other important press characteristics include the daylight (maximum platen separation), which is associated with the stroke, and the platen size (15 cm x 15 cm or ≈ 6 in x 6 in to over 1 m x 2 m or ≈ 3 ft x 6 ft). The platens of small presses sometimes have built-in heating and cooling features, allowing the use of simpler non-heated molds, particularly for laboratory purposes.

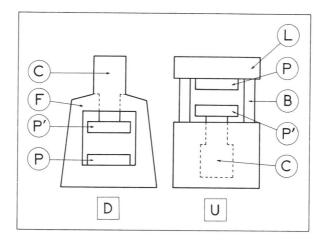

Figure 5.129 · **Compression molding presses** · [D] Downstroking; [U] Upstroking; (P) Stationary platen; (P′) Moving platen; (F) Frame; (C) Clamping cylinder; (L) Bolster plate; (B) Tie bar

5.11.3 Tooling

Compression molds for thermosetting resins and vulcanizable rubbers are heated to temperatures typically in the range 140-200°C ($\approx$ 280-400°F) and are subjected to high forces and pressures. They are generally made of tool steel, and cavities are often chrome-plated. Electrical resistance, steam, or oil heating can be used.

In compression molding, it is the closing of the two-half mold that shapes the material charge and establishes the pressure required to obtain a good molded part. Two very different mold configurations, generally referred to as "flash molds" and "positive" (or "fully positive") molds, can be used, as well as intermediate configurations ("semi-positive" molds).

Flash molds are illustrated in Figures 5.130 and 5.131. Figure 5.130 shows the configuration during curing, and Figure 5.131 illustrates the loading [L] and unloading [U] stages. The diagrams feature the cavity (C), the parting line (J), the stationary half (T), the moving half (T'), the material charge (M), and the molded product (P). The blow-up of the important area at the edge of the cavity, in Figure 5.130, shows the

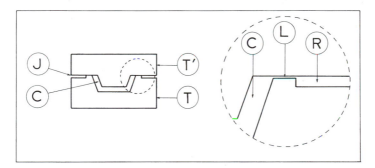

Figure 5.130 · **Flash compression mold** · (C) Cavity; (J) Parting line; (T),(T') Mold halves; (L) Flash land; (R) Flash recess

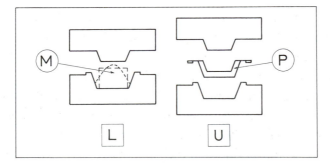

Figure 5.131 · **Flash molding** · [L] Loading; [U] Unloading; (M) Material charge; (P) Product

flash land (L) and the flash recess or groove (R). A slight excess of material is placed in the open mold; as the mold closes, this excess must overflow through the land, which, as it is oriented perpendicular to the mold closing direction, becomes gradually thinner, offering more resistance to flow and thus causing a rise in the cavity pressure. After the relatively rapid curing of the thin material in the land, the mold clamping force may reflect the compression of the flash web, rather than the actual pressure in the cavity. The removal of the flash web is an essential, and sometimes complicated, task that may involve direct sanding for rigid thermosets, or freezing and sanding for rubbers. Part dimensions are relatively difficult to control accurately in the mold closing direction, but the mold fabrication is generally relatively simple. Flash molds tend to be used for flat or shallow products.

Positive (or fully positive) molds are illustrated in Figure 5.132. The upper part of the mold (T') plays the role of a piston to exert a positive pressure on the material charge. The gap (G) must be sufficiently thin to prevent significant material leakage, and the mold fabrication and handling require special care. Part dimensions in the mold closing direction are directly dependent on the amount of material in the charge, as well as on possible leakage.

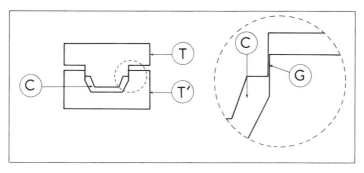

Figure 5.132 · **Fully positive compression mold** · (C) Cavity; (T),(T') Mold halves; (G) Gap

Figure 5.133 illustrates possible cavity edge configurations that combine flash mold and fully positive mold features in, so-called semi-positive molds. Case [I] is referred to as an internally landed configuration" and case [E] as an "externally landed configuration." Such compromises are widely used in commercial compression molds.

Compression molds, like injection molds, often feature ejection systems, but movable parts or any but sturdy inserts are often avoided, because the material charge tends to exert strong forces on such items during the mold closing stage. Compression mold dimensions take into account cure and cooling shrinkage allowances, which are in the range 0.001-0.008 (0.1-0.8%) for phenolic systems, for example.

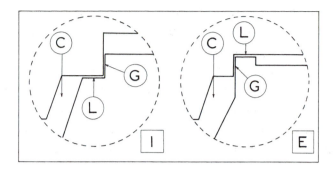

Figure 5.133 · **Semi-positive compression mold details** · [I] Internally-landed; [E] Externally-landed; (C) Cavity; (L) Land; (G) Gap

5.11.4   Auxiliaries

The starting material for compression molding is often in powder form for thermosetting systems such as phenolic resins and amino resins. For convenience in sizing and handling, powders are often compacted into preforms (pellets, pills, biscuits, bricks).

The commercial molding of small parts calls for the use of multiple cavity molds, which may be loaded simultaneously through loading boards (feedboards).

Material charges are generally preheated to temperatures somewhat below those initiating rapid curing (100-150°C or ≈ 200-300°F). Infrared (IR) radiation is used for thin layers or powder, as well as dielectric or high frequency (microwave) heating for compacted preforms.

Screw devices are also used to produce hot plasticated slugs as material charges; this technique is intermediate between conventional compression molding and injection molding.

5.11.5   Materials

Temperature-activated thermosetting plastics most commonly processed by compression molding include phenolic, amino and alkyd resins, and diallyl phthalate (DAP), as well as unsaturated polyesters (UP) and epoxy resins (EP). They are often associated with particulate fillers and fiber reinforcement.

Vulcanizable (millable) rubbers are most commonly processed by compression molding. In this case, the material charge (stock) is deformable, and preheating is not essential.

The compression molding of thermoplastics would require cooling of the mold after shaping the part (temperature cycling) and is not normally commercially attractive. Exceptions include the molding of extremely viscous thermoplastics (e.g., PTFE or UHMWPE), or special products such as phonograph records.

5.11.6 Products

A large number of compression molded thermoset products are found in electrical and electronic applications. Other applications are often associated with heat resistance (utensil handles, knobs, buttons, closures, dinnerware, etc.), and with structural resistance, when associated with glass fiber reinforcement. As indicated earlier, parts must generally be relatively simple in shape, without thin wall areas or fragile inserts.

Compression molded rubber products are innumerable. Many products involve metal inserts that form strong bonds with the rubber and are used to attach the products to structures (rubber mounts). Tires are molded to their final shape by compression molding.

Phonograph records, one of few commercial thermoplastic compression moldings applications, are made by pressing a screw-preformed vinyl slug (biscuit) between heated nickel-based mold halves, made by an electrolytic process from the master recording, and subsequently cooling the mold. For such thin parts, cycle times can be as low as about 1 minute.

Two compression molding machines are shown in figures 5.134 and 5.135.

Figure 5.134 · Hydraulic vacuum compression molding press (five 24 in. x 21 in. platens or four openings; electric heating and water cooling) [TMP]

Figure 5.135 · Large compression molding press (SMC composite molding of chair seat) [DANIELS]

5.12 TRANSFER MOLDING

Transfer molding is often associated with compression molding, because it is used with the same two classes of materials, temperature-activated thermosets, and vulcanizable rubbers. There are, however, important differences between the two processes.

5.12.1 Principle

In transfer molding, a softened temperature-activated thermoset, or a vulcanizable rubber, is "transferred" through a narrow gate into the closed cavity of a heated mold, where it cures to a solid state.

5.12.2 Equipment

Hydraulic presses similar to compression molding presses are used (Fig. 5.136). In addition to the main (clamping) ram or cylinder (C), an auxiliary (transfer) ram (C′) may be used.

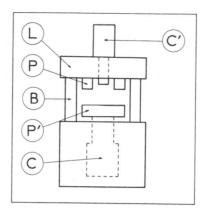

Figure 5.136 · **Transfer molding press** · (C) Clamping cylinder; (P′) Moving platen; (B) Tie bar; (P) Stationary platen; (L) Bolster plate; (C′) Transfer cylinder

5.12.3 Tooling

There are two basic methods for transfer molding, which are generally referred to as "plunger transfer molding" and "pot transfer molding."

In plunger transfer molding (Fig. 5.137), the material charge (M) is first placed in a loading well (W), which extends to the mold parting line ([L]). The plunger (R) then transfers the material to the cavities (C), through distributing channels (D) and gates (G) ([M]). The material left at the bottom of the loading well, known as the "transfer pad" (cushion, cull), is essential for pressure control, but should be minimal.

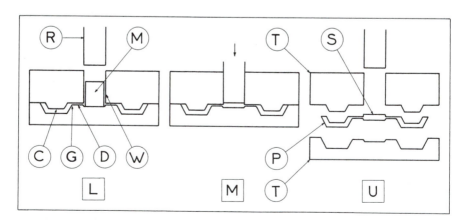

Figure 5.137 · **Plunger transfer molding** · [L] Loading; [M] Molding; [U] Unloading; (W) Loading well; (D) Distributing channel; (G) Gate; (C) Cavity; (R) Plunger; (M) Material charge; (T′) Stationary mold half; (S) Cull (scrap); (P) Product; (T) Moving mold half

Products (P) and a certain amount of material (S), to be scrapped, are ejected after mold opening ([U]). Plunger transfer molding normally requires the use of an auxiliary transfer ram to drive the plunger, while the main ram handles the mold clamping. The process is not normally suitable for single part molding.

In pot transfer molding (Fig. 5.138), the material charge (M) is loaded into the pot (chamber) (L), and subsequently transferred through the sprue (S) and gate (G) into the cavity (C). The press stroke can normally assure both mold clamping and material transfer functions, without a need for an auxiliary transfer ram. The press opening stroke can be arranged to cause a two-way opening of the tooling with the sprue and transfer pad system (S) separated from the product (P) at the gate (G), pulled by the transfer piston (R) fitted with a dovetail (undercut), and subsequently laterally ejected. Multicavity molding is possible through the use of distributing channels.

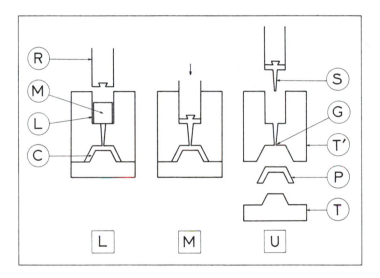

Figure 5.138 · **Pot transfer molding** · [L] Loading; [M] Molding; [U] Unloading; (C) Cavity; (L) Pot; (M) Material charge; (R) Transfer piston; (S) Sprue (scrap); (G) Gate; (T),(T′) Mold halves; (P) Product

5.12.4 Materials and Products

Transfer molding is normally used with materials that have fairly high pre-curing fluidity, facilitating the flow from the loading area to cavities. This also permits the molding of complex parts, or parts featuring fragile inserts. Cavity pressure can be controlled accurately and set at high levels (500-800 atm or ≈ 7000-12,000 psi). Products do not feature hard to remove flash, and they can have accurate dimensions. A transfer molding apparatus is demonstrated in figure 5.139.

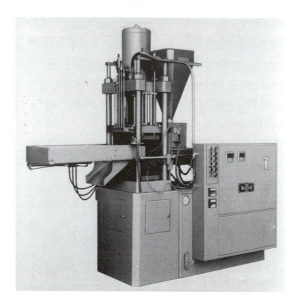

Figure 5.139 · Small transfer molding press (12 in. x 12 in. platens, 30-ton clamp and 7.5-ton transfer capacities) **[WABASH]**

5.13   INJECTION MOLDING

The injection molding process involves the rapid pressure filling of a specific mold cavity with a fluid material, followed by the solidification of the material into a product. The process is used for thermoplastics, thermosetting resins, and rubbers. The major part of this section concerns the case of thermoplastics; the cases of thermosetting resins and rubbers are discussed specifically at the end. A special case of injection molding leading to polymeric products is discussed separately as reaction injection molding (RIM).

5.13.1   Principle

The injection molding of thermoplastics can be subdivided into several stages, which are illustrated in Figure 5.140, in the case of the most common reciprocating screw machine. At the plastication stage [P], the feed unit [F] operates pretty much as an extruder, melting and homogenizing the material in the screw/barrel system. The screw (S), however, is allowed to retract, to make room for the molten material in a space at the cylinder head, referred to here as the material "reservoir" (R), between the screw tip and a closed valve (V) or an obstruction of solidified material from the previous shot. At the injection stage [I], the screw is used as a ram (piston) for the rapid transfer of the molten material from the reservoir (R) to the cavity between the two halves [(T) and (T')] of the closed mold. Since the mold is kept at a temperature below the solidification temperature of the material, it is essential to inject the molten material rapidly to ensure complete filling of the cavity. A high holding or packing pressure (10,000-30,000 psi or 600-2000 atm) is normally exerted, to partially compensate for the thermal contraction (shrinkage) of the material upon cooling. The cooling of the material in the mold is often the limiting time factor in injection molding, because of the low thermal conductivity of polymers. After the cooling stage, the mold can be opened and the solid product removed (ejection stage [E]).

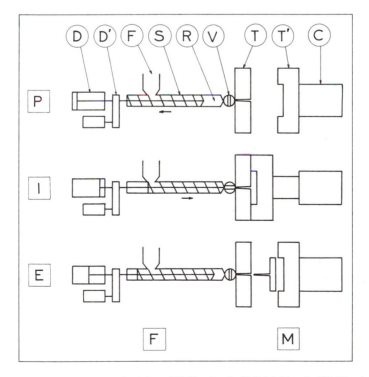

Figure 5.140 · **Injection molding principle** · [F] Feed unit; [M] Mold unit; [P] Plastication stage; [I] Injection; [E] Product ejection (demolding); (D) Axial Screw Drive; (D') Rotation screw drive; (F) Feed hopper; (S) Reciprocating screw; (R) Material "reservoir"; (V) Valve; (T),(T') Mold halves; (C) Mold clamping device

5.13.2 Equipment

Injection molding machines were initially of the plunger/torpedo type. They sometimes involve separate plastication (screw) and injection (piston) functions, and are then referred to as "pre-plasticator screw machines." They are now most commonly of the reciprocating screw type, as illustrated in Figure 5.141.

Two distinct units referred to as the "feed unit" [F] and the "mold unit" [M], are mounted on a frame (F'). The operation is primarily hydraulic with pumps (H) driven by electric motors (M), used in conjunction with hydraulic cylinders, motors, valves, accumulators, and tanks. Sophisticated computer- based control systems are now increasingly used to improve the quality and uniformity of products.

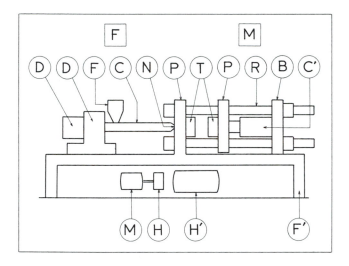

Figure 5.141 · **Injection molding machine** · [F] Feed unit; [M] Mold unit; (D) Axial screw drive; (D') Rotation screw drive; (F) Feed hopper; (C) Plastication/injection cylinder; (P) Stationary platen; (T) Mold; (P') Moving platen; (R) Tie bars; (B) Back platen; (C') Mold clamping mechanism; (F') Machine frame; (H') Hydraulic accumulator; (H) Hydraulic pump; (M) Electric motor; (I) Injection unit

The feed unit [F] consists of the plastication/injection cylinder (C) [screw, barrel, and feed hopper (F)], the axial screw drive (D), and the rotation screw drive (D'). The whole unit (I) is sometimes mounted on a carriage for limited axial displacement along the machine frame (F'). The screw tip is normally fitted with a non-return valve, one type of which is illustrated in Figure 5.142, in which the sliding of a ring (A), between a sealing surface (B) and a grooved stop (B'), permits the forward flow of material from the screw channel to the reservoir (R) when the screw retracts during the plastication stage [P], but blocks it when the screw moves forward during the injection stage [I].

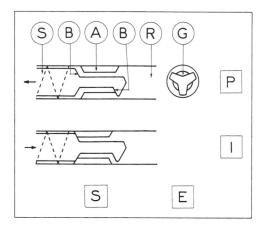

Figure 5.142 · **Screw-mounted, non-return (check) valve** · [P] Plastication configuration; [I] Injection configuration; (S) Screw; (B) Sealing surface; (A) Sliding ring; (B′) Grooved stop; (R) Material "reservoir"

The mold unit [M] generally consists of two stationary vertical platforms (platens) (P) and (B), connected by four cylindrical bars or columns (tie bars) (R), and a moving platen (P′) driven by a clamping mechanism (C′). The stationary and moving halves of the tool (T) are fastened to the platens (P) and (P′), sometimes referred to as "front" and "rear" platens, respectively. Clamping mechanisms, most commonly mechanical or hydraulic systems (Fig. 5.143), first produce a relatively fast motion (traverse) associated with a low force, followed by relatively slow motion and high "locking" force in the last stage of mold clamping. In mechanical types, such as the double toggle [M], this involves a set of links (L) actuated by a device (D), while in hydraulic types [H] a small diameter traverse cylinder (C) is associated with a large lock cylinder (C′); both systems are shown in the mold-open [O] and mold-closed [C] configurations.

While injection molding machines may occasionally be dedicated to the molding of a single product, a machine is normally used with a variety of tools (molds), which may imply frequent mold changes and the associated costly set-up period. The unproductive (down) time can be considerably reduced by the use of increasingly popular quick-mold changing (QMC) systems and computers for the storage and retrieval of process data.

Injection molding machines are available in a broad range of sizes. They are normally rated by their maximum clamping force, with normal ranges from about

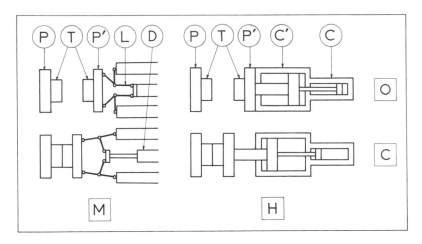

Figure 5.143 · **Mold clamping mechanisms** · [M] Mechanical (double toggle); [H] Hydraulic (dual cylinder); [O] Mold open configuration; [C] Mold closed configuration; (P) Stationary platen; (T) Mold; (P′) Moving platen; (L) Link; (D) Toggle drive; (C′) Lock cylinder; (C) Traverse cylinder

25-150 tons for "small" machines, 150-750 tons for "medium-size" machines and 750-5000 tons for "large" machines; the current maximum is 10,000 tons. There is generally a correlation between the rated clamping force and other machine characteristics. Representative figures for a 150-ton machine are as follows: screw diameter about 2 in ($\approx$ 5 cm); platen size about 27.5 in x 27.5 in ($\approx$ 0.7 m x 0.7 m); molding capacity about 0.7 lb ($\approx$ 0.3 kg); plasticating capacity about 150 lb/h ($\approx$ 70 kg/h); drive power about 30 hp, and heating power about 12.5 kW. Corresponding figures for a 750-ton machine are about 4 in ($\approx$ 10 cm); about 60 in x 60 in ($\approx$ 1.5 m x 1.5 m); about 6 lb ($\approx$ 3 kg); about 750 lb/h ($\approx$ 350 kg/h); about 30 hp and about 35 kW. The 10,000-ton machines are reported to have a molding capacity as high as 170 kg ($\approx$ 375 lb) for a maximum mold size of about 2.5 m x 5 m ($\approx$ 8 ft x 16 ft).

5.13.3   Tooling

The interchangeable injection molding tool, the mold, must provide a cavity corresponding to the geometry of the product and must allow the removal of the product after its solidification (ejection). Product removal involves a primary mold opening, an ejection system in most cases, and sometimes retractable secondary mold sections.

Primary mold opening is achieved by fastening one-half of the mold to the stationary platen (P), as in Figure 5.144, and the other half to the moving platen (P'). The stationary mold half (T) is sometimes referred to as the "front, "cavity," or "negative block," and the moving mold half (T') as the "rear," "force," or "positive block." The two mating surfaces form the parting surface, which is preferably planar and perpendicular to the primary mold opening axis, although many products require more complex parting surfaces. The trace of the parting surface in axial mold cross sections is referred to as the "parting line." The centering of the two mold halves (T) and (T') is generally achieved through leader (guide) pins or dowels (P) and associated bushings (B), as illustrated in Figure 5.144 [L] in closed [C] and open [O] configurations.

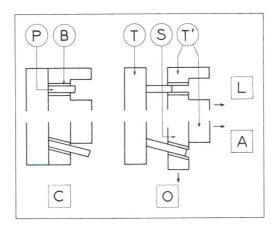

Figure 5.144 · **Pin/bushing** · [L] Centering pin; [A] Angled pin; [C] Mold closed configuration; [O] Mold open configuration; (P) Pin; (B) Bushing; (T) Stationary mold half; (S) Secondary mold section; (T') Moving mold half

The removal of a product from a cavity surface requires, in addition to an ejection system, a suitable surface finish and an appropriate taper or draft. It should not normally require the use of a release agent.

During injection, the material flows from the nozzle at the tip of the injection unit to the single cavity, or each of several cavities, through what is referred to here as the "feed system" (F), generally comprising sprues (S), runners (R) and gates (G), as illustrated in several figures (Fig. 5.145-5.149, 5.151-5.156). The material in the feed system (F) is generally cooled along with the products, to form what is referred to here as the "feed appendage" (F'), ejected with the products. Material suppliers provide specific recommendations for dimensioning feed systems for their products. Many considerations are involved in the design of a feed system for a multicavity mold and some of them are discussed below.

Figure 5.145 illustrates possible arrangements for an eight-cavity mold. The [L'] arrangement is superior to the [L] arrangement in terms of filling all cavities simultaneously, while the [R'] arrangement is better than the [R] arrangement in terms of providing cold slug wells (W). Figure 5.146 illustrates certain alternatives for the molding of thin rectangular plates perpendicular to the machine axis. Single-cavity

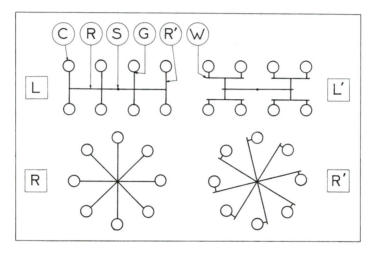

Figure 5.145 · **Multicavity molding** · [L],[L'] Linear arrangements; [R],[R'] Radial arrangements; (C) Cavity; (R) Main runner; (S) Sprue; (G) Gate; (R') Secondary runner; (W) Cold slug well

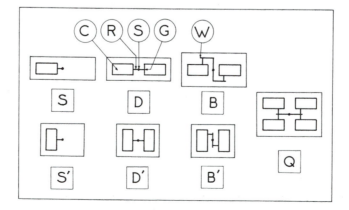

Figure 5.146 · **Plate molding alternatives** · [S],[S'] Single cavity; [D],[D'],[B],[B'] Double cavity; [Q] Quadruple cavity; (C) Cavity; (R) Runner; (S) Spue; (G) Gate; (W) Cold slug well

arrangements [S] and [S'] are undesirable for their lack of symmetry. Double-cavity arrangements [D] and [D'] involve direct end-gating or lateral gating, respectively. Double-cavity arrangements [B] and [B'] involve what is often considered a more desirable gating, with cold slug wells (W). The quadruple-cavity arrangement [Q] combines several desirable features.

A simple two-plate mold is illustrated in Figure 5.147 for a multicavity situation. The material flows to cavity (C) through the sprue (S), runner (R), and edge gate (G). After mold opening (ejection [E]), the products remain attached to the feed appendage (F'). The same products can be molded in a more complex three-plate

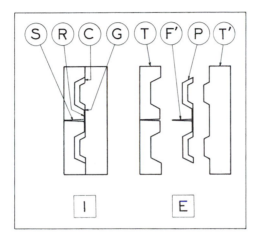

Figure 5.147 · **Two-plate multicavity molding** · [I] Injection configuration; [E] Ejection configuration; (S) Sprue; (R) Runner; (C) Cavity; (G) Gate; (T) Stationary mold half; (F') Feed appendage; (P) Product; (T') Moving mold half

mold, as illustrated in Figure 5.148, which involves flow through main sprue (S), runner (R), secondary sprue (S') and pinpoint center gate (G). The cavities (C) are formed between the moving plate (T') and an intermediate (floating) plate (I). At ejection [E], the products (P) are automatically separated from the feed appendage (F').

In most cases, injection molded products need to be removed from one mold half by an ejection (knockout, stripping) device. This device is normally incorporated in the moving mold half. Shrinkage of the product over cores, or deliberate slight undercuts, are among the reasons for product retention. The operation of an ejection device is illustrated in Figure 5.149 for a simple cup-like product (P). After mold opening [O], the product remains held on the core of the moving mold half (T'); at ejection [E], the part is pushed out by ejectors or knock-out pins (E), moved by a drive mechanism (D) through an ejector plate (bar) (B). Ejectors are usually cylindrical (pins), but valve-shaped pins, plates, bars, blades, rings and sleeves are also used. Ejectors can be driven mechanically by the mold motion itself (stroke) or by independent mechanical, hydraulic, pneumatic and electromagnetic devices. The injection of compressed air through suitable cavity ports is occasionally used to eject parts.

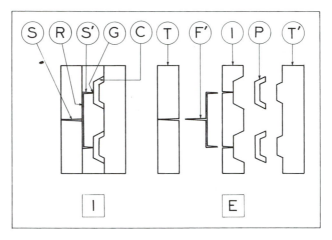

Figure 5.148 · **Three-plate multicavity molding** · [I] Injection configuration; [E] Ejection configuration; (S) Main sprue; (R) Runner; (S') Secondary sprue; (G) Gate; (C) Cavity; (T) Stationary mold half; (F') Feed appendage; (I) Intermediate plate; (P) Product; (T') Moving mold half

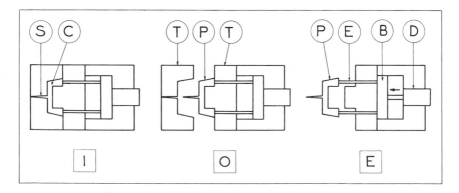

Figure 5.149 · **Product ejection device** · [I] Injection configuration; [O] Mold open configuration; [E] Ejection configuration; (S) Sprue; (C) Cavity; (T) Stationary mold half; (P) Product; (T') Moving mold half; (E) Ejector; (B) Ejector plate; (D) Ejector drive

Retractable secondary mold sections may be required when products feature undercuts, re-entrant shapes, internal or external threads, etc. They may include sliding blocks, collapsible cores, or unscrewing devices. The retraction may be effected by mechanical devices associated with the mold motion (stroke), as illustrated in Figure 5.144 [A], where an angled pin (finger) (P) drives the secondary mold section (S) sideways; the name "cammed section" may then be used. It may also involve independent hydraulic, pneumatic, or electromagnetic drives.

A mold configuration for a product (P) featuring undercuts and re-entrant shapes is illustrated in Figure 5.150. Injection takes place in the cavity (C) of the closed mold ([C]); after the primary mold opening [O], the product cannot be ejected; secondary mold sections (S) and (S') are retracted in stage [O'] and the product can now be ejected ([E]).

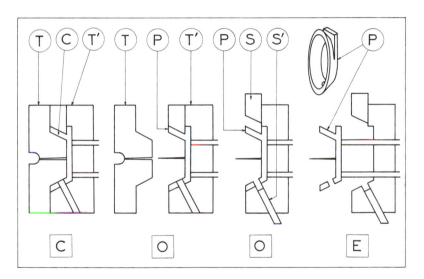

Figure 5.150 · **Retractable secondary mold sections** · [C] Mold closed configuration; [O] Primary mold opening; [O'] Secondary mold sections retraction; [E] Product ejection; (T) Stationary mold half; (C) Cavity; (T') Moving mold half; (P) Product; (S),(S') Secondary mold sections

Runners are machined in mold halves, next to the parting surface (J) (Fig. 5.151). Ideally, they would be fully round [F] for optimum flow and to minimize cooling during injection. A trapezoidal section [T], with a 5-7° taper machined in a moldhalf, is often used rather than a half-round section [H]. There is a growing trend toward feed systems that do not have to be cooled and ejected as feed appendages. One solution, applicable to chemically stable thermoplastics, consists of having large runners cooled in such a way that a sleeve of insulating solid plastic forms around a molten core, where the intermittent injection flow takes place; this method is referred to as "insulated" or "Canadian" runner molding. Another solution referred to as "hot runner molding" involves a heated runner, or manifold block, and is often used in conjunction with valve gating.

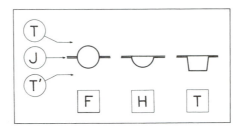

Figure 5.151 · **Runner cross-sections** · [F] Fully round; [H] Half round; [T] Trapezoidal; (T) Stationary mold half; (J) Parting plane; (T′) Moving mold half

Gates serve several purposes in injection molding. Their easily altered, smaller cross-section permits a convenient control of the flow of the molten material, the rapid freezing of the material to shut off the cavity after injection, and the easy separation of the products from the feed appendage (degating).

Edge (side) [E], fan [F], tab [T] and flash (web) [F′] gates are illustrated in Figure 5.152. Fan and flash gates spread the flow of material over a wider area, sometimes reducing warpage problems. Tabs avoid a direct jetting of material into the cavity.

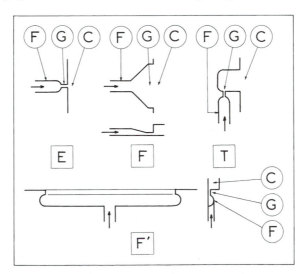

Figure 5.152 · **Gate types (1)** · [E] Edge gate; [F] Fan gate; [T] Tab gate; [F′] Flash gate; (F) Feed channel; (G) Gate; (C) Cavity

Sprue [S], pinpoint [P] and spider (spoked) [S'] gates, often used for axisymmetric products, are illustrated in Figure 5.153. Sprue gates tend to leave a major gate mark (scar) and pinpoint gates are often associated with secondary sprues (S') in three-plate molds (Fig. 5.148).

Diaphragm (disk) [D], internal ring (wafer) [R] and external ring [R'] gates, as illustrated in Figure 5.154, are used when axisymmetric filling of a cavity is desirable; they ensure roundness and avoid weld-lines associated with spider gating, for example.

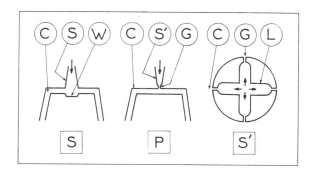

Figure 5.153 · **Gate types (2)** · [S] Sprue gate; [P] Pin gate; [S'] Spider gate; (C) Cavity; (S) Diverging sprue; (W) Cold slug well; (S') converging sprue; (G) Gate; (L) Spider leg

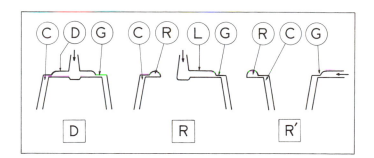

Figure 5.154 · **Gate types (3)** · [D] Diaphragm gate; [R] Internal ring gate; [R'] External ring gate; (C) Cavity; (D) Disk; (G) Gate; (R) Ring; (L) Spider leg

An interesting type of gate illustrated in Figure 5.155 is referred to as the "submarine" or "tunnel" gate [T']. Upon ejection of both product (P) and feed appendage (F'), separation (degating) takes place automatically, as the runner flexibility is sufficient to clear the undercut.

Important savings can be made by using hot runners. They normally require valve gating, as illustrated in Figure 5.156, with an externally-actuated needle (N) and an insulating element (I) between the heated runner block (B) and the tool (T).

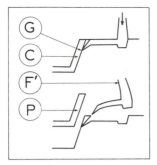
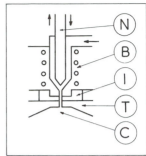

Fig. 5.155   Fig. 5.156

Figure 5.155 · **Submarine gate** · (G) Gate; (C) Cavity; (F′) Feed appendage; (P) Product

Figure 5.156 · **Valve gate** · (N) Needle; (B) Heated Runner block; (I) Insulation; (T) Mold; (C) Cavity

Several molding alternatives are illustrated in Figure 5.157 for a moderately complex product [P]. Mold opening can, in principle, be associated with either one of three orthogonal directions [X], [Y], or [Z]. In each case, the stationary and moving mold halves (T) and (T′), the parting surface (line) (J), and secondary retractable mold sections (S) and (S′) for holes (H) and boss (C) are shown. Each orientation has advantages and disadvantages that must be weighted; solution [Z], for example, appears simpler, but ejection may be difficult without a significant draft on the faces of the wings (W).

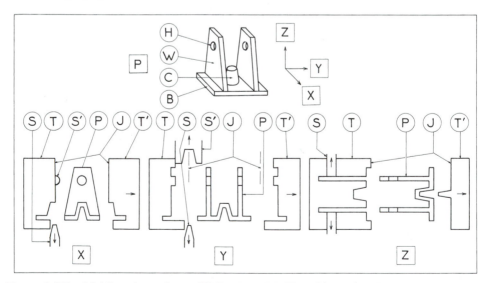

Figure 5.157 · **Molding alternatives** · [P] Product; [X] "X" mold opening; [Y] "Y" mold opening; [Z] "Z" mold opening; (S),(S′) Retractable secondary mold sections; (T) Stationary mold half; (P) Product; (J) Parting line; (T′) Moving mold half

Commercial products often involve several different components made of the same material. It may appear attractive to mold all components in the same mold (family mold). Such a method, however, has shortcomings associated mainly with the lack of symmetry. Different cavities may fill at different rates unless gate and runner geometries are designed to compensate; forces on the mold will be higher around the larger cavity. If one component of a set is unsatisfactory, the whole set must be discarded or reprocessed.

The maximum pressure in injection molds is normally in the range 4000-12,000 psi ($\approx$ 300-800 atm), corresponding to a clamping force per unit projected area of cavity and feed system in the range 2-6 tons/in^2 ($\approx$ 0.3-0.9 tons/cm^2). Injection molds must also feature channels and cavities for fluid cooling, as well as moving elements such as ejectors and retractable secondary sections discussed earlier.

The construction of injection molds requires materials with a combination of good heat conductivity and resistance to mechanical wear and abrasion. Prototype molds (about 10 moldings) can be cast from low melting alloys (Kirksite, Kayem, etc.). Short-run molds (about 1000 moldings) can be machined in aluminum or mild steel. For medium runs (about 10,000-100,000 moldings), tool steel is normally used. Long runs involving millions of moldings require special hardened and chrome-plated steels.

A variety of techniques are used to form mold cavities. They include cutting (machining) of a solid block or of sections of a "fragmented" mold, often with duplicating machines working with scaled patterns and, increasingly, with computer-aided machining centers (CAM). Hobbing (cold forming) is often used for multiple cavities. Electrochemical machining (ECM) and electrical discharge machining, or spark erosion (EDM), are used to form complex cavities. Electroforming, plating and etching (texturing) are other techniques associated with mold cavity forming. Cast cavities of beryllium/copper alloys are also used for moderate runs.

An important consideration in mold cavity dimensioning and forming is the material shrinkage during cooling. Cavities are cut somewhat larger than the desired product, with typical linear shrinkage allowances in the range 0.2-5% (0.002-0.050 in/in) for amorphous or highly crystalline thermoplastics, respectively.

5.13.4 Auxiliaries

Many thermoplastic resins require thorough drying prior to molding, to avoid the formation of voids or a degradation of the material at molding temperatures; continuous hopper dryers are often used.

Mold temperature control is often achieved by the circulation of a fluid through a separate heater/chiller device.

With increased interest in automation, robots have been introduced for the removal of products and feed appendages from open molds, and for separation (degating) and sorting.

Feed appendages, start-up scrap and occasional production scrap are normally reground in granulators and recycled as a fraction of the feed material.

5.13.5   Materials

All thermoplastics are, in principle, suitable for injection molding, but since fast flow rates are needed, grades with good fluidity (high melt index) are normally preferable. Significant differences in ease of molding, and the resulting structure and properties of products are found between amorphous and crystallizing thermoplastics; they concern problems such as shrinkage, warpage, sink marks, flashing, and short shots.

The moldability of a resin is sometimes assessed through global tests, such as the spiral flow test, which reflects the melt flow as well as the solidification behavior.

5.13.6   Products

A major advantage of injection molded products is the incorporation of fine details such as bosses, locating pins, mounting holes, bushings, ribs, flanges, etc., which normally eliminates assembly and finishing operations.

The numerous applications can be broken down into broad categories. Microproducts are molded in multiple cavity molds on small precision machines and include components for watches, and microelectronics. Medium-size products can be molded continuously in very large numbers in dedicated machines (e.g., disposable items) or in relatively small runs (e.g., highly technical parts). Large products including dashboard frames, garden furniture, and small boat hulls require very large machines corresponding to very large investments.

5.13.7   Related Processes

5.13.7.1   Bi-Injection Molding

The expressions bi-injection, bi-component injection, co-injection or two-shot molding are used when two distinct polymeric materials are involved in the molding of a single part. The two materials may just have different colors, one may contain a reinforcement or gas cells (cellular material or foam), or they may be entirely different to provide different properties in different locations (e.g., strength and low friction, rigidity and flexibility). The process requires two distinct feed units and a single mold unit.

Two methods of bi-injection are illustrated in Figure 5.158. The part [P], which features materials (M) and (M'), is reminiscent of a two-color calculator or typewriter key. In the first molding method [l], material (M) is first injected in cavity (C) (stage [I]), and then two movable sections (S) and (S') are retracted to open cavity (C'), through which material (M') is injected (stage [I']). In the second molding method [2], material (M') is first injected in cavity (C') (stage [I']), the mold is then opened and mold half (I') is replaced by mold half (I), freeing cavity (C), through which material (M) is then injected (stage [I]).

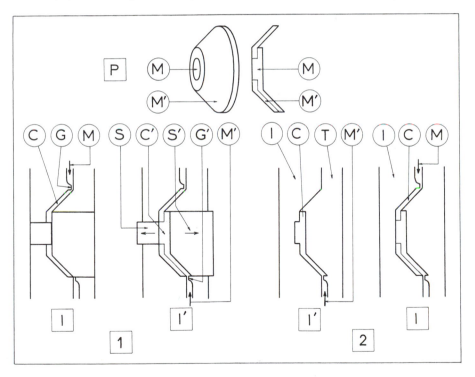

Figure 5.158 · **Bi-injection molding alternatives** · [1] Retractable mold sections method; [2] Indexable mold halves method; [P] Product; [I] Injection of material M; [I] Injection of material M'; (M) Inner material; (M') Outer material; (C) Cavity; (G),(G') Gates; (S),(S') Retractable mold sections; (C) Expanded cavity; (I') First moving mold half; (I) Second moving mold half

Figure 5.159 corresponds to a bi-injection technique aimed at forming a product with a core and a skin made of different materials. At stage [S], material (M) is injected with the distributing sleeve (D) in the lower position, and the cavity is partially filled. At stage [C], material (M') is now injected and pushes forward the molten core of material (M). A skin/core structure is formed with (M') and (M) as skin and core materials, respectively. This technique, which could be referred to as "sequential single cavity bi-injection," is currently used extensively with cellular (foam) core/solid skin products. Simultaneous injection of the two materials has also been used.

When a plastic part previously molded in a specific mold is introduced in another mold, in the same way as a metal insert, and a different plastic is molded over it, the expression over-injection is sometimes used.

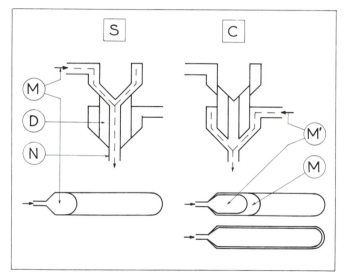

Figure 5.159 · **Core/skin bi-injection molding** · [S] Skin material injection; [C] Core material injection; (M) Skin material; (D) Distributing sleeve; (N) Nozzle; (M') Core material

5.13.7.2   *Injection Molding of Thermosetting Resins*

Thermosetting resin systems, such as phenolics (PF) or unsaturated polyester (UP), often used with fillers or reinforcements, are increasingly injection molded at relatively high speeds. The material is usually fed to the machine in pellet (granule) form, and its consistency may require the use of a "stuffing" (loading) cylinder (L), as illustrated in Figure 5.160. The reciprocating screw unit (S) does the plastication and pre-heats the material in preparation for the injection into a continuously heated mold (T). The temperature and residence time in the screw unit must be limited to avoid premature curing.

Curing, which involves chemical reactions, takes generally much longer than the injection, and multi-mold machines are thus often used with shuttle or rotary systems. Figure 5.161 illustrates an arrangement with two molds, and a single injection/curing station, while Figure 5.162 illustrates a system with four stations, each featuring a clamping mechanism; injection [I] is followed by curing [C] and ejection [E].

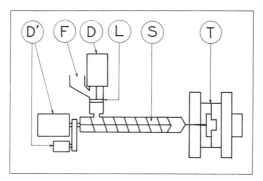

Figure 5.160 · **Thermoset/rubber injection equipment (1)** · (D') Screw drive; (F) Feed hopper; (D) Loading cylinder drive; (L) Loading cylinder; (S) Screw; (T) Mold

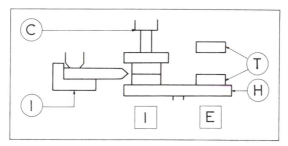

Figure 5.161 · **Thermoset/rubber injection equipment (2)** · [I] Injection station; [E] Demolding station; (I) Injection unit; (C) Mold clamping mechanism; (T) Mold; (H) Revolving or shuttle platform

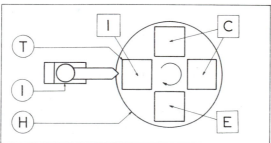

Figure 5.162 · **Thermoset/rubber injection equipment (3)** · [I] Injection station; [C] Curing stations; [E] Demolding station; (T) Mold; (I) Injection unit; (H) Revolving table

5.13.7.3 Injection Molding of Vulcanizable Rubbers

Injection molding is increasingly used for producing relatively small rubber products significantly faster than by compression molding and, normally, with a smaller amount of scrap and a better dimensional accuracy. As in the case of thermosetting resins, a heated mold is needed for vulcanization (curing). The unvulcanized rubber compound (stock) is often fed in ribbon form, and the plasticating and injection functions may be separated, as shown in Figure 5.163, with a three-way valve (V), first transferring the plasticated material to the storage/injection cylinder (I), and subsequently from that cylinder to the mold (T).

Various injection molding devices are shown in figures 5.164-5.183.

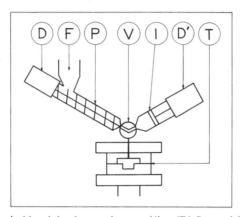

Figure 5.163 · **Thermoset/rubber injection equipment (4)** · (D) Screw drive; (F) Feed hopper; (P) Plasticating unit; (V) Valve; (I) Injection unit; (D′) Cylinder drive; (T) Mold

Figure 5.164 · Small injection molding machine (15-ton) **[BOY]**

Figure 5.165 · Medium size injection molding machine (180-ton) **[KAWAGUCHI]**

Figure 5.166 · Large injection molding machine (two injection units) **[BILLION]**

Figure 5.167 · Very large frame-type injection molding machine (10,000-ton with multiple injection units) **[BILLION]**

Figure 5.168 • Thermoset injection molding machine (with vertical "stuffing" cylinder) **[BUCHER]**

Figure 5.169 • Vertical clamping rubber injection machine (440-ton) **[DESMA]**

Figure 5.170 • Injection molding of a large tub (300-liter capacity) **[ITALSTAMPI]**

Figure 5.171 · Single cavity compact disc molding [ENGEL]

Figure 5.172 · 250-ton injection molding machine with automatic parts handling equipment [HUSKY]

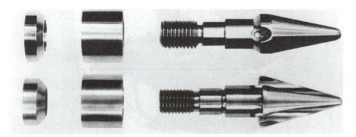

Figure 5.173 · Screw tip valves

Figure 5.174 · Hot runner and value gate devices **[MOLD MASTERS]**

Figure 5.175 · Machining of cavity block for injection molded sailboard hull **[SMTP]**

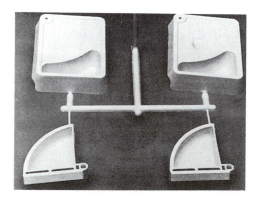

Figure 5.176 · Family mold (pair of dishwasher detergent holding set)

Fig. 5.177   Fig. 5.178

Figure 5.177 · Sequential co-injection of video cassette case (pigmented ABS and transparent SAN in three-plate mold) **[SUMITOMO]**

Figure 5.178 · Piping T-mold (three retractable cores)

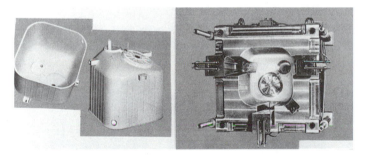

Figure 5.179 · Washing machine tub and mold

Figure 5.180 · Injection mold with multiple retractable secondary mold sections

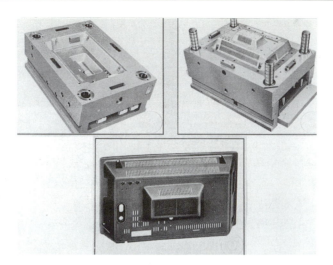

Figure 5.181 · TV rear pannel and injection mold (four-point hot channel feed)

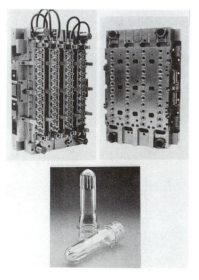

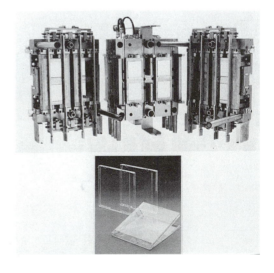

Fig. 5.182   Fig. 5.183

Figure 5.182 · Injection of pet blow molding preforms; (48-cavity, valve-gated, hot runner mold) **[HUSKY]**

Figure 5.183 · Hot-runner stack mold for compact disc display boxes (2 x 4 - cavity) **[HUSKY]**

5.14   REACTION INJECTION MOLDING

5.14.1   Principle

Reaction (or reactive) injection molding (RIM) is a relatively new process that involves the rapid mixing, in precise proportions, of two or more highly reactive low-molecular-weight liquid components and the immediate injection of the mixture in a closed mold. Polymerization and/or molecular network formation take place in the mold in a very short time (typically 30 s or so), yielding a solid product in a total cycle time of the order of 1-2 min. The RIM process was developed with urethane resins and is still used primarily with these materials. It is particularly suited to the production of large, relatively thin part, capital investment and operating costs being much less than those for thermoplastics injection molding. The process is energy efficient, but requires good control of complex reactions.

5.14.2   Equipment

RIM process equipment involves two, and sometimes more, components, each one corresponding to a stream up to the mixing head. In addition to a number of appropriate valves, each stream features several major elements, depicted schematically in Figure 5.184.

A suitable batch of each component is held in a material tank (R) (day tank, work tank), which is pressure-rated (about 7.5 atm or $\approx$ 110 psi). Typical capacities are

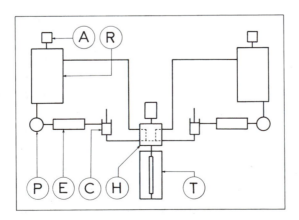

Figure 5.184 · **RIM equipment** · (T) Mold; (H) Mixing head; (E) Heat exchanger; (P) Recirculating pump; (R) Material tank; (A) Stirrer; (C) Metering cylinder

about 250 l ($\approx$ 65 gal). Tanks generally feature a nitrogen gas overlay (blanket) to protect the chemicals from oxygen or moisture, and a vortex-free stirrer (agitator), particularly for materials containing filler particles.

A high pressure pump (P) (300 atm or $\approx$ 4400 psi) is used for circulating (recirculating) the liquid component.

A cylinder-piston unit (C) of the lance-displacement type is used for the rapid and accurate dispensing (metering, dosing) of the component, through a servo-hydraulic drive system. Typical capacities are in the range 2-40 l($\approx$ 1-15 gal).

The mixing head (mixhead) (H) accomplishes the rapid mixing of the components, by impingement, during the injection phase [I] (Fig. 5.185), and allows the recirculation of each component [inlet (I) to outlet (O)], the rest of the time ([R]). Mixing heads are generally self-cleaning.

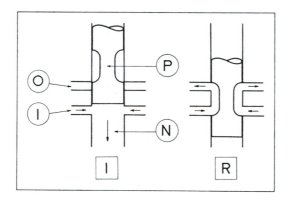

Figure 5.185 · **Mixing head** · [I] Injection configuration; [R] Recirculation; (I) Inlet; (O)Outlet; (P) Distributing piston; (N) Nozzle

A heat exchanger (E) permits the control of the temperature of each component. The two halves of the mold (T) are mounted on the platens (P) of the molding press (mold carrier), which often allow rotation or tilting of the mold or booking (alligator) opening (Fig. 5.186). Platen sizes can be as large as about 0.8 x 1.4 m (4 x 9 ft) and, in view of the relatively low maximum in-mold pressure (4-8 atm or $\approx$ 50-100 psi), the clamping (locking) force is moderate (300 tons for large presses). Some systems feature shuttle or carousel-type mold carriers, with a single injection unit.

Polyurethane resins are often processed near ambient temperature (up to 65°C or $\approx$ 150°F), but some resin systems (polyamide systems in particular) require much higher processing temperatures; corresponding equipment featuring jacketed tanks and lines is often referred to as "heat-traced" (HT) equipment.

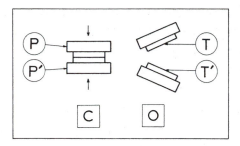

Figure 5.186 · **Booking press** · [C] Closed; [O] Open; (P),(P′) Platens; (T),(T′) Mold halves

5.14.3   Tooling

RIM molds do not have to withstand high pressures (4-8 atm or ≈ 50-100 psi), and for most polyurethane systems their temperature remains moderate. Depending on the number of parts required, mold materials can range from epoxy, metal-coated epoxy (nickel is common), kirksite, aluminum, and steel. Mixing heads are attached to the mold, which often features a baffle-type aftermixer. Laminar flow through runner, gate and cavity is desirable to minimize air bubble entrainment. Product release from the mold requires internal or mold-applied release agents, which may have a negative effect on subsequent paint adhesion. The throughput or overall injection rate (all components) can be as high as 5 kg/s (≈ 10 lb/s).

5.14.4   Materials

Urethane resin systems (RIM-PUR) are most widely used. Processing normally takes place near ambient temperature. Parts are often slightly cellular in the core, to minimize sink marks and to ensure good mold reproduction. Related isocyanurate and triazathane systems are also used.

Urea resin systems (RIM-PUA) have been developed with a superior temperature resistance which makes them suitable, for example, for automotive body components subjected to high temperature paint ovens (see Chapter 6).

Amide (nylon) resin systems (RIM-PA) have been introduced, which feature caprolactam/catalyst and caprolactam/prepolymer components. A thermoplastic block copolymer is formed, which features alternating stiff polyamide-6 (PA-6) and soft polyether blocks. The system is sometimes referred to as RIM-NBC for nylon block copolymer. The components must be processed at temperatures above about 85°C ($\approx$ 185°F), and the mold temperature must be over 140°C ($\approx$ 285°F).

Epoxy systems, featuring a low molecular weight resin component and a catalyst, are generally used as an impregnating matrix for continuous glass reinforcement (RIM-EP).

Unsaturated polyester systems are being developed for use in fast RIM-type equipment, also in connection with fibrous reinforcement (RIM-UP).

A two-component reactive system, leading to an olefinic thermoset (polydicyclopentadiene), is being marketed (RIM-OL). An acrylic system has also been mentioned (RIM-AC).

5.14.5   Products

Because of the low-viscosity fluid involved and the low mold pressure, the RIM process is particularly well suited to the fabrication of large thin parts, which include exterior automotive body panels such as front-end fascias and fenders, as well as furniture, electronic cabinets, and window frames.

5.14.6   Related Processes

When small particulate reinforcement is added to one of the components, and thus becomes part of the stream, the process is called "reinforced RIM" (RRIM). Long chopped glass fiber or short milled glass fiber can lead to anisotropic (oriented) products, which do not have optimal dimensional stability. Flake reinforcement can reduce this problem (glass or mica flakes).

The use of a RIM system to impregnate a fiber preform, placed in the mold prior to injection, has been referred to as "structural RIM" (SRIM). The difference with the resin transfer molding (RTM) process, discussed in section 5.15.3.6, appears to lie primarily in the speed of injection.

If a resin system of the RIM type is sprayed against the surface of an open mold, the expression reactive spray molding (RSM) is used. The technique has been used for the rapid fabrication of large parts that require only one finished surface (shower stalls, boat hulls, camper canopies, etc.).

The rapid injection of reactive liquid silicone resins to form elastomeric parts is often referred to as "liquid injection molding" (LIM). Similar systems could include liquid butadiene-based resins. Equipment for RIM is shown in figures 5.187-5.189.

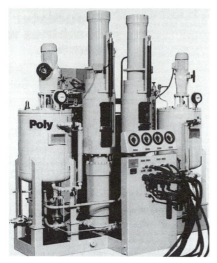

Figure 5.187 · Two-cylinder rim injection unit **[BATTENFELD]**

Figure 5.188 · RIM mold carrier **[BATTENFELD]**

Figure 5.189 · RIM booking press with bus bumper mold **[ADMIRAL]**

5.15   COMPOSITE MATERIALS, PROCESSING, AND PRODUCTS

5.15.1   Materials

5.15.1.1   Introduction

Fiber-reinforced plastics, referred to as "FRP," "structural composites" or simply "composites," are associated with products in which a polymeric matrix is combined with reinforcing fibers. FRP products have now acquired a high reputation for structural applications. The composition, as well as the processing of FRP materials, permit considerable flexibility in tailoring the material structure to the end use and, in particular, to the product loading pattern.

The polymeric matrices used in FRP are primarily of the thermosetting type and include unsaturated polyesters, vinylesters, and epoxies, which are discussed in Chapter 3.

The reinforcing fibers include glass, carbon/graphite and aramid fibers; glass is, by far, the most common type. Reinforcing fibers are discussed primarily in Chapter 2.

Forms of fiber reinforcement, fiber preforms, fiber prepregs and fiber molding compounds are discussed below.

5.15.1.2   Fiber Reinforcements

Continuous filament reinforcement is manufactured in the form of wound cylindrical packages of untwisted roving, which are held stationary for center pull, or mounted on creels (spindles) for tangential pull. Wound tubes of twisted yarn are normally used for fabric weaving. Uniaxial glass reinforcement can make up to 80-90% of the composite weight.

Biaxial or bidirectional reinforcement can be achieved with continuous filaments by using woven roving or yarn-based woven fabric. The weight of woven roving is in the range 0.3-0.75 kg/m^2 ($\approx$ 9-24 oz/yd^2), that of woven fabric in the range 0.05-2 kg/m^2 ($\approx$ 2-50 oz/yd^2) and the thickness of one layer (ply) of woven fabric-based composite is in the range 0.1-2.5 mm ($\approx$ 0.004-0.100 in) with a weight percent of glass commonly between 45 and 55% and occasionally up to 75%. Fabric-like continuous roving assemblies are also available, which involve stitching with a polymeric thread.

Random or multidirectional reinforcement can be achieved with mats of discontinuous chopped strands ranging in length from 5 to 50 mm ($\approx$ 0.25-2 in) or with mats of continuous strands (swirl mats). Such mats have weights in the range 0.3-0.9

kg/m^2 ($\approx$ 1-3 oz/ft^2). The glass content in corresponding **FRP** products is commonly between 25 and 35% and occasionally up to 50% by weight. Lighter surfacing or overlay mats (veils) are used to form resin-rich surface layers, containing no more than about 20% by weight of glass, which help improve appearance and chemical resistance.

A special form of composite fabrication aid which is now widely used in aerospace and other advanced applications is the honeycomb structure. Such structure, initially made of aluminum, now increasingly consists of reinforcing fibers embedded in a thermosetting resin. Honeycomb structures in thicknesses around 3/8 in ($\approx$ 10 mm) are used primarily as a light, yet stiff, spacer element between bonded composite skins.

The fiber-resin interface plays an important role in the composite behavior and fibers are treated with coupling agents that help form a good fiber-resin bond. Silanes, titanates and zirconates are used as coupling agents with glass fibers.

5.15.1.3 Fiber Preforms

Fiber preforms are preferable to conventional planar fiber mats and fabrics for the molding of complex shapes in processes such as resin transfer molding (**RTM**) discussed in section 5.15.3.6. They ensure an appropriate distribution of the reinforcement, and help minimize its displacement during the resin flow phase. Preforms normally consist of a mat of fibers held together by a binder and having the shape of the mold cavity. Dry preforming techniques (Fig. 5.190) involve the placement of a mat of chopped strands (**F**) (2.5-5 cm or 1-2 in) over a suitably-shaped perforated preform screen (**S**) with the help of air aspiration (suction) (**A**) through the perforations. A liquid resin binder (**B**) is spread over the mat, and its subsequent hardening in a curing oven gives the preform its strength. Chopped strands are either

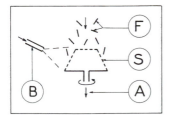

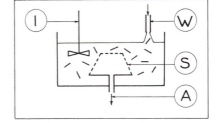

Fig. 5.190   Fig. 5.191

Figure 5.190 · **Dry preforming** · (B) Binder; (F) Fibers; (S) Screen; (A) Aspiration

Figure 5.191 · **Wet preforming** · (I) Impeller; (W) Fiber/water slurry; (S) Screen; (A) Aspiration

projected (blown) onto the screen with an orientable gun (directed fiber method) or fed to a rotating fiber distributor in a chamber and, subsequently, fall onto the screen (plenum chamber method). A wet preforming technique (water slurry method), depicted on Figure 5.191, involves the aspiration (suction) (A) of a stirred suspension (slurry) (W) of chopped strands in water, onto the perforated preform screen (S). A small amount of cellulosic fibers, flexible in the wet state but quite rigid in the subsequent dry state, is used as the binder. The use of preforms allows glass loadings of about 35% by weight.

Conventional flat cut strand or continuous strand fiber mats featuring a thermoplastic binder can be preformed by a heating/shaping/cooling process.

5.15.1.4   Fiber Prepregs

Any form of reinforcement can be obtained in the form of preimpregnated ribbons, tapes, or sheets (prepregs), in which a thermosetting resin is pre-cured to a semi-solid state, which facilitates the fabrication of parts. Curing of the resin at an elevated temperature and under an appropriate pressure, a time-consuming operation, must follow. Thermoplastic-based prepregs are being introduced that involve only shorter heating, fabrication and cooling stages.

5.15.1.5   Fiber Molding Compounds

Combinations of discontinuous fibers and temperature-activated thermosetting resins, such as unsaturated polyesters, directly suitable for compression or injection molding in hot molds, are often referred to as "molding compounds." A number of commer- cially-important types are discussed below.

BMC

Bulk molding compounds (BMC) result from the mixing (blending) of about 25% by weight of chopped glass fibers and a thick resin system in a blade-type mixer. The compound has the consistency of modeling clay (putty, dough) and is often extruded into logs or rope for easy cutting into suitable molding charges. The mixing process tends to reduce the length of the chopped fiber strands, but what is lost in properties can be turned to advantage in processing, since the material can flow well into fairly complex shapes (ribs, bosses, etc.). Compression molding, transfer molding and even injection molding can be used with such compounds. The expression dough molding compound (DMC) is also used for this type of compound.

ZMC

A new comprehensive molding technology, referred to as ZMC, is claimed to produce injection molded parts with particularly long fibers, owing, in particular, to a special injection unit.

PMC

Molding compounds have been introduced, which are in the form of "dry" free-flowing (free-running) pellets, in contrast with the generally "tacky" BMC or DMC. Such compounds, which have been referred to as "pelletized molding compounds" (PMC), are intended primarily for injection molding.

SMC

Sheet molding compounds (SMC) generally involve the combination of about 25% by weight of relatively long chopped glass fibers (1-5 cm or ≈ 0.5-2 in) with a high viscosity thermosetting polyester resin matrix (paste). The paste-like consistency of the resin is partly associated with the use of magnesium oxide (MgO) as an additive/filler. The manufacture of sheet molding compounds is normally a continuous operation and the rolled material can be stored or shipped for subsequent molding. SMC manufacture (Fig. 5.192) generally involves a polyethylene carrier film (web) (F) on which a layer of resin paste (P) is applied by means of a doctor blade (D). The carrier film is supported by a wire mesh belt (B). Glass fiber roving (G) is cut with a rotary chopping device (C) into strands that fall in a random pattern on the paste layer. A polyethylene cover film (web) (F′) also coated with resin paste is overlaid, and the glass-resin system is compacted (kneaded) between the underlying belt (B)

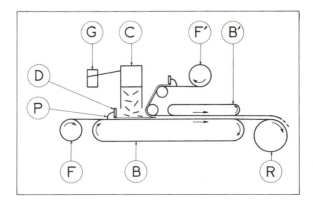

Figure 5.192 · **Sheet molding compound (SMC) fabrication** · (B) Carrier belt; (F) Carrier film; (P) Resin paste; (D) Doctor blade; (G) Glass roving; (C) Chopping device; (F′) Cover film; (B′) Cover belt; (R) Wind-up roll

and a roll/belt device (B') to ensure a good penetration of the resin into the fiber strands. The SMC sheet is then wound up into rolls that, after a resin-maturing stage, can be used in compression molding. A representative production rate is about 3000 kg/h/m of width ($\approx$ 200 lb/h/ft). SMC compounds are particularly suited to the manufacture of large, relatively thin parts such as automotive body components. The sheet material can be cut to the desired shape and placed in the mold, after stripping off the polyethylene carrier and cover films. To accommodate larger or variable thicknesses, the sheet material can be layered. Sheet molding compounds are compression molded into heated molds (around 150°C or $\approx$ 300°F), the curing time ranging from about 1 to 5 min, depending on the part thickness. In-mold pressure is relatively high (15-150 atm or $\approx$ 250-2000 psi) and thus sturdy steel molds and large presses are required for large parts such as automotive body components. The cost of an SMC press, however, can be only one-fifth that of a corresponding metal stamping press. Contraction of the resin after curing and cooling can give a somewhat uneven part surface; this problem can be countered by the use of so-called low-shrink (low-profile) resin additives. A technique referred to as "in-mold coating" (IMC) has also been developed to inject a lacquer into the mold, at an intermediate stage, to obtain the sort of finish (class A) that is desirable, for automotive body components, for example.

TMC

A special technique has been introduced that permits the preparation of thick, SMC-like, compounds (up to 5 cm or 2 in). It is referred to as "thick molding compounds" (TMC). In this case, the chopped glass fibers are combined to the resin at the nip of two counter rotating rolls, from which the resulting sheet-like material is stripped, and subsequently formed, and compacted into the thick final compound. Thick molding compounds can be compression molded into thick products and they can also be used as feed material for injection molding.

XMC

For applications such as large panels, which involve little deformation of an initially flat molding compound during molding, but call for high mechanical properties in the product, a special sheet molding compound has been developed. It features a high loading of continuous glass strands laid in a cross-pattern (hence the name "XMC"), supplemented by either chopped strands or continuous swirled strands to provide resistance in directions other than the major fiber directions. Helical winding on a large cylindrical mandrel is used to place the continuous fibers.

5.15.2   Open-Tool Processing

A number of techniques for manufacturing fiber-reinforced parts have in common the use of a single tool surface to give a part its shape. They are often globally referred to as "open-tool (mold) processing." They include the so-called contact molding, such as hand lay-up and spray-up, as well as filament winding, and centrifugal casting.

5.15.2.1   Contact Molding

The expression "contact molding" is often used for processes that involve the placement of fiber reinforcement, impregnated with resin, against a tool surface (mold). The surface is often concave (negative), as in the fabrication of a boat hull, but it may also be convex (positive), as in the case of a swimming pool. The surface of the cured part away from the mold is normally inferior in quality to the mold side surface. The mold side surface can be even better if a surfacing resin layer (gel-coat) is first applied. Contact molding is particularly convenient for making large parts (tanks, pools, hull, etc.), and room temperature-curing resins are thus most frequently used. Resin consistency, as well as gelling and hardening times, must be adjusted to each situation.

Hand Lay-Up

The simplest method of fabrication, which involves the manual placement of mat or fabric reinforcement and batch-mixed resin on the mold surface, is referred to as "hand lay-up" or "hand laminating." It is often necessary to place several successive layers of reinforcement, each layer being compacted with the help of brushes, rollers (flat or finned), and squeegees (rubber blades). The method is well suited to the incorporation of other elements, such as foam cores, and fasteners, but it is very labor intensive. Molds are often made of reinforced plastic when room temperature cure is used. Preimpregnated reinforcements (prepregs) can also be placed manually, but heat cure is then required.

Spray-up

Faster production rates can be achieved with the spray-up method, which involves the projection against the mold surface of chopped glass strand and atomized, continuously catalyzed liquid resin (spray-up gun). Compaction is often required between successive passes (layers). Spraying and compaction can be automated for relatively rapid production rates, particularly in the case of simple convex shapes such as cylindrical tanks.

Pressure Assistance

Several pressure-assisted techniques are used to improve the quality of contact moldings.

The vacuum bag technique involves the use of a flexible plastic film, such as polyethylene, to wrap the part after hand lay-up or spray-up. After sealing the edges, a vacuum is drawn in the resulting "bag" and atmospheric pressure (1 atm or $\approx$ 14.7 psi) helps compact and densify the laminates through complete curing.

In the pressure bag technique, a rubber sheet may be placed and sealed over the laminate. Higher hydrostatic pressures can be applied (about 3 atm or $\approx$ 50 psi). The use of this technique also allows the fabrication of parts such as seamless necked tanks with a good external surface, using a negative (concave) mold with an extractable collapsible pressure bag (bladder).

Laminates protected by a temperature-resistant vacuum or pressure bag (e.g., polyamide or polyester film) can be placed in an autoclave for curing under high temperature and pressure (200-250°C or $\approx$ 400-500°F and 3-7 atm or $\approx$ 50-100 psi). Molds must have appropriate thermal resistance. This more costly technique, subject to size limitations, is widely use for advanced (high performance) composites for aerospace applications.

5.15.2.2   Rigidized Thermoformed Sheets

Several techniques have been developed to combine thermoformed sheets (as skin) and fiber-reinforced thermosetting resins (as backing) to form laminated parts, referred to here as "FRP-rigidized thermoformed sheets." Acrylics, ABS, and PVC are most commonly used as skins, while chopped glass-reinforced polyester resins with room temperature or moderate temperature-curing characteristics are used for backings. The thermoplastic skin offers an alternative to a gel-coat to give a good surface finish, and appropriate materials can impart excellent weatherability, as well as superior abrasion and impact resistance.

If the FRP backing is applied by hand lay-up or spray-up, the thermoformed sheet can serve as an open mold with minimal support, even in conjunction with a vacuum bag technique. This is suitable when the FRP surface is not apparent in the finished product, and for large parts.

The technique of resin transfer molding (RTM) can also be used after placing a matching thermoformed sheet in the mold. The major mold surface need not be as good as in the conventional RTM process.

The use of a thermoformed sheet, placed in the mold prior to cold press molding, corresponds to the process sometimes referred to as "comoforming" (cold molding/thermoforming).

Applications of rigidized thermoformed sheets include bathroom components, outdoor table tops, motor vehicle body components (panels, tops, domes, caps), small craft hulls and decks, swimming pool elements, and caskets.

5.15.2.3 Filament Winding

Filament winding is perhaps the FRP processing technique that can best use the potential of composite materials. It involves the mechanical wrapping (winding) of resin-impregnated continuous filaments (strands, rovings) over a convex tool (mandrel, core).

The basic elements of a filament winding machine (Fig. 5.193) normally include a filament-dispensing station (F) (multiple creels, spools, packages), a resin bath (B) to impregnate the continuous strands, a carriage-mounted guide (G) (comb, eyelet, etc.) that defines the delivery (feed, payout) point and whose axial motion is controlled through a screw mechanism (S), and, finally, supports and a drive spindle for the rotating tool (mandrel) (T).

After winding and curing the composite material (room temperature, infrared heating, autoclave, etc.), the part can be mechanically stripped from cylindrical or

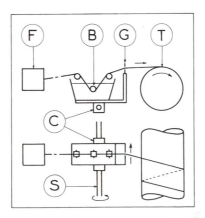

Figure 5.193 • "Wet" filament winding • (F) Filament stock; (B) Impregnation bath; (G) Filament guide; (T) Tool (mandrel); (C) Carriage; (S) Feed screw

tapered mandrels. Temporary mandrels (plaster), collapsible or inflatable mandrels, and hollow forms that remain as part of the product are also used.

Filament winding can be subdivided into three basic methods, depicted in Figure 5.194, which involve increasing complexity. In circumferential (or hoop) winding [C], the mandrel rotates while the filament guide travels relatively slowly, giving a fiber angle of about 90° to the axis. Hoop resistance of the product is high, but longitudinal resistance is very low unless additional reinforcement, such as a sprayed-up random mat of chopped fibers, is simultaneously applied. The method is widely used for vertical tanks and stack liners that do not undergo axial tension. Helical winding [H] involves the appropriate control of the rotation and axial speeds of the mandrel and guide, respectively, to lay down the fibers at a desired angle, such as 54.5° to the axis for optimum resistance of pressure tubes. The need to reverse the motion of the guide at the end of a pass to obtain a symmetrical fiber pattern creates "dwell" regions that may have to be trimmed off. Polar winding [P] corresponds to applications where it is desirable to wind the ends (caps, closures) of a vessel, together with the rest of the vessel (seamless pressure vessels). One such situation involves a cylindrical/ hemispherical combination. Polar winding can be accomplished through the simple rotation of the mandrel and the use of a whirling arm to carry the guide or by a "tumbling" motion of the mandrel (axial, as well as end-over-end rotations). Polar winding is the most complex method and requires computer-controlled equipment; it is normally reserved for high performance applications such as the fuel tanks and motor cases of rockets.

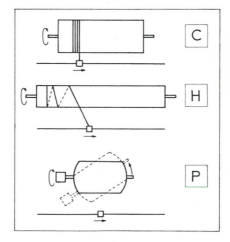

Figure 5.194 · **Filament winding methods** · [C] Circumferential; [H] Helicoidal; [P] Polar

Winding rates can range from about 5 kg ($\approx$ 10 lb) of composite per hour for complex parts to as much as 250 kg ($\approx$ 500 lb) per hour for large tanks.

Large size applications involving filament winding include horizontal and vertical storage tanks (chemicals, oil, fuels, etc.) and stack liners or structures. Pressure- or crush-resistant tubings, pipes, and conduits, as well as pressure bottles, tanks and vessels, rocket motor cases, and shotgun barrels, are also made by this process. Parts that require axial reinforcement, such as hollow beams, and propellers, can be made by winding tapes featuring transversely oriented reinforcing strands held together by stitched polymeric fibers (weft-tapes).

5.15.2.4 Pultrusion

Pultrusion is a special processing technique that combines continuous reinforcing fibers (roving yarn) and a resin matrix in a suitable tool (die), to produce uniaxially reinforced profiles with outstanding longitudinal resistance. Modifications to the basic process now allow the incorporation of some transverse reinforcements, either continuous (by winding) or discontinuous (as mat).

The basic elements of a pultruder (Fig. 5.195) include a filament-dispensing station (F), a resin bath (B) for fiber impregnation, a guiding device (G) to position the numerous strands, and a heated forming/curing tool (die) (T) where the fiber/resin system acquires the desired shape and cures to a solid state under pressure. The process requires the application of a rather strong pulling (dragging) force, which is applied to the solid pultruded profile by a gripper/puller device (P). The device features two or more pairs of contoured clamps mounted on endless tracks and taking turns pulling a distance, releasing and returning. The heart of the process, the die, is typically 75 cm (30 in) long, and the relatively high pressures involved, as well as frictional forces, require hardened steel construction; a tapered entrance facilitates the compaction of the composite. Pultrusion speeds are primarily limited by curing within the die, and thus rather slow (about 1-2 m/min or $\approx$ 3-6 ft/min). Pre-curing in the

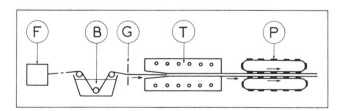

Figure 5.195 · **Pultrusion** · (F) Filament stock; (B) Impregnation bath; (G) Guide; (T) Tool (die); (P) Gripper/puller device

die, followed by final curing in a suitable tubular oven, can speed up the process, particularly for thick cross-sections. Large pultrusion machines can involve pull load capabilities as high as 10 tons.

Products of the basic process are straight, with a uniform cross-section, but modifications can be made to produce slightly curved or twisted products.

Applications include cylindrical products (rodstock), such as fishing poles (rods), golf clubs and arrow shafts, antennas, and oil well sucker rods; basically rectangular products (flat stock), such as sail battens and snowmobile track stiffeners; channel profiles, such as guard rails, cable trays, and ladder rails; hollow profiles, such as ladder rungs, pole-line or cherry-picker booms, and windmill blades.

The technique referred to as "pulforming" forms a heated, but not fully cured "pultrudate" in suitable molds mounted on endless tracks or on a carousel. The cross-section area of the product must be nearly uniform along its length, but the cross-section shape can be varied significantly. This is of particular value in the case of leaf springs, for example, where the moment of inertia can be widely varied to match the bending moment.

Rolltrusion is another pultrusion-related technique that forms profiled, continuous fiber-reinforced products in the gap between contoured counter rotating heated rollers. The drag is considerably less than in the stationary die pultrusion process, but the forming zone is short and most of the curing must take place in the absence of compacting pressure.

5.15.2.5   Centrifugal Casting

Products such as tubing, pipes, and tanks (excluding end-caps), which have a circular-cylindrical shape, can be made of FRP by a process generally referred to as "centrifugal casting" (Fig. 5.196). In the case of discontinuous fiber reinforcement, a mix (M) of chopped fibers and pre-catalyzed liquid resin is dispensed along the axis of a rotating cylindrical tool (mold) (T). As the material falls on the mold surface, it is entrained, and centrifugal forces help compact it into a uniform layer, also keeping

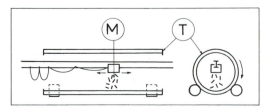

Figure 5.196 · **Centrifugal casting** · (M) Fiber/resin mix; (T) Tool (mold)

it in place during cure. Thickness can be built up by successive passes along the length of the cylinder. The final inner surface, although not as good as the outer surface is reasonably smooth, and features can be formed in the outer surface, (flanges, threads, ribs, etc.) if the mold is made of suitable sections to allow the extraction of the finished part. The process can be modified to allow continuous pipe production.

In an extension of the process, large pipes have been made that involve the successive formation of an external FRP layer, a rigid foam core layer, and an internal FRP layer. Such pipes have outstanding insulation and crushing properties, in addition to pressure resistance.

5.15.2.6 Continuous Laminating

Fiber-reinforced panels can be made by continuous laminating processes. Such flat or corrugated panels, which can be made translucent, find use in construction or as electrical insulation material. The process involves the impregnation of individual layers of glass fiber mat or fabric in a resin dip or with a doctor blade, and their gathering between temperature-resistant carrier and cover films (cellophane, polyester, or polyamide). The laminate is then compacted by squeeze rolls and cured. Corrugations are produced by special rollers or mold sections (shoes). The typical glass content is about 30% by weight and thicknesses range from about 1 to 5 mm ($\approx$ 0.040-0.200 in). Production speeds can be as high as 20 m/min ($\approx$ 60 ft/min).

5.15.3 Closed-Mold Processing

Several processing techniques involve the formation of a part in the cavity of a mold. This is referred to as "closed-mold," "matched-mold," or "matched-die" processing. In the case of fiber-reinforced thermosetting systems, one can distinguish between hot-mold processing, which corresponds to temperature-activated thermosetting resins, and cold-mold processing, which corresponds to catalyst-activated or mixing-activated resin system.

There are two basic ways of managing a fiber/resin system prior to closed-mold processing.

Fiber reinforcement and resin can be combined prior to their introduction into the mold. The combinations prepared by molders just prior to molding are often called "premixes," while the combinations developed and prepared by specialized compounders and supplied as ready-to-mold stock, with appropriate molding instructions, are generally called "compounds."

Fiber reinforcement and resin can also be combined within the mold cavity (at-press or in-mold combination). In this case, the reinforcement is placed in the mold, either in the form of cut pieces of mat or woven fabric, or as preforms prepared in advance. A suitable amount of resin can be placed under, or poured over the reinforcement just prior to closing the mold (hot or cold press molding), or a low viscosity resin can be injected into the closed mold containing the reinforcement [resin transfer molding (RTM) and structural reactive injection molding (SRIM)].

5.15.3.1   Compression Molding

Compression molding of glass reinforced systems in flash molds requires certain adjustments to the basic process to accommodate, in particular, the fact that reinforcement trapped in the flash land area may prevent the build up of a suitable pressure; some molds are thus fitted with telescoping shear pinchoffs. Bulk molding compounds (BMC) and sheet molding compounds (SMC) are processed by compression molding. The process is discussed in section 5.11.

A special compression molding process uses a deformable rubber plug on one side of the mold cavity to facilitate the rearrangement of the charge when the mold is closed.

5.15.3.2   Batch Laminating

High pressure batch laminating, the process used to make laminates in thicknesses up to 15 cm ($\approx$ 6 in), is a compression molding-type process carried out in presses that are often equipped with multiple platens. The fiber content for glass reinforcement is often as high as 60% by weight. Formica/Arborite- type laminates involve paper reinforcement with phenolic and amino-resins.

5.15.3.3   Transfer Molding

Transfer molding, which is particularly suitable for multicavity molds, can be used with premixes and compounds with good flowability. The process is discussed in section 5.12.

5.15.3.4   Injection Molding

Injection molding requires some adjustments associated in particular with the flow of the short fiber-filled material and abrasion associated with glass fibers in particular.

Premixes or molding compounds of the BMC/DMC, ZMC and PMC types can be suitable. The injection molding of reinforced thermoplastics (RTP) is very similar to that of unreinforced thermoplastics and the injection molding of thermoset-based premixes and compounds requires equipment designed for thermosets. The injection molding process is described in section 5.13.

5.15.3.5 Cold Press Molding

Cold-mold compression molding (cold press molding) generally uses a mat or preform reinforcement placed in the open mold and over which a catalyst-activated resin is poured. Because of low temperatures and moderate pressures, relatively inexpensive molds can be used. This process, however, is slow and thus suited to the small volume production of large parts.

5.15.3.6 Resin Transfer Molding (RTM)

Resin transfer molding (RTM), sometimes called "resin injection molding," first involves the placement of a well-bound fiber mat (continuous or discontinuous reinforcement) in the cavity of a mold.   A low-viscosity, catalyst-activated thermosetting resin is subsequently pumped into the cavity under moderate pressure [up to 5 atm ($\approx$ 80 psi)]. Simultaneous evacuation of the cavity is often used. Displacement of the reinforcement (washing) by the resin must be minimized by an appropriate choice of resin and reinforcing mat, continuous strand (swirl) mats being particularly suitable. The glass content in final products is generally around 20% by weight. Curing times are normally fairly long (10-20 min). Mold construction is relatively simple, and the use of a flexible perimeter gasket, associated with a suitable number of quick-release perimeter clamps, can eliminate the need for a press. Large parts can be produced in small runs at a small fraction of the cost of hot-mold or even cold-mold compression molded ones. Gel-coating prior to the placement of the reinforcement, or in-mold coating (IMC), are compatible with the process.

If a fast-reacting, mixing-activated, RIM-type thermosetting resin system is used, cycles can be much shorter. This process is sometimes referred to as "structural reaction injection molding" (SRIM).

Three somewhat related processes: elastic reservoir molding (ERM), thermal expansion resin transfer molding (TERTM) and ultimately reinforced thermoset reaction injection (URTRI) have been described in the literature.

Composite materials, processing equipment, and products apparatuses are shown in figures 5.197-5.227.

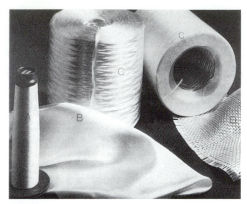

Figure 5.197 · Glass reinforcement-1 (yarn, woven yarn or fabric, roving, woven roving)

Figure 5.198 · Glass reinforcement-2 (continuous strand mat, surfacing mat, chopped strand mat, woven roving/chopped strand mat combination)

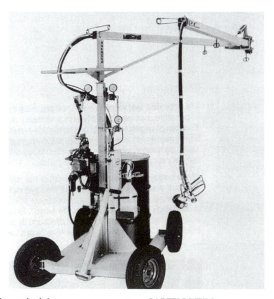

Figure 5.199 · Mobile resin/glass spray-up system [AVENGER]

Figure 5.200 · Curing autoclave (thermosetting matrix) **[LIPTON]**

Figure 5.201 · Helical pipe winding (start-up) **[VETROTEX]**

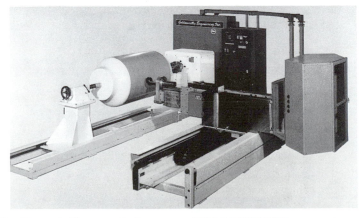

Figure 5.202 · Four-axis filament winding system **[GOLDWORTHY]**

Figure 5.203 · Polar filament winding of a rocket motor pressure vessel

Figure 5.204 · Robotic filament winding of a piping t-joint **[AUTOMATED DYNAMICS]**

Figure 5.205 · Pultrusion of construction panels **[CREATIVE PULTRUSIONS]**

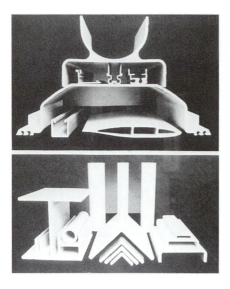

Figure 5.206 · Pultruded profiles
[PULTEX]

Figure 5.207 · Pultruded "cherry-picker"
boom [MORRISON]

Figure 5.208 · Centrifugal casting of pipe [VETROTEX]

Fig. 5.209   Fig. 5.210

Figure 5.209 · Cold press molding-1 (reinforcement and resin loading) **[VETROTEX]**

Figure 5.210 · Cold press molding-2 (cured product) **[VETROTEX]**

Figure 5.211 · Injection molded automobile
rear hatch (ZMC, BX model, 1982)
[CITROEN]

Figure 5.212 · CN Tower TORONTO (composite upper tower cover and radome)

Fig. 5.213

Fig. 5.214

Figure 5.213 · Injection molding in vertical press (ZMC composite) **[BILLION/ SPIERTZ]**

Figure 5.214 · Composite bicycle frame (SMC) **[GITANE]**

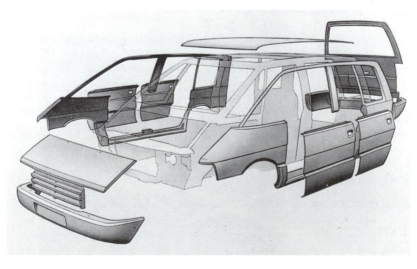

Figure 5.215 · All composite body elements (SMC or RTM composites, Espace model, 1984) **[RENAULT]**

Figure 5.216 · Formula I racing car, composite skin and structure **[McLAREN]**

Figure 5.217 · All-composite voyager aircraft **[RUTAN]**

Figure 5.218 · All-composite business aircraft (Starship model) **[BEECHCRAFT]**

Figure 5.219 · Filament wound aircraft fuselage (Starship model) **[BEECHCRAFT]**

Figure 5.220 · Filament-wound "geodesic frame" aircraft fuselage **[GOLDWORTHY]**

Figure 5.221 · Helicopter blades and rotor head (Dauphin model) **[AEROSPATIALE]**

Figure 5.222 · Composite helicopter rotor head (starflex) **[AEROSPATIALE]**

Figure 5.223 · Composite helicopter rotor head **[SIKORSKY]**

Figure 5.224 · All composite helicopter prototype

Figure 5.225 · All-composite mine sweeper hull (120-ton vessel) **[VETROTEX]**

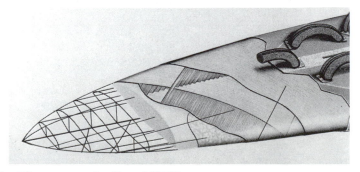

Figure 5.226 · Filament-wound sailboard **[JAD]**

Figure 5.227 · All-composite catamaran hull (Jet Service, 18m-long) **[VETROTEX]**

5.16   APPENDIX 5

Alphabetical List of Processing Equipment Suppliers - United States

AAA	DRYPOLL
ACCURATIO	DUPLEX
ACCUSNET	EEMCO
ADMIRAL/UPJOHN	EMHART
AKRON EXTRUDER	ERIC
AMESBURY	EX - CELL - O
AMUT	EXTRUDYNE
ARMAC	FARREL/ANSONIA/EMHART
BAKER-PERKINS	FJELLMAN
BELOIT	FMC
BELOIT	FRENCH
BRABENDER, C.W.	GLOUCESTER/GLOENCO
BRAMPTON	HESTA
CANNON	HOOVER/UNILOY/UNIVERSAL
CARVER	HPM/KOERING/PRODEX
CINCINNATI-MILACRON	IMPLANTI
CLIFTON	IRWIN
DAKE	JACO
DAVIS STANDARD	JOMAR
DEACON	KANNEGIESSER

KILLION
KOSTUR
LYLE
MAS
MAUSER
MCNEIL
AKRON/EMS/FEMCO/ROTOCAST
NATIONAL RUBBER MACHINERY
(NRM)
NEWBURY/IMPCO
NRM
PATHEX
PENNWALT
PLASTI-VAC (PVI)
POLYMER MACHINERY
PTA - SWEETS
PU TECHNOLOGY
R & B TOOL
RAINVILLE
REED - PRENTICE
RIET
ROCHELEAU/ROSADE

ROMMELAG
ROTODYNE
ROTOTRON
SANO
SAUM
SCHIESSER
SENTINEL
SHUMAN
STERLING/STERLCO
STOKES - PENNWALT
SYBRON
TYLER
VERSON
WABASH - STERLCO
WABASH/STERLCO
WELDING ENGINEERS (WE)
WELEX
WHEATON
WILLIAMS/WHITE
WINDSOR/KLOCKNER - FERROMATIK
ZED

Outside the U.S.

ADS
ALPINE
ANDOUART
ARBURG
AUTOMA
BARMAG
BATTENFELD
BAUSANO
BEKUM
BERSTORFF
BIPEL
BOY
BROWN
J./LEESONA/EGAN/CUMBERLAND
BUCHER-GUYER
BUSS-CONDUX
CREUSOT-LOIRE/SOMI
DANIELS
DESMA
DIEFFENBACHER
DK-CODIM
DOLCI
DSM
ELASTOGRAN

ENGEL
EPCO
GABLER
HARTIG
HAYSSEN
HENNECKE
HENSCHEL
HUSKY
ILLIG
JOHNSON
JAPAN STEEL WORKS (JSW)
KAUTEX
KAWAGUCHI
KIEFEL P.
KLOCKNER-FERROMATIK
KRAUS-MAFFEI
LEISTRITZ
MAILLEFER
METALMECCANICA
MIR
MORIYAMA
NEGRI BOSSI
NIIGATA
NISSEI

OMIPA
PLACO
PLASTIMAC
REIFENHAUSER
REINHARDT
REP
SAMAFOR
SANDRETTO
SCHULER

SMTP-BILLION/KAUFMAN/SIDEL
THYSSEN
TOSHIBA
TRIULZI
TROESTER
VOITH-FISCHER
WERNER-PFLEIDERER
WINDMOELLER-HOELSCHER

Processing Equipment Suppliers (by Technique)

►EXTRUSION (section 5.2)
GLOUCESTER/GLOENCO
STERLING/STERLCO
FARREL/ANSONIA/EMHART
EGAN/LEESONA/J. BROWN
NRM
WELEX
HPM/KOERING/PRODEX
KILLION
EXTRUDYNE
WE
DK - CODIM
KAUFMAN - SMTP
MAILLEFER
BUSS - CONDUX
TROESTER
BERSTORFF
HARTIG
WERNER - PFLEIDERER
REIFENHAUSER/NABCO
KRAUSS - MAFFEI
OMIPA
TOSHIBA
SAMAFOR
ANDOUART
THYSSEN
LEISTRITZ
DAVIS - STANDARD
BAUSANO
AKRON EXTRUDER
BATTENFELD
AMUT
BAKER - PERKINS
SCHIESSER

►EXTRUSION COVERING (section 5.3)
STERLING

SANO
REIFENHAUSER/VAN DORN
KILLION
HPM
DAVIS STANDARD
BRAMPTON
BRABENDER C.W.
BATTENFELD/PURNELL

►FILM BLOWING (section 5.4)
BARMAG
ALPINE
GLOUCESTER/BATTENFELD
DOLCI/FMC
KAUFMAN/SMTP
REIFENHAUSER/STEIGLER
WINDMOELLER & HOELSCHER
KIEFEL, P.
PLACO
EGAN/BROWN
DAVIS - STANDARD

►CALENDERING (section 5.5)
BERSTORFF
FARREL
EMHART
GLOENCO

►SHEET THERMOFORMING (section 5.6)
BROWN/LEESONA
SHUMAN
AAA
PVI
KOSTUR
ZED
FMC
GLOUCESTER

SENTINEL
HAYSSEN
IRWIN
DRYPOLL
RIET
TRIULZI
LYLE
ARMAC
ILLIG
GABLER
KIEFEL, P.

►BLOW MOLDING (section 5.7)

Extrusion blow molding

HOOVER/UNILOY/UNIVERSAL
NRM
GLOUCESTER/GLOENCO
ROCHELEAU/ROSADE
R & B TOOL
BEKUM
KAUTEX/KRUPP
HAYSSEN
HARTIG/MIDLAND -
ROSS/SOMERSET/WALDRON
VOITH - FISCHER/BATTENFELD
SIDEL/SMTP
BROWN/LEESONA
AUTOMA
STERLING
MAUSER
BELOIT
HESTA
ROMMELAG

Injection blow molding

NISSEI
HOOVER - RAINVILLE
SAUM
JOMAR
BEKUM
WHEATON
FARRELL

Injection - stretch blow molding

CINCINNATI - MILACRON

NISSEI
RAINVILLE
ADS
HUSKY

►ROTATIONAL MOLDING (section 5.9)
MCNEIL
AKRON/EMS/FEMCO/ROTOCAST
SYBRON
ROTODYNE
ROTOTRON
REINHARDT

►COMPRESSION MOLDING (section 5.11)
DIEFFENBACHER
PATHEX
EEMCO
DAKE
BIPEL
CARVER
WABASH/STERLCO
DANIELS/BROWN
SCHULER
ERIC
WILLIAMS/WHITE
VERSON

►TRANSFER MOLDING (section 5.12)
POLYMER MACHINERY
FRENCH
FJELLMAN
DAKE
DANIELS/BROWN
CLIFTON
STOKES - PENNWALT
WABASH - STERLCO

►INJECTION MOLDING (section 5.13)

Thermoplastics

REED - PRENTICE
CINCINNATI - MILACRON
NEGRI -
BOSSI/LEESONA/BROWN/EPCO
NEWBURY/IMPCO
BELOIT
BOY
DEACON

DUPLEX
FARREL EMHART
NATCO
ENGEL
HUSKY
CREUSOT - LOIRE/SOMI
BILLION - SMTP
NISSEI
NIIGATA
KAWAGUCHI
WINDSOR/KLOCKNER - FERROMATIK
BATTENFELD
ARBURG
KRAUSS - MAFFEI
JACO
VAN DORN
REIFENHAUSER
JSW
SANDRETTO
PLASTIMAC
DSM
METALMECCANICA
TRIULZI

Thermosets

PENNWALT
BILLION
FARREL
BUCHER - GUYER
BATTENFELD/BERGES
BIPEL

Rubbers

DESMA/KLOCKNER - FERROMATIK
WERNER - PFLEIDERER
REP
MAS
DANIELS BROWN

Structural foam

BATTENFELD

►REACTION INJECTION MOLDING
(section 5.14)

BATTENFELD
DESMA
KRAUSS - MAFFEI
HENNECKE/BAYER/MOBAY
ELASTOGRAN/BASF/EMB
CINCINNATI - MILACRON
CANNON
ADMIRAL/UPJOHN
PTA - SWEETS
ACCURATIO
AMESBURY
PU TECHNOLOGY
KANNEGIESSER
TYLER
ACCUSNET
EX - CELL - O
IMPLANTI
REINHARDT

Chapter 6

APPLICATIONS

6.1 INTRODUCTION

Applications of polymeric materials (plastics, rubbers, or composites) are numerous and steadily growing. Many applications are mentioned throughout Chapters 3, 4, and 5.

Conventional breakdowns by types of applications (or markets), for polymeric materials, often include packaging (adhesives, containers/lids/closures, coatings, films and sheets); building/construction; electrical/electronics; transportation (land, air, space); housewares; furniture; appliances (major, small, radio, TV), and toys.

Other categories are sometimes added or substituted, such as consumer/institutional products, agriculture, corrosion-resistant equipment, and aircraft/aerospace/military.

Specialized markets that often involve interesting products include, for example, recreational products and health/medical products.

A thorough review of all types of applications is clearly impossible in a single textbook. Instead, the author has chosen to discuss, in some depth, two distinct topics.

First, a modern recreational product, the sailboard, is considered, which is viewed as a remarkable example of the variety of polymeric materials and processing techniques that have been commercially used for its fabrication. The discussion of this topic is largely self-contained and does not require prior knowledge of other sections of this book.

Second, a product that everybody is familiar with, the automobile, is reviewed for its polymeric components. This section is written for those who are already quite familiar with the rest of the book (particularly Chapters 3 and 6), and thus makes use of a number of abbreviations for materials and processes to lighten the text.

The last section of this chapter discusses some basic considerations associated with the design of polymer-based products.

6.2   A CASE STUDY: THE SAILBOARD

6.2.1   Introduction

The sailboard is an increasingly popular recreational product. The board itself, the major component of the sailboard, is a particularly good example of the variety of materials and processing techniques that can be successfully used to make a polymer-based product. As most other components of sailboards are also based on polymers, a comprehensive discussion of the sailboard system provides a good opportunity to illustrate concretely the use of polymeric materials and processes.

The origin of sailboarding has been traced back to the 1920s in France and the early 1960s in the United States (Darby), but it is really in the late 1960s that Drake and Schweitzer developed in California the global system that is still generally in use. "Windsurfer" is a tradename associated with the company formed by Schweitzer, while "sailboard" is the most commonly used general name.

The principal components of a sailboard system are illustrated in Figure 6.1.   An all-purpose board (float) is about 4 m ($\approx$ 12 ft) long and 70 cm ($\approx$ 27 in) wide; it weighs about 20 kg ($\approx$ 43 lb) for a volume of about 200 l ($\approx$ 2.2 ft^3). It always consists of a shell whose upper part (topside) forms the deck and lower part (underside) forms the hull. The shell is normally filled with a lightweight cellular material (foam) that imparts rigidity and buoyancy. The deck must have a nonskid surface either molded in or subsequently applied as a coating and must be resistant to severe impact loading from the mast-wishbone system in particular. The hull can have quite a variety of shapes (flat, rounded, V-shaped, partly concave, channeled, etc.); it must be resistant to the impact of concentrated loads (rocks) or distributed loads (waves) and must have a smooth, abrasion resistant surface (sand, etc.). The entire shell must be resistant to weathering under severe sun exposure.

Many different polymer types have been used by companies around the world to make board shells, in conjunction with many different processing techniques. Economic and technical considerations are involved in the choice of material and process, with some combinations more suited to high performance boards and others better for recreational models. Many companies have offered a line of boards manufactured by different material-process combinations.

Board shells are most commonly manufactured either as two separate half shells that are subsequently fastened or bonded together, or as a single hollow part (one-piece shell). In the first case, the cellular material can be formed separately as a block of suitable shape and inserted between the halves, or it can be foamed in place after closing the half shells. In the second case, the cellular material must be foamed in place.

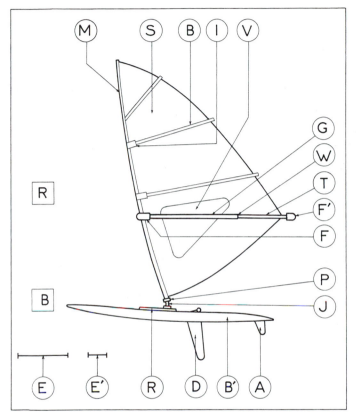

Figure 6.1 · **Sailboard elements** · [R] Rig; [F] Float (board); (E) 1 m-scale; (E′) 1 ft-scale; (M) Mast; (S) Sail; (B) Batten; (I) Camber inducer; (V) Window; (G) Boom grip; (W) Wishbone (boom); (T) Boom tube; (F′) Rear boom fitting; (F) Front boom fitting; (P) Mast foot; (J) Swivel joint; (A) Skeg; (B′) Board; (D) Retractable centerboard; (R) AST track

6.2.2 Board Materials

Resins

Polymeric resins used in the commercial fabrication of boards involve both thermoplastics and thermosetting resins.

Thermoplastics include resins such as polystyrene (PS), polycarbonate (PC), acrylonitrile-butadiene-styrene (ABS) and acrylonitrile-styrene-acrylic (ASA)

copolymers and alloys, polyethylene (PE) and polypropylene (PP). Thermosetting resins, which include polyurethane (PU) resins, epoxy (EP) resins, and unsaturated polyester (UP) resins, undergo a chemical reaction (curing) during processing.

The specific gravity of thermoplastic or thermosetting resins is approximately in the range 0.9-1.3, and their modulus (stiffness) is in the range 0.2-0.5 Mpsi (1.4-3.5 GPa).

Fiber Reinforcements

Continuous or relatively long fibers are used as reinforcement, primarily in conjunction with thermosetting resins. They include glass fibers, carbon/graphite fibers, and aramid fibers.

Glass fibers have the highest specific gravity ($\approx$ 2.5) and the lowest modulus (stiffness) ($\approx$ 10 Mpsi or 70 GPa), but they are also much cheaper than the others.

Carbon/graphite fibers have a lower specific gravity ($\approx$ 1.8) and a high modulus (40-60 Mpsi or 275-420 GPa).

Aramid fibers have an even lower specific gravity and an intermediate modulus; they are often referred to under the tradename Kevlar (DuPont).

6.2.3   Board Fabrication Methods

The following comprehensive survey of the major fabrication methods, used by a wide variety of manufacturers since the early 1970s, includes rotational molding, thermoforming, injection molding, and blow molding, that are associated with thermoplastic resins, and a number of fabrication techniques which use composite materials, that is, combinations of thermosetting resins and reinforcing fibers.

Appendix 6 features a list of materials and associated sailboard manufacturers and distributors, which corresponds to the early 1980s, a period that saw a peak for the variety of materials and fabrication methods used concurrently.

6.2.3.1   Thermoplastic-Based Fabrication

Rotational Molding

The rotational molding technique (Fig. 6.2) involves a two-part mold often made of a thermally conductive metal such as aluminum. The wall thickness of the mold is normally small to facilitate heat transfer, and mold rigidity is achieved through ribs or an external frame. A load of powdered thermoplastic resin, most commonly polyethylene, is placed in the mold. The mold is then closed and mounted in a device which allows its slow rotation around the board axis, as well as a 10-20° longitudinal

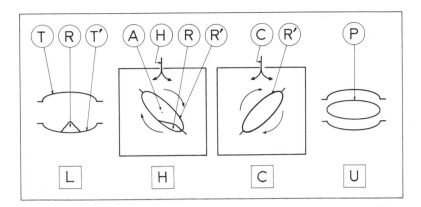

Figure 6.2 · **Sailboard - rotational molding** · [L] Loading; [H] Heating; [C] Cooling; [U] Unloading; (T),(T′) Mold halves; (R) Powdered resin; (A) Axis of rotation; (H) Heating medium; (R′) Fused resin; (C) Cooling medium; (R″) Solidified resin; (P) Product (one-piece shell)

rocking motion. The assembly is placed in a chamber that is first heated by steam, fuel burning, or electrical power. Heat conduction, through the wall of the mold, raises the inner mold surface temperature to the point where thermoplastic resin particles, brought in contact with it by the rotation, fuse and adhere to form a continuous layer of resin. Further heat conduction through the less conductive resin layer leads to a uniform thickness increase until the entire resin load is consumed. The chamber is subsequently cooled, by water jets, for example, to cause the solidification of the resin layer. The final product is a seamless one-piece shell, which is then filled with expanded polyurethane foam, as discussed later.

The sequential introduction of different resin systems can be used to form a multilayered shell structure, featuring, for example, fiber reinforcement or a cellular structure beneath the outer surface layer. It is also possible to induce cross-linking of the polyethylene to improve its temperature resistance in particular. The rotational molding technique was the original commercial method for board production (Windsurfer).

Thermoforming

A simple thermoforming technique (Fig. 6.3) first involves the heating, between infrared heaters, of an extruded plastic sheet held in a frame. The softened elastic sheet is first slightly inflated (prestretched) and then formed (retracted) over a cooled positive (male) mold with the help of a vacuum. After solidification and suitable trimming around the periphery, the resulting half shell can be bonded to a matching half shell, usually through adhesives, and the resulting full shell is subsequently filled

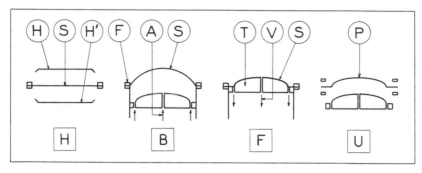

Figure 6.3 · **Sailboard - thermoforming** · [H] Heating; [B] Blowing; [F] Forming; (H),(H′) Heaters; (S) Plastic sheet; (F) Clamping frame; (A) Air pressure; (T) Positive mold; (V) Vacuum; (P) Product (half shell)

with expanded polyurethane. It should be noted that the external surface of the shell does not come in contact with the mold, which thus does not need a good finish and can be rather inexpensive. The introduction of this technique led to major production cost reductions and the rapid expansion of the sport in Europe in the late 1970s, illustrated by the success of the Dufour Wing, for example. ABS resins, and now ASA resins, which have a better resistance to outdoor exposure (i.e., weathering), have been used primarily for their good combination of processability, surface finish, rigidity, and impact resistance.

A currently popular thermoforming-based method, sometimes referred to as dual thermoforming (Fig. 6.4), involves the simultaneous forming of two matching half

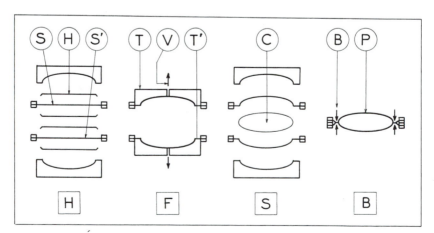

Figure 6.4 · **Sailboard - dual thermoforming** · [H] Heating; [F] Forming; [S] Core insertion; [B] Bonding; (S) First sheet; (H) Heating panel; (S′) Second sheet; (T),(T′) Negative molds; (C) Foam core; (B) Peripheral bond; (P) Product (finished board)

shells into cooled negative (female) molds, the rapid insertion of a molded foam core and the peripheral pressure-bonding of the half shells while they are still hot. The method requires more costly surface-finished molds, as well as complex processing equipment. The cores, usually of the expanded polystyrene type, must be molded separately, as discussed later.

The sheets used for thermoforming techniques are produced by an extrusion process (Fig. 6.5). Particles of the thermoplastic material are fed to a screw, rotating in a heated barrel, which causes their melting, pressurization, and conveying into an extruding die. The molten plastic, emerging from the die outlet slit, is passed between cooled polished rolls to give it a glossy finish, and then into a final cooling bath.

A modification of the process, referred to as coextrusion (Fig. 6.6), permits the formation of sheets consisting of layers of distinct materials fed by separate extruders.

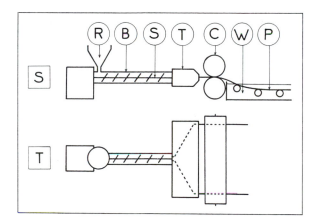

Figure 6.5 · **Sailboard - sheet extrusion** · [S] Sideview; [T] Topview; (R) Resin feed; (B) Barrel; (S) Screw; (T) Die; (C) Finishing rolls; (W) Cooling bath; (P) Product (blank for thermoforming)

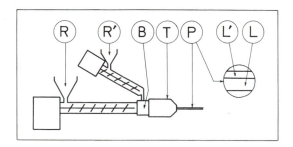

Figure 6.6 · **Sailboard - sheet coextrusion** · (R) Substrate resin; (R') Skin resin; (B) Combining feedblock; (T) Die; (L) Substrate layer; (L') Skin layer; (P) Product (blank for thermoforming)

Coextruded sheets can feature an outer layer (skin) that is particularly resistant to weathering, abrasion, and impact, while the substrate layer confers rigidity at a moderate cost. Polycarbonate (skin) and ABS (substrate) are used as coextruded sheets in commercial board shells.

Injection Molding

Injection molding of thermoplastics is a process characterized by the very fast production of complex and accurate parts. It involves plastication, injection and ejection stages as illustrated in Figure 6.7. The rapid expansion of the sailboard market in Europe in the early 1980s suggested that a mass-produced board would justify the heavy development and capital costs. Several companies conducted extensive studies of the process, but it appears that only one commercial model, the Dufour Sun,

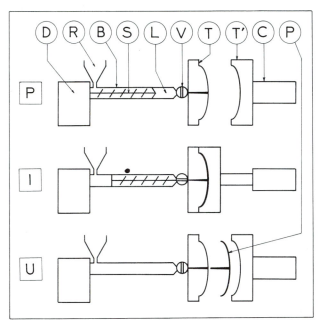

Figure 6.7 · **Sailboard - injection molding** · [P] Plastication; [I] Injection; [U] Unloading; (D) Screw drive; (R) Resin feed; (B) Barrel; (S) Screw; (L) Injection load; (V) Valve; (T),(T') Single cavity mold halves; (C) Mold clamping system; (P) Product (half shell)

was ever marketed. The two half shells, as well as a structural insert, in lieu of a foam core, were molded simultaneously (Fig. 6.8). The very large mold dimensions, and the high injection pressure needed, called for the use of the largest injection machine available, a 10,000-ton-capacity press. Polypropylene was the resin chosen, probably for its moldability, dimensional stability, and moderate cost.

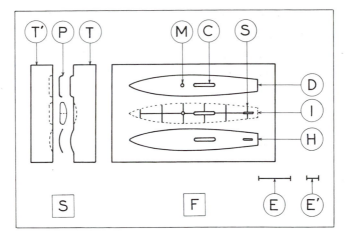

Figure 6.8 · **Sailboard - injection mold** · [S] Mold sideview; [F] Mold front view; (E) 1 m-scale; (E′) 1 ft-scale; (T),(T′) Mold halves; (M) Mastfoot socket; (C) Centerboard well; (S) Skeg box; (D) Deck; (I) Insert; (H) Hull; (P) Product (all board elements)

Blow Molding

The blow molding process (Fig. 6.9) is widely used to make hollow containers. An extruder and an annular extrusion die are used for the vertical downward extrusion of a tubular preform called the "parison." The hot parison is pinched, at the top and the bottom, between the two halves of a mold. Air pressure is then applied through a pipe port to inflate the parison until it conforms to the shape of the cooled mold. After solidification of the plastic, the hollow seamless shell is extracted, to be subsequently filled with expanded polyurethane. Polyethylene is most commonly used for the blow molding of boards. The process is associated with large capital costs but fast production rates. The exceptionally long parison involved, represents a major challenge for resin and equipment specialists.

6.2.3.2 Composite-Based Fabrication

Several manufacturing techniques involve the combination of reinforcing fibers with thermosetting resins: the resulting material is termed a "composite." The fibers discussed earlier under "Materials" are used as unidirectional reinforcement (roving) or as multidirectional reinforcement (mat, woven cloth, etc.)

Many techniques have been used commercially for the production of composite sailboards. Three distinct methods are discussed below that correspond to different investments and production rate potentials. They are referred to here, in short, as "contact molding," custom building, and resin transfer molding.

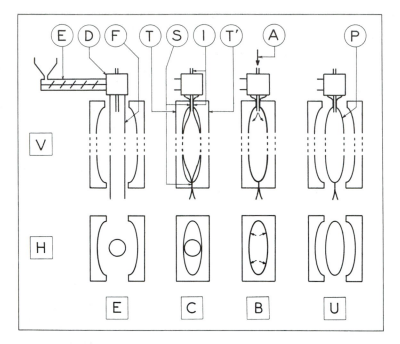

Figure 6.9 · **Sailboard - blow molding** · [V] Vertical section; [H] Horizontal section; [E]Extrusion; [C] Mold closing; [B] Blowing; [U] Unloading; (E) Extruder; (D) Die; (F) Parison; (T),(T′) Mold halves; (S) Pinch areas; (I) Air injection pipe; (A) Air pressure; (P) Product (one-piece shell)

Contact Molding

The method referred to here as "contact molding" (Fig. 6.10) is well suited to the fabrication of a limited number of units. Two half shells are made independently in

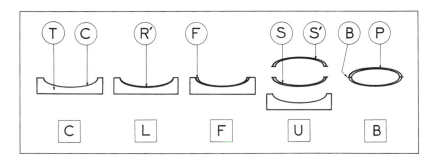

Figure 6.10 · **Sailboard - contact molding** · [C] Gel coating; [L] Laminating; [F] Pre-foaming; [U] Unloading; [B] Bonding; (T) Mold; (C) Gelcoat; (R′) Resin and reinforcement; (F) Dense foam; (S) half shell; (S′) Matching half shell; (B) Bond; (P) Product (half-shells)

two molds that are often made of reinforced plastic molded over a pattern. A layer of catalyzed liquid resin, referred to as the "gelcoat," is first applied on the mold surface, which is pre-treated with a release agent. After suitable hardening of the gelcoat, the resin-impregnated reinforcement is applied all over the mold surface in a suitable pattern, and properly compacted. After hardening, a layer of dense expanded polyurethane is often applied around the edge to facilitate the subsequent bonding of matching half shells. Core filling with lighter polyurethane foam is the final step. The technique is quite labor-intensive, and the need to keep the resin in a fluid state during the building process is associated with long curing times, unless heat can be used to speed up the reaction.

Custom Building

The method of custom building (Fig. 6.11) is particularly suited to the fabrication of a single unit or prototype. A block of rigid foam, usually the polyurethane type, is carved to the intended board shape with the help of suitable precut gauges. Fiber reinforcement, impregnated with a liquid catalyzed resin that is often of the polyester type, is placed around the shape in the desired configuration. Multidirectional fabric or long fiber mat is normally used all over, but unidirectional roving can be added at suitable locations and in appropriate directions to maximize the strength and stiffness. The impregnated reinforcement is compacted and smoothed out before a finishing impregnated mat is applied. After the resin has hardened at room temperature, the surface is sanded to smooth out imperfections. A suitable protective and decorative resin coating is subsequently applied as the last step. This labor-intensive method is used primarily to construct short sinker-type boards that do not feature the relatively complex centerboard well. It is the most suitable fabrication method for amateurs.

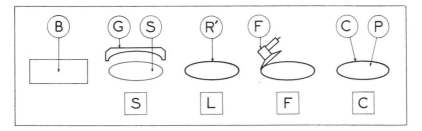

Figure 6.11 · **Sailboard - custom building** · [S] Shaping; [L] Laminating; [F] Finishing; [C] Coating; (B) Foam block; (G) Template; (S) Shape; (R′) Resin and reinforcement; (F) Finishing tool; (C) Final coating; (P) Product (finished board)

Resin Transfer Molding

The process of resin transfer molding (Fig. 6.12) requires a larger investment and is intended for relatively large-production runs. The starting point is a molded foam core around which nonimpregnated reinforcement is wrapped or positioned at specific locations. The wrapped core is then placed in a slightly oversized mold. A catalyzed liquid resin, dispensed by a fast-mixing device, and often preheated, is injected at suitable points in the gap between core and mold, while a vacuum is pulled at suitable vent points. The liquid resin travels through the reinforcement and eventually impregnates it thoroughly. Hardening can be quite rapid, particularly if the mold is heated. The final product is a seamless board with the exact shape of the mold. It may be noted that polyester resins cannot be used with polystyrene foam since they contain styrene monomer which would dissolve polystyrene; epoxy resins are compatible with polystyrene foam. Of historical interest is a board that featured continuous reinforcement wrapped around a foam core by a sophisticated filament winding process (JAD-Aerospatiale) with, presumably, subsequent resin transfer molding.

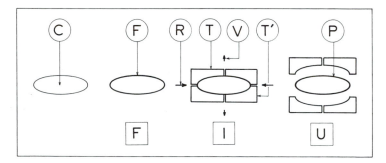

Figure 6.12 · **Sailboard - resin transfer molding** · [F] Reinforcement placement; [I] Injection; [U] Unloading; (C) Molded foam core; (F) Fiber reinforcement; (T),(T′) Mold halves; (R) Resin injection; (V) Vents; (P) Product (finished board)

Simple resin transfer molding does not normally give a perfect surface finish and the presence of reinforcement very near the surface tends to make it impact- and abrasion-sensitive. Thermoforming combined with resin transfer molding (Fig. 6.13) involves the same initial step of wrapping a molded foam core with nonimpregnated reinforcement; however, at the time of insertion into the resin transfer mold, two independently thermoformed thermoplastic liners are placed between the mold surface and the reinforcement. Resin injection takes place between the liner and the foam core. The liner becomes an impact- and abrasion-resistant skin that also imparts a good finish to the final product. Good adhesion between the skin and the underlying resin is, of course, essential.

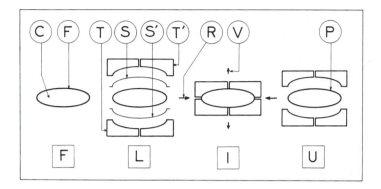

Figure 6.13 · Sailboard - thermoforming/resin transfer molding · [F] Reinforcement placement; [L] Loading; [I] Injection; [U] Unloading; (C) Foam core; (F) Fiber reinforcement; (T),(T′) Mold halves; (S),(S′) Thermoformed sheets; (R) Resin injection; (V) Vents; (P) Product (finished board)

6.2.3.3 Foam Core Formation

The techniques discussed above for the fabrication of sailboards involve two distinct methods of formation of foam cores. In one method, a finished shell is filled with foam that is normally of the expanded polyurethane type. In the other method, the foam core is first molded to shape and a shell is subsequently formed or fitted around it; either expanded polyurethane (EPU) or expanded polystyrene (EPS) can be used in this case. In the following, the filling of a shell with EPU is first described; the molding of EPU as a core would be similar, except for the absence of the shell and the use of a mold release agent. The molding of an EPS core, a very different process, is then discussed.

Expanded Polyurethane Shell Filling

Expanded polyurethane shell filling (Fig. 6.14) may involve the injection of a relatively small amount of a liquid reactive thermosetting urethane resin system in the shell constrained by a mold. A gas is liberated by the reaction, the decomposition of a chemical blowing agent, or the vaporization of a physical blowing agent, and the foam gradually rises and hardens. The process may also involve the incorporation of a physical blowing agent such as nitrogen, under high pressure, followed by the transfer of the fluid foam into the cavity. In both cases, a denser skin may result where the foam contacts the shell, or when it contacts the mold surface in the case of core molding.

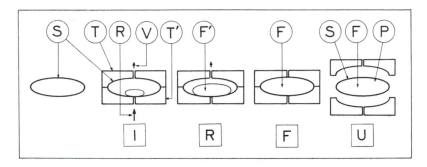

Figure 6.14 · **Sailboard - expanded polyurethane shell filling** · [I] Injection; [R] Foam rise; [F] Final foaming; [U] Unloading; (S) Board Shell; (T),(T′) Constraining mold; (R) Liquid resin injection; (V) Vents; (F′) Rising foam; (F) Final foam; (P) Product (finished board)

Expanded Polystyrene Core Molding

Expanded polystyrene core molding (Fig. 6.15) starts with tiny compact beads of thermoplastic polystyrene containing a dissolved, but volatile, physical blowing agent such as pentane. The beads are first preexpanded through the application of heat, which softens the polystyrene and vaporizes the blowing agent, but leaves them free running. A suitable mold is then filled with preexpanded beads, and steam is passed through the system to complete the expansion and to fuse the beads together.

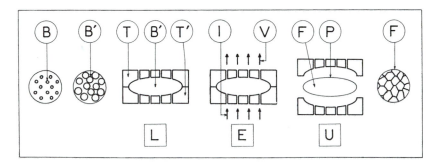

Figure 6.15 · **Sailboard - expanded polystyrene core molding** · [L] Loading; [E] Expansion; [U] Unloading; (B) Expandable beads; (B′) Pre-expanded beads; (T),(T′) Mold halves; (I) Steam injection; (V) Vents; (F) Final bead configuration; (P) Product (core for dual thermoforming, resin transfer molding or custom building)

6.2.4 Other Sailboard Elements

Most other components of the entire sailboard system are made entirely or primarily of polymeric materials.

6.2.4.1 Centerboard, Skeg

Directly associated with the board itself, the centerboard used to be of the sliding type (sabre daggerboard); it now pivots (semiretractable to fully retractable types) in the centerboard well, which is normally a separate injection molded part fastened to the board. Centerboards have been made of solid or laminated wood, aluminum, or composite material with glass or carbon reinforcement, but most commonly they are injection molded of a thermoplastic resin. Many centerboards have been made of polypropylene, which has the interesting advantage of good flotation in water. Other thermoplastics cited are polyethylene, polystyrene, polyamide, and ASA. The structural foam injection process has been used also for lighter products.

At the tail part of the board, a skeg provides directional stability. Opaque skegs are often molded from polyamide or polypropylene, while transparent ones are generally molded from polycarbonate. High-performance short boards do not have a centerboard, and their skegs are sometimes made of laminated composite for maximum rigidity. Interchangeable skegs are fastened to a molded skegbox that is permanently fitted to the board.

6.2.4.2 Mast

The mast must be light and relatively flexible as it is significantly curved when a modern sail is hauled. It has to be strong to resist severe impacts during falls and very high bending stresses in strong winds. It is now always hollow and tapered. Some high-performance masts are made of aluminum alloys, but the vast majority are made from composites of epoxy resin and glass fiber, occasionally supplemented by carbon fibers. A typical construction involves a circumferentially wound inner layer, a middle layer with longitudinal reinforcement, and a circumferentially wound outer layer. Such construction provides good longitudinal rigidity and lateral crushing or buckling resistance.

6.2.4.3 Mastfoot, Track

The low end of the mast is connected to the board through a complex device (mastfoot) that allows the sail system to swivel freely over the deck of the board. The key element of the mast foot is either a mechanical joint, generally featuring molded plastic parts and metal pins, or the now more common hourglass-shaped elastomeric joint.   The latter joint involves conventional rubber (such as neoprene), or polyurethane, which is strongly bonded to metal plates, using established rubber mounts technology; the plates are, in turn, fastened to the plastic elements of the mastfoot. A third system, using a flexible polyurethane rod-shaped element, primarily subjected to tension, (tendon) was also used. In all cases, the mastfoot design must allow free rotation of the mast around its axis.

In most cases, the point of attachment of the mastfoot on the board is now longitudinally adjustable along a mastfoot track, with a mechanism allowing shifting to different positions during sailing. Another mechanism generally allows the safety release of the mast-board connection. The track and mechanisms, which previously featured anodized aluminum elements, are now increasingly made almost entirely of plastics.

6.2.4.4 Sail

Modern high performance sails involve a complex construction. The characteristic airfoil shape is achieved by a suitable assembly of precisely cut panels, with the frequent use of battens and other devices to control the camber.

The sleeve (boot, sock) for the attachment to the mast, and the foil itself, involve woven sailcloth (generally based on polyester fibers) and, increasingly, laminates of woven sailcloth with a polyester film (Mylar) to reduce air permeation and sail distortion.

The window is commonly made of plasticized PVC, although thin polyester films, laminated with a loose grid of fibers (scrim construction), can be significantly lighter.

Lightweight battens are often made of unidirectional fiber composite by a pultrusion process. They are fitted in pockets and sometimes used in conjunction with molded plastic camber inducers on the mast side.

6.2.4.5 Wishbone

An essential part of the sailboard rig is the double boom (wishbone), which has a symmetrical tear-drop shape.

The wishbone, originally made of laminated wood, now almost always features two anodized aluminum alloy tubes of circular cross-section. The aluminum tubes must be partially coated or covered with a soft sleeve (sheathing) to provide a good and comfortable handgrip. Rubber (neoprene), plasticized PVC or polyurethane, in compact or cellular form, have been used for this purpose.

On the mast side, the two tubes are connected through a front boom fitting, which has multiple functions. It serves to attach the boom to the mast through an in-haul line. It also features a handle, as well as the point of attachment of the up-haul rope (line), which can be used to lift the rig from the water. The front boom fitting used to be a rigid plastic part with added rubber bumpers. It is now increasingly molded from a relatively flexible plastic, such as a thermoplastic polyurethane, to reduce the stress concentration in the part itself and in the mast. The rear boom fitting serves as the hauling point for the sail outhaul. It sometimes incorporates pulleys and a clamcleat.

It is important to realize that small or relatively small plastic components are normally made by injection molding. This implies the fabrication of a rather costly mold (single- or multiple-cavity) for each component, and the use of an expensive injection molding machine. While the cost per part can be very low when tens of thousands are molded, it is prohibitive if only a few parts are needed.

The mastfoot involves a minimum of four distinct polymeric components and an all-polymer mastfoot track involves a minimum of eight such components. The total number of small distinct molded polymeric components in a modern sailboard is probably between 30 and 40.

The small, or relatively small, molded sailboard components are often made of tough engineering plastics such as toughened nylon or thermoplastic polyurethanes, or stiff short glass- fiber-reinforced plastics when impact resistance is not critical. Resistance to weathering is, of course, a major consideration.

Figures 6.16-6.29 show various applications of polymer technology in manufacturing of sailboards.

Figure 6.16 · Sailboarding, speed sailing [WINDSURF/R. MYERS]

Figure 6.17 · Sailboarding, wave jumping **[T. KING]**

Figure 6.18 · Board rotational molding, loading of a mold; (polyethylene HDPE) **[TEN CATE]**

Figure 6.19 · Board rotational molding, mold closing **[TEN CATE]**

Figure 6.20 • Board thermoforming, positive mold and thermoplastic sheet (ABS resin) **[PLASTIQUES-OUEST]**

Figure 6.21 • Board thermoforming, sheet formed over mold **[PLASTIQUES-OUEST]**

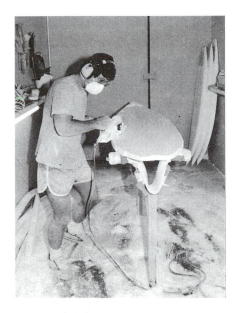

Figure 6.22 • Board blow molding, downward extrusion of tubular preform between mold halves (polyethylene HDPE) **[HIFLY]**

Figure 6.23 • Board custom building, shaping of a foam core (polyurethane PU) **[SEATREND/T.KING]**

Fig. 6.24

Fig. 6.25

Figure 6.24 · Board shell foam filling, injection of the fluid resin (polyurethane PU)

Figure 6.25 · Mechanical mast/board swivel joint (injection molded thermoplastic components) **[TEN CATE]**

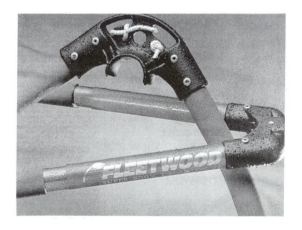

Fig. 6.26

Fig. 6.27

Figure 6.26 · Wishbone, front and rear boom fittings (injection molded thermoplastic) **[FLEETWOOD]**

Figure 6.27 · Hourglass-shaped elastomeric mast/board swivel joint (compression molded and metal-bonded rubber)

Fig. 6.28   Fig. 6.29

Figure 6.28 · Centerboard (injection molded thermoplastic such as polypropylene PP) Two piece centerboard well (injection molded thermoplastic such as ABS RESIN)

Figure 6.29 · Fins (injection molded polycarbonate PC) Fin box (injection molded thermoplastic such as ABS resin)

6.3   A FOCUSED SURVEY: AUTOMOTIVE PRODUCTS

6.3.1   Introduction

Plastics and rubbers have long been used in the automotive industry for such applications as electrical insulation and flexible elements, but in the past two or three decades in particular, their use has grown considerably in volume and sophistication.

This section presents a systematic review of important elements of an automobile to illustrate the increasingly important role played by polymeric materials (plastics, rubbers, and composites). This review is preceded by some background information on volumes and patterns of use of polymeric materials in automotive applications.

Data on volumes and patterns of use of polymeric materials in automotive applications occasionally appear in technical publications. They are based on information released by material suppliers or automobile manufacturers. Since many factors and variables are involved, such data can be seen as having only a rough indicative value.

When assessing the extent and growth of the usage of polymeric materials in automobiles, it is important to bear in mind the general downsizing trend that has been so significant for North American cars over the past decade. The 1985 representative (average) car weight was about 3200 lb ($\approx$ 1450 kg), and it is expected to drop further to about 3050 lb ($\approx$ 1390 kg) in 1990 and about 2850 lb ($\approx$ 1300 kg) in 1995.

In absolute terms, automotive usage of polymeric materials in general, and plastics in particular, has grown rapidly over the past decade. Representative data or predictions for North American cars are as follows: 1970: about 75 lb ($\approx$ 35 kg); 1975: about 110 lb ($\approx$ 50 kg); 1980: about 165 lb ($\approx$ 75 kg); 1985: 180-275 lb ($\approx$ 80-125 kg); 1990: 250-450 lb ($\approx$ 100-200 kg); 1995: 275-650 lb ($\approx$ 125-300 kg). Such figures correspond to the following approximate weight percentages (wt%): 1985: about 6-9 wt%; 1990: about 8-15 wt%; 1995: about 10-23 wt%. On a volume basis, the figures are much higher since the specific gravity of polymeric materials, including composites, is roughly in the range of 1-2, while that of ferrous metals, for example, is around 7.5.

An automobile is made primarily of the following three classes of materials: metals, which comprise steel as formed sheets or machined parts, as well as cast iron and aluminum alloys; polymers (or organic materials), which include plastics, rubbers, paints, varnishes, and textiles; and finally glass. Representative weight-based percentages (wt%) for 1980 automobiles were as follows: steel (sheets): 45-55; steel (parts): $\approx$ 15; cast iron: 10-20; rubber: $\approx$ 5.5; plastics: $\approx$ 4.5; aluminum alloys: $\approx$ 1.5; textiles: $\approx$ 0.5. Through the 1990s, the relative use of cast iron is expected to decline most dramatically (perhaps by 50%), while the use of aluminum alloys and plastics could double and the use of glass and rubber would remain stable. Such conservative predictions do not appear to take into account any major breakthrough in the use of plastics and composites for vehicle frame, and body panels in particular.

The weight-based percentage of use of polymeric materials in automobiles can be broken down into plastics (about 40 wt%), elastomers, including tires (about 40 wt%), and paints and varnishes (about 15 wt%). Tires are estimated to account for about 80 wt% of the automotive elastomers.

The relative amounts of the various plastics used in automobiles can be significantly different in North American and European vehicles, for example, or for small and large vehicles. Representative figures in terms of weight-based percentage (wt%) were as follows for North American automobiles around 1980: PU: 21-24; PP: 18-25; FRP: 9.5-12; PVC: 10.5-18; PA: 3-7; ABS: 6-10.5; PE: 4-6; acrylics: 2-2.5; POM: $\approx$ 1.5; PF: 1-2; PC: $\approx$ 1.2; PAT: $\approx$ 1.5; PPO: $\approx$ 1.1.

It has been reported that a typical car of the 1970s contains about 1000 plastic parts, of which about one-half are different in design. About 80 n % (number-based percentage) of the parts are made by injection molding of thermoplastic resins; about

10 n % are produced in the form of sheet or film, and about 5 n % are made by extrusion or blow molding.

The automotive industry is still a relatively small user of plastics in terms of quantities. Figures cited indicate that only about 3-5 wt% of the total plastics consumption is associated with the automotive industry (about 0.7×10^6 tons out of a total of 20×10^6 tons in 1984). Automotive applications, however, are generally more technical and involve more added value than do those in the packaging or construction markets, which, together, consume almost 50% of the plastics produced.

6.3.2   Major Structural Elements

6.3.2.1   Body Frame

Automobiles previously were manufactured with a rigid and heavy metal chassis onto which the body was attached. Currently, most automobiles have a self-supporting body frame consisting of pressed and welded sheet metal onto which sheet metal body panels are attached. As indicated in the discussion of exterior components, polymeric body panels are rapidly being introduced. Following the rapid growth of the use of polymer-based composites in the aerospace industry, composites are being evaluated for body frames in the automotive industry.

Increasing concern for occupant's safety is associated with the search for a very resistant and undeformable occupant's space frame (box) (O), as shown in Figure 6.30, combined with front (E) and rear (E') end-frames that support functional elements

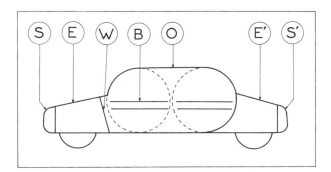

Figure 6.30 · **Automobile frame and related structural elements** · (S) Front shield; (E) Front end-frame; (W) Crash wall; (B) Lateral intrusion beam; (O) Occupants space frame; (E') Rear end-frame; (S') Rear shield

and can collapse in a controlled manner, in the case of a severe impact, with the maximum possible absorption of energy.

One promising avenue involves filament-wound composite occupant's space frames to which molded composite front and rear end-frames would be fastened. Wrap-around shields (bumpers) (S) and (S') attached to the front and rear end-frames, a crashwall (W), and composite lateral (door) intrusion beams (B) would complement the occupants protection.

Body frame molding is shown in figures 6.31-6.34.

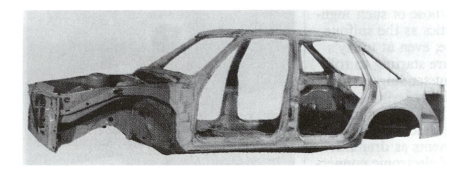

Figure 6.31 • Prototype composite frame subsequently bonded to steel underchassis. Frame consists of bonded RTM-fabricated elements (vinylester resin + glass fiber preforms) **[BUDD/CHRYSLER]**

Figure 6.32 • Elements of composite passenger cell molded from SMC (polyester resin + glass fiber) **[MENZOLIT]**

Figure 6.33 · Roadster-model floor pan molded from thermoplastic composite (thermoplastic + glass fiber mat) **[GE/BMW]**

Figure 6.34 · RTM-molded composite front cross-member for mini-van model (vinylester resin + glass fiber preform) **[FORD]**

6.3.2.2 Bumper System

Bumper systems are designed to meet two major mechanical constraints. They must show little or no sign of damage after a minor impact and must contribute adequately to a protection of the front or rear end integrity upon impact at speeds of 2.5 or 5 mph (≈ 4 or 8 km/h).

All-metal, chrome-plated bumper systems have been practically eliminated, and a variety of distinct designs involving polymeric materials have been introduced.

One of the first nonmetal bumpers systems was introduced in the 1960s (Renault 5) as an SMC "shield" with PU foam crush blocks. Many early designs in North America involved a metal beam with a flexible cover (e.g., **PU-RIM**), which sometimes extended to form the body front end and spoiler (flexible fascia).

The two-element, mixed materials construction is still widely used, with high-impact PP (HIPP) in particular, for the cover. The metal beam has sometimes been replaced by a lighter FRP pultruded beam.

The trend seems to be for all-plastic (integral) designs that are injection-molded from a variety of high performance resins capable of withstanding impacts even at low temperatures. These include PAT, PBT, A(PC/PBT), A(ABS/PC), PC, PA-6, HIPP, and ABS. Energy absorption is often achieved through the honeycomb-type design of a back element that is easily molded. Multicomponent box-beam systems can be assembled by friction or ultrasonic welding, as well as chemical bonding or electrofusion. Early examples include Ford Escort (PC/PBT), Austin Maestro (PAT), Mercedes (PP), and Peugeot (ABS).

Bumper system applications are shown in figures 6.35-6.39.

Figure 6.35 · R5-model (1972), bumper/shield (sheet molding compound SMC) [RENAULT]

Figure 6.36 · Auto fascia backing, molded energy absorbing honeycomb (EVA copolymer) [DU PONT]

Figure 6.37 · 928-model rear fascia (polyurethane UR foam/skin) [PORSCHE]

Figure 6.38 · Taurus/Sable-models rear bumper, mold on 4000 ton press **[FORD]**

Figure 6.39 · Mold for bumper element

6.3.2.3 *Suspension System*

The design of a good suspension system is a very complex problem; one basic rule is to try and minimize the unsprung weight.

A suspension system may be viewed as consisting of two elements (Fig. 6.40): the suspension mechanism (M), which controls the geometry of the wheel displacement, and the suspension unit (U), which controls the amplitude of the displacement and its damping. In some cases, the two elements may be indistinguishable.

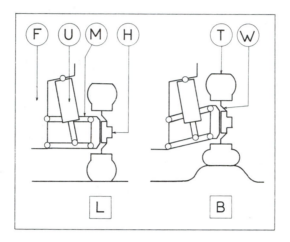

Figure 6.40 · **Automobile suspension system** · [L] Level ground; [B] Bump; (F) Vehicle frame; (U) Suspension unit; (M) Suspension mechanism; (H) Hub; (T) Tire; (W) Wheel

Traditionally, metals have been used almost exclusively for suspension elements, including the all-important springs.

Notable early exceptions include Citroen's pneumatic/hydraulic system, from the mid-1950s, which incorporates an important elastomeric element, as well as Austin in the 1960s with the Moulton system.

Once popular metal leaf springs were almost totally replaced by metal coil springs and torsion bars, but there is now much development going on with polymer-based composite (FRP) springs, spearheaded by General Motors (Corvette) in the early 1980s, with variable cross-section leaf springs made by special filament winding or pultrusion (pulforming) processes. Corrugated FRP springs, somewhat equivalent to coil springs in terms of their possible location, are being evaluated also.

It seems likely also that polymeric materials and their associated fabrication techniques will facilitate the implementation of sophisticated, yet inexpensive, pneumatic/hydraulic systems which have the best potential for comfort and road holding compromises.

See figures 6.41-6.43 for examples of polymer based suspension components.

Fig. 6.41

Fig. 6.42

Figure 6.41 · Front suspension element (epoxy-glass) **[VETROTEX]**

Figure 6.42 · Molded element of hydropneumatic suspension for CX and BX models (reinforced thermoplastic RTP) **[CITROEN]**

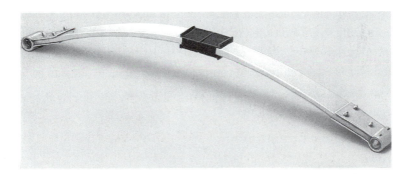

Figure 6.43 · Rear leaf spring on traffic-model van (epoxy-glass) **[RENAULT]**

6.3.2.4 *Vibration and Noise Control*

Engines are mounted on appropriate elements of the body frame through rubber mounts, normally consisting of a rubber block sandwich-bonded to two metal mounting plates. The viscoelasticity of the rubber and the geometry of the block are carefully designed to "filter" engine vibrations and noise. NR and CR rubbers are most commonly used for this purpose. Other noisy or vibrating elements, such as the exhaust system, are also "insulated" from the body frame through rubber mounts.

Undesirable sounds (noises) also have their origin in other elements of the vehicle (tires, cooling fan, vibrating panels, aerodynamic flow, etc.). Sound-deadening coatings, which previously was based on asphalt, increasingly involve polymers such as PVC, EVA, EPDM, and IIR, which are frequently combined with inorganic fillers.

In the interior, rubber floor mats or floor carpets and their backing material contribute to noise abatement, and it is expected that the introduction of polymer-based floor panels will have a favorable effect on noise reduction.

6.3.3   Powertrain and Underhood Elements

"Powertrain" is the term used here to designate the elements from engine to tires which serve to move and stop a car. Engine and transmission are major elements of the powertrain: the rest is referred to as the "driveline."

The engine compartment (underhood space) of modern downsized automobiles tends to be small and packed with the engine, as well as a large number of mechanical and other elements. The operation of modern high performance engines, and the exhaust system, generates much heat and, even with adequate cooling and ventilation, ambient temperatures of the order of about 200°C ($\approx$ 400°F) can be encountered. In addition, a variety of aggressive chemicals (gasoline, battery acid, detergents, antifreeze additives, etc.) can come in contact with components located in the engine compartment. In this review, various underhood components are discussed as part of the functional system they belong to.

6.3.3.1 Engine

Most car engines are reciprocating piston, internal-combustion engines involving explosive combustion (gasoline fuel) or, less commonly, progressive combustion (diesel fuel). The high temperatures involved, and the dynamic forces associated with modern fast revolving engines, constitute challenges and opportunities for polymeric materials and composites.

Much publicity has been made around the experimental Polimotor "plastic engine," which makes considerable use of polymers (e.g., PAI) and fiber reinforcement (e.g., Carbon), for a variety of elements including the engine block itself. Such construction, however, is not yet suitable for inexpensive, mass-produced engines. Polymers are nevertheless increasingly used in production engines.

Elements illustrated in Figure 6.44, such as the cam (valve) cover (C) and the oil underpan (C'), are molded or stamped from glass-reinforced plastics (e.g., PA, PAT, RIM-Epoxy). Light-weight plastic or composite construction is particularly promising for reciprocating parts such as molded piston skirts (P') (e.g., PEEK), filament wound/pultruded connecting rods (R), pultruded valve stems (V) or push rods, and, possibly, valve springs. Timing gears and sprockets (W) are commonly molded from RTP plastics (e.g., PA, PP, PMO, PAT), with cord-reinforced elastomeric belts (B) increasingly replacing chains.

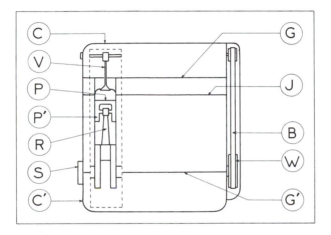

Figure 6.44 · **Automobile engine elements** · (C) Valve cover; (V) Valve stem; (P) Piston crown; (P') Piston skirt; (R) Connecting rod; (S) Crankshaft seal; (C') Underpan; (G) Valve cover gasket; (J) Main engine gasket; (B) Timing belt; (W) Timing gear/sprocket; (G') Underpan gasket

Elastomeric low-pressure gaskets or seals [(G), (G'), (S) in Fig. 6.18] have long been used (crankshaft, valves, valve cover, underpan, etc.). Resistance to oil must now be achieved at higher temperatures in the presence of different additives (engine-oil-lubricated gearbox, turbocharged engines). High performance or specialty conventional elastomers are used (e.g. CR, FKM), and the newer high-performance thermoplastic elastomers are likely future contenders. The high-pressure main engine gasket (J) normally involves a thermosetting binding resin.

Some polymer based engine components are shown in figures 6.45-6.47.

Figure 6.45 · Piston skirts, intake valve stems and oil rings in polimotor engine (polyamideimide PAI and carbon fiber) **[AMOCO]**

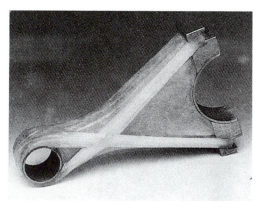

Fig. 6.46

Fig. 6.47

Figure 6.46 · Filament-wound connecting rod (thermoset and glass fiber) **[IKV]**

Figure 6.47 · Toothed timing belt (thermoplastic urethane TPU and reinforcing cords) **[BAYER]**

6.3.3.2 *Transmission*

Plastics, even in reinforced form, are unlikely to compete with metals for compact torque-transmitting gear systems in either manual or automatic transmissions. They are used, however, for some molded internal control parts (e.g., PMO, PA). Reinforced thermosets are used for thrust converter reactors in automatic transmissions that may involve temperatures as high as 200°C ($\approx$ 350°F), as well as for reverse clutch cones in manual transmissions. Transmission covers and underpans are also now made of molded or stamped reinforced plastics with elastomeric gaskets and seals.

6.3.3.3 Driveline

The major elements of what we refer to here as the "driveline" (Fig. 6.48) are the drive shaft [S], the braking system [B] and the wheels [W]. The steering mechanism is also discussed in this section.

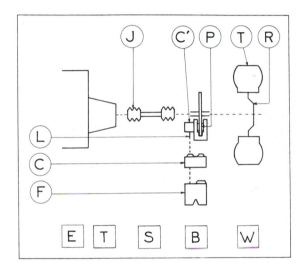

Figure 6.48 · **Automobile power train** · [E] Engine [T] Transmission; [S] Driveshaft; [B] Braking system; [W] Wheel; (J) CV joint; (C′) Brake cylinder; (P) Brake pad; (L) Brake line; (C) Brake master cylinder; (F) Brake fluid reservoir; (T) Tire; (R) Rim/flange

Driveshaft

A majority of modern cars feature front-wheel drive (FWD), which is associated with short driveshafts and the compulsory use of constant-velocity (CV) axle joints (J) (universal, cardan). Composite driveshafts (glass and graphite/carbon) are successfully replacing long metal shafts in vans or trucks for weight-saving as well as noise, vibration, and harshness (NVH) reduction, but these advantages are less significant in FWD cases. Composite flexible driveshafts have been developed, which involve the combination of fiber reinforcement wound at a suitable angle with a matrix of relatively low stiffness, and could eliminate the need for axle joints in the case of rear-wheel drive with independent wheel drive, for example.

FWD axle joints require bellow-shaped flexible covers (boots), which contain the lubricating grease and are subjected to large cyclic stresses and deformations. For this application, high performance conventional rubbers (e.g., CR, Silicone) are being challenged by new thermoplastic elastomers that are associated with faster production methods.

See figures 6.49-6.53 for examples of polymer based driveline components.

Fig. 6.49   Fig. 6.50

Figure 6.49 · Boots for front wheel drive constant velocity joints (thermoplastic elastomer HYTREL) **[DU PONT]**

Figure 6.50 · Brake fluid reservoir molded and bonded elements (polyamide PA + glass) **[DU PONT]**

Figure 6.51 · Molded brake blocks (phenolic PF binder + filler) **[REICHHOLD]**

Figure 6.52 · Green (uncured) tires. Bias (left), radial (right) **[GOODYEAR]**

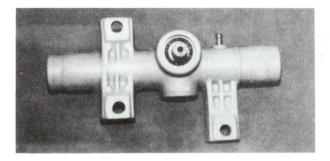

Figure 6.53 · Rack and pinion steering mechanism housing (thermoplastic polyester PET structural foam with metal inserts) **[DU PONT]**

Braking System

Automobiles feature hydraulic braking systems [B], which are now increasingly of the disk type. The master brake cylinder unit (C) and the brake fluid reservoir (F) are subjected to the normal underhood environment, while individual brake cylinders (C′) and brake pads (P) can be subjected to high braking temperatures. Brake fluids and their additives are aggressive to certain polymers.

Brake fluid reservoirs are now made of translucent blow molded plastics (e.g., HDPE, PA); injection- or transfer-molded plastic master brake pistons, cylinders, and valves are being introduced (e.g., PA, PMO, PF).

Rigid metal brake lines (L) are being challenged by plastic tubings (e.g., PA), and flexible brake hoses normally involve a rubber/cord braided construction to withstand the fluid pressure, as well as road hazards.

Thermoset plastics (e.g., PF) have been introduced for brake cylinders, and pistons and are also used as binders for brake pads.

For hand brakes, plastic cable conduits (sleeves) can help reduce rust problems associated with road salt.

Wheels

Wheels [W] consist of a rim (rim/flange) (R) fitted with a tire (T) and, as unsprung elements, they should be made as light as possible.

Rims are most commonly made of pressed steel welded elements or, occasionally, of cast aluminum alloy. Compression-molded FRP rims were developed and used in a top-line production car in the early 1970s (Citroen SM), and, after a long lapse, renewed interest is currently expressed for the introduction of FRP wheels in mass-produced vehicles. The low conductivity of composites is a factor to be considered in view of the temperatures induced in the wheels by braking (about 140°C or ≈ 285°F).

Tires (Fig. 6.54) are most interesting elements of an automobile with their multiple role for cushioning, steering, traction, and other functions. Conventional tires are made by a complex tire building process that involves different rubber compounds for the tread (T), the shoulders (S), the sidewalls (L), the bead area (B), and the innerliner (or innertube) (I), as well as a carcass of reinforcing cords arranged radially and circumferentially (belts) in modern "radial" tires [R] or at an angle in "bias" tires [B]. Polymeric tire cords have been used throughout the long tire history (natural cotton, rayon, nylon-PA, polyester-PET, aramid-Kevlar). The use of nonpolymeric tire cords (steel or glass) has been limited primarily to belts in "radial" tires. Periodically, publicity is made about revolutionary, unconventional tires made by a "casting" process, rather than the "building" process and involving a single material such as PU. A number of factors have not yet permitted a significant growth of such product that should not, however be permanently discounted.

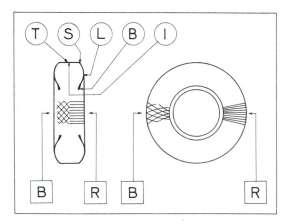

Figure 6.54 · **Automobile tire** · [B] Bias-type carcass; [R] Radial-type carcass; (T) Tread; (S) Shoulder; (L) Sidewall; (B) Bead; (I) Innerliner

Steering Mechanism

Engineering polymers are already used appreciably in steering mechanisms and offer a particularly interesting potential. A notable current application involves pleated elastomeric covers (boots) associated with the growing use of large displacement rack and pinion steering systems. The concept of flexible drive shafts has an interesting potential for the reduction of mechanical joints in steering columns.

6.3.3.4 Fuel/Air System

Although compressed gaseous fuel is sometimes used, liquid fuel is, by far, the most common source of energy in internal combustion engines.

Regular gasoline contains lead-based additives, while unleaded and "premium" gasolines feature more aromatic fractions. Fuel injection, requiring fuel recirculation, introduces hydroperoxides ("sour" fuel). Gasohol fuels contain a fraction of alcohol for cost-reduction and octane-rating boosting. The resistance of materials to such aggressive media must be carefully evaluated, particularly in the case of polymeric materials. Permeation of volatile fuels through polymeric materials must also be considered in the light of existing regulations.

The expanding use of fuel injection and turbocharging tends to make higher demands on material properties and constitute a challenge for the best high-performance polymers.

The major elements of a fuel/air system are represented in Figure 6.55. Fuel tanks [T] were traditionally made of two joined metal half shells. Plastic fuel tanks were introduced in the early 1970s (Volkswagen Passat/Dasher). High-density PE is used primarily, normally in combination with the extrusion-blow molding process, which produces a one-piece product. Reduction of fuel permeation can be achieved by fluoridation, sulfonation, chlorosulfonation or irradiation of the PE or by introducing barrier polymers as blends or coextrudates. Plastic fuel tanks are considerably lighter than their metal conterparts and easier to manufacture in space-saving contoured shapes; in a number of respects, they are also considered safer.

For safety reasons, filler necks (N) (e.g., PE) are normally connected to the tanks through flexible connecting hoses (S) made of fuel-resistant elastomers. Fuel caps (F) are often made of plastic (e.g., PA-RTP). The level indicator device (I) now features plastic elements such as a metal-coated tape (e.g., PI).

Rigid metal fuel lines (P) are increasingly being replaced by semirigid extruded plastic lines (e.g., PA-11, 12). Fuel filters [F] feature a plastic housing (e.g., PA) and a polymeric filtering medium (e.g., PVDC). Fuel pump [P] housings and diaphragms or impellers, depending on the type, may involve engineering plastics (ex: PMO, PBT). Fuel hoses (P') must be flexible and involve higher pressures; they often consist of an inner liner (veneer) of fuel-resistant rubber (e.g., NBR, FKM), a fiber reinforcement (braid), and a rubber cover (e.g., CR, CSM).

Carburetors [C] with their intricate shapes are likely candidates for a switch from cast metal to plastics. Nonautomotive carburetors have already been made with plastic bodies (e.g., PAT) and floats (e.g., PMO). Automotive carburetor outer linkage mechanisms (L) are already molded from plastics, reducing the number of parts and the assembling time (e.g., PA, PMO).

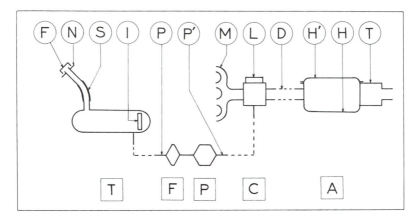

Figure 6.55 · **Automobile fuel/air system** · [T] Fuel tank; [F] Fuel filter; [P] Fuel pump; [C] Carburettor; [A] Air filter; (F) Fuel cap; (N) Filler neck; (S) Flexible connection; (I) Level indicator device; (P) Fuel line; (P') Fuel hose; (M) Air intake manifold; (L) Carburettor linkages; (D) Air duct; (H') Air filter cover; (H) Air filter housing; (T) Thermostat-controlled flap

The major element of the engine air intake system is the air filter (cleaner) [A]. Both housing (H) and cover (H') are now commonly made of plastic (e.g., PP, PA, PBT), often with a reinforcing filler. The thermostat-controlled flap (T) and its mechanism are also increasingly made of plastics.

The flexible air-intake duct (D) is normally made of an elastomeric polymer and often involves bellows, easily formed by blow molding in the case of a thermoplastic.

For the complex rigid air intake manifold (M), reinforced plastic materials (e.g., PA-RTP, BMC) have been evaluated for injection or transfer molding with fusible metal cores.

The use of high temperature and corrosion resistant plastics (e.g., PPS, PI) in exhaust systems is likely to be first restricted to relatively small mechanical parts in EGR (exhaust gas recirculation) or ECD (emission control device) systems. Figures 6.56-6.60 depict several applications of polymer technology in automotive fuel/air system design.

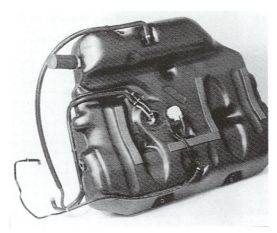

Fig. 6.56   Fig. 6.57

Figure 6.56 · Blow molded plastic gas tank (polyethylene HDPE) **[LANDRY]**

Figure 6.57 · Air inlet manifold, fusible core molding (polyamide PA + 33% glass fiber) **[PORSCHE/VW/ICI]**

Figure 6.58 · Fuel pump (acetal PMO) **[HOECHST]**

Figure 6.59 · Air filter housing (polypropylene PP + glass fiber) **[FORD]**

Figure 6.60 · Oil pump, water pump and turbocompressor components for Ferrari F-1 racing engine (polyetheretherketone PEEK) **[ICI]**

6.3.3.5 *Liquid Cooling/Heating System*

Most automotive engines are now liquid-cooled. This method is superior to air cooling in terms of noise and temperature control, and is also convenient for heating the occupants' space. Since sealed liquid cooling systems are becoming the norm, the liquid must have permanent antifreeze properties for cold weather. Ethylene glycol, for example, which is widely used with water, can be aggressive to metals in particular, calling for the addition of corrosion inhibitors, which, in turn, can be aggressive to other materials. Materials are normally chosen to resist temperatures as high as 120-135°C (≈ 250-275°F).

The construction of radiators [R] (Fig. 6.61) has changed radically with the introduction of injection-molded plastic and end-caps (headers) (E) in the early 1970s (e.g., PA or PPO-RTP). At about the same time, glass yielded to blow molded transparent or translucent plastic for expansion tanks (T) (e.g., PP).

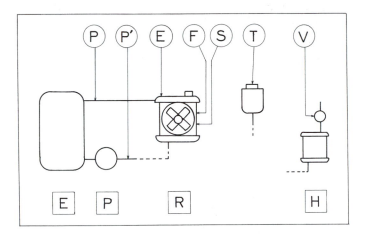

Figure 6.61 · **Automobile liquid cooling/heating system** · [E] Engine; [P] Water pump; [R] Radiator; [H] Heater heat exchanger; (P),(P′) Liquid circulation conduits; (E) Radiator end-caps; (F) Fan; (S) Fan shroud/support; (T) Expansion tank; (V) Heater control valve

Fans (F), now mounted on thermostat-controlled electric motors, are generally injection-molded one-piece plastic units (e.g., PP or PA-RTP). Molded plastic fan shrouds (S) often incorporate motor-supporting brackets (e.g., PP or PA-RTP).

Molded plastics are being introduced for water pump [P] housing and impeller (e.g., PF). Liquid circulation conduits (P) and (P′) preferably have a large diameter and smooth inner surface to reduce drag and must have adequate flexibility and a specific contoured shape. Thermoplastic elastomers (TPE) are increasingly competing with conventional rubbers. On the suction side, collapse must be prevented by built-in convolutions (corrugations) or embedded stiff spirals.

The engine cooling liquid is also used for interior heating; a valve (V), increasingly made of injection molded plastic elements (e.g., PA-RTP), controls the flow of hot liquid through the heat exchanger (heater) [H], analogous in construction to the radiator [R].

See figures 6.62-6.64 for liquid cooling/heating system applications.

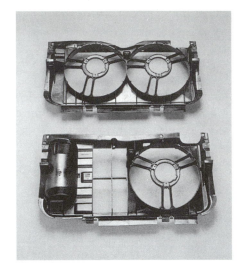

Fig. 6.63

Fig. 6.62

Figure 6.62 · Radiator end caps (polyamide PA + glass) **[DU PONT]**

Figure 6.63 · Fan shrouds and supports for 205-model (polyamide PA + glass) **[PEUGEOT]**

Figure 6.64 · Cooling fan, heater fan, cooling liquid surge tank (polypropylene PP) **[MONTEDISON]**

6.3.3.6 *Electrical Systems*

Most automotive electrical circuits operate under low voltage (12 V), sometimes with high intensities (starter motor, forward lighting); electrical resistance is then of primary concern. The ignition circuit, on the contrary, involves high voltages; thus, arc and track resistance become important properties.

The storage battery [B] (Fig. 6.65) consists primarily of the case (H), which formerly was made of hard rubber and is now almost exclusively made of high-impact PP; easy molding resins have allowed much thinner walls, as well as built-in separators, for more compact batteries. The cover (H'), as well as vent caps and the tray (T), are also made of plastics.

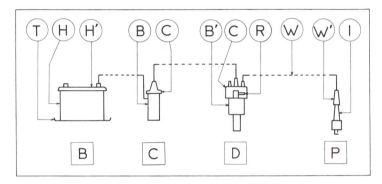

Figure 6.65 · **Automobile electrical ignition system** · [B] Battery; [C] Ignition coil; [D] Distributor; [P] Spark plug; (T) Tray; (H) Battery case; (H') Battery cover; (B) Coil tower; (C) Coil cap; (B') Distributor housing; (C') Distributor cap; (R) Rotor; (W) Ignition wire; (W') Spark plug boot; (I) Spark plug body

Average automobiles feature over 100 m (≈ 300 ft) of wires and cables. Low-voltage insulation (jacketing) is normally made of PVC; PA is occasionally used. Individually insulated wires are normally gathered into wiring harnesses, but the use of multi-conductor tapes is likely to grow. Associated molded connectors often involve PA resins with or without glass.

Thermosetting resins (e.g., PF, alkyd, epoxy), which were traditionally used for a variety of electrical components (voltage regulator, switches, fuse boxes, relays, coil forms, terminal blocks, electric motor brush holders, lamp bases or sockets, printed circuit boards PCB, etc.), are increasingly yielding to thermoplastics (e.g., PA, PAT, PP, PC, PSU), with or without glass.

The high-voltage ignition system consists of several elements. The ignition coil [C] involves the tower (B), often made of PF thermoset, and the cap (C). The distributor

[D] with its housing (B'), cap (C'), and rotor (R), traditionally involved cast metal and thermosetting resins (e.g., PF, alkyd); they are now increasingly molded of glass-reinforced PAT. The ignition wires (W) are now generally jacketed with silicone or other specialty rubbers. The ceramic insulating body (I) of spark plugs [P] is a potential application for high temperature-resistant plastics such as PI. Rigid insulating caps are already made of plastics, such as PPS or DAP, while silicone rubber is often used for the elastomeric boot (W').

See figures 6.66-6.68 for electrical system applications.

Figure 6.66 · Battery case and cover (polypropylene PP)

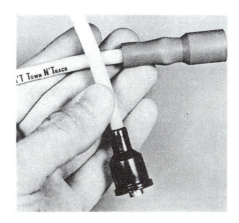

Fig. 6.67   Fig. 6.68

Figure 6.67 · Distributor cap, rotor and other electrical components (thermoplastic polyester PBT) **[GAF]**

Figure 6.68 · Ignition cable, outer jacket, inner dielectric covering, conductive rubber core (silicone rubbers) **[DOW]**

6.3.4   Interior Elements

Demands on car elements located within the occupants' space (passenger compartment) are quite different from those for underhood or exterior elements, but not always easier to meet. Major preoccupations include the behavior at temperatures that can range from -40°C (-40°F) to over 90°C (≈ 200°F), the effect of sunlight; wear-and-tear resistance, and aesthetic considerations.

6.3.4.1   Dashboard Area

The dashboard [D] (Fig. 6.69), which extends across the occupants' compartment, under the windshield, plays a multiple role: it hides and shields functional elements such as electrical and climate control systems; it holds sub-elements such as the instrument cluster (I), various control panels and knobs (C), vents (V), smoking accessories (L), (A), glove box (G), etc.; finally, it is an important passive safety element designed to minimize injuries to occupants in cases of head-on collisions.

Audio elements and some controls, including the gear lever, are sometimes housed in a lower console [C], and aircraft-style roof consoles have been introduced.

The interior elements of the steering system [S], associated with the dashboard, comprise the steering wheel itself (W), a crash (horn) pad (P), the steering column and shroud (S), and column-mounted controls (C).

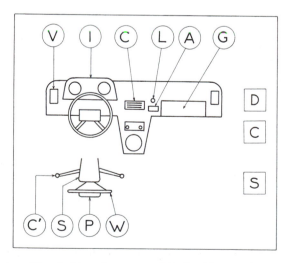

Figure 6.69 · **Automobile dashboard area** · [D] Dashboard; [C] Console; [S] Steering wheel/column; (V) Vent; (I) Instrument cluster; (C) Climate controls; (L) Cigarette lighter; (A) Ashtray; (G) Glove box; (C′) column-mounted controls; (S) Column shroud; (P) Crash pad; (W) Steering wheel

Dashboard

The dashboard construction increasingly consists of a complex injection molded plastic frame (e.g., PS, PP, ABS, PC, often in RTP form), supporting a semi-flexible PU foam padding covered with a thermoformed, weather-resistant, plasticized PVC skin. Moderate impacts are absorbed by the skin/padding system, while the controlled collapse of the frame can help absorb energy in severe collisions.

Climate control systems (ventilation and heating) now make extensive use of plastics that must be dimensionally stable at fairly elevated temperatures. Hidden fans and ducts often involve filled or reinforced molded resins (e.g., PP, PA), while vent grille, louvers and surrounds are molded to attractive finishes (e.g., PA, PPO, ABS). Control panels and mechanisms increasingly use plastics for facings, levers, cable conduits, etc.; a shift toward electronic controls involving pushbutton or even membrane switches is probable in the near future.

Ashtrays and cigarette lighters, which require temperature and incandescence resistance up to 600°C or ≈ 1100°F, have been penetrated by suitable plastics (e.g., PF and PI), replacing metals and even ceramics.

Examples of dashboard area elements are shown in figures 6.70-6.75.

Figure 6.70 • R5-model dashboard; flexible skin/foam backing (plasticized PVC/polyurethane PU) **[RENAULT]**

Figure 6.71 • Espace-model dashboard; fabric-textured skin/soft backing **[RENAULT]**

Figure 6.72 · AX-model molded dashboard (polyalloy A(PC/PET)) **[CITROEN]**

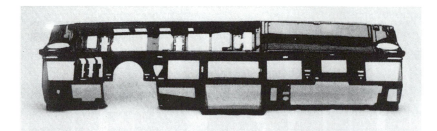

Figure 6.73 · Molded dashboard frame (polyphenylene oxide PPO) **[GENERAL ELECTRIC]**

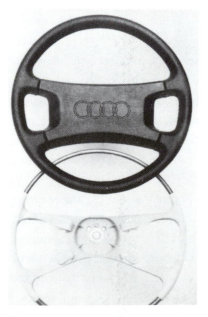

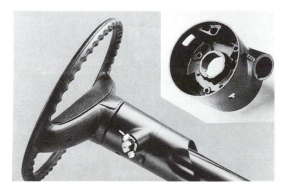

Figure 6.75 · Molded steering column lock housing (polyamide PA + glass) **[DU PONT]**

Figure 6.74 · Quattro sport-model steering wheel; metal frame, plastic molding, soft cover (polyamide PA + glass, foam core/skin polyurethane PU) **[AUDI/BASF]**

Instrument Cluster

The instrument cluster is often a separate element that consists of a housing (e.g., PS, ABS, PPO, PMO) and a transparent facing (e.g., acrylic), surrounded by a bezel. The increasing use of electronic LED-type visual displays, sometimes associated with fiber optics, is said to have raised the temperature requirements and, consequently, require more engineering-type plastics.

Conventional mechanical instruments (speedometer, odometer, tachometer) make considerable use of engineering plastics, ideally suited to such lightly loaded applications and requiring no lubrication (e.g., PMO, PA, often in RTP form).

Steering

Conventional steering wheels consist of a metal frame over which rigid (e.g., PP, CAB) or semirigid (e.g., PVC) plastics are molded; "friendly" soft steering wheels are increasingly used, which feature a self-skinning PU foam cover. Plastic and composite steering wheel frames are being introduced.

In the steering column, injection-molded plastic functional elements are now competing with conventional die-cast zinc alloy parts (e.g., PA-RTP). Shrouds (cover plates) have long been made of molded plastic (e.g., ABS).

Steering column-mounted controls now feature molded plastic hollow shafts with a larger cross section and multifunction knobs (e.g., PMO).

6.3.4.2 Seating

Automobiles now almost exclusively feature front bucket seats with adjustable (reclining) backs. Rear seats are following a slower but similar trend, with folding backs (50/50 or 40/60) popular in hatchback or stationwagon versions, and it is probable that partial reclinability for rear seat backs will gain ground in future cars. The general downsizing of cars and the example set in the 1960s for excellent seating comfort in small inexpensive cars (e.g., Renault), call for light, thin (low profile), adjustable, and comfortable seats.

A typical bucket-type seat (Fig. 6.76) features the horizontal seat [S], the reclining back [B], and the headrest [H]. Each element of a conventional seat comprises a rigid metal frame (F); a metal suspension (S) often consists of flat snake-like metal springs, a cellular (foam) elastomeric padding (cushion) (P), and a protective/aesthetic covering (upholstery) (C). A cellulosic liner (L) is often inserted between padding and covering.

Some of the early inexpensive, yet comfortable, car seats featured elastomeric bands instead of metal springs (e.g., Citroen, Renault); recent innovations include the

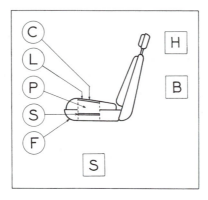

Figure 6.76 · **Automobile seat** · [S] Seat; [H] Headrest; [B] Back; (C) Cover; (L) Liner; (P) Padding; (S) Suspension; (F) Frame

introduction of a hammock-like elastomeric fabric suspension (e.g., Ford Aerostar). Shell-shaped frames (e.g., FRP or RRIM), completely filled with single or dual stiffness PU foams, have been introduced (e.g., Chevrolet Corvette). Foam padding is a very large market that is certain to see a lot of competition and possibly the introduction of polymers other than the dominating molded PU. Coverings currently show a trend away from leatherette (PVC- or PU-coated fabrics), toward wear-resistant woven or knitted fabrics, and velvets (e.g., acrylics). Major changes should be expected in the mechanisms for front-seat longitudinal and vertical adjustment; this could include the incorporation of suitable tracks into molded composite floors, for example.

A seating design is shown in figure 6.77.

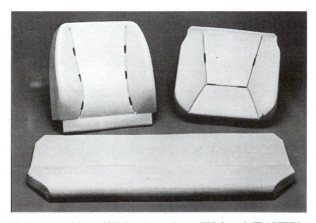

Figure 6.77 · Molded seat cushions (RIM polyurethane PU foam) **[BAYER]**

6.3.4.3 Interior Panels

Interior panels (Fig. 6.78) comprise primarily door panels (D), roof liner (headliner) (R), roof pillars (posts) covers (P), and window surrounds (W). The combination of fiberboard substrates and plasticized PVC skins is being phased out, and door panels, for example, are increasingly molded from impact-resistant plastics (e.g., ABS, PP); this permits the incorporation of features such as latch, ashtray or speaker recesses, arm rests, map racks, etc. Roof liners tend to be one-piece elements, comprising a semirigid foam backing and a formed skin, which are bonded to the roof.

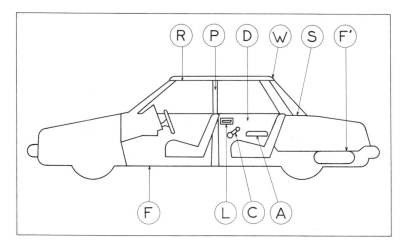

Figure 6.78 · **Automobile interior elements** · (R) Roof liner; (P) Pillar cover; (D) Door panel; (W) Window surround; (S) Parcel shelf; (F′) Trunk floor; (F) Passenger area floor; (L) Door latching system; (C) Window opening system; (A) Armrest

6.3.4.4 Interior Accessories

Door latching systems (L) are increasingly making use of engineering plastics, sometimes in RTP form or with chrome plating for classical appearance (e.g., PA, PAT, PMO). Bezels, handles, strikers, and even keylocks, are now made of plastics.

Door window opening devices (C) (regulators, cranks) also increasingly make use of plastics. Besides handles, the internal mechanisms now include much lighter plastic brackets and levers, and a novel system has been introduced that involves a perforated plastic tape and sprocket wheels. Examples of polymer based automotive interior accessories are shown in figures 6.79-6.80.

Figure 6.79 · Taurus-model window crank handle molded structural element and cover (left) Earlier design with metal element (right) **[FORD]**

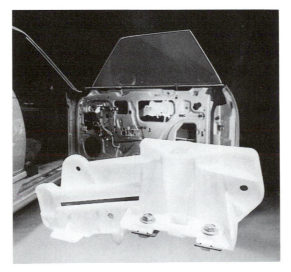

Figure 6.80 · Window mechanism bracket (acetal PMO) **[DU PONT]**

6.3.4.5 *Flooring*

Traditional floor mats (F) made of heavy conventional rubber stock (e.g., SBR) are most conveniently produced in flat form and may become less essential with the introduction of molded reinforced plastic floor panels that are resistant to corrosion. Floor carpets can now be made with a thermoformable backing to give them the appropriate contour. Fibers and backing are resistant to winter salt and slush in particular and are fully washable (e.g., PP, PA).

6.3.4.6   *Cargo Areas*

Rear cargo areas in stationwagons (see example in figure 6.81), hatchbacks, or minivans, and luggage compartments (trunks) in sedans, need sturdy load floors (F'), which were traditionally made of sheet metal as part of the car body. Molded or stamped fiber-reinforced and ribbed plastic load panels are being introduced, particularly when it is desirable to be able to remove them occasionally (spare wheel well or storage compartment covers, convenience trays, shelves, or decks) (e.g., HDPE, PP, RRIM).

Figure 6.81 · Taurus-model station wagon load floor (Stamped polypropylene PP + glass fiber mat) [FORD]

6.3.5   Exterior Elements

Exterior elements or components include body panels, as illustrated in Figure 6.82, which were traditionally made of sheet metal and can be subdivided into horizontal panels, such as the hood (H), cowl vent (P), roof (R), read deck (P'), and trunk lid (L) and vertical panels, such as the front end (E), front fender (F), doors (D), rear fender/quarter panel (F'), and rear end (E'). Upper panels normally require a better surface finish (class A) than do lower panels, such as valance (V) and rocker (U) panels.

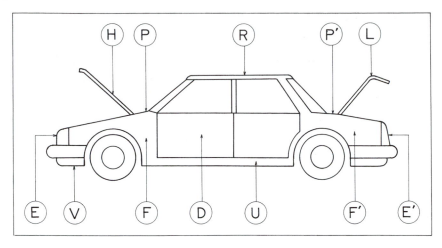

Figure 6.82 · **Automobile exterior body panels** · (H) Hood; (P) Cowl panel; (R) Roof; (P′) Rear deck panel; (L) Trunk lid; (E) Front end panel; (V) Valance panel; (F) Front fender; (D) Door panel; (U) Rocker panel; (F′) Rear fender/quarter panel; (E′) Rear end panel

Other exterior components, accessories, glazing, and trim elements are illustrated in Figure 6.83: front (B) and rear (B′) bumpers, forward or head (L) and rear or tail (L′) lighting assemblies, grill (G), and license plate assembly (R), and in Figure 6.84: windshield (W), side (lateral) windows (L), sun roof window (R), rear window (W′) and associated window surrounds (G) and window cleaning system (C), front (S) and rear (S′) spoilers, wheel covers or hub caps (H), rearview mirror (M), door handle (D) and bezel (D′), side or other moldings (T), and mudflaps (B).

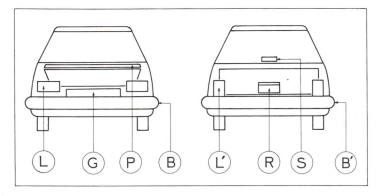

Figure 6.83 · **Automobile front and rear exterior elements** · (L) Forward lighting; (G) Grille; (P) Cowl vent; (B) Front bumper; (L′) Rear lighting; (R) License plate assembly; (S) high-mount stoplight; (B′) Rear bumper

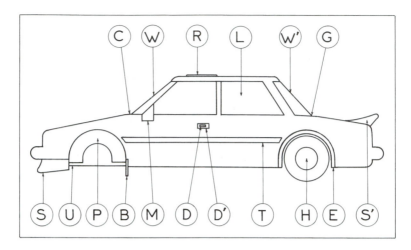

Figure 6.84 · **Automobile glazing, exterior accessories and trim elements** · (C) Window cleaning system; (W) Windshield; (R) Sunroof; (L) Lateral window; (W') Rear window; (G) Window surround; (S) Front spoiler; (U) Underbody fairing; (P) Fender liner; (B) Mudflap; (M) Rearview mirror; (D) Door bezel; (D') Door latch; (T) molding; (H) Hubcap; (E) Fender extension; (S') Rear spoiler

Exterior components are subjected to severe conditions, which include atmospheric agents (sunlight, acid rains, hail, etc.), road salt, gasoline spills, and cleaning and polishing agents, as well as mechanical abuse (car washes, road projections, and a variety of impacts associated with driving and parking).

One current major constraint inherited from the use of metals is related to painting. Conventional car bodies are currently subjected to high temperatures for the baking of various coatings. Electrostatically applied primers (dip) require temperatures in the range 350-450°F ($\approx$ 175-230°C) for 30 min., while "on-line"-applied top coats correspond to a range of 250-300°F ($\approx$ 120-150°C) also for about 30 min.

Solvent-based lacquers are being replaced by solventless enamels of the alkyd or urethane types, which tend to require lower baking temperatures. It is expected that required oven temperatures could drop to the 200-250°F ($\approx$ 90-120°C) range by 1990, greatly facilitating the use of polymers for exterior components. A number of plastic parts are currently painted off-line and subsequently mounted. They may have to be removed for touch-up or bodywork operations.

Since polymeric materials can have molded-in colors, it is likely that the evolution will be toward unpainted exterior panels with a surface texture suited to plastics rather than sheet metal fabrication. Such evolution is already nearly complete in the case of bumpers; chrome finishes have practically disappeared.

6.3.5.1 Body Panels

Large body panels classified as horizontal panels are generally considered more difficult challenges than vertical panels, partly because they are more visible (hood, in particular) and because they are more likely to become distorted under their own weight or as a result of temperature changes. Movable parts (hood, trunk lid) normally have stiffening back elements bonded to the main panel. Examples of plastics used for hoods include SMC (Pontiac Fiero, Ford Aerostar, Cadillac 87), PBT, and PA with suitable fillers. FRP roofs were first used in the 1950s (Citroen DS) and, at one point, vinyl-upholstered roofs became fashionable. Integrated roof racks (carriers) are introduced for certain categories of vehicles (PAT, PA, PVC). Cowl vent panels (screen, grille) are now routinely made of injection-molded thermoplastics which are particularly suited to the complex shapes. SMC has been used for rear decks (Pontiac Fiero).

Large vertical body panels include front fenders, door panels and rear quarter panels; they do not require the same rigidity and dimensional stability as horizontal panels. Besides such all plastic-bodied vehicles as the inexpensive Citroen Mehari of the 1960s (thermoformed ABS body panels) and the classy General Motors Corvette introduced in the mid 1950s (FRP and SMC body panels), a variety of materials and processes have been used recently such as RRIM-PU (Oldsmobile Omega 1981, Pontiac Fiero), other RIM systems, RTM (Renault Espace), SMC, and new engineering thermoplastics blends based on PC, PA, and ABS for injection molding.

In the 1970s, plastic fender liners were introduced as a protection for metal fenders against road projections (e.g., HDPE and PP-RTP).

With the current emphasis on good aerodynamics to reduce fuel consumption at high speeds, the introduction or generalization of underbody fairings (U) is very likely with light, impact-resistant plastics in areas sufficiently distant from the exhaust system.

Front-end and rear-end vertical panels often have similar requirements. Rigid panels normally serve also as structural elements to support forward and rear lighting systems, grille, license plate holder, etc. In such cases, they can be made of SMC, as well as PA-RTP or PC-RTP, RRIM, etc. In the case of "soft" fascia, commonly made of RIM, rigid back panels are required, which are not visible.

Valance and rocker panels, because of their low location, are particularly subject to impacts. In speed-oriented vehicles, valance panels are replaced by front spoilers (air dams), which are even more exposed. Valance panels and front spoilers are sometimes integrated in the bumper system or part of the whole fascia. A thermoplastic elastomer is used for the rocker panels of the Pontiac Fiero.

The grille, which was traditionally a chrome-plated major component of the front end, went from plated die cast metal to plastic (ABS, PBT, etc.) a number of years ago, but with the current emphasis on sleek aerodynamic shapes, its size is rapidly shrinking and it tends to become an integral part of the front end panel, that is, to disappear in its traditional form.

Rear gates (lift gates) of hatchbacks or stationwagons have been made of modified BMC or ZMC (Citroen BX), SMC (Ford Aeostar), and engineering plastics blends (PPO, PA). Such parts, which carry the heavy rear window, as well as accessories such as a window wiper system, often feature a bonded two-piece boxed or ribbed construction.

Side doors represent a special challenge with the need to house vertically retractable windows and the associated mechanism, as well as provide adequate passenger protection (intrusion beam). Combinations of rigid reinforced plastic frames and semi-rigid panels are likely to be introduced soon.

Various body panel designs are shown in figures 6.85-6.90.

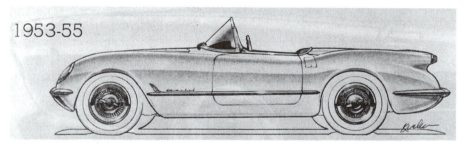

Figure 6.85 · 1953 Corvette-model body (fiberglass) **[GENERAL MOTORS]**

Figure 6.86 · 1963 Le Mans-model body (fiberglass) **[ALPINE/RENAULT]**

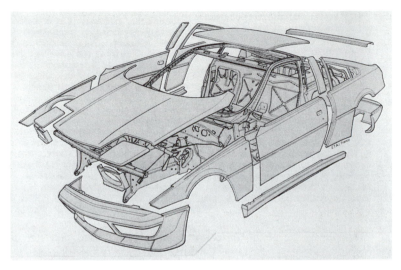

Figure 6.87 · 1980 Murena-model body (polyester resin + glass fiber molded by RTM) **[MATRA]**

Figure 6.88 · 1984 Fiero-model body panels on metal frame (SMC horizontal elements, PU-RRIM vertical elements) **[GENERAL MOTORS/PONTIAC]**

Figure 6.89 · 1987 Le Sabre-model, injection molded front fenders (A(PPO/PA) polyalloy) **[GENERAL MOTORS/BUICK]**

Figure 6.90 · 1984 Espace-model; galvanized metal frame with molded panels doors, bumpers molded by SMC; side panels, rear door, hood and roof molded by RTM (polyester resin + glass fiber) **[MATRA/RENAULT]**

6.3.5.2 *Exterior Accessories and Trim*

A variety of small elements associated with the body and its protection have long been made of polymeric materials (Fig. 6.84). They include fender extensions (E) (wheel opening flares, wheel arch "eyebrows") made of thermoplastic PU, PA, or SMC and mud flaps (B) made of conventional rubbers or thermoplastic elastomers.

Door handles and bezels are now commonly made of plastics that are often metal-plated (e.g., PET/PBT, PA).

Rearview mirrors increasingly feature a streamlined housing (cowl), mounted flush with the body (e.g., ABS, PA-RTP) and a mechanism for adjustment from the interior, for which engineering plastics are rapidly replacing die-cast zinc alloys.

Wheel covers (hubcaps) are now commonly made of plastics (e.g., ABS, PA, PPO) which must resist braking heat and, preferably, baking oven temperatures.

Styling has long involved the use of decorative trim strips that were first made of chrome-plated metal, then of polished aluminum covered with plastic (e.g., CAB), and now often of plastics alone. They include weld seam strips, roof guttering strips, wheel arches strips, side moldings, bumper strips, and window and light surrounds. They were initially clipped through holes in body panels, for example, but are now increasingly adhesion-bonded.

See figures 6.91-6.98 for examples of polymer based exterior design.

Figure 6.91 · 1982 BX-model, SMC-molded hood (thermoset + glass fiber composite) **[CITROEN]**

Figure 6.92 · 1982 BX-model, ZMC-molded hatchback door (thermoset + glass fiber composite) **[CITROEN/BILLION]**

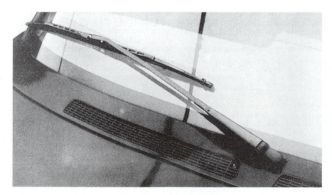

Figure 6.93 · Cowl vent panel (polyamide PA) Wiper blade frame (thermoplastic polyester PBT) **[CITROEN]**

Fig. 6.94

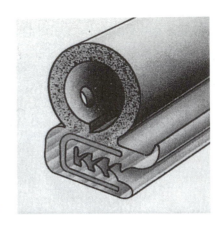

Fig. 6.95

Figure 6.94 · Door bezel (mineral-filled polyamide PA) **[CHRYSLER]**

Figure 6.95 · Body/door seal, dual hardness rubber (sponge/dense) with metal carrier **[SHELLER-GLOBE]**

Figure 6.96 · Anti-laceration laminated safety glazing (glass/polyvinylbutyral PVB/glass/polyurethane or polyester) **[ST-GOBAIN/DU PONT]** ·

Figure 6.97 · Headlamp frame and indicator light reflector (thermoplastic polyester PBT + 30% glass fiber) **[BAYER]**

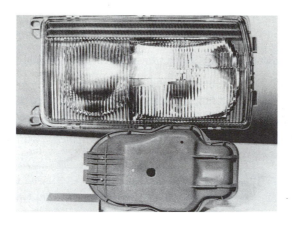

Figure 6.98 · Front lamp housing (polypropylene PP + glass beads) **[MERCEDES/POTTERS]**

6.3.5.3 *Weatherstripping*

Air and water tightness around doors, window openings, and the trunk lid is achieved through the use of weatherstripping. Weatherstripping most often consist of an elastomeric foam (sponge) material that may involve a resilient core (e.g., NR) and a weather-resistant skin (e.g., CR). High deformability can be achieved through a tubular structure. Weatherstripping is normally made by extrusion. It is held in place through a built-in clipping strip or, sometimes, by bonding. (See figure 6.99)

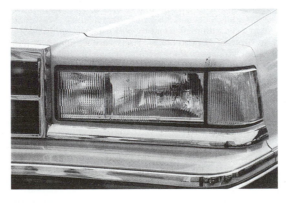

Figure 6.99 · 1987 Dynasty-model, headlamp, park and turn signal lamp lenses and reflectors (polycarbonate PC) **[CHRYSLER]**

6.3.5.4 Glazing

Glazing, i.e. transparent panels or windows, have traditionally been made of glass panes; fixed windows are mounted in molded rubber sealing surrounds (gaskets). For obvious safety reasons, side and rear windows are made of tempered safety glass, while windshields normally consist of laminates featuring a polyvinylbutyral (PVB) interlayer, sandwich-bonded between two glass panes. Safety glass, featuring a scratch- and abrasion-resistant PU film on the inside surface, is being developed, which should afford a better protection against lacerations.

A considerable weight advantage could result from the adoption of plastic glazing for, at least, side and rear windows; polymers such as PC or acrylics with suitable surface treatment or coatings (silicones, PU), which are already used for sun roof windows, are likely candidates.

The generalization of flush-mounted glazing has led to the gradual disappearance of conventional molded rubber sealing surrounds in favor of bonding techniques. In some cases, a suitable polymeric surround is molded directly over the glass panel (RIM process). (see figure 6.100)

Figure 6.100 · 1987 New Yorker-model taillamp housing (A(ABS/PC) polyalloy)/Tail lamp lens (polycarbonate PC) **[CHRYSLER]**

6.3.5.5 Window Wiper/Washer System

Windshield or rear window wiper blades have always been made of an elastomeric material, but conventional rubbers (e.g., NR) are being challenged by some thermoplastic elastomers. Wiper arms are now increasingly molded in plastic (e.g., PET/PBT).

Window washer systems make extensive use of detergent- and antifreeze-resistant plastics for the bottle (e.g., PE), the tubing (e.g., PVC), and the motor/pump device.

It is likely that the generalization of the new types of forward lighting lenses will promote the use of associated wiper/washer systems.

6.3.5.6 Lighting Systems

Considerable changes have affected the design and fabrication of forward lighting systems (headlights). Aerodynamic and styling considerations are leading to the replacement of conventional North American glass-based sealed beam systems by combinations of interchangeable conventional or halogen lamps (bulbs) with socket, reflector, housing, seal, and lens that can all be made of plastics. Examples include PSU (lamp socket); ABS/PC (housing); PAT and PA (reflector); and PC, PES, and PAR (lens). Some challenging problems associated with forward lighting systems involve high temperatures (215°C or ≈ 420°F), i.e. thermal stability; the metallization of the reflector; and abrasion and impact resistance of the lenses.

Rear lighting systems (tail lights) involve lower temperatures, and polymeric materials used include acrylics, PC (lens), PP-RPT, ABS, and PAT (housing).

Sidemarker lights now tend to be incorporated into forward and rear assemblies, but new high-mount stop lights are being introduced that are often interior-mounted.

In the interior, courtesy lights are straightforward, but major changes are taking place in the area of indicator lights, with the introduction or generalization of LED displays and fiber optics that are reported to increase local temperatures.

6.3.6 Future

Over the past decades, the use of polymeric materials (plastics, rubbers, and composites) in automotive applications has grown steadily. The areas of application have expanded from such classical ones as electrical insulation or elastomeric components to include appearance and functional elements, many of them highly technical, which now abound in the occupants space and under the hood.

The introduction of large polymeric exterior components, initiated on a large scale in the 1970s, is rapidly gaining ground, and the 1990s will probably see a real breakthrough with massive conversion to polymeric body panels. The 1990s are also likely to see polymer-based composites widely introduced as structural materials for vehicle frames and other structural components, while high temperature-resistant plastics and composites will play an increasing role in engine construction.

6.4   PRODUCT DESIGN PRINCIPLES

The design of a product for a certain application is generally a complex undertaking, and it is perhaps especially complex in the case of polymeric materials, because of the great variety of materials and processes that are, in principle, available.

Experienced designers rely heavily on accumulated knowledge, and thus can often bypass a fully rational approach to the problem.

In this introductory textbook, the following discussion of product design principles is intended for newcomers to the field who have become reasonably familiar with the contents of the various chapters.

When a product is needed for a specific application, certain requirements, referred to here as "constraints," can be defined. It is convenient to subdivide the constraints into three types. Geometry constraints involve the shape and dimensions of the product and may be dictated by aesthetic, functional, or other reasons. Property constraints are associated primarily with the material and the environment (loads, chemicals, etc.), and Chapter 5 gives a good idea of the wide range of properties that may be relevant. Finally, economy constraints correspond to possible limits on the cost of the product, and are often closely tied to the volume of production.

It is essential to realize that geometry, property, and economy constraints are quite interdependent in their role on product design.

The design of a polymer-based product for a specific application normally results in the specification of a geometry choice for the product (shape and dimensions), a material choice (a commercially available polymer or polymeric system with details regarding the specific grade and possible curing conditions for thermosets or rubbers), and a process equipment choice (commercially available processing equipment fitted with a product-specific tool).

Geometry, material and process choices are also largely interdependent, and the design procedure must thus be an iterative process.

A strict geometry constraint may impose the general process (narrow-neck-bottle/blow molding). An economy constraint (volume of production) may further dictate a choice between extrusion blow molding and injection blow molding for a narrow neck bottle. In the case of a wide-neck jar, injection molding may be a viable alternative. The geometry constraint may be limited to the shape; materials of different properties in appropriate thicknesses are equally suitable. It is important to realize that shape changes, which do not affect the functional role of a product, can reduce considerably the complexity of a tool and thus its cost and reliability. It is always preferable for product designers and tool designers to collaborate closely.

A strict property constraint may impose the material and, as a consequence, the process (high-temperature elastomeric seal/vulcanizable rubber/compression molding). A similar, but less stringent, property constraint (moderate temperature elastomeric seal) may offer two alternatives (vulcanizable rubber/compression molding or thermoplastic elastomer/injection molding).

Property constraints for a given application are generally multiple, and a central problem is the assessment of their relative importance. If possible, it is desirable to distinguish between primary property constraints, which must all be met at a certain level, and secondary property constraints for which some "trade-off" may be acceptable. In the absence of past experience, it is often difficult to judge whether a 10% increase in a certain secondary property is worth a 20% decrease in another one. In the end, only actual product performance in service can provide answers.

Different economy constraints, coupled with similar geometry and property constraints, may dictate different processes associated with the same generic material, but very different grades (small-run snowmobile gas tank/rotational molding/RM grade of polyethylene or high production tank/blow molding/BM grade).

Economy constraints can be met through the judicious choice of geometry, material, and process, keeping in mind that the unit product cost is affected almost directly by the material price and by the process operation cost, but only indirectly by the tool price (significant for short runs, minimal for very long runs).

Inexperienced newcomers to the field, such as students, can do "preliminary" product design based on information in this introductory textbook. More realistic product design requires access to handbook or encyclopedia information. In the end, it is only with commercial literature on materials and processing equipment, supplemented by discussions with company representatives and, if possible, plant visits, that reliable product design can be achieved. I have systematically included product design projects in his polymer engineering courses to expose students to real industrial problems.

The development of computer-based databases on commercial polymers, and their properties, prices, processing conditions, and known applications, is likely to have a profound effect on the procedure of product design. A vast amount of information can be scanned rapidly to yield at least a pre-selection of candidate materials and processes. The scanning can even be automated if the constraints are specified in an appropriate manner. It is felt that after such pre-selection, the conventional product design procedure, with its combination of experience, reference to detailed commercial literature, and personal contacts, will still be essential to reach a satisfactory final design.

The mechanical design of a part, which was not the subject of this section, is another area where computers are making great inroads. Besides the convenient geometric definition of parts (Computer-Aided Drafting), the distribution of stresses in a loaded part can be determined through Finite Element Analysis, and lead to an optimization of shape and dimensions (Computer-Aided Design).

6.5   APPENDIX 6

THE SAILBOARD (section 6.2)

Board Shell Materials and Associated Brands (early 1980s)

Polyethylene (PE)
ALPHA
BIC
EON
FANATIC
GULF
HIFLY
JEANNEAU
JET
MAGNUM
MISTRAL
MYSTERE
O'BRIEN
STARSURF
SURFPARTNER
TENCATE
TIGA
VINTA
WAYLER
WINDSURFER

Polyethylene (PE) - glass fibers
SURFPARTNER

Polypropylene (PP)
BIC-DUFOUR

Acrylonitrile-Butadiene-Styrene (ABS)
AMF
BIC
CRIT
CURTIS
DUFOUR
F2
JEANNEAU
JET
OCEANITE
PELICAN
SAILRIDER
SAINVAL
SPEEDY
TIGA
WINDFLITE

Acrylonitrile-Styrene-Acrylic (ASA)
BIC
BROWNING
F2
FANATIC
MYSTERE
SAILBOARD
WINDGLIDER

Unsaturated polyester (UP) resin - glass fiber
AMF
CRIT
HOWMAR
MAGNUM
MARKER
MARLIN
OCEANITE
REIX
SAINVAL
SPEEDY
WINDGLIDER

Epoxy (EP) resin - glass fiber
F2
HIFLY
MISTRAL
SAILBOARD
TENCATE

Polyamide (PA)
TENCATE

Epoxy and polyester resins - aramid fibers
BROWNING
CRIT
MARES/AMF
REIX

Chapter 7

HISTORY, ECONOMICS, INFORMATION, AND EDUCATION

7.1 HISTORY

Natural polymers (vegetal or animal) have always been around, but the so-called man-made, artificial, or synthetic polymers made only modest debuts in the second half of the nineteenth century; they developed significantly between World War I and World War II and literally exploded after World War II.

Most often cited early landmarks for the polymer industry include the discovery of sulfur vulcanization of natural rubber (1839, Goodyear), the fabrication of billiard balls with cellulose nitrate (1869, Hyatt) and the development of phenol-formaldehyde resins (1909, Baekeland).

It is now generally recognized that major polymer discoveries may be over for a while, as the large companies who can afford the research have already systematically investigated the promising avenues. The period 1940-1960 is considered the most prolific period for the development of large-volume materials. In the 1960s, 1970s, and 1980s, more specialized and expensive engineering materials were developed. Currently, much emphasis is placed on modifications and combinations of existing types of polymers, and the efforts appear to be very successful in producing materials tailored to specific applications, at reasonable cost.

The modern development of synthetic polymeric materials involves several stages. Usually as a result of focused research, a discovery is made by chemists in the laboratory, followed by a preliminary evaluation of the material for its commercial potential, and a patent may be sought. A pilot plant is then built to produce enough material for its evaluation on an industrial basis; it involves a close collaboration between chemists and engineers. A full-scale plant is then designed and built to fulfill anticipated commercial supply needs.

The following review of discovery, development and commercialization dates for polymeric materials follows the order of presentation of materials in Chapter 3. The information presented should be viewed as indicative of the historical development of polymers, but not always perfectly accurate, since dates vary significantly from source to source.

Olefinics. Polyethylene (PE) was discovered as LDPE around 1933 (Fawcett, Gibson at ICI). It was commercialized after 1937. HDPE was first made around 1953

(Ziegler at Hoechst) and commercialized around 1955. Ionomers were introduced around 1964. Polypropylene (PP) was discovered around 1957 (Natta at Montecatini). Polyallomers (block copolymers) were introduced around 1962. Polybutene, discovered around 1954, was commercialized around 1964. Polymethylpentene was discovered around 1955 and commercialized around 1965.

Vinylics. Most vinylics were developed and commercialized in the 1930s, often by German chemical firms. Polyvinylchloride (PVC) was discovered around 1835 (Regnault), but commercialized only after 1927. Polyvinylidenechloride (PVDC) was commercialized after 1939. Polyvinylacetate (PVAC), polyvinylalcohol (PVAL) and polyvinylacetal (safety glass layer) were introduced around 1936, 1924, and 1938, respectively.

Styrenics. Polystyrene (PS) was discovered around 1839 and commercialized in the 1920s. SAN copolymer, discovered around 1936, was commercialized around 1955.

Acrylonitrilics. Polyacrylonitrile was discovered around 1894 and developed into fibers in Germany around 1929. Acrylic fibers were introduced in the U.S. around 1950.

Acrylics. Polymethylmethacrylate (PMMA) was discovered around 1901 (Rohm) and commercialized after 1927. Cyanoacrylate adhesives were commercialized around 1958.

Miscellaneous Copolymers and Polyalloys. ABS resins were introduced after 1946.

Cellulosics. Regenerated cellulose was discovered around 1891 (Chardonnet); fibers (Rayon) and films (Cellophane) were commercialized after 1910. Cellulose nitrate, and resins plasticized with camphor, were introduced around 1869 (Hyatt in the U.S.). Cellulose acetate was discovered around 1905 and turned into fibers and plastics after 1924. CAB and CAP cellulose esters were introduced in 1938 and 1945, respectively. Ethyl cellulose was commercialized around 1933.

Polyamides. Nylon 6 (PA-6) was discovered around 1938 (Schlach at BASF), and commercialized around 1939. Nylon 6,6 (PA-6,6) was discovered around 1929 (Carothers at du Pont) and commercialized around 1935 as fiber material. Nylon 11 was discovered around 1946 (Zelner, Genas at ATO). Amorphous nylons were introduced around 1974. Aromatic polyamides (aramids) were introduced around 1961 (Nomex) and 1972 (Kevlar).

Thermoplastic Polyesters, Polycarbonate. PET was discovered around 1941, and fibers were introduced around 1950. PBT was introduced around 1969 and became widely used for injection molding around 1974. Aromatic polyesters were introduced around 1974 and polyarylates around 1978. Polycarbonate PC was first discovered around 1898, but commercialized only after 1957 (at Bayer and General Electric).

Sulfone Polymers. Conventional polysulfone (PBSU) was introduced around 1965

(Union Carbide).   Polyarylsulfones were commercialized in the period 1967-1976. Polyethersulfone was commercialized around 1972 (ICI).

Imide Polymers. Polyimide resins, primarily of the thermosetting type, were developed after 1953 and became commercially available around 1963 (du Pont, Rhone-Poulenc). Polyamide imide was introduced around 1976 (Amoco) and polyetherimide around 1982 (General Electric).

Ether/Oxide Polymers. Polyphenyleneoxide (PPO) was discovered around 1956 (Hays at General Electric) and commercialized in blended form after 1960. Polymethyleneoxide (acetal) was discovered around 1859 and commercialized after 1956.   Chlorinated polyether was discovered around 1950, commercialized around 1959, and withdrawn around 1972 (Penton, Hercules).

Ketone Polymers. Polyetheretherketone (PEEK) was discovered around 1977 (Victrex at ICI) and commercialized gradually from 1978 to 1983. Other ketone polymers have since been introduced, such as PAEK in 1987.

Fluoropolymers. Fluoropolymers were first discovered in the form of PTFE around 1938 (du Pont).   Development and large-scale commercialization took place over the period 1943-1950. PVDF was introduced around 1961. The copolymer P(E-TFE) was introduced around 1970 and PFA around 1972.

Miscellaneous Heterochain Polymers.   Polyphenylenesulfide (PPS) was discovered around 1967 and commercialized around 1973 (Ryton by Phillips). Parylene resins were introduced around 1965.

Formaldehyde Systems. Phenolic thermosetting resins (PF) were discovered around 1872 and commercialized around 1907 (Baekeland). Urea aminoplasts (UF) were first investigated around 1884, patented around 1918, and commercialized around 1920. Melamine aminoplasts (MF) were discovered around 1935 and commercialized around 1938.

Allyl Systems.   Diallyl phthalate resins DAP were discovered around 1941 and commercialized around 1950.

Alkyd Systems.   Alkyd resins were discovered around 1926 (General Electric) and commercialized in 1927, mainly for paint applications.

Unsaturated Polyester Systems.   Unsaturated polyester resins UP were discovered around 1933 (Ellis) and commercialized around 1942 (Pittsburgh Plate Glass).

Epoxy Systems. Epoxy resins were first commercialized around 1943 (Araldite, Ciba).

Urethane/Urea Systems. Polyurethanes were first developed for fiber applications around 1938 (Bayer). They were first used as elastomers around 1946, as plastics around 1950 and as foams around 1953.

Diene and Related Elastomers.   Natural rubber saw its properties considerably improved by the discovery of vulcanization around 1839 (Goodyear). Synthetic polyisoprene (PI) was first produced around 1954. Polychloroprene (CR) was discovered around 1931 (Duprene/Neoprene). Polybutadiene (PB) was discovered around 1932 (USSR) and commercialized in the U.S. in the late 1950s. Polyisobutylene (PIB) was discovered around 1937 and commercialized around 1942. The first synthetic rubber was probably methyl rubber (2,3 dimethylbutadiene) discovered around 1910, but no longer used.

Elastomeric Copolymers. SBR rubber was discovered and commercialized in Germany around 1927 (Buna-S). Its large scale production in the U.S. was undertaken during World War II to counter the shortage of natural rubber. Nitrile rubber NBR was introduced in Germany around 1930 (Buna-N), and in the U.S. around 1939. Carboxylated versions were introduced in the early 1960s. Ethylene-propylene rubber was introduced around 1963 (Nordel, du Pont).

Ethylene-Related Elastomers. Chlorinated polyethylene, discovered around 1938, was commercialized around 1967 (Dow/Bayer). Chlorosulphonated polyethylene (Hypalon by du Pont) was commercialized around 1952. Ethylene-vinylacetate EVA flexible resins were introduced around 1964. Ethylene-acrylic rubber was commercialized around 1975.

Fluoroelastomers. Fluoroelastomers were developed from 1940. P(VDF-HFP), for example, was commercialized around 1957 (Viton, du Pont).

Silicone Polymers. Silicone polymers were first developed during World War II (Dow-Corning, General Electric).

Miscellaneous Other Elastomers. Acrylic rubbers were discovered around 1940 and commercialized around 1948. Epichlorohydrin rubbers were introduced around 1965. Polysulfide rubbers were developed and commercialized in the period 1923-1932 (Thiokol). Polypropyleneoxide rubber was introduced around 1964. Polynorbornene was introduced around 1977.

7.2 ECONOMICS

7.2.1 Material Volumes and Markets

The production and use of plastics has grown remarkably over the past quarter century. Reported volumes in million tons (M tons) for the United States were approximately as follows: 2.9 M tons (1960), 5.4 M tons (1965), 8.8 M tons (1970), 10.7 M tons (1975), 19.5 M tons (1980), and 21.1 M tons (1985). The early 1970s (oil crisis) and 1980s (recession) were periods during which growth slowed down somewhat.

In considering material volume statistics, one becomes aware of differences, sometimes trivial, sometimes significant, between production, sales, consumption, and use figures. Such differences may be associated with accumulated stocks, as well as imports or exports, which may fluctuate with time.

The consumption of plastics in individual countries is a function of the population and of the degree of industrialization. Around 1977, the breakdown of a total consumption of about 33.5 M tons of plastics in Western countries was approximately as follows: United States, 38%; Federal Republic of Germany, 15%; Japan, 12.6%; United Kingdom, 6.6%; France, 6.5%; Italy, 6%; Spain, 3.1%; and Canada, 2.8%.

The following brief review of sales figures for individual plastics is based on one of the convenient sources of compiled information (*Modern Plastics*, January 1987), and corresponds to the situation in the United States in 1986. The discussion follows the order of presentation of materials in Chapter 3.

Olefinics. The polymeric materials discussed in the section on the olefinic group account for almost half (45%) all plastic sales. Polyethylenes correspond to about 7.2 M tons or 7200 k tons and, assuming a strict split between LDPE and HDPE, the proportions are 55% and 45%, respectively. Polypropylene, with about 2700 k tons, accounts for 27% of olefinics.

Vinylics. Vinylics account for about 17% of all plastics, and PVC forms over 87% of this group with about 3300 k tons.

Styrenics. Styrenics account for about 11.5% of all plastics, and PS forms about 80% of this group with about 2000 k tons.

Acrylics. Acrylics account for just over 1% of all plastics or about 260 k tons.

Miscellaneous Copolymers and Polyalloys. This group is mainly represented by ABS plastics with about 490 k tons (2.2%).

Cellulosics. Cellulosics form a very small group (about 50 k tons or 0.25%).

Polyamides. Polyamides, like other engineering plastics, have relatively small specialized markets, and their volumes are thus relatively small (about 190 k tons or less than 1%).

Thermoplastic Polyesters, Polycarbonate. One must distinguish between engineering PET/PBT and packaging grade PET, with fractions of 7.5% and 92.5%, respectively. The total volume is about 750 k tons or 3.4%. Polycarbonates correspond to about 150 k tons or less than 1%.

Ether/Oxide Polymers. PMO (acetal) corresponds to about 53 k tons, and PPO/PPE to about 73 k tons, i.e. a fraction of 1% for each.

Formaldehyde Systems. The total volume of formaldehyde systems is about 1860 k tons or 50% of thermosetting resins, which breaks down into 65% phenoplasts and 35% aminoplasts.

Alkyd Systems. The alkyd systems correspond to about 130 k tons.

Unsaturated Polyester Systems. Unsaturated polyesters correspond to about 560 k tons or 15% of thermosets.

Epoxy Systems. Epoxy systems correspond to about 170 k tons or about 30% of unsaturated polyesters.

Urethane/Urea Systems. Urethane systems, associated primarily with cellular varieties (flexible and rigid foams), have a volume of about 1060 k tons, i.e. 28% of thermosets and about 5% of all plastics.

As indicated in Chapter 3, most polymeric materials, and certainly all of the high-volume plastics, have multiple suppliers. At the end of 1986, for example, the manufacturing capacities of the leading U.S. suppliers of the four major materials were as follows: polyethylene, USI ($\approx$ 1500 k tons/year); poly-propylene, Himont ($\approx$ 650 k tons/year); polyvinylchloride, B.F. Goodrich ($\approx$ 700 k tons/year); and polystyrene, Huntsman ($\approx$ 450 k tons/year). In all four cases, the leading supplier's capacity is about 20% of the total U.S. capacity.

Rubber sources are sometimes subdivided into natural rubber, synthetic rubbers, reclaimed rubber and thermoplastic elastomers. Volumes in the U.S. for 1986 are approximately as follows: natural rubber $\approx$ 700 k tons (21%); synthetic rubbers $\approx$ 1900 k tons (58%); reclaimed rubber $\approx$ 300 k tons (9%) and thermoplastic elastomers $\approx$ 400 k tons (12%), for a total volume of about 3300 k tons, which is approximately 15% that of plastics.

A representative volume breakdown of synthetic rubber used in the U.S. around 1986 is approximately as follows: SBR ($\approx$ 47%), PB ($\approx$ 21%), EPDM ($\approx$ 9%), PIB ($\approx$ 5%), PI ($\approx$ 4%), CR ($\approx$ 4%), NBR ($\approx$ 3%), CSPE ($\approx$ 1%), and SI ($\approx$ 1%).

A breakdown of eight major markets, associated with the use of about 13 M tons of plastics in the United States in 1986, is discussed below. Packaging ($\approx$ 40%) is the biggest market; HDPE for containers and LDPE for films account for 27% and 25% of this market, respectively. The second largest market is building/construction ($\approx$ 34%) where PVC accounts for about 32% in pipes, fittings, and conduits. Transportation (6.5%), as well as the other markets, are much lower in volume, although often more technically sophisticated; PU foam accounts for about 26% of the transportation market. Electrical/electronic markets ($\approx$ 6%, excluding automotive and appliances) use PVC extensively for about 28% of this market. Housewares ($\approx$ 4%), appliances ($\approx$ 3.5%), furniture ($\approx$ 3%) and toys ($\approx$ 2.5%) are dominated by LDPE ($\approx$ 34%), ABS ($\approx$ 19%), PU foam ($\approx$ 57%), and PS ($\approx$ 30%), respectively.

The group of high performance or engineering plastics corresponds to an estimated worldwide volume of about 1.6 M tons in 1985, of which about 25% is used in the United States. The biggest market is for electrical/electronic applications, with transportation and building/construction accounting for about 50% and 30% of the electrical/electronic market, respectively. The volume of engineering plastics was about 7.5% of that of all plastics in 1985. Since the price of engineering plastics is roughly four times that of commodity plastics, their value was thus about 30% that of all plastics.

A breakdown of markets for composites based on unsaturated polyesters was approximately as follows for the United States in 1986: building and construction (25%), marine (20%), corrosion resistance such as in the chemical process industry (20%), transportation (12.5%), consumer goods (8%), appliances and business equipment (5.4%), electrical (3.2%), and aircraft/spacecraft (2%). The corresponding total volume was about 0.7 M tons.

Thermoplastics (PA, PP, and PET/PBT, in particular) are increasingly used with short-fiber reinforcement (mostly glass). The volume for the United States in 1986 was about 0.23 M tons, which is roughly one-third that of conventional (longer fiber/-thermoset) composites.

Main markets for elastomers include tires and inner tubes, belting, footwear, waterproofed fabrics, and shock-absorbing devices.

7.2.2 Material Prices

In a textbook on polymeric materials, it is appropriate to give some information about material prices. Considering fluctuations in the economy and the wide variety that characterizes polymeric materials, this is not an easy task. A thorough review of price information published in the 1970s and 1980s has revealed significant discrepancies and inconsistencies resulting from attempts to oversimplify this question.

Before giving material price information, it is important to review the many factors that affect material prices.

Material prices, most commonly quoted on a weight basis (e.g., U.S. $/lb), depend on the quantity of material sold; they are usually quoted for bulk quantities (e.g., hopper car). The location of the delivery point may also have an effect on prices.

For a given type of polymer, numerous grades are often available. Differences may involve molecular weight, copolymers, fillers, reinforcing fibers, plasticizers, additives, or blends with other polymers. Prices can vary quite considerably (e.g., 50% for polyethylene or polyamide-6, 100% for ABS) for the range of grades. One can usually define a base resin with a price at the low end of the range and this is the sort of price that will be considered subsequently in this section.

Material prices can vary considerably in time as a result of economic factors. In the 1970s and 1980s, there was a general upward trend in prices, associated primarily with inflation, but there can be also significant fluctuations, which may have several causes. Fluctuations in feedstock prices (primarily oil) affect the price of polymers. The general health of the economy (boom or recession) affects the market demand and, depending on the corresponding supply capacity, market prices may be adjusted up or down from list prices.

New materials are often commercialized under a monopoly situation (single supplier). A change in this situation, created, for example, by patent expiry, can drive prices down.

There is a fairly general relationship between material price and volume of production. This arises primarily from the fact that a material that is easy to produce, and thus inexpensive, is more likely to find large markets justifying large volumes of productions. One must realize also that for any material, the production cost can be a significant function of the volume; large-scale plants are more economical to run. The opening of large markets can thus drive the price of a material down significantly.

The reasons presented in the general introduction for not giving systematic simplistic lists of material properties applies equally well for material prices.

The only reliable and unequivocal source for material prices is the supplier. Useful compilations (updates) of material prices are regularly published by various sources (*Chemical Marketing Reporter, Modern Plastics* magazine, *Plastics Technology* magazine, etc.)

Some considerations that can help give material price information a general and lasting value are discussed below.

Over the 1970s and 1980s, the base prices of the five major polymeric materials (LDPE, HDPE, PP, PVC, and PS) have fluctuated somewhat, but at any time they have remained comparable, that is, within less than 15% of the average. The base price of the highest-volume material, LDPE, is representative of this average, and its value at a time t is denoted here P^1_t. If the price P_t of another material, at the same time t, is divided by P^1_t, a price factor denoted F_t is obtained, which turns out to be generally rather insensitive to time, except for materials subject to severe marketing changes.

This implies that if a material price P_{t1} at a time t1 (for instance, 1987) is known, and the base prices of LDPE are known at time t1 and at another time t2 (e.g., 1992), the price P_{t2} of the material at time t2 can be estimated through $P_{t2} = P_{t1} \times (P^1_{t2}/P^1_{t1})$.

Several categories of material prices can be associated with values of the price factor F, for example, very low price (F < 1.25), low price (1.25 < F < 2.00), medium price (2 < F < 4), high price (4 < F < 8), and very high price (F > 8).

The following discussion of prices of specific polymeric materials is based on one of the convenient sources of compiled price information (*Plastics Technology*, mid-1987). The discussion follows the order of presentation of materials in Chapter 3. Prices quoted correspond to large bulk quantities and to market prices that are equal to, or sometimes lower than, list prices. Prices P are quoted as numbers that correspond to U.S. \$/lb [e.g., P ≈ 1.75 (average or representative figure) or P ≈ 0.75-1.25 (range)]. To get a rough idea of prices P_* in a different system of currency and mass (e.g., for example, £/kg), one can also assume that the price factor F defined earlier does not depend strongly on the currency. The price P_* can then be estimated through $P_* = Px(P_*^1/P^1)$ if the base prices of LDPE P_*^1 and P^1 are known in the two systems.

Olefinics. For general-purpose molding or extrusion grades of polyethylene, the base price is $P = P^1 = 0.36$; for a powdered PE for rotational molding, P ≈ 0.57; for a blow molding grade of HMW-HDPE, P ≈ 0.38; and for UHMWPE, P ≈ 0.95-1.00. Ethylene copolymers prices range from P = 0.46-0.70 for EVA to P = 2.41 for EVOH. Ionomer resins are relatively expensive (P ≈ 1.00-1.40). For general purpose polypropylene homopolymer, P ≈ 0.43, and the price is just slightly higher for copolymer grades with improved low-temperature impact (P ≈ 0.44). Glass-fiber-reinforced grades are much more expensive (P ≈ 0.81 for 30% glass). The price of polybutylene (PB-1) can range from P = 0.84 for general-purpose grades to P = 1.30 for hot water grades.

Vinylics. The price of general purpose polyvinylchloride (PVC) homopolymer is P ≈

0.35 with relatively little variation for different grades. CPVC is much more expensive ($P \approx 0.92$). PVDC, the barrier material, is even more costly ($P \approx 1.15$).

Styrenics. The price of general purpose polystyrene (PS) is currently relatively high ($P \approx 0.53$); high-heat, high-impact grades are only marginally costlier ($P \approx 0.56$), but fire-retarded grades can reach $P \approx 0.82$. Styrene-acrylonitrile copolymers sell around $P \approx 0.73$ and styrene-acrylic copolymers, around $P \approx 1.02$.

Acrylics. General-purpose acrylic resins sell around $P \approx 0.85$ and impact modified grades, as high as $P = 1.20$.

Miscellaneous Copolymers and Alloys. The price of a medium-impact ABS resin is around $P \approx 0.80$, but flame-retarded grades can be as high as $P = 1.20$. Polyalloys of ABS with a low-priced resin are only moderately more expensive [$P \approx 1.00$ for A(ABS/PVC)]. If more expensive resins are used, the cost is higher [$P \approx 1.20$ for A(ABS/PC) or $P \approx 1.70$ for A(ABS/PA)].

Cellulosics. Cellulosics are relatively expensive materials ($P \approx 1.30$ for cellulose acetate or mixed esters CAB and CAP).

Polyamides. Currently, unreinforced PA-6 is less costly than PA-6,6 ($P \approx 1.37\text{-}1.78$ vs. $P \approx 1.77\text{-}1.97$). Glass-reinforced grades have similar prices; the lower cost of glass is balanced by the cost of compounding. Types 11 and 12 are considerably more expensive ($P \approx 3.35$). Transparent (amorphous) polyamides are also quite expensive ($P \approx 2.50\text{-}3.60$).

Thermoplastic Polyesters, Polycarbonate. Injection moldable PBT correspond to the range $P = 1.30\text{-}1.70$. Glass-reinforced grades are slightly more expensive. PET grades for bottle blowing are considerably cheaper ($P \approx 0.54$), partly because of the volumes involved and the well-established fiber related chemical technology. Polyarylates are slightly more expensive ($P \approx 2.00\text{-}2.80$). Polyester-based liquid crystal polymers (LCP) are very expensive ($P \approx 12.00$ in unfilled extrusion grades). The price of unreinforced polycarbonate (PC) is moderate ($P \approx 1.61$) and increases significantly for glass-reinforced grades (up to $P = 2.45$), fire-retarded grades (up to $P = 2.23$), or optical grade for compact discs, for example (up to $P = 2.30$).

Sulfone Polymers. Regular polysulfone (PSU) is quite expensive ($P \approx 3.80$). Interestingly, low glass-reinforced grades (10%) are slightly more expensive, while high glass grades (30%) are slightly less expensive than the base resin, illustrating the relative effects of compounding costs and lower material cost for glass (P under 1.00). Polyethersulfones and polyarylsulfones are costlier than regular PSU ($P \approx 4.25$ and $P = 4.65$, respectively).

Imide Polymers. Unmodified polyetherimide (PEI) is highly priced ($P \approx 4.45$), but still much cheaper than unmodified polyamideimide PAI ($P \approx 15.00$).

Ether/Oxide Polymers. Acetal (polymethylene oxide) has a price comparable to that of regular polyamides ($P \approx$ 1.50-1.60 in unreinforced grades). Unreinforced polypropylene oxides (or polyphenylene ethers) are moderately priced ($P \approx$ 1.10-1.39 for injection, $P \approx$ 1.40-1.81 for extrusion); glass reinforced grades are significantly more expensive.

Ketone Polymers. PEEK resins are very highly priced in unreinforced form ($P \approx$ 23.00) and only slightly less expensive with glass fibers ($P \approx$ 20.50 for 30% glass). The less crystalline PEK is even costlier at this stage ($P \approx$ 32.00).

Fluoropolymers. All fluoropolymers are quite expensive, starting with PTFE ($P \approx$ 5.55-6.05) and culminating with PCTFE ($P \approx$ 30.00). In order of increasing price, various types rank as follows: PTFE, PVDF, FEP, P(E-CTFE), P(E-TFE), PFA, and PCTFE.

Miscellaneous Heterochain Polymers. Polyphenylene sulfide (PPS) is not sold in unreinforced form, due to its high inherent brittleness. Glass-fiber-reinforced grades for structural applications are reasonably priced ($P \approx$ 3.20 for 40% glass). The addition of inexpensive fillers can reduce the cost to rather low levels for nonstructural applications ($P \approx$ 1.50-1.90).

Formaldehyde Systems. Phenolic molding compounds are low-priced ($P \approx$ 0.43-0.54). Dark urea resins are slightly more expensive ($P \approx$ 0.50-0.57), while light-color urea or melamine resins are much more costly ($P \approx$ 0.70-0.75).

Allyl Systems. Diallyl phthalate resins are quite expensive ($P \approx$ 2.51-4.97) and in the same price range as high-performance engineering thermoplastics.

Unsaturated Polyesters. Orthophthalic-type general purpose thermosetting polyester resins are quite inexpensive ($P \approx$ 0.65). Other types can be much more costly (up to $P = 1.30$).

Vinylester Systems. Vinylester thermosetting resins for corrosion or corrosion and heat resistance are quite expensive ($P \approx$ 1.26-1.38).

Epoxy Systems. General purpose epoxy thermosetting resins are about twice as expensive as corresponding unsaturated polyester resins ($P \approx$ 1.16-1.26). Special compounds for electrical applications can be much more expensive (up to $P = 2.70$).

Urethane/Urea Systems. Thermosetting urethane resins involve the combination of an isocyanate with a polyol. The combined costs correspond to about $P \approx$

Silicone Polymers. Silicone molding compounds are in a high price range ($P \approx$ 5.80-6.40).

Thermoplastic Elastomers. The range of prices for the various thermoplastic elastomers is quite broad. Styrenics start at $P \approx$ 0.63; olefinics are in the range $P \approx$ 0.98-1.35; polyurethanes correspond to $P \approx$ 1.60-2.50 and polyester-types to $P \approx$ 2.00-3.10.

7.2.3   Processing Equipment Prices

In this section, examples of equipment prices are given for both testing and processing equipment. In the absence of full details about the equipment, the prices can only be considered as roughly indicative. It is suggested that readers refer to the photographic illustrations of chapters 4 and 5 when reading this section. Multiples of $1000 are indicated as $k ($1000) and $M ($1,000,000). The prices are representative of the U.S. market in the late 1980s. Prices for very basic equipment are relatively stable but with the fast growth of control and automation systems, the cost of sophisticated models is rising rapidly.

7.2.3.1 Testing Equipment

Materials and Test Specimens. A thermoplastic injection mold for four standard test pieces costs about $8k. A die cutter for sheet samples is slighly under $1k, while the associated stamping press is about $3.5k.

Short Term Conventional Mechanical Testing. A floor model universal testing machine with a minimum of controls and accessories costs about $50k. A simple flexural stiffness tester costs about $3.5k.

Hardness. A simple Durometer tester costs about $0.2k and a Barcol impressor about $0.3k.

Friction, Wear, Abrasion. A simple slip tester costs about $5k, about the same as a two-station abrasion tester.

Impact. The simplest pendulum impact tester costs about $5k but the price can rise to over $15k for electronically-controlled models. The price of an Izod notcher is about $3k. The simplest drop weight tester costs about $3k and one with residual energy measurement is about $5.5k. A sophisticated high rate impact tester can cost as much as $150k.

Long Term Static Loading. A multi-station dead-weight creep apparatus costs about $8k.

High Temperature Softening. A five-station manual tester costs about $10k while an automated version can be as high as $30k.

Weathering. An accelerated weathering apparatus costs about $45k.

Flammablility/Combustion. An oxygen index apparatus of the simplest kind costs about $3k while a heated version is over $15k. A smoke density chamber costs about $30k and a radiant panel apparatus about $16k.

Gas/Vapor Permeability. A three-cell gas transmission rate tester costs about $15k while a two-cell water vapor transmission tester costs about $6k.

Optical Properties. A simple gloss meter costs about $5k, a haze meter about $18.5k, and a spectrocolorimeter about $20-25k.

Density. A commercial six-column density measuring apparatus costs about $15k.

7.2.3.2 Processing Equipment

Extrusion. A simple 1 inch screw costs about $1.5k while a 6 inch screw is about $6k. The cost of sophisticated screws (barrier, etc.) can jump by a factor x 2.5. A simple plate for profile extrusion is in the range $0.5-1.5k and the back assembly about $3.5k. A complete die for exterior wall siding would cost about $20k, not comprising the cooling/sizing accessories. Prices for standard extruders range, roughly, from about $40k for a small 1.5 inch model to about $100k for a 3.5 inch model. An 8 inch-wide laboratory sheet line costs a total of about $40k with about $16k for the extruder, $4k for the die and $20k for the take-off system.

A 65 inch-wide sheet die costs about $45k and it would be matched with a 3.5 inch extruder costing about $100k. A large sheet coextrusion set-up with four extruders, a five feet die and the appropriate take-off equipment represents an investment of over $1M. The cost of a standard tubing die (diameter about 6 inch) is around $20k but for a huge thick pipe, four or five feet in diameter, it could approach $1M.

Extrusion Covering. The price of a crosshead die for building wire insulation would change by a factor x 10 ($3.5k to $35k) if ceramic guiders are used instead of plain steel ones.

Film Blowing. The complete blown film extrusion line associated with a 3 inch extruder would cost about $0.75M. A 24 inch multilayer film blowing die costs about $200k and the complete corresponding line around $2M.

Calendering. A small four-roll laboratory calendar with four DC drives costs about $175k. A large four-roll (36 inch diameter, 136 inch length) calender would cost about $2.5M, to which $1-1.5M should be added for auxiliary take-away equipment. The cost of installing such equipment could be as high as $0.75M.

Sheet Thermoforming. A small single station thermoformer costs about $16k while a large shuttling oven thermoformer is about $100k, about the same as a roll-fed, in-line thermoformer. A production mold for a refrigeration liner would cost about $50k and one for the low volume production of the deck of a sailboat would be only about $20k.

Blow Molding. Single cavity molds for handled bottles or automobile ducts cost about $10k. Machines to extrusion-blow mold three or four bottles in an automated way would cost around $300k and the molds around $50k. The molding of an automobile gas tank or a sailboard shell corresponds to molds costing as much as $75k and machines costing over $1M. The investment for even larger tanks could exceed $2M.

Rotational Molding. The cost of a rotary arm machine is as high as $100k. A mold to make simultaneously two small boats at low production rates would be almost $50k.

Compression Molding. A relatively small compression molding for the press stack molding of for printed circuit boards costs about $50k. Molding of SMC chair seats would require a $200k mold and a machine in excess of $500k.

Transfer Molding. A small transfer molding press (30-ton clamp, 7.5 ton transfer) costs about $30k.

Injection Molding. A very small basic machine (15-25 tons) costs about $20k. A medium size unit (180 tons) costs about $80k. Large machines (2000-4000 tons) cost well over $1M, the largest ones (10,000 tons) representing investments around $5M. Thermoset or rubber injection machines around 500 ton capacity cost about $250k. The mold for the injection of a very large tub with side-moving sections could be as high as $300k. The total investment for a compact disk manufacturing facility would be over $1M per unit; the 60-80 ton injection unit would cost around $100k and the mold over $60k. A 250-ton machine with sophisticated controls and part removal/packaging accessories would cost about $650k. The use of hot runners generally adds 10-20% to the cost of a mold. A system for the co-injection of a video cassette case would cost about $500k with about $300k and $200k going for the mold and machine respectively. The mold featuring three moving secondary mold sections for a washing machine tub could cost as much as $150k but the less complicated mold for a TV rear pannel could cost under $40k. A 48-cavity hot runner mold for PET bottle preforms costs about $150k, about the same as an eight-cavity stack mold for compact disk display boxes. An inexpensive piping T-joint requires a mold with three retractable cores costing ove $30k.

Reaction Injection Molding. A small two-cylinder injection unit (100 lb or 36 l/min) costs about $125k (base model) to $175k (more sophisticated model). A very large unit (1800 lb or 720 l/min) would cost between $275k and $350k. A booking press for an automotive fascia would cost about $350k and a steel mold for large production volume about $500k, a price similar to that for a thermoplastic injection mold of a similar part.

7.3   INFORMATION

7.3.1   Professional Organizations

A number of professional organizations are directly associated with polymeric materials (plastics, rubbers and composites). Most industrialized countries have one or several such organizations. Three representative American organizations are introduced below.

The Society of Plastics Engineers (SPE) is formed of individuals working in the plastics field. It has a central office with a permanent staff and local sections throughout the country. It is organized with divisions corresponding to specific areas of interest (injection molding, vinyls, thermosets, etc.). Activities include the publication of magazines and journals, the organization of short courses, conferences, and monthly local section meetings. SPE encourages student participation through its student chapters.

The Society of the Plastics Industry is a regroupment of companies to assist and promote the industry. It also involves a number of specialized divisions. Besides the organization of conferences, it collects and distributes information and participates in regulatory or standardization programs.

The Rubber Division of the American Chemical Society regroups individuals active in the rubber field. It organizes conferences, as well as short courses or correspondence courses. It publishes a journal and maintains an extensive library reference system.

7.3.2   Conferences and Exhibitions

Conferences offer excellent forums for the exchange of knowledge, and thus the development of the field. Over a period of several days, many contributors present their recent work, which can be followed by immediate discussions with attendees. Written papers are normally printed in *Proceedings* for later reference. Three major polymer-related conferences regularly held in North America are discussed below; they attract international participation.

The annual technical conference of the Society of Plastic Engineers (ANTEC) is held every spring and attracts hundreds of contributors and thousands of attendees. Topics include material and process developments, and economics.

The annual conference of the Composites Institute of the Society of the Plastics Industry, held early each year, is devoted to reinforced plastics, and their technologies and applications.

Meetings of the Rubber Division of the American Chemical Society are held twice a year for rubber scientists and engineers.

Many smaller conferences on specialized subjects are held regularly and announced in trade publications.

Suppliers of materials and processing equipment have opportunities to promote their goods at a number of major exhibitions held regularly in North America, Europe, and Asia. Such exhibitions offer a fascinating opportunity for newcomers to become quickly acquainted with the field.

The major North American plastics exhibition isreferred to as the "National Plastics Exposition" (NPE) and is held in Chicago every three years.

Kunststoffe (K) is an even larger German exhibition held every third year in Dusseldorf.

7.3.3 Trade Publications

A fairly large number of trade publications are dedicated to polymeric materials (plastics, rubbers, or composites). They contain technical and economic news, review articles written by the editors, and solicited or reprinted technical articles. They also feature announcements for conferences, short courses, and employment, as well as advertisements by material and equipment suppliers. Some trade publications are published by professional organizations (e.g., *Plastics Engineering* by SPE) and others by publishing firms (e.g., *Modern Plastics* by McGraw-Hill or *Kunststoffe* by Hanser). They are generally monthly publications. Many individuals or companies subscribe to one or several trade publications, and they can generally be found in technical libraries.

A representative list of North American and European polymer-related trade publications is given in Appendix 7.

7.3.4 Scientific and Engineering Journals

A fairly large number of scientific and engineering journals is devoted to polymeric materials and their processing into products. Such journals feature articles submitted by researchers, which have been approved by expert reviewers. Individuals do not normally subscribe to such journals, which are kept in fairly large technical libraries for consultation. Some of these journals specialize in the chemistry and physics of materials, while others deal primarily with engineering aspects. Many other journals, which are not polymer-specialized, contain polymer-related articles.

Several systems permit the retrieval of articles published on a specific subject. They are generally based on the use of appropriate keywords, in conjunction with index books or computerized banks. The systems provide relevant references in standard form [author(s), title, journal details] and the articles can then be consulted. *Chemical Abstracts* and *Engineering Abstracts* are examples of such systems.

A representative list of polymer-related scientific and engineering journals is given in appendix 7.

7.3.5   Books

Many books have been published that are related to polymeric materials and processing. One broad classification could distinguish three classes, although boundaries are somewhat subjective. Introductory descriptive books are intended for newcomers and those with minimal technical background (e.g., T.A. Richardson, *Modern Industrial Plastics*). Technology-oriented specialized books are valuable, in particular, for people facing industrial production problems (e.g., I.I. Rubin, *Injection Molding: Theory and Practice*). Science and engineering oriented books were used primarily by those involved in advanced research and development, but with the rapid increase in the use of mathematical modeling in industrial contexts, their use is likely to spread (e.g., J.L. Throne, *Plastic Process Engineering*).

A representative list of classical and recent polymer-related books is given in appendix 7.

7.3.6   Compiled Data Sources

A number of publications, often referred to as "encyclopedias" or "handbooks," regularly compile information and specific data on polymeric materials, modifiers, additives, processing equipment, tooling, etc. This information originates with suppliers and is presented by the publications in their own format and style. Generally, enough qualifying information is given in such publications to make the data truly valuable to designers, as opposed to most short tables of data given in many books which are only roughly indicative, and sometimes rather misleading. *Modern Plastics Encyclopedia* is a widely used example of such a publication.

7.3.7   Company Literature

I feel strongly that company literature is the ultimate source of information on materials, process equipment, and tooling. Material suppliers are generally the ones who have gathered the most information about their own materials, the ones who are aware of their strengths as well as their limitations. It is not normally to their long-term advantage to withhold honest information or advice from a current or potential client. The technical and visual quality of company literature is known to be a strong factor in the perception of the company by its clients and in helping achieve client satisfaction with a minimum of costly personal technical consultation.

Company literature can take a variety of forms. General brochures briefly describing materials and products, with major examples of applications, may be useful to newcomers. Some booklets give a broad overview of an area in textbook style (e.g., *An Introduction to Fiberglass-Reinforced Plastics/Composites*, 39 pp., Owens/Corning Fiberglas). Extensive booklets may be devoted to product design (e.g., *ZYTEL Nylon Resins-Design Handbook*, 186 pp., du Pont), to a molding process (e.g., *LEXAN Polycarbonate Resin Injection Molding*, 27 pp., General Electric), to a specific product (*Gears of DELRIN and ZYTEL*, 16 pp., du Pont), or to a specific area of application (*HALON TFE for Critical Chemical Processing Applications*, 13 pp., Allied). Many companies issue regular newsletters regarding their products (e.g., *Spotlight KYNAR*, 6 pp., Pennwalt). All of this literature is available free of charge to potential users. It should be noted that when there are several suppliers for a type of polymer, it is advisable to obtain literature from all suppliers.

Since it has been stressed in this book that properties depend on not only on the type of material but also its grade, as well, grade-specific data sheets should eventually be obtained from suppliers.

7.4   EDUCATION

7.4.1   Short Courses and Self-study

Specific information or a broader education on polymers can be sought by attending short courses, sometimes referred to as "seminars," which are sponsored by several professional organizations (e.g., SPE), publishing companies, or educational institutions (e.g., Stevens Institute).

Short courses are most commonly 1-day affairs taught by a single instructor. Longer courses (2-5 days) are sometimes taught by multiple instructors. Instructors are sometimes academics, but, more commonly, they hold a position in industry or consult privately. Short courses are often scheduled to coincide with conferences or exhibitions, but they are also organized to fulfill local needs, and are sometimes presented as in-house or in-plant courses. Short courses are regularly announced in trade publications.

There does not appear to be many polymer-related correspondence courses, a notable exception is the course entitled "Rubber Technology," conducted by the Rubber Division of the American Chemical Society, and based on a collaborative textbook (M. Morton, ed., *Rubber Technology*).

With the fast-growing availability of video equipment, it is likely that the development and use of educational video programs will increase significantly in the years to come. Interactive computer-based educational programs offer very good prospects for the longer term.

7.4.2   Educational Institutions

Traditional education of young generations is likely to remain the major method of training competent people to carry over the responsibility of advancing the science and technology of polymeric materials and their processing.

The coverage of polymeric materials in educational institutions has generally been less extensive than would seem justified by their current importance. This is related to the fact that their market penetration and their recognition as performance materials are relatively recent.

Four major levels of education can be distinguished which, although different as to their goals and expectations, are all important to the economy.

Schools, often referred to as "vocational schools," train students as specialized operators with the prospect of getting foreman responsibilities. Other schools, often referred to as "community" or "technical" colleges, train students as technicians with subsequent supervisory prospects. Undergraduate programs in universities and colleges train students who intend to go into laboratory or production work (B.Sc., B.Eng.). Graduate programs in universities and colleges train graduate students for research careers (M.Sc., M.Eng., Ph.D.).

The differences outlined above are not really so strict for all institutions and students, but they represent a useful rough classification.

Two approaches can be taken by any institution to incorporate polymer-related training.

"Unspecialized training" implies that a certain number of specialized courses and laboratories are incorporated into conventional programs.   In undergraduate engineering programs, for example, students in chemical engineering may be able to take an elective polymer engineering course. At the other extreme, fully specialized training would involve, for example, the creation of a polymer engineering program with a curriculum involving a sufficient number of fundamental general courses supplemented by a variety of polymer-oriented courses. An intermediate solution is associated with broader Material Science or Material Engineering programs in which polymeric materials form a major element.

There are relatively few places in North America that offer fully specialized programs at the university/college undergraduate level (e.g., University of Lowell) or at the community/technical college level (e.g., Farris College). This has been more common at the university/college graduate level (e.g., University of Akron).

While at some point in time, many thought that specialization involved some risks, it seems now that polymeric materials as a class are here to stay and grow, and that, consequently, a reasonable number of specialized programs is justifiable.

7.5 APPENDIX 7
TRADE PUBLICATIONS

Automotive Engineering (SAE)
Canadian Plastics
Elastomerics/Rubber Age
European Plastics News
European Rubber Journal
Kunststoffe - German Plastics
Materials Engineering
Modern Plastics
Plasticheskie - Massy - Soviet Plastics
Plastics And Rubber International
Plastics Compounding
Plastics Design Forum
Plastics Engineering (SPE)
Plastics Industry News
Plastics Machinery And Equipment
Plastics Technology
Plastics World

Plastiques Modernes Et Elastomeres
Revue Generale Des Caoutchoucs Et
Plastiques
Rubber And Plastics News
Rubber World
Textile World
Other Sources of Information on Polymers
Hydrocarbon Processing, Petrochemical
Handbook
Materials Engineering, Materials Selector
Issue
Modern Plastics Encyclopedia
Rubber Red Book, Directory of the Rubber
Industry
Textile World, Man-Made Fiber Chart

SCIENTIFIC AND ENGINEERING JOURNALS

Advances in Polymer Science
Advances in Polymer Technology
British Polymer Journal
Composite Structures
Composites
Composites Science and Technology
European Polymer Journal
Fiber Science and Technology
International Journal of Polymeric Materials
Journal of Applied Polymer Science
Journal of Cellular Plastics
Jounal of Composite Materials
Journal of Composites Technology &
Research
Journal of Elastomers and Plastics
Journal of Elastoplastics
Journal of Macromolecular Science
Journal of Materials Science
Journal of Plastic Film & Sheeting
Journal of Polymer Engineering
Journal of Reinforced Plastics and Composites
Journal of Rheology
Journal of Testing and Evaluation

Macromolecules
Mechanics of Composite Materials
Plastics and Rubber Processing and
Applications
Polymer
Polymer Composites
Polymer Engineering and Science
Polymer Journal
Polymer News
Polymer-Plastics Technology and Engineering
Polymer Process Engineering
Polymer Science and Technology
Polymer Science USSR
Polymer Testing
Polymeric Materials Science and Engineering
Rubber Chemistry and Technology
Textile Research Journal

Book List (since 1980)

J.G. WILLIAMS
Stress Analysis of Polymers
ELLIS HORWOOD, London (1980) 2nd ed.

J.D. FERRY
Viscoelastic Properties of Polymers
JOHN WILEY, New York (1980) 2nd ed.

R.W. HERTZBERG, J.A. MANSON
Fatigue of Engineering Plastics
ACADEMIC PRESS, New York (1980).

R.D. BECK
Plastic Product Design
VAN NOSTRAND-REINHOLD, New York
(1980) 2nd ed.

R.L.E. BROWN
Design and Manufacture of Plastic Parts
WILEY-INTERSCIENCE, New York (1980).

G.V. VINOGRADOV, A. YA. MALKIN
Rheology of Polymers
SPRINGER-VERLAG, Berlin (1980).

R.T. FENNER
Principles of Polymer Processing
CHEM. PUBL. CO., New York (1980).

S.W. TSAI, H.T. HAHN
Introduction to Composite Materials
TECHNOMIC, Lancaster, Pa. (1980).

M.R. PIGGOTT
Load Bearing Composites
PERGAMON PRESS, New York (1980).

B.D. AGARWAL, L.J. BROUTMAN
Analysis and Performance of Fiber
Composites
J. WILEY, New York (1980).

R.B. SEYMOUR, C.E. CARRAHER, JR.
Polymer Chemistry
M. DEKKER, New York (1981).

K.J. SAUNDERS
Organic Polymer Chemistry
RYERSON/CHAPMAN AND HALL (1981).

R.J. YOUNG
Introduction to Polymers
CHAPMAN AND HALL-METHUEN, New
York (1981).

R.J. CRAWFORD
Plastics Engineering
PERGAMON PRESS, Oxford (1981).

B.S. BENJAMIN
Structural Design with Plastics, 2nd ed.
SPE SERIES (1981).

E. MILLER, Ed.
Plastics Product Design Handbook
Part A: Materials and Components
MARCELL DEKKER, New York (1981).

R.P. BROWN, Ed.
Handbook of Plastic Test Methods
G. GODWIN/TECHNOMIC, Lancaster, Pa.
(1981) 2nd ed.

D. HULL
An Introduction to Composite Materials
CAMBRIDGE UNIVERSITY PRESS, U.K.
(1981).

J.A. BRYDSON
Flow Properties of Polymer Melts
ILIFFE, London (1981) 2nd ed.

F.N. COGSWELL
Polymer Melt Rheology
J. WILEY, New York (1981).

S. LEVY
Plastics Extrusion Technology Handbook
INDUSTRIAL PRESS, New York (1981).

J. MONK, Ed.
Thermosetting Plastics: Practical Molding
Technology
TECHNOMIC, Lancaster, Pa. (1981).

H. ULRICH
Introduction to Industrial Polymers
HANSER PUBLISHERS, New York (1982).

A. RUDIN
The Elements of Polymer Science and
Engineering
ACADEMIC PRESS, New York (1982).

F. RODRIGUEZ
Principles of Polymer Systems
MCGRAW-HILL, New York (1982) 2nd ed.

S.L.ROSEN
Fundamental Principles of Polymeric Materials
J.WILEY, New York (1982).

J.A. BRYDSON
Plastics Materials
BUTTERWORTH, Stoneham, Ma. (1982) 4th
ed.

A.W. BIRLEY, M.J. SCOTT
Plastics Materials: Properties and
Applications
CHAPMAN AND HALL-METHUEN, New
York (1982).

S.S. SCHWARTZ, S.H. GOODMAN
Plastics Materials and Processes
VAN NOSTRAND-REINHOLD, New York
(1982).

L. MASCIA
Thermoplastics: Materials Engineering
ELSEVIER, New York (1982).

E. MILLER, Ed.
Plastics Product Design Handbook
Part B: Processing and Production
Techniques
M. DEKKER, New York (1982).

J.B. DYM
Product Design with Plastics
INDUSTRIAL PRESS, New York (1982).

F.J. LOCKETT
Engineering Design Basis for Plastics Products
HMSO BOOKS, London (1982).

W. SCHNABEL
Polymer Degradation
HANSER PUBLISHERS, New York (1982).

C.J. HILADO
Flammability Handbook for Plastics
TECHNOMIC, Lancaster, Pa. (1982).

C.M. BLOW, C. HEPBURN
Rubber Technology and Manufacture
BUTTERWORTH, Stoneham, Ma. (1982).

C. HEPBURN
Polyurethane Elastomers
APPLIED SCIENCE PUBLISHERS, London
(1982).

M.J. FOLKES
Short Fiber Reinforced Thermoplastics
RSP-J. WILEY, New York (1982).

R.P. SHELDON
Composite Polymeric Materials
ELSEVIER, New York (1982).

G. LUBIN, Ed.
Handbook of Composites
VAN NOSTRAND-REINHOLD, New York
(1982).

J.M. DEALY
Rheometers for Molten Plastics
VAN NOSTRAND-REINHOLD, New York
(1982).

A. WHELAN
Injection Molding Materials
APPLIED SCIENCE PUBLISHERS, London
(1982).

T.A. RICHARDSON
Industrial Plastics: Theory and Applications
BOBBS-MERRILL, Indianapolis (1983)

J.A. BIESENBERGER, D.H. SEBASTIAN
Principles of Polymerization Engineering
J. WILEY, New York (1983).

P.C. POWELL
Engineering with Polymers
CHAPMAN AND HALL-METHUEN, New
York (1983).

I.M. WARD
Mechanical Properties of Solid Polymers
J. WILEY, New York (1983) 2nd ed.

A. J. KINLOCH, R.J. YOUNG
Fracture Behavior of Polymers
APPLIED SCIENCE PUBLISHERS, U.K.
(1983).

S. TURNER
Mechanical Testing of Plastics
TECHNOMIC, Lancaster, Pa. (1983) 2nd ed.

J. TROITZSCH
International Plastics Flammability Handbook
HANSER PUBLSIHERS, New York (1983).

H. SAECHTLING, Ed.
International Plastics Handbook
HANSER PUBLSIHERS, New York (1983).

J.H. BRISTON, L. KATAN
Plastics Films
TECHNOMIC, Lancaster, Pa. (1983) 2nd ed.

C.J. BENNING
Plastic Films for Packaging
TECHNOMIC, Lancaster, Pa. (1983).

M. HOLMES, D.J. JUST
GRP in Structural Engineering
APPLIED SCIENCE PUBLISHERS, U.K.
(1983).

M. GRAYSON, Ed.
Encyclopedia of Composite Materials and
Components
TECHNOMIC, Lancaster, Pa. (1983).

J.R.A. PEARSON, S.M. RICHARDSON, Eds.
Computational Analysis of Polymer Processing
ELSEVIER, New York (1983).

F. MARTELLI
Twin Screw Extruders
SPE-SERIES (1983).

E.C. BERNHARDT
Computer Aided Engineering for Injection
Molding
HANSER PUBLISHERS, New York (1983).

F. JOHANNABER
Injection Molding Machines
HANSER PUBLISHERS, New York (1983).

H. GASTROW, K. STOECKHERT, Eds.
Injection Molds
HANSER PUBLISHERS, New York (1983).

K. STOECKHERT, Ed.
Mold-Making Handbook
HANSER PUBLISHERS, New York (1983).

R.G.W. PYE
Injection Mold Design
TECHNOMIC, Lancaster, Pa. (1983), 3rd ed.

R.B. SEYMOUR, C.E. CARRAHER, JR.
Structure-Property Relationship in Polymers
PLENUM, New York (1984).

F.W. BILLMEYER
Textbook of Polymer Science
J. WILEY, New York (1984) 3rd ed.

H.G. ELIAS
Macromolecules
Vol.1: Structure and Properties
Vol.2: Synthesis, Materials and Technology
PLENUM, New York (1984) 2nd ed.

G.R. MOORE, D.E. KLINE
Properties and Processing of Polymers for
Engineers
PRENTICE-HALL, Englewood Cliffs, N.J.
(1984).

J.E. MARK, A. EISENBERG, W.W. GRAESSLEY, L. MANDELKERN, J.L. KOENIG
Physical Properties of Polymers
AMERICAN CHEMICAL SOCIETY, Washington, D.C. (1984).

J.G. WILLIAMS
Fracture Mechanics of Polymers
HALSTED-J. WILEY, New York (1984).

C. MACDERMOTT
Selecting Thermoplastics for Engineering Applications
M. DEKKER, New York (1984).

G.W. EHRENSTEIN, G. ERHARD
Designing with Plastics
HANSER PUBLISHERS, New York (1984).

S. LEVY, J.H. DUBOIS
Plastics Product Design Engineering Handbook
CHAPMAN AND HALL-METHUEN, New York (1984) 2nd ed.

V. SHAH
Handbook of Plastics Testing Technology
WILEY-INTERSCIENCE, New York (1984).

J.C. HALPIN
Primer on Composite Materials: Analysis
TECHNOMIC, Lancaster, Pa. (1984) 2nd ed.

W. MICHAELI
Extrusion Dies: Design and Engineering
HANSER PUBLISHERS, New York (1984).

A. WHELAN
Injection Moulding Machines
ELSEVIER-APPLIED SCIENCE PUBLISHERS, London (1984).

J. FRADOS, Ed.
Plastics Engineering Handbook of the Society of the Plastics Industry
VAN NOSTRAND-REINHOLD, New York (1985).

R. GACHTER, H. MULLER, Eds.
Plastics Additives
HANSER PUBLISHERS, New York (1985).

J.M. MARGOLIS, Ed.
Engineering Thermoplastics
M. DEKKER, New York (1985).

R.J. CRAWFORD
Plastics and Rubbers Engineering Design and Applications
MECHANICAL ENGINEERING PUBLICATIONS, London (1985).

N. SCHULTZ
Fire and Flammability Handbook
VAN NOSTRAND-REINHOLD, New York (1985).

D.H. KAELBLE
Computer-Aided Design of Polymers and Composites
M. DEKKER, New York (1985).

R.I. TANNER
Engineering Rheology
SPE-SERIES, (1985).

J.R.A. PEARSON
Mechanics of Polymer Processing
ELSEVIER, New York (1985).

M.J. STEVENS
Extruder Principles and Operation
ELSEVIER, New York (1985).

D.V. ROSATO, D.V. ROSATO
Injection Molding Handbook
VAN NOSTRAND-REINHOLD, New York (1985).

R.W. MEYER
Handbook of Pultrusion Technology
CHAPMAN AND HALL-METHUEN, New York (1985).

V. GOWARIKER, N.V. VISWANATHAN, J.
SREEDHAR
Polymer Science
J. WILEY, New York (1986).

R.B. SEYMOUR, G.S. KIRSHENBAUM
High Performance Polymers
ELSEVIER, New York (1986).

D. MORTON-JONES, J.W. LEWIS
Polymer Products
CHAPMAN AND HALL, London (1986).

J.M. MARGOLIS, Ed.
Advanced Thermoset Composites
VAN NOSTRAND-REINHOLD, New York
(1986).

C. RAUWENDAAL
Polymer Extrusion
HANSER PUBLISHERS, New York (1986).

G. MENGES, P. MOHREN
How to Make Injection Molds
HANSER PUBLISHERS, New York (1986).

L.H. SPERLING
Introduction to Physical Polymer Science
J. WILEY, New York (1986).

H.S. KATZ, J.V. MILEWSKI, Eds.
Handbook of Fillers for Plastics
VAN NOSTRAND-REINHOLD, New York
(1987).

J.V. MILEWSKI, H.S. KATZ
Handbook of Reinforcements for Plastics
VAN NOSTRAND-REINHOLD, New York
(1987).

M. MORTON, Ed.
Rubber Technology
VAN NOSTRAND-REINHOLD, New York
(1987) 3rd ed.

T. RICHARDSON
Composites: A Design Guide
INDUSTRIAL PRESS, New York (1987).

J.L. THRONE
Thermoforming
HANSER PUBLISHERS, New York (1987).

J. FLORIAN
Practical Thermoforming - Principles and
Applications
M. DEKKER, New York (1987).

J.B. DYM
Injection Molds and Molding
VAN NOSTRAND-REINHOLD, New York
(1987) 2nd ed.

J.H. DUBOIS, W.I. PRIBBLE, Eds.
Plastics Mold Engineering Handbook
VAN NOSTRAND-REINHOLD, New York
(1987) 4th ed.

F.M. SWEENEY
Reaction Injection Molding, Machinery and
Process
M. DEKKER, New York (1987).

K. KIRCHER
Chemical Reactions in Plastics Processing
HANSER PUBLISHERS, New York (1987).

M. CHANDA
Plastics Technology Handbook
M. DEKKER, New York (1987).

Z.H. STACHURSKI
Engineering Science of Polymeric Materials
ROYAL AUSTRALIAN CHEMICAL
INSTITUTE, Victoria (1987).

G. GRUENWALD
Thermoforming: A Plastics Processing Guide
TECHNOMIC, Lancaster, Pa. (1987).

N.P. CHEREMISINOFF
Polymer Mixing and Extrusion Technology
M. DEKKER, New York (1987).

S.W. TSAI
Composites Design
THINK COMPOSITES, Dayton, Oh.(1987)

P.K. MALLICK
Fiber-Reinforced Composites
M. DEKKER, New York (1987).

N.G. McCRUM, C.P. BUCKLEY, C.B.
BUCKNALL
Principles of Polymer Engineering
OXFORD UNIVERSITY PRESS, Oxford
(1988).

F.D. PALMER
Thermoforming
HOPPLE PLASTICS (1988).

INDEX of CHEMPLATES (Chapter 3)

VA vinyl'acetate (3.4.2.3)

V vinyl (3.4.2.5)

VDF vinylidene'fluoride (3.2.2.14)

SUBJECT INDEX